RUNNING ALL OVER THE WORLD

50 Marathons in 50 Countries

JIM MANFORD

COPYRIGHT

RUNNING ALL OVER THE WORLD (50 Marathons in 50 Countries)

Copyright 2021, JIM MANFORD
Self-Publishing
Jim Manford asserts the moral right to be identified as the author of this work in accordance with the Design and Patents Act 1988

ALL RIGHTS RESERVED. Any unauthorised reprint or use of this material prohibited. No part of this book may be reproduced or transmitted in any form or by any means either electronic or mechanical, including photocopying, recording, or by any information storage and retrieval system without express written permission from the author/publisher

Cover photos

ISBN: 9798472729062
Imprint: Independently published

For my Grandson Bobby.

"Only those who will risk going too far, can possibly find out how far they can go."

About the Author

Jim Manford has been an active sportsman all his life; first as a competitive soccer player and later through the racquet sports of squash and tennis. In the early 1980s while training on the beaches of Australia for the forthcoming soccer season he discovered that the longer he ran the more he enjoyed it. This led to him entering his first marathon, the Perth Marathon in Western Australia in 1985. Since then he has completed over 300 marathons in 58 countries across 5 Continents (and counting!) These days he considers himself a dedicated Marathon Tourist – one who enjoys combining a love of running with a love of travel and who uses the marathon as the focal point that allows him to visit new cities in new countries on a regular basis.

Jim continues to run each day on the long sand-dune beaches near his homes in Northumberland and Spain. This is his thirteenth book about his favourite hobby.

By the same author:
Memories of a Marathon Man 2013
Marathon Tourism 2014
Marathon Tourism in Spain 2016
Marathon Tourist's Guidebook 2016
Marathon Bucket List 2016
Marathon Tourism USA 2017
Marathon Tourism in Europe's Capitals 2017
Marathon Tourism in Eastern Europe 2017
Marathon Tourism Down Under 2018
Island Marathons 2019
World's Most Exotic Marathons 2019
Marathon Tourism in Africa and Asia 2021

CONTENTS

Pages
7 Foreword
13 NETHERLANDS. Amsterdam Marathon
27 SPAIN. Barcelona Marathon
39 GERMANY. Hannover Marathon
49 NORWAY. Oslo Marathon
63 SLOVAKIA. Bratislava Marathon
75 PORTUGAL. Porto Marathon
85 MOROCCO. Marrakech Marathon
97 AUSTRIA. Linz Marathon
105 HUNGARY. Budapest Marathon
119 CZECH REPUBLIC. Prague Marathon
133 POLAND. Gdansk Marathon
145 ICELAND. Reykjavic Marathon
157 ESTONIA. Tallin Marathon
169 DENMARK. Hans Christian Andersen Marathon
179 BELGIUM. Brussels Marathon
191 GREECE. Athens Marathon
203 CYPRUS. Limassol Marathon
215 CANADA. Vancouver Marathon
231 LATVIA. Riga Marathon
245 FINLAND. Helsinki Marathon
257 AUSTRALIA. Sydney Marathon
273 REPUBLIC OF IRELAND. Dublin Marathon
283 TURKEY. Istanbul Marathon
299 MALTA. Malta Marathon
313 RUSSIA. St. Petersburg Marathon
329 CROATIA. Zagreb Marathon
343 SWITZERLAND. Lausanne Marathon
353 FRANCE. French Riviera Marathon
365 ITALY. Florence Marathon
379 EGYPT. Egyptian Marathon
395 ISRAEL. Tel Aviv Marathon
407 UNITED STATES OF AMERICA. Boston Marathon

419 NORTH MACEDONIA. Skopje Marathon
431 LUXEMBOURG. Luxembourg Night Marathon
445 SWEDEN. Stockholm Marathon
459 LITHUANIA. Kaunas Marathon
471 SOUTH AFRICA. Capetown Marathon
485 ROMANIA. Bucharest Marathon
503 SLOVENIA. Ljubljana Marathon
517 CUBA. Havana Marathon
529 UNITED ARAB EMIRATES. Dubai Marathon
539 FAROE ISLANDS. Torshavn Marathon
549 BELARUS. International Friendship Marathon
565 UKRAINE. Kiev Marathon
581 BULGARIA. Sofia Marathon
591 SERBIA. Novi Sad Marathon
599 MONTENEGRO. Podgorica Marathon
609 MOLDOVA. Chisinau Marathon
617 CHINA. Shanghai Marathon
633 MALAYSIA. Penang Bridge Marathon
643 Epilogue

FOREWORD

I've been running marathons around the globe since 1985 when I ran my first overseas marathon in Perth, Western Australia. In subsequent years work and family commitments (not to mention a severe shortage of money) meant that my overseas excursions were few and far between. Instead I contented myself with travelling the length and breadth of the UK in order to fulfil my goal of reaching the 100th marathon landmark. During that time I managed the occasional overseas adventure to marathons close to home like Amsterdam, Paris, Belfast and Dublin, while wishing I was in the position to travel further afield. Retirement in 2005 with its twin benefits of a healthy lump sum and a regular income provided the financial freedom to expand my running horizons. The purchase of an apartment in Spain on retirement inspired the idea of running a marathon in each of that country's 17 autonomous regions (similar to English counties). The next few years found me travelling the length and breadth of Spain, just as I'd done in the UK previously, running marathons in Barcelona, Madrid, Seville, Valencia, Bilbao, Zaragoza, Tenerife, Gran Canaria, Lanzarote, San Sebastian and so on and so forth. (I could go on but I think you get the gist). If not, the journey towards achieving that ambition is documented in my 2016 book 'Marathon Tourism in Spain.'

Within a few years I'd just about exhausted all the Spanish marathon possibilities and was once again looking for a new running adventure. By this stage I'd also reached the twin goals of running 200 marathons in over 20 different countries. I thought it unlikely, though not impossible, that I'd reach the 300 marathon mark. (I did!). I knew I didn't particularly want to keep on repeating the same old UK and Spanish marathons over and over again. I needed a new motivation. It came in the form of concentrating on running my marathons in countries I'd not yet visited. I'd always derived a great deal of pleasure in running in new cities in different countries; observing alternative cultures, lifestyles, sights, sounds and sampling the local food and drink (in the case of the latter, providing the opportunity to continue my never-ending search for the perfect strong, dark beer!). There's a whole world of marathons out there waiting to be explored, opening the door to a whole range of new experiences. Using the marathon as the focal point, what better way is there to sample the delights of a foreign city than to travel it on foot: all 26.2 miles of it - a kind of 'Marathon Tourism' if you like, the perfect combination of a love of travel and a love of running. Even the planning involved before travelling was enough to give me a buzz. I'm a firm believer in what Ernest Hemingway once said, 'It is good to have an end to journey toward; but it is the journey that matters in the end.'

As I documented in the introduction to my first book on overseas events, 'Marathon Tourism,' I'd been encouraged to write this in the form of a runner's guidebook by an article that had appeared in Runner's World magazine. Entitled '20 Races to do before you Die' it went on to list, by continent, a series of 20 races, 'sure to inspire you to add a few more races to your to-do list.' Basically, that's all it was: a list of 20 races, including the usual suspects like Paris, Berlin, Athens in Europe and New York, Chicago and Boston in the States among others. I'd done some of these and wouldn't necessarily have included them on my personal list of essential to-do events. As I wrote at the time, 'There was no explanation in the article as to why whoever had written it had chosen these events, no suggestion that the person involved had actually run any of them. It appeared more like a space-filling, lazy man's guide to running marathons; almost as if someone had trawled through a marathon calendar and simply written down the names of marathons that he or she thought should be included on the basis that most people would have heard of them.' Comments to this effect soon began to appear in the magazines Forum pages. Usually I ignore most of this cyber hot-air, finding that the comments of anonymous serial bloggers, unprepared to even use their real names, usually contribute little to meaningful debate. However, on this occasion the responses of someone rejoicing under the pseudonym of 'Cake' seemed to hit the nail right on the head. Our friend Cake felt that while it was all very well listing these 20 must-do events, what was needed was more information other than a link to the event's website, to help runners plan out a programme to get to each event. His suggestion was that Runners World should sponsor an 'every-day runner' on an all-expenses-paid visit to each of the 20 events to report back on the logistics involved. Unsurprisingly, he unselfishly volunteered himself for the job. His offer was never taken up, but it did get me thinking. Without moving Cake from his comfort zone and leaving him in peace to enjoy his confectionary pleasures, I decided to attempt to fill the void by reporting on all my future overseas marathons from the point of view of his mythical every-day runner.

This provided just the motivation needed for me to continue on my marathon globetrotting journey. As soon as the 'Marathon Tourism' book was published it was back to the drawing board: the endless hours on the computer analysing race calendars for suitable overseas events, pouring over maps on Google of how to get there, dissecting airline timetables for convenient and inexpensive flights as well as researching hotel booking sites for reasonably priced accommodation. Hard work, but nonetheless a labour of love. As I progressed with the planning a predictable pattern started to emerge. For each and every new marathon I considered going to, certain information needed to be known: how to get to the place itself, how to get from the airport to the city centre, where to stay, where and when to register, where were the best places to eat and drink from a runner's perspective, what exactly was the local cuisine and the best local beer and, most importantly of course, what was the marathon itself really like. How convenient it would have been if there'd simply been a 'Runner's Guide' available for each city, that specifically catered for runners' needs on their visits in the same way that there's guidebooks available for various other interest groups. While 'Marathon Tourism' made no claims to be anything like the type of guidebook described, I decided that for every new marathon I entered I'd attempt to answer the questions I personally would have liked to have known the answers to before setting off. Rather than simply state the facts under guidebook style headings, a careful read of the following chapters will see that I've attempted to cover most of the points I mention within the narrative.

At this stage of my running career I thought of, and described myself, as a 'Marathon Tourist' – a collective term for runners who, like me, espoused a lifestyle philosophy of combining their love of running with their love of travel and visiting new countries. Gradually, I found myself accompanied on my travels by a number of like-minded runners, mainly from the UK 100 Marathon Club. It seemed only a matter of time before someone recognised the ever-expanding interest in running overseas marathons and channelled this into a more formal structure. In 2015 a new club, Marathon Globetrotters, was born to 'Promote global friendships among those who run marathons in many countries.' I joined later that year and can now officially describe myself as a Marathon Globetrotter. (Though, I'm just as comfortable with the term 'Marathon Tourist.' The two are virtually interchangeable and are used as such in this book). I've currently completed well over 100 overseas marathons in 58 different countries (and hopefully still counting). Most of these have been in the 10 years between 2009 and pre-Covid 2019. This is a mere drop in the ocean compared to the tallies of some of my Globetrotter club colleagues, many of who have completed marathons in much more than 100 different countries around the world. I take my hat off to them for their achievements. I've a long way to go to catch up with them!

In the meantime, to keep busy during the various lockdowns we've been forced to endure, I've produced this compilation of the 50 favourite marathons I've run in 50 of the different countries I've visited. Those of you familiar with all the books in my 'Marathon Tourism' series will recognize many of these from their reading. Where possible I have attempted to update what was written previously to reflect changing circumstances. Although care has been taken in trying to provide accurate, up-to-date information, marathons frequently change their entry requirements, arrangements at the start and at the finish, courses, sponsors and Expo locations so always double-check to see if what I've written is still in place. All errors of a factual nature are entirely my responsibility.

It's Official! 50 Countries Certificate

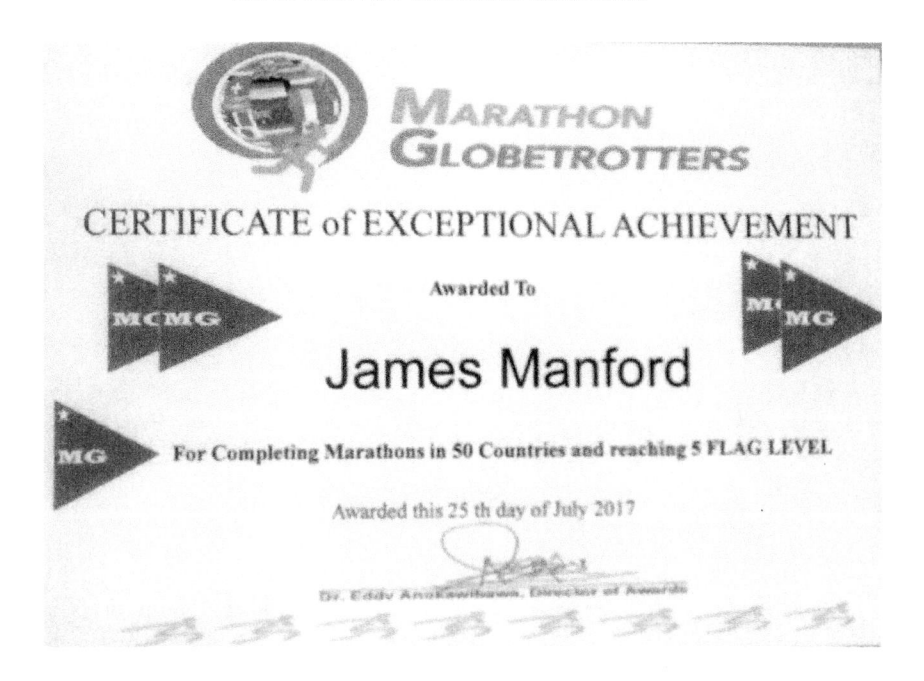

MARATHON GLOBETROTTERS

CERTIFICATE of EXCEPTIONAL ACHIEVEMENT

Awarded To

James Manford

For Completing Marathons in 50 Countries and reaching 5 FLAG LEVEL

Awarded this 25 th day of July 2017

Dr. Eddy Anakaviharan, Director of Awards

THE NETHERLANDS

AMSTERDAM MARATHON

This was to be my first marathon outside the UK since running in Perth, Western Australia some 16 years previously. The time had come to dip my toes into the waters of overseas marathons and Amsterdam, with its proximity to my home near Newcastle, was a cheap and cheerful option with which to start my Marathon Globetrotting journey. Though I went initially in 2001, the description that follows is mainly about my return visit to the city in 2013.

Before we start let's clear a couple of things up. Many people confuse Holland with the Netherlands. They think they're interchangeable. They're not. The Netherlands (officially the Kingdom of the Netherlands) didn't come into existence until after Napoleon in the 19th century. At that stage, two of the twelve provinces in The Netherlands had the name Holland, specifically North Holland and South Holland. The major cities of Amsterdam, Rotterdam and The Hague are located in these two provinces. The confusion arises from the time of the Dutch Golden Age of exploration in the 17th century when most ships came from the two provinces now called North Holland and South Holland. As the Netherlands did not exist at that time, when the sailors where asked where they came from they would respond with the name of their province – 'Holland'. Ever since Holland has been a synonym for the area that would later be called The Netherlands. A similar confusion arises over which city is considered to be the nation's Capital. Some will say Amsterdam, others nominate Den Haag (The

Hague) - on the basis that a nation's capital is usually the city in which the government resides. This is not so in the case of the Netherlands. According to the Dutch constitution, Amsterdam is the capital of the Netherlands, although the parliament and the Dutch government have been situated in The Hague since 1588, along with the Supreme Court and the Council of State. Surprisingly, the only reference in the Constitution stating that Amsterdam is the capital came as recently as 1983 when that year's revision of the Constitution specifically mentioned that 'the King shall be sworn in and inaugurated as soon as possible in the capital city.' Sorted! I'm rather pleased that Amsterdam and not the Hague is the capital – I've not got round to running The Hague's own marathon yet.

The 2013 version of the event wasn't on my original to-do list. I'd already run the event in 2001 and wasn't in any hurry to go back when there were so many other marathons in other countries I'd yet to run. The itinerary I'd mapped out for 2013 had the Bergen Marathon in Norway down for the same weekend. I'd probably have ended up there too, had a friend not phoned to say that he'd an Amsterdam entry he was unable to use due to illness. As Bergen was entry-on-the-day and I hadn't yet booked the flights or finalised arrangements to go, I asked for 24 hours to consider taking his place in Amsterdam as an alternative. (By that stage I couldn't enter Amsterdam in my own name as online entries had already closed). To tell you the truth, I wasn't too happy with both the cost of the Newcastle – Bergen flight and the fact that I'd have to spend long hours in Stavanger waiting to change planes both there and back. Weekend flights from Newcastle to Amsterdam appeared both a lot less costly and a lot more convenient. So it was off to Amsterdam instead. This would be the first time that I'd run any sort of race wearing someone else's number. It's not something I'd normally advocate or condone. As a Race Organiser, I've seen at first hand some of the problems it can cause. After our first Newcastle Town Moor Marathon I'd had to deal with the aftermath of a young-looking 20-something coming in first place wearing the number of an entrant in the Vet 50 category. It plays havoc with the results as well as annoying fellow runners who end up being wrongly placed in their age groups. There wasn't much chance of that happening on this occasion though. My friend with the spare race number was in a category many years younger than mine. There was, as they say, no way I was going to trouble the scorers in Amsterdam. I half expected to have to come clean at Registration when they requested identity on picking up the number; but no one bothered to ask.

I'd been to Amsterdam twice previously – once as a tourist and on the second occasion to have my first crack at the city's marathon. Both visits had been many moons ago and, while I was familiar with the basic layout of the city I expected to see changes on this occasion. My first visit in the early 70s had been at the height of the hippy culture with which the city became rightly or wrongly associated. There was a permissiveness about the place that reflected its citizens' live-and-let live, philosophy towards life. That attitude appeared to have been well and truly exploited by the unscrupulousness of drug dealers and pornographers who, allowed to flourish, had begun to tarnish the city's image and reputation. Public attitudes and official policy is said to have hardened in recent years and I understand that the municipal government has since taken action to reduce some of the worst excesses. Nonetheless, I found on my second visit in 2001 that there were still aspects to Amsterdam's character able to shock the unprepared visitor. Many people, however, choose to come to Amsterdam because of its reputation for open-mindedness. Prostitution, for example is legalised, licensed and still very visible in Amsterdam. Likewise, the sale, possession and use of cannabis, though technically illegal is tolerated under the policy of 'gedogen' (I think this translates as 'turning a blind eye') I was to find plenty evidence of both during this latest visit.

Amsterdam derived from 'Amstelredamme' (or 'dam across the River Amstel') is the country's largest city and its financial, cultural and creative centre. It has come to be known as the Venice of the North because of its extensive canal system, traditional architecture and over 1,500 bridges - taking one of the many canal boat cruises is a recommended way to see the best of this canal-threaded city.

Beginning life as a small fishing village in the 12 century, Amsterdam became one of the world's most important trading centres during the Dutch Golden Age of the 17th century. It rapidly expanded following the construction of the Canal Belt neighbourhoods and its cultural significance was eventually acknowledged when it became a UNESCO World Heritage Site in 2010. Though now a huge, sprawling urban area with its satellite outer suburbs, the Amsterdam most of us experience on our visits is the semi-circular inner area of six concentric canals with the Central Station and Dam Square at its apex.

The Central Station was to be my first port of call after arrival at Schiphol Airport late on the Friday night. I needed to get from there to my room at the Hotel de Paris near Leidseplein on the 6th of these canals and knew, from previous visits, that the best way of doing this was by tram from the station. Schiphol, one of the world's busiest airports is situated some 13km south west of the city centre. Direct trains taking 20 minutes to the Central Station run at frequent intervals and cost approximately 4 euros from a machine, (50 cents extra at a counter). Remember to buy a single, second class that is valid on Sprinter, Inter City and night trains – but not the Thalys. The station at Schiphol is located underground – be careful though, there's two separate rail lines. Make sure you get the one going to Amsterdam Centraal, usually platform 3, and not to Amsterdam Zuid. Once at the Central Station it's a simple matter to take one of the many trams from the terminus there to your eventual destination. All tram stops have an easy-to-follow detailed map of the system and the surrounding area. Most trams have conductors on the rear of the tram from whom 1 or 24 hour tickets can be bought. You have to punch the ticket when boarding or alighting the tram. There's also a four line metro system serving the neighbourhoods of the South East. The marathon's organisers suggest taking Metro line 51 from Central Station towards Amstelveen Middenhoven, changing at station Zuid/WTC then Sneltram number 50 towards Isolatorweg and getting off at Amstelveenseweg for the Olympic Stadium start on the Sunday.

This sounds complicated to me. Fortunately I'd chosen a hotel within reasonable walking distance of the start.

I'd arrived too late on the Friday night to do anything but head straight to the hotel for a good night's sleep. The plan was to register early next morning, leaving myself the remainder of the day for sightseeing. Registration took place on Saturday from 9am until 7 pm in the giant Sports Hall, (Sportshallen Zuid), part of the Olympic Stadium complex. This was an approximately 2.5km walk from my hotel via the very autumnal Vondelpark, Amsterdam's largest park, which we were to run through twice the next day. Even an early start didn't fail to avoid the crowds that were already beginning to gather. The Expo there was a much bigger affair than normal, with numerous other European marathons represented and a wide selection of retailers pushing their running-related products. I even managed a couple of freebie samples of food and drink. On presentation of our registration letter, (or in my case someone else's), we were given our number, chip and a rather decent Mizuno T-shirt. There was even a separate version of the shirt for female entrants. I decided against the Pasta Party later that day, backing myself to find somewhere not only less crowded but also better value-for-money than the 15 euros wanted by the organizers. Entry alone had already cost me 65 euros.

I re-traced my steps back to Leidseplein, this time along De Lairessestraat to Museum Square, home to three major museums: the Stedelijk, Museum of Modern Art, the Van Gough and the Rijksmuseum. The latter is one of Amsterdam's major highlights (for those who like museums). It had recently re-opened after major renovation and the building is a vast neo-Gothic palace containing the national art collection of the Netherlands. Apparently it's a veritable treasure house of paintings, applied art, porcelain, silver and Asiatic sculpture. Having been informed that it's far too big to absorb in one visit I gave it the once-over while scurrying past! My itinerary for that afternoon involved taking the number 5 tram up towards the station area and having a look around the city centre and its canal streets.

The lively Central Station is worth a visit in its own right. It bustles with the combined energy of people on the move: there's cafes, shops, buskers, barrel-organs, bicycles, commuters, tourists, backpackers, junkies and pickpockets. In short, it's the perfect place for a bit of people-watching – one of the fundamental pleasures of being a marathon tourist. Designed by the same architect who designed the Rijksmuseum in the same neo-Gothic style, it opened in 1889, having been constructed on three artificial islands in the IJ channel. It's my favourite place in Amsterdam. The Japanese liked it so much they even modelled their Tokyo Station on it. A short walk away is Damrak, not to be confused with Dam Square. Now a duck pond this is all that remains of the city's original harbour. Dam Square, or as the locals call it 'the Dam,' was the original dam built in the 13th century to protect what was then a fishing village. As the city expanded, flood defences were built further afield and the Square, with its Royal Palace, became the political, commercial and ceremonial heart of the city.

Though Amsterdam is a fairly compact city to walk around there's two much better alternative ways of seeing the sights. One of these is to hire a bike and pedal your way around. I did that last time I was there and thoroughly enjoyed it. This time I wanted to see it from the water via the hop-on-hop-off Canal Bus system that takes you through all the famous canals, past the typical canal houses, houseboats and beautiful bridges. It's much more marathon-tourist friendly than either walking or cycling, in keeping you off your feet the day before a marathon. The Canal Buses operate on the same principle as London's get-on, get-off sightseeing buses with no reservations required; just a ticket. This could be bought online at the time for 18 euros for a day ticket or 19.80 euros for 24 hours. I bought the former which is interchangeable on any of the 4 colour-coded lines, (green, red, blue and orange), serving 19 stops in total. The green line for example, visited among other places the Central Station, Ann Frank's House, the Rijksmuseum, Leidseplein, Rembrant Square, City Hall and Rembrandt's House. I spent a happy few hours chugging along listening to the commentary, alighting initially to pay a visit to the house in which the Frank family hid with friends for two years during the Nazi occupation. This provides an unsettling glimpse of the claustrophobic lives the family led. Seeing Ann's diary, sitting behind a glass case, is a particularly poignant reminder of a tragic life. I got off a couple of more times to break the journey before changing over to the blue line to visit the Passenger Terminal and Transport Museum. After that I changed again for another water-based form of transport and took one of the free GVB ferries from the north side of the station on the 15 minute service over the River IJ to NDSM Werf. A great way to spend an afternoon.

I returned in the evening to Leidseplein, knowing that I was bound to find somewhere suitable for a pre-race pasta meal among its numerous Italian restaurants and pizza houses. This is a really vibrant section of the city pulsing with bars, restaurants, clubs and theatres. This large open square was developed in the 17th century as a wagon park for farmers to leave their horses and carts before entering the city centre. The name comes from the fact that this used to be where the road from Amsterdam to Leiden began. A couple of restaurants had been recommended as suitable; the Incanto on Muntplein and the Saturnino next to the Flower Market. Both looked a little pricey for my needs and I eventually settled on the 3 course pasta menu at a small Italian restaurant just off the Square on Hobbemastraat before retiring for a fairly early night.

Next morning it was back through the Vondelpark for the first of four times that day for the 9.30 am start at the Olympic Stadium. This stadium bears little resemblance to the modern structures built recently for the Sydney, Beijing and London Games, having been constructed initially for the 1928 Olympics. It's certainly seen some changes over the years. Its initial capacity of approximately 32,000 was doubled in 1937 by the addition of an extra ring following the completion of a rival stadium in Rotterdam. AFC Ajax actually used it as their home ground until 1996 and in 1962 the European Cup Final was held there – I'm old enough to remember Benfica beating Real Madrid 5-3 on that occasion. 1987 saw it listed as a national monument, leading to a complete renovation in 1996 where the second ring was demolished and the capacity reduced to around

22,000. It's now primarily a track and field venue, no longer suitable for football matches. I've mentioned in other books how much I enjoy finishing on an athletics track. Here we were going to start on one as well.

The sense of occasion built up as supporters started to fill up the grandstand and runners poured on to the track to take up their places behind the designated pacers. These had been arranged in 15 minute intervals from 3 hours and 15 minutes to 4 hours 30 though, surprisingly, there were no slower groups considering the 6 hour time limit for the race. It was a special feeling to realise that you were on the same track as athletes who'd actually started an Olympic marathon on that spot. The runners in the other two main events that day; the Half Marathon at 1.20pm and the 8k at 10.10am were not to have that privilege. Both of these started in the streets outside the stadium with only their finishes on the track. The Amsterdam Marathon is certainly a huge international event with over 17,000 overseas athletes, representing 82 different nationalities, registered among the 41,000 runners in the series of races held on the day. It turned out that well over 11,000 started the marathon, 14,000 the Half and over 4,000 the 8k. There were also a number of children's races making up the numbers. This was to be the 38th edition of what has become an IAAF Gold Label event.

I felt a bit more confident in myself for this one than I had in my previous marathon two weeks earlier. The illness that had laid me so low for that event had been diagnosed as a nasty kidney infection for which I'd since been treated with strong antibiotics. Unfortunately, the doctors found a large kidney stone engulfing my left kidney - the cause of the infection, for which I've been waiting several months at the mercy of the NHS to have surgically removed. When that happens the running will have to come to a stop, hence my concern to keep on running while I still can. Because of this I'd set myself no time-specific goals for this event though I did hope that I could manage a sub-4 hour 30 minutes finish. After taking over 10 minutes to pass the Start line before jogging a half lap of the athletics track, we emerged into the broad Amstelveensveg for the first loop of the two-lap course. This wasn't so much a loop as a square of about 7km, taking us around the points of the compass and back to near the start. At the top of Amstelveensveg we turned east to run through Vondelpark for the first time before a sharp turn at the Rijksmuseum had us heading south to cross the canal shortly after 5k. We then ran westwards again along the wide Stadium Way to the Sportspark and a mini-loop up Marathon Way to turn us around and back from whence we'd just arrived. This meant heading back along the other side of Stadium Way with runners running in both directions. Crowd support here was excellent and by this stage the runners had begun to thin out allowing space to look around and take it all in instead of having to watch where you put your feet.

The second, much larger loop of 35km started at the eastern end of Stadium Way. This took us initially along streets named after former world leaders, Churchill and Kennedy to the southern end of Martin Luther King Park and the River Amstel at about 13km. There then followed what was to me the best bit of the course. For next 12 to 13km we ran on both sides of the river in first a southerly and then, after a bridge turn, in a northerly direction against a strong headwind. It was nice to be out of the city and to have views of fields and windmills instead of buildings and concrete. The one downside was that you could see exactly where you were in the scheme of things with the faster runners surging ahead on the opposite bank.

Leaving the river at 26km we spent the next 7km running through the most uninspiring part of the course; an industrial landscape consisting largely of factories, warehouses and railway lines. I found myself flagging at this point, even the bands playing en route couldn't keep me going and I started the first of a series of run/walk breaks after stopping at the 30k drinks station. These stations were at regular intervals throughout with water, lemon sports drinks and sponges at all of them supplemented by bananas after 16km and with energy gels at 30km and 38km – so no complaints there. Things began picking up again on emerging beside a canal at 33km. I don't know whether it was being beside water again or the fact that we'd only got single figures to go, but I was able to continue at a steady running pace. At 35km we turned westwards again for the final slog towards the finish, encountering supportive crowds once more on our way through the city streets. First came Mauriskade and then Stadhouderskade, both long, straight avenues, with the latter taking us back to the Rijksmuseum for the second time. All that remained was to re-negotiate the Vondelpark again, this time from the opposite direction, to pass the 40km mark just before its exit. From here on in you could sense the approaching stadium and hear the noise from its sound system and the cheering of the crowd within. A final part-lap of the track and it was over. I'd finished within the hoped for four and a half hours; mission accomplished and another one done and dusted. Mind you, I'd have been disappointed to have taken much longer on what, given Amsterdam's below sea-level, location, was a perfectly flat course throughout. Armed with my medal, a couple of sports drinks and a banana I left immediately for a hot hotel shower. The return took me back the way I'd just run and through the Vondelpark for the final time that day, shouting encouragement to the back-markers as they negotiated their final few kilometres.

That night I headed back into town for a bite to eat and a walk on the wild side; after all no visit to Amsterdam would be complete without a wander through its famous Red Light District, (purely for observational purposes, of course). Unless your expertise involves cheese, the Netherlands doesn't appear to have a distinctively Dutch cuisine. What it does have is some pretty good Indonesian restaurants, the legacy of its former colonisation of the Dutch East Indies. Most of these offer a range of 'rijstafels' (rice tables) - set menus consisting of from 15 to 45 different dishes served with rice and a hot chilli sauce called 'sambal' I found what I wanted in the Kantjil restaurant on Suistraat serving Indonesian fare at a reasonable price. The Nasi Rames, a mini –rijstafel, was particularly good value.

A short walk from here takes you into the heart of the Red Light District. This part of town is known as 'De Wallen' (The Walls), after the city walls that once stood here. The two canals in which it's largely contained; Oodezijds Voorburgwal and Achterburgwal are lined with lovely 16th and 17th century houses, many of them put to uses their Calvinist builders would definitely find objectionable. Despite the minimal risks of going there, the area remains an essential part of the Amsterdam experience, as evidenced by the large number of tour groups wandering its streets at all times of the day. Be mindful though that tourists are strongly advised not to photograph the women as both they and their minders tend to react strongly to this. (It's just as well that I forgot to pack my camera on this trip). The red-light district is a pragmatic solution to a perennial problem. Under Dutch law, soliciting is illegal but what the girls and their clients do in the privacy of what is regarded as their home is considered to be their own business. Hence, the large number of 'rooms to rent' signs around the place: officially the money that changes hands is room rent and not payment for services rendered. These services complement a whole range of live shows, peep-shows, massage parlours, video libraries and assorted sex shops all concentrated into a small area. Ironically, the neon-lit setting looks even more colourful at night and I spent an interesting hour or so taking in the scene before heading to a couple of the nearby canal-side bars. In the first of these bars, the aptly named Red Light Bar and Coffee Shop on the corner of Monnikenstraat, I was able to sit by the window with my pint of Amstel and look across the canal to windows full of girls and their gawking potential customers. (This marathon tourism certainly gets you to some strange places)

As a footnote I have to say that Amsterdam was not the place to continue my quest for the perfect dark beer. (It's a long story!) I was disappointed with the range of beers offered in the Red Light Bar. These seemed to consist mainly of lager brands commonly found in the UK. The bar at Café Remember further along the canal was no better either. It seems that the Netherlands specializes largely in pale lagers brewed by the likes of Heineken, Grolsch and Amstel who account for 95% of the country's total beer consumption. Even the most common alternative is called 'witbier' (white beer) – definitely not in the dark category. The quality of the beer certainly didn't spoil the quality of the day. A visit to Amsterdam has to be an essential component of every marathon tourist's itinerary.

The Rijksmuseum. Photo courtesy of jennieramida (Unsplash)

Programme for my first overseas marathon: Amsterdam 2001

SPAIN

BARCELONA MARATHON

I followed the 2001 Amsterdam Marathon with a couple of memorable trips to the Paris Marathon in 2002 and 2004. (This event has been so well-documented that I've decided to include one of my other French marathons in this compilation). My next overseas marathon wasn't until the Barcelona Marathon of 2007. It's an event that I've returned to again and again since then. It's become one of my 'local' events while staying at my apartment in Spain, being a reasonably cheap four hour train ride up the coast from Alicante. The route has become one I'm familiar with since purchasing the apartment in 2005, having used it also for marathons in Valencia, Castellon, Benidorm and, more recently, Tarragona. I'm always happy to make Spanish inter-city rail journeys. Their trains, with on-board videos and plentiful leg-room, are so much more comfortable and relaxing than their British counterparts. The train drops you off at the Barcelona-Sants station just a short walk from Registration and the race's Start at the Plaza Espana. Those coming by air have the choice between frequent bus and train services for the thirty minute journey into Sants from El Prat airport. The Aerobus service will also take you into the Placa de Catalunya in the very heart of town. At the time of writing, single tickets cost 6 euros by bus and 4 euros by train. Once in the centre there's an excellent Metro service to get you to wherever you need to go. You can buy tickets for individual metro journeys for 2.15 euros. However, if you're staying for more than one day or planning on making more than 5 journeys on any form of public transport, by far the most cost-effective thing to do is to purchase a T10 ticket costing 9.95 euros. Available for purchase from outside any metro station, this will entitle you to 10 journeys on metro, bus, train or tram – saving you 11.55 euros if used in full.

I wish I could say that I've been equally as happy with the accommodation I've used when arriving in Barcelona. On one occasion Mo and I splashed out on the 4-star Hotel Derby in a quiet part of town, figuring we'd get a good night's sleep there on the night before the race. We hadn't bargained on the same venue playing host to a noisy bunch of American cultural exchange students whose ideas on culture seemed to mainly involve partying all-night long. On another visit we rented an apartment for the weekend in what was regarded as an up-market area. Instead of meeting us with the keys on arrival as arranged, the landlord's agent kept us waiting outside on the pavement for over an hour. His excuse would have shamed the naughtiest of naughty schoolboys and was not well received. Neither were we happy on waking next morning to find vagrants, having by-passed the 'secure' entry system, sleeping in numbers on the stairs. The next time, being on my own and with minimal expectations, I simply took pot-luck on accommodation available and, paying homage to one of my favourite groups, booked a couple of nights at the low-price Hotel California. Located just off La Rambla, the city's most famous thoroughfare, this proved the best place yet to stay on any of my visits.

Barcelona is undoubtedly one of the most vibrant and exciting cities in Europe. With an urban population of 1.6 million it's the capital city of the autonomous community of Catalonia and the second largest city in Spain. Founded initially as a Roman city, it later became an important city in the Crown of Aragon. Having been besieged several times during its history, it has a rich cultural heritage and is now one of the world's leading tourist destinations containing a number of UNESCO World Heritage Sites. There's an awful lot about the city that makes it a unique place to visit. It contains some outstanding examples of Gothic and Art Nouveau architecture, particularly the buildings of Antoni Gaudi – the city's most famous son, as well as a number of important art museums dedicated to the likes of Picasso and Joan Miro. In a city noted for its passion for sport, the award of the 1992 Olympics was not only an important boost to its status, but also led to the regeneration of much of Barcelona's infrastructure. Today, it's influence in commerce, education, media, fashion, science and the arts all contribute to its status as one of the world's major global cities. It's certainly a city that should be on any marathon tourist's itinerary. It even boasts a beach that was rated by National Geographic at number one in a list of the top ten city beaches in the world.

Despite its size, Barcelona is a surprisingly easy place to explore on foot. Most visitors make immediately for La Ciutat Vella (the Old Town) – the medieval heart of the city, characterised by its narrow streets and historic buildings. This area spreads northwest from the harbour for 1.5 kilometres, bisected by everyone's favourite street: the Rambla. (This actually consists of five separate streets linked into one).The name derives from the Arabic 'rambla' meaning torrent and is a reminder that the street marks the course of a once seasonal river. In the dry season the channel created by the water was used as a road linking the harbour with the old town. Eventually it was paved over, trees were planted and the surroundings landscaped so that today it provides a pedestrianised refuge in a city choked with traffic. It's a great place to stroll along and observe all that's taking place, from stalls selling everything under the sun to con men, tricksters, buskers and pavement artists. As with many places in Barcelona you should keep a close eye on your wallet – the city has an unfortunate reputation for pickpockets and petty crime.

Barcelona has hosted a marathon since 1978 when the race started in the coastal village of Mataro,, located on the Costa Brava to the northeast of the city. These early marathons were not pure city courses like today but provided the prototype for that run during the Olympic Games in 1992. On that occasion the race ended in the Olympic Stadium on Montjuic, the hill overlooking the present Start and Finish. From 2001, the marathon changed to become a pure city marathon. In 2005, however, following disagreement over the route it was relocated into an area between

Castelldefels and the resort of Sitges. The following year after cooperation between the organisers and the city authorities, the race returned to the city centre. Since then the Barcelona Marathon has consolidated itself as the fourth largest marathon in Europe behind London, Berlin and Paris and ahead of rivals Stockholm and Rome. From just over 10,000 finishers in 2010, a high of over 16,000 finishers was reached in 2012. Since then finishing numbers, particularly of overseas runners, has declined somewhat. It currently ranks in the Top 15 on the list of world marathons.

The current, staggered entry fee structure makes it best to commit early for the race. Being among the first 10,000 to enter in 2015 cost me 61.50 euros. It then increases to 73 euro for entrants between 10,000 and 17,000 and to 84 euros after that. According to the website there were 19,179 entries that year. Hotels in the city, convenient for the race, also sell-out early on marathon weekend so, again, it's best to get in early if you don't want to find yourself in some out-of-town location. Registration takes place on the Friday and Saturday at a giant Sports Exhibition in Pavillion 8 of the Fira de Barcelona, outside of which the race will start and finish. There's also a free Saturday morning Breakfast Run for the first 2,000 to enter, (the marathon alone is enough for me.) The Fira is Barcelona's trade fair institution and one of the most important in Europe. Every year it brings together numerous trade shows and congresses, allowing leading companies from different economic centres to showcase their products. On marathon weekend there are more than 200 exhibitors of a running related nature, attracting over 60,000 to the Expo. A Saturday number pick-up is best avoided unless you particularly want to make use of your free Pasta Party pass for runner and guest. I usually go to this despite the crowds – the food served is always good value, plus it provides a chance to catch up with running friends.

The area immediately surrounding the Fira, totally taken over by the marathon on race day, is an interesting one to visit in its own right. Looming over the proceedings is the steep hill of Montjuic, by far the largest green area in the city. Its name is derived from the Jewish community that once lived on its slopes and there's been a fortress on its heights since the mid-seventeenth century. It served as a prison, often holding political prisoners, until Franco's time. The eastern side of the hill forms a sheer cliff, giving it a commanding view over the harbour below. Since being selected for the site of the 1929 World's Fair, Montjuic has become Barcelona's greatest cultural asset. There's so much to see and do on the hill it's best to allocate a full day for any visit. The surviving buildings from the Fair include the grand Palau Nacional, the Olympic Stadium, the ornate Magic Fountains, (switched on for the start of the marathon), and a grand staircase leading up from the foot of the hill (usually littered with exhausted marathon runners after the event). The Poble Espanyol, meant to replicate a typical Spanish village, also survives and is a much visited attraction.

The hill also holds a certain fascination for lovers of sport. The Olympic Stadium, for example, was intended to host an anti-fascist alternative Olympics in opposition to Hitler's Berlin Games of 1936. These plans were scuppered by the outbreak of the Spanish Civil War. In 1992 the stadium was extensively refurbished to host the athletic events of the Summer Olympics as well as the opening and closing ceremonies. Around it an 'Olympic Ring' of sporting venues was constructed, including an indoor arena, venues for swimming and diving plus a centre for sports science. The main stadium remained the home of La Liga football club Espanyol until 2008. I was fortunate to attend one of their matches there on one of my previous visits to the marathon. A less well known fact about the hill is its use in the past as motor racing venue. The roads on the slopes facing the city were once the Montjuic Formula One racing circuit, hosting the Spanish Grand Prix on several occasions. Unfortunately, a fatal accident in 1975 that saw one of the cars crash into the stands, killing four people, resulted in the Grand Prix moving elsewhere. For those runners wanting to save their legs for the race, the top of the hill can be reached using a funicular railway that operates as part of the Barcelona metro system. There's also an Aerial Tramway connecting Montjuic with the Barceloneta beach area.

The marathon starts outside the Feria at 8.30am in the Avenida de la Reina Maria Cristina linking Montjuic to the Placa d'Espana. The atmosphere begins to build up to a crescendo long before then with loud music, fireworks and noisy tannoy announcements. Runners are segregated according to finishing times over the 6 hour time limit with pacemakers in attendance to achieve quarter- hour time goals between 2 hours 45 and 4 hours 30 minutes. Runners finally set off to the strains of Freddie Mercury's epic 'Barcelona' and huge cheers from the thousands lining the start area. It's a wonderful spectacle for over 20 minutes or more before the final runner clears the start line. What follows is a Marathon Tourist's dream of a course as the route deliberately takes us past the best that the city has to offer.

Almost immediately we pass between the twin Venetian Towers at the junction with the Placa d'Espana. Modelled on the campanile of St Mark's Basilica in Venice, they were constructed in 1929 as part of the areas redevelopment for the World Fair. They serve an ornamental function to mark the entrance to the exhibition district now known as the Fira. Now registered as protected structures of local interest, they were originally open to the public, who were allowed to climb the internal stairs to the viewing galleries. As we stream through the Placa d'Espana heading inland, it's a sobering thought to remember that it was built on a site once used for public hangings. Today it's the junction of several major and very busy thoroughfares, including the Gran Via and the Av. Del Parallel, along which we were both yet to run.

The crowds start to thin out after the first couple of kilometres though the course remains uncomfortable and congested. Though it's heralded as a flat, fast course capable of producing fast times, I'm never happy in crowded big-city events where every bit of space has to be fought over with fellow runners. It's probably the main reason why I've never really achieved a decent finishing time in Barcelona. These days I simply relax and enjoy the sights. Next up at 6km is the New Camp stadium, home to Barcelona FC since 1957. The route takes us through the car park of the giant stadium, capable of holding over 99,000 fans, making it the largest football venue in Europe and the fourth largest in the world. It has hosted numerous international matches and two UEFA Champions League finals as well as the 1992 Olympic Games final. Unlike its fierce rival, the Bernabeu Stadium in Madrid, it has changed little over the years and lacks many of the modern facilities common in most stadiums today. For many years the club has been investigating the options of either redeveloping the stadium or constructing a new one elsewhere. Many runners with a love of soccer make the effort to take one of the self-guided tours on offer. Entitled the Camp Nou Experience, this includes a walk through the stadium with audio guide plus a visit to the club's museum.

The route then turns for 2km into the Av. Diagonal, one of the city's broadest and most important avenues dividing the city between west and east. At this point on-course conditions start to get a little less congested. Then just after 10km we make our way east along Av. Tarragona back towards the Placa d'Espana from whence we started. Located in the Parc Joan Miro on our left is one of the more unusual sights on the course. This is the huge 22-metre high sculpture Dona i Ocell (Woman and Bird) whose phallic-like appearance usually provides some degree of mirth among the runners. The sculpture is part of an artwork trilogy commissioned from the sculptor Joan Miro to welcome visitors to Barcelona. The first of the trilogy is at the airport, the second in La Rambla but neither have become as famous (or should that be infamous) as this one. The work uses some of Miro's recurring themes of women and birds. Apparently, the Catalan word for a bird is also a term for a penis and the sculpture was originally titled 'The Cock' until the city authorities suggested otherwise!

After the levity near the Parc, the route takes another turn – this time to the north along the Gran Via towards the enormous and constantly overcrowded Placa de Catalunya. This gigantic square functions as a hub for the city's public transport network. Below the square lies the main subway junction; three metro lines and a city railway line. Many of the city's buses, as well as the airport express and tourist buses stop at the square. It's a place best avoided if possible. No less than nine streets emanate from the square including the Passeig de Gracia into which we now turn at 14km into the race. Here we're confronted for the first time by one of the city's remarkable buildings designed by Antoni Gaudi. The building is the Casa Mira, commonly nicknamed La Pedrera (The Quarry) the last civil work designed by Gaudi and built between the years 1906 and 1910.

Gaudi's work is admired internationally for its distinctive and unique architectural styles. Influenced more by forms of nature than traditional architectural ideas, they appear radically different from those of his contemporaries. Natural curved construction stones, organic-like shapes and twisted ironwork are all characteristic traits of Gaudi's work. His use of coloured mosaic tiles also added a refreshing visual dimension to the many, stunning examples of his architecture that enrich Barcelona's city centre. Not everyone approved of his work. La Pedrera's unconventional style provoked much criticism with many claiming it would lower the price of land in their area. To me, it looks fantastic! Before seeing it for the first time I never realised that buildings could be fun as well as functional.

Waiting round the corner at the 16km mark is Gaudi's most noted work; the internationally-famous Sagrada Familia. Begun in 1892 by public subscription, Gaudi devoted his last years to the project before being run over by a tram in 1926. By this stage the work was less than a quarter complete. Today, the church remains unfinished, though amid great controversy work restarted in the late 1950s and is still continuing with completion date now said to coincide with the anniversary of Gaudi's death in 2016. The scale of the building is enormous. Eight spires, likened to everything from perforated cigars to celestial billiard cues, soar to over 100 metres. For Gaudi they were symbols of the Twelve Apostles. He also planned to build four more above the main façade and to add a 180 metre tower topped with a lamb and surrounded by a further four smaller towers symbolising Matthew, Mark, Luke and John. La Sagrada Familia attracts around 3 million visitors a year, whose entrance fees pay much of the annual 25 million euro cost of continuing its construction. Gifts from private donors make up the rest. The building has a mesmerising effect on all who see it. Many runners stop at this point to take selfies of themselves next to the iconic building. (The next time I witnessed so many runners stood motionless during a race was to be when running over the Harbour Bridge during the Sydney Marathon). Both La Pedrera and the Sagrada Familia are listed World Heritage Sites.

After the wonder of the Sagrada Familia there's little else of note before reaching the turn at 20km and running back on the opposite side to emerge at the northern end of the Gran Via. There follows another long, undistinguished out-and-back from 26km to 31km on the Av. Diagonal. Crowd support is minimal on both of these long stretches and it's rather dispiriting to see faster runners running away in the opposite direction. During the latter stretch we run first towards and then away from the skyscraper tower of Torre Agbar which marks the gateway to the city's new technological district. Since opening in 2005, this huge tower has become an architectural icon and is now the venue where thousands of locals choose to congregate for New Year celebrations.

Things improve on finally reaching the coast at 32km. We run along here for 3kms or so, taking in the sea views before making a sharp right turn at the twin Mapfre Towers. After this the route passes a number of the more interesting sights in the Old Town quarter. Here, the crowds of spectators are supplemented by thousands of tourists and locals stopping to watch the procession of runners streaming past. First up is the Parc de la Ciutadella, for decades the only park in the city. Within its 70 acres is the Parliament of Catalunya, a lake, a modern art museum and Gaudi's imposing Cascada monumental Baroque fountain. The Park is perhaps most famous for being the home to the city's zoo. For many years until its death in 2004, the zoo's main exhibit was Snowflake, a unique (in captivity) pure-white albino gorilla.

We head out of the Park at 36km and run through Barcelona's own version of the Arc de Triomf (Catalonian spelling), built as the main access gate for the 1888 World Fair. The combination of red brick with the series of friezes around the arch, make it a singularly beautiful landmark - though this is not necessarily apparent while in a state of near exhaustion in the latter stages of a marathon. It is well worth going back to look at these after the race if time permits. The frieze facing you as you approach shows Barcelona presenting medals to the World Fair participants while, on the opposite side, a frieze depicts the city welcoming the nations taking part.

On approaching the Placa Catalunya for the second time in the race, the course heads back to the coast at 40km and the 60 metre tall Columbus Monument at the lower end of La Rambla. Also built for the 1888 World Fair, the monument serves as a reminder that Columbus reported to Ferdinand and Isabella in Barcelona after his first voyage to the New World. At the top of the monument a giant statue of the man himself points towards the new continent with his right hand while holding a scroll in the left. I prefer to think he's pointing towards the finish line.

The final 2km are something of an interminable uphill struggle back to the Venetian Towers. It's good to feel the support of the crowds with little children holding up signs reading 'Nearly there' in three languages. As you turn the final corner Freddie is still belting out a rousing version of 'Barcelona' to welcome you back. Those responsible deserve credit for their near flawless organisation of the race. Considering the numbers involved the registration and baggage drop/pickup works more efficiently than similar marathons in Spain, live athletic tracking is provided on the website and results are posted almost immediately. The actual race is equally well-organised, from the Expo to the on-course support. As Barcelona can get quite hot even in March, drink stations are frequent and well-stocked with both water and isotonic drinks. In the later stages there are also plenty of gels, bananas and oranges. It's a race and a city that I know well and one I'll enjoy coming back to whenever I can.

Barcelona Marathon Start Area

Photo by paciana, CC BY 3.0, via Wikipedia Commons

My first Barcelona Marathon

37

GERMANY

HANNOVER MARATHON

I was persuaded in 2009 to travel to Hannover by friend and fellow founder of the North East Marathon Club, George Routledge. Just like the lads in the popular BBC series 'Auf Wiedersehen Pet,' in the late 60s George had swopped an uncertain future in the declining North East job market for guaranteed full employment in the burgeoning German economy and was keen to revisit old haunts. As I'd also spent time hitchhiking solo around Germany during that era, by-passing Hannover en route, I was interested in seeing what I'd missed. (First of all let's clear-up the spelling: it's 'Hanover' in English and 'Hannover' in German. As the marathon is promoted by a German company, and obviously takes place in a German city it would be obtuse not to use the latter spelling).

Hannover is the capital of Lower Saxony in north-western Germany and is situated on the Leine River and the Mittelland Canal, where the spurs of the Harz Mountains meet the North German Plain. The marathon's slogan, 'Hannover: running in the heart of Europe,' alludes to the city's strategic position in the centre of Germany. Due to its location, Hannover has good connections from all major cities in Germany through Deutsche Bahn, the German rail service. Leaving Hannover the high speed Inter City Express Trains can take you all over Germany to places such as: Frankfurt, Hamburg, Stuttgart, Munich, Cologne, and Berlin. The trip to Hannover from Berlin takes 1:30, from Hamburg 1:20, from Frankfurt 2:20, and from Munich 4:30. There are also direct trains to the Netherlands, Switzerland, France, and Austria several times a day.

During World War II about three-fifths of Hannover was destroyed, but from the ruins arose a planned, modern, and highly industrialized city. It is a financial, administrative, and commercial centre with highly diversified industries, including the manufacture of motor vehicles, machinery, synthetic rubber, electrical engineering equipment, electronics products, chemicals, and foodstuffs. The German Industries Fair (first held in Hannover in 1947), now called Hannover Fair, has had great influence on the city's post-war development. In 2000 Hannover hosted Expo 2000, the World's Fair when a huge exhibition complex was built in the city. This has led to Hannover being dubbed the 'Expo City,' one of the two nicknames under which it attempts to promote itself. The other is the 'Garden City,' for reasons which will become obvious from my description of the marathon route. Despite Hannover's reputation as a highly industrialized city, post-World War II planning preserved parks, public gardens, and woods. Notable are the Great Garden (laid out in the 17th century in geometric fashion), the great Hannover woods (Eilenriede), the Maschsee (an artificial lake), the Hermann-Lons Park, the Stadtpark, and the zoological gardens. We were to run through, or past, many of these during the race.

Hannover is not a typical European city. Don't expect to see beautiful centuries-old buildings on your visit - the city was one of the hardest hit during World War II leaving it with only a few historical landmarks. Even the Old City (Altstadt) area is new, all the old houses left standing after the war (around 40) were taken from throughout the city and deposited here. Reconstructed buildings include the old town hall, the Leibniz House, where the philosopher Gottfried Wilhelm Leibniz lived from 1676 to 1716, the opera house, the Marktkirche (Market Church; 1349–59), the Neustadter Church (which contains the tomb of Leibniz), and the Kreuzkirche (Church of the Cross; 1333). The central area in which these are located is surrounded by grey 1950's buildings that contrast sharply with their reconstructed neighbours.

George and I flew out from Newcastle for a 2-night stay in Hannover with TUI Airlines, the official sponsor of that year's event. I say two nights but our late evening flight didn't get us into

Hannover airport until well after midnight on the Friday night/Saturday morning and we were scheduled to return straight after the marathon on the Sunday evening. Return flights cost £34 each. There is a train that runs twice-an-hour (called the S-Bahn) from the airport to the central station (Hauptbahnhof). A 2-Zone ticket costing 2.50 euros at the time was needed for the 17 minute journey from the airport to city centre. There are no trains between 1:30 am and 4 am and, after passport formalities, we were lucky to catch the last train of the day – otherwise it would have been a 20 euros taxi fare. Fortunately, we'd chosen to stay close to the station in the nearby Mercure Hotel. Our comfortable twin-bedded room cost a reasonable 55 euros per night without food. This was a lot less than the 138 euros a night at the marathon's partner hotel, the MARITIM Grand Hotel, recommended on the website.

George and I were up bright and early the next morning for a spot of sightseeing following 'The Red Thread,' a 4.5 kilometre route guiding visitors to 36 notable buildings and monuments in central Hannover. This self-guided tour starts at the tourist information centre opposite Hauptbahnhof Station and continues along walkways that are painted with a red line. Along the way, you can stop at historical sites such as Market Church, the Opera House, Museum August Kestner, and the New Town Hall. You can get a brochure from the information centre for about 3 euros, which includes detailed information about each landmark and an additional 45-minute route along the banks of Lake Maschsee. I'm not saying that we visited everything on the list of attractions – there wasn't enough time for that – but it was enough to satisfy our curiosity.

It was then on to Registration in the Marathon Fair tent in the grounds of the imposing Neues Rathaus (New Town Hall). This magnificent building is a grand palace-like structure in Trammplatz, about a 5-minute walk away from the Old Town. Established in 1913, several halls within the building have been converted into museums, which hosts a variety of exhibits all year long. It was interesting to study the 4 scale models depicting Hannover's cityscape during the Middle Ages, pre-World War II, 1945, and the present day – each giving a sense of how the city has progressed through time. Outside, in the extensive grounds, there was a whole camp of tents for the kids, a giant inflatable bouncy castle, and everything needed to make the day of the Children's Races a lot of fun. Around the other side of the town hall a music stage had live bands playing while a variety of food stalls supplied every type of German sausage available: Bratwurst, Currywurst and Knockwurst in particular. There was even a beer stall with a giant inflatable beer bottle dispensing free pints of Erdinger (one of the event's main sponsors). Given the warm sunshine, the whole place had a relaxed friendly, carnival-like atmosphere that was difficult to leave. We sat for several hours watching the Children's races while working our way through the various sausages on offer supplemented with a thick and tasty bean stew served cheaply and generously from a huge vat. And, yes, of course we had a few beers too. We were still there at 4pm – just in time to be among the first into that evening's Pasta Party in the same venue. The packet pickup including timing chip was seamless and ruthlessly efficient, as you would expect from the Germans, and very friendly – again: as you would expect from them. I was already beginning to think that my 41 euros race entry fee had been money well spent. What had turned out an excellent day was rounded-off by locating the city's Irish Bar (every city has at least one of these) to watch Barcelona thump their great rivals Real Madrid by 6 goals to 2 in the last of that season's 'El Clasicos.'

Next up was the big day itself. The Hannover Marathon is an annual road running event featuring races over the marathon, half marathon and 10 km (run and Nordic walk) that has been held in May since 1991. The 29th edition took place in 2019 (the 2020 and 2021 editions of the race were cancelled due to the COVID pandemic). According to the race organisers the marathon has played a leading role in making Hannover one of the foremost sporting cities in the country. The flat course, with only 17 metres of difference in elevation, attracts runners from far and wide who want to improve their personal best times. Generally, up to 20,000 people take part in the day's races with the half marathon attracting the highest number of entries from the public (over 5000). The marathon race typically features up to 2000 runners annually. When I took part in 2009 there were 1437 marathon finishers. Numbers had increased somewhat by 2019 when 2223 runners completed the full marathon distance. The marathon race holds IAAF Silver Label status and it is part of the German Road Races group. The race is these days officially known as the HAJ Hannover Marathon, as Hannover Airport is the current title sponsor. As well as runners from over 80 different countries, there is a friendly mix of professional and casual runners which adds to the atmosphere of the race. At the elite German, East African and Eastern European runners have been the most successful in the marathon category. South Africa's Lusapho April has the men's best of 2:08:32 hours since 2013 while Racheal Mutgaa (KEN) ran 2:26:15 for the women's record in 2019. Natalia Galushko has won the race the most times, with three straight wins from 1995 to 1997, while Stephan Freigang and Andrey Gordayev are the most successful male runners, having both had two back-to-back wins.

The heat of the weekend continued into Sunday morning as we revisited the New Town Hall for the 9am start to the marathon. The half marathon left two hours later at 11am with 10km runners setting-off at noon, twenty minutes before the Nordic Walkers. Marathon runners had 5 hours and 30 minutes to negotiate their way around a course that resembled the shape of a medieval battle-axe - with the first 16km run up and down the handle of the axe and the remaining distance around the blade. The course was obviously designed to highlight the best that Hannover can offer, with enough attractions to impress the most discerning of Marathon Tourists. The first kilometre took us past the striking Waterloo Monument a 46.31 metre high Victory Column. The memorial commemorates the victory in the Battle of Waterloo, which Great Britain , Hannover and Prussia won together against Napoléon in 1815. The building rises above a six-step base with a cube-shaped substructure with the dedication: 'THE HEROES OF WATERLOO THE GRATEFUL FATHERLAND.' A spiral staircase with 189 steps leads through the hollow fluted shaft of the column to the square viewing platform with the figure of Victoria standing on a drum and a ball.

Within 2km of the start we were running past the Niedersachsenstadion (Lower Saxony Stadium), a football stadium home to Bundesliga football club Hannover 96. The original 86,000 capacity stadium was completed in 1954 and has since been rebuilt several times for various major football events. It hosted the 1974 FIFA World Cup and 1988 European Championship and was also one of the venues for the 2006 FIFA World Cup when it was renamed FIFA World Cup Stadium, Hannover. Aside from football, the stadium has been the scene of several German athletics championships, the German Turnfest (a sports festival), field handball finals, concerts, rugby & American football. After undergoing extensive redevelopment the stadium has developed into the leading open-air concert venue in Northern Germany. Artists of the calibre of The Rolling Stones, Madonna, Michael Jackson, U2 and Bruce Springsteen have all appeared there in recent years.

The route continued along the shoreline of the Maschsee, a huge artificial lake created in the Leinemasch swamp between 1934 and 1936. With its proximity to the centre of Hannover, the Maschsee is a popular recreation area for the city's walkers and joggers. In 2005 a 6 km long route around the lake was mapped out by the German Athletics Association. This track runs along the footpath, closer to the water than the asphalt-coated cycle path. The lake hosts regattas and other boat races, including the annual dragon boat race, and is also suitable for a wide range of other water sports. One of the main events of the festival season in Hannover is the annual Maschseefest, when around two million visitors transform the city's idyllic lake into a social party scene for just under three weeks of the year.

On leaving the Maschsee, from 10km to 16km we ran up the other side of the axe's 'handle,' back towards the city passing en route the Dohrener Turm, part of the fortifications on the old city wall (11km), the Opera House (15km) and the Kropckeuhr Kropcke (15.5km). The latter is Hannover's central square named after

Wilhelm Kropcke, one of the owners of the former Café Robby, which was erected on the then-nameless square in 1869. Kropcke leased the café in 1876, changed the business's name to Café Kropcke and operated the café until 1919. Eventually, the square adopted the name from the café and in 1948 was officially named Kropcke by the city of Hannover. One of its notable features is the Kropcke clock, a replica of an 1885 clock that was scrapped after World War II.

After passing the city's Central Station at 16km, we entered the Eilenriede ('alder moor'), the largest urban city forest in Germany at nearly twice the size of Central Park. This huge forested area encloses the southern area of Hannover all the way from the northeast to the Maschsee in the south. The entire area is covered by a 130 kilometres long road network of which 80 km is reserved for hiking, 38 km for cycling and 11 km for horse riding. Despite the presence of ramblers, joggers and bikers, a multitude of forest animals live in the Eilenriede, among them deer, foxes, hares, martens, and bats. The shade from the thousands of trees in this green lung in the heart of the city provided a welcome escape from the increasing heat. Slap bang in the middle of the forest at around the 19km mark we ran past the city's Erlebnis ('Adventure') Zoo, where themed zones re-create some of the world's most spectacular wildlife destinations - from Canada's Yukon Bay to the African Savannah or the Australian Outback with more than 3,000 animals—all within the city limits.

The next few kilometres were largely around the city streets, with little of interest to grab our attention. At 33km we passed the Lutherkirche (exactly what the name suggests), a once prominent landmark destroyed by an aerial bomb during one of the last air raids on Hannover. 35km brought us to the imposing Welfenschloss, a former castle which has been the seat of the Technical University of Hannover (today the LUH University of Hannover) since 1879. At 37km we arrived in the Herrenhausen Gardens, one of Hannover's most famous attractions and a striking example of grand horticultural style for more than 300 years. The Great Garden with its baroque figures and magnificent fountains attracts visitors from all over the world. Its centrepiece is the impressive Herrenhausen Palace, a former royal summer residence of the House of Hannover. The original palace was destroyed by a British bombing raid in 1943 and subsequently reconstructed between 2009 and 2013. The 39km mark brought us to The Wilhelm Busch Museum, built in honour of the German humourist, poet, illustrator, and painter of the same name who became famous for his wildly innovative illustrated tales of the 19th century.

Entering the city at 41km we passed the 'Nanas', three colourful, plastic outdoor sculptures by Niki de Saint Phalle that have stood on the banks of the Leine since 1974. The figures depict distorted female bodies in motion. The sculptures led to protests and controversy when first introduced. Today they are considered one of the landmarks of the city. (To be honest, I didn't know what to make of them. Are they meant to be taken seriously?) At 42km we arrived at our final landmark, The Leineschloss (Leine Palace), situated on the River Leine. Not only is it considered to be one of the city's most beautiful buildings, but it is also a monument to the political history of the region. In the past, the building was home to the House of Hannover royal family, a dynasty that had absolute power over its people. This reconstructed Neo-classical palace is now the home of the Lower Saxony parliament.

All that was left was the long and tiring final kilometre back to where we'd started at The New Town Hall. Here, just like the previous day, the festivities were in full swing. I finished in just over 4 hours and was lucky enough to have over an hour to myself in the sun, enjoying the atmosphere (and the beer and sausages) while waiting for George to finish. Then it was a mad dash out to the airport for our early evening flight back to Newcastle. It had certainly been an interesting and enjoyable short stay in Hannover. The Marathon had lived up to the organization and precision that Germans are known for. It was very well organized, fast, full of spectators, and with lots of entertainment along the way. Apart from the heat (which was nobody's fault), the only negative I would mention was that there were numerous races going at the same time. The fact that the half marathon started at 11am and the 10K at noon meant that runners from all three races were running the final stages of their races simultaneously. This led to tiring marathon runners being jostled by their much fresher counterparts from the shorter distance events. I've had worse things happen to me during a marathon, so no real complaints there then.

Hannover. In front of The New Town Hall

Enjoying free beers after the Race!

48

NORWAY

OSLO MARATHON

I first ran the Oslo Marathon in September 2009 and came away with the impression of a picturesque though bland city: a pretty place with prosperous citizens where nothing really exciting seemed to happen. These impressions were shattered less than two years later when Oslo hit the headlines for all the wrong reasons. In July 2011 right-wing fanatic Anders Breivik detonated a car bomb damaging the offices of the Norwegian Prime Minister and killing 8 people in the process. Then, posing as a policeman, he went on to massacre 69 participants at a Labour Party Youth Camp on the nearby island of Utoeya. When brought to trial Breivik stated that he was 'defending Norway from multi-culturalism.' I could hardly believe what I was reading. It was difficult to reconcile the descriptions of the scenes of carnage with the quiet, peaceful Oslo I remembered.

Since 2009, I'd also become an enthusiastic reader of what the critics like to call 'Nordic Noir.' This is a genre of crime fiction made popular by the likes of Stieg Larsson with his Millenium trilogy and Henning Mankell of 'Wallander' fame. Though both these writers are Swedish, Norway has my favourite exponent of this genre in Oslo's Jo Nesbo. Nesbo is an ex-professional footballer and current lead singer of a rock group who has written a dark and compelling sequence of novels featuring his fictitious Oslo detective, Harry Hole. Hole is an alcoholic, non-conformist, anti-authoritarian who solves crimes by battling gangsters, bank robbers and serial killers in authentic and easily recognised Oslo locations. The novels, with their characters of drug-dealers and prostitutes, concentrate on the squalid and seedier side of Norway's capital. Sales of Nesbo's books now exceed 20 million worldwide and an enterprising couple now offer a 'Jo Nesbo's Oslo' guided walk to cater for the legions of Harry Hill devotees. (Kr 200 for 2 hours if you're interested – though I'm told the 'Rebus Walks' around Edinburgh, based on the Ian Rankin novels, are much more informative) I'd no intentions of forking out good money (£1 bought Kr 11.5 then) to be led through the streets of Oslo visiting sights I could easily find on my own.

The Breivik massacre combined with Nesbo's descriptions on his home-town had forced me to rethink my first impressions of Oslo. I was now beginning to see the city in a different light and approached my second marathon there in 2014 with a more open frame of mind. As Oslo has a Saturday marathon, the complexities of the Ryanair timetable meant that, to take advantage of the cheapest fares, I had to fly out from Edinburgh on the Thursday (£32.99) and return via Manchester on the Sunday evening (£22.99) In keeping with Ryanair's tradition of flying to where landing fees are cheapest, as opposed to passengers' intended destination, both out and back flights involved flying to and from Oslo Rygge airport some 66 kilometres south-east of the city. The Rygge-ekspressen bus service to and from Oslo Bus Terminal is timetabled to meet all international flights. The one hour journey can be booked cheapest online with return tickets costing Kr300 (Kr 140 for seniors like me!) The return trip leaves Oslo 2 hours and 40 minutes before each flight departure. All-in, the whole journey had turned into something of an endurance test before taking the marathon into consideration.

From the bus terminal, directly in front of the Central Station, it was an easy ten minute walk to the single room I'd booked for 3 nights in the Anker Hostel on Storgata. Though officially a hostel this spotless, modern building is run more on the lines of a hotel and at £158 for 3 nights is reasonably cheap by Oslo standards. Even better for those on a budget, is the fact that cooking equipment can be hired for a small fee and, with a supermarket nearby, considerable savings can be made on the huge cost of eating out in Oslo. I'd stayed there in 2009, been happy with the facilities and, given its proximity to the Start and Finish, saw no need to look elsewhere.

Oslo is the capital city, and with a population of about 650,000, also the most populous city in Norway. It occupies an arc of land at the end of the Oslofjord in a beautiful setting, surrounded by green hills and mountains and with 40 islands within the city limits. The origin of its name has been the subject of much debate though modern linguists generally interpret the original 'Oslo' to mean either, 'Meadow at the Foot of a Hill' or 'Meadow Consecrated to the Gods' According to the Norse sagas, the city was founded in around 1049 by King Harald Hardrade and eventually became the capital city during the reign of King Haakon V, the first monarch to reside in the city. Unions with Denmark and then later with Sweden, both in which it was the weaker partner, significantly restricted Oslo's influence. In the 17th century, fire destroyed major parts of the city on several occasions. So much so that King Christian 1V decided that the city be rebuilt anew in a different location and renamed Christana in his honour. In 1925 it reverted to its original Norwegian name of Oslo.

Today, Oslo is the economic and governmental centre of Norway as well as the hub of Norwegian trade, banking, shipping and industry. Its population is currently increasing at record rates making it the fastest growing major city in Europe. To Mr Breivik's chagrin, most of this growth is due to international immigration as well as to Norwegians moving to the capital to live. It seems though that the immigrant population in the city is growing faster than the Norwegian population. In the inner city it is reported to be more than 25% of the total. Many of Oslo's citizens are employed in the maritime sector and the city is home to some of the world's largest shipping companies, shipbrokers and maritime insurance brokers. Oslo was ranked number one in terms of quality of life among European large cities in 2012. In recent years it has also been placed as the second most expensive city in the world for living expenses after Tokyo. (I'll vouch for that!)

Visitors will find Oslo a compact city and one easy to explore on foot. Most of its main attractions are confined in a narrow area bordered by the Central Station to the east, Karl Johans Gate to the north, the Royal Palace in the west and the harbour and fjord to the south. Those wishing to travel further afield must use Ruter's integrated transport system. Single tickets allowing free transfer/return within one hour, can be used on Oslo's buses, trams, metro, trains and ferries. These are best bought in advance from in front of the Central Station, in most Narvesen stores, from 7-Eleven shops and ticket machines as they cost Kr 20 more if purchased on board. 2015 prices are Kr 30 for one hour, Kr 90 for 24 hours and Kr 240 for a 7-day ticket. If you are caught travelling without a ticket the fine if paid on the spot is Kr 950. If you're planning on travelling extensively or intend visiting numerous museums, the best option might be to buy an Oslo Pass. This gives free travel on all public transport, free entry to over 30 museums and outdoor swimming pools as well as a whole range of discounts at other attractions. Passes can be purchased for 24, 48 and 72 hours costing Kr 320, 470 and 590 respectively. As I was planning on making a nostalgic return to the out-of-town Holmenkollen Ski Jump and Vigeland Sculpture Park I'd first visited on a hitch-hiking tour around Europe as long ago as 1966, I settled for one of the Oslo 24-hour passes. I figured that I would also be able to use this for the ferry across to the Bygdoy peninsula to visit the Norwegian Folk Museum, the Polar ship Fram and the Viking Ship Museum – places I hadn't found time for on my last trip.

Holmenkollen National Ski Arena is one of Norway's most visited tourist attractions and even has its own line on the Oslo metro system. The line is the only one with platforms for six carriages, allowing up to 9,000 people to visit each hour. (It can get busy at times) The Arena includes a Ski Museum, Jump Tower, shops, café and a ski simulator. The jump raises about 60 metres in the air with the viewing platform at the top affording spectacular views across Oslo and the Fjord. I've a photo somewhere of myself standing on top of it in 1966 – well, not exactly the same jump as the entire ski jump area and arena was rebuilt before the 2011 Nordic World Championships. Completed in 1892, Holmenkollen continues to host World Cup events every winter. Inside the ski jump is the world's oldest ski museum with an interesting 4,000 years of ski history on display.

Much nearer the city and also reachable by metro or Tram 12 is the Vigeland Sculpture Park. I'd been intrigued on my first visit by the life-size statues of naked human figures in virtually every position imaginable. Nothing smutty here, this is Art we're talking about. I wanted to see if they still had the same effect on me after all these years. They did. The 200 plus bronze and granite sculptures represent the lifetime's work of Gustav Vigeland, who was also in charge of the design and architectural layout of what is the world's largest sculpture park. It's quite some achievement. The most impressive of the sculptures entitled 'The Monument' is the park's most popular attraction. More than 180,000 people attended its unveiling in 1944. Over 14 metres high, the Monolith is composed of 121 human figures rising towards the sky. It is said to represent man's desire to become closer with the spiritual and divine and portrays a feeling of togetherness, with the figures embracing one another as they are carried towards salvation. They would say that wouldn't they. It's still worth a visit if time allows.

Later that day I returned to the city and took the B9 ferry to Bygdoy and the Viking Ship Museum. The museum displays the world's two best-preserved Viking ships built in the 9th century as well as small boats, sledges and other artefacts from the Viking period. The museum is most famous for the completely whole Oseberg ship excavated from the largest known ship burial. The skeletons of two women were found in the grave with the ship though it is not clear which was the most important in life or whether one was sacrificed to accompany the other in death. The opulence of the goods found in the burial site suggests that this was a burial of very high status.

Nearby is yet another museum featuring a Norwegian sailing vessel. This is the Fram Museum honouring Norwegian Polar exploration in general and three great Norwegian polar explorers in particular: Nansun, Sverdrup and Amundsen. The centrepiece is the original exploration vessel 'Fram' with its intact interior that visitors are allowed to walk through. As you do so you leave the comfort zone of 21st century living with a reminder of how harsh conditions were for the crew and their dogs. Even more realistic is the polar simulator where you can experience both the cold and the dangers of polar exploration over a hundred years ago. I came away full of admiration for their efforts. I could also have popped into the Kon-Tiki and National Maritime Museums on the same site but figured I'd already seen enough of all things nautical for the day.

The final visit on the peninsula was to the Norwegian Folk Museum. I'd seen something similar while in Stockholm for the marathon there the previous year. With collections from around the country, the museum aims to show how people lived in Norway from 1500 to the present. The 160 buildings in the Open-Air Museum represent different regions in Norway, different periods of time as well as differences between town and country and social classes. The Gol Stave Church dating from 1200 is one of five medieval buildings you're able to visit. I much preferred the 1865 tenement building transported from the centre of Oslo. Several of the flats show typical interiors from various periods of the 19th and 20th centuries, including my favourite: a flat inhabited by an immigrant Pakistani family as recently as 2002.

As Registration was open until 8pm on both Thursday and Friday nights I still had plenty time to return to the city and take a look around before going to the Expo. This took place opposite the ferry terminal adjacent to the Radhuset, the City Hall. It was the usual mix of retail (shops) and administrative facilities (number pick-up). I was taken though by the organiser's description of the Expo on the event website. They were at least open and honest about the Expo's function. Without any of this pretence about it being for the runners' benefit the blurb, addressed to potential exhibitors, explained that, 'It is a unique opportunity to promote and sell products and services for your company focused on consumers with a strong buying consumption' Got it in a nutshell! I picked up my number, T-shirt and storage bag and made a quick exit.

We were all back outside the City Hall next morning for the 9.30am start of the marathon, (or 9.35am, depending on which start-wave you'd been assigned to). This was to be the first of several events on the day. Of the other main events, a Half Marathon left at 1.40pm and a 10k at 4pm. Both had much bigger fields than the 3,000 marathon limit – a number always reached well in advance of the day despite the high cost of entry. My online entry cost Kr800, plus Kr15 Administrative Fee, plus Kr50 for a Licence Fee. Not sure why I needed the latter when I'm already licensed to UK Athletics. Never mind; the Kr915 total worked out at something like £80. The Half had a limit of 13,000 runners while the limit for the 10k was set at 9,000. The organisers were anticipating upwards of 50,000 participants over the course of the day. Doing the maths it means that there must have been a heck of a lot of children in the Children's Races. For those only visiting Oslo for the day or who were without friends and relatives to assist, changing and baggage facilities were located close to the Start.

City Hall Square, from where we were starting and were due to finish, contains one of Oslo's most famous buildings. On December 10th each year, the anniversary of Alfred Nobel's death, the City Hall hosts the Nobel Peace Prize ceremony with the Norwegian Royal Family and Prime Minister in attendance. The fact that it was voted Oslo's 'Structure of the Century' with over 30% of the popular vote adds prestige to the start to the race. When I ran it in 2009 both start and finish were at the Akerhus Fortress further along the waterfront. This was also to be a different course to the one we ran in 2009. On that occasion we wound our way around what was a huge construction site involving some fairly serious roadworks and building projects to the east of the city centre. These ongoing developments are all part of Oslo's 'Fjord City' programme. This is a major project involving the extensive renewal of Oslo's waterfront. The City Council approved the project in 2008 with the aim of making Oslo's waterfront accessible to all its citizens. In addition to plans for future development, it subsumed some projects already completed like the popular Aker Brygge wharf, built on a former industrial site and the recently finished neighbourhood of Tjuvholmen – both of which we were due to run through. The most exciting changes are scheduled for Bjorvika, an area to the west that we struggled through in 2009 as contractors worked to remove the rail and road barriers and old container terminals that had separated the city from the fjord. The area is still in the process of being completely transformed: a new seafront promenade now runs along the coast, the construction of a new public library has just started and a new museum for Edvard Munch's art is to be built shortly. There's even to be a new city beach, built over the sunken motorway. I wasn't sure how much of the development we'd see on the new two-lap course, but I was looking forward to it.

After moderately successful warm-up attempts by a troupe of dancers and a bellowing MC, we set off along the waterfront heading westwards. Much of the first 3 kilometres followed an opulent looking, tree-lined street full of beautiful houses – several of them home to various foreign embassies. The crowd support here was minimal. Shortly after 3k a left turn took us over the Ring Road and down towards the waterside. Here we ran along a multi-purpose footpath-cum-cycleway with magnificent views over the fjord. At this stage we virtually had the path to ourselves – it was to become much busier second time around as the locals came out for the day. Shortly after reaching the Colour Line passenger terminal to Kiel at 6k the path turned away from the waterfront and back toward the start area. At 7k we were taken through Tjuvholmen, a former dockyard area taken over by private developers and now part of the Fjord City urban renewal programme. The development features some pretty swanky apartments (1,200 in total) as well as a Museum of Modern Art and a popular Sculpture Park. Next up was Aker Brygge, another redeveloped dockyard area that is now the place to be seen in Oslo for those with the money to enjoy its myriad of expensive bars and restaurants. As is typical of such new, boutique-style developments there are lots of statues and artworks on the streets – many of these involve naked ladies. (What is it with Oslo and nudity?) An iconic clock in the shape of a lighthouse, once belonging to the original shipyard on the site, marks the entrance to the Brygge It was a place I visited each evening while in the city, but only to stroll around observing the well-heeled crowds.

We returned to the start area at 8k, running along the waterfront under the ramparts of the impressive Akershus Castle and Fortress. This medieval castle is one of Oslo's earliest surviving buildings. Its main claim to fame is that it has successfully survived all sieges, primarily by Swedish forces over the centuries. It did surrender without combat to Nazi Germany, however, in 1940 when the Norwegian government evacuated the capital in the face of an unprovoked German assault. Several citizens were executed here by the German occupiers while, after the war, eight Norwegian traitors, sentenced to death for war crimes were also executed in the fortress. Among these was the infamous traitor Vidkun Quisling. As was apparent during its use as marathon HQ in 2009, the Fortress is still a military area, but one open to the public. Many come to visit the two military museums as well as the Royal Mausoleum on the site.

At 10k we approached the more recent developments in the Fjord City project. The first of these is the harbour-front Opera House. This striking building has an angled white exterior that appears to rise directly out of the water. Visitors are allowed to climb its roof to enjoy panoramic views of the city and fjord, while large-scale windows at street level provide glimpses of rehearsals and workshop activities. It's a beautiful building but will never rival the one in Sydney. Opposite the Opera House is the controversial Barcode development of high-rise apartment blocks. Designed by different firms of architects, the buildings are long and narrow with spaces in between so that they jointly resemble a barcode. They reminded me of the Lego-block architecture I'd seen at the Rotterdam Marathon. The height of the buildings located so close to the fjord have radically redefined the skyline of a city that had previously taken pride in being considered low-rise. The project has caused an unprecedented stir among citizens, and the designs and heights of the Barcode buildings have not met with universal approval.

The next four kilometres took us eastwards and out and back through what had been mainly a building site in 2009. This time though we weren't taken so far out of the city before turning to head back and conditions weren't as bad as previously. Arriving back at the Barcode at 14k we ran inland to make a loop around the city's Botanical Gardens. These contain two further museums of note: the Natural History and the soon to be re-sited Munch museums. If you're getting the impression here that Oslo is full of museums, you're not wrong. That's why the Oslo Pass is such good value provided, of course, you're a fan of museums. The Natural History Museum contains extensive exhibits on zoology, botany and geology while the Munch Museum displays the life's work of Norway's most famous artist. Munch's greatest painting 'The Scream' has been the target of several high-profile art thefts. You have to be impressed by the bravado of two villains who stole The Scream from the National Gallery in 1994, leaving a note saying, 'Thanks for the poor security.' The painting was recovered months later when, after refusing to pay a ransom request, the gallery set up a sting operation with assistance from the British police and the Getty Museum. It disappeared again in 2004 when masked gunmen entered the Munch Museum and stole both it and Munch's 'Madonna' after forcing the guards to lie on the floor. Again, the paintings were recovered, this time two years later, after which the Museum was closed for ten months for a much-needed 'security overhaul.' While passing it on the second lap I was ready to perform my own version of The Scream and would have quite happily have lain on the floor if anyone had asked me to.

    Returning to the Barcode again after 18k we passed in front of the Central Station to enter the cobbled main thoroughfare of Karl Johans Gate just before Cathedral Square. I was reminded in passing of the newsreel pictures following the Breivik massacre showing tens of thousands of Oslo's citizens gathering there to honour the victims of the shootings. Karl Johans Gate contains three of the city's major landmarks in Stortinget, (Norway's Parliament) and the National Theatre before ending at Slottet (the Royal Palace). The Stortinget is an easily approachable, impressive grey building with two lion statues at its main entrance. The Parliament was established in 1814 when Norway got its own constitution, many years before the country's independence.

Guided tours are free but unfortunately only on Saturdays (race day) during September. There's an interesting story about the lions. Apparently these were carved by a convict from the nearby Akershus Fortress who, having initially been sentenced to death for murder, subsequently had this commuted to life imprisonment. Public appreciation of the lion sculptures paved the way to his freedom in 1872 for 'services to Norway's National Assembly' He started his new life by migrating to the USA. Given what happened in the city in 2011, I was surprised by what seemed an obvious lack of security around both the Parliament and the Palace.

Although the course didn't take us right up to the Palace gates it was an imposing presence on our route. Set in a huge landscaped park the 173-room palace is still the official residence of the present Norwegian monarch. Equally imposing is the city's National Theatre building, situated equidistant between the Palace and the Parliament. The theatre is renowned for featuring the plays of Henrik Ibsen, Norway's most famous playwright, the most frequently performed dramatist in the world after Shakespeare. His 'Doll's House' is said to be the world's most performed play. We turned just before the theatre at the 20k mark to take a convoluted route through the main part of Oslo and back to where we'd begun and the start of the second lap.

I'd taken things fairly easy for the first lap and had come in around the 2 hour 10 minute mark having, attempted both to sightsee and take photos en route. Even so, I was already beginning to flag and knew already that the second half would take much longer. I think there's a negative psychological effect in knowing that you have to go around exactly the same course for a second time. There's nothing different on the horizon to look forward to. Maybe that's just excuses for not running particularly well. I had no expectations of breaking 4 hours 30 so none were broken. I'm not sure about the Oslo Marathon. I can't put my finger on what it is exactly but it seems to be lacking something: atmosphere perhaps. I'm not convinced the people of Oslo appreciate their marathon in the same way as other cities I've run in. Apart from the short stretches around the wharf area and through the main part of the city centre there was a noticeable lack of crowd support around the course. I don't fault the organisers. The route was well-marked and marshalled and there were plenty of drink stations and bananas. They also did their best to provide entertainment and live music on the way around, yet the whole thing felt a bit flat – and I'm not talking about the course here.

After picking up my fairly average medal it was time to commence the search for the perfect dark beer. I was hoping to get reacquainted with at least one drink of the awesome Mikkeller Black Hole Imperial, coming in at an incredible 13.1% AVB, that I'd found after running the Stavanger Marathon. No such luck, and maybe it's just as well as I doubt if I would have been able to afford it. Remember that this is one of the most expensive cities on the planet where even a pint (500ml) of your average weak-as-water, bog standard lager will cost as much as £6 or £7 depending on how far away you are from the waterfront. I think I would have needed to take out a bank loan to drink in some of the establishments on Aker Brygge. As for sampling the local cuisine, that was out of the question for the same reason. I'd tried it when in Stavanger for the marathon and hadn't been particularly impressed. I did consider eating at Schroeders, Harry Holes favourite restaurant on Wldemar Thranes Gate, but walked away on seeing that I'd have to pay approaching £30 for Onion Soup and Sirloin of Beef – neither of which represents traditional Norwegian cuisine. Anyway, I had self-catering and a local supermarket to keep expenditure realistic.

Strangely, I'd enjoyed the tourism aspect of the trip considerably more than the marathon itself. Usually I find it an equal combination of the two. Culturally, Oslo is an interesting city, home to world-class museums and galleries rivalling anywhere else in Europe. It's also set in a stunning natural location between fjords and mountains, turning such easy delights as a waterfront stroll into a real pleasure. The anorak in me even had the consolation of stumbling across at least a dozen of the Harry Hole locations I'd read about in Nesbo's novels. I came away, though, reflecting on the following comment often made about the place, 'Oslo is a nice city. It would be even nicer if they ever get it finished!'

Certificate from my first Oslo Marathon in 2009

Aker Brygge. Oslo. 2009 Marathon Start
(Photo by Meriç Dağlı on Unsplash)

SLOVAKIA

BRATISLAVA MARATHON

Following the fall of the Iron Curtain and the cessation of conflict in the Balkans a number of new states were created in Europe at the beginning of the 90s. Two big countries, Czechoslovakia and Yugoslavia, broke into several smaller states. Two of them have similar names: Slovakia and Slovenia. They're the two countries in the world that cause the most confusion; more than the two Congos or Niger and Nigeria in Africa. I'd never been to either of them before 2011 but both their capital cities hosted increasingly popular international marathons that I'd planned to run. I needed to discover more about both. Though the names might be similar, these countries have very different pasts. Slovakia rose from the Czechoslovakia, Slovenia from Yugoslavia. While Slovakia separated from its Czech neighbour in a peaceful way, Slovenia arose from war in the Balkans. These countries don't share borders, they never did. Slovakia is situated directly in Central Europe with no access to the sea. Slovenia, on the other hand, is surrounded by Austria, Hungary, Croatia and Italy and is a coastal country on the border of the Balkans and Central Europe. The capital of Slovakia is Bratislava and the capital of Slovakia is Ljubljana. I was to find them two interesting but very different places. While Slovakia has a population of about 5.4 million, Slovenia is much smaller with only about 2 million inhabitants. Both countries are members of the European Union and NATO and both are members of the European Monetary Union – the so-called Euro Zone. To avoid confusion I found that the easiest way to remember the difference between the two was to remind myself that when Czechoslovakia split in

1993, they really just split the word in half. The Czech Republic went in one direction, Slovakia went the other. This helps me remember the geography of Slovakia - I know it's next to the Czech Republic, not one of the former pieces of Yugoslavia. Slovenia isn't as conveniently named after the country it sprung from, but process of elimination reminds me it was a part of Yugoslavia. Simples!

Slovakia was the first of the two countries I visited when, together with a former colleague from the North East Marathon Club, I travelled to Bratislava in March 2011 for the 6th edition of the city's marathon. Ryanair had only recently introduced Bratislava to its route network so fares were remarkably cheap. We flew out with them on the Friday from Edinburgh, returning on the Monday via Stansted. Both fares cost 37 euros with taxes. The connecting rail fares to the airports were almost as much. On arrival at M. R. Stefanik Airport, Bratislava we took the number 61 bus for the 12 kilometre journey to the city's main Hlavana train station. Fares cost as little as 50 cents for a 15 minute journey or 1 euro for the 30 minute ride into town. Bus drivers don't sell tickets in Bratislava so you need to get tickets in advance. Use the vending machines at the bus stop but note that you will need euro coins as the vending machines don't take notes (there are also two big red ticket machines in the terminal building close to arrivals, which accept banknotes). You can also buy tickets in the tourist and exchange offices in the terminal, but they have only limited working hours. Be aware that the airport shops and kiosks are not very helpful when it comes to changing bills into coins. A screen in the arrivals hall displays actual departure times of the next public transport buses. Unfortunately, the main train station is something like 2 kilometres outside the city centre so it's quite a walk into town. We'd booked a twin room for 3 night's bed and breakfast at the city's quirky Hotel Kiev for a paltry £42. Though the hotel appeared set in a time-warp with an ex-police Trabant on display in the lobby, it was nonetheless more than adequate for our requirements with a breakfast selection I haven't found in much more expensive establishments. The staff were very helpful, with suggestions for all the best-value places to eat and drink. I'd have no hesitation in recommending it to fellow budget-conscious Marathon Tourists.

With a population of about 450,000, Bratislava is Slovakia's capital and the country's largest city. It's situated in southwestern Slovakia, occupying both banks of the River Danube and the left bank of the River Morava and is the only national capital that borders two sovereign states independent countries: Austria and Hungary. Bratislava is geographically accessible, too with the Czech border only 60km away, Vienna 60km to the west and Vienna Airport is even closer. Both cities lie on the Danube River and the Hungarian capital Budapest is only 200km further downriver. Bratislava's location in central Europe and its proximity to these larger cities has given it a varied history reflected in the three different names by which it is still known. The city received its contemporary name as recently as 1919 but Hungarians call it Pozsony while in German it is known as Pressburg, and at different periods in the past they have both claimed it as their own territory. Only 100 years ago the city's population was 42% German, 41% Hungarian, and just 15% Slovak. Czech army occupation after the First World War drove many Hungarians out, and there was a similar exodus of Germans after World War II when Czechoslovakia became part of the Soviet bloc and Slovakia part of the Czechoslovak Soviet Socialist Republic. By then the city's population was 90% Slovak. In 1968, after the unsuccessful Czechoslovak attempt to liberalise the Communist regime, the city was occupied by Warsaw Pact troops. Shortly thereafter, it became capital of the Slovak Socialist Republic, one of the two states of the federalized Czechoslovakia. Anti-Soviet sentiment continued and the city became one of the foremost centres of the anti-Communist Velvet Revolution in 1989. Finally, in 1993, the city became the capital of the newly formed Slovak Republic. Independence brought a strong cultural impact to Bratislava as well as economic buoyancy, resulting in a construction boom and many new public buildings. Bratislava is the political, cultural and economic centre of Slovakia. It is the seat of the Slovak president, the parliament and the Slovak Executive. It is home to several universities, museums, theatres, galleries and other important cultural and educational institutions. Many of Slovakia's large businesses and financial institutions also have headquarters there. Today, the advent of low-cost airlines has contributed to the city is becoming a popular destination for weekend travellers from European countries and stag party groups.

Bratislava has a very pleasant medieval inner city with narrow, winding streets. The dominant feature of the town is Bratislava Castle, a hill-top castle next to the river Danube, providing excellent views over the Old Town. This historical area is centred on two squares, Hlavne namestie (Main Square) and Hviezdoslavovo namestie (Hviezdoslav Square, named after a famous Slovak poet). Virtually everything that's worth seeing in Bratislava from a tourist's viewpoint is situated either in, or within walking distance, of the Main Square containing the iconic Old Town Hall. The Main Square is the venue of many concerts, performances and markets while the area nearby is full of beautiful historic palaces, museums, galleries, small cafes and romantic alleyways. It's well worth seeing for yourself. Of a rather different architectural character are some of the communist-era buildings found in the modern parts of the city; a prime example is the Petrzalka housing estate, the biggest Communist-era concrete block housing complex in Central Europe, which stretches on endlessly just across the river. Surprisingly, the majority of the marathon route was to take us in this direction with only the last couple of kilometres of each of the two laps being run anywhere near the historic city centre.

On Saturday morning we set off early for Registration in a tented village next the Eurvea Galleria, a modern shopping centre on the banks of the Danube. Registration is open to 7pm on the three days before race day as well as from 7am to 8.30am on the Sunday morning. We were handed two bibs for both the front and back as well plus an ankle chip that came with a warning of a 20 euros penalty for non-return. We were also given one of the best quality T-shirts from any marathon – a plain black, dressy affair that mercifully hadn't been smothered in awful corporate logos. It's one of the few that I'm still proud to wear these days. The T-shirt alone was worth the 25 euros I'd paid to enter the event. Entry fees remain remarkably cheap. In 2017 it still only costs between 32 and 42 euros to enter, depending on how soon you get your entry in. A free Pasta Party was scheduled in the same location from 2pm to 6pm that afternoon. Our initial plan for the day had been to take a trip on one of the boats that ferry passengers the short distance upstream to Vienna and back. We'd seen prices advertised for these from 27 euros return for the 90 minutes each-way journey (expensive when compared to a return train ticket for less than 15 euros). Unfortunately, we'd arrived out of season and the boats weren't operational until the following week, (April). In subsequent years the marathon has taken place on the first Sunday in April so the ferry to Vienna would have been an option for participants. Somewhat disappointed we decided instead to take a long walk along the riverside paths on either side of the river. This too proved a bit of a let-down with the southern bank in particular being untidy and undeveloped. Apparently there are major plans afoot for new buildings. Just before leaving for Bratislava one of those irritating property programmes on daytime TV in the UK had featured the city as the next 'In' place in which to invest. It was now time for some serious sightseeing. Isn't that what Marathon Tourism is all about? (As well as the marathon, of course)

In Bratislava, the best way to start is by concentrating on the historic old town. It's easy to find, downhill from the hill-top dominating medieval castle, and past the tall spire of St. Martin's Cathedral. The maze of cobblestone streets are mostly limited to pedestrians.'Korso' is the name given to the main pedestrian zone running through the heart of the city centre leading from St Michael's Gate to the Main Square. Today, the cafes, bars and restaurants in the zone are a meeting place for people of all ages, just as they were a century ago. The route of the Korzo is illuminated each night by a coloured laser ray that adds a modern touch to the historical centre. Virtually every building on the Main Square is worthy of attention. The one that stands out most, though, is the square's main landmark – the Old Town Hall. The rebuilt Bratislava's Town Hall on the Main Square began to be fully used in 1434. Prior to 1442, an underpass was built to enable entering the Town Hall from the Square. Fortunately, this remarkable architectural element has been well preserved. A plaque with a line marking the water level of the Danube River during disastrous floods in February 1850 is placed on the wall. An exposition of the history of the city and feudal justice of the Bratislava City Museum is on show in the Old Town Hall building. Throughout Bratislava's history it was the main market place, an area for public gatherings, welcoming ceremonies to sovereigns and other renowned personalities.

St. Michael's Tower is another of the not-to-be-missed essential symbols of Bratislava. Only the gate on St. Michael's Tower has been preserved out of the original four gates that were gateways for entering the fortified medieval city. We were to enter the city via this gate on both laps of the marathon course A zero kilometer sign, which counts the distance of selected cities in the world from Bratislava, is located under the tower. A view of the entire rest of St. Michael's Street (Michalska ulica), which is one of the oldest in the city, opens up from St. Michael's Gate. Michael's Gate is the only gate that has been preserved from the medieval fortifications, and it ranks among the oldest of the town's buildings. What is said to be the narrowest house in Europe with a front facade only 130 centimetres wide is attached to the tower. A kebab shop on its ground floor now replaces the spot where guards once stood.

For those interested in religious history or architecture three institutions, all within walking distance of one another, stand out. These are the Franciscan Church and Monastery, St. Martin's Cathedral and St. Elizabeth's Church. The Franciscan Square in which the first of these is situated, constitutes a quiet contrast to the lively Main Square. Encircled by ancient historical buildings, the Square's name is derived from one of the oldest churches in Bratislava – the Franciscan Church with a monastery from the 13th century. Meetings of the Hungarian magnates were once held in the monastery with its main claim to fame being the election of Ferdinand 1 as Hungarian king within its walls. The royal theme can be continued by visiting St. Michael's Cathedral, a 15th century Gothic church in which no fewer than eleven Hungarian kings and eight consorts were crowned between 1563 and 1830. Inside the Cathedral is a replica of the Hungarian crown, weighing an unbelievable 300 kilogrammes. St. Elizabeth's Church by contrast owes its fame mainly to its colour. Known as the 'Blue Church' it is characterised by the prominent blue colour of its exterior walls. It's said to be a unique example of Art Nouveau church architecture.

While you're walking around don't forget to look out for three of the more unusual attractions in the centre. My favourite among these is 'Rubberneck' a statue of a man's head and shoulders arising out of what appears to be a manhole cover. I've no idea of the statue's origins but it provides tourists with much amusement. Apparently, Rubberneck has already lost his head twice due to careless drivers, prompting the local authorities to erect a road sign behind the statue. There's also a curious statue commemorating an eccentric local dandy dressed in a top hat and tails. It seems that at the beginning of the 20th century he was often seen around the Korso handing out flowers to ladies. These days he would be arrested as a nuisance! Finally, there's the strange figure of the 'Taunter' – a stooping man on the facade of a house in Panska Street. There are various explanations as to its origins. One of them says it is intended to ridicule the owner of an adjacent house who used to enjoy spying on his neighbours.

Of course, no stay in Bratislava would be complete without visiting the ancient castle that stands on a strategic site above the Danube. The site was inhabited as far back as Celtic and Greater Moravian times. The aristocratic Palffy family completed extensions that make for today's 'upside-down table' appearance of four peaked corner towers on the building. In 1811 a fire in what was then a barracks left the castle an abandoned hulk, and restoration was to start only in the 1950s. Serving briefly as seat of government for independent Slovakia in 1993, the castle today serves as museum and special events venue, notably as the site of the Bush-Putin summit in February 2005. The courtyard of the castle as well as the Treasury are open to the public.

With sightseeing over for the day we returned to the hotel to hear familiar voices calling out while passing the bar. Sure enough, although having just arrived, Martin Bush, Pete Morris and Brian Mills of the 100 Club had already found the 1 euro per litre local brew to their liking. The three of them had plans to do the 5k fun run to be held later that afternoon as part of the marathon weekend, (Martin loves collecting medals no matter where they're from). As it was such a nice, sunny day we decided to go along and watch them finish. It was a popular event attracting a huge field of local runners. Martin and Pete, in their Manchester United and Chelsea kits with 'Rooney' and 'Lampard' on their backs stood out like sore thumbs among the numerous family groups. Brian, covered head to toe in tattoos, simply stood out.

Next morning saw us all line up in front of the Eurova building on Pribinova Street for the 10am start to the marathon, half marathon and four-person half marathon relay run. The previous year, with participation steadily increasing there had been a total of 3,677 people registered over all events; including 440 in the Marathon and 1021 in the half. The others were inline-skaters, or were in the half marathon relay, fun run, kids' runs and toddlers' competition. Just to show how far the event has progressed since then, in 2017 the 12th edition of the Bratislava Marathon sold out with 12 000 participants well before race day. With 5 hours in which to get around, we crossed the Danube on Novy Most (New Bridge), featuring a UFO-like tower restaurant. Close by but high above the bridge, on a rocky outcrop of the Little Carpathians, looms the massive rectangular bulk of Bratislava Castle. Marathon runners cross the Danube twice in each direction, and half marathon runners once each way. By looking up we got a good view of this prominent landmark which now houses the Slovak Parliament. The New Bridge connects the centre of the city to the south-west suburb of Petrzalka, an enclave of systems-built housing from the 1970s. For the next 16 kilometres of each loop the course was fairly non-descript and boring. My colleague and I ran together every step of the way, churning out even paced 9:15 minute miles and telling each other jokes as we tried to maintain our interest through the drab surroundings. It was only on entering the Old Town for the last couple of kilometres of each lap that things began to improve as we passed many of the landmarks described earlier. I'm pleased to see that the organisers have now abandoned the southern section of the course. The new route goes twice through the northern suburbs of the city before coming back to the centre each time. I'm not familiar with this area of Bratislava so am unable to comment on the suitability, or otherwise, of the new route. I was happy with my finishing time of 4 hours 7 minutes in the knowledge that I could almost certainly have improved on this if I hadn't been conscious of having to face a difficult off-road ultra marathon the following Saturday.

That evening we made the same journey we'd taken on the previous two nights back to the favourite bar/restaurant we'd been recommended on arrival. I'd like to give it its correct name but the notation made on our city map by the hotel receptionist has become unreadable over time. We'd asked for somewhere that served both Slovakian cuisine and the best local beer (the words 'strong' and 'dark' may even have been mentioned). He wrote what looks like Scovae (maybe Scouae) Pub on the map with directions of how to get there. He wasn't wrong about either the food or the beer. Built with a labyrinth of rooms heading off in all directions, the place certainly had atmosphere. Before leaving the UK I'd read that the food in Slovakia is quite hearty, including lots of meat (especially pork) with potatoes, dumplings, cheese, and thick sauces. Our previous visits to the pub had proved this assessment to be accurate. There weren't too many vegetables on offer, other than healthy portions of cabbage in the form of sauerkraut. On previous visits we'd tried the spicy cabbage soup for starters followed by a huge plate of goulash - excellent value for around 5 euros. Though the latter is traditionally more of a Hungarian dish, it is also well received in Slovakia. On our final evening I tried the Bryndzove Pirohy, a heavy entree of potato dumplings made from potato dough, filled with special slovak bryndza (sheep) cheese and topped with smotana (like sour cream), spring onion and bacon. For a main course I went with the Masove Gulky, or Slovak-style meatballs made from potato dough and served over steamed cabbage topped with roasted onion. Again, the whole meal was delicious for very little cost.

Slovakia has a number of breweries and a rich beer culture. Since the fall of communism, most large commercial breweries have been privatized and subsequently bought by foreign multinational companies. Today most are owned by either Heineken or SABMiller. While we did find some good dark beer in Bratislava none of it was particularly strong. Brews in Slovakia usually range between 3.8 and 5.0% alcohol content, and are classified further according to their colour. We were recommended to try the Saris brewery's products as a well-known and trusted brand. Though they're now being produced by the brewery-giant SABMiller, the original recipes have not been touched. Bohemian pilsner at an ABV of 5% is the pride of the Saris brand and available in most places. Better than that though is Saris Tmavy at ABV of 4.1% - a tasty dark beer brewed from four kinds of malt and the best hops. And, just like the food in Bratislava it's ridiculously cheap.

St Michael's Gate. Bratislava
(Photo by Maksym Harbar on Unsplash)

Bratislava Marathon Memorabilia

PORTUGAL

PORTO MARATHON

Porto was to be my first marathon in Portugal. Though I'd been to the country on numerous occasions it was generally to spend a holiday in one of the many touristy spots on the Algarve coast. The farthest north I'd been was to Lisbon, some 175 miles south of Porto on the Atlantic coastline. Porto is one of the oldest European centres. Its settlement dates back many centuries, when it was an outpost of the Roman Empire. Its combined Celtic-Latin name, Portus Cale, has been referred to as the origin of the name Portugal. Some historians have argued that the name derives from the Greek word 'kallis' meaning 'beautiful' (referring to the beauty of the Douro valley); others believe that the word 'Cale' comes from the Latin and means 'Warm Port.' Some say it's most likely a Celtic word for 'port,' – as in the place where boats dock. Whatever the origin, 'Portus Cale' evolved to 'Portucale,' which eventually became Portugal. During our visit I discovered that the people of Porto are known as 'Tripeiros' because of a dish they created called 'Tripas a Moda do Porto.' It seems that back in the 15th century, when Infante D. Henrique's armada needed supplies for its Conquest of Ceuta (Portugal's first stronghold in Africa), the citizens of Porto provided them with every last bit of meat they had. Only the tripes were left behind. From these leftovers, the people of Porto created this dish: thus earning themselves the strange nickname.

World-famous for its port wine, Porto is Portugal's second largest city and is the commercial and industrial centre for the zone north of the Mondego River. The historic centre of Porto was designated a UNESCO World Heritage site in 1996. Among the architectural highlights, Oporto Cathedral is its oldest surviving structure, together with the small Romanesque Church of Saint Francis, the remnants of the city walls and a few surviving houses. In more recent times other interesting monuments have been added to the landscape of the city like the magnificent Palacio de Bolsa, (Stock Exchange Palace), the buildings in Liberty Square, the tile-adorned Sao Bento Train Station and the gardens of the Crystal Palace. The present-day city lies chiefly on the Douro's north (right) bank, sprawling outward from the older riverside district known as the Ribeira. Today it is best known internationally for the production of the world famous port wine - a popular fortified wine usually served after meals. The red-tiled warehouses of the town of Vila Nova (New City) de Gaia, where vast quantities of port wine are blended and stored, are on the south bank of the Douro. The trade in port was begun in 1678 and was firmly established under the terms of the Methuen Treaty (1703) between England and Portugal. An act of 1906 defined port as a wine produced in the Douro district and exported from Porto with an alcoholic strength of more than 16.5 percent. A sizable proportion of the population is still engaged in the manufacturing of this product with fisheries and tourism also important components of the city's economy. Long considered as Lisbon's ugly sister, a rejuvenated Porto has been growing in popularity in recent years. Now, the city's river banks are crowded with hip new bars and cool pavement restaurants. In 2014 and 2017, Porto was elected The Best European Destination by the Best European Destinations Agency.

    A colleague and I from the North East Marathon Club went to the 2011 Porto Marathon via Stansted. Not a good place to travel to on a Friday afternoon when the motorways of England seem increasingly incapable of coping with the volume of weekend traffic. We'd travelled down by train from Newcastle to Stevenage thinking it would be a simple matter to connect with a National Express coach from Stevenage to the airport. What we hadn't considered was that our coach would get stuck in a motorway pile-up on it's way from Birmingham. We stood helpless at the bus stop while the minutes ticked away into what seemed like hours. Finally, just as we were heading off to find a taxi, the coach arrived. We weren't the only ones in danger of missing a flight so to a chorus of 'put your foot down,' to which the driver duly complied, we arrived for the flight with literally minutes to spare. We eventually arrived in Porto late on a damp and rainy evening. Porto Francisco Sa Carneiro Airport is located around 11km from the city and provides three methods of transport to get you into the centre. The quickest method is by taxi. The Porto airport taxi ride takes approximately 20 minutes and cost around 23 euros. There are also multiple local bus lines that run from the airport to various locations in the city, costing approximately 2 euros and taking around 30 minutes. Finally, you can take the Metro (we did) taking 25 minutes at a cheap rate of around 2.45 euros.

We found the Metro to be the best way to get around the city during our visit. The Metro do Porto is not an underground railway like London, New York or Lisbon. It's a network of six tram or light-rail lines, running on the surface in the suburbs, then converging to run under the city centre in tunnels. The website has comprehensive information, much of it in English. Trains run every 15 - 30 minutes on each line from 06.00hrs until around 01.00hrs. Through the central section from Senhora da Hora to Estádio do Dragao that means a train every 5 or 6 minutes most of the day. Four of the lines radiate out to the western and north-western suburbs and the airport. Line D, runs north to south from the Hospital Sao Joao across the Douro River to Santo Oviedo, in the city of Gaia. Line F extends eastwards through the Rio Tinto area into the neighbouring city of Gondomar. Ticketing is fully integrated with most buses, trams and much of the local rail network under the 'ANDANTE' banner. Zonal fares are used, so make sure that you buy a ticket for the correct number of zones for your journey. Day passes are available and you can choose how many zones you want. Tickets are ridiculously cheap by UK standards; a two zone (Z2) ticket covers most central city journeys and is only 1.20 euros. A two zone (Z2) day pass is 4.15 euros - this covers the whole of the central city area. (All prices as at 2021).

Arriving in the city centre, the place appeared to be both closed and deserted as we made our way towards our chosen hotel – the Hotel Peninsula – a quirky, somewhat outdated, older building with interior wooden balconies. At 26 euros per night for a single room we got exactly what we paid for. Not much! This was a bad start to the weekend. We wandered the wet streets later that night looking for somewhere, anywhere, with a bit of life, but, as we realised the next day, we'd been looking in the wrong area. From there on things picked up considerably. Saturday started sunny & bright making sightseeing easy and presenting what turned out to be a beautiful city in an altogether more favourable light - with its narrow, medieval streets leading down to the River Douro, its numerous public squares, magnificent churches and impressive public architecture.

The Porto Marathon has been held in October or November every year since 2004 (apart from 2020 when it was cancelled due to the Covid pandemic). The race is held in conjunction with a 15K event and a 6K Fun Run. Numbers participating on all 3 events on the programme have increased dramatically over the years – from 317 in 2004 to 4042 in 2014 when, with runners from over 40 different countries, it set a new national finishers' record, confirming the event as the largest Marathon in Portugal. When last held in 2019, 3836 runners took part in the event. Cost of entry fees have remained remarkably stable over the years. I paid 45 euros in 2011 (with a free Pasta Party). Ten years later, early-bird entry for 2021 is still only 50 euros (the Pasta Party now costs 3 euros). Registration in the old Customs House by the river was easy to find and the pre-race goodies among the most generous ever: t-shirt, quality rucksack, cap and, best of all, a specially commissioned, commemorative Porto Marathon 750ml bottle of port. Sadly, because it wasn't possible to bring this back to the UK it had to either be consumed or given away. No prizes for guessing which option was taken by most of us. My colleague, being a non-drinker, attempted unsuccessfully to sneak his bottle back home in his luggage as a present for his Dad. It was removed from his hand luggage during the security search and inceremoniously dumped into a large basket under the desk. The bucket was full to the brim with confiscated bottles of Port. I wonder who got to drink all of these! Many years later while at the Expo for the Warsaw Marathon, I got talking to the Porto race organiser who was there promoting his event. I described the difficulties most foreign competitors carrying hand luggage only had in taking their souvenir bottles home to their countries of origin. I got the impression that it was the first time that anyone had ever mentioned the problem to him. Following Registration we were able to spend our lunchtime in a pub by the river watching the Newcastle v Everton match before returning later that afternoon to the Custom's House for the free Pasta Party. Once again the generosity of the organisers was overwhelming with unlimited spaghetti bolognese, jellies and as much as you wanted of the local Super Bok lager.

Race day was beautiful with clear blue skies with steadily rising temperatures. I managed to meet up at the start with friends Paul Richards and Dave Goodwin, both of whose recent 100 marathon celebrations I'd attended in Jersey and Palma respectively. The race started at 9am, together with the 15K event, on the outskirts of the city centre, because the centre itself is about as hilly as any major city can be. The Marathon does well to avoid it. By combining the Atlantic seacoast and the Douro River estuary the course is remarkably flat. It passes through three cities and crosses the river out and back on the lower level of the Eiffel Bridge. We ran a switchback first kilometre before the course turned westward along Boavista Boulevard and gently declined to meet the Atlantic Ocean. That made for some fast early kilometres, during which we passed by the finish area after about 6km. We hit the seafront at 7km and followed a short out-back section to the north, the turning point of which was marked by a sculpture, suspended above a roundabout of a fishing net about to be cast. We then turned and ran south, passing fortresses to the seaward side. The prevailing wind is from behind along this section, so at 10km the pace was still fast, before runners turned into the steep-sided and more sheltered Douro estuary to begin a tour of the city's World Heritage waterfront. We lost the shorter distance runners after 10km and after that the course was largely flat, fast and scenic as it headed out and back along both sides of the river past the port distilleries and the iconic suspension bridge that's used as the race's logo.

At 14km we passed under the high-level bridge, before running landward of the old customs building at 15km. With the city now up above us (apart from the old waterfront warehouses) we passed under a tunnel before emerging back on the riverside to cross to the south side of the Douro by a low-level bridge. The following out-and-back section, westwards towards the Atlantic along a narrow road at the foot of the steep riverbank, was marked with a turn at the half marathon point. We then retraced our steps back over the low level bridge to the north side, turning eastward, further upriver, to another turn point at 28.5km. I ran with my colleague until this point until he upped the pace and took off for a sub 4 hour finish. The course then turned back towards the Atlantic, reaching there at around 36km. I then teamed up with Dave Goodwin for the final few miles to the finish. The sting in the tail was a bit of headwind and a climb over the final 1500m. Turning off the Boavista Boulevard we hugged the periphery of the City park, and turned on to level ground for the final 100m red carpet finish in the company of a host of those completing the Fun Run event. I finished in 4 hours 12 minutes – a time I'm sure I could have bettered had the temperature not risen so much. For a well-prepared runner there is a definite potential here for a personal best time. The course record of 02:09:05 was set by Robert Chemonges of Kenya in 2018.

The finish too provided yet more goodies for the luggage home – a specially minted medal, another canvas bag, another t-shirt, sports drink and yet another free, help-yourself Super Bok bar. There were also free buses laid on to take us back to Town - all excellent value for money. The four of us rounded off a great day by finding a restaurant on the quayside specialising in Porto's culinary speciality, the Francesinha. This consists of thick bread stuffed with cured ham, roast meat covered with melted cheese and a hot thick tomato and beer sauce served with French fries, (delicious!) After that it was on to the ubiquitous, local Irish pub to fortify us for the long journey back via Gatwick the next day.

There were negatives, but this was such a great marathon event it seems churlish to dwell on them. For example the queues at Registration were unnecessary and could easily have been avoided with a little more thought. There was also confusion over the buses at the Finish that a couple of simple, well-placed signs would have prevented. Also, three-quarter miles of the route through the old town went over cobbles causing many runners to chance their luck with the pedestrians on nearby footpaths. None of this would stop me from doing the race again, however.

I loved Porto. It's a must visit city, with stunning views, incredible architecture, deep history and a great nightlife. There are some things you simply can't not-do on any visit there. You really can't go to Porto and not drink Port given the city's reputation as the port wine capital. The cellars are in Vila Nova de Gaia, a 5 minute walk from Ribeira across the Douro river. There are so many different Port wine houses to try, some you need to queue for, some you have to book ahead of time. We weren't in Porto nearly long enough to experience enough of them, I went to Sanderson's on the Saturday afternoon. In retrospect it maybe wasn't a sensible thing to do. I should have gone after the event but by then I had my own souvenir bottle of Port to finish before going home.

Another area not to be missed is Ribeira - one of the most beautiful and liveliest districts in Porto's historic centre. As its name suggests, the district is situated on the riverbank (Ribeira in Portuguese stems from the word river). Filled with the hustle and bustle of tourists and locals alike, this part of town becomes alive at nighttime and is the perfect place to spend your evenings. Ribeira is full of market stalls, cafes, shops and traditional restaurants with lively terraces where you can savour some of Portugal's delicious typical dishes while, at the same time, enjoying views over the Dom Luís I Bridge and across to Vila Nova da Gaia with its cellars lit up. When it opened in 1886, the iconic Dom Luís I Bridge held the record for the longest iron arch in the world. The double-story bridge is an excellent place to admire the views of the river and the city below. The metro crosses the upper deck, whilst cars pass at the bottom under the arch. Pedestrians can use either levels.

Finally, if time allows, another must-do is to take a cruise upriver. There are numerous options for exploring the Douro River. Whether you'd prefer a luxurious wine tour or a simple boat ride to admire the landscapes you can pay as little as 10 euros for a 50 minute trip, or choose a day-long cruise for a higher price. Most of the cruises leave from the Vila Nova de Gaia side of the river with some offering discounts for port cave tours or port purchases. Maybe next time?

Posing under the iconic Dom Louis 1st Bridge

Postcard given out at Registratiom

MOROCCO

MARRAKECH MARATHON

The Marrakech Marathon was arranged as part of a double celebration to mark Mo and I's 40th Wedding Anniversary. We'd spent the previous week in the Canary Islands where I'd taken part in the Gran Canaria Marathon on the Sunday. We then flew directly from there to Madrid before changing planes for Marrakech. I'd really been looking forward to this event. Apart from my very first marathon in Australia (where I was living there at the time) this was to be my first ever marathon outside the continent of Europe. I knew that Marrakech is one of the busiest cities in Africa and a major tourist destination with an interesting reputation. Over the years the city's energy and proximity to Europe have drawn generations of affluent European travellers. Winston Churchill visited regularly, as did Edith Piaf, Maurice Chevalier and Yves Saint Laurent. I recalled that by the late 60s, Morocco was fast becoming an essential stop-off point on that decade's new hippie trail. It was a place frequented by seekers of all types, from travellers and the more adventurous tourists through to artists, writers, fashionistas and rock stars. They were all drawn by the exotica of this exotic corner of North Africa, wIth its promise of spiritual enlightenment and plentiful hashish to help to melt away the conventions of the West. In 1966, for example, Graham Nash of Crosby, Stills & Nash fame made a pilgrimage of his own, one that sparked off one of his most famous songs, 'Marrakech Express.' On a break from touring as leader of The Hollies, Nash bought himself a ticket and hopped on board a train from Casablanca to Marrakesh. 'I was in first class and there were a lot of older, rich American ladies in there, who all had their hair dyed blue,' Nash recalls today. 'and I quickly grew bored of that and went back to the third class of the train. The place was full of chickens, pigs and goats. It was fabulous; the whole thing was fascinating.' Likewise, beset by legal issues in the UK, the Rolling Stones moved to Marrakech in 1967. Though the album that was inspired by their visit, 'Their Satanic Majesties Request' is generally considered as one of their worst, the Stones set the trend for others, intent on escaping to a magical, distant place, to follow. Before continuing, I better explain the differences in spelling. While the common English spelling is Marrakesh' (as in Graham Nash's song title), the French spelling 'Marrakech' is also widely used. As this is the official name of the marathon (organised by a French company) this is the one I'll continue to use. The name Marrakech originates from the Berber words amur (n) kush, which means 'Land of God.'

Marrakech is the third largest city in Morocco, after Casablanca and Fez and the first of Morocco's four imperial cities. It lies in the centre of the fertile, irrigated Haouz Plain, south of the Tennsift River. The city is divided into two distinct parts: the Medina, the historical city, and the new European modern district called Gueliz or Ville Nouvelle. The Medina is full of intertwining narrow passageways and local shops full of character. In contrast, Gueliz plays host to modern restaurants, fast food chains and big brand stores. The ancient section of the city (the Medina) was designated a UNESCO World Heritage site in 1985. Surrounded by a vast palm grove, the medina in Marrakech is called the 'red city' because of its buildings and ramparts of beaten clay, which were built during the residence of the Almohads (a Berber confederation that created an Islamic empire in North Africa and Spain during the 12th century). The heart of the medina is Djmaa el-Fna square, a vibrant marketplace. Nearby is the 12th-century Kutubiyyah (Koutoubia) Mosque with its 253-foot minaret, built by Spanish captives. The 16th-century Saʻdī Mausoleum, the 18th-century Dar el-Beïda Palace (now a hospital), and the 19th-century Bahia royal residence reflect the city's historical growth. Much of the medina is still surrounded by 12th-century walls; among the surviving gates to the medina, the stone Bab Agnaou is particularly notable. The modern quarter, called Gueliz, to the west of the medina developed under the French protectorate.

Marrakech is famous for its parks, especially the Menara olive grove and the walled 1,000-acre (405-hectare) Agdal gardens. An irrigation system built in the 12 century is still used to water the city's gardens. Popular for tourism and winter sports, the city is a commercial centre for the High Atlas Mountains and Saharan trade and has an international airport. It is connected by railway and road to Safi and Casablanca. Tourism is strongly advocated by the reigning monarch, Mohamed 1V, with the goal of doubling the number of tourists to 20 million by 2020. The city is particularly popular with the French and many French celebrities have bought property there in recent years. Despite the tourist boom, however, the majority of the city's inhabitants are still very poor and this contrast between the obvious wealth of a minority with the poverty of the majority is one of the most fascinating aspects of any visit there. Every year the city, with its own blend of tradition and modernity, plays host to the Marrakech International Marathon - making it an ideal location for runners in search of a winter escape to the sun.

We flew into Marrakech on the Wednesday evening for a 5-night stay at the Hotel Agdal in the newer part of town. Perfectly adequate Bed and Breakfast for the 5 nights cost a reasonable 32 euros per night. Marrakech's modern international airport has direct scheduled flights from London, Dublin, Oslo, Copenhagen, Stockholm, Paris, Madrid, and many charter flights arriving from all over Europe. From the UK, easyJet flies to Marrakech from Manchester, Bristol, London Stansted and Gatwick Airport (and also from Madrid and from Lyon). One of the problems we had on arrival concerned the Moroccan dirham (MAD). The dirham is officially designated a closed currency, meaning it can only be traded within Morocco. This meant queuing up on arrival to change currency for the bus fare/taxi ride into town. Terminal 1 (the international terminal) has two money changing outlets in the Arrivals hall and one in Departures. (£1 = MAD12.39) As we queued we were assailed from all sides by dodgy-looking 'taxi drivers' circling us like vultures around a corpse. 'Welcome to Marrakech,' muttered one knowing fellow traveller! You're advised to keep the receipts of currency exchange, as these will be required for the conversion back to foreign currency before departure, when you can change as many dirhams as you have left. At the airport the exchange rate is very similar to that in the town centre, so there is not much lost in waiting to the last minute to change your remaining dirhams. Once through to embarkation you can no longer spend dirhams, only foreign currency, so make sure you have no unwanted dirhams left. As the airport is only about 5km from the city and we'd no intention of getting fleeced by one of the dodgy taxi drivers, we decided to take the airport bus. The No 19 Airport express bus is MAD30, with a free return trip if it is within 2 weeks of the initial purchase (keep your receipt). It serves all the major hotels and is a great way to go from the airport to the hotels. You can easily find its departure stop, to the left of the road immediately outside of the Arrivals Hall. The bus leaves the airport every half an hour between 07:00 and 21:30. The bus has no particular stops except Djema El Fna Square and can stop anywhere on the route - the driver has a small map to hand out and you can tell the driver the hotel you're heading to. Although it was dark by this stage the only trouble we had in locating our hotel was in fending-off the inevitable touts waiting at the bus stop, ready to pounce on gullible travellers. This was to be a recurring theme of our stay.

They say Marrakech is a bit like Marmite, you either like it or loathe it. Most of the negatives we'd heard about the place seem to centre on this continual harassment of northern Europeans perceived to be 'rich' by elements of the local community. In certain parts of the city you are continually accosted by people wanting to: be your guide, sell you their wares, sell you their grandmothers, pose with their pet monkey, pay to watch them make snakes dance out of a basket, or simply just hand them dirhams because you look as if you could afford to. Most of this activity takes place around Djemaa-El-Fna, the central square, and the nearby Souks. Away from there, however, there are sections of the city that are both affluent and cosmopolitan and a match for any area of your average European city. During the 4-plus hours that I was running the marathon Mo was able to walk freely around all parts of the city without unnecessary harrassment. I liked the place.

The Marrakech Marathon, organised under the High Patronage of His Majesty King Mohammed VI, is surprisingly one of nine AIMS (The Association of International Marathons and Distance Races) events in Morocco. The country has assumed a leading role in road racing in North Africa and the Arab world for the last 10 years through the efforts of Rachid Ben Meziane, who was recently appointed an AIMS ambassador. The inaugural race was held in 1987. Frenchman Jacques Boxberger won the men's race while the women's event was won by Morocco's 14-year-old Nadia Colombero – an achievement not to be repeated since 18 years has become accepted as the lower age limit to run a Marathon. Marrakech celebrated the silver anniversary of its marathon in 2014 with 7,000 runners participating and coming from all over the world to do so. With blue skies and a mild temperature of around 15C at the start of the race, the Marathon boasts an impressive course record of 2:06:35 (at the time of writing).

When I ran this event in 2012 Registration for the marathon was about as low-key as you can get. It took place between 10am and 6pm from Thursday to Saturday in a tent near a busy roundabout close to the Central Post Office. We were simply handed a number and a T-shirt. No written instructions, no explanations, no route maps – just turn up and run. So that's what I did. The start was elsewhere in the wide Ave de la Menara on the southern edge of town. There were few portaloos and, as far as I could see, nowhere secure to leave baggage. That year they'd decided to start the approx. 2500 half marathon runners at 8.30am, half an hour before the 500 of us in the marathon. This at least gave us the course to ourselves for the full distance. (I understand that start times have subsequently been changed to 8.30am for the Marathon and 9.30am for the Half)

It was a perfect cloudless, crisp, sunny morning as we set off with 5 hours and 30 minutes in which to complete our journey. We all knew that meant a hot, sticky final few miles for anyone still running after four hours. After a small detour up to the Gare de Marrakech the route then took us on a huge anti-clockwise circle around the perimeter of the city. For the first few miles, heading south through olive groves, we were treated to some quite breathtaking views of a wall of snow-covered Atlas Mountains in the near distance. Returning back to the city we then followed the ancient city walls along the aptly named Rue des Remparts. The course passes several historic sites and landmarks unique to the 'Red City' – red mud buildings and 12th century fortifications. This was the only part open to traffic, leading to some interesting encounters with men on donkeys, angry motorists and whistle-mad policemen.

We were then taken north east on a beautiful traffic-free stretch through La Palmerie, the green lung of Marrakech. This is a real oasis on the outskirts of the city. This beautiful area covers 13,000ha and is a literal forest of palm trees (about 150,000 of them) surrounding a few upmarket hotels. The route then headed past manicured and well-watered golf courses to hit the main Casablanca road back towards town and the finish. By then the digital roadside thermometers were showing 26 degrees and the day was warming up. The road surface was excellent throughout, there were refreshment stations water bottles every 5k on the course along with whole oranges and little bags of raisins and dates - though no gels or sports drinks. At the finish there was quite a nice medal and a friendly greeting from fellow club member David Parry who'd managed to get round in under 4 hours.

At 60 euros this marathon was twice the cost and half the value of the week before in Gran Canaria. There was no pasta party, no isotonic drinks, no goody bags; in fact no extras at all. It was a totally different experience though and one I'll long remember. It's also one I'd definitely like to repeat if only to pay another visit to the beautiful Atlas Mountains. We travelled there on the day after the race in a small group of four and an experienced and very knowledgeable tour guide. This was undoubtedly the highlight of the whole trip. The peacefulness of the mountain valleys is about as far removed as you can get from the hustle and bustle of Marrakech itself. For anyone contemplating going to the marathon, make sure your itinerary also includes a visit to the mountains while you're in the area. The Atlas Mountains are about 65km outside Marrakech and run across Morocco for about 1000 km, separating the mild Atlantic and Mediterranean coastlines from the harsh Sahara desert in the south. The mountains are home to arid desert landscapes dotted with burnt-orange rock, pines, cedars, snow-capped peaks and lush green valleys, often interspersed with the clay homes of the nomadic Berber population. The guided tour into the Mountains offered access and insight into Berber culture that would be difficult to get on your own. We visited local Berber villages, explored the local souks of Tahanaout, and stopped for what we were told was a typical Berber lunch at the home of a Berber family. We also had time for a 1.5 hour walk into one of the empty mountain valleys where the air was as clear as a bell and it seemed like time had stood still. The hassle-free round-trip transport from our hotel cost around £32 – well worth the expense.

Our visit to the mountains was our only excursion outside the city limits. We spent most of our time in the area around Djemaa-el-Fina Square and the endless labyrinths of souks (bazaars) and alleyways covering all of the Medina. The carnival atmosphere of Djemma El-Fna is a must-visit attraction. The square and its open-air space may be touristy but is unlike any other place on Earth. There's always something to see there day and night whether it be snake charmers, ('charming cobras in the square' – 'Marrakesh Express'), acrobats, sooth-sayers, or the musicians and food stalls. At night the square really comes to life as people navigate toward the exotic aromas and the entertaining sights. As the evening darkens, the hustle and bustle rages on and the exotic music appears louder and even more hypnotic. Smoke rises from hundreds of barbecues and storytellers, Gnawa musicians, acrobats and fortune-tellers attract throngs of visitors out to experience the 'real' Marrakech. The square is undoubtedly the highlight of any

Marrakech night. Musicians, dancers, and story tellers pack the square filling it with a cacophony of flutes, drum beats and excited shouts. Scores of stalls sell a wide array of Moroccan fare (some overcharging heavily) and you will almost certainly be accosted by women wanting to give you a henna tattoo or the photo of yourself with a monkey on your shoulder. You can stand and watch the shows, but be prepared to give some dirhams for the pleasure. By day it is largely filled with snake charmers and people with monkeys, as well as some of the more common stalls. It makes sense to ignore anyone who offers you something that you do not want or be prepared to move away. It's inevitable that they will be asking you shortly for (too much) money. If you don't want to pay dearly for that henna tattoo or the monkey photo, you need to have an excuse prepared before the seller approaches.

The souks (marketplaces), whose various entrances are tucked behind and above restaurants and cafés at the edges of the square are where you can buy almost anything. Thousands of stall holders sell anything from cactus silk scarves to aromatic herbs, from spices to shoes, jellabas to kaftans, tea pots to tagines, Arabian-style lamps and much, much more. Each quarter of the souks focuses on a separate trade and as you wander through the back alleys the air rings with the sounds of carpenters, metalworkers, fabric dyers and cobblers working hard on their craft. Seeing what goes on behind the scenes in the souks leaves you with a greater appreciation for the goods you barter for. We both thoroughly enjoyed just wandering around, occasionally getting lost, taking in the atmosphere. Mo even managed to barter her way into buying a Moroccan belt and drum for her dancing class. I still think she was robbed!

The other major attraction worth a visit is the Koutoubia Mosque, across the road from Djemaa El-Fna Square. This is named after the booksellers market that used to be here. It is said that the minaret of the Koutoubia mosque is to Marrakech what the Eiffel Tower is to Paris. At night, the mosque is beautifully lit. Admiring it from the tranquillity of the park in which it's situated provides a welcome diversion from the mayhem taking place in the square.

Unfortunately, as with most mosques in Morocco, non-Muslims are not allowed inside.

If you want to eat well during your stay in Marrakech, it's best to do what the locals do and eat at the food stalls in the square. It is a common misconception that these stalls are here for the tourists. They have been in existence long before Marrakech became a tourist destination. We were told that all of the stalls can be regarded as perfectly safe to eat at. They are strictly licensed and controlled by the government, especially now it's a popular destination for tourists. Each night in the Djemaa El-Fna rows of street stalls are set up under giant white tents. These establishments serve similar fare and have menus printed in French, Arabic and usually English. With dishes such as: Spicy snail broth, skewered hearts, bubbling tajines, flash-fried fish: the Djemaa food stalls are the ideal place to try Moroccan culinary specialities. Stalls have numbered spots and are set up on a grid. (The spicy snail dishes are on the eastern side of the square). Our favourite (and least expensive) dishes were tajine, couscous, brochette and harira (a cheap, hearty soup made of tomatoes, onions, saffron and coriander with lentils and chickpeas). Despite alarmist warnings from some of the more conservative guests in our hotel, our stomachs were fine the next morning. I'm sure that most travellers are soon aware that the restaurants employ rather insistent 'greeters' who are very aggressive in getting customers for their stall.

Thinking that we'd be lucky to find any alcohol in such a strict Muslim country, Mo and I took the precaution of bringing our own spirits from the duty free at Madrid airport. After all, it was our Wedding Anniversary. We needn't have bothered. We found a (very limited) selection of places selling alcohol in the Medina. The best of these was the Chesterfield Pub in the Hotel Nassim on Avenue Mohammed V. The pub provided an unusual experience. Described as an 'English pub' it serves Moroccan lager (no perfect dark beer here) and has an outside pool in a courtyard with palm trees – not at all your authentic English experience.

The city of Marrakech was beautiful, chaotic and strikingly different from the European norm. For anyone looking for a fast course, the Marrakech Marathon provides a good option (although be prepared for the temperature rise as the race progresses). While there's not much in terms of any pre-race activities or Expo associated with the event, this is more than compensated for by the character and atmosphere of the delightful old city with its winding narrow passageways, food stalls and souks. It's a place, and a race, to which I'd love to return.

Poster from 2012 Marrakech Marathon

Jamaa El-Fna Square. Marrakech
(Photo by Selina Bubendorfer on Unsplash)

AUSTRIA

LINZ MARATHON

I discovered this event while searching for an alternative venue to the London Marathon weekend in April 2012. When London, with its marathon monopoly of a UK April weekend no longer appeals, it's necessary to look farther afield for somewhere new to run. The previous year I'd gone to Madrid. This time, having never run in Austria, I decided to give Linz a try. After the Vienna City Marathon, the Linz-Danube Marathon is the second largest marathon in Austria and a popular alternative with local runners to the 'big brother' in Vienna that takes place earlier in the same month. According to the pre-race publicity, around 20,000 participants, over 100,000 spectators and a fast running course passing the most beautiful places in the city make the Linz Marathon a great running festival every year. In addition to the classic distance, the Linz-Danube Marathon also features a half marathon, a quarter marathon over 10.5 km, a relay marathon and competitions for hand bikers and inline skaters Before setting out I realised that I only knew three things about Linz. Firstly, that it was Austria's third largest city. Secondly, that Adolph Hitler spent much of his youth living there and thirdly, that it had also been the home of Anton Bruckner, the famous composer. The pictures of the city on the event website looked both attractive and interesting. Why not go and see it for ourselves?

Linz lies along the Danube River 100 miles (160 km) west of Vienna. The city has a long and interesting history, having been founded by the Romans, though the first references to the name Linz date back to AD 799. Having originated as the Roman fortress of Lentia it became an important medieval trading centre. Lying on a direct rail route between the Baltic and Adriatic seas, as well as on the Danube, Linz has extensive docks and a busy river-transit trade. The city was heavily industrialised during the Second World War, but in modern times, its industrial legacy is beginning to fade, with tourism coming more to the forefront of trade and commerce. The city is made up of several districts, home to an extensive old town with beautiful historic buildings, which include the old castle, St. Martin's Church, the early Baroque town hall, the 13th-century Main Square with a monument to the Holy Trinity, the 13th century City Parish Church, the Old Cathedral (1669–78), the 13th century Minorite (Franciscan) Church and the 16th-century Landhaus ('State House'). The Danube River and the surrounding hills give Linz a pleasant ambience which is always popular with visiting river cruisers. Linz has also established an international reputation due to its extensive cultural life. This is most evident in a park alongside the river referred to as 'Kulturmeile' (culture mile) which stretches from the Brucknerhaus concert hall and the Lentos art museum and the Ars Electronica Center on the northern bank of the river. Having been awarded the European Capital of Culture award in 2009, Linz hosts numerous concerts and during the summer it hosts regular concerts and performances, including many taking place in the public places such as the town squares,

With no direct flights to Linz from any of our local airports Mo and I were forced into making an overnight stay in Gatwick before catching an early Saturday morning flight to Austria, arriving in Salzburg by 9am. Salzburg, Austria's second largest city, offers an abundance of interesting, impressive and historically significant sights, among them: the Mirabell Palace, Salzburg Cathedral, Salzburg Fortress, Mozart's Residence and Birthplace, the Festival District and St. Peter's Abbey. Wanting to see as much as possible of the place during our short stopover we'd gone online and pre-booked a cheap, one-hour Salzburg Panorama City Tour before leaving the UK. Trips leave on the hour from outside the Mirabell Palace (whose famous gardens are featured in 'The Sound of Music'). Salzburg's W.A. Mozart airport is only 4km from the city centre. Bus service 2 runs between the airport and the Central Station every 10 to 20 minutes; the journey takes approximately 20 minutes and a single ticket costs 2.50 euros. As we were running to a tight schedule we took a taxi instead. From memory this cost around 17 euros and allowed us to catch our 10am tour bus with minutes to spare. Salzburg is a beautiful city and, having enjoyed what we'd seen, it made me determined to revisit and run the city's own marathon at some stage in the future. There are approximately 40 trains per day that make the 67 kilometre journey from Salzburg to Linz. Having paid 37.40 euros for a return ticket for two, Mo and I boarded the midday train for a one hour scenic journey along the valley to Linz where for 137 euros we'd booked a 2-night stay in the 4-star Austria Trend Hotel Schillerpark located in the center of Linz, a 12-minute walk from the marathon finish in the main square and a 10-minute walk from Linz Central Station. Incidentally, the race organisers are currently offering Hotel Packages under the heading 'Enjoy 2 Nights – Pay Just 1' for the 2021 edition of the event. The free additional night is bookable at selected hotels with your registration confirmation for the Marathon. A free 1-day-LinzCard is included as well. Among Partner hotels in Linz that offer a free second night in the city are: Amedia Hotel, Courtyard by Marriott, Hotel Donauwelle, Ibis styles, and Park Inn by Radisson.

With the rest of the afternoon free we went off in search of any evidence of Hitler's time spent in Linz. Unsurprislingly, the local tourist office wasn't keen on promoting its unavoidable link with evil dictators or mass murderers (Notorious Holocaust architect Adolf Eichmann also spent his youth in Linz). Hitler too spent most of his youth in the Linz area, from 1898 until 1907, when he left for Vienna. The family lived first in the village of Leonding on the outskirts of town, and then on the Humboldtstrasse in Linz where Hitler was enrolled in the high school, (as was the philosopher Ludwig Wittgenstein). Until the end of his life, Hitler considered Linz to be his hometown and, when installed as Fuhrer, envisioned extensive architectural schemes for it – including a massive new Fuhrermuseum to house his collection of looted art. He wanted it to become the main cultural centre of the Third Reich, and to eclipse Vienna, a city he hated. To make the city economically vibrant, Hitler also initiated a major industrialization of Linz shortly before, and during, the Second World War. Near the end of World War II, he became enamored of the musical compositions of Anton Bruckner another noted citizen of Linz who spent the years between 1855 and 1868 working as a local composer and organist in the city's Old Cathedral. Hitler planned to convert the monastery of St. Florian in Linz – where Bruckner also played the organ, and where he was buried – into a repository of Bruckner's manuscripts. Today a magnificent Classical concert hall on the banks of the Danube built in 1974 called The Brucknerhaus is named after him. It holds about 200 performances per year and is home to the Ars Electronica festival and Brucknerfest. In conjunction with an Austrian broadcasting company it also organizes the Linzer Klangwolke, an annual musical event. The Brucknerhaus Linz with its unique location on the Danube, range of superb classical, jazz and world music concert events and timelessly elegant Finnish - styled architecture is regarded as one of the leading concert halls in Europe. It's also where Registration for the marathon takes place.

    Having paid 52 euros to enter the event, Mo and I visited on the Saturday afternoon to collect my bib and information for the next day's race. After looking in on the Pasta Party we decided to give it a miss. At an extra six euros for a tiny plate of spaghetti plus another two euros for bottled water, it appeared very poor value for money. Instead, we spent what was left of a beautiful Spring afternoon sitting in glorious sunshine by the banks of the Danube watching a succession of children's races and fun runs, all part of the marathon weekend. The river looked so appealing that we made enquiries about the possibility of taking the 5-hour boat trip along the Danube from Linz to Passau in Germany at 27 euros per head, including food. While it's possible to come back the same way, it seems that those on a tight schedule take the option of returning by train. Sadly, our return flight times on the day after the marathon didn't allow sufficient time to make the journey.

Marathon day started much cooler with a continual threat of rain that didn't materialise. I was surprised at how big this event is with over 15,000 of us lining up together on the Voest Bridge about a 15 to 20 minute walk along the Danube from the Main Square. (For those arriving on the day, free shuttle buses to the start run from Linz railway station). The various events started at intervals with the estimated 1,000 marathon runners being the last to leave at 9.30am. We were given 5 hours and 30 minutes to complete the race for which course records are held by Alexander Kuzin of Ukraine (2:07:33 in 2007) and Lisa-Christina Stublic of Croatia (2:30:45 in 2011). As pacemakers were provided my intention was to attempt to follow the green 4hr 15 minute balloons initially and then to see how I felt from there. I won't do this again. This strategy lasted only a couple of miles before the balloons disappeared skywards in the strong wind and the pacemaker himself became invisible in the seething throng - next to be spotted arriving at the finish as I was making my way back to the hotel. Maybe he'd been looking for his balloons!

The course is difficult to describe. Consisting largely of a series of unremarkable urban roads, there was little of interest to be seen for most of the way around. We completed a variety of loops around the City with the first 10km going through the northern suburbs before re-crossing the Danube shortly after 9km for a further 10km loop to the west. The half marathon then left us in the main square as we were treated to a much larger, convoluted loop of the southern suburbs, including a pleasant section through a scenic park. Finally, just after 40km we returned to the city centre for the long straight stretch up the Landstrasse – the cobbled, tram-lined, main street, where we were encouraged by cheering crowds all the way into the finish in the Hauptplatz (The Main Square). The square is one of the largest enclosed squares in Austria with an impressive 20-metre-high column, completed in 1723, as its centrepiece. Made of white marble, the column is dedicated to the Holy Trinity and was built in gratitude for having survived disasters and as protection against fire, war. The Hauptplatz is enclosed by the striking facades of buildings with an important historical background such as the Old Town Hall (the seat of Linz's mayor), the University of Arts and Industrial Design and Feichtinger-Haus which houses the famous Glockenspiel that changes its melody depending on the season – from Christmas carols to the national anthem or masterpieces by Mozart, Haydn or Bruckner. Filled with noisy spectators, it was certainly an impressive place to finish a marathon.

The crowds were, in fact, a constant in a well-supported race organised with typical Austrian efficiency throughout. Drink stations were numerous and well stocked with copious amounts of Powerade, cola, bananas, water and other unknown consumables that I didn't have the courage to try. There were live bands, dancing cheerleaders, flags and bunting all around the route giving it the feel of a big city marathon on the day. There was even a possee of Kenyans (presumably too slow to get into London) running for big bucks at the head of the field. At the finish we received an excellent medal, technical t-shirt plus loads of free food and real alcoholic beer. Not a bad day out and, even if it is a bit of a long way to go, it was still a nice change from running around the streets of London for the umpteenth time.

Normally, when visiting somewhere new, we make an effort to sample the local cuisine. I left for Linz with thoughts of tucking in to platefuls of Tafelspitz (a boiled beef broth considered to be Austria's national dish). Or maybe even Wiener Schnitzel or Vienna Sausage followed by the lovely Apfelstrudel (layers of thin pastry surrounding a filling of apple, usually with cinnamon and raisins). That was not to be. Most of the restaurants we looked at would have necessitated taking out a bridging loan to pay the bill. We settled instead on fast food outlets like the local McDonald's, conveniently placed on Landstrasse, and Big Joe Falafel just around the corner in Graben. There were compensations though in the form of a couple of good Irish pubs within spitting distance of the Main Square: the Chelsea Pub on Domgasse and The Old Dubliner, tucked away in a nearby back street. So, all in all, things didn't turn out too bad in the end.

Start and Finish of Linz Marathon

Photos: Linz Marathon / Klaus Mitterhauser www.klaus-mitterhauser.at

HUNGARY

BUDAPEST MARATHON

Completing the Budapest Marathon in 2012 achieved the first of the twin targets that I'd set myself for that year; to have run a marathon in 20 different countries and to reach 200 marathons within the year. Never having run in Hungary before, this was my 20th country. Ironically I had entered this event six years earlier but the race was cancelled at the very last minute due to civil unrest in the capital over the Government's proposed economic reforms. We were offered free entry to the next edition but I was never in a position to take it up. Of course, the money wasted on airfares and hotel expenses was never recovered. Six years down the line easyJet had long abandoned its unprofitable Newcastle – Budapest route making the getting there all the more difficult. This time Mo and I made the long train journey south to fly from Gatwick, returning via Manchester with an unwanted overnight stay at an airport hotel. How much easier it would have been had we gone in 2006.

Still, Budapest was a city I was determined to visit. As someone old enough to recall the black and white TV images of Soviet tanks rolling into the city to quell anti- Soviet uprisings in 1956 the place had always held a certain fascination. I'd even gone-on to study the subject as part of a university course module on 'Communism' many years later. I wanted to see the place for myself. With a population of about 1.8 million, Budapest is often cited as one of the most beautiful cities in Europe. It has variously been ranked as the most liveable Central and Eastern European city on EIU's quality of life index and 'Europe's 7th most idyllic place to live' by Forbes.

Throughout its history it has been occupied at times by the Celts, the Romans, the Hungarians, the Mongols and the Ottomans before emerging as the co-capital of the powerful Austro-Hungarian Empire in the 19th century. The year 1872 stands out as a milestone inthe city's history as this was when the three separate settlements of Pest, Buda and Obuda ('Old' Buda) were united into one city with a population of more than 150,000. Budapest officially became the capital city of Hungary, and underwent rapid growth in size and eminence. This was the city's golden age, and coincided with the Hungarian millennial celebrations in 1896 when the continental Europe's first underground railroad was opened. Towards the end of the Second World War, in the autumn of 1944, Budapest became a front-line town and suffered severe damage, especially in the castle quarter where units of the German army were barricaded in. From 1945 onwards Soviet troops controlled the whole of Budapest and thereafter it was ruled along strict Soviet lines. In the autumn of 1956 political turmoil and economic hardship fuelled popular uprisings which were savagely put down by Hungarian and Soviet forces of law and order. The inner city presented a picture of devastation. In the 1960s and 1970s much inner-city building and reconstruction took place, such as the opening to traffic of the Elisabeth Bridge, extension of the underground network, renovation of the old city centre, especially the castle quarter, and the building of large luxury hotels both in the castle quarter and on the Pest bank of the Danube. What soon became known as 'goulash communism' encouraged an upsurge in tourism, and visitors from both Eastern and Western Europe as well as the US in particular visited the city in ever-increasing numbers. In 1989 political changes in Hungary finally led to the Iron Curtain on the Hungarian-Austrian border being pulled down, cementing Budapest's popularity as an attractive tourist destination.

A major tourist attraction is the 60 hectare section of Budapest spanning the bridges either side of the Danube. This area contains the impressive architecture of Government buildings, museums, markets, Palaces, Baroque churches plus the bridges themselves. In 1987 the UNESCO World Heritage Committee listed the view of the

Danube embankments and the Buda Castle District - which is one of the most beautiful and romantic parts of the city of Budapest - as a World Heritage site. The Castle District is an ancient town, giving home to some of the most important historical monuments in Hungary. While nearly 800 years passed since it has been originally founded, its beauty still stands unparalelled, despite earthquakes, fires, sieges and world wars. The buildings themselves in Budapest bear tell-tale signs of recent and ancient history. Both the Pest and Buda embankments of the Danube stretching from the Liberty Bridge all the way up to the Margaret Bridge, the area encompassed by the Chain Bridge and some of the buildings belonging to the Technical University, the Gellert Bath, the Gellert Hill with the Statue of Liberty and the Citadel, the Castle of Buda, the Baroque churches and Turkish baths of the so-called Water Town are all parts of the World Heritage today. On the Pest embankment of the Danube, the listed items are the Parliament building, Roosevelt Square, the Academy of Sciences and the Gresham Palace (now the Four Seasons Hotel). In 2002 Heroes' Square along with its surroundings, and Andrassy Avenue with the Millenium Underground Railway were added to the World Heritage List. There's certainly enough to satisfy the most discerning of Marathon Tourists.

Our outward journey to Budapest proved to be something of a disaster. A two-hour delay in leaving Gatwick meant that I was never going to be in Budapest in time for the 6 pm closing of Registration on the Saturday evening. I was aware that I was cutting it fine in booking an afternoon flight but knew that, if the worst came to the worst, there was always the option of picking my number up between 7 and 9 am on race morning. On landing at Budapest Terminal 1 there are two main options of getting into the centre of town: either by taxi or by public transport. We invariably (and in this case, wrongly) choose the latter. At the time, the official provider of taxi services from the airport was an outfit named Fo Taxis who have their own booth within the terminal offering prices to the city centre for about 6,000 to 6,500 HUF (Hungarian Forints) or 22 to 25 euros depending on exchange rate and quoted fare by zone. The official currency is the Hungarian Forint (HUF) in Hungary though euros are accepted at several places. At the time of writing £1 buys approximately 357 Forints. In a misguided attempt to save a few euros we ignored the taxis and went instead for the much more complicated option that involved first taking the 200 E bus from the terminal to the Blue Line metro terminus at Kobanya/Kisbet station. It's necessary to purchase separate tickets for each individual journey – not an easy thing to do when ticket machines are out of order. At the time single tickets, whether for bus, metro, tram, trolley bus as well as suburban railway within city boundaries all cost the same price of 320 HUF (about £1) Every ticket has to be validated immediately on entry, or just before entry to the tracks of the metro. Ignore this at your peril. Ticket inspectors are everywhere and we watched as several of our fellow passengers on the metro section were handed what appeared to be quite hefty fines. After a long and awkward commute we eventually arrived in the centre of Pest at the Deak ter station. All three of the city's metro lines intersect at that stop (and only at that stop) and, if necessary, you can use your metro ticket to transfer to another line. All we now had to do, or so we thought, was to find our way down to the Danube and follow the river along to our pre-booked accomodation on the Boat Hotel Fortuna moored close to one of the bridges. Unfortunately Deak ter is an extremely complicated area once you surface above the ground. Roads head-off in all directions with signs in undecipherable Hungarian, it's not easy to find your bearings and many first time visitors simply get lost. We got lost! After wandering about in the dark for ages we eventually gave in and flagged down a passing cab no more than a stone's throw from where we wanted to be. We were charged the minimum set fare. We should have taken the taxi option at the airport. The consolation was that our floating hotel was ideally situated within walking distance of all amenities and with outstanding views from its decks of the city's iconic buildings, particularly when lit up at night. We considered it excellent value for 120 euros for the 3-night stay with a good breakfast provided each day.

Exhausted by the long journey and with a marathon to run next day we spent our first night admiring the views from the boat before arising early next morning and taking the Yellow Line metro to Registration in the city's Heroes' Square. The Square sits at the conclusion of Andrassy Avenue, the city's main thoroughfare. The two and a half kilometre long Andrassy Avenue is the Hungarian Champs-Elysees. Named after a former Prime Minister of Hungary, it was built for the millennial celebrations of 1896 and connects Varosliget and Heroes' Square to the downtown area. Heroes Square is the biggest and most impressive square in Budapest. In the middle stands the Millenium Monument, with Archangel Gabriel on top, holding the double cross of Christianity and the Holy Hungarian Crown. It was constructed to mark the 1000th anniversary of the arrival of the Magyar tribes. The pedestal below is occupied by the ornate horseback statues of the seven Hungarian leaders who led the Hungarian nation into the Carpathian Basin in 896 AD. The middle of the square is dominated by the Tomb of the Unknown Soldier, wreathed by all heads of state when officially visiting Hungary. Behind Heroes' Square, the City Park Lake offers the capital's citizens boating in the summer and ice-skating in the wintertime (apparently the ice is artificial and of good quality). The entertainment and cultural facilities of the City Park (Budapest Zoo, Funfair, Municipal Circus, Vajdahunyad Castle, the museum of Agriculture and Transport, the Petofi Cultural Hall and the Szechenyi Thermal Bath) are among the most sought after tourist sights in Budapest.

Mo and I were fortunate to have arrived early enough that morning to have time to have a good look around. We returned to the area on the Monday to catch up on what we'd missed. It's an impessive loction for a marathon. These days Number pick-up takes place in the Square from the Thursday before the race and those running their first marathon are encouraged to wear a second bib on their back inscribed with 'My First Marathon.' Everyone is given a technical T-shirt and a race bag when registering. There's also a free-to-runners Saturday afternoon Pasta party as part of the deal (HUF 1,000 for non-runners) Our delayed flight meant that we missed out on this. We also missed out on the free 3.3km fun run on the Saturday morning but, as I rarely bother with these events, it was of no consequence. My race entry cost 55 euros way back in 2012. For the current edition entry fees go up in stages from 65 euros in April to 90 euros in October with on-site entries costing 100 euros. In addition, runners without their own championship chip have to pay a refundable deposit of 1,000 HUF (about £3) for the single-use chip provided. The organisers will only accept a HUF 1,000 note for this – it's not possible to pay by any other means. I was glad to have had my own chip on seeing the lengthy queues of those seeking to reclaim their deposit back at the end of the race. Some simply gave up and walked away in disgust.

The Budapest Marathon has an interesting history and can trace its origins back to 1984 when, having been inspired by the success of events in cities like London and New York, a few Hungarian sports organisers dreamed of staging a people's marathon in Budapest. Though Marathons had previously been held in Hungary for decades they had only catered for limited fields of mainly professional runners. In the very first popular Budapest Marathon 625 male and 25 female runners finished the race, coming from 18 countries. Five years later in 1989 the Budapest Sports Office, founded at the beginning of that year, became the organisers of the marathon for the first time and the race is still held under their direction. Runners came from 29 countries and the Guest of Honour was Fred Lebow, founder of the New York City Marathon. Lebow, who had lived his childhood years in Arad (a town in the Hungarian-speaking part of Romania) ran the half marathon. In 1994 and 1995 there was a hiatus: the Marathon had not been organised at a sufficiently high level to attract adequate financial support. The city government showed no interest in helping and private companies in the emerging Hungarian marketplace were initially reluctant to become involved. In 1996 the SPAR group stepped in to become the title sponsor of the marathon. The relationship has developed as the event has grown and this highly successful partnership has now endured for over 20 years. Since 1996 the half marathon has become a separate event held a month before the marathon and the date of both races has moved to autumn. Then in 1998, following a suggestion by Fred Lebow, the City Park next to Heroes Square, became the start and finish area of the marathon, signalling a new era in the history of the event: one in which the quality of the services provided began to improve year by year. The last decade in particular has been one of continuous growth. Hungarians have come to appreciate their own marathon and foreign runners have begun to discover quite how gorgeous a course Budapest offers. Participating in the marathon is essentially a running sightseeing tour of Budapest. The course leads through the centre of the city, down the famous Andrassy Boulevard and across the Chain Bridge. Runners are able to admire the views of Buda Castle from the Danube banks and marvel in the panorama of Pest as well as Europe's third largest Parliament Building. The number of participants is increasing rapidly and Budapest has been described by Distance Running magazine as 'Europe's new favourite running city.'

When I ran in 2012 it was the 27th edition of the event and included over 19,000 runners in a variety of races including the marathon, a 30km race, a mini marathon, fun run and marathon relay. Apparently over 2,600 of the entrants were from outside Hungary. Since then it has attracted over 27,000 in all the distances with more than 6,000 in the marathon. In 2016 there were more than 4,300 foreign runners including 2,500 in the marathon from 79 countries. With the slogan 'All for the run and the run for all' the organisers have attempted to create a running festival offering the chance of participating to those who are not yet ready for the full marathon distance. Today the Budapest Marathon is part of a 2-day festival of running with Sunday the focus is on the marathon, a 30km, marathon relay or 10km events while on Saturday the focus is on shorter distances.

The Marathon and Marathon Relay set off at 9.30am in four separate waves on an unseasonably hot and humid Sunday for October. (We didn't know it at the time, but the oppressive conditions were the precursor to the mother and father of a thunder and lightning storm later that evening, bad enough to cause the abandonment of Ferencvaros' televised football match late in the second half). We were given five and a half hours to complete the course. Rather unusually, those in the 30km event joined in exactly 12.195km into the main race. There was no mass start for this event – runners were encouraged to begin at a time interval according to their planned finishing time so that their pace coincided with the marathon runners they were joining. I'm not convinced that what sounded ideal in theory actually worked in practice. Shortly after the start I found myself passing someone dressed entirely as a giant Rubic Cube. Apparently this guy has become an instantly recognisable, permanent fixture in the marathon. So much so that the organisers have started to use him in promotional literature for their event. He finishes in quite a decent time too despite his self-imposed handicap.

As previously mentioned, the marathon has been designed as 26-mile sightseeing journey of the city and the Danube. On leaving Heroes' Square the first two kilometres heads directly towards the river before making a short three kilometre loop around city streets. In this section we ran past the infamous House of Terror, the former headquarters of the dreaded secret police. This picturesque building has a ghastly history – it was here that activists of every political persuasion before and after WWII were taken for interrogation and torture. The walls were apparently of double thickness to muffle the screams.It is now a museum focusing on the crimes and atrocities of Hungary's fascist and Stalinist regimes in a permanent exhibition called Double Occupation. The years after WWII leading up to the 1956 Hungarian Uprising get the lion's share of the exhibition space (almost three-dozen spaces on three levels). The reconstructed prison cells in the basement and the Perpetrators' Gallery, featuring photographs of the turncoats, spies and torturers, are chilling. The tank in the central courtyard makes for a jarring introduction and the wall outside displaying metallic photos of the many victims speaks volumes. Also in this section we pass the Hungarian State Opera House, one of the most important 19th century landmarks as well as one the most beautiful buildings in Budapest. It's basically a smaller version of the Paris Opera House on which it was modelled. In fact, the entire area in which it is situated was modelled on Paris during a major rehabilitation project. Its facade is decorated with statues of muses and opera greats such as Puccini, Mozart, Liszt and Verdi, while its interior is littered with marble columns, gilded vaulted ceilings, chandeliers and near-perfect acoustics. It's possible to join one of the three daily tours with tickets available from the souvenir shop inside the lobby.

The Danube was reached just after the 6km mark where a right turn introduced us to the first of the more than 30 kilometres to be run on both sides of the river. We passed Liberty Bridge, the third permanent bridge of the city to link the towns of Buda and Pest. The bridge was built between 1894 and 1896 to the plans of Janos Feketehazy and was opened in the presence of Emperor Franz Joseph. The last silver rivet on the Pest abutment was inserted into the iron structure by the Emperor himself, and the bridge was originally named after him. Our floating hotel was moored close to the bridge. Thoughts turned to sitting out on deck later that evening with a nice bottle of Hungarian wine but there was still a lot of work to do before then. After the 9th kilometre the course passed between Corvinus University and the The Great Market Hall. Also known as the Central Market Hall this is the largest and oldest indoor market in Budapest. It's located at the end of the famous pedestrian shopping street Vaci utca and on the Pest side of the Liberty bridge at Fovam Square and offers a huge variety of stalls on three floors. The entrance gate has a neogothic touch. During the World Wars it was completely damaged and then closed for some years. Throughout the 1990s restoration works brought back the market to its ancient splendour. The building was awarded the 'Prix d'Excellence' in 1999 and has become one of the most popular tourist attractions of the city. The market hall is frequently visited by tourists and there are stalls selling fruits and vegetables, Hungarian meats, fish, local cheeses, Hungarian herbs and spices, Hungarian wines and spirits, clothing, purses, accessories, and souvenirs. For those like me who like to try local dishes the market specialises in langos, a yeast-based dough deep fried in oil and topped with different things like sour cream, cheese, and garlic.

Across on the Buda side of the river at 10km we gazed upwards to Gellert Hill one of the most peaceful and attractive parts of the city. Gellert Hill, a 235m high hill overlooking the Danube was named after Saint Gerard who was thrown to death from the hill. Now an affluent residential area, a number of embassies and ambassadorial residences line the streets which wind up the hill. A prominent feature on the Hill is The Citadel, a fortress erected in 1854 by the Habsburg emperors after overcoming the Hungarian army in the revolution of 1848-49. Other sights on the hill include the sculpture of the bishop St. Gellert, the St. Gellert Cliff Church and the Liberty Statue. The latter was first erected in 1947 in remembrance of the Soviet liberation of Hungary from Nazi forces during World War II. Its location upon Gellert Hill makes it a prominent feature of Budapest's cityscape. The 14 metre tall bronze statue holding a palm leaf stands atop a 26 metre pedestal with several smaller statues present around the base.

Next up at 13km we made the first crossing of the Danube via the iconic Chain Bridge which, together with the magnificent Parliament building, is the most instantly recognisable symbol of Budapest. The Chain Bridge was the first permanent bridge between Buda and Pest and also the first one across the Danube. It was built between 1839 and 1849, in the period when Budapest started to evolve from a dusty Central-European town to a vibrant metropolis and has symbolized the connection between East and West, progress and development. It has played an enormous part in the city's economic, social and cultural life, prompting comparisons with the role of the Brooklyn Bridge in the history of New York, After the bridge it was just one gigantic slog along a series of interminably long straight, airless stretches back and forth along the river bank under the former Royal Palace and by Gellert Hill. One such stretch went from 18 to 28km, proving somewhat dispiriting for us slower runners as the faster guys headed in the opposite direction. The course recrossed the river over the Elizabeth Bridge at the 30km mark. This slender, white cable bridge connects downtown Pest with the Gellert Hill. The bridge was name after Elizabeth of Bavaria, the popular queen who was assassinated around the time the construction works began. It was finished in 1903. In World War II, all the bridges of Budapest were destroyed, including the Elizabeth Bridge. It was rebuilt in a slightly modified version 1964. The next highlight was passing the imposing Houses of Parliament, built in Neo-Gothic style on the bank of the Danube as the permanent seat of the National Assembly. The building complex, the biggest of its kind in Hungary, was erected between 1884 and 1904 with 691 rooms and a dome 96 metres high. Since 2000, the Hungarian coronation symbols —St. Stephen's crown, the sceptre, the orb and the Renaissance sword— have been on display in the Parliament. Tours in eight languages run for 45 minutes. Turning away from the river at around 38km all that remained was to head towards the Budapest Zoo and finally to the finish and the medals in Heroes' Square.

I finished in a disappointing 4:42, much, much slower than I was used to running at the time. I'd no excuses; I just couldn't handle the humidity on the day. After 26 previous editions the organisers had got things virtually spot on. There was entertainment all along the route with rock, choral or orchestral music at regular intervals. The 16 drink stations, sporting a variety of food and drink meant that, even in the high humidity sustenance was never too far away. The course had also been deliberately designed to allow spectators to follow the runners by easily changing viewing positions, so crowd support was constant throughout. To me, the only negative aspects were the inclusion of the relay runners and, to a lesser extent the 30km race, in the main event (don't you just hate it when someone fit and fresh pushes you out of the way after 20 miles) plus the insistence of Spar, the major sponsors, to plaster their corporate logo all over an otherwise excellent medal and t-shirt. There was lots going-on in the Square at the end: food stalls, charity stalls, free massages and a stage with entertainment. We didn't hang around, our main concern was to get back to the shelter of the boat before the inevitable thunderstorm hit. And hit it did, with surprising ferocity. For the second night in a row we found ourselves marooned on board as the ferocity of the storm kept us prisoners. So much for our plans of finding a local restaurant specialising in Hungarian cuisine. Instead, we had to satisfy ourselves with a couple of kebabs from a nearby dockside stall while sitting on deck as the lightning lit up the views along the river.

The next morning started sunny and bright – it was time for some proper sightseeing. Mo and I both love being close to water; which was why we'd chosen to stay on a boat hotel in the first place. We'd been intrigued by the comings and goings of all manner of craft on the Danube, from luxury river cruisers to small ferryboats making their way up and down the river. Water travel remains an integral part of life in Budapest and ferryboats still faithfully ply the riverfront providing a relatively slow means of commuting but an extraordinarily enjoyable way of appreciating the city's beauty. BKK public-transport company maintains multiple ships that zigzag back and forth between more than a dozen stops in both Buda and Pest, travelling from the city's southern section toward the northern outskirts and back. A single adult ticket for a one-way ferry ride of any duration was 750 forints. We'd worked out that by taking a boat from one terminus to the other we'd enjoy a journey lasting almost two hours when travelling upriver, and about 90 minutes going downriver. So that's what we did, along the way delighting in spectacular views over every major waterfront landmark of Budapest – including Gellert Hill, the Buda Castle, and the Parliament House – while passing under all of the downtown bridges. I'd recommend it to any fellow Marathon Tourist. In the afternoon we took advantage of the 50% discount offered to all marathon entrants by the Hop On Hop Off Budapest City Tours. All you had to do was show your Bib Number (Mo 'borrowed' one) This way we were able to take a more leisurely look at virtually all the major tourist attractions I'd passed on the marathon route: especially the House of Terror, The Great Market and the Opera House.

That left us with time in the evening to sample both the local cuisine and continue the never-ending search for the perfect dark beer. We made for a restaurant we'd spotted close to the city centre advertising Hungarian dishes at reasonable prices. We didn't just want to go down the obvious route of ordering a traditional goulash dish – you can get them anywhere these days. We were looking for something a little more exotic. I tried the Porkolt, one the most popular meat dishes in Hungary. This is a ragout made from pork, beef or mutton, or chicken with onions and Hungarian paprika powder mixed with sour cream to add a nice creamy texture to the meal. Mo went for one of the range of pasta dishes that are peculiar to Hungarian cuisine. On offer were the savoury pastas Turos csusza (pasta with cottage cheese) and Kaposztas teszta (egg squares with braised cabbage.) She settled instead for the sweet pasta dish of Turogomboc (cottage cheese dumplings) which were a little too sweet for my taste. With beer the bill came to less than 20 euros for the two of us. Dreher Classic is the beer most readily available found mainly on draught and occasionally in bottles in Budapest. Despite being a lager-type beer it's still quite drinkable but not anywhere near as nice as Dreher Bak, a dark bottled beer with a burned toffee taste. Though this turned out to be my favourite of the Hungarian beers, I'm reluctant to put in the 'perfect, dark' category – it simply wasn't strong enough!

Budapest. Parliament, Bridges and Danube
(Photo by Krisztian Tabori on Unsplash)

Budapest Race Programme and Medal

CZECH REPUBLIC

PRAGUE MARATHON

Variously described as 'The City of a Thousand Spires,' the 'Belle of Bohemia' and 'The Golden City,' Prague has a lot to do to live up to all the hype. It survived intact and unharmed after both World Wars, while its own Velvet Revolution of 1989 came and went without a single shot being fired to affect the city's infrastructure. The end result is that what remains is a stunning city with a picture-postcard centre complete with medieval streets showcasing its Gothic, baroque and art nouveau architecture. For those of us of a certain age, it's hard to believe that the city was virtually off-limits to westerners just over two decades ago. Since the Czech Republic joined the EU in 2004, the new, cosmopolitan Prague has established itself very much as one of the must-see cities on the eastern European tourist trail.

Prague has been a political, cultural and economic centre of central Europe for all of its 1,100 year existence during which time it has been not only the seat of the Holy Roman Empire but has played a major role in the Protestant Reformation, the Thirty Year's War, and in both World Wars and the decline and fall of the Communist Bloc. Today, with its population of over 1.2 million it is the capital and major city of the recently formed Czech Republic; which used to be joined to Slovenia until the 1993 split. The Vlatava River, running from south to north through the city centre defines the areas in which tourists spend most of their time. Those of you who've run the Budapest Marathon will see the similarities with the way in which the Danube separates Buda from Pest on the opposite bank. In Prague, the right bank contains the Old Town and its famous Square. North of the Old Town Square lies the Jewish Quarter while to the south is the equally imposing Wenceslas Square, home to the aforementioned Velvet Revolution. On the other side of the river is what is known as the Lesser Quarter, an equally atmospheric area of narrow streets leading up to Hradcany, a district totally dominated by the imposing Prague Castle.

Having decided that this was a race I'd like to enter in a city I'd like to see, I logged on to the Prague Marathon website in early January 2013. This proved an informative site with attractive pictures of happy crowds of runners streaming past iconic buildings and along the charming banks of the Vltava. The website blurb certainly increased my interest with its description of the event as 'one of the most beautiful international marathons in the world'. It boasted of the race's IAAF Road Race Gold Label award, its start and finish in the Old Town Square in the historic centre of the city with the course 'leading through the heart of the medieval metropolis, along the Vltava River and crossing the Charles Bridge – arguably the most beautiful Gothic bridge in the World!'

That was enough for me – two 'beautifuls' in the same description. I was hooked and just had to see all this beauty for myself. The next stop was on to the Jet2 website to see if it was possible to get there from Newcastle. Sure enough there were flights there and back on Thursdays and Sundays at reasonable prices. (From memory the whole thing cost something in the region of £240 return for my wife, Mo, and I). The main drawback was the return flight left Prague at 8:30 pm on the day of the marathon – not something I'd normally contemplate but with a 9am start and a 7 hour time limit I reckoned that even I could make it back to the airport on time.

So, four months later, after a couple of scares along the way Mo and I presented ourselves at Newcastle airport on a Thursday afternoon ready to head off to Prague. In the interim, between booking and leaving, I'd had nagging back pain subsequently diagnosed as a particular nasty form of kidney stones. Having been advised not to run or travel abroad fearing complications from movement of the stones, I'd already missed out on a couple of marathons and a trip to Nice. I couldn't face the prospect of missing this trip too so had sought a second opinion from my Consultant at Newcastle's Freeman Hospital. This took the form of neither a yes nor a no, more like a 'on your head be it'. This time, although I'd been able to do little or no proper training since first diagnosed, I was determined not to miss out on yet another marathon. Especially one I'd already paid out good money for.

Before leaving Mo and I were made aware by our two sons (who know about these things from personal experiences) of Prague's reputation as a destination for stag party groups. We reckoned that this wouldn't bother us. As we sat at the airport, however, waiting for the flight we became conscious of an increasingly raucous noise from the bar area. Looking across, it was apparent that a large group of similarly dressed young men were intent on having a few pre-flight thirst quenchers. The departure board showed flights heading off soon to Malaga and Amsterdam. Surely they were getting on one of those. Unfortunately not. Further investigation showed them all to be sporting T-shirts with the legend, 'Andy's Stag Night. Prague May 2013'. They were destined for our flight. Their T-shirts were incredible – I don't think I've seen anything like them before. Initially I thought the large picture on the rear was that of a gorgeous, naked, Asian lady reclining, legs apart, in such a way that a prostrate male figure was able to cover the sensitive area with a strategically placed forearm. Wrong! As I boarded the plane's steps behind them the picture was revealed to be no female, but that of an attractive Asian Lady Boy. The forearm was no forearm but a very large protruding private part of the said person and the prostrate male wasn't attempting to spare anyone's blushes by covering it from view, more enjoying it with his tongue. In no way can anyone describe me as a prude, but how on earth they were able to go about wearing it in the presence of families with children I'll never know. For the duration of the flight they happily wandered up and down the aisle so that everyone could receive full shock value. Andy the groom, meanwhile roamed the aisle resplendent in a head-to-toe canine outfit complete with dog lead attached to his handler for the occasion. I think he missed a trick here. Surely to complete the scenario he should have been outfitted in full Lady Boy gear. I got one of them to pose so that I could take a picture of the T-shirt, thinking I might feature it in this book. I'm sitting looking at it now but there's no way that it would pass censorship laws. We bumped in to some of them in the city centre the next night, still wearing the same T-shirts. They didn't have them on during the flight back though. Actually, they weren't a bad set of lads. Despite almost drinking the flight dry they remained good-natured as opposed to offensive. On the way back they were unrecognisably subdued and drank only Diet Coke and Iron Brew. One of them was missing!

After an eventful flight we finally landed in Prague early on the Thursday evening. For those who've never been, getting into the city can be complicated. Like Budapest, whose marathon I'd ran the previous October, there's no direct metro link to the city centre. Like Budapest, it's necessary to take a combination of bus and metro – in this case the 119 bus from outside the terminal to the station called Dejvicka at the western end of the green metro line. From there it's a mere three stops on the metro to Staromests Bridge, or four to Mustek, (for the Old Town/Wenceslas Square area).

Prague actually has quite a decent and cheap integrated city transport system that is easy to understand and use. A 32 Czk crown ticket, (approx £1), will get you 90 minutes on metro, tram or bus. You must buy your ticket before boarding and validate them by punching into a ticket machine on first use. You can then use the same ticket on each form of transport as long as the 90 minutes is not exceeded. They can be purchased in kiosks (at the airport for example) or at metro stations. The 3 interconnecting metro lines are colour-coded and easy to follow. Prague though is such a compact, pedestrian friendly city with most of its attractions within walking distance of one another, that most of it is best seen on foot.

We reached our hotel, the Charles Bridge Palace by 7pm with the evening to look forward to. As the name suggests, it was right next to the iconic Charles Bridge with the word 'palace' not entirely a misnomer. It was certainly one of the most opulent hotels I've stayed in on any of my marathon trips, finding myself normally down in the budget range. However, we got such a good deal on this one we couldn't resist. We paid 319 euros in total for the 3 nights with buffet breakfast. The same room was going for £1,121 two days before we left. I say room, but it was more like a suite located on two floors, with space in which to swing most of the world's cats. The big plus for me was its proximity to the marathon start, a short walk away on the Sunday morning.

On arrival all we had to do was cross the road to find ourselves on the terrace of a riverside restaurant overlooking the main weir on the Vlatava. This, being impassible to traffic, was the place where all the cruise boats turned. We enjoyed a warm relaxing couple of hours simply sitting watching the boats as the sun set over the Royal Palace on the opposite bank of the river. One of the great things about being a marathon tourist is that, as well as seeing new countries and new cultures, you also get to try out their own particular specialities in food and drink. That evening we had our first taste of their famous spicy cabbage soup and dark Czech beer. Both were delicious and, despite the riverside location of the restaurant, not especially expensive. The remainder of the evening was spent getting our bearings - crossing the historic, statue-lined Charles Bridge, still busy with tourists long into the night and walking past the numerous outdoor restaurants lining the streets to the Old Town Square.

The bridge has become the symbol of the marathon and is used on all of its promotional literature. It's easy to see why – it's a spectacular edifice and one that has witnessed more than 600 years of processions, battles, executions and, increasingly these days, film locations. Built in Gothic style, its most distinguishing features are the two defence towers at each end and its gallery of 30 statues of saints and other religious figures installed to encourage the masses back to the church. Nowadays it is plagued by the ubiquitous touts and beggars but does provide interesting entertainment on occasions. We spent quite a bit of one afternoon listening to a local 3-piece blues band whose young bottle-neck guitarist's renditions of old Robert Johnson and Mississippi Fred McDowell numbers were so professional it made you wonder what he was doing playing on a bridge.

I'd seen famous Town Squares at previous marathons in ex-Communist bloc countries, (Poznan in Poland for example is based around its square), but have not been as impressed with any of them as much as this one. Apparently a market place has been located here since the 11th century and the square is surrounded by ancient buildings like the Gothic Tyn Chrch and the Baroque Church of St Nicholas with its Astronomical Clock. During the day, on the hour, bells ring, cocks crow and 15th century statues dance while the necks of the tourist hordes stiffen below. Today, the Square has a very lively atmosphere with cafe tables, horse and carts waiting to ferry tourists and street hawkers selling their wares. We stood and watched them erecting the advertising hoardings and space age video screens and gantries for the marathon. They all looked strangely out of place in such a medieval setting.

Equally out of place, but a little more discreetly tucked away in a far corner was the George and Dragon English pub right next door to another of the ubiquitous Irish bars. I think this one was called Flannigan's - it seemed to be the favourite of our friends with the T-shirts. Ice Hockey is a popular sport in the Czech Republic so for the first two days both pubs were showing wall-to-wall matches from some tournament or other. They did manage to switch these over to the FA Cup Final on the Saturday night. I've misplaced the note I took of the particular brand of dark beer served in the Irish bar (possibly 'Kelt' - from one of the local breweries) but it was delicious and meant that we were a regular visitor there.

Those of you that enjoy a drink or two as part of your rehydration strategy will probably already know that Czech beer is world famous. The Czech Republic is officially the No. 1 beer drinking nation on the planet, with an annual per capita consumption of some 156 litres and beer is served almost everywhere in Prague, even in breakfast cafes. Most beers are light beers, served chilled and with a tall head. When ordering draught beer ask for 'male pivo' (small beer – 0.3 litre) or 'pivo' (large at 0.5litre) The average price of a large beer in a typical city centre pub away from the main square appeared to be between 35czk and 40czk, (£1.20 - £1.35) The best known is Pilsner Urquell, though in Prague itself the local Staropramen brand tends to dominate. Staropramen is also one of the major sponsors of the marathon and, whether by accident or design, we were twice treated to the rather captivating smells emanating from their brewery as we ran past it on an out and back section of the course. If you've enough time to spare on your visit there are organised tours visiting all three of the major local breweries. Despite the 'free' tasters, these did appear quite expensive at over 1200czks for a three and a half hour visit. After a few beers in the centre, though, beware the food stalls lining the square on the opposite side to the Irish pub. On our first visit we stuck to the highly seasoned sausage and mustard for 60 Czech crowns. This seemed good value so anxious to try all the local food we returned a second time for the 35 crown potato and bacon stew with what we thought was a small portion of ham at 80 crowns. Avoid the ham at all costs – you'll be ripped off. They have no intention of cutting you a small slice of ham and you'll end up paying something like 400 crowns instead, unless you refuse their giant portions. Having been once bitten we were ready the next time we went out to eat, confining ourselves to the beef goulash served in a hollowed out circular loaf, (no plate) Though tasty and traditional it certainly wasn't anything to write home about. Oh well, having tried all the local dishes on offer it was back next time to that time-honoured stand-by of marathon runners everywhere: the universal kebab and chips. Not a local dish, I know, but certainly fuel enough to get you round anyone's marathon course. Europa Kebabs, half way between the Bridge and the Square, provided the most nourishing meal in town for the princely sum of 99 crowns.

Getting back to the marathon, Friday was registration day for me. In truth I could have registered any day from Thursday onwards but decided I neither wanted to pay extra for the Saturday afternoon Pasta Party nor get mixed up with the huge crowds I knew would attend that day. Unfortunately, Friday was the day it never stopped raining and registration was located over two miles out of town at some National Exhibition Centre we had to attend. To be fair, as far as pre-race exhibitions go Prague is one of the better ones with merchandise galore and numerous other European marathons well represented. We received our race number including timing chip and a rather useful running rucksack with the 'Run Czech' logo. T-shirts were extra and appeared to be plain white with the Volkswagen sponsors logo more prominent than that of the event. I didn't like it and was pleased not to have ordered one. I can't help thinking the Expo's location was designed to suit the purposes of the various corporations trying to sell us their wares rather than for the convenience of the individual runner. The organisers had already erected a sort of tented village they called the Technical Area in the spacious St.Wenceslas Square just around the corner from the start. There were all sorts of facilities there for use both before and after the race. I could see no reason, other than corporate convenience, why we couldn't have registered there too. As it was, Mo and I, and virtually everyone else, ended up thoroughly soaked getting to the Exhibition grounds. We'd set off to walk – much the best way of seeing a new city – thinking that the rain would soon stop. It didn't, it got worse and our first full day in Prague ended with us like two drowned rats. Ironically, had we realised it we could have taken the number 17 tram there from outside our hotel. We certainly took it back. In fact, to get our money's worth we ended up riding it all the way to its final destination along the river and out into some far-flung southern suburb. We then got straight back on at the terminus and rode it back to the hotel. This manoeuvre is actually recommended in the guide book under 'What to do in Prague on a Rainy Day'.

The plan was by registering on Friday to leave the Saturday free for sightseeing. I won't bore you with all the places we went to but will say that Prague is rightly regarded as one of the most beautiful cities in the world as well as being the historical jewel of Europe. Since 1992 the historical heart covering an area of 866 hectares has appeared in the UNESCO World Cultural and National Heritage list. No visit would be complete, without including at least, Charles Bridge, the Old Town, Wenceslas Square and the area across the river including the Royal Palace and St Vitus' Cathedral. Having already spent time at the first two of these we set off to take a good look at Wenceslas Square.

This huge rectangle (it's not actually a square) named in honour of Bohemia's patron saint originated as a horse market and has often been the scene of important events. The most recent was in 1989 when crowds gathered to celebrate the end of Communism. Today, it's lined on either side by exclusive shops, hotels and restaurants. Unfortunately the high volume of tourists has attracted many of the cleverest of the city's pickpockets. Its southern end is dominated by the huge edifice of the National Museum, shelled in 1968 by invading Warsaw Pact troops who mistook it for the Czech Parliament.

The hill across the river is dominated by the Palace and Cathedral – a weary climb the day before a marathon but worth it nonetheless. We were in time to catch the ceremony involving the changing of the Palace guards. Crowned by the distinctive spires of St Vitus' cathedral within its grounds, the castle is the historical throne of the Czech lands and at one stage became the capital of the Holy Roman Empire. Today it is home to the country's President. While entrance to the Cathedral is free, the huge crowds, as in the rest of Prague, deterred us from joining the queues to get in. By this stage I'd had enough of this sightseeing lark and was thinking about the marathon tomorrow.

Over the past 19 years Prague has built up its event to be one of the top international marathons on the calendar, earning itself an IAAF Gold Standard award in the process. For comparison purposes London and Berlin are also Gold standard, Madrid and Turin are Silver and UK events like Edinburgh and Brighton are Bronze. I've just been learning about the criteria behind the grading system. For those of you interested, there appears to be six main requirements for a Gold award. These are, briefly: that the course is designed to minimise ecological damage, that it complies to course measuring standards and has electronic timing, that the event is broadcast live, that there are a minimum of five nationalities among the elite runners, that the route is traffic free and finally, that there's gender equality in prize money and bonuses. I'm surprised at Prague's status given the number of cobblestones, tram lines and kerbs encountered on the course. The potential for personal, never mind ecological, damage was more of a concern to me on the day. Then again, in football, Qatar was awarded the FIFA World Cup so who knows what really influences the officials of these worldwide sporting federations.

This year the marathon hosted 9700 runners from 78 different countries – quite an exercise in logistics and a test of organisational skills. I don't usually enjoy these mass participation events involving thousands of runners battling one another for somewhere to place their feet. Give me the solitary spaciousness of a smaller field. They had us organised into pre-race holding pens marked from A to K dependent on projected finishing times. There were two different routes to the start- pens depending on which pen you were meant to reach. I'd taken the time to study the literature about this but, given the size and swell of the crowds, there was no way that I could reach my allocated pen without being sent the wrong way and having then to fight through everyone to get to my place. The start, in fact, was simply one big uncomfortable jostle with runners tripping both over each other and the cobbles. Things did finally become more sensible after a few miles and despite not having been able to train properly for three months I actually started to enjoy myself. I was pleased to be able to maintain a steady sub 10 minute mile pace throughout.

Leaving the Town Square we headed straight towards the river, crossing the Czchuv Bridge before turning back on ourselves to re-cross the river before 3km were up at the iconic Charles Bridge – possibly the high point of the race. At 3km we crossed once again, using the Manesuv Bridge this time before heading north on a long stretch to the Libensky Bridge at 8km. This continued to be the theme of the race. They could have called it the Prague Bridges Marathon' but there again bridges tend not to pay out sponsorship money. The course was basically a large H shape with legs of about 5km up one side of the river and then back again with the central bridges acting as the bar in the H. As many of the city's famous buildings are located on or near the river this was marathon tourism in its truest sense with the whole course providing an interesting sightseeing experience, (as I'm sure the organisers intended it to be).

Fortunately the rain of the previous two days had given way to warm sunshine. Unfortunately, with so much moisture drying in the air the day became quite humid and unsuited to fast times. Being next to the river had a cooling effect and meant that the course was almost perfectly flat with the only inclines being on the bridges' on and off-ramps. It also meant that you were constantly in view of other runners, both faster and slower, running in the opposite direction. At the 5km point I caught up with a Scouse friend Gary O'Brien, escorting a first-time marathon running mate of his around the course. I'm not sure what they were doing ahead of me at this stage, given that Gary's intention was simply to steer his friend around at a walk/run pace for his first marathon. Gary is a real character, an experienced marathoner with a typical Liverpudlian sense of humour, quite capable of running a fast time if necessary. It seems that, unlike me, they'd decided to ignore the rule of having to be in a certain starting pen and simply vaulted the fences to start near the elite runners. They were now in the first of one of their walking stages and were quite happy to relax and catch up with what we'd all been up to since Gary's last appearance at the Druridge Bay marathon I used to organise on the Northumberland Coast every April.

My own pre-race strategy had largely been one of indecision. I was hoping that I still had sufficient miles in the bank since February to allow a 9 minute mile pace for at least the first 10 miles. That would have got me to 1 hour 30 minutes with 16 miles to go. I knew I could do those 16 mile regardless, at a fast-walk, 15 minute-mile pace if necessary, bringing me home in 5 hours 30 minutes – well inside the 7 hour time limit. I'd have been perfectly happy with that. Two things happened that changed my plan. Firstly, my old and worn Garmin Forerunner 205 gave up the ghost on the start line meaning that I had to run without a watch. Secondly, the congested start had me running more at 10 minute than 9 minute pace for the first few miles. That proved quite a blessing in disguise. I found myself quite comfortable with this pace and simply kept it up like a metronome for the remainder of the race. It did help, though, that the distance was measured in kilometres instead of miles. The kilometre boards seemed to appear with such ease and frequency that counting them off gave a real psychological lift. At my age, marathons are less about pain, effort and being obsessively concerned with time and more about a pleasurable day out, finishing comfortably having enjoyed a fulfilling sightseeing experience with exercise. I don't think I'll be in any hurry to replace the Garmin. While recognising its usefulness, I've never been a big fan of new technology – sometimes I think there must have been a Luddite somewhere in my family tree. Prior to purchasing the Garmin a couple of years ago I'd managed to successfully complete well over 100 marathons without tying myself to some time-obsessed routine involving satellites. I much prefer to run without a watch, relying instead on the natural rhythms of the human body.

On finishing Mo and I headed off back to the hotel for a change and a wash. We still had time to have a quick meal and a beer before returning to the main square to watch the 6-hour finishers coming in. By then it had started to rain and we had to abandon plans for one final sit-out drink in the restaurant overlooking the weir where we enjoyed our first evening in Prague. We set off, instead, walking back along the course en route to the airport metro just in time to see Gary and friend wisecracking their way to the finish, challenging the marshals, (who hadn't a clue what they were talking about), to race them up the final straight. With only 300 metres to go and 30 minutes to get there they knew they could afford to have a laugh. Knowing Gary, though, he'd have acted like this the whole way round. You don't have to do a good time to have a good time. Enjoyment is the main thing – otherwise, why bother.

Prague is a fascinating city, well worth a visit, particularly for the slower runner or someone looking to run an atmospheric first marathon. Provided you don't mind crowds – both in the streets and in the race; it's full of attractions to entertain the visitor with its historic monuments, value-for-money restaurants and comfortable pubs. Beware though the stag night hordes with their constant nocturnal, drunken chanting until dawn. Or at least, do what I did, and make sure you pack a good quality pair of ear plugs before you set off.

Prague Marathon Finish Line

Photo by SilkTork, CC BY-SA 3.0 via Wikimedia Commons

2013 Prague Marathon Medal

POLAND

GDANSK MARATHON

I had compelling personal reasons for going to this event. My late father-in-law Fred Unwin, a man who I greatly respected and admired, had spent a large portion of his five years as a prisoner of war in what was formerly known as Danzig before being changed after the war to Gdansk. Having been captured by the Germans very early in the conflict, Fred had been initially assigned as slave-labour filling barges with coal on the Motlawa River running from Gdansk out into the Baltic Sea. Anxious to make his way to freedom in Sweden, Fred made three serious escape attempts from the camp in which he was held. These included disguising himself as a German soldier, the inevitable digging of a tunnel and then finally hiding under the coal stacked on one of the tenders leaving the port. On this occasion he was spotted burying himself under the coal by an informer so, at the next port of call, armed guards were waiting – thrusting bayonets into the stack to flush him out. Weary of Fred's constant attempts to escape the authorities decided to transfer him to the nearby cement works on the basis that at least the heat of the cement would discourage any further burying attempts to escape!

Fred was a very special man, who despite years of deprivation, held no animosity whatsoever towards his German captors. In fact he went out of his way to make friends with German citizens while on holiday. His attitude was that the average German soldier was, just like him, an average family man, served up as cannon fodder to satisfy the ambitions of corrupt politicians. To his death he maintained a healthy disrespect of politics and politicians. Perhaps that's why I got on so well with him. It was a special moment when, on the second day of our visit, Mo and I were able to take a ferry upriver to the very spot where her Dad had spent so much of his young life in captivity over seventy years ago. The fact that we were able to combine this sentimental visit with a very modern marathon just made the whole trip extra special.

The marathon in question was to be the 19th edition of the Solidarity Marathon running through the streets of what is known as the 'Tricity' (the three cities of Gdynia, Sopot and Gdansk), held in commemoration of the 44 striking shipyard workers killed by the Communist Government in December 1970. The second objective of the marathon is stated as 'the popularization and propogation of running as the easiest form of leisure'. In common with other Polish marathons the organisers of this one are deadly serious in their intent with low entry fees and large cash prizes on offer in every age-group category. Competitors like myself, over 60 years of age, are offered free entry, and accommodation is provided free to anyone who wants it in a nearby sports hall. It's all excellent value and something definitely worth the cost of the airfare there. The marathon is held annually on the 15th August regardless of which day of the week on which it falls. This year it was a Thursday.

Mo and I flew to Gdansk on the Monday immediately after our organising our fourth highly successful Northumberland Coast Marathon – reckoning that we needed a break from all the hard work that we have to put into the event. Flights from Doncaster/Sheffield with Wizz Air cost about £77 each return for the less than two hour flight. The Information Office within the Lech Walesa Airport sold us tickets for the half-hourly 210 bus to Gdansk Glowny, (Central Station), for a very cheap 3.60zl for the 40 minute journey. (At the time of writing the rate of exchange was 4.3zl to the £ - I found it easier to work on the principle that a 20zl note was about the equivalent of a fiver). After that it was a simple 15 minute walk to the Dom Aktora, our hotel for the next four nights.

Gdansk is actually quite an easy city to find your way around, with the central tourist area being condensed into a square mile or so of parallel streets between the station and the river. Before leaving home we were initially concerned that we'd chosen badly and even considered changing hotels at the last minute having done a virtual walk' around the area on Google Street View. It just goes to show how misleading Street View can be – what looked a somewhat seedy and out-of-the-way location turned out to be just about the perfect place to be. The Dom Aktora, though in need of an update in places, possessed a character and charm not found in more modern hotels. The Polish staff was, without exception welcoming and helpful and the apartment-like rooms contained not only a lounge area but a well-stocked kitchen in which we could cook our own food if necessary. (Very useful, given that it rained heavily on two of the days – we at least had somewhere to retire to for a couple of hours and make ourselves cups of coffee). Despite the cooking facilities the owners still insisted on providing everyone with a very generous buffet breakfast each morning. The clincher though, was its location within a spitting distance of the beautiful river promenade and less than a stone's throw from Dlugi Targ (the Royal Way) containing most of the city's important buildings. We thought it was good value for £75 per night.

Of the three cities in the Tricity through which the marathon is run, Gdansk is by far the most historically important. To describe its past as eventful would be a major understatement. The city has been fought over continuously throughout its history and at least two of the significant events in recent European history have their origins there. For example, the Second World War started in Gdansk when the German battleship Schleswig-Holstein fired the first shots on the Polish military post at Westerplatte, (through which we were also to run during the race – more later) During the Nazi occupation that followed both Polish citizens and British POWs like my father-in-law were used as forced labour on the dockside. When the Red Army arrived in 1945 the fierce fighting that ensued resulted in the almost total destruction of the city centre. What we see of Gdansk today is the end product of a post-war rebuilding programme that has followed a stone-by-stone approach to restoring many of its finest old buildings to their former glory.

Nowhere else in Europe has such a large area of a historic city been reconstructed from the ground upwards.

The second, more recent event of historical significance, followed on from the shipyard workers' strike of 1970 on which the marathon is focused. Though brutally stamped out by the authorities this protest signified the first major crack in Eastern Europe's communist wall. A decade later a Gdansk shipyard electrician named Lech Walesa led a further series of strikes resulting in the formation of the Solidarity movement and eventually to democracy for Poland, with Walesa as its first President. Most Poles will argue that this movement was the catalyst for the overthrow of Communism in Eastern Europe.

Gdansk's jewel in the crown is its Main Town which now looks the same as it did some 400 years ago, during the height of its prosperity. The major east west facing streets of this area all appear to finish in a decorative arched gate leading to the river at their eastern end. By far the most attractive of these is the Green Gate at the end of the Royal Way and intended as a residence for visiting royalty. The less imposing Golden Gate is situated at the other end of the Way. Along the Royal Way itself is a whole array of tourist attractions, if you can get near them for camera-toting visitors. These include the Prison Tower from where prisoners were taken for public execution, the impressive Town Hall, Neptune's Statue and the Golden House with its covering of gilt stone carvings. Dominating the heart of the Main Town is the colossal St Mary's Church, the largest brick church in the world which can comfortably accommodate over 25,000 people, (or so they say)

We were fortunate in that our visit also coincided with Gdansk's biggest fair, the Dominican Fair, held in the city for three weeks from the last Saturday in July from the year 1260. During this time the city's streets are lined with stalls selling all manner of wares. There's food stalls: stalls selling dubious antiques, bric-a-brac and general craft items – all making for a very lively atmosphere during our stay. My favourite activity during our visit was to follow the cobbled promenade running alongside the Motlawa River – an excellent location to eat and drink or simply to watch the world go by or to visit another of the city's main attractions; the 14th century wooden crane reputed to be the largest in medieval Europe. The river is also home to the numerous public ferries and tourist boats offering river trips as well as longer journeys up the coast to Sopot or Gdynia, or even across the Gulf of Gdansk to the Hel Peninsula. In fact, apart from the marathon itself, the highlight of our trip has to be the two hour voyage to Hel on our second day. (I'll refrain from making the obvious comment about the name – it doesn't have the same meaning to the Poles who, I'm sure, are sick to death of hearing the same old jokes every time an English-speaking person buys a ticket there). The Hel Peninsula is a 34km long crescent-shaped sandbar stretching out into the Baltic Sea. It's an interesting place; a mere 300 metre wide at its base, expanding to 3km at the end where its capital, Hel, is situated. Strangely 2013 has been a bit of a year for visiting sandbars as far as I'm concerned. I spent a week in June on La Manga on the Mar Menor in Spain. At 38km this is Europe's longest sandbar making it some 4km longer than Hel and, in my opinion, seems the perfect place to have a marathon. If only someone would get up off their backside and arrange it.

Once a prosperous fishing village Hel has now re-invented itself as a tourist trap and, being mid-summer, I'm afraid Hel was crowded on the day we arrived, (it wasn't very hot though – in fact it was raining). Never mind, a short walk out of the main port centre took us to a large wooded area near the very tip of the sandbank that had been turned into some sort of living museum featuring the legacy of its strategic wartime location. Huge walk-in concrete bunkers, gun emplacements, underground sleeping quarters and the remnants of a horrible past were to be found everywhere – perhaps the place was trying too hard to live up to its name. I couldn't help speculating that Fred may well have helped supply the cement involved in what remained of these concrete monstrosities. Having had enough of Hel for one day, we decided to take the boat back across the Gulf to Sopot and then travel from there back to Gdansk by train.

Sopot is equidistant between Gdansk and Gyynia and very much the junior partner in the Tricity. It is also very different to the other two in that it is an up-market, fashionable beach resort very popular with both Poles and international visitors alike. We arrived from Hel onto the famous Molo, Europe's longest wooden pier jutting 515 metres out into the Bay of Gdansk before making our way past two long, sandy beaches to the chic Heroes of Monte Casino Street. This crowded pedestrianised thoroughfare, running from the railway line to the pier, is full of expensive bars, eateries, designer shops and the inevitable poseurs sunning themselves in what is the place to be seen. I've read reports in which Sopot is described as a cross between Brighton and Eastbourne. This does it a grave injustice – it's far more attractive and has much more class than either of the English resorts. It had me looking forward to running through it in a couple of days.

The next day meant a journey up to Gdynia for Registration. The best way to do this is via a commuter train known as the SKM, (Fast City Train), which runs constantly between Gdansk and Gdynia Glowna. Tickets cost 5.70zl for the 35 minute trip, (25 minutes to Sopot for 3.40zl). You buy tickets at the station and it's important to validate them in the big yellow boxes at the platform entrance before setting off or prepare to be fined if you don't! Disembark at the station before Gdynia Glowna called Wzgorze, cross under the road via the underpass and you'll find the registration in the Youth Community Centre next to the park on your right. You'll also not fail to notice the large Victims of December 1970 Monument from where the race starts on the following day.

I found the Registration somewhat disappointing. It was a long trip simply to pick up a number and an unattractive white T-shirt in the foyer of a building. It did, however, give me the chance to meet up with the inevitable fellow-member of the 100 Club and seemingly the only other English-speaker in the race. This turned out to be an American member named Robert Bishton, better known for some reason as 'Cowboy Jeff' on account of his trademark wearing of a cowboy hat in every marathon in which he participates. Robert/Cowboy Jeff was heading off to run the

Helsinki Marathon on the Saturday immediately after this one. There was a Pasta Party to be held that afternoon in the Hotel Rezydent, Sopot (I guess they had to let Sopot feel as if it too was part of the event) but as it was 28zl to enter and involved yet another train ride, I didn't bother to go.

Gdynia, though very much the ugly sister to Gdansk's charm and Sopot's chic, is nevertheless an interesting place in its own way. Today it's a thriving port city with the highest reputed per capita income in Poland. Its industrial infrastructure leaves it largely ignored by tourists though. The heavy rain meant I didn't see as much of it as I would have liked but Mo and I still enjoyed a leisurely, wet walk along a pleasant sea-front promenade up to the port's main square.

Marathon day dawned dry and sunny after the rain of the previous two days and it was back on board the train again for another trip up to Gdynia. Before the 10am start to the race itself we had what the organisers called the 'Ceremonial Start' in front of the Victims Monument at 9.45am. This was a solemn affair in which some of the older local runners took part along with various dignitaries, speeches and the laying of wreaths – all in front of the TV cameras.

Then we were off – following a circuit of Gdynia's main shopping streets before turning and heading south towards Gdansk. For the next 19km or so we ran along an uninspiring closed section of motorway with minimal crowd support. Without thinking, I found myself among the sub 4 hour pacer's group for much of this stretch. This obviously convinced a friendly Polish runner called Peter that I must have been aiming for a sub 4 hour finish. I wasn't. I don't make plans like that anymore, simply preferring to run at how my body feels at the time. Peter, it seems, decided to adopt me as someone he could assist and someone who he could practise his English on. The problem was, he was not only 25 years younger than me but a lot fitter too. Eventually, approaching the half-way point just outside Gdansk it took all my powers of persuasion to get him to go on ahead and leave me to my own pace. By this stage the combination of trying to maintain a conversation in broken English and the increasing warmth of the day was beginning to tell.

We continued through the busy cobbled streets of the city centre, packed with crowds celebrating their Public Holiday (the Assumption), before crossing the river for a 20 km out-and-back stretch along the Westerplatte peninsula. At this point an amusing incident occurred; I'd brought gels with me but had forgotten to pack my gel bag to keep them in so had arranged with Mo that she'd hand me a gel at a designated point in the city centre. I'd gone past the point without seeing her so had simply continued running before hearing my name being shouted out from behind. On turning I was confronted by the sight of a woman in a blue anorak racing up the course waving a gel, while at the same time being pursued by burly policemen trying to block her progress. Sad to say, she was actually catching up with me. Anyone who's met Mo knows how determined she can be. I got my gel.

Westerplatte turned out to be a big disappointment – a lonely, desolate stretch with little signs of activity. Being a public holiday all the shipyards and factories were closed and all we had for company was an empty, endless dual carriageway. The turning point at 32km was, I believe, meant to show us yet another monument. I missed it, I'm afraid. The finish though was spectacular – entering the Royal Way via the Golden Gate and running past cheering crowds along its length to finish outside the magnificent Town Hall.

I'd enjoyed the run and had managed to maintain a sub 10 minute per mile pace for all the second half, stopping only to take on isotonic drink, banana and sugar lumps at the 25km mark. (These had been provided at 5km intervals throughout) Unfortunately, apart from the couple of kilometres within Gdansk city centre and especially the final sprint down the Royal Way the course had been dreary and unexciting throughout – not at all conducive to fast times, though this didn't seem to affect the leading Kenyan who was virtually back in the city before I'd left it for Westerplatte. I ended up 512th out of 739 finishers, almost an hour and a quarter within the strictly imposed five and a half hour time limit. The final results showed that I was one of only four

Britons to finish, together with the same number from the USA. The heavy, double medallion at the end was excellent though – one of the best I've received – as too was the warm food that followed. Though no expert on Polish food, I believe we were given Bigos (Hunter's Stew), a traditional dish consisting of meat, cabbage, onion and sauerkraut. Whatever it was, it was very welcome.

As usual on my visits abroad I'd made it my business to try the local cuisine. On a previous visit to Poland I remember being disappointed with some over-priced dumplings and a dish of unappetising beetroot soup. This time I tried zurek (sour rye soup with sausages and potatoes) and golabki (boiled cabbage leaves stuffed with beef, onion and rice). Mo had beef broth with home-made noodles followed by placki, (potato pancakes, sour cream and sweet cabbage.) This meal, including a couple of beers, in a Polish restaurant away from the main drag came to approx. 90zl, (just over £20) Not bad value for money I suppose. Though the guide books will have you believe otherwise, there's really only so much you can do with a cuisine that relies heavily on a combination of sausages, onions and potatoes. So, yet again I came away somewhat unimpressed. Mind you, there's nothing much wrong with some of the dishes sold by local street vendors. I can certainly recommend the Pajda – onions, mincemeat and gherkins on a slap of rye bread, very filling for only 12zl. The smoked herring sold on the street barbeques in Hel not only smelt nice but was also particularly tasty.

The final word on the trip has to be about my eternal quest for the perfect dark beer. I almost thought I'd found it in Prague but had limited success here. Most of the beer on sale in bars appeared to be Tyskie, a light but drinkable brew at between 5 to 7zl, for 500 ml. The rule seems to be the nearer the city centre and the more up-market the bar, the higher the cost. My favourite though was a 6.5% malt ale produced by the Warka brewery. Now that's a drink I'd definitely recommend to anyone visiting Gdansk.

I'm aware of the economic reasons why Poles come to the UK in such large numbers. However, as one of the few English speakers returning on the plane to Doncaster the next day, I couldn't help but wonder how reluctant my fellow Polish travellers were to be leaving the beauty of Gdansk and Sopot for the grim reality of some British industrial town.

Local runners lay wreaths at the pre-race ceremony

Finished – in the Royal Way.

ICELAND

REYKJAVIK MARATHON

From a very early age mere mention of the word 'Iceland' had captured magical mental images of marauding Vikings, exploding geysers, glaciers, sagas and trolls. It was a distant, mythical place I'd always wanted to visit. In more recent times these images have been replaced in turn by those less entrancing: like cod wars, volcanic ash, failed banks, extortionate prices and drunken revelry. It's held a quite a decent marathon there since 1984 so, when easyJet started flying from Edinburgh to Reykjavik for the first time in 2013 I was determined to go. Mo and I paid £135 each for a Thursday to Monday flight arguing that, with it being a Saturday marathon, we'd have at least a couple of days free to look around.

All international flights to Iceland land at Keflavik Airport some 52 kilometers from the capital Reykjavik and, expensive taxis apart, the only way to get to the city on arrival appears to be via the local operator FlyBus which guarantees to provide a bus leaving 45 minutes after each incoming flight. Like everything else in Iceland, it's not cheap. Mo and I pre-booked our tickets online for 1950 Icelandic kronas, (ISKs) each. At the exchange rate of 170 ISK to the pound, that amounted to an outlay of approximately £11.50 each for a single 50 minute journey into the town's BSI (long-distance) bus terminal. It's also possible to buy a ticket for an extra 550 kronas each way to be dropped off and collected from the hotel at which you're staying. We noticed that most of our fellow passengers on the flight had chosen that option. These consisted of a happy gang of guys in kilts (they should have checked the weather forecast before leaving) heading for their second consecutive

Reykjavik Marathon, plus half a plane's worth of more serious runners from two of Scotland's well-known athletic clubs. Buses back to the airport leave hourly from the terminal for the return flight.

We arrived to driving rain and zero visibility, dumped onto the bleak, semi-vegetated moonscape of the Reykjanes Peninsula on which the airport is situated. It took 30 minutes of travelling along the lunar landscape before we encountered our first tree until the scenery improved on approaching the capital. It's a strange introduction to a major city, merely confirming the fact that, in Iceland, nature is king. The very name Reykjavik translates from the Viking as 'smoky bay' on account of the geysers they encountered on first sighting the area.

The city itself is situated between two water features: the harbour and the Pond with Austurvollur Square containing the historic Parliament and Cathedral plum in the centre. Across the road and up the hill is Laugavegur, the main shopping street. Towering over the city is the soaring steeple of Hallgrimskirkja; a useful guide to getting your bearings. The other landmark of note on the skyline is Perlan, (the Pearl), sitting above the city's hot water tanks. Beyond the city lies the vast emptiness of Iceland's weird and wonderful volcanic countryside.

As the world's most northerly capital, Reykjavik is by far the largest city in Iceland with a population in the urban area of around 200,000 as well as being home to the vast majority of Icelandic citizens. It's very much the centre of culture of the island, and the main focal point for tourism, (more on that later). Though the outer area consists largely of a variety of sprawling suburbs, the city centre itself is quite compact and a leisurely walk of an hour or so will easily get you round most of the important sites. With that in mind, Mo and I decided to simply find our own way to our hotel on foot from the bus terminal undeterred by the persistent rain, seeping mist and strong winds that had greeted our arrival on the island.

And what a little gem the Hotel Orkin turned out to be at, around £90 a night for the room. I say room but it was more like having our own apartment for 4 nights. We didn't know it when booking, but the room consisted of stairs up to a mezzanine floor with two beds, plus a comfortable lounge area below containing a heating system that we were able to control - given the days of rainfall to follow, this was to prove a Godsend. Also, in one of those weird co-incidences of fate that you couldn't make up, it turned out that the receptionist was a native of Gdansk where I'd run the marathon the previous week. She'd been in Iceland for five years and, by this stage, was thoroughly homesick and anxious to hear about our visit to her home city. As our new best-friend she couldn't do enough for us and went out of her way to make our stay memorable. That, combined with the great breakfasts included in the price and the glorious views we had out of our room over the sea to Mount Esja, (Reykjavik's own volcano), meant that we had a really enjoyable stay. The Orkin is only 10 minutes' walk from Registration in one direction and 20 minutes to the Start/Finish in the other making it a definite recommendation for anyone looking for somewhere to stay for the marathon. It also provided unlimited free coffee and cake at all hours of the day. While there we also had the company of Jeremy Haslett, a Norwich based marathon runner very much in the same mold as myself. Like me, Jeremy enjoyed the idea of marathon tourism; experiencing new cities in new countries with the marathon as the impetus and focal point of the trip. He'd run 77 marathons in total, most of these in some pretty exotic parts of the world. Isn't it great to unexpectedly meet others on your travels with similar motivations for keeping-on running.

Next day, (Friday), was registration day for the event. This was held between 10am and 7pm in a huge sporting complex in an area known as the Laugardalur Valley some 3 kilometres west of the city centre. The area is best known as the site of Iceland's premier sports ground as well as a superb outdoor swimming complex, botanical gardens and zoo. The fact that it was very much one of the newer suburbs soon became apparent from the architectural style of the buildings: everything appeared all straight lines and sharp edges, almost as if a succession of concrete oblongs had been speared into the ground. On our early morning walk there we encountered no other pedestrians, no one cycling – the streets were deserted with no signs of litter, dog poo or graffiti – in fact, it all just seemed too sterile and antiseptic from the point of view of someone coming from the UK. I was later to find that these chrome and glass structures in the form of expensive apartment blocks continue along the seafront for most of the way both west and east of the city centre. It's only in the streets away from the front that you find Reykjavik's true atmosphere and character with brightly painted houses of corrugated iron and tin. I found these areas quite appealing.

We arrived early for registration hoping to beat the inevitable queues of later in the day, (last year there were over 13,000 entrants in the 5 events on offer). Unfortunately, our plans for a quick exit were thwarted by a computer malfunction in the verification of our timing chips, resulting not only in us having to stand in a long queue waiting for things to be sorted, but also being unable to use our own chip for the race. Our goody bag contained a rather nice official T- shirt and two vouchers: one for a free Camelbak drink bottle and the other for a free swim in any of the city's seven thermal pools. The bottle ended up being left at the hotel and the swim voucher went unused – I'm afraid the idea of swimming in the open air in the incessant pouring rain simply just didn't appeal. Unlike Gdansk the previous week, however, there was a proper sports expo accompanying registration with stalls selling all manner of clothing and equipment plus some very generous hand-outs of yoghurt, chocolate milk, coffee and assorted treats to supplement our pre-race diet. It was with some apprehension that we returned to the sports hall later that afternoon for the Pasta Party, fully expecting the place to be packed to the rafters with heaving wet bodies. Our fears were unfounded, not only were family and friends allowed in for free, we were served immediately with a full plate of pasta, salad and bread and allowed to return for refills as many times as we wanted (Greedy me managed three servings). Given the exorbitant cost of a meal in Reykjavik city centre this was a real bonus.

The marathon start was at 8.40am the next day (no, I don't know why) and, unbelievably, it was still raining. In fact, the mist was even further down to the ground than when we arrived – so much for the beautiful pictures of runners in the sunshine in the event literature. This was the 30th edition of the race in which the number of participants has grown each year from the 214 entrants in 1984. Apparently 14,272 registered this year. I don't have a full breakdown of the figures for 2013 but last year 806 ran the full marathon, 116 ran in the marathon relay, 2,004 ran the half, 5,177 ran the 10km while almost 2,000 entered the 3km Fun Run and 3,379 took part in something called the Lazy Town Run, (don't ask!) At 62 to 80 euros to enter, depending on date of entry, the marathon itself is obviously the minority event in this little lot. Within all these figures we're told that there were altogether 1,693 foreign entrants representing 63 different nationalities – making it a nice little earner for Iceland's booming tourism industry.

While sheltering in the over-crowded baggage/changing area near the start line I was delighted to bump into Kate Taylor, a long-time running friend from Yorkshire. Kate is a fellow marathon tourist and very independent-minded lady who often travels alone to some of the most far-flung marathons around the world. This was to be her 98th marathon and with the Ypres Peace Marathon next on her agenda, she'd planned October's Munich Marathon for her 100th. She'd actually travelled to Reykjavik for the marathon in 2007, only to have to stand and watch others run due to a troublesome knee injury requiring surgery. Kate was determined to make up for that lost opportunity this time round. Engrossed in catching up with what each of us had been up to since last meeting, we almost missed the start altogether and ended up sneaking in at the very back of the field with thousands ahead of us. Never mind, they say it's good to talk and neither of us were intent on breaking any world records.

The race started in conjunction with the half marathon outside Reykjavik Junior College on Laekjargata in the heart of the city centre. The 10km set off approx. one hour later. The first kilometre took us alongside Tjornir, the lake bisecting the city on which the new Town Hall is built, before crossing the lake and heading in a southerly direction to the fjord across the peninsula. On our way there we passed both the National Museum and the University of Iceland. There followed a 10km loop around the shoreline back to Harpa, the monstrosity of an Opera House, close to where we had started. The course then headed eastwards along the Atlantic shoreline to approximately 16km: past the iconic Sun Voyager aluminum sculpture resembling a Viking ship designed to commemorate the city's 200th anniversary in 1990, past Hotoi – the house in which Reagan and Gorbachev met in 1986 to try to find a resolution to the Cold War and finally to the International Shipping Terminal where a recently arrived boatload of American passengers had to wait patiently in their tour buses for the runners to pass before they could head off on one of their day tours.

Running back towards the city at 18km we finally lost the half marathoners as they made their way back to the finish. At this point we were able to see Videy Island, first inhabited soon after the discovery of Iceland in 870, before heading inland to the half-way mark in the aforementioned Langardalur Valley. Up to this point we had largely been running on closed roads. The rest of the route was to take us mainly on good walking/cycle paths all the way to where we'd started in the centre of town. From 24 to 25km we ran through Ellioaardalur, a nature reserve containing a salmon river and a lovely mini waterfall before crossing the southern ring road over a footbridge at the 29km mark near to Nautholsvik, Iceland's only serviced beach. This is a partly man made facility where the water is held at a constant temperature of 20 degrees, being a mixture of the cold Atlantic Ocean and hot spring water. As we ran past, the temperature on the course was a mere 8 degrees in the horizontal rain and I was feeling more in need of a hat and gloves rather than a swim in the sea by this stage.

We continued on the footpath beside the shoreline behind Reykjavik's domestic airport before heading out at 36km to Grotta, another nature reserve and protected birdlife area from where we turned eastwards again for the long run-in past the Icelandic Prime Minister's Office and Catholic Cathedral to the finish line and the prospect of at last getting dry. I have to admit, though, that I didn't really mind the cold and wet. I enjoyed the course, showing us as it did so many of the city's tourist sites. It was largely flat and scenic with most of it being within sight of the ocean and I invariably run best in colder weather. I later discovered that I'd finished as 2nd Vet 65 in a time of 4 hours 11minutes – some five and a half minutes behind the first runner in that category. Whether or not I could have made up that deficit by starting further up the field and not stopping at the half-way portaloo is open to conjecture – I very much doubt it. It's all academic anyway as there were no prizes on offer in that age-group category; the organizers preferring to lump everyone between 60 and 70 into the same age bracket – hardly fair to those at the older end of that scale who find themselves competing with someone who could be up to 10 years younger. The only consolation was that my time would have won the Vet 70 category by over 20 minutes. Perhaps I'll go back next year. On finishing we were handed a medal (Mo swears that the half marathoners got the same medal – I hope she's mistaken) a banana, a bun and a bottle of water.

Having got the marathon over and done with my thoughts could now turn to investigating the local food and drink and considering where we could go on the almost two full days that remained of our stay. The marathon is timed to coincide each year with Reykjavik's Culture Night. This is defined in the literature as ' an annual event in the city since 1996, offering the chance to enjoy a variety of activities, ranging from guided tours, exhibitions, traditional shows and more unusual happenings' We were warned that it attracted huge crowds and that the city centre and its restaurants were likely to be full. The night also finishes with a huge firework display down by the harbour. I hope it didn't turn out to be a damp squib. With that in mind we decided that our best bet would be to eat somewhere outside of town. Kate was to join us before leaving early the next day. I'd done some research beforehand on what constituted authentic Icelandic food. This seemed to consist largely of fish dishes, particularly Plokkfiskur, a type of stewed fish, Ponnukokur, (Icelandic pancakes) and Kjotsupa, a traditional meat soup containing lamb, (there's more sheep than people in Iceland). In the event we ended up at an out of town Mexican restaurant called the Red Chilli eating burritos and enchiladas, not at all very Icelandic. The food was tasty and well-presented costing Mo and I 5,200 ISK, (£30), for the main course plus a couple of beers.

The next night we were determined to sample some of the local dishes and had been recommended to visit the Icelandic Fish and Chips restaurant down by the harbour. It was meant to serve a wide variety of fresh seafood straight from the boats and the idea of eating a filling plate of cod and chips seemed very appealing. We knew we'd made the wrong decision the minute we stepped through the door and spotted the logo 'organic bistro' straight out of Pseud's Corner. Can someone please tell me what on earth that means other than an excuse to hike up prices and make you feel they're doing you a favour by letting you buy their over-priced culinary efforts. Despite this, the place was packed with queues out the door. I abhor all forms of food snobbery, seeing food essentially as fuel to keep the body moving rather than some exotic art form, to be shaped and sculptured for admiring 'connoisseurs.' I should have run out of the premises there and then but, instead, allowed us to be shown to some dingy table opposite the toilets. I wasn't having that and insisted on waiting for a more suitable spot with a harbour view. Eventually we got one but still had to rejoin the long queue to place our order, (no such thing as waitress service in an organic bistro). On reaching the counter we were informed that they didn't serve chips - so what's with the name, it definitely read 'Icelandic Fish and Chips' on the sign. Instead we needed to order, and, of course, pay extra for, 'roasted crispy potatoes' with some sort of green stuff sticking on them. When the food finally arrived it was the tiniest portion I'd ever seen, consisting of a small, oblong plate, (even the plates have sharp edges in Iceland), sporting about 8 of the aforementioned roasted crispy thingies and two cigar shaped pieces of cod – all for 4,00ISK, (£12 each), without drinks. As someone who could eat for England, particularly after a marathon, the amount on the plate was an insult to a grown man's appetite. Resisting the urge to scream out words such as 'Robbery' and 'Rip-off' I was persuaded by Mo to accept what I'd been given and put it all down to experience, which I did. Our next meal consisted of a very filling Cheeseburger and loads of proper chips plus a 500ml bottle of coke for 890 ISK, (£5), in our local greasy spoon café.

Our experience with the local alcoholic beverages was a different matter altogether. We arrived forewarned about the high cost of drinking in the local bars, armed with a litre bottle of whiskey from Edinburgh airport's duty free shop. Apparently, even the locals get tanked up at home before joining the weekend 'runtur' (literally translated as pub-crawl) in the city's bars. There's even a state-owned liquor store in the main street known as Vinbuo where alcohol can be bought for, what in Iceland, passes as a reasonable price. For example, the main local brews Viking and Gull can be purchased at about 350 ISK per 0.5 litre can. I couldn't resist trying the 7% Purs Striker for that price though avoided the 10% version for 645 ISK. Because of the prohibitive cost we only tried one bar while we there. This was the Dubliner near the main square where, even during Happy Hour, a pint of draught Gull cost 1,000 ISK, (£6) The place lacked atmosphere and I'd be in no hurry to return. The unimaginatively titled English Pub on the main street looked a much better bet.

One of the big disappointments of our stay was Reykjavik's seemingly over-reliance on tourism. Last year Iceland had twice as many visitors as it has inhabitants. It appears to have taken the concept of tourism to another level and, rightly or wrongly, I formed the impression that the country was prepared to sell its soul in the quest for the tourist dollar. So much so that, if it's not careful, it'll end up destroying the very things that tourists come to see. (Who wants to travel all the way to Iceland just to see other tourists?) Everywhere you went, everything you read, appeared to be pointing you in the direction of some organized tour or other. Even the government funded Tourist Information Centres seemed to serve as mere conduits for the tour operators. None of these tours were cheap. In fact, the cost of many was prohibitive. For example, we arrived determined to visit the 'must see' Blue Lagoon, between the city and the airport, with its geothermal springs, swimming pool and spa. On enquiry it was going to cost us 9,500 ISK each with FlyBus plus another 800 ISK for towel hire – a combined total of 20,600 ISK, or a whopping £121 for a couple. This just seemed an obscene amount to sit in water, regardless of its origin, while yet more water plummeted on our heads from the sky above. We gave it a miss and took the ferry across to the island of Videy instead for a more reasonable 1,100 ISK each. The island, which is actually the top of an extinct volcano, has a number of designated walking trails leading to its various historical sites. Strangely, it is also home to Yoko Ono's 'Imagine Peace Tower' conceived as a beacon to world peace. This structure emits a powerful beam of light illuminating the Reykjavik sky every night between October 9th (John Lennon's birthday) and December 8th (the anniversary of his death). Unfortunately, once again the torrential rain limited our enjoyment of what, on sunnier days, must be a beautiful place.

   I cannot emphasise enough the part the atrocious weather played in souring our experience of Iceland. It rained virtually from the minute we arrived to the minute that we left. The only variation was in its intensity. Sometimes it would be light drizzle and mist that slowly soaked you to the skin. At other times it would be an all-out downpour that quickly soaked you to..... I'm sure you get the picture. I kept telling myself how much nicer it would be to come in the summer before remembering that I was, in fact, there in summer. We knew that we were surrounded by a beautiful landscape of mountains, hills and sea – it was just that we never got to see any of it for the low cloud, mist and rain. Personally, I'd be reluctant to go back without a guarantee of dry weather from the Icelandic Tourist Board and even then I'd be sure to pack plenty changes of waterproof clothing. I wonder what the Viking word is for 'soggy bay.'

It was raining before the race

And it was still raining long after we finished in Reykjavik!

ESTONIA

TALLINN MARATHON

As someone growing-up during the Cold War era, the idea of travelling to any of the Baltic States simply wouldn't have come under consideration. At that time they were among the many satellite states of the former USSR and very much, no-go areas, where tourism was actively discouraged. Not only that, but the local inhabitants were prevented from leaving themselves by the infamous KGB. It's only since gaining their independence after the fall of the old Soviet Union in the early 1990s that Estonia, Latvia and Lithuania have appeared on the tourist map. Suddenly, what had been provincial backwaters became serious European countries with their own identities, currencies, airlines and, above all, recognition on an international basis. Nowadays, all three countries have their own established annual marathons in their respective capital cities. Tallinn, (Estonia) and Vilnius (Lithuania) hold theirs on consecutive weekends in September while Riga (Latvia) hosts a mid-May marathon. My youngest son Ross has twice visited Tallinn and returned with glowing reports on each occasion. I thought it was time to visit the place for myself especially as it was in a country that figured prominently on my marathons to-do list.

With Estonia in the north, Latvia in the middle and Lithuania in the south, the Baltic States are situated on the southeastern shore of the Baltic Sea, bordered in the south by the Russian territory of Kaliningrad, Poland and Belarus. Estonia is the smallest of the three, while Latvia and Lithuania are roughly of the same size. Their three capital cities are home to almost a quarter of the region's seven million inhabitants. These three cities, while joined by many historical ties, each have a distinctly different character: from the medieval grandeur of Tallinn, to the Art Nouveau architecture of Riga and the Baroque of Vilnius. At some stage I hope to complete the full-set of each of the cities' marathons. I suppose the best way of doing this is to stay in the region for a week or more in early September, combining both the Tallinn and Vilnius marathons with some general sight-seeing and then to return to Riga the following May. Had I realized how beautiful the weather was to be, I might well have been persuaded to extend my trip. Though I didn't have time to visit the coast on this occasion, I found on a subsequent trip that their long western coastline consists of a seemingly endless unspoiled beaches broken only by beautiful resort towns such as Palanga, Parnu and Jurmala, (memories of the beautiful Sopot from the Gdansk trip spring to mind here).

Estonia itself has had a troubled history, resulting from its geographical situation at the crossroads of Eastern and Western Europe. It has been fought over by both Sweden and Russia on several occasions. Despite years of recent Russian domination many of its citizens consider themselves more of Swedish, than Russian origin, and look westwards rather than eastwards for inspiration. (Certainly most of the girls have that long-legged, blond, Swedish look). Despite finding itself in state of near economic collapse following its independence from the Soviet Union, Estonia is now regarded as an example of how to modernize rapidly while preserving a distinct cultural identity built on its historic architecture and natural landscapes. You'll find it often referred to as e-Estonia due to its reputation for technical innovation. In recent years it has grown into a major travel destination for western Europeans: the young flock there for their stag-parties while many Finns prefer to cross the Baltic on the frequent ferries from Helsinki to do their shopping in Tallinn. Tourism has, without doubt, been fundamental in Estonia's advance to a thriving economy with the marathon weekend helping in no small part by attracting visitors from over 40 different countries to its series of events.

The influence of tourism is particularly noticeable in Tallinn itself. In a little over a decade it has grown from a relative backwater to a dynamic and modern city. Apart from the architectural beauty of the Old Town, Tallinn also sports some outstanding examples of modern architecture as symbols of its new-found prosperity. I found it to be a hybrid combination of pristine, medieval architecture at its centre surrounded by what appeared to be a rapidly developing, dynamic city. But, as my hotel receptionist was keen to point out; it was not all brightness and light. She was concerned that tourists only ever saw the beautiful medieval core and that the city's more downtrodden suburbs continued to be ignored by her government.

Unfortunately for me, the journey there and back was to be long and circuitous and certainly not without incident. With no direct connections from either Newcastle or Edinburgh I was forced into taking an early morning flight from Manchester, returning via Gatwick. Isn't it strange that things can go so badly wrong at the outset of a journey but you can still return with great memories of the trip! I'd planned to meet up with my 100 Club friend Dave Goodwin for the 6 am flight from Manchester airport. Dave had chosen to drive up from his home in the Midlands the night before and stay overnight at the airport Travelodge. Knowing that I'd need to be up by 3 am I decided that as I was unlikely to get much sleep anyway I might as well travel down on the overnight train from Newcastle. That's when things started to go wrong big time! Firstly, my train to Manchester simply conked out in the middle of nowhere, losing all power and leaving us passengers sitting in the pitch dark for ages - not knowing whether the problem could be fixed in time for the flight. It was, but there was no sign of Dave at the airport where, by chance, I met up with old friend Gary O'Brien (of Prague fame/notoriety) who was also travelling to the marathon. We boarded the flight just assuming that Dave was also somewhere in the queue. This consisted largely of a boisterous stag party already well-oiled after an early morning drinking session in the airport bar. No crude T-shirts this time, just lots of fairly crude banter. I'm beginning to think that Friday to Monday flights to destinations known to attract stag parties should be avoided at all costs. Dave wasn't in amongst the stags. On arrival in Tallinn there was a text message from Dave, disgusted with himself for oversleeping his wake-up call. Never mind, Andy Glen from the 100 Club was also on our flight so we'd already got the basis for a good social drinking team for the coming weekend.

The journey into town was via a short 1.60 euro bus ride on the number 2 bus that leaves every 20 minutes from directly outside the passenger terminal. We hadn't realized though that this wasn't exclusively an airport service. It travels in from one of the outer suburbs and can already be quite full on reaching the terminal. Our journey in was hot, uncomfortable and probably contravened all known health and safety regulations. If you're travelling in company it's probably better just to pay the 8 euros taxi fare. You don't really need public transport to get around in Tallinn, but if you want to go further afield the central bus terminal in Viru Keskus, the main shopping mall, serves most routes. There's also nine trolleybus lines serving residential areas and four tram lines running across the four compass points of the city. The same tickets, bought from the driver, can be used on all three systems. Our early morning flight meant that we were in the Town Hall Square before 11 am, (Estonia is 2 hours ahead of BST). As none of us could get into our respective hotels until 2 pm we thought it best to pick up our numbers at Registration before the crowds arrived. This was easily accomplished by a short stroll in the hot sun to the registration marquee in Freedom Square; Tallinn's showcase square full of national symbolism and civic pride. The square is dominated by a huge pillar with a cross known as The Monument to the War commemorating Estonia's battle for independence from Russia from 1918 to 1920. As well as receiving our numbers with incorporated chip, we were also handed a rather disappointing grey T-shirt that didn't even include the word marathon anywhere on it (I'd seen last year's shirts and they were of a much more appropriate design), a free ferry ticket to either Helsinki or Stockholm and a discounted pasta restaurant voucher. (Neither of the latter two was used even though the ferry voucher was valid until the following May.) There were also a couple of sports retailers' tents but, with us being among the first visitors, they were as yet unopened. So with still over 2 hours to go before hotel check-in the sensible idea seemed to be to enjoy the sunshine with a couple of beers and a bite to eat in one of the many outdoor restaurants lining the main Town Hall square.

Andy had run the marathon last year and knew all the best places to go and, of course, one thing led to another and with lots of catching up to do, a couple of beers soon became a whole lot more – setting the pattern for what was to prove a very boozy weekend. It's great to spend time with fellow marathon tourists that you haven't seen for awhile and to hear their stories of some of the things that have happened to them on their marathon travels. What should have been an early, became a very late check-in at the Hotel Bern. It probably wouldn't have been my first choice but, as a last minute entry, I was very lucky to find anywhere at all so conveniently located within the city centre. Gary's low budget hotel, appropriately named the Economy, (where Dave was also supposed to be staying), was fully booked. Within the region of 20,000 entrants spread over the series of races in the marathon weekend, early booking for this event is definitely advisable. However, I was happy with my double room in the 3 star Bern, (same price as a single at 238 euros for three nights), and found it quiet, clean, comfortable and convenient. I'd only to roll out of bed on the Sunday morning and I was virtually on the start line. I even had time for their 8 am breakfast of scrambled egg, meat balls, pickled herring, salmon and a selection of meats and cheeses. Obviously I didn't eat them all on marathon day but I certainly did on the other two that I stayed.

Before leaving home research on Tallinn's Old Town had described it as 'one of the best-preserved examples of medieval architecture in Northern Europe with its winding cobbled streets and rows of elegantly gabled facades'. Having recently been impressed with the medieval centres of both Prague and Gdansk I was anxious to see how Tallinn compared, so I'd left the following day (Saturday) to do the full tourist routine. There are, of course, organized guided tours and tour bus companies to relieve you of your money but by far the best way to see things is to explore on foot with a free map from one of the Information Centres. Tallinn is a compact city with most of the important sites concentrated in and around Town Hall Square and the nearby Toompea Hill. This whole area is distinguished by a series of narrow cobbled streets and alleyways, museums, courtyards with spired churches dominating every vista. I won't bother you by describing everything there is to see. I'm aware of the axiom, 'once you've seen one church/museum/bridge/square etc you've seen them all' so I'll just mention a few of the places I enjoyed visiting.

Perhaps the best place to start is Toompea Hill, looking down on the town and offering an excellent vantage point with panoramic views out to the Baltic. In the old days the nobles living on the hill would look down- both literally and figuratively on the merchants and artisans residing below. From the free viewing platforms you get great views of the city's fairytale walls and towers as well as St Olav's Church and the harbour. Also on Toompea and well worth a visit, if only to stand in awe of its internal opulence, is the Russian Orthodox Cathedral of St Alexander Nevsky. With its colourful onion domed towers and heavy Russian influence the cathedral looks out of place amongst its medieval neighbours. Finally, Toompea also contains the castle that has been the seat of power in Estonia since the 13th century. An impressive building, it's today home to the nation's Parliament.

Below the hill, in the Old Town, the magnificent Town Hall Square; littered today with numerous bars and restaurants all competing for the tourist dollar, has served as a marketplace for centuries. The Town Hall itself is the best preserved Gothic building in Northern Europe. Nearby, there's the Holy Spirit Church, a spectacular structure with Tallinn's oldest timepiece, an elaborate painted clock on its façade. There's also a Dominican Monastery, St Olav's Church – a major Tallinn landmark with an interesting story of how it came to be built and once the tallest building in the world and the Viru Gates that have become the symbol of the Town. I could go on – if you're interested in history and architecture there's just so much to see. Personally, I'm not a city person, preferring seascapes and mountain views to buildings any day. I think what I enjoyed most of all about the city was its closeness to the coast. I spent a happy few hours in the warm sunshine watching the sleek, giant ferries leaving the harbour on their journeys to Helsinki and Stockholm. Certainly, if I'd been able to stay an extra day I'd have taken advantage of the free ferry voucher and joined the early morning ferry for a 2 hour voyage to Helsinki, returning late that evening. I also thoroughly enjoyed a long, leisurely walk along the Baltic shoreline later that day, following part of what was to be the next day's marathon route.

With sightseeing over for the day, I could now begin to think about the run at last. This year's event was dedicated to the 100th anniversary of Estonian marathon running. Apparently the first running competition in Estonia took place on 28th April 1913 over the old distance of 40.2 kilometres and was won by a Russian athlete in the time of 3 hours 23 minutes 45 seconds, (I guess that's a poor time for a short course). The organizers seemed to make a great deal out of their marathon being the best attended of those in the Baltic States – hardly surprising I suppose if you insist on counting the large numbers of children who participate in their Saturday afternoon races with age groups going upwards from 2 to 12. This year the numbers broke the 20,000 mark for the first time. This consisted of: 2,077 in the marathon, 2,728 in the half, 7,689 in the 10k, 7,201 in a Nordic 10k and 2,661 in the children's races. The children's events culminated on the Saturday evening with an Official Opening Ceremony on a large stage in Freedom Square from 6 to 7 pm. This started with all the elite runners in the 3 main events being introduced to us individually on stage. These were, of course, largely Ethiopian and Kenyan athletes. As their personal best times were displayed electronically on screen behind each runner, I couldn't help thinking that there was little to choose between the three favourites in the men's race. This proved correct the next day when the same three came flying past me with scarcely a hair's breadth between them. All three finished within seconds of each other. After the introductions came the speeches from various suited and booted dignitaries. As it was all in Estonian I hadn't a clue what they were on about. Then it was 30 minutes of a rather old-fashioned looking and sounding rock group, (a cross between Frank Ifield and the Seekers if any of you are old enough to know who they are). The curtain finally came down with a decent fireworks display. As I left the Square the temperature on digital display was still showing 19 degrees. It had been a hot day and, at 25 degrees, it was tipped to be even hotter for tomorrow's race.

Despite having had 15 years in Australia in which to acclimatize, I still don't run well in the heat. That night I had a decision to make. – should I forgo the pleasures of a convivial, boozy evening with Gary, Andy and Martin Bush or should I have an early night and try for a decent time the next day. No prizes for guessing what happened. – either those boys are very persuasive or I'm easily persuaded, (probably the latter). The upshot was, I left Mad Murphy's after 1am knowing that I'd be standing on the start line with up to 2000 other, more sober runners, in less than 8 hour's time. Not unnaturally, I struggled badly with the combination of heat and hangover, coming in some 35 minutes later than my time in Reykjavik two week's previously. I'm realistic enough to know though that my suffering was all self-inflicted. I had a choice and even with hindsight wouldn't have changed my decision. I'd had a bad day at the office but a great night out on the town. At this stage of my running career it's become more important to me to have a good time than to run one.

At the 9am start next morning we were policed into pens according to our race number, before heading out of the city centre for two laps of the half marathon course along a fairly flat out-and-back route, following the Baltic shoreline to the 9km mark. Incidentally, the half marathon set off two and a half hours later at 11.30 am and the 10km had a 13.30 start. It meant that, after having the roads to ourselves for most of the race, many of us were overtaken by pushing and jostling half marathoners as the race progressed. The endless stretches of long straight roads could have been monotonous had it not been for the views of the open sea and giant Helsinki and Stockholm ferries on the return leg. With about 3km to go before the finish of each lap we were directed along narrow, cobbled streets around the perimeter of the ancient city walls before entering the welcome shade of Toompea Park en route to Freedom Square. I managed to keep going at a steady pace until the 25km mark but it wasn't getting any better and, from thereon in, I opted for a walk/run strategy to the finish. It wasn't worth killing myself just to come in a few minutes earlier – I wanted to go out on the town again that night! On finishing we each received a heavy, distinctive marathon medal before being led past numerous stalls handing out bananas, isotonic drinks, water, snickers bars and all manner of assorted free offerings. The best was yet to come, however. Discreetly tucked away around the corner was a marathon runners-only enclosure to which runners from the other events were barred from entering. Here we given hot food and drink in the form of unlimited amounts of tasty, thick soup, pasta, rolls/bread, pastries, tea and coffee. There was a furnished marquee in which to sit and eat too. An added bonus was the free bar where pints of the local Saku 4.7% beer were handed out as many times as you cared to visit. I'd planned on using my Pasta restaurant discount voucher that evening but managed so much to eat and drink on finishing that I didn't need another meal that day. Unfortunately, many of the marathon finishers I spoke to later hadn't known about the free area and missed out on the treat. Gary and Martin for example were sitting in a nearby bar paying for their post-race beverages while Andy and I were filling our boots for free. They weren't pleased to hear about what they'd missed when we all met up later that night.

I have to say this is a really well organized and value for money marathon, up there with the best as far as both aspects are concerned. In particular, the spacing of the drinks stations every 2 km worked really well on such a hot day. Each of these had isotonic drinks and bananas as well as copious amounts of water. There were even free gels at the 12 and 33km marks so the four gels that I'd paid 2 euros each for before the race were saved for another time.

The marathon cost from 20 to 35 euros to enter depending on date of entry but we certainly got our money's worth. The generic T-shirt we were given was selling to non-runners for 15 euro, the pasta ticket saved approx. 5 euros, four gels saved 8 euros and I must have had at least 20 euro worth of free food and drink at the post-race marquee. Factor in the free ferry ticket, (it's something like 60 euros return to Helsinki), do the maths and you'll see that we got a good deal. I'm not even including several free bottles of sports drink, a couple of bottles of coke, a bar of snickers etc. etc. There were also prizes in every 5 year age-group category up to M75. (The 100 Club's Dave Ross, who I met up with later that evening took the V45 trophy home with him). I do hope some of those greedy UK race organizers currently charging over £50 for their marathons and giving so little back in return read this and take note.

For those who like their food and drink I'm afraid that I found little in Estonia to distinguish it from many of the other Eastern European locations I've visited. Like other Eastern Bloc countries their cuisine is heavy and filling, consisting largely of meat (particularly pork), potatoes and rye bread designed largely for hard work and harsh winters. I tried the local Seljanska; a meat and pickled vegetable soup followed by a tasty mutton goulash in an Estonian pub, the Hell Hunt in Pikk street – good value for only 10 euros. The other local fish specialities like pickled herring were already on offer on my hotel's breakfast menu. I did notice a restaurant in the main square offering Elk Soup followed by Wild Boar that I would have liked to have tried but, like all restaurants within the square, the cost was off-putting.

Investigation of the local beer produced more encouraging results. Andy was able to remember the Hell Hunt from his time here last year and took us there on the first day. Not only did they serve dark beer they also brewed it themselves in an off-premises micro-brewery. I'd thoroughly recommend the 5% Hell Hunt Tume at 3 euros a pint. Our other venue of choice was the rather better than normal Irish bar, Mad Murphy's above the Town Hall Square. This sold a range of local beers and, at 2.80 euros a pint, was over a euro cheaper than in the bars below. It also showed all the international sports programmes as well as hosting some pretty decent blues and rock bands later in the evening. Initially we drank the A La Coq Premium, a light beer from Tartu, Estonia's second city. Tallinn's own brewery, Saku, that supplied the free beer at the marathon, appears to be the most popular brand on sale in the city. After a couple of nights of getting to know the barman in Murphys's he put us on to another very drinkable 5.3% bottled dark beer called Konig Ludwig Weissbier – soon to become a major contributor to my poor performance in the race.

I really enjoyed every minute of my time in Tallinn and would certainly go back for the marathon again. Next time, with the correct preparation, I'm sure I could acquit myself well. The weather for the full four days was as hot and cloudless as Reykjavik had been damp and cold. There was a general feel-good factor about the place which, combined with the low-cost outdoor life style, makes it a pleasant place to spend a few days. I'd visited an exhibition depicting Estonia's history of struggle and suffering and found it hard to equate what I was reading with what I could see around me. Having been impressed with one of the Baltic States, it made me want to experience what Latvia and Lithuania have to offer. I'm not just talking about their marathons here, but what ideal vehicles on which to focus a visit. Don't you just love marathon tourism!

After the crowds have gone

Gary, Andy and I do a spot of refuelling in Tallin's Old Town Square.

DENMARK

HANS CHRISTIAN ANDERSEN MARATHON

This one definitely goes down in the quirky/different category. I found myself with three reasons for wanting to run this marathon in Odense, Andersen's birthplace and Denmark's third largest city. (Hands up if you can name its second largest). Firstly, I'd not yet got round to running a marathon in Denmark: my initial plan had been to go there for the Copenhagen marathon the following May but, at the time, that seemed such a long way away. (I finally made it to Copenhagen to run my 300th marathon in May 2019). Secondly, I'd been looking through some of my back copies of Distance Running and come across a very favourable article about the event. Finally, like most kids, I'd grown up on a diet of Hans Christian Andersen fairytales. Stories like 'The Little Mermaid', 'The Ugly Duckling' and, particularly 'The Emperor's New Clothes' had held a fascination for me as a child and had stimulated my imagination at the time. Years later I'd read these along with others such as 'The Snow Queen,' 'The Fir Tree,' 'The Tinder Box' and 'The Little Match Girl' to my own two children, deriving as much pleasure from their timeless stories as an adult as I had all those years ago. Of course, as an adult I was more aware of the sophisticated moral messages which Andersen had deliberately included in his stories for more mature readers. (He was acutely conscious of the fact that it would be the adult who had to read the fairy tale to the child). As a child I couldn't understand why the Emperor's courtiers continued to admire his non-existent outfit. That was before I understood the meaning of satire and Andersen's use of it to attack sycophancy and deference. A closer analysis of his writing shows a dark, anarchic and fatalistic element typical of the man himself. I was to learn during my visit that Andersen, far from being the genial character portrayed in the Danny Kaye film, was in fact a sad and troubled man with a dark and complicated private life. Most Danes I spoke to would allude to this, almost with a nudge and a knowing wink, but showed a reluctance to discuss precisely what Andersen's problems were. Nevertheless, Andersen, it would seem, achieved something unusual in creating tales that are read and loved by successive generations despite the overwhelming sadness that permeates most of his work. I can remember how, even as a child, this element of sadness was what struck me most about his stories. For example, The Little Match Girl dies, the Fir Tree is thrown away after Christmas and the Little Mermaid is betrayed by her Prince. Those of you who've read his stories will know that even those that end happily like 'The Snow Queen,' 'Thumbelina' and 'The Ugly Duckling' contain more than their fair share of suffering and unhappiness along the way. It would seem that in real life Andersen himself was the Ugly Duckling, born to poor parents and shunned throughout his career by the social class whose acceptance he was so desperate to enjoy. Despite that, his fairytales, having been translated into more than 125 languages, continue to inspire writers and artists to this day. In fact, the most prestigious award in children's literature is called the Hans Christian Andersen Medal.

For those unsure of Odense's exact location, it's situated in the middle of the large, central island of Funen one of the over 400 islands making up the Kingdom of Denmark. Only 72 of these are inhabited, however, with more than 40% of Denmark's population living on the island of Zealand which contains the capital, Copenhagen. Connected by the south of the large Jutland peninsula to Germany in the west, Denmark is the only Scandinavian country physically connected to the European mainland, serving as the bridge between Scandinavia and the rest of the continent. In recent times it has also been physically joined to Sweden by the magnificent Oresund road and rail bridge across to Malmo. I recall that when I last visited there in the 1960s it was necessary to travel north of Copenhagen and take the ferry across Oresund from

Helsinger to Helsingborg on the Swedish mainland. On discovering a suitably cheap Friday to Monday evening flight from Edinburgh to Copenhagen with easyJet, my plan was to go to Odense, run the marathon and find out more about the man after whom it is named, while satisfying the 'tourism' aspect of the trip with a stay in Copenhagen before and after the race. I'd last been to Denmark's capital over 47 years ago while on a month long hitch-hiking trip around Europe. My memories of that occasion were of spending a whole day visiting the two main breweries there; Tuborg in the morning and Carlsberg in the afternoon. The day ended in a panic on discovering that I'd lost my passport at one or other of these places. Early next morning I retraced my steps of the previous day and fortunately found the passport waiting for me at Carlsberg's reception desk, my second port of call. I've liked their beer ever since. My other big memory of the place was of making a special trip to the outer harbour to see the statue of Andersen's Little Mermaid. I thought it would be nice to go back and see if she remembered me.

It's a short 14 minute journey from Kastrup Airport by either train or metro to the centre of Copenhagen. Fares cost 36 DKK, approx. £4.25 at 8.42 Danish kroner to the £ (I found it easier mentally to work on the basis that 100 DKK was approx. £12, 50 DKK = £6, 25 DKK = £3). I'd divided my three nights stay into one night in Copenhagen and two in Odense, staying in all three in Hotel Cabinn – a new chain of eight identical hotels in five Danish cities. The chain's motto is along the lines of 'All you need to sleep' and that's precisely what you get. The rooms are based on the cabins of a ship with many having bunk beds – though they do stretch to 'Captain' and 'Commodore' class whatever they are, (perhaps you can get room to swing an extra-large cat in them). Though space is limited they were nevertheless clean, comfortable and functional with unlimited free tea and coffee via a kettle in the room. At 495 DKK per night for a twin room they're not cheap but are certainly value for money by Danish standards and I'd no complaints. The Copenhagen Cabinn is right next to the famous Tivoli Gardens and that's where I spent my first evening. The Tivoli, the world's most popular city park, is a huge amusement park with roller coasters, merry-go-rounds, a miniature railway, theatre, concert hall and landscaped gardens. The park prides itself on the over 100,000 specially designed lights that illuminate it in the evenings as well as on the exotic architectural style of Moorish facades and Oriental towers. If, like me, you enjoy people-watching, it's fun to simply sit in one of the many cafes and observe the crowds enjoying themselves in the magical evening light reflected off the lake while sipping a beer or two, (Carlsberg, of course) The evening ended with a firework display just to add a bit more colour to the proceedings.

Next day, Saturday, I had to be in Odense before Registration for the marathon closed at 6pm so time was limited in the capital. I wanted to see, in the light of day, how much Copenhagen had changed since I'd last been there in the 1960s. It's a very compact city despite its 625,000 inhabitants and, for the visitor, easily walkable or bicycle-friendly. The Danes cycle in their thousands: men in suits, students galore, some pulling cart extensions, some carrying pets. Every time the lights change there's a virtual peloton heading towards you at pace, so you've got to be pretty nimble on your feet. I'd decided that apart from a general walk-around looking at the sights, there were two places I wanted to revisit from years ago. I gave up on the idea of the first of these, a return to the Carlsberg Brewery, on being told that they no longer brewed beer on site these days and that all that remained was an official Visitor Centre with talks and displays. That just didn't appeal, although my passport would probably have been safe. My other intention was to go and visit the Little Mermaid again. I'd dug out an old photo of a young me with an even younger her just before leaving home. I wanted to see how much we both had changed. The plan was to follow Hans Christian Andersen Boulevard to the Langbro Bridge and then take the riverside footpath along Inderhavnen some 3.5 km to the statue at Yderhavnen, (I think these mean Inner and Outer Harbour, but I could be wrong). That plan was also abandoned when riverside works meant unwanted detours inland. Fortunately, Copenhagen has an excellent integrated transport system where a cheap 2 zone ticket allows transfers between buses, trains, metro and river ferries provided the transfer is made within an hour. It was an easy matter to jump on to one of the blue and yellow harbour ferries; the 991/992 sails from the Opera House downstream to near the Little Mermaid. I recognized her immediately, though I doubt if the feeling was reciprocated. She didn't seem to have moved at all, (though I had heard she'd been touted around China for some reason recently), and was still staring forlornly out to sea. She looked as young as ever. I looked my age.

I guess Copenhagen has changed a lot since I was last there. The old quarter around the station area has been pedestrianised, the docks have been rejuvenated and a number of impressive modern buildings such as the Black Diamond, the Opera House, the Royal Danish Playhouse, Concert Hall and Blue Planet Aquarium have appeared on the skyline. In fact, a whole new downtown area has been created from nothing on Amager Island, while large scale regeneration of the suburbs is continuing to take place. There's even a brand new Metro expansion working towards completion in 2018, incorporating 17 new city-centre stations.

I took the inter-city train to Aarhus for the 1 hour 35 minute journey to Odense not realizing that weekend fares are considerably more expensive than those in mid-week. Even with an over-65 discount it cost me a well over budget 290 DKK to get there as opposed to only 140 DKK to return to the airport on Monday. Having dropped my bag off at the hotel I made immediately for the Saturday afternoon registration at the local Sports Park some 2.5 km walk out of town. (I later found that I could have taken the number 31 bus, but fancied the walk anyway). This area reminded me very much of the registration facilities at Reykjavik: in a sports hall with expo on a huge campus containing a running track and major football stadium. Unfortunately there weren't the same freebies available – just some tiny containers of the sponsor's beer, the delightful Vestfyen 5.3% Chocolate Brown. I hadn't even had to go looking for Denmark's perfect dark beer, it had found me instead. I couldn't resist taking up their offer of 25 DKK for three 500ml cans of the stuff for later that night.

We were handed a rather nice grey Newline T- shirt with V neck together with a ticket for that afternoon's pasta party taking place in a large marquee nearby. This proved excellent value with as-much-as-you wanted pasta and mincemeat with sausages plus chocolate mousse. There was also a choice of bottled beer or water to drink while a local band 'Cutting Grass' provided bluegrass and country to aid digestion. They were so good, in fact, that I stayed until they'd finished both of their sets – saving myself the cost of an expensive dinner later that evening. With plenty of time left before dark, it was time to do a spot of sightseeing around Odense.

Odense is the main city on the island of Funen which lies between the larger Zealand Island and the Jutland peninsula. With a population of 185,000 it is one of the oldest cities in Denmark, having celebrated its 1,000 anniversary in 1988. Its name derives from 'Odins Ve' meaning Odin's shrine, (Odin is, of course, the famous God of Norse mythology) Not only is Odense synonymous with Hans Christian Andersen it would appear to be heavily dependent on his legacy to attract visitors, in much the same way that Stratford-on-Avon relies on Shakespeare to draw the crowds. (As opposed to the Lake District, for example, to which people would flock regardless of Wordsworth and Beatrix Potter). In many ways Odense reminded me of Stratford with its quaint architecture and picture postcard riverside. It seemed almost mandatory to visit the house in which Andersen was born, the H C Andersen Museum, the H C Andersen Park and the H C Andersen statue. To me though, the best bit about the place was the local Odense River and the use the city had made of it for landscaped parks, cycle paths and river cruises. One of the cruises went downstream to the Odense Zoo – one of the largest in Denmark. Can you guess what they called the boat that made the journey there? Other attractions, some of which I visited but others I ignored, are the Town Hall, City Museum, Cathedral of King Canute and, strangely, the Danish Railway Museum. The city centre itself consisted of a smattering of cobbled, pedestrianised streets in a compact area between the railway station and the river. Saturday night found it crowded with outdoor restaurants, all full and doing good business. On Sunday evening it was as dead as a door-nail. Initially I thought that Sunday closing must be compulsory before finding the inevitable Irish bar, Ryan's, full to the fake rafters. Everyone in there appeared to be wearing a Manchester United shirt and to be in deep mourning. It turns out that their team were being hammered by, at that stage, four goals to nil in the local derby with Manchester City. Not a single soul was in City's colours. As soon as the match ended at 7 pm they all stood up and soundlessly walked out leaving me virtually on my own to finish my pint of the local Odense Pilsner, (35 DKK) I neither liked nor disliked Odense – it was just one of those cities that looked pretty but didn't appear to have a great deal of life or vivacity. I found it an inoffensive but uninspiring place and wouldn't be in any hurry to go back.

The marathon there is promoted as 'The Fairy Tale Marathon' for obvious reasons. 2013 was the 14th edition of the event and each year finishers are presented with a medal bearing the portrait of Hans Christian Andersen with a representation of one of his famous stories on the rear. To my delight, this year's medal showed a scene from 'The Emperor's New Clothes.' Entry fees were between 550 and 650 DKK depending on the date of entry with entries being taken right up to the 6 pm closing of registration on Saturday. As far as I am aware the event is unique in holding a Women's only Half Marathon separate from the main race starting at 9 am. The full marathon together with the men's half marathon both started at 10 am. Numbers have continued to increase over the years with 2013 featuring approx. 800 in the women's half, another 800 in the men's half and approx. 1,400 in the marathon itself. Those of us in the marathon were to run two laps of the half marathon course. Given the distance from the city centre to the start line, the organizers had thoughtfully provided a free shuttle bus to and from Odense central station both before and after the race. Baggage and changing facilities with hot showers and post-race massage were available inside the stadium building. The finish was to be in front of the grandstand in the adjacent Athletics Stadium following one lap of the track itself, making it an ideal venue for spectators to watch the runners come in.

It had been a sunny weekend in Denmark and the warm weather and stiffening, blustery wind were to be a factor in the race. Fortunately there were well-stocked feed stations every couple of kilometres so we never wanted for food or drink throughout on the somewhat unexceptional course. This took us on a clockwise, circular route through residential streets and uninspiring industrial areas, the monotony only being broken by a 2km stretch through the streets of the city centre from between the 13 and 15 km marks of each lap. At least on these sections we had some vocal crowd support and interesting sights to see. After crossing the river and running for a short distance through one of the riverside parks we were soon back into the residential street routine again. Personally, I found it difficult to maintain concentration knowing what we were faced with again on the second lap and, having tried and failed to stay with the 4 hour 15 minute pacers after 28 km, simply settled for a comfortable finish. I always enjoy the feeling of entering a big athletics stadium and finishing the race on the track.

On finishing we were given our medals, plus flowers for all the female competitors, (a nice touch), before being led into what they described as the depot – basically a free-for-all of bananas, apples, water, energy drink and yet more Vestfyen bottled beer. It was nice to relax in the sunshine and have a couple of beers with some of my Danish fellow runners, all of whom spoke perfect English and had the good manners to converse in my language while I remained in their company. As far as I could see I was the only runner from the UK entered in the marathon. I doubt if I'd go all that way to run it again though. I'd succeeded in my objective of adding Denmark to the list of countries in which I've run a marathon. I also fulfilled a desire to revisit Copenhagen, this time as a marathon tourist. I did hear some excellent reports of the North Sea Beach Marathon held on a beautiful 26 mile stretch of beach north of Esjberg on the last weekend of June each year. Now that sounds like a plan.

As usual when I visit a different country I try to sample the local cuisine as well as the local brew. There was, however, very little that I saw on any menu to distinguish the food from what we see in the UK. Like us, their menus largely consist of sturdy filling dishes of carbohydrates, meats and as befits a seafaring nation - fish. The one restaurant I visited in Odense offered a choice between two traditional Danish dishes: Frikadeller – the national dish consisting mainly of meatballs and Stegte Sild – fried herring in vinegar. I went for the meatballs. The free food at the previous day's pasta party tasted better and was twice as filling! As for Danish beer, well there was quite a bit of choice particularly in the supermarkets where I found a Carlsberg 8.2% Porter, something you don't see in the UK, for 20 DKK (approx. £2.40 per can) and Albani, the local Odense brewery's 10% Giraf Beer for 23 DKK. Yes I did try it, purely for research purposes of course, and live to tell the tale but I'd already found my favourite in the aforementioned Chocolate Brown and was happy to stick with that.

I found the Danes I met to be a tolerant and independent-minded bunch, who were without exception very friendly and welcoming to me as a visitor. They all seemed happy and at ease with their lot in life. This is hardly surprising when you consider that their country is frequently ranked as the happiest country in the world in cross-national studies of happiness as well as having the highest social mobility, income equality and one of the world's highest per capita incomes. Some country!

Ps. Aarhus is the second largest city in Denmark and the boat was, of course, called 'H C Andersen.'

Checking out the Start Line before the race

This would have been a dangerous place to finish running!

BELGIUM

BRUSSELS MARATHON

I'd previously run the Night of Flanders Marathon in Torhout, Belgium but had never before visited Brussels. My curiosity about the place had been aroused the previous winter when my two sons and their friends had been there on what would have to go down as the ultimate in bad-taste Stag party. Much to the bemusement of the local citizens, clueless as to who he was supposed to represent, Scott my eldest and future groom-to-be, had paraded around Brussels for days in full Jimmy Savile regalia complete with cigar and blond wig.

I'm not sure that those in my sons' party realized that taking paedophiles to Belgium is a bit like taking coals to Newcastle. The Belgians have had their own notorious paedophiles to worry about. Does anyone remember the recent case of the truly unspeakable Marc Dutroux? The stories of police cover up and conspiracy, plus allegations of involvement of some in high office, that caused so much anger and frustration in Belgium have echoes of what occurred later in the Savile case. But I digress. The accounts of Brussels my sons brought back persuaded me that I should follow my own particular brand of tourism (the marathon type) across the Channel to the city.

Brussels is, of course, the capital of Belgium as well as being the headquarters of many European institutions. With a population of just over 1 million, the Brussels Capital Region is made of 19 separate communes. The city of Brussels and its 150,000 citizens is merely one of these communes. Brussels is also considered to be the de facto capital of the European Union because of its long history of hosting its institutions within its own European Quarter, (from where the marathon was to start) Though the EU has no official capital, Brussels hosts the official seats of the European Commission, the Council of the European Union, the European Council, as well as a second seat of the European Parliament. As a consequence 27% of its population is made up of foreigners with over 40,000 EU employees, 4,000 from NATO plus those from over 300 permanent representations such as embassies and press corps. Unsurprisingly, English is widely spoken everywhere you go. The question of language, though, is a very divisive issue in Belgium. Brussels is a bilingual city with both French (80%) and Flemish (20%) are official languages. Consequently, something to be aware of is the fact that all the streets have two names that often look and sound very different. For example, I found it confusing that the main square in which the marathon finishes is referred to as both La Grand Place and de Grote Markt. Despite so many diverse influences making it the archetypical melting pot, Brussels, as I was to find out, still retains its own unique character.

With Brussels Airways having pulled out of the Newcastle to Brussels route shortly after my sons' stag party flights (a pure co-incidence - I hope) I decided to travel there by Eurostar for the marathon in October 2013. One of the hidden benefits of being a frequent traveller on the East Coast service between London and Edinburgh is that you gradually amass a number of rewards points that can be redeemed eventually for free tickets. I decided to use mine to treat myself to free travel on the connecting trains between my local station at Alnmouth and the St Pancras' Eurostar terminal; saving a fortune in the process. Eurostar trains arrive in the huge Gare du Midi on the southern edge of the city while anyone arriving at Brussels main airport will need to take the train which runs every 15 minutes into town – taking about 20 minutes for the approximately 8 euros journey. Several budget airlines including Ryanair and Wizzair fly to Brussels South Charleroi airport entailing a one hour drive by shuttle bus running at 30 minute intervals to the Gare du Midi (14 euros single/22 euros return)

On arrival on the Saturday afternoon I was left with less than two hours to make my way to the giant Parc du Cinquantenaire on the eastern side of the city and pay my money to enter the event. (I'd missed the September 23rd online deadline). Fortunately, Brussels has an excellent integrated city transport system involving bus, tram and metro with metro lines 2 and 6 calling at the Gare du Midi to take me up to the Arts-Loi station to connect with lines 1 and 5 to Schuman metro station near the entrance to the Parc. The metro system in Brussels is quite clean and safe compared with some other cities and can be recognised by the big 'M' signs in blue and white with the station names written underneath. Single tickets called Jump 1 cost 2 euros if pre-purchased, (2.50 euros from the drivers on the bus and tram) Tickets, valid for one hour, must be validated in the small orange machines in the bus and tram or at the entrance to the metro. You can interrupt your ride and change between the types of transport but must re-validate the ticket each time. Jump 5 and Jump 10 tickets are available for 5 and 10 journeys respectively, plus there's also a one day pass called a 'Jump 1 jour' ticket. All tickets can be purchased either at staffed windows or nearby kiosks.

The Parc du Cinquantenaire (or Jubelpark) where the registration for the marathon is held is a national landmark in Brussels. The name meaning 'Park of the fiftieth anniversary,' was built during the reign of Leopold 2nd to commemorate 50 years of Belgian independence. Symbolically, the park is also built in the shape of a pentagon, like the inner and outer rings of the city and sits just outside the inner ring close to the European Quarter. At the south eastern point a giant arch with two arms extending out to house various museums, rests behind a fountain marking the grand entrance. As the entire area is populated by workers from the various European institutions, the park plays host throughout the year to a large number of concerts, club nights, festivals, drive-through cinemas and above all, is the starting line for the annual Brussels Marathon.

The Registration itself was a huge disappointment with none of the bustle found at a big city marathon. There were no crowds, few exhibitors, no freebies and very little of interest. I guess most of the locals simply pitched up pre-race on the Sunday morning. I was annoyed at having to pay out a hefty premium for a last minute entry, (a whopping 80 euros), and even more annoyed to see that all I got for my money was a plain white T-shirt of dubious value. Given that I'd been feeling unwell during the week before the event and wasn't at all marathon-fit, I was almost tempted to settle for entering the 30 euros/no T-shirt half marathon instead. It was touch-and-go, in fact, whether I made it to this one. I'd already paid the hotel and Eurostar up-front when, with days to go, I came down with something connected to a recurrent kidney problem that resulted in feverish sweating and shivering that no amount of antibiotics was going to shift. Not travelling to Brussels wasn't an option given the money I'd already paid out, but I knew I hadn't the strength to actually run the full marathon distance. The real options boiled down to either going as a non-running tourist, (perish the thought), going and simply entering the half or, perhaps, finding some way in which I could get my body around within the strictly imposed 5 hour time limit. The organisers had posted the ominous warning that, 'those who run slower than a finish time of 5 hours will be taken out of the race' (by force, no doubt). I'd never before gone over 5 hours in a normal road marathon and didn't want to start now. This involves maintaining an even 7 minute per kilometre pace throughout the race, something that wouldn't normally have been a problem at my usual 6 min/km pace.

This time though I knew that I'd be reduced to walking at some stage so set about working on a strategy to get me round within the limit. With that in mind I headed off to my local track to time how long it would take to walk a kilometre at a steady pace. It took 8 minutes 30 seconds. Too long. A bit more experimentation showed that if I ran the first 3 minutes of each kilometre and walked the remainder it would take about 7 minutes. Desperate times need desperate measures and, I was desperate to finish. I reckoned that if I ran the first 10k at my normal 6 min pace, I could follow the run/walk scenario for the next 32k, leaving myself with a bit to spare at the end. That's exactly what I did and, as predicted, it brought me home in 4 hours and 44 minutes. Nothing to shout about, I know, but it at least saved me the indignity of being hauled off the course and into the following sweeper bus. The only downside, (apart from not feeling like a marathon runner), was having to fend off the solicitous enquiries of fellow runners convinced that there was something wrong with me and continually shouting, 'Courage, mon brave!' – or something similar. Next time, if there is a next time, I think I'll have a T-shirt printed on the back with the words, 'Please don't be concerned. I'm simply following my own personal adaptation of Jeff Galloway's Run/Walk Marathon Plan.' Only problem is, if I'm in Belgium, I'd have to have it printed in Flemish, French and English so I'll need a pretty big T-shirt. Anyway, I caught up with most of these people before the finish. This strategy of taking walking breaks before you're tired enough to need to certainly works. I started each new kilometre with something in the tank and had energy to spare on the final stretch.

This was the 10th edition of the Brussels Marathon that also incorporates a half marathon setting off 90 minutes after the main event. I say main event, but there were only 1,800 of us in the full as opposed to 8,000 in the half which followed a separate route. It made a nice change from having to run the same course twice. Both races started in the Parc du Cinquntenaire and finished on the cobbles of the Grand Place, the medieval square in the centre of town. Despite being well organised with lots of drink stations and enthusiastic marshals, somehow or other Brussels didn't seem to have the same feel as a big city marathon. I think it was down to the lack of atmosphere on much of the course which followed an, at times, uninspiring loop along closed and deathly silent long and straight dual carriageways. Between 20 and 35km this took the form of a large section of out-and-back along the Ave. de Tervueren. It was dispiriting to see the faster runners so far ahead of us on the other side of the road. Relief from the monotony came in the form of a couple of beautiful parks and lakes we passed en route. The finish was spectacular though. It was a great feeling to be running through cheering crowds at last as we entered the square. We weren't short-changed on the finisher's medal either. This was a solid, heavy affair depicting the runners in the Grand Place. Unfortunately, unlike my latest marathons in Tallinn and Odense there was no free beer or hot food on finishing, just a couple of bottles of a very watery tasting sports drink and some sort of honey biscuit. Value for money it was not. As my hotel was nearby, I rushed back to collect the camera hoping to take a few photos of the last runners coming in. Guess what! By the time I returned they'd already started dismantling the finishing gantry. I timed it as 15 minutes after the 5 hour cut-off. These people weren't messing around: they meant what they said. The main thing was, I did it, ending up feeling no worse than when I started. Another city to add to the list, but I won't be back. Next time I'm in Belgium it'll be for the Antwerp Marathon.

With the marathon over and with the camera already in hand it was now time to get down to the tourism aspect of being a marathon tourist. What I hadn't realized about Brussels before going there was that it began life as a group of little islands on a marshy river. Legend has it that a church was built on one of these islands around which a settlement grew. The name Bruocsella (later Brussels) meaning 'house on the swamp' is first mentioned as long ago as 966. The river, called the Senne, ran through the city until the 19th century approximately along the line between the Gare du Midi and the Gare du Nord until, becoming such a health hazard following another outbreak of cholera, it was finally covered over. Apparently it can still be glimpsed in places although I failed to spot it as I made my way around. Today the city of Brussels is neatly contained within a clearly defined shape called the Pentagon formed by a busy ring road named the Petite Ceinture. This road follows the path of the old city walls some 6 miles in length of which the old city gate, the Porte de Hal is the only remaining structure. Most of historic Brussels is contained within this pentagon, including both the commercial and popular districts of the Lower Town and the aristocratic quarter of the Upper Town. As a result Brussels is still very much a compact city that can be walked across in little over half an hour, passing most of its tourist spots en route.

I'm not a great one for visiting the insides of dusty museums and ancient churches, preferring instead to simply walk around a city taking in the sights and sounds while indulging in my favourite pastime of people watching. The Grand Place, being perpetually full of people is the obvious place to start. The buildings in the square are almost breathtakingly beautiful, like something you'd see on the top of a wedding cake. Lit up at night they're almost magical in their appearance. They're a mixture of styles from over the centuries: Gothic, Baroque, Neo-Classical and Neo-Gothic but their proportions are in perfect harmony with each other. Like most medieval squares it started life as a market place while its Town Hall has been the seat of the city's government since 1402. Today the Grand Place is a designated UNESCO World Heritage Site and the jewel in Brussels' tourist industry.

I guess the other must-see tourist venue is the nearby world famous statue of Manneken-Pis. This cheeky little chap standing naked and urinating on a street corner certainly draws the crowds. I found it difficult to get near him no matter what time of day due to the hordes of camera-wielding visitors attempting to pose so that the stream of water appeared to be directed into their mouth or hands. How weird! The statue's actions obviously appeal to something of the child-like naughtiness within us all. According to legend this mini-hero extinguished the fuse of a bomb by peeing on it and was rewarded by the building of a fountain in his honour. Though normally naked he does own a star's wardrobe of over 800 different outfits in which he is dressed for festivals and official visits. The first time I passed he looked like a Spanish nobleman for some reason. After that he remained as naked as the day he was built.

The only other two places I actually took time to visit, as opposed to simply walk past and stare at during the limited time I was there were the Eglise Notre-Dame de la Chapelle and the Porte de Hal both of which were conveniently on my Monday morning walk from the hotel south to the Gare du Midi. The former is a large atmospheric church, like something out of a Brueghel painting – aptly so since Peter Brueghel the Elder is buried there. The Porte de Hal, of course, is the sole surviving gate of the old city walls mentioned earlier. I did consider taking the metro out to the European Parliament building but, unsurprisingly, found more interesting things to do with my time.

One of these involved a pilgrimage to the 250 Belgian Beers shop in the street linking, and to the north of, the Bourse and the Grand Place. This was an Aladdin's cave of great bottled beers, (most of the best beers in Belgium come in their own individually shaped bottles). This had to be the place to take my search for the perfect dark beer. Belgian beers have become fashionable in recent years with official estimates suggesting that there are over 700 of them to choose from. The best of these appear to be treated with the reverence normally afforded to a fine wine. The country's beer-making history goes back centuries to when the Cistercians, a silent order of Trappist monks, first started brewing beer as an alternative drink to the unsanitary water at the time. Today the Trappist brands are produced commercially by five breweries with close ties to the monasteries. Other abbeys also produced beer, but unlike the Trappists monasteries, many have licensed them to commercial breweries. Leffe, for example, brewed in Leuven just to the east of Brussels is now closely connected with the brewery chain of InBev. After a few sample tastes of various beers in the shop I settled on Leffe as my favourite brand. Its strong and malty beers, coming in two main varieties, can be found in most of Brussels' bars. Leffe Blond is a lighter, slightly orangey flavoured beer while Leffe Brune is dark, aromatic and full of body at 6.5% No prizes for guessing which one was my favourite. A look at the label showed that it had been brewed at the Abbey de la Abdij Van since 1242. The Brune could be bought for about 4 euros for a 33cl bottle in the local bars or for 2.50 euros per 50cl can at the local supermarket. It was so tasty, I simply had to bring a couple of cans back with me on the Eurostar.

For those of you who like your food there's a great variety of restaurants in Brussels. The restaurant scene is lively and filled with both Belgians and foreign workers most nights of the week. I'd been warned though to avoid the tourist-trap areas around the Grand Place and Avenue Louise metro where, though the menu meals appear inexpensive, the drinks are overpriced and low quality. It appears that Belgian cuisine reflects the cuisines of neighbouring countries like France, Germany and the Netherlands. I'd read one comment to the effect that Belgian food is served in the quantity of German food but with the quality of French cuisine. Unfortunately, I didn't have the budget to check this out for myself. I was more interested in two of the less expensive food items for which Belgium has developed a unique reputation. The first of these was the Belgian frites, (chips to you and me). Belgians have raised the status of the humble chip to something approaching haute cuisine. There's an abundance of Friteries (Chip Shops) in Brussels, easily recognizable by the queues outside them at all hours of the day. I visited two of them during my stay: one on the south-east corner of the Bourse to see what all the fuss was about and later at one on Duquesnoy, behind the Town Hall, because I'd enjoyed what I had the first time. As someone steeped in the fish and chip traditions of North East England I was surprised at the quality of the chips, (sorry, frites), on offer. They really were nourishing and with added sauce made for a filling meal at only 2.50 or 3.20 euros with a selection of Belgian sauces. The locals seemed to favour them served with mussels. Moules-frites is virtually the national dish.

The other low-budget food item popular in Belgium is the Brussels Waffle. A waffle is a leavened batter or dough cooked between two iron plates. These were served warm, covered in icing sugar, on most corners of the city by street vendors. For an extra few cents you could have them topped with whipped cream, soft fruit or chocolate spread. I found that provided you were prepared to walk from one venue to the next, you could easily get by in Brussels on a satisfying but inexpensive meal consisting of waffles and frites.

Finally, I suppose no visit to Brussels can go by without mention of Belgium's most famous food export: Belgium chocolates. The country is noted for its high quality chocolate and has over 2,000 chocolate shops, or chocolatiers, most of which seemed to be in Brussels. It was impossible to walk more than a few metres down any of its main streets without facing a window full of the stuff. Belgium's association with chocolate apparently goes back to when the country was under Spanish occupation. Don't ask me why. I live for part of the year in Spain and rarely come across a Spanish chocolatier. Anyway, it seems that the country had the advantage in more recent times of being able to import cocoa from its former colony, the Belgian Congo. I'm told that what makes Belgian chocolate unique is not only the quality of ingredients, adherence to traditional methods and lack of vegetable fat but, also, the fact that much of it is laboriously hand-made. Seafood pralines, (the ones shaped like sea shells), appeared to be the most popular with tourists. As I haven't got a sweet tooth and generally end up with a LIDL's box of these at Christmas, I gave them a miss on this occasion.

For those thinking about going to the Brussels Marathon I'd definitely recommend booking a hotel near the centre of the city. When booking I was faced with the choice of a suitable hotel in the European quarter convenient for the start of the race or staying in the Ibis a short walk from the city centre finish. After some deliberation I chose the latter and was pleased with the result. I ended up right in the middle of the action with pubs, restaurants and places to visit bang on my doorstep. It was no problem getting the metro to the 9 am start. The European quarter by contrast, though quiet, is too far removed from the buzz of the centre. I also enjoyed the ride on the Eurostar much more than if I'd gone by plane. Clean, comfortable and punctual it whisked us from city centre to city centre in just over two hours without any of the hassles usually associated with airports. That's the way to do it.

Brussels Marathon Finish in the Grand Place

Registration for the Brussels Marathon

GREECE

ATHENS MARATHON

I was once not so politely informed by someone who'd been there, done it and was wearing the T-shirt, that I couldn't call myself a true marathon runner as I'd never run the Athens Marathon. Considering that I'd already run over 200 marathons at the time I simply laughed off his remark. He had a point though; not to run Athens during a marathon career would be inexcusable. More so than any other event, Athens with its hoary old story of Pheidippides is the one marathon to which all others should pay their dues. There'd be no Boston, no New York, no London and none of the hundreds of other marathons throughout the world without Athens and its marathon legacy. I'd be surprised if anyone interested in distance running wasn't familiar with the legendary 40km run of the Greek soldier Pheidippedes in 490BC from the battlefield on the plain of Marathon to Athens, to inform the king of victory over the Persians. After allegedly pronouncing the immortal word, 'Nenikekamen' ('We are victorious') he is said to have promptly collapsed and died. Most people are also aware of the celebration of this 'achievement' beginning in 1896, by the inclusion of a long distance race of around 40km along the route used by Pheidippedes, as part of the first Olympic Games. What people are less familiar with is the fact that, even before the battle, Pheidippedes had been sent the 250km from Athens to Sparta to enlist the Spartans' help. According to the ancient Greek historian Herodotus, he actually arrived in Sparta the next day. Some runner! This feat has been commemorated in September each year since 1984 by the increasingly popular ultra-distance race the Spartathlon which attracts the cream of ultra-runners from around the world attempting to run the 246 kilometres in a mere 36 hours. Not many manage it. So really we're indebted to our Greek friend with the long name for not just one, but two, excellent long distance running events.

I'll never run the Spartathlon, but the Athens Marathon has been on my radar for some years now. In 2013 I got the opportunity to go for the first time. Athens, as we all know, is the capital and the largest city in Greece. At some time or another we've all been schooled in the belief that Greece is the cradle of Western civilization, the origin of drama, history and philosophy and, above all, the birthplace of democracy. I guess it's hard to imagine what civilized life would be like today without the influence of ancient Greece: without the geometry of Pythagoras, the logic of Aristotle and Plato, the wisdom of Socrates, the poetry of Sophocles, the fables of Aesop and the architecture of those who built the Acropolis and the Parthenon. The list of ancient Greek greats appears endless. The Greek language too, has enriched so many other languages with so many words and concepts, like music, architecture and geometry to name but three. The Greeks also gave us the first Olympic Games, with their spirit of world-peace and brotherhood. It all made me anxious to see for myself the legacy of the country's heroic past.

Unfortunately, in more recent times, Greece's image has suffered from some pretty bad press; most of it connected with the economic meltdown the country has been going through for the past few years. Within days of entering the event the papers were full of the rioting currently taking place in the streets of Athens against the Government's austerity measures. These measures had been forced on the populace to counteract an unemployment rate of 28% in a country with a huge international deficit that had seen its economy contract by 25% since 2008 – a decline not experienced by any advanced western economy since the 1929 Wall Street crash. Headlines like, 'Greece today is at the door of the madhouse' and 'Democracy is endangered' featured prominently in the press in the weeks before the race. Unfortunately, the attempt to recreate and revive its Olympic legacy in 2004 played a significant part in the country's economic decline. Though the 2004 Olympics successfully regenerated the city's infrastructure, with a greatly enhanced metro and the pedestrianisation of many of its central streets, in the rush to be ready on time many of the works went way over budget. Meanwhile costly, rapidly deteriorating stadia have simply become embarrassing, hardly-used white elephants. It seems the citizens of Greece will be paying for these mistakes for many years to come. Ironically, economic considerations did not seem to affect the pricing structure for the Athens Marathon. Even with the entry fee set at a ridiculously high 90 euros the event was filling up fast. It was against this background of economic uncertainty and political chaos that five of us from the North East Marathon Club flew out from Edinburgh on the Thursday before the race. Apart from myself there were the Lonsdale sisters, Adele and Davina - veterans of such exotic events as the Las Vegas and Miami marathons; Stevie Matthews, an experienced ultra specialist still holding her own in the Vet 60 category and recently returned from New Zealand's 5 Bridges Marathon plus fellow 100 Clubber Ivan Field working his way slowly to his 300th marathon.

We'd carefully chosen to book ourselves into the Arethusa Hotel near the famous Syntagma Square, the city's main square with its metro line connection to the airport. Our thinking was based on the fact that in previous years Registration for the marathon had been held in the nearby Zappeion building while both the finish in the Panathenaic Stadium and the very early morning buses to the start in Marathon were also within easy walking distance. This year though, as we were subsequently to find, only two out of these three applied. For some reason the organizers had decided to move Registration away from the inner-city convenience of the Zappeion and out to the distant TaeKwonDo Exhibition Centre on the coast. The hotel was also ideally based for the short walk into the Plaka, the city's oldest and most picturesque neighbourhood of largely traffic-free streets nestling at the foot of the Acropolis. Though something of a tourist trap, we were to find it an area of welcoming serenity in an otherwise bustling and aggressive city with an excellent choice of inexpensive restaurants and tavernas in which to pass the time.

Getting from Athens International Airport to Syntagma is a fairly straightforward affair. The metro station is reached from arrivals by crossing the road and taking an elevator up to the next level. Tickets to the city cost 8 euros but there's a discount system in operation for every additional person. For example, you'll only pay 14 euros for two people or 20 euros for three. Trains run every 30 minutes, (on the hour and half hour), and take 40 minutes to reach Syntagma Square. Be careful though when returning to meet a flight deadline! We were fortunate on our journey back to the airport to be already on board what turned out to be the last available metro when the announcement was made that the remainder of that evening's scheduled services had been unexpectedly cancelled without notice. For those wishing to take the bus, the X95 service costs 5 euros and takes about an hour to Syntagma. For marathon entrants, however, journeys on all forms of public transport turned out to be free in the end. We weren't informed of this by the organisers before setting off but, on arrival, volunteers representing the marathon were in attendance at the airport to meet all flights and hand out free transport passes covering the three days prior to and after the event. I calculated that this saved us at least 25 euros in transport costs during our stay.

The first thing that you notice about Athens on arrival is that it's a seething mass of traffic and people. The city has a population of approximately 700,000 and virtually every one of them seems to have a vehicle of some kind. Noisy scooters together with the thousands of bright yellow taxis are particularly noticeable. The seemingly endless hooting of horns down the wide boulevards and the drone of vehicles making painfully slow progress through the narrower streets raises noise levels; and in a city with so many apartments and so little parking it's no surprise that footpaths have become places for leaving vehicles and pedestrians risk life and limb by walking on the roads. There's also a strange paradox created by the meeting of ancient and modern in the same crowded environment. The historic sites of ancient Greece like the Acropolis and the Parthenon stand in regal splendour amongst an ugly tangle of high-rise blocks, dirty apartment buildings and highly congested streets. Immediately apparent is the polluted atmosphere created by the never-ending procession of horn-tooting vehicles producing a brown smog that hangs over the city and is easily visible from any high point.

Our late arrival on the Thursday night left us little time to look around and be more selective about where we wished to eat. I'd been warned beforehand to stick to the simple rule of never to eat anywhere where someone stands outside to entice you in. With that in mind, we found an excellent, authentic Greek restaurant on the edge of the Plaka where we were able to tuck in to some of the more recognisable local dishes like tzatziki, (yoghurt, cucumber and garlic dip), kalamari, (fried squid), gyros, (pork strips on pitta bread), moussaka, (aubergines and mince), and souvlaki, (meat on a skewer) I'm sure that most of these dishes are very familiar to anyone who's ever visited any of the Greek Islands on holiday. The bill, including a few glasses of a nice red wine came to something like 15 euros per head, which in the circumstances seemed perfectly reasonable.

In an attempt to avoid the crowds at Registration, Friday morning saw us up early for the number 4 tram from Syntagma Square to the Exhibition Centre on the coast at Delta Falirou. After gathering our bib numbers with attached chips plus a rather fetching dark grey and blue event T-Shirt and hand towel, we were walked through corridors of no less than 55 exhibitors' stalls selling everything from the latest go-faster lycra offerings, to nutritional and dietary supplements, science technologies (whatever they are), hot yoga and handmade jewellery. The old adage incorporating the words 'fool' 'money' 'soon' and 'parted' spring readily to mind. While my colleagues were busy splashing the cash I concentrated my attentions on locating the freebies on offer. There weren't many.

While at the Expo we met up with a group of friends of mine from the 100 Marathon Club: Roger Biggs, Jack Brooks, Gina Little, Les

Pullen and Paul Holgate of whom only Roger had run the event previously. This year an injured Achilles meant that he was in Athens as a spectator rather than a competitor but he was able to pass on some valuable tips about the course over a cup of coffee on the beach nearby. A lot of what he said about the hilly nature of the route did nothing to inspire confidence for what lay ahead. After the cold of the UK, the weather in Athens was something of a shock to the system with temperatures throughout our stay in the mid to high 20s – perfect beach, (if not running), weather. Both the beaches and the sea next to the Exhibition Centre were full of bronzed Athenians for whom summer was simply continuing as before. It was hard leaving them to return to the city centre but we all fancied a look at the old Olympic Stadium in which we were to finish on Sunday. What a beautiful place this turned out to be. The horse-shoe shaped Panathenaic Stadium, to give it its proper name, is a 19th century reconstruction on Roman foundations, located between pine-covered hills a short walk from Syntagma. During Roman times it was adapted for an orgy of blood sports, with thousands of wild beasts slaughtered in the arena in front of crowds in excess of 60,000.Its reconstruction dates from the modern revival of the Olympic Games in 1896 and its appearance – pristine whiteness and perfect symmetry - closely resembles how it was under the Romans. Though its bends are too tight for major modern events the stadium is still used by local athletes and has been the finishing point of the Athens Marathon for some years now. The sense of history gained from standing within the stadium looking down on to the track has to be experienced to be believed.

That night saw us make another excursion into the Plaka district in search of pre-race sustenance. This time we neglected the advice about men standing outside restaurants and were foolishly lured into one where we suffered accordingly and were systematically ripped off. Having been lured inside we were then totally ignored by the waiting staff. Maybe because it was Friday night, the place was busy and there were more people eating, but the food we were presented with was cold, we had to virtually beg for what we thought were essential accompaniments to what we'd ordered (like sauces and parmesan cheese) the red wine was straight out of the fridge and the service, to say the least, was totally indifferent. The only time the waiter showed any interest was when looming over us while we sorted out the bill – a bill that showed no itemised items, just a series of figures. Needless to say we left no tip. It was left to me to tell him our reasons for this. Even then my measured words had no effect. The only thing we could do was make a mental note not to return for our final evening. (It's the restaurant on the south-west corner of the intersection of Plessa and Navarchou – avoid it like the plague).

Saturday was to be our final day for sightseeing and rather than face a long, dusty ramble through the traffic-choked streets the day before the race, three of us decided to make use of the hop-on hop-off tourist buses for which we got a marathon runners discount. The other two settled for yet more retail therapy. I have to say that I normally try to avoid such obvious touristy-type experiences but, given the energy-sapping heat, this proved the best thing to do on the day. We were able to sit in the sunshine, listening to a commentary in English about all the historic sites we visited while some other poor soul had the unenviable task of negotiating the horrific traffic encountered en route. For an extra couple of euros we were able to combine the two separate routes on offer. The first of these took us, among other things, from Syntagma Square to the Acropolis Museum, Temple of Zeus, Parliament and National Gardens, Panathenaaic Stadium, (again), National Library, Omonia Square and City Hall. The two routes then intersected at the foot of the Acropolis from where a second bus headed off on a huge loop around the coast before finally reaching the port of Pireaus and its international passenger terminal. This was somewhere I'd last disembarked in 1974 following a long sea voyage from Australia and I was anxious to see if it revived any long dormant memories. So, while my two companions indulged their passion for coffee and sandwiches, I headed off to explore the streets nearby. 39 years is a long time and, sad to say, very little looked familiar. Finally, after missing one bus while my companions waited for the sandwiches to be prepared, (this is Greece, after all and waiters aren't called 'waiters' for no reason), we ended up where we started near the foot of the Acropolis.

No visit to Athens can be complete without visiting the city's prime attraction – the magnificent Acropolis. We were convinced that, as marathon entrants, we were entitled to a discount on the 12 euros entry fee. Unfortunately, the guy at the ticket office knew nothing about this and charged Ivan and Stevie the full price. He couldn't avoid letting me in for half price though once I showed him my passport to confirm I was indeed over 65. The name Acropolis means 'upper city' and it was the focal point of Athenian life from the very foundation of the city. Situated on a huge rock crowned with temples, the Acropolis is visible from almost everywhere in central Athens, standing timeless and proud above the bustle of the streets below. The effect is comparable to a first glimpse of the Pyramids or the Eiffel Tower with the massive Doric temple, the Parthenon, being for most people the enduring symbol of Athens. Fortunately, by the time we arrived late in the afternoon most of the crowds as well as the heat of the day had gone, leaving us time to explore at our leisure. Again I'd last visited this site 39 years earlier and, on returning home, made a point of comparing the two sets of photographs I'd taken then and now. The Parthenon hadn't changed. I had.

After our disappointing experience the previous night we settled for the more reliable pizza and pasta carbo-load before an early night. It was to be a very early wake-up call the next morning with the first buses to the Start at Marathon leaving in front of the Parliament Building facing Syntagma Square at the ungodly hour of 5.30am. I'd found myself worrying for most of Saturday evening about the fact that I hadn't brought a hat with me for what was forecast to be another very hot day. Incredibly, I spotted exactly what I wanted while passing a kiosk on my way to the bus. Where else in the world can you buy a very cheap baseball cap suitable for running in at 5.40 in the morning of a major marathon. I'm convinced that, given the 27 degrees temperature on the course, I'd have struggled to finish the race without my newly acquired head-covering. Just like the rest of the organisation for the event the arrangement for the buses was spot-on, (just as it should be after 31 years of practice). There were no crowds or queues and we arrived in comfort in Marathon some 40 minutes later to be met by a veritable army of volunteers pointing us in the right direction. The pre-race facilities in the town were excellent: loads of toilets and portaloos, changing rooms, a café for hot drinks – even a warm-up track for those so inclined. The town was also home to the only museum that I've seen dedicated to the history of marathon running. Of course, I had to pay it a visit. Sadly, on the one day of the year that the town played host to thousands of marathon runners, the museum was closed. Shortly before 9am and to a background of colourful exploding fireworks, approximately 6,000 of us were released from our time-allotted starting pens according to the race's Wave Start System. This meant that only the elite runners actually started at nine. The second block commenced one minute later, the third block started two minutes after the second wave, with all other blocks down to the Power Walkers commencing in increments of four minutes. Sounds complicated but it worked. We were given a very generous 8 hours in which to drag ourselves over the finish line 26.2 miles away in Athens.

In the AIMS commemorative supplement produced in 2010 to honour the 2500th anniversary of the Battle of Marathon, David E Martin describes how over the years several different organizations have attempted to create an annual competitive race using the classic Marathon-to-Athens course, all with varying degrees of success. He believes that no other marathon course on the planet has been used by so many such groups such as: the Balkan Games, the European Athletics Championships, the Mediterranean Games, the Olympic Games and several IAAF events – all of which have taken place on what has become known as the 'classic' route – virtually unchanged since 1896. It is a measure of the course's difficulty that the Kenyan winner's time of 2 hours 13:50 was over 8 minutes slower than that recorded by the winner of my previous marathon in Amsterdam. Because of this Athens rarely attracts the cream of the marathon elite. In fact, the course profile displayed in the official programme is not for the faint-hearted; seeming to climb endlessly but steadily for a large part of the race. We knew on setting off, that once the sun rose above the surrounding hills, we were in for a testing day out.

The first 4 kilometres leading away from Marathon are imperceptibly downhill and lead to a further 2km circular route around the area of the Marathon Tomb, (War Memorial). The course remains reasonably flat to the 10km mark and then the climbing begins in earnest until the 17th km. There follows a short, steep descent and then it's the most difficult uphill part to 20km. Passing through the district of Pikermi the course undulates until 25km. By this stage the sun was high above us and directly in our faces and I, for one, was beginning to wonder if the uphill gradient was ever going to end. The sounds of the passing ambulance sirens, picking up those who'd already succumbed to the heat did nothing to improve spirits. I'd already decided that survival was the most sensible strategy and begun the race/walk procedure that had got me safely around at Brussels during illness. The passage through the city of Pallini with its cheering crowds and Zorba the Greek dancers was again uphill for a further 3 kilometres to the 28th km mark. The last and most difficult part started at Gerakas, finishing at Stavros Junction between 30 and 31km. This steep ascent was thankfully followed by an equally steep descent leading to the Agia Paraskevi Square. After that I'd like to say it was easy but by then exhaustion had well and truly set in and nothing seemed easy at the time. It was a great feeling to wave goodbye to the hills at long last and plough on through the crowds of spectators lining the streets as we approached the inner suburbs of Athens. Eventually we passed the American Embassy, the Athens Music Hall and the Park of Liberty with the final feeder zone at 40km. Shortly after that we were able to hear the cheering from inside the Stadium. The final kilometre was sheer bliss compared to what had gone before; a long downhill stretch past the Presidential Residency and the National Gardens before turning a sharp left at the bottom to enter the Stadium and the 100 metres or so to the finish line with Queen belting out 'We Will Rock You' at full volume. Within minutes of crossing the line I'd met up with the three ladies from our group –

we'd all finished in a 9 minute time-span from 4hours 32 to 4 hours 41 with yours truly bringing up the rear. (My excuse was that I did have the Valencia Marathon the next weekend but, in truth, I couldn't have gone any faster). Ivan had sprinted home in 4hours 02.

Without doubt, entering the historic Panathenaic Stadium in the footsteps of all those great marathon runners from 1896 onwards had to be the highlight of the whole race, (and not just because I'd finished!). I'd also enjoyed soaking up the atmosphere at Marathon before the start – those eight magical letters have come to play such a significant part in my life and mean so much to me still. I guess it was only the bit in between that wasn't so nice. However, I'm prepared to put that down to the heat. I'm sure the hills wouldn't have appeared half as demanding on a cooler day. Hats off to the organizers; they got just about everything right, particularly the regularity and availability of seemingly limitless amounts of water when needed. There were isotonic drinks and bananas too at frequent intervals, together with the occasional gel and energy bars; so no complaints there. The heavy duty finisher's medal with its depiction of the Stadium on one side and Greek hero on the other was appropriate for an event of Athens' stature and one that I'll long cherish. Post-race we were supplied with Powerade, water, orange squash and energy bar to take away with us plus there were massage areas and a sponsor's village to visit if we were so inclined. I had a couple of beers demanding my attention in the hotel fridge. Not of the perfect dark beer variety I'm afraid; I couldn't find anything of that nature in Athens, it was all Mythos and Amstel in the bars and ouzo and wine in the restaurants. Never mind, I wasn't going to let the lack of a strong dark-coloured beer sour what had been an excellent three days in the sun. I'll be back as soon as they get those hills flattened.

A group of us at Registration for the Athens Marathon

In front of the Olympic Flame at Marathon before the race

CYPRUS

LIMASSOL MARATHON

This was to be my first attempt at running any sort of distance since kidney surgery. It transpired that I'd effectively been operating on only one kidney for some time. The operation turned out more difficult than anticipated and the Consultant was adamant that there should be no running whatsoever for at least ten weeks. After three frustrating months without any form of exercise, I finally got the letter from my surgeon I'd been waiting for. This contained the magic words, "Mr Manford can now resume his marathon running." Great! Though my first few outings saw me shuffling around like a lead balloon with the handbrake on; I was nevertheless determined to enter this event. I'd had to cancel the Cyprus Marathon in Paphos last year when the kidney problem was first diagnosed and this had also meant missing out on a week's holiday in the sun. I'd promised Mo that we'd make up for that this year. Ideally, I would have preferred to run this year's (2014) Paphos Marathon on March 9th as that was where we were based for our holiday. That had a 5 hour time limit; something I was not confident of achieving after my months of inactivity. March 16th's Limassol event, on the other hand, had a 6 hour limit and I was confident that I could haul myself around in that time, even if it meant walking for most of the way – I've long since stopped being too proud to finish among the back-markers. 'Rest is Rust' so they say, and I was starting to gather a fair coating of the stuff. I'd never before run a marathon in Cyprus; I couldn't pass up the chance – there wouldn't be another one there for a further 12 months.

Just a word about booking the holiday: given that we'd only made up our minds to go a few days beforehand, we went looking for one of those widely advertised, last-minute, cheap deals. They didn't exist; at least not as far as we could see via the obvious sources of Thomas Cook, Thomson, easyJet and Jet 2. We were able to find better deals ourselves by combining charter flights with self-booked accommodation. Thomson Holidays had a mid-week, flight-only option from Newcastle cheaper than any of the low cost airlines involving long journeys to either Edinburgh or Gatwick; provided that is you weren't persuaded by any of the myriad of add-ons they tried their best to sell you. After all, who needs the champagne and chocolates option when flying to Cyprus? Who cares if they allocate your seats next to the toilets in an attempt to persuade you to pay extra for selected seats? You simply get up and move to a suitable empty seat straight after take-off. Also, as anyone who has visited Malta for its February marathon will tell you, islands in the Mediterranean have enormous unused capacity through the winter months and reduce prices to ridiculously low levels just to keep hotel staff in employment. So, off we went on the Wednesday before the race for five nights self-catering in a one-bedroom apartment next to Paphos harbour for a mere £25 per night, followed by two nights bed and breakfast in a 3 star Limassol hotel either side of the race for only £16 per night each. Cheap as chips!

The important strategic position of Cyprus at the crossroads of Europe, Asia and the Middle East means that the island has had a long and chequered history. Geographically, it is the third largest island in the Mediterranean Sea, after the Italian islands of Sicily and Sardinia. It is 149 miles long and 62 miles wide with Turkey, 47 miles to the north as its nearest neighbour. Mainland Greece lies almost 500 miles away, while the Middle East's 'Big Two' of Egypt and Israel are 236 miles and 124 miles distant respectively. The island itself is divided into four main segments with the southern two-thirds of the island belonging to the predominantly Greek speaking Republic of Cyprus. The Turkish Republic of Northern Cyprus occupies the northern third with a United Nations controlled buffer zone and the sovereign British bases of Akrotiri and Dhekelia making up the rest. Physically, the island is dominated by two mountain ranges; the Troodos Mountains in the south and west and the Kyrenia Range in the north

Cyprus is divided culturally between the two distinct cultures of Greece and Turkey with each community maintaining its own cultural identity at all costs, leading to very little cultural interchange. While the Greek influence has been present on the island since antiquity, the invasion by the Ottoman Empire in 1570 introduced cultural differences that have caused problems to this day. It is difficult to overestimate the degree of bitterness that divides the two main, Orthodox Christian Greek and Muslim Turkish, communities. Even during the British occupation from 1878 to 1960, no distinctive Cypriot national identity managed to emerge. Following independence in 1960, long-dormant rivalry between the two principal ethnic groups led to widespread violence. The Greek military junta's attempt to unite Cyprus with Greece in 1974 finally gave the Turkish government the excuse it needed to step in and invade the island. International pressure led to a ceasefire after three days by which time 37% of the island had been taken over by the Turks and 180,000 Greek Cypriots had been evicted from their homes in the north. This situation, which has dominated and defined Cypriot politics for the past four decades, remains virtually unchanged today. The separate communities in north and south of the island are mutually isolated, having developed over time into parallel societies.

Since the time of the Turkish invasion, the south of the island in particular has witnessed a massive growth in tourism and property development. The Cyprus economy has also diversified into areas such as shipping and financial services and become prosperous in recent years. In 2012, however, it became badly affected by the Eurozone financial and banking crisis; leading to a 10 million euro bailout from the European Commission and International Monetary Fund. This resulted in stringent cuts being imposed on uninsured bank deposits, many of these held by Russian investors using the island as a tax haven. The repercussions from these unpopular measures are still a major cause of concern. In short, both politically and economically Cyprus is in a right mess at the moment.

It certainly looked messy on our early evening arrival at Paphos airport where we were greeted by torrential rain and strong winds – quite a contrast to the warm sunshine we'd left behind in the UK. We took the regular 1.50 euro local bus service 612 into the resort, (for those going direct to Limassol there's a less regular connection costing 9 euros). It's important here to make the distinction between Kato Paphos, (Paphos harbour) where we were staying and the old town of Paphos, 3 kilometres inland and uphill. The former is the much nicer place. On arrival the young receptionist at our apartment block, himself a keen runner, seemed a little put out that I hadn't chosen to run that Sunday's Paphos event instead of Limassol. My explanation of concerns over the 5 hour time limit didn't appear to impress. I could already see him writing me off as some form of no-hoper. Within a matter of minutes I was even less impressed at finding our room without hot water or a working television. Not for the first time, our accommodation turned out to be nothing like it showed in the brochure. It took the threat of cancellation to be given an upgrade.

Walking around that evening we thought we'd made a big mistake. In the rain, the place had the depressing air of an out-of-season seaside resort down on its luck. Shops were shuttered, bars were empty and restaurants deserted. We seemed to be the only ones around. I guess the largely older-aged visitors occupying our plane had settled for the cosy comforts of their 5 star, all-inclusive hotels lining the eastern fringes of the resort. After a good soaking we decided to cut our losses and retire back to the apartment with a bottle of the local KEO brandy. Consoling ourselves that it couldn't possibly get worse we hoped for that the next day would bring an improvement. It did. The sun shone, (and continued to shine for the remainder of our stay), bringing out the crowds and showing us what a lovely little gem of a place Paphos really is. It's both low-key and low-rise – none of the buildings are over four stories high. There's something refreshing about a place where the palm trees are higher than the buildings. It's definitely one of the more pleasant of the modern, manufactured resorts along the Mediterranean coastline. Best of all, from a runner's perspective, it has miles of well-paved pedestrian pathways stretching in both directions from the ancient castle at its centre. It was here that we met up with 100 Marathon Club friends Danny Kay and Andy Glen staying in Paphos for the Paphos/Limassol Marathon double on consecutive weekends. The company of Danny's wife Marion allowed Mo an escape from the constant marathon-chat of the three men.

The entire town of Paphos is a listed UNESCO World Heritage Site. It was the capital of Cyprus for a long period in antiquity before repeated earthquakes relegated it to something of a backwater. It is presently on the short-list of cities for the 2017 European Capital of Culture. I hope it gets it. As I've probably mentioned, I'm not big on visiting museums and historical sites. Paphos is different, however. There are at least three interesting archaeological sites there well worth a visit. Next to the harbour is the world-famous Kato Paphos Archaeological Park containing marvelous mosaic floors of four Roman villas from the 2nd to the 5th century. Nearby is the equally famous 'Tombs of the Kings' – monumental underground tombs carved out of solid rock in the 3rd century and decorated with remarkable Doric pillars. Also worth seeing are the Christian Catacombs beside the main road up to the old town. You'll know you've found them when you reach a tree festooned in what looks like pieces of ribbon. This 'sacred' tree is believed to cure anyone who hangs a personal offering on its branches. Beneath the tree is a small underground complex of chamber tombs visited by medieval pilgrims. Among the graffiti cut into the plaster are the names of 13th century Crusaders who stopped off in Paphos en route to the Holy Land. Finally, you've got to see the iconic ancient castle that dominates the harbour and is, incidentally, the finishing point of the Paphos Marathon. Originally a Byzantine fort it was, in turn, demolished by the Venetians, rebuilt by the Ottomans who used the ground floor as a dungeon and then taken over by the British for use as a salt warehouse. The roof offers unrivalled views of the port and town up to the hills beyond.

Sadly, Limassol where we arrived on the Saturday for Registration, was as crowded and noisy as Paphos had been peaceful and calm. I'd last been there 20 years ago for a holiday with my family and had memories of a sprawling, dusty city without an obvious centre. It hadn't changed. The first mistake we made was to remain on the Paphos to Limassol intercity bus, (tickets 4 euros), until it reached the terminus at the New Port. This proved to be 3km away from where we should have alighted at the Old Port. The driver hadn't helped matters; confusing every English speaking passenger with his instructions. Just by 'chance' there happened to be a fleet of taxis waiting like the proverbial vultures to swoop us back to where we should have been told to get off in the first place. Collusion or what? We walked. And that wasn't the end of our problems: not a single person we asked seemed to have heard of the Evagoras Linitis Centre where the Registration was being held. (For the record, it's across the road from the Old Port on the western side of Castle Square).

The Registration set-up was a big disappointment: the computers were out of action, there was no Exhibition to enjoy, no written information about the event available, no Start List, very few people and no maps of the course on display. The goody bag contained 500g of spaghetti and a gel. On requesting a map, (I wanted Mo to know where she could see me en route in case I was forced to pull out), I had to wait ages for the computers to come back on before they could print one out. It wasn't until getting back to the hotel that I realized that the map they'd given me was for the 10k course. At least the Pevkos Hotel was everything promised in the brochure. The only downside being that it was a 20 minute walk away through a run-down residential area with pavements blocked by vehicles but without facilities such as pubs and restaurants nearby. Danny and Marion had already booked themselves into one of the sea-front hotels; possibly a better option for anyone contemplating running this event. As it turned Andy Glen was booked into the room opposite ours in the Pevkos so we at least had someone to team up with during our stay.

I found Limassol to be a strange place. Though not without a certain charm in its old Levantine centre of stone buildings and narrow alleyways, this is overshadowed by the ugly and unsightly ribbon of tourist-orientated development stretching endlessly to the east of the town. This Benidorm-like development has to be one of the eyesores of the Mediterranean and we were due to run the length of it tomorrow; a pity really, because there are one or two decent historical sites said to be worth visiting in the area. I'd done the full tourist-thing while on holiday here twenty years ago. Limassol Castle, for example, now home to the city's Medieval Museum used to serve as a prison during the Ottoman rule. Richard the Lionheart is said to have married and been crowned 'Lord of Cyprus' and his wife 'Queen of England' within its walls. Also the ancient city of Amathus, (the turning point of the marathon), is one of the oldest imperial cities on the island. Legend has it that the city was built by one of the sons of Hercules, who was worshipped as a God there. There was always a natural harbour at Limassol, with potable spring water and surrounded by extensive agricultural plantations; mainly olives and grapes. It took the invasion of 1974 with the closing of significant ports like Famagusta, plus the advent of mass tourism, to bring it to its present-day prominence. Today it's the largest municipality in Cyprus with a population of over 105,000 and has progressed into one of the most important ports in the Mediterranean as well as a busy tourist, maritime, commercial and service centre. It's now the business and financial centre of Cyprus and home to a large number of local and international companies. But pretty, it is not. I was relieved that we'd chosen to stay there for the marathon weekend only and would be returning to our base in Paphos for the remainder of the holiday.

Still, I won't complain too much. The fact is I was just happy to be standing on the start line of a marathon again at 9am on the Sunday morning. Given the rustiness of a three month lay-off, I was full of apprehension, having no idea as to how the body would perform. At least, for the first time in over a year, I'd be operating on two functioning kidneys this time round. The farthest I'd managed in the handful of attempts at running I'd had recently was a very slow six miles. On that basis I'd a strategy in mind based on a worst-case scenario of duplicating that six miles within an hour, leaving me twenty more miles to complete in the five hours before the time limit expired. This meant fast-walking them if necessary at 15 minute mile pace. I was confident I could manage that. DNF was not an option.

On what was a warm, sunny morning, the organisers lined us all up on the main promenade next to the Port according to event. The 200 marathoners were placed at the front, followed by 325 in the half marathon with the largest group of 450 in the 10k at the rear. (There was also a Corporate 5k in there somewhere that apparently turned out to be a bit of a disaster). I'm not sure that the placement was such a good idea given that the faster, shorter distance runners inevitably had to jostle their way to the front of the field. From the Old Port the route took us 14km eastwards along a closed coastal dual-carriageway to the first of three turns at what was left of the ancient royal city of Amathus. This stretch was what constituted the resort's tourist strip; replete with tacky bars, fast-food outlets and every type of tourist accommodation. I guess the majority of the tourists were still eating their breakfasts as the place was deserted for most of the early miles. We then crossed over to the other side of the carriageway and retraced our steps all the way back to where we'd started from. There was bottled water and isotonic drink in cups every 2.5km. Without turns, corners or inclines and only more of the same on a long straight road ahead of us into the distance, most of us found this monotonous and uninspiring. The literature encouraged us to 'Run with a Smile' and 'Run along the Waves.' The former was difficult; the latter totally impossible given the number of rather large buildings between us and the seafront.

The course then continued westwards for a further 3 km to a large roundabout at the totally deserted New Port area before heading back past the start again to the 38km mark. We turned yet again for the final 4km back along the same road yet again to the finish on the promenade. There we were handed our medal and a bottle of water. There were no T-shirts; despite the 50 euros entry fee these had to be purchased separately at 9.90 euros for a plain white cotton affair or 19.90 euros for a more colourful, light blue, technical running vest. I saw a number of the vests but very few T-shirts being worn.

From what I've said it might seem that I didn't enjoy it. I did. It was great to be back in the saddle so to speak. I even surprised myself with my finishing time, doubling my distance run recently by going well past the planned 6 miles of running to over half way in 2 hour 7 minutes, before having to succumb to a walk/run strategy. Even then I managed to get round in 4 hour 40 without any form of discomfort. I guess, as marathon runners, we must retain a residue of fitness for longer than expected. It says something about my state of mind that, given the circumstances, I took greater satisfaction from my time here than I did from achieving my PB over a quarter of a century ago. Both Danny and Andy finished within a minute of their times at last weekend's Paphos Marathon – remarkable consistency.

This was the 8th edition of the Limassol Marathon that started with a field of a mere 70 runners first time out. It now styles itself an 'International' marathon and has pretentions to be recognised as such. The website sets out the mission statement 'to establish it as one of the most popular marathons in Europe.' I'm afraid it has quite a bit of work to do to reach that goal. For a start there were no kilometre markers apart from at the drink stations. The marshals were mainly teenagers and though plentiful, appeared distracted and disinterested at times. The roads were meant to be closed to traffic but that didn't seem to stop whole streams of death-by-lycra cyclists from taking advantage and using the course for training runs. As the day progressed these were joined by roller skaters and skateboarders – an accident waiting to happen. Would I do it again? Of course I would; next time as a double-header with Paphos. (In fact, I attempted to do this in March 2020 and flew to Cyprus only to have both events cancelled at the last minute due to the deteriorating Covid situation).

The food on offer in Cyprus was very similar to what we'd found while in Greece for the Athens Marathon. Much of it was typical resort food: a blend of generic Middle East and British cooking with a chips-with-everything approach. You really need the advice of someone who's spent some time there for recommendations as to how to avoid this indiscriminating tourist fare. Andy, who likes his food, had already been there a week to find the best places to eat. He pointed us in the direction of the Cypriot-owned Argo restaurant behind the main tourist drag in Paphos. Every Tuesday and Saturday the restaurateur fires up his outside oven to produce the tasty national dish of Kleftiko, a slab of lamb roasted until tender and served with vegetables. The same restaurant also provided a decent set menu 3 course meal for 12.50 euros. Mo had the Halloumi, (grilled ewe's cheese), followed by Moussaka and salad with Greek yoghurt and honey for dessert. I settled for Stuffed Tomatoes, Stifado, (beef stew) and Pancakes. The disappointment was in having to pay 9.50 euros for an indifferent carafe of village red wine with the meal. Mo and I are spoilt by comparison given what we can get for much less money in the local restaurants where we have our apartment in Spain. There the 9 euros four-course menu is far more extensive, much better quality and includes a litre carafe of wine, (two if you want it!), in the price. There were cheaper options along the tourist stretch to the east of the harbour. There, in an attempt to be competitive, virtually every restaurant advertises a psychologically priced 9.90 euros set menu starting with traditional Cyprus dips like tzatziki, tahini and taramosalata plus the aforementioned main courses of kleftiko, stifado and pork afelia, (chunks of meat in coriander seed sauce) The Phivos restaurant is perhaps the best of those we tried. Whatever you do though, don't be tempted by the touts trying to lure you in to the places fronting the harbour. Their locations are wonderful; their prices wondrous.

Limassol was a much more difficult place to find somewhere decent to eat. We virtually gave up trying after the first night but post-marathon hunger pains forced a re-consideration. Most of the locals seemed to frequent the indoor/outdoor restaurants on all four sides of Castle Square next to where Registration was held. In the end we settled on Ousa restaurant in the Square: I managed Pork Souvlaki, (on a skewer) and couscous while Mo had a very tasty roast aubergine smothered in fetta cheese and tomato. The bill came to a reasonable 20 euros.

Yet again the search for the perfect dark beer had to be put on hold for this trip. There's little demand for such heavy northern European beers on sun drenched islands in the Med. The market seems to be dominated by the giant Limassol based KEO brewery whose bottled and draught, light lager brew appears to be everywhere. With its ideal climate and soils, Cyprus tends to favour wine production, (and drinking), over beer consumption. Again, KEO produces Afrodite, a medium dry cheap white, Rosella, a dry, dark rose and Othello, a full-bodied red. All are quite palatable. However, Mo and I both preferred to finish our evenings with a glass or two of the local brandy. Metaxa 5 star and KEO, (again), ended up as our favourites. Like everywhere these days, it worked out far cheaper taking the bottle back to the hotel as opposed to paying inflated prices in the harbourside bars.

With Andy Glen at Registration

Finished in Limassol, but maybe not with a smile!

CANADA

VANCOUVER MARATHON

Over forty two years ago, just before getting married, Mo and I had plans to start our new life together by emigrating to Canada. We'd completed all the necessary immigration documents and were summoned to Manchester for interview by the Canadian authorities. I'm not sure whether the guy interviewing us had got out of the wrong side of the bed that day but he was certainly anything but friendly and helpful. His attitude was that while we'd be granted permission to go to our chosen destination of British Columbia, he didn't fancy our chances of finding work there. It seemed that, at the time, British Columbia was more in need of lumberjacks and construction workers than couples like us with a university degree in Social Sciences and a qualification in laboratory work. The interviewer was so negative and pessimistic that we came away feeling quite flat. The feeling didn't last long though; three doors further down the same street was the Australian Immigration Office displaying enticing posters of life Down Under, just inviting us to walk in and look around. The attitude of the Australian officials couldn't have been more different from that of their Canadian counterparts. Far from being discouraging, they were most welcoming with their easy-going, 'no-worries mate' approach. Basically all they wanted to know was when did we want to go and whether we wanted to go by boat or by plane. More importantly for an impecunious couple like Mo and I, unlike the Canadian government, they were even prepared to pay our fare. So, instead of becoming Canadian citizens, we ended up as £10 Poms, (the best thing that ever happened to us). We've tried a couple of times during the past forty two years to make it out to British Columbia to see what we'd missed. On both occasions fate intervened, resulting in last minute cancellation of plans. This time, thanks to a spot of marathon tourism courtesy of the Vancouver Marathon, we were finally on our way; having found ourselves a good, discounted deal with Canadian Affair that allowed us to split our 15-day holiday between stopovers in both Vancouver and the neighbouring city of Victoria. Unfortunately, despite searching desperately, I was unable to find another marathon in the vicinity during our time away. (The Victoria Marathon is not until October 12th).

Our first port of call in May 2014 was Vancouver where it didn't take long to realize how fully deserving it was of its reputation as one of the world's most beautiful cities. Separated by the rest of Canada by the Canadian Rockies, Vancouver is renowned for its incomparable natural beauty and cultural diversity and for favouring a lifestyle more akin to its American West Coast neighbours of Seattle and San Francisco to the south than to its eastern Canadian counterparts of Toronto and Quebec. Located on the southwestern corner of British Columbia, it is bounded on three sides by water: Burrard Inlet in the north, the Strait of Georgia to the west and the Fraser River to the south. Looming overhead, the Coast Mountains, rising to more than 5,000ft, preside majestically over the city. The mountains and seascape make Vancouver an outdoor playground for hiking, skiing, sailing, cycling and, of course, running. The cultural scene is equally diverse, reflecting the makeup of the city's ethnic population. The whole attractive package brings more than eight million visitors a year to the city.

The history of Vancouver is essentially linked to the taming of the western Canadian wilderness. In 1792, Captain George Vancouver first explored the Burrard Inlet on which the city stands and in 1827 the Hudson Bay Company set up a trading post on the Fraser River. It took the subsequent discovery of gold in the 1850s to bring an influx of European settlers to the region. When the Canadian Pacific Railway chose the then ramshackle site of Granville as its Pacific terminus the citizens were inspired to incorporate the site as a city, changing its name in 1886 to Vancouver in honour of its first explorer. The importance of the railway to Vancouver's development cannot be overstated. The railway, along with Canadian Pacific's fleet of clipper ships, gave Vancouver a week's edge over the blossoming Californian ports in shipping tea and silk from the Orient to New York. Timber, fish and coal – resources that are still the backbone of the area's economy, left Vancouver for world markets. The same ships and trains returned with immigrants from all corners of the earth. This is reflected in the fact that today 52% of the population does not speak English as their first language. Almost 30% of the city's inhabitants are of Chinese origin with significant numbers also coming from India, the Philippines, Japan and Korea as well as Vietnam, Indonesia and Cambodia. The 2011 census recorded over 600,000 people in the city making it the eighth largest Canadian municipality. It has consistently ranked as one of the top five worldwide cities for livability and quality of life. Unfortunately, it has also been ranked as one of the most expensive cities in which to live, (better take a lot of pocket money on your visit).

First impressions on landing at Vancouver International Airport about 10 miles south of the city weren't particularly good. After a nine and a half hour flight arriving at what would have been bed-time in the UK, we were subjected to a ridiculously long wait at Immigration Control; being herded like cattle into a series of holding pens before finally having our passports intensely scrutinized. And that wasn't the end of it: despite carrying only hand luggage we were compelled to join the carousel crowds channeled through a narrow, manned, exit gate where our immigration cards were collected. (Why couldn't we have simply handed them in at passport control?) Despite their signs to the contrary, the system appeared neither efficient nor welcoming. The airport has recently been voted as the best in Canada – heaven help the rest. To add insult to injury the fares for what was for a long time the fastest and cheapest way to travel to our Downtown hotel via the Canada Line, (the newest addition to the city's rapid-transit system) have recently been subjected to the imposition of a $5 tourism tax. Instead of it being the 2-Zone price of $4 it is now a whopping $9. The station is inside the airport, on level four, between the international and domestic terminals. Trains leave every six minutes from the airport and every three minutes from the city for the return journey.

Central Vancouver is located on a peninsula, which makes it compact and easy to explore on foot, particularly as most streets are laid out on a grid system. All streets have east and west designations and are numbered; the higher the number, the farther away you are from Burrard Inlet. (If in doubt; remember that the mountains are to the north). We had no problems finding our hotel on Davie Street after alighting from the train at the Yaletown Roundhouse station. The public transport system is easy and efficient to use. It's a mix of bus, ferry and the fully automated 3-line system known as the Sky Train, with transfer tickets allowing travel between the different modes of transport. Fares are based on zones: one zone within the city limits costs $2.75, two zones to the North Shore or Richmond and the Airport cost $4. If you intend travelling a lot within the city it's probably best to purchase an all-zone Day Pass for $10. You'll need the exact change for bus travel, though Sky Train and SeaBus ferry tickets can be purchased from automatic machines. At the time of our visit £1 bought $1.75 (Canadian dollars). For ease of calculation I worked on the principle that $10 equated to £6.

The main focus of our trip, aside from the marathon, was to take advantage of the wonderful natural scenery and the emphasis placed on a healthy, outdoor lifestyle by both of our major stopover destinations. The nicest thing that can be said about both Vancouver and Victoria is that in neither of them do you feel like you're trapped inside the stereotypical concrete and traffic-filled metropolis. While Vancouver is a large cosmopolitan city with a huge ethnic population, Victoria, by contrast, is smaller, quieter and very much more anglicised. Both, however, place the same government-backed emphasis on taking full advantage of their breathtakingly beautiful locations. Surrounded by water and overlooked by snow-capped mountains, (Vancouver has the Coast

Range: Victoria the Olympic Mountains to the south), both cities have built a series of interesting pedestrian trails and traffic-free cycle paths around their more scenic parts. Our intention was to utilize these as much as possible during our stay.

Even the journey between the two cities can be a bit of an adventure. Pacific Coach Lines have several services each day from downtown Vancouver to the ferry terminal at Tsawwassen before boarding BC Ferries for the one and a half hour voyage to Swartz Bay on Vancouver Island. (It is possible to do the whole trip by using public transport but it's a time-consuming journey involving too many changes to make it a comfortable trip). The coach then continues for a further thirty minutes or so into Victoria. En route the ferry crosses the Strait of Georgia separating Canada from the USA and negotiates the narrow channels between several of the incredibly beautiful Gulf Islands that litter the Strait: home to writers, artists, craftsmen as well as log-cabin vacationers from the mainland. We were lucky to have clear blue skies while sailing in both directions and the views on both occasions were spectacular. If time had allowed it would have been a great place to explore.

The place we really wanted to visit, however, was the iconic Stanley Park; a one thousand acre wilderness park only blocks away from the centre of Vancouver containing fir and cedar forests, beaches and First Nations sculptures with magnificent views of the ocean, inlet and North Shore mountains. Vancouverites use it in their thousands to walk, jog, cycle, rollerblade, play tennis and watch outdoor theatre. I don't think I've ever seen as many people jogging as can be found on the 9 km paved shoreline path, known as the Seawall, skirting its perimeter. Next to them, in a totally separate lane, whole hordes of cyclists peddle furiously around in a rigidly observed anti-clockwise direction. It was here that I first experienced the phenomenon of the Canadian Female Runner. After a couple of visits to the park both Mo and I formed the opinion that the number of female joggers on the paths far outnumbered the males – it didn't matter what time of the day you went, there always seemed to be more females running than males. We decided to test our theories on this by having a head count.

(No, we don't need to get a life – it was an easy thing to do to sit in the sun with a beer and count the runners as they came past by the dozen). Within 15 minutes we'd counted 63 females in the first 100 runners. We did it again. This time there were 65 females to 35 males. I'm not sure where else in the world I'd find these ratios. The ratios were reflected in the results for the Vancouver Sun 10k, Canada's biggest road race, held the weekend before the marathon. Of the more than 45,000 entrants, 25,384 were females as opposed to only 20,383 males. I was actually in Victoria that weekend and was surprised to find that it was also hosting a major road race, the Times Colonist 10k. This is Canada's third largest 10k with over 11,500 entrants. As it was the 25th edition they'd decided to include a half marathon for the first time. I went to enter for this but walked away on being asked for $75 for the privilege. I don't pay that sort of money for a mere training distance race – not when Mo and I could have dined out for three nights on the entry fee. As it was only 378 took part in the half marathon.

Anyway, getting back to Vancouver's Seawall; on leaving the park it continues a further kilometre along the waterfront via up-market Coal Harbour to the white sails of Canada Place, designed to represent the style and dimensions of a luxury ocean liner. This is Vancouver's main cruise-ship terminal - a sort of less grandiose version of the Sydney Opera House. (By the way, has anyone seen a cruise ship with sails?) From English Bay at the south side of the park, the Seawall stretches a further 28 km along the waterfront to the University of British Columbia: an ideal scenic training run. We were to make use of most of it during the coming marathon.

Victoria too has a no-less impressive array of footpaths around the inner harbour that extend into trails along the southern coastline. I enjoyed exploring these on short training runs during our six day stay there. What we were most interested in, however, was cycling part of the longer distance, 88 km Galloping Goose Trail that follows the course of former railway lines linking Victoria with the settlement of Sooke and beyond, extending 55 km west, and the ferry terminal at Swartz Bay, 33 km north. The trail is actually part of the Trans Canada Trail linking every province and territory throughout the country. The 'Galloping Goose' was what the locals nick-named the gas-powered passenger railcar that carried mail and 30 passengers daily between Victoria and Sooke in the 1920s. With a whole range of cycle hire options available, Mo and I paid $35 each for a touring bike and headed off on a glorious sunny day to pedal the 40 km there and back through farmland and rugged wilderness to the beautiful Sooke Basin. I'm sure this would have made a better harbour for the early settlers if it hadn't been for the mile-long Whiffenspit guarding its entrance. The day was definitely one of the highlights of the whole trip.

Equally memorable was the day spent in Whistler, Canada's premier ski resort and location for the 2010 Winter Olympics. I'd advise everyone visiting Vancouver to include a trip to Whistler in their itinerary. Just 120 km north of the city, Whistler is easy to get to by scheduled Greyhound services from the Pacific Central depot and the scenery en route will virtually take your breath away. The Sea-to-Sky Highway gets you there in around two hours, passing along the length of the fjord-like Howe Sound with the mountains growing taller by the mile. As you drive north make sure you sit on the driver's side of the coach to see the best views. (Whatever you do, don't fall into the trap of booking one of the ultra-expensive coach trips offered in all hotels – just book the Greyhound online, you'll save hundreds of dollars). Whistler is an expensive place designed to attract, and frequented by, the money-to-burn brigade in search of the perfect ski/après-ski lifestyle. The cost of a single gondola ride up to the slopes is enough to make serious inroads into your holiday spending money. That's not to say that mere mortals on a budget can't still enjoy the same outstanding scenery by making use of the many clearly marked hiking trails in the vicinity. Foremost among these is the Valley Trail, a 45 km path linking Whistler Village to Alta and Nita Lakes. Mo and I spent half a day on this and would have stayed longer had it not been for a certain marathon looming large on the horizon.

Next day it was back to Vancouver for pre-race registration. This took place in one of the large Convention Centres inside the Canada Place building. May is the beginning of the cruise season in British

Columbia and for the first time this year the building was flanked by two giant cruise vessels ready to take on board the first of the thousands of tourists sailing the Inner Passage to Alaska. Arriving at what we thought was way too early for the Friday morning 11am opening we were greeted by orderly queues already in place. Given that there were 5,000 marathon entrants plus 10,000 in the Half Marathon and a further 2,500 in a separate 8 km event the queues shouldn't have been unexpected. These figures provide an interesting comparison to the numbers in the city's first marathon in 1972. On that occasion a mere 51 runners turned up to run a five-lap circuit of the Seawall around Stanley Park. Though the organizers had dubbed it as a 'Health, Sports & Lifestyle Expo,' the registration process appeared no different to those experienced at other marathons throughout the world. We were handed our personalized number and chip, a canvas bag, pair of gloves and a lovely bright yellow T-Shirt and were then left to wander around the usual stalls of exhibits. I'd say Vancouver is a little more generous in giving out freebies than many of my most recent marathons. Containers of chocolate milk and yoghurts were handed out freely and there were lots of other goodies to be sampled without charge. Before leaving we were issued with transport passes to enable us to get to the out-of-town start before the event.

The travel pass certainly proved useful. After two days of hot sun Vancouver was hit on marathon morning by one of those monsoon-like rain squalls that frequently blow in from the Pacific. I've not experienced rain so cold and so persistent for a long, long, time, (the Shakespeare Marathon of 2012 comes to mind – and they cancelled that one on the start line). This was a point-to-point course with the start being in the Queen Elizabeth Park in the outer suburb of Oakridge. We'd been advised to take the Sky Train to Oakridge station and then walk to the park. It turned out to be an exceedingly wet walk of close to thirty minutes with most of us arriving in the park already feeling like drowned rats. Worse still: there didn't appear to be any shelter whatsoever near the start line. The 10,000 half marathoners had already left from there at a very early 7am and their sodden discarded clothing and empty drink containers still littered the area. Those of us arriving later were faced with the unsightly scenes of thousands of runners sheltering in the lee of buildings or shivering beneath trees. It's not as if there weren't any venues in the park that couldn't have been opened for us. I spotted what looked like a Racquets Club and a baseball stadium where shelter could perhaps have been made available. Ironically, one of he local runners informed me that before the start of last year's event the competitors were seeking the same shelter under buildings and trees; but from the heat of the sun.

The organizers had us placed on the Start Line in coloured 'corrals' (their word) according to estimated finishing times. I was in the grey corral for the staggered start with a start time scheduled for 8.38am; eight minutes after the elite runners had set off. I was still standing there at 8.44am, shivering uncontrollably in the never-ending downpour. I'm afraid that's just not good enough for what prides itself on being a major world marathon. (The organizers made much of the fact that it was named as a Top 10 Destination Marathon by Forbes.com and one of the world's most 'exotic' marathons by CNN Travel). Finally we were off; with space in front of us in which to stretch our legs – the runners in the red corral were, by now, well up the road. My plan was to try to stick with the 4hr 15 'pace bunnies' (their words again) until finding out that all pacers regardless of finishing time were under orders to run 10 and then walk 1 minute all the way around the course. I find it difficult to stop running when I don't need to, preferring instead to take my run/walk breaks only when I'm too tired to continue at a running pace. They were right, I was wrong, as I was to find to my cost when the 4:15 group came past me before the finish.

On leaving the park we continued south for three kilometers down the long, straight Cambie Sreet, past the Oakridge Sky Train station we'd left what seemed like hours ago. The first turn took us west down a slightly downhill gradient for a further five kilometres when, just past the 8 km mark, we encountered the one and only hill on the course. The crowds standing out in the rain were really encouraging as they cheered our efforts to get to the top. The route then entered the beautiful Pacific Spirit Park, continuing westwards past the imposing campus of the University of British Columbia, before emerging at 16 km near the Seawall on Marine Drive. We followed this past the half-way mark with tantalizing glimpses of the ocean and Locarno and Jericho beaches on our left until reaching the trendy seaside suburb of Kitsilano at 24 km. At this stage, cooled by the rain and with a breeze on our backs, I was still running strongly and anticipating a sub-4hr.15 finish. As anyone who's run a marathon knows, however, it's a big mistake to count your chickens too soon. Within the next few kilometres I was to be reduced to my own version of the run/walk philosophy.

The beachside suburb of Kitsilano, (affectionately known as Kits), is an interesting place. Originally inhabited by the Squamish people, it became a haven for Vancouver's hippies in the 60s and 70s, but has now gone very much up-market with many of its former timber homes being upgraded and restored for the yuppie brigade with their fashionable shops and chic galleries. Not that we could see much of any of this in the mist, wind and rain. I was lucky to see my watch.

By 30 km we were finally heading back into the city over the Burrard Bridge leading us along English Bay to meet the Seawall path as it entered Stanley Park at 32 km. Now I was on familiar territory having run around the Park earlier in the week. As our hotel was nearby Mo was waiting there as arranged with the camera, a couple of gels and some encouraging words. Had we known how bad the weather would turn out to be I think we may have cancelled this arrangement: we were given gels en route and the photos only accentuated what a dreadful day it was. Actually, the torrential rain was less of a problem for the runners, (as long as you kept running), than it was for the poor spectators who'd committed themselves to offer support. They say you can't do anything about the weather. They're right, you can't.

We should have been enjoying the best views on the course during the final 10 km around Stanley Park. On a clear day you look over the Inlet, past the lined-up oil tankers, to the wide Pacific with stunning vistas of snow-capped mountains on Vancouver's North Shore. This year it wasn't to be. At 39 km we came round the final bend in the Seawall to be confronted by the white sails of Canada Place at what seemed an arm's reach away. Unfortunately we still had a further 3k to go past the display of totem poles in the Park, past Vancouver Yacht Club and, finally, the Rowing Club before turning eastwards into town along Georgia Street, the city's main thoroughfare.

We finished in West Pender Street, a non-descript skyscraper canyon. I couldn't help thinking that the organizers had missed a golden opportunity here to showcase their marathon. A major international marathon needs a recognizable, iconic finish location to show to the world, (think London, think New York etc.) It's not as if Vancouver doesn't have such a location: Canada Place with its white sails was just around the corner – in fact, anywhere on the nearby waterfront, only metres away from where we finished, would have made for a better end to the race. I'm sure the organizers have considered this and that there are sound logistical reasons for finishing where we did but, nonetheless, it was a disappointing anti-climax. At this stage, having stopped running, most of us were shivering and just wanted a warm bath and some warm clothes after receiving our medals and a generous collection of food and drink. On leaving I saw runners collecting their clothing, which had been placed in clear plastic bags, from tables standing out in the rain. I hope their clothes were dry! Incidentally, 2,118 females completed the race as opposed to 2,817 males. Not quite the 60/40 split seen in the shorter distance events but still a higher than average number of female runners than are found in most marathons.

That night it was time for a celebration meal. The problem was we were spoilt for choice as to where to eat. Vancouver's culinary landscape is as diverse as its population with virtually every imaginable world cuisine represented among its wide range of restaurants. Stepping outside our hotel on Davie Street we could virtually throw a blanket over the following ethnic restaurants, all in the same street: Japanese, Korean, Philippine, Himalayan,

Malaysian, Indian, Chinese, Greek, Vietnamese, Mexican, Egyptian – and I've probably missed out or two out here. We'd tried to work our way through a few of these during our stay but had never managed to get into our nearest venue: Stepho's Greek Taverna. While most of the others on the street were near empty at times, Stepho's always has a long queue outside. We'd see people emerging carrying brown paper bags and had assumed they were take-way meals. When we finally got in that night we realized that they were actually doggy bags – the quantity and quality of the food served for $10 or so was so good that it was difficult to eat everything on the plate. Stepho has the perfect business plan; provide lashings of tasty food in a cosy atmosphere at reasonable prices and customers will return for more. We certainly did. He also has a similar restaurant on nearby Robson Street – make one of these your first call for food if you're ever in Vancouver. I'd recommend, however, that you give the city's Chinatown, much heralded as the oldest in Canada, a miss. Before our visit we were looking forward to spending time eating there but were disappointed with both the variety and quality of restaurants available. The whole area looked seedy and run-down – there's a better choice of Chinese food in Newcastle's Stowell Street. Incidentally, a survey carried out during our stay showed that Vancouver had no fewer than 600 Sushi restaurants; more than any other city in Japan except Tokyo.

Canada is an excellent country in which to continue the never-ending search for the perfect dark beer. British Columbians, in particular, are very choosy about their alcohol and drink, per capita, more microbrewed ales than anywhere else in the country. Perhaps the best one we found was Canada's oldest licensed brew pub; Spinnaker's Brew Pub Victoria. We spent much of the afternoon of Mo's birthday in there enjoying panoramic views of the harbour while sampling their delicious Cascadia Dark Ale at 6.5% Even tastier was the malty Nut Brown Ale at 5.2%. Both ales cost $6.50 per pint. Back in Vancouver, at the end of our street we found our way into the 'Three Brits' pub overlooking Burrard Inlet. The local Granville Island Brewery supplied this outlet with a very nice

Granville Island lager at $3.50 for a measure somewhere between a half and a pint. If your preference is for something stronger the heavier River Pilot ESB (Extra Special Brew) at $6.40 per pint will fit the bill nicely. Don't expect to purchase beer or wine from the supermarket though; alcohol can only be bought in licensed premises. You'll have to locate the nearest BC Liquor Store. If it's cans you're after, I'd recommend a 6-pack of the Pacific Western Brewing Co's 'Ironhorse' 6.4% at $8.00 per carton. British Columbia is also slowly developing an international reputation as a wine growing region. Though we didn't drink a lot of wine during our stay, we found the local Peller Estate's Cabernet Merlot and Pinot Grigio an excellent red/white combination at $7.99 a bottle each.

Though the weather ruined the marathon it certainly didn't ruin the rest of our holiday. We were impressed by British Columbia; not only by the wonderful scenery but especially by its people. Without exception, everyone we met was friendly, good-natured and anxious to help. And it wasn't that superficial, false, 'have a nice day' type of friendliness you come across in some cultures. British Columbians seemed to have a respect for their environment, for others and, most of all for themselves. Throughout our stay we saw no sign of dog-dirt or graffiti and very little litter. People went out of their way to make us feel welcome. Three examples: first, the bus driver on seeing us walking down the street looking at a map stopped his bus, asked us where we wanted to go, told us to get on the bus then altered his route to take us there without accepting any fare. Second, seeing us taking photographs of one another, strangers would come up to us and offer to take photos with both of us together. Third, we thought we'd made the mistake of getting on a local bus at the wrong time when it stopped outside a High School to pick up a crowd of teenagers. Instead of the usual high jinks and foul language every single one of them behaved impeccably; giving up their seats to the elderly and thanking the driver when they got off. Imagine that happening with the pupils of an inner-city Comprehensive in the UK. There were many other examples of their in-built politeness too numerous to mention here. My only complaint would be with their overuse of the words 'like' and 'awesome.' I lost count of the number of times we heard the repetition of, 'I'm like…..Oh my God!' and 'It's like….Awesome!' Never mind, I can put up with that. It seems we may have been unlucky forty two years ago in our immigration interview in having the misfortune to come up against a rare example of an unpleasant Canadian. If we hadn't, who knows, we may have been Canadians ourselves by now. I don't think I would have minded that.

At 32km in Vancouver. How wet can you get?

Finished!

LATVIA

RIGA MARATHON

After Gdansk and Tallinn, the 2014 Riga Marathon was the third of the Baltic coast marathons I had on my 'to-do' list and I still had Stockholm and Helsinki to run that year with Vilnius and St. Petersburg already planned in the near future. The whole Baltic coastal area has held a fascination for me since being compelled to study the Hanseatic League during A Level History many moons ago. For those of you who don't have a clue what I'm on about, the Hanseatic League was a powerful 12th century economic and defensive alliance within the cities of North Germany and the Baltic that left a great cultural and architectural inheritance. It tickled me that the guy who set it up rejoiced in the unlikely name of Henry the Lion.

My original plan had been to take the 5.50pm Ryanair flight to Riga from Prestwick in Scotland airport on the Friday before the race, thus allowing myself a leisurely lunchtime train journey up to the airport. The very day that I'd booked the train tickets an email arrived from Ryanair announcing a change of flight departure time: not of one or two hours as you might expect, but of a whopping nine and a half hours. The flight was now scheduled to leave at 8.35am on the Friday morning but there was no way I could get to Prestwick for that without an overnight stopover. Of course, Ryanair offered us our money back but by this stage it was impossible to get an alternative flight at anywhere near what I'd paid for the original; and I'd already lost the money I'd just paid for the train tickets and would now have to buy new ones, as well as fork out for an overnight stay in Glasgow. Don't you just love the way certain low-cost airlines treat their paying customers with such total disdain. Ironically, that same day's Daily Mail of February 22nd 2014 carried the front page headline, 'Mutiny at the Airport.' It explained that, 'Furious passengers stranded on a Ryanair flight called police from the tarmac after being left for hours without food or drink.' The article concluded by stating, 'The drama comes weeks after Ryanair boss Michael O'Leary pledged to treat passengers better and stop p****** people off unnecessarily.' Need I say any more.

The stock reply I've had from friends on telling them I was running in Riga has generally been one of, 'Where's that?' On explaining that it was in Latvia I was generally given the same, 'Where's that?' response. The best answer I could give was that it was the meat in the sandwich between the other two newly independent Baltic States of Estonia to the north and Lithuania to the south. 'Never heard of either of them,' was one memorable reply. Either my friends need to brush up on their geographical knowledge or the Baltic States need to work on their tourism marketing strategies. Latvia, the largest of the Baltic States, is situated on the Baltic Sea in Northern Europe. It shares its borders with Estonia, Lithuania, Russia and Belarus as well as a maritime border to the west with Sweden. It's a democratic parliamentary republic, established in 1918, with Riga as its capital and with a population of just over two million inhabitants. Despite foreign rule by, in turns, Sweden, Germany and the USSR from the 13th to the 20th centuries, the nation has maintained its identity via its language and cultural traditions. Latvian and Lithuanian are the only two surviving Baltic, (Indo-European) languages and help cement relationships between these two neighbours, while both Latvia and Estonia share a long common history of Soviet exploitation. During the Second World War Latvia was forcibly incorporated into the Soviet Union, then invaded and occupied by Nazi Germany before being re-occupied by the Soviets to emerge as the Latvian Soviet Socialist Republic for the next fifty years. In 1991 it re-gained independence with the dissolution of the Soviet Union. Today

Latvia is a member of the European Union, NATO and the United Nations. In January of 2014 it finally replaced its currency of the Latvian lat with the Euro – not without causing some problems for those of us who were trying to pay the entry fee for the Riga Marathon at the time.

As I was to discover, the Soviet legacy is still a touchy subject within Riga particularly as, due to the russification policies of the USSR, the Latvians nearly became a minority within their own country. In an attempt to quell rebellion, tens of thousands of Latvians were deported to Siberia during and after the War and replaced by a deliberate influx of Russian speakers. Jobs became open only to those who spoke Russian, the Latvian language was actively discouraged and the local inhabitants effectively became second class citizens. Today the Russian presence is notable everywhere in Riga; they make up around a third of the nation's population and outnumber Latvian natives in the capital itself. Their continuing influence is a bone of contention and the concern of the Latvians is fully understandable given recent developments in eastern Ukraine.

Riga, Latvia's capital, with around 700,000 inhabitants is the largest city in the Baltic States and houses more than one third of the country's population. The city was founded in 1201 as a base for the Northern Crusades and subsequently developed as the trade hub of the Baltic during the time of the aforementioned Hanseatic League. After the fall of the League, Riga became a part of first the Swedish then the Russian Empires before becoming capital of independent Latvia in 1918. Today its historical centre is a UNESCO World Heritage Site noted for its Art Nouveau architecture and 19th century wooden buildings. The city is divided by the Daugava River which flows another 15 km north into the Gulf of Riga. Old Riga, the historic heart of the city (commonly referred to as the Old Town) is a mixture of cobbled streets, church spires and crooked alleyways that stretch 1 kilometre along the river's eastern bank between Valdermara iela (street) to the north and 13 Janvara iela to the south. As Valdermara moves away from the river it turns into Brivibas bulvaris (Freedom Boulevard) with its narrow ribbon of parkland and scenic canal. This is an inner-city oasis protecting the medieval centre from the grand boulevards just beyond. The substantial, copper-topped Freedom Monument in the middle of the park provides the unofficial gateway into the city centre. At its perimeter the European grandeur begins to fade into unsightly, suburban, Soviet-style housing blocks.

Riga is considered one of the key economic and financial centres of the Baltic economy. Almost half the jobs in Latvia are in Riga and the city generates over half the nation's GDP as well as around a half of its exports. Its main exports are in wood products, IT, food, beverages, pharmaceuticals and metallurgy. In recent years, tourism has also become a growth industry in Riga as many large-scale restoration projects in the city, combined with its reputation for an exciting nightlife, have made it an increasingly attractive destination for foreign visitors. Nevertheless, it would seem that stereotypes about former communist-bloc cities die hard and Riga has yet to enjoy the type of tourism renaissance enjoyed by the likes of Budapest and Prague.

Getting into the city from the airport is a very easy matter as the number 22 leaves every fifteen minutes or so from across the car park outside the terminal building. The bus takes 30 minutes to arrive at a stop near the central bus and rail terminals with the fare a mere 1.20 euro, paid to the driver on entering. The city owned Rigas Satiksme controls the buses, trams and trolley buses all of which charge the same 1.20 fare, if paid to the driver, regardless of distance travelled. (A transfer requires payment of two fares; though if you use a vehicle on the same route and in the same direction within the hour, your ticket is still valid and you won't be charged again). To save 50% of the fare, however, make sure you purchase in advance a re-loadable e-talon card from ticket offices, vending machines or Narveson shop. If you plan on frequent use of the local transport it's best to buy either a 3-day card for 7 euros or a 5-day card for 8 euros. Activate the cards when first boarding. As most of Riga's attractions are condensed into the small, easily walkable, central core, I found little need for public transport to get around.

I'd carefully chosen the 4-Star Hotel Garden Palace for its proximity to the Start and Finish of the marathon on the riverbank in the busy 11 Novembra Krastmala running between the two road bridges across the Daugava. Disappointingly, I was to find that though filled with runners of all nationalities, it appeared to be about the only hotel in the city that hadn't the gumption to serve an early breakfast on marathon day. In all other respects it was an excellent choice, located right next to the river between the transport hub and the delights of the Old Town.

Given Riga's compactness, sightseeing didn't take long. The city is most famous for possessing the largest concentration of Art Nouveau architecture in the world, (ornate buildings with asymmetrical shapes and extensive use of arches and curves). This is due to the fact that at the end of the 19th and beginning of the 20th century, when art nouveau was at the height of its popularity, Riga experienced major financial and population growth making it the fourth largest city in the Russian Empire after Moscow, St Petersburg and Warsaw as well as its largest port. This increased wealth was ploughed into the construction of over 800 luxurious art nouveau apartment blocks in and around the Old Town. As you wander around the city you can't fail to be impressed by the grandeur of the many examples of chocolate box architecture at every turn.

The local Tourist Office guidebook lists over twenty 'top sites' and If time is pressing most of these can be seen within an hour or two's walk; in fact, there is a recommended 'Old Town Walk' that takes you past most of them through the labyrinth of cobbled streets. If I had to pick a must-see selection from these I'd go for the following: St Peter's Church, The House of the Blackheads, Freedom Monument, Dome Square, Riga Castle and the Central Markets. St Peter's Church, mentioned for the first time in 1209 is one of the best examples of Gothic architecture in the Baltics. The church tower appears to be jinxed, having been burned down and rebuilt many times over the centuries. Rumour has it that in 1667 the builders threw glass down from the spire to test how long the spire would last; the more shards, the longer the life. The glass landed on a pile of straw and failed to shatter – a year later the tower went up in flames! The unlikely named House of Blackheads, first mentioned in 1334, is another beautiful building. The Blackheads was an organisation of unmarried foreign merchants existing in several Baltic medieval towns. Apparently, the building was famous in its early years for the wild parties held there by the bachelors. It was totally destroyed during the war, but rebuilt as an exact copy of the original, for Riga's 800th anniversary in 2001. Riga's major landmark, the tall Freedom Monument constructed in 1935, is an important symbol of Latvian Independence. The bronze casting of a woman at the top of the monument (fondly named 'Milda' by the Latvians) holds up three golden stars in her hands which symbolize the three Latvian regions. A guard of honour stands at the foot of the tower each day. Surprisingly, the Soviet overlords neglected to demolish the tower during their time in Latvia, decreeing instead that it was a symbol of their own occupation; with the three stars representing their possession of the three Baltic states of Latvia, Estonia and Lithuania. They nevertheless decreed the statue off-limits to the local populace and anyone seen placing flowers at its base was summarily arrested and transported to Siberia. We were to pass it four times during the course of the marathon.

In the heart of the Old Town lies Dome Square around which the city's best outdoor cafes and restaurants are situated. The square's current appearance only dates back to the 1930s when a portion of its medieval buildings were torn down. At its edge is Dome Cathedral, rebuilt on several occasions to result in a strange mixture of Romanesque, early Gothic and Baroque architectural styles. One of the most striking features of Riga's classic skyline is the Castle which has served as the seat of various rulers throughout the centuries. After the country's independence was restored in 1991, the castle became the primary workplace of the President of Latvia and the home of the country's National History Museum. Totally different and separate from the rest, tucked away behind the main railway station, is Riga's Central Market. As one of the largest and oldest markets in Europe it's well worth a visit, with five food pavilions located inside the enormous, converted Zeppellin hangars. These were transported in at great cost from the town of Vainode in Western Latvia. In stalls around and between them, everything from clothes to flowers is sold. It's always busy and a great place to observe the locals and sample local produce. They say that going to Riga without seeing the Central Markets is like going to Paris without visiting the Louvre. I made sure I visited.

Marathon apart, the highlight of my trip took me away from the city for a day and out to the seaside resort of Jurmala, about 25 kilometres west of Riga. Saturday, the day before the race, was exceptionally hot and ideally suited to a day on the coast. To get there I took a two and a half hour ferry ride upriver on the Dauvaga leaving at 11 am from close to the marathon start. The 20 euros single fare was well worth the money. On reflection, the journey was an hour longer than it had taken to cross the Strait of Georgia between Vancouver and Victoria two weeks earlier. Leaving Riga behind the views improved the farther we travelled as we passed the Passenger Terminal, the shipyards, industrial sites and ugly apartment blocks to arrive at pristine, wooden shorelines with timbered vacation homes and tempting river beaches. Jurmala itself is a gorgeous resort town, considered the Baltic's version of the French Riviera, sandwiched between the river and the Gulf of Riga. Its 33 km stretch of white, hard-packed sandy beach is one of the longest stretches of beach I've ever seen – I only wished I'd had more time to explore along it. While Latvia was part of the Soviet Union, the town was a favourite destination for high-level Communist Party officials, particularly Leonid Brezhnev and the infamous Nikita Krushchev. Holidays there were also given as rewards for top Union officials but while Riga has advanced rapidly after the Soviet departure, Jurmala is only now beginning to receive the recognition it deserves. Russians are now subject to strict visa requirements and, while its beaches have yet to attract significant numbers of European visitors, Jurmala is starting to recover. Many celebrities and successful businessmen are buying up properties near the beach and a number of different festivals and tourism initiatives are bringing more and more people to the town each summer. I was taken in by the place and very reluctant to leave. However, my friend Dave Goodwin was arriving later that day so, forsaking a return by boat, I boarded the thirty minute regular train journey back to Riga for the princely sum of 1.40 euros.

After the sightseeing it was time to get down to the main purpose of the trip and start thinking about the next day's marathon. The race organizers had been very good in keeping us informed about developments by sending out regular emails in the preceding months. They'd even warned us about the high temperatures forecast for race day and provided sensible advice as to how to cope. However, they'd delayed notification of the venue for registration until shortly before I left the UK. This was to be held at the Olimpiskais Sports Centre some 3.3km from my hotel. Unfortunately, as no information was given as to how best to get there by public transport; it proved a long, hot and tiring walk there and back alongside busy roads. Frankly, it wasn't worth the bother. I was less than impressed by the absence of stalls at the Expo and, other than picking up number and chip and a few bits of tat, there really wasn't any incentive to go there. (There was a facility in place to pick numbers at the Start line on the morning of the race; I'd do this next time). I'd paid a very reasonable 35 eurs to enter and had decided against paying an extra 25 euros for an event T-shirt on seeing on the website that all previous year's shirts had been white in colour. This year was no different; the 25 euro would have bought another white T-shirt with, believe it or not, the design of a snail on the front and a few undecipherable words in Latvian on the rear. The organizers promoted it as if it was a work of art. How's this for an entry in Private Eye's 'Pseuds Corner?' 'The design of this year's official adidas supernova T-shirt has been created by Ilmars Blumbergs, one of the most famous contemporary Latvian artists of all-time. And he has chosen a typical Latvian country creature-snail- a slow and optimistic one as the symbol for this year's marathon. Mr Blumberg's irony is very evident - he is trying to say that we should relax, should not be afraid to be slow and just enjoy the race!' I didn't need to be told that, nor did I need to be wearing one of Mr Blumberg's 25 euro creations to run like one of the creatures on it.

As predicted, race day started out hot and humid. Standing on the Start Line at 8.30 am with a headache and a hangover, I knew that a torrid time lay ahead of me. For Mr Blumberg's information, I wasn't afraid to be slow; I just didn't want it to hurt. Steve Bruce and Arsene Wenger were to blame for my predicament. I'd met up with Dave as planned early the previous evening and after a couple of beers headed into Paddy Whelan's at 7 pm to watch the Cup Final. The fact that neither Hull nor Arsenal could finish each other off in the normal 90 minutes meant that instead of returning to our hotels only slightly the worse for wear, the extra two rounds consumed during extra time ensured that we ended the night very much the worse for wear (or at least, I did – not a great way to be with a marathon to run early next morning.)

The marathon has been popular in Riga since the mid-1980s. The first races were based on the idea of Latvian independence and were known as The Folk Song Marathons. The course in those days was in multiple laps and runners were invited to cover as much of the distance as they were capable. On finishing they received a part of a Latvian national symbol (a fragment of the national costume for example) giving the participants the feeling that they'd run for the independence of Latvia. The first official Riga Marathon, organized by the City Council, took place in 1991 just before independence from the Soviets was achieved. Initially only several hundred took part but in recent years the race has gained in popularity in the international running community. In 2007 it became a member of AIMS and in 2012 was upgraded to the IAAF Road Race Bronze Label, the first race in Northern Europe to receive this award. Apparently the course has changed each year so there is no official course record to compare performances to. 2014's attendance for the four distances on offer broke all previous records with a combined entry of over 23,000 runners of whom 2,500 were international athletes from 61 different countries. This made Riga the Baltic's biggest running festival with 1,485 of us in the Full and 3,715 in the Half Marathon that started simultaneously.

There were 5,666 in the 12.30 pm 10k and a whopping 12, 327 in a 5k race starting at 1.30 pm – basically a full day of running to keep the spectators' interest.

This was yet another marathon where the shorter distance half marathoners were set off behind the full marathon competitors. Very soon the inevitable happened and the faster runners from the half were pushing and shoving their way to the front. Things got worse every time the half marathon pacemakers with their posse of followers wanted to get through. Surely it's not beyond the bounds of human ingenuity to devise a system where say, the 2 hour half marathoners start with those hoping for a 4 hour marathon time, the 1 hour 45 group starts with the 3 hour 30 marathoners and so on. Anyway, it was chaos at first. In view of the previous night's alcohol intake I was determined to drink as much and as often as possible at the water stations. Unfortunately, I was running on the left hand side of the road at the first station and simply couldn't fight my way across to the drinks placed on the right hand side. I stayed on that side for the next one and guess what? While approaching, an English voice on the tannoy announced that those seeking refreshment should run on the left hand side of the course. I missed out again. At the third station the drinks were on the right, I was on the left as instructed. Some might think this inconsequential: not if they were at risk from dehydration on such a hot and humid day.

After that things settled down and there were no more problems. In fact, I was impressed with the organizational infrastructure put in place. Vast quantities of water were available every two kilometers and there were also isotonic drinks, bananas and oranges at every station after 8.5km. Gels were meant to be handed out at 15.5 and 28.5 km but both Dave and I were unable to find these on the second occasion.

The course itself, though artificial and manufactured, had some interesting points. We started running along the river initially before turning inland back towards, then through, the city centre before making our first crossing of the Dauvaga River via the Vansu Bridge at 4 km. Returning to the bridge again at 10 km we were taken back through the city before turning at the 14 km mark and running a further 5 km in the opposite direction along the river bank. After losing the half marathon runners, a much quieter second lap kept us in the outer suburbs and away from the river until going back over the bridge at 32 km. Presumably in an attempt to minimize road closures where possible, we often found ourselves running along one side of the road before turning and running back in the opposite direction. Some I spoke to afterwards hadn't liked that aspect of the course. It didn't bother me; in the high humidity I was just intent on finishing! I guess I must have sweated the hangover out of me. Everyone was totally lathered after a few kilometres and I was actually running ok until about 30 km when, yet again, I had to resort to a run/walk to the finish. At this stage even repeating to myself the mantra, 'I do this to have a good time, not to get a good time,' wasn't any help. I was only kidding myself. Feeling dreadful while struggling to run is no one's idea of a good time – not even mine. The fact that I'd enjoyed myself last night was no consolation for how I was feeling during the last few miles of this race. I longed for the days when I could go from start to finish in sub 8 minute miles without breaking stride. The marathon is a distance that has to be accorded the respect it deserves. I'd disrespected it on this occasion. A mental note was made to treat it more seriously in future.

One of the interesting innovations in the race worth mentioning was the integration of the 'Culture Kilometre of Brivibas iela' into the marathon programme. Brivbas iela is the main street in which, during the run, there was a special programme of Latvian themed music, performances and traditionally dressed guards of honour on raised plinths. As we passed on each of the four occasions something different was taking place. It provided an interesting diversion and something to look forward to on the way around.

At the finish we were presented with an excellent heavy-duty medal, one of the best I've received, depicting most of Riga's iconic buildings mentioned earlier. We were also handed a canvas Riga marathon bag containing a variety of drink and foodstuffs. Within the finish area there was a virtual mini-village with shower and massage facilities, food courts, stages, scaffolds and stalls catering from everything from having your medal engraved to help-yourself free beer. Fortunately, marathon runners only were allowed access to the beer supplied by Aldaris, Riga's premier brewery. The Mezpils Tumais – a strong dark beer went down a treat. Meeting up with Dave that evening we both agreed that despite one or two organizational errors the event had been enjoyable and one that we'd both be keen to repeat.

It was now time to think about food. For dietary purposes my friend Dave avoids spicy, exotic food and is very much a pie and pint man. That's what we had the previous night and very good it was too. My tastes are more extensive and I was very keen to try the local Latvian cuisine. However, since this is an amalgam of several other national cuisines it is difficult to draw the line where it starts or ends. There were a number of restaurants in Riga's city squares advertising Latvian food that seemed to contain menus similar to those of other nationalities. I'm told that truly Latvian cooking would consist of cheap self-grown ingredients like dried peas and cheap cuts of pork and bacon with few spices and high in calories. With that in mind I ordered the Solanka soup containing cabbage and potatoes, followed by an unpronounceable dish which seemed to consist of pieces of pork loin wrapped in eggs and breadcrumbs. The salad that accompanied it contained potatoes, bacon and pickled cucumber. It proved quite a filling combination for less than twelve euros. Being on the Baltic coast, fish dishes are also popular and plentiful. I made a point of tucking in to the smoked mackerel, herring and sardines on the hotel menu.

Like its neighbour Estonia, Latvia is an ideal place to continue the search for the perfect dark beer. Beer is by far the most popular alcoholic drink in Latvia; the country has a rich brewing history and there are plenty of different styles on offer. Wherever we went the beer pumps offered the choice of either a pale or a dark beer. (Gaisais is pale; tumsais is dark) In the two Irish bars we mostly frequented, Paddy Whelans served up the tasty 4.9% Usavas Tumsais dark beer produced in the nearby town of Ventspils for 3.20 euros per pint. I preferred this to Donnegan's version of a dark beer, the Mezpils Tumsais at 3.50 euros – this was the same beer from Riga's Aldaris brewery that we'd be given at the end of the marathon. Other major players in the Latvian beer scene include Cesu Alus, the second largest brewey after Aldaris, and Lacplesa. Though I didn't get round to sampling them, I'm told that both of these also produce excellent dark beers.

Riga made a big impression and I left reluctantly, determined to return at some stage. I'm not convinced that it lived up to its reputation as 'The Paris of the North,' (I think Tallinn is more deserving of that accolade) nevertheless, there was enough of interest to make you want to re-visit. Before that though, I'll be interested to see what the rest of the Baltic States have to offer.

Sailing from Riga on the boat to Jurmala

Feeling hungover at the Start. Never again!

FINLAND

HELSINKI MARATHON

Three o' clock on what is generally a hot August afternoon seems an unusual time of day to hold a major city marathon. A week before travelling out to the Helsinki Marathon in 2014 weather reports showing afternoon temperatures as high as 27 degrees in the city had me wondering what I'd let myself in for. Before leaving I'd tried, without success, to uncover the logic behind an afternoon start in the middle of August. The two low-key UK marathons I'd recently completed had both been run in very hot, (for the UK) weather and I'd suffered in both. The humidity in Dundee, a city not known for its tropical climate, had a number of us struggling around its course at the end of July – an experience I was not hoping to repeat. This was to be the 34th edition of the Helsinki event, however, so there's obviously a valid reason for the organizers to retain the same claiming date. Not only had I'd never previously ran a marathon in Finland, I'd never even visited the country and, other than having read about the exploits of Paavo Nurmi and followed the careers of ex Liverpool footballers Sami Hyypia and Jari Litmanen, I knew virtually nothing about the place. For those who aren't aware; Nurmi, dubbed 'The Flying Finn' is considered to be the greatest Finnish sportsman and one of the greatest athletes of all time. He excelled at distance- running, winning no less than nine Olympic gold medals between 1920 and 1928, setting 22 official world records in the process. Just to show my life isn't a total cultural desert, I was also aware that the composer, Sibelius, was another famous Finn; his work 'Finlandia' played an important role during the country's struggle for independence. On a lighter note, I did recall reading somewhere about two of the more eccentric pastimes enjoyed by the Finns. As the home of the mobile phone giant Nokkia, it seems that Mobile Phone Throwing World Championships are held there on a regular basis, as too is the very competitive Wife Carrying World Championship. The winners of each are obviously those who throw the phone or carry the wife furthest: uncomplicated but weird, as well as a great way to take out your frustrations towards both modern technology and a nagging spouse. It was time to get the guide books out and conduct some research. This Marathon tourism business is much more enjoyable with prior knowledge of the country to which you're travelling.

I'd mistakenly believed given its cultural and historical links, that Finland was part of Scandinavia. Technically that is not the case. It seems that this area only refers to Norway, Sweden and Denmark and that Finland should, instead, be referred to as a 'Nordic' country, bordered by Norway to the north, Sweden to the west, Russia to the east and Estonia to the south across the Gulf of Finland. With a population of around 5.5 million, it's the eighth largest country in Europe and the most sparsely populated in the EU. It is described as a land of lakes and islands with Europe's largest forested area as forests cover almost 86% of its land mass. It is also one of the world's most northernmost countries with Reykjavik being the only major capital city situated further north than its capital Helsinki.

Historically, the geographical area we now call Finland was a political vacuum until the 12th century with both its western Catholic neighbour, Sweden and its eastern Greek Orthodox neighbour, Russia competing for possession. Until 1809 most of the area came under Swedish control with that country imposing both their legal and social systems on Finland. During its period as a great power in the 17th and 18th centuries Sweden extended its influence around the Baltic and managed, due to the weakness of Russia, to push the Finnish border further east. With Sweden's subsequent decline, Russian pressure increased and it finally conquered Finland in 1809. While under Swedish rule Finland had merely remained a group of provinces and not a national entity, the Russians gave Finland extensive autonomy thereby creating the Finnish state. The Finnish nationalist movement gradually gained momentum during the rule by Russia leading in 1917 to what is now the independent republic of Finland. It remained largely an agrarian country until the 1950s before developing an advanced economy while building an extensive welfare state. This has resulted in widespread prosperity and one of the highest per capita incomes in the world. Finland is now a top performer in numerous studies of national performance like education, quality of life, civil liberties and economic competitiveness. It was recently voted by Newsweek as 'The best country in the World.'

Helsinki, Finland's largest and most cosmopolitan city with a population of about 575,000 inhabitants, was founded in 1550 by King Gusta Vasa Sweden as a Hanseatic (them again!) trading post to compete with the then Danish city of Tallinn. It replaced Turku as the county's capital following Russia's victory over Sweden and was then developed by the Tsars along the lines of a miniature St. Petersburg. Architects were commissioned to construct a city of grand proportions in the Empire style predominant in the Russian city. The city's Lutheran Cathedral, completed in 1852, is the most obvious legacy of this rebuilding programme. As a consequence, modern-day Helsinki reflects the influences gained from its occupiers straddling both eastern and western cultures. It remains officially bi-lingual, with an 86% Finnish-speaking majority and a visible 6% Swedish minority. Many of the city's street signs are shown in both languages while, staff in the large department stores often wear flags representing the languages they speak. Helsinki today appears a vibrant, modern city surrounded by nature at almost every viewpoint. On arrival, the city's architecture appeared to be the usual mix of the old and the new; with the older buildings reflecting the city's unique character while the newer ones were of the type that can be found in virtually every other modern city. Half the city appears to be water with its approximately 100 kilometres of shoreline of bays, inlets and islands cutting into the land. The core of the city is the area around the Central Railway Station, a destination that most visitors, whether coming by train, long-distance coach or airport-link, will reach on arrival. This area, used as a hang-out by the city's younger crowd, can get quite noisy in the evening and presents a real contrast to the up-market Esplanadi, where the rich and famous go to see and be seen, a couple of blocks away.

Mo and I travelled by plane from Edinburgh to Helsinki via Arlanda airport in Stockholm for a three day stay. All international flights land at Helsinki-Vantaa airport situated about 19 kilometres from the centre of town. Taxis cost about 40 euros but the cheapest option is to take the 40 minute bus ride on Regional Bus 615 to the Central Station. The 4.50 euros fare costs slightly less than the faster Finnair Airport Bus priced at 6.30 euros. As our hotel, the Cumulus Kasaniemi, was located just around the corner from the Central Station we simply took the 615 in both directions. Incidentally, this hotel cost us approximately the same amount as we'd paid for our recent accommodation for an aborted marathon attempt in Stockholm; but there the similarity ends. Unlike in Stockholm the rooms were not only above ground and with windows but were also comfortable and spacious with an excellent all-you-can-eat buffet breakfast. It also contained that essential ingredient of Finnish culture; a public sauna. (Apparently there are 3.3 million of these in a country of only 5.5 million people). I was hoping that this might prove particularly useful in banishing some of the post-race aches and pains.

Helsinki is yet another compact city, easy to explore on foot, with most of the major attractions situated in a rectangular area of a dozen or so streets between the Central Station and the Harbour. If you get footsore or short on time there is a good, reasonably inexpensive public transport to take advantage of. A single ticket, valid for an hour and costing three euro allows you to hop on and off trams, buses and the metro within the city area. Likewise, Day Tickets are available for unlimited use on public transport for 1-7 days. They can be purchased from ticket machines, from the Tourist Information offices or from the Helsinki City Transport service point in the Central Station. Both sorts of tickets are also sold by the drivers. Anyone wanting a simple and affordable way to explore Helsinki should ignore the highly priced tourist buses and simply hop on board tram routes 2 and 3 (it's the same tram; only the number changes half way round). The routes make a giant figure-of-eight in either direction and take in many interesting sights such as the Market Square, Senate Square, Finnish National Opera House and the Olympic Stadium. Make sure you pick up a 'Sightseeing on 2 and 3' brochure before boarding as this includes descriptions of what you pass along the route. Each loop takes approximately one hour and the tram can be boarded at any stop along the way. An even more interesting trip is to take the SparaKOFF, a historic tram that has been converted into a pub offering a unique sightseeing tour of Helsinki in summertime. A lap of the city leaving from Railway Square takes about 40 minutes while beer, cider, sparkling wine and soft drinks are served to passengers. Look out for a red tram with the word 'Pub' displayed in the front and rear destination windows. (Koff is the name of the brewery involved)

For those who like the water, money can be saved by ignoring some of the 20 euros plus boat cruises and taking the 5 euros return public ferry across to the UNESCO World Heritage site of Suomenlinna, a 15 to 20 minute ride away from the Market Square. Known as 'The Gibraltar of the North,' this is a must-see venue for any visitor to the city. Founded on a group of islands off the coast of Helsinki in 1748, the Suomenlinna sea fortress is regarded as a cultural treasure to be preserved for future generations as a prime example of the military architecture of its time. Its significance in the defence of three separate states; Sweden, Russia and Finland, gives the fortress its own special importance. Mo and I spent a lovely sunny afternoon there the day before the race, sitting drinking beer in the sunshine as the giant passenger ferries sailed past on their way to Stockholm, Tallinn and St Petersburg. It was hard to believe that, in the winter months, the same waters have to be cleared by ice-breakers for the ferries to pass through. There's a designated tourist walking route – the Blue Route – that can be followed around the islands with information signs telling you all about the sights and their history. The whole place is a living museum with cafes, theatres and restaurants and still occupied with about a thousand inhabitants living their daily lives among the old fortifications, tunnels and cast iron cannons.

Sailing back towards South Harbour the skyline is dominated by the striking white dome of Helsinki Lutheran Cathedral, the unofficial symbol of the city. Completed in 1852 and recently refurbished, the building towers over the nearby Senate Square and is the focal point for all the city's sightseeing buses. The statues of the twelve apostles on the roof are reputedly the largest set of zinc sculptures in the world. I was more interested, however, in what was going-on in the adjacent Market Square. Always crowded with tourists, the Square features a host of market stalls selling everything from fresh fish, fruit and vegetables, handicrafts and souvenirs. There's also a motley collection of outdoor cafes housed in tents where it's possible to buy meals of reindeer meat and Baltic salmon. The 9 euros dishes of reindeer stew sold by the Lapland Food stall were rather tasty and filling. Other buildings worth looking at in this area include the long, low, bluish-grey City Hall and the former Presidential Palace, purchased as the residence of the Russian tzar on his visits to the city and now mainly used for the prestigious presidential reception held each year on 6th December, Independence Day. What I found most interesting was the harbourside Old Market Hall with its colourful array of stalls selling delicatessen- style foods, including such things as bear meat, cheeses, bakery products and sushi. Having looked all over Helsinki for an ALKO store – the only place where alcohol over 5% can be purchased, I was surprised to locate one of these outlets in such a boutique-style environment.

After the day's sightseeing thoughts had now to be focused on the following day's marathon. Registration for this was open from 12 noon on the Friday and until 1pm on the Saturday in the Toolo Sports Hall on the appropriately named Paavo Nurmi Street, immediately in front of the Olympic Stadium. There was even a large bronze statue of the great man at the entrance to the stadium car park. Remembering his battles with our own Brendan Foster, I was even more delighted to find, in front of the sports hall, a smaller statue of that other great Finnish distance runner, Lasse Viren, winner of double gold at 5,000 and 10,000 metres at successive Olympics in 1972 and 1976. It's about a 30 minute walk along the main road from the Central Station to the stadium, but this can be avoided by taking the number 4 or 10 tram. I preferred the more scenic stroll on the pathway through Hesperia Park by the side of Toolonlahti Lake, particularly as we were to run that way during the race. Registration was an easy matter as the crowds hadn't yet built up – I'm told it's more congested on the morning of the race. There was little in the Expo of any real interest, just the usual merchandise and representatives from marathons I'd already completed. The event Pasta Party as such, wasn't so much a party as an offer of a 6.90 euros discounted meal on production of your race number at Vapiano, a city-centre restaurant. As it seemed to be full every time I passed, I decided to stick with the reindeer meat. Within minutes I was outside and on my way with number, chip, purple T-shirt, 250ml. of shower gel that went in the bin and a carrier bag full of paper and assorted tat. My main interest lay in taking a look at the nearby Olympic Stadium where the next day's race would finish on the track.

The Stadium has a fascinating history. It was completed in 1938, after the Finns – flushed with their athletic successes of the 1920s resolved to seek the ultimate prize of playing host to the 1940 Summer Olympics. These Games were initially given to Tokyo but, due to threats of a boycott over Japan's war with China, Helsinki was asked to step in and take over. Unfortunately the Second World War intervened and the 1940 Olympics were cancelled. It wasn't until 1952 that the Games finally arrived in Helsinki. The most memorable moment of the 1952 Olympics was when the torch was brought into the stadium and the identity of the torch-bearer was finally revealed to a rapturous reception from 70,000 people, as Paavo Nurmi himself. The stadium houses the Finnish Sports Museum, open to the public daily, as too is the 72 metre Stadium Tower which offers excellent views over the city and – on a clear day – right across the Gulf of Finland to Tallinn in Estonia. The tower's height is based on the gold-medal winning distance the

Finn, Matti Jarvinen, threw in the 1932 Olympics. There's even a Youth Hostel situated within the stadium for those who like to sleep next to the ghosts of their sporting heroes. Since inauguration the stadium has been the venue for the first World Athletics Championships in 1983 as well as those in 2005. It hosted the European Athletics Championships in 1971, 1994 and 2012. Nowadays, like many similar stadiums, it largely hosts large-scale pop concerts and can count Michael Jackson, Bruce Springsteen, U2 and Madonna among the artists appearing there. Strangely, since March 2007, a Eurasian Eagle-Owl has been spotted living in and around the stadium. It even delayed play for ten minutes by perching on a goalpost during a Euro 2008 qualifying match, much to the amusement of Helsinki's citizens who subsequently christened it Bubi and voted it as the city's Resident of the Year. I decided to keep an eye out for Bubi while finishing in the stadium the next day.

We were all back outside the stadium again the following afternoon watching the last of the thunderclouds rolling away out to sea. After the rain came the heat and, even worse, the humidity. As someone whose performance is badly affected by this, I knew I was in for a torrid afternoon. A children's Mini-Marathon earlier in the day had already been and gone and, fortunately, with no simultaneous Half Marathon or 10k to contend with, we were going to have the whole course to ourselves. Apparently over half of the route follows the Helsinki waterline so hopes built up of cooling breezes to come We were told that there were approximately 6,200 of us from 54 different countries by the announcer who then proceeded to take up a great deal of time by thanking each of the 54 countries individually. Then we were off – on a 3km loop around the back of the stadium initially and then alongside the Toolanlahti Lake mentioned earlier. After crossing the main road, the next 2 km took us westwards towards the coast. At this stage crowds were both large and vocal; a huge contrast to what we were to encounter as the course followed the perimeter of the Bay. The next 10km were largely run on what were, at times, congested cycle tracks around the coastline with traffic thundering by on adjacent roads.

At 15km we crossed a bridge over a dual carriageway to head back eastwards towards the town. My memory of landmarks here is a bit of a blur even though the next stretch between 15 and 21km was the main out and back section of the course. I can only think that, at this stage, the humidity was beginning to take its toll. Things perked up a bit after half-way when we reached a beautiful, large, landscaped park affording breath-taking views out to sea and a host of tiny islands. Having turned a corner at 23km, we were running towards the South Harbour and our first views of the city and, in particular, the iconic Lutheran Cathedral. To our right could also be seen the Russian onion-domed Uspenski Cathedral – each of the five domes is said to be topped with 22-carat gold. Ironically placed nearby is a large ferris wheel and a rather weird statue of what looks like a giant alien having a pee. This brought us past the Old Market Hall, the ferry landing and the market stalls with their enticing food smells; through enthusiastic crowds to emerge onto a lap of the nearby Esplanade Park.

The Esplanadi is Helsinki's most emblematic park and, with its two quite different streets on either side, is always a magnet for locals and visitors alike. The northern side is home to boutique shops, expensive bars and cafes including the popular Esplanade Café, while the southern side houses much larger institutions that replaced the older, wooden buildings in the 19th century. I'd arranged to meet Mo in the middle of the park by the statue of J L Runeberg, the poet who wrote the lyrics for the national anthem. She could see I was struggling and as well as offering encouragement, also mentioned that, if I felt like pulling-out, our hotel was only around the corner. I was sorely tempted but, having got to 25km, I knew I could manage a run/walk to the finish from there. It was a case of head down and retrace our footsteps back to where the 33km mark on the return journey met the 15km mark on the outward leg. From there the course took a delightful detour across the Bay that we'd ran round earlier, crossing a couple of wooden bridges that joined up the islands in the middle of the water. There was even a pleasant trail section through woods before rejoining the cycle path that took us to the 38km point. I'd spotted a runner of about my age wearing a Melbourne Marathon vest, an event I'm down to run shortly. It helped the kilometres pass quickly having someone with whom I could have a natter. I'd long ago given up all thought of the 4 hour 15 minute time that I set out hoping for. Though the temperature had now dropped to something approaching acceptable, the damage had been done by the humidity levels earlier in the race.

From 38km it was back towards the city and along the pavement next to the main Mannerheime Road until a footbridge took us into the park at the rear of the stadium at 41km. It's an unbelievable feeling entering the tunnel to emerge onto the track of a famous Olympic Stadium. Despite the 5 hour finish there was still quite a large crowd cheering us on and you couldn't help but attempt to pick up the pace for a faster finish. (No sign of the owl though).

On finishing we were handed a substantial medal before being led past a succession of stalls handing out goodies such as bananas, energy bars, yoghurts, crisps, packets of rye bread and, best of all after consuming water and isotonic drink for 26 miles, were the hot cups of coffee on offer. I have to congratulate the organizers on a brilliantly organized event. After 33 years of practice they'd really had everything well worked out with 16 well-marshalled drink stations at regular intervals along the course plus sponges and shower sprays to combat the heat. Free massages were offered both pre and post race and there was even free swimming facilities for runners in a complex nearby. I'd paid 77 euros to enter and considering everything this seemed reasonable value compared to similar events.

Having already tried the reindeer meat, Mo and I went out that evening in search of another example of Finnish cuisine. As in Stockholm, the cheapest menus are usually offered at lunchtime. I'm told that this is because many Helsinki businesses supply their workers with luncheon vouchers, leading to restaurants cutting their prices to compete for these. Certainly every restaurant we saw advertising 'Finnish Cuisine' had prices that would make your eyes water. In the end we settled for a middle-of-the-range restaurant offering the fish dishes we were looking for. I tried the fried vendace, (a sort of whitebait), with garlic sauce while Mo went for the smoked Baltic herring. Both dishes came with potatoes and a small salad. Berries of all kinds are also a popular desert dish in Finland – they were served at breakfast each day in our hotel. We each finished our meal with bilberries and ice cream and two unavoidably expensive glasses of wine. The bill made a huge dent in our travel budget.

Back in our hotel we had waiting for us some examples of the Finnish beer we'd bought earlier from the aptly named ALKO store in the Old Market Hall. Before leaving the UK I'd discovered that the largest Finnish brewers are Sinebrychoff, Hartall and Olvi so had tried to find a sample of each of their products. As in most places these days there's also a number of small micro-breweries springing up around the city – we came across two of them without even looking: on the fortress island of Suomenlinna and on the first floor of the giant Kamppi shopping complex. That evening we worked our way through a 5.2% Olvi Export, a 4.5% Hartwall Porter and a 7.2% Koff Porter, (well, we were sharing!) The last two easily fulfilled the Manford criteria for an excellent dark beer. Surprisingly though, perhaps the nicest beer we found in Helsinki wasn't even brewed in Finland. Our nearby supermarket, with its strict 'no strong beer' restrictions still managed to sell a really malty dark lager from the Czech Republic; the 4.7% Litovel, at a cheap, by Finnish prices, of 2.39 euros per can. (We can get 10 cans of the local lager for the same price at our local supermarket in Spain but I guess you shouldn't think like that when you're travelling.)

We'd enjoyed a great weekend in Helsinki and were sorry to leave. It's an ideal size for a capital city with a central core containing most of its attractions that is easy to negotiate your way around. Being so close to water on all sides certainly helps too – at no stage do you get the feeling of being hemmed in. Despite what I'd heard about the reserved nature of the Finnish people, everyone we met came across as friendly and genuinely helpful. I'd certainly recommend this marathon to all fellow marathon tourists particularly those who can handle a hot afternoon's start.

Paavo Nurmi's statue in front of the Olymic Stadium

Moral support from Mo before the Start

AUSTRALIA

SYDNEY MARATHON

My main focus in 2014, apart from attempting to run in as many different countries as possible (I managed 10 that year) had been to combine a visit to my son Ross, now living in Sydney, with an attempt on what the Australian 100 Club call 'The Australian Sweep.' This involves completing a marathon in each of the country's 6 States and its 2 Territories, (Northern Territory and ACT). I'd worked out an itinerary that would allow me to run in each of the eight regions during what constitutes the Aussie winter/spring period between July and October. As usual when you make plans, fate intervened and, at the last moment, Ross decided to come to Europe in August for a friend's wedding in Sweden. This meant us delaying our visit by several weeks and by the time we arrived in Australia there were only three marathons on the calendar that my itinerary allowed me to run: Sydney, Western Sydney and Melbourne. I entered all three. Completion of 'The Sweep' will have to be put on hold until another year.

Mo and I eventually headed Down Under at the beginning of September, having arranged a two-day stopover in Dubai en route. The city plays host to an increasingly popular marathon in mid-January and, always on the look-out for new countries in which to run, I wanted to check it out. The idea of combining it with a beach holiday, when temperatures settle into the mid-20s as we suffer the UK winter seemed appealing initially. That was until I visited the place. Dubai in the summer is not for me. We arrived to 42 degree heat to find ourselves the only ones seemingly prepared to venture outdoors. Everyone else was living in an air-conditioned bubble;

moving only from air-conditioned homes to air-conditioned cars, to air-conditioned offices and in the evening to air-conditioned shopping malls. The whole place seemed like a nightmare vision of a futuristic hell on earth: of cities judged on how tall they can erect their skyscrapers and how fast, straight and congested they build their motorways. I found out that the marathon course simply runs down the straightest of Dubai's motorways, turns around at half-way and then comes back down the other side – like running up and down the M1, but with buildings. My initial reaction was, 'I think I'll give it a miss.' (As things turned out I ended up returning to Dubai in 2017 and thoroughly enjoyed completing that year's Dubai Marathon.)

It was a relief to arrive in the relative sanity of Sydney. No one can accuse this city of lacking character. I've been visiting it on and off now for over forty years and on each occasion have never failed to be taken-in by the splendour of its location. Its spectacular waterside setting ensures that it has few rivals for the title of one of the 'World's Most Beautiful Cities.' Sydney is fortunate to be built on one of the world's greatest harbours, where its twin icons of the Bridge and the Opera House are complemented by a myriad of vessels from great ocean liners, to historic ferries and colourful sailing boats all vying for space on its clear, blue waters. At times, standing by the harbour at Circular Quay, hemmed in on three sides by the city's skyscrapers, you have to pinch yourself to believe that it was just over 200 years ago that the First Fleet of 1,000 people (736 of them convicted felons) arrived at that very spot to kick-start the European colonization of the Continent as a penal colony - all in conditions of great brutality and despair. These days Sydney is a dynamic, international city; the epitome of sophistication and cosmopolitan charm. Its citizens now enjoy an enviable lifestyle in one of the most multicultural cities in the world with Australia having long ago abandoned its 'White Australia' policy and accepted its true geographical position and the proximity of its Asian neighbours. Almost one-third of Sydney's 4.5 million citizens were born overseas; many from China, India and Vietnam and these newer migrants have contributed significantly to Sydney's current position as a global, cultural and economic centre.

For most of the six weeks of our stay Mo and I were based in a rented apartment in Manly, just around the corner from our son. For those of you who've never heard of the place, Manly is a rival to Bondi as Australia's most famous surf beach. Situated on an isthmus, surrounded on three sides by water, a half hour's ferry ride from the centre of Sydney, Manly is an affluent suburb within an affluent city, within an affluent country. You need deep pockets to meet both its rent and restaurant costs - even the beer prices are inflated compared to elsewhere in the city. With the Aussie dollar strong against the pound, I wasn't sure how I'd cope. It's mainly inhabited by young professionals working in the city on six-figure salaries or by those flaunting their inherited wealth. Nowhere I've visited has the old Jewish expression along the lines of, 'It's fortunate that his father was born before him,' appeared more appropriate. Rightly or wrongly I got the distinct impression that some people I met were so full of themselves that it never crossed their minds to appreciate how lucky they were to be living in such a beautiful place. A recently retired friend, looking for voluntary work tells the story of how he approached the local library offering to assist migrants with their reading of English, only to be informed that, 'We don't have migrants in Manly.'

Most mornings during my stay I ran along the beautiful mile-long surf beach. When the tide was in I was left with no option but to run along the adjacent promenade. There I came into contact with the beautiful people and their perfect bodies: a tribe of narcissists that congregated there each day. I found it interesting to observe the strange protocols that appeared to be part of their daily ritual. Even before 7am the place was like Piccadilly Circus during the rush hour. Hordes of swimmers from the Manly Surf Club would disappear into the waves for their morning safari around the bay to Shelly Beach and back. Meanwhile, the really serious athletes would be pounding the pavement before heading off on the ferries to work. Next came what Mo and I called the, 'Pink and Blacks' – a large contingent of fashionistas; female runners all clad head to toe in a uniform of boutique running gear as if by prior arrangement. It wasn't a club, most of them didn't seem to know each other, yet each somehow had managed to equip themselves in the same designer outfits expressing the same fashion statement, like something out of Aldous Huxley's 'Brave New World.' Headgear was a black peaked cap, preferably with a blond ponytail trailing through the hole at the back. Then came the chic, pink lycra vest, the state-of-the-art, black, knee-length compression tights finished off with the latest-in-pink Nike trainers. Virtually every one of them came complete with wires dripping out of their ears leading to mobile phones strapped on to one arm and heart-rate monitor on the other. Some of them could run, some seemed more content to be part of an unofficial fashion carnival.

After 9 am, having got their husbands off to work and their older children to school, the buggy brigade appeared: a collection of pram-pushing mothers determined to keep in shape regardless. Woe-betide anyone who got in their way as, heads down, they careered their streamlined chariots along the prom; sometimes three-abreast. The majority of these adhered to the same uniform as the Pink and Blacks. The final group was to be found standing in circles on the nearby grass in front of what was usually a male figure barking out instructions. These were those with so many disposable dollars they preferred to pay others to show them how to exercise. The personal trainer usually sported an expression that can only be described as 'laughing all the way to the bank.'

The activities I've described up to now usually took place during the week. The weekends were an entirely different kettle of fish and, if the tide was in, it was better to avoid the prom at all costs. While the above groups were all still in action they were joined by a whole phalanx of out-of-schoolers and their dangerous toys. The younger ones rode scooters into your Achilles with reckless abandon while their teenage counterparts crashed skateboards into your calves as you tried to run. Surfers of all ages attempted to weave their twelve-foot surfboards through the throng while those on bikes simply refused to adhere to the rule of giving way to pedestrians. There was even a guy who insisted on riding his penny farthing among the crowds. While I loved Manly as a place, the problem was that nearly everyone else in Sydney loved it too and made a bee-line there when free at weekends. At such times I longed to be back running along the deserted beaches of my Northumberland coast. Relief of sorts could be had later in the day after the crowds had all gone home. At these times it was a pleasure to stroll unmolested along the prom. Each day I'd pass a succession of plaques either commemorating those who'd died tragically in the surf, or that simply celebrated the lives of those who'd spent time there. One such plaque always caught my attention. It was in memory of a young Manly triathlete named Saxon Bird who'd been tragically killed while competing in an Ironman contest in 2010. It read, 'Only those who will risk going too far, can possibly find out how far they can go.' This simple epitaph resonated so much with my own philosophy on life that I found it difficult to pass without stopping to reflect.

After two weeks of attempting to train in these congested conditions I was glad when the day of the Sydney's Marathon finally arrived. With approximately 5,000 entrants I expected there to be a degree of congestion but was confident that scooters, skateboards, surfboards, buggies and cycles would be banned. Registration for the marathon was open from the Wednesday prior to the event. As it was being held in the basement of Sydney Town Hall on George Street; the building in which Ross works, I was looking forward to attending the Expo there. Other than the fact that it allowed us to meet him for lunch afterwards, the whole registration process turned out to be a huge disappointment; the least said about which the better. I've already made my views clear elsewhere on the marketing aspects versus the captive runners' theme. This was the worst of the lot. I felt sorry for those out-of-town entrants who'd been dragged into the city to what was basically an Asics' shop and then simply handed a bib with a chip attached. There was little there except highly-priced Asics' merchandise and a stall for some obscure Japanese marathon. Melbourne, an equally prestigious but less costly marathon, had already posted out the same number/chip combination meaning that we could travel there at our own convenience and not that of the race organizer. Given its $135 entry fee I'm sure Sydney could have afforded to absorb the cost of the postage too. The only positive feature about the Registration was the facility to leave baggage there for collection after the race.

Sunday's race day started cool and showery: a welcome change from what had been a very hot week in Sydney. Our race numbers were meant to give us free public transport to the Start under the northern end of the famous Harbour Bridge. What the organizers had neglected to mention was that, given the 7 am start, public transport for such an early hour on a Sunday was virtually non-existent from some of the outer suburbs. So, after a very expensive taxi ride we lined up under the Bridge itself, a short stroll away from Luna Park, Sydney's version of Blackpool Pleasure Beach. A Half Marathon had already set off from there an hour earlier and, later that morning, a well-attended 9km Bridge Run plus a Family Fun Run were to leave from the same spot. Altogether there were over 35,000 runners entered in the four events with everyone wanting to make the most of the once-a-year closure of the Bridge.

Almost as much as Paris, Sydney is a Marathon Tourist's dream in that the course takes you on a tour of most of the city's iconic and historic sights. Before setting off I took the opportunity to reacquaint myself with Luna Park, the city's longstanding amusement centre at the harbour's edge. I recall that during the time I'd been living in Australia in the late 70s, there'd been a major fire on the Ghost Train ride, which killed six children and one adult. After this, most of the park was demolished and a new amusement park constructed. When I last visited it a dozen or so years ago this new park had fallen into disrepair and appeared in urgent need of refurbishment. After another redevelopment in 2004, Luna Park reopened in its current format. It contains popular rides such as the Hair Raiser, the Wild Mouse Rollercoaster and the FerrisWheel that continue to attract thousands of Sydneysiders each week. The Park is also one of only two amusement parks in the world that are protected by government legislation with several of its buildings listed on the NSW State Heritage Register.

Leaving the street adjacent to Luna Park at 7am the route took us uphill initially before levelling out on the northern approach to the charismatic Harbour Bridge. Standing proudly above the harbour and instantly recognizable as an iconic symbol of the nation, the Bridge is the world's tallest steel arch bridge. Since 1932 it has connected the northern suburbs of Sydney with the city centre, making it a vital link in the city's transport infrastructure: more than 20,000 cars travel across the bridge each day on its 8 road lanes. It also carries 2 rail tracks as well as pedestrian and cycle ways. There's an interesting story about the Bridge's opening. Just as Jack Lang, the Labour Premier of New South Wales was about to cut the ribbon to officially open the Bridge, a man in a military uniform rode up on horseback, slashing the ribbon with a sword and declaring the Bridge open in the name of the people of New South Wales. The intruder was Francis de Groot, a member of a right-wing paramilitary group, the New Guard, opposed to Lang's leftist policies and angry that a member of the Royal Family had not been asked to the opening ceremony. De Groot successfully appealed against his £5 fine for offensive behaviour and was subsequently awarded an undisclosed out of court settlement for unlawful arrest.

Running across the Bridge reminded me very much of crossing my local Tyne Bridge during the Great North Run but on a much bigger scale. The views too were much more spectacular. Behind us sat Admiralty and Kirribilli Houses; the official residences of the Governor General and the Prime Minister respectively. Ahead of us across the water the world-famous Opera House, our final destination, awaited us some 40 kilometres later. The only obstacles were those caused by fellow runners stopping mid-stride to take the inevitable selfies of themselves in such a famous setting. They would have got better views by forking out the $260 or so to take part in the organized Bridge Climb where every ten minutes, groups of 12, tied together with safety ropes, are taken to the very top of the bridge. Apparently celebrities such as Matt Damon, Sarah Ferguson and Kylie Minogue have all done the climb. Imagine following behind Kylie all the way to the top! Personally, I prefer the view from below, aboard one of the harbour ferries, (costs less too).

After about 4km we left the Bridge behind and headed along the Cahill Expressway, parallel to busy Circular Quay. This is the home of the gold and green city ferries: the workhorses that take both tourists and commuters to all points on the harbour's compass. A train station and nearby bus terminus complete the set to make this area one of the city's major transport hubs. On the eastern side of the Quay lies the controversial Opera Quays development of mega-expensive high rise apartments that somehow managed to get built fifteen years ago despite protestations that they obscure the views of both the Opera House and Botanic Gardens. The locals have dubbed them 'The Toaster' due to their resemblance to the kitchen accessory of that name. The Aussies have an amusing tendency to give nicknames to buildings: the Bridge is 'The Coathanger,' an ungainly apartment block in Manly has been dubbed 'The Toilet Bowl' and, best of all, a shipping facility that regulates the docking of vessels in the harbour, is known as 'The Pill' (because it controls the berths).

Leaving Circular Quay we turned right into historic Macquarie Street where in 2000 I'd stood and watched cyclists in the first Olympic Triathlon flashing past. The street is named after Governor Lachlan Macquarie who was instrumental in setting the course of development in the colony's early years. It was designed as a ceremonial thoroughfare leading from the harbour to the vast expanse of Hyde Park through which we were later to run. Among the buildings commissioned by Maquarie that we were to pass en route were the original Sydney Hospital, Hyde Park Barracks, the State Library, Parliament House, the Mint and St Mary's Cathedral. Some of these buildings including the Barracks have been preserved largely unchanged. Today, the street is the location of the main governmental institutions of New South Wales and the term 'Macquarie Street' is often used as a metonym for the State's government in the same way that 'Whitehall' is used for its British counterpart.

At 5km we were taken into the beautiful Botanic Gardens, a haven of peace and tranquility for office workers and tourists alike in the midst of a busy city. The Gardens occupy 30 hectares of land between the Opera House and Farm Cove where the early settlers struggled to grow vegetables for the hungry colony. As well as providing examples of trees and plants from all over the world, the Gardens also present some of the most stunning views of the harbour. As we made our way around the perimeter of the Gardens a giant, white cruise liner chose that moment to berth alongside our route. The views past the ship back to the Opera House and the Bridge were simply breath-taking. While running we passed Mrs Macquarie's Chair, a well-known local landmark carved out of a rock ledge, where legend has it, the wife of the Governor used to sit forlornly looking out to sea, waiting for ships to arrive.

At 8km we passed the Domain, once the Governor's private park, but now a popular picnic spot with the Art Gallery of NSW and a well-used outdoor swimming pool. 10km brought us out of park and alongside the huge Gothic-style St Mary's Cathedral. A short out-and-back section then took us into Hyde Park, named after its London equivalent. This is the oldest public parkland in Australia and was used in the early days mainly as a venue for sporting contests: particularly cricket, rugby, boxing and even horse racing. These have long since moved elsewhere and today the park is best known for its spectacular Archibald Fountain, designed in honour of Australia's contribution to World War 1. There's also an Anzac War Memorial, a Pool of Remembrance and even a giant chess set on leaving the park.

We then entered on an unremarkable long, straight section taking us out of the city along Oxford Street, (home to Sydney's gay community), Flinders Street and into Moore Park Road. At this point I was running and chatting with Bob Fickel, Chairman of Australia's 100 Marathon Club. On his 229th marathon that day, Bob was four ahead of me. Recognising kindred spirits we managed to keep in touch. Bob was subsequently kind enough to invite me to his club's post-race celebration after the following month's Melbourne Marathon. Moore Park at 14km is the home to some of Sydney's premier sporting and entertainment arenas. The first stadium we passed, the Allianz Stadium, is home to the Sydney Roosters Rugby League team, the Waratahs Rugby Union team and Sydney FC Soccer club. The previous evening I'd watched on TV one of the season's rugby preliminary finals being played there in front of a sell-out crowd. We also passed the Horden Pavillion, an important entertainment venue, next door to the Royal Hall of Industries, (fondly remembered in my time in Oz as the Showbag Pavillion in the days of the annual Royal Easter Show). Most impressive of all though, was to run past the famous Sydney Cricket Ground: the ground where Bradman scored his record 452 not out and where England caused controversy with their bodyline bowling tactics in the 1930s. The ground is also home to the notorious Hill where, fuelled by alcohol, the rivalry between Australian and English supporters often reaches boiling point.

Next came a giant loop around yet another park; this time Centennial Park, where the half-way point was reached. Emerging from the park at 23km there followed a slightly uphill drag back along Anzac Parade, Flinders and Oxford Streets, back again through Hyde Park and on through the near deserted Central Business District to arrive again at Circular Quay. At this stage I was running quite well and had managed to maintain an even 6km per minute pace up to 32km. The final 10km were, as usual, the hardest part of the race. Passing the liner-shaped International Passenger Terminal we made our way under the southern side of the Bridge. The area around here is known as the Rocks and was where Captain Phillip of the First Fleet proclaimed the establishment of Sydney Town in 1788. It's the historic heart of convict era Sydney and home at one time to the notorious 'pushes' – gangs of louts who brawled continuously and mugged passers-by. It still retains something of its original character and, for those who like their pubs with atmosphere, it's a great place to visit. We headed there immediately after the race, to the upstairs bar of the Glenmore Hotel with its sweeping views across to the Opera House and the back-markers arriving at the finish line. The food there was pretty basic pub fare but, with lashings of carbohydrate, just what I needed after finishing a marathon.

The final 8km out and back to Darling Harbour along Hickson and Sussex streets were the least scenic on the course; the views being obstructed by the multi-million dollar Barangaroo development of high-rise apartments and casinos designed to attract future, mainly Chinese, high-rollers. Darling Harbour itself was once a grimy, industrial docks area until the State Government decided on its regeneration as part of the 1988 Bi-centenary project. Today, its numerous attractions make it a favourite place for Sydneysiders to spend their leisure time. Returning back under the Bridge at 40km we enjoyed a pleasant run-in along the harbour to the finish at the Opera House steps. I was delighted to see Mo, Ross and his partner Hayley among the huge crowds cheering us on as we turned the final corner at Circular Quay. The World Heritage listed Opera House, such an icon of the nation, was an excellent place to end the race, with its white roofs evocative of full sails complemented by the sparkling blue water of the harbour. I'd first visited this in 1973 shortly after completion and recall being spellbound by its appearance on that occasion, never thinking that 41 years later I'd be finishing a marathon on its forecourt. I'd even got to see inside this time too as Ross had managed to secure tickets for my favourite musician, the legendary Bob Dylan, as a surprise Father's Day treat two weeks earlier.

I was satisfied with my run and pleased to finish well under my targeted 4 hour 30 minutes. Under the steps there was a dedicated marathon recovery area where we were handed our medal and T-shirt. There were also the usual freebies to be had. Nearby in the Botanic Gardens, a whole tented village had been erected incorporating all sorts of stalls selling food and drink, (including Manly's local Four Pines Brewery stall), allowing runners to sit out in the sun with their families and celebrate. We headed off to the Glenmore and the Rocks.

As you can imagine, travelling and socializing for six weeks in Australia involved an awful lot of eating (and drinking!) out. Australia has come a long way from the days when it appeared to survive on a combination of meat pies smothered in sauce and giant steaks sizzling on a BBQ; all washed down by copious quantities of cold lager. Sydney has become one of the great restaurant capitals in the world, offering a wide range of sophisticated restaurants catering for every imaginable cuisine. Many ethnic areas reflecting the city's diverse immigrant communities have become noted for that community's particular food speciality. For example, Sydney has a large, central Chinatown district near Haymarket for those who enjoy Chinese cooking. East Sydney is known for its Italian cuisine, Anzac Parade for Indonesian food, Surry Hills for Turkish and Lebanese cooking while, rather surprisingly, the famous beach area of Bondi contains a number of Jewish restaurants. I'd like to say that I sampled the food in each of these places. I didn't; there was no need to when each of these cuisines could be found within walking distance of our Manly apartment. I did make a point though of taking the ferry across to the world famous Doyle's restaurant in Watson's Bay, a place I'd last visited some 40 years earlier when, even then, it had a reputation as the haunt of the rich and famous. With the likes of Russell Crowe having been spotted there recently, I wasn't surprised to find that my plate of fish and chips (except they didn't call it that) was over two and a half times more expensive than what I was paying in Manly.

Before leaving for Australia we'd received many warnings from both friends and family who'd recently returned about the excessive cost of eating out. We found most main courses in mid-range restaurants to come within the $20 to $25 mark; not a great deal different from what you'd pay in the UK. What we did find expensive was the cost of a half-decent bottle of wine to go with our meal; this was often more than the cost of the meal itself – ridiculous really when you consider that the wine is produced right on the doorstep. It had us nostalgic for the golden days we spent in Perth when a 5-litre flagon of good Australian wine could be purchased for the princely sum of $2. Times certainly have changed and not necessarily for the better. We soon learned to avoid any restaurant that didn't offer BYO (bring your own wine) and to nip into Coles Liquorland for a bottle of the on-special $6 Cabernet Sauvignon to go with our meal.

Of course, with the country's booming economy and the rise of the A$ against the £GB, Sydney certainly is an expensive city for UK citizens to visit these days. However, a lot of the expense can be avoided by anyone sensible and frugal with their money. We were able to save on food costs by shopping in the big supermarkets and cooking at home in our apartment. Likewise, though the price of a schooner, (425 ml) of beer was in the $6 to $7 range in local hotels, a 30 can case of 'Hammer and Tongs' lager could be bought for $30 in Coles supermarket. (We did a lot of our shopping in Coles!) Even eating out needn't to be that expensive. Many of the restaurants we frequented offered mid-week specials of which to take advantage. Monday evening's goulash in an Eastern European restaurant could be bought for $11, Tuesday and Wednesday's Thai menu in Manly's 'Pat Ploy' was priced at $10.95, (it was hard to get our friend Ross James out of there). On Wednesday the local Four Pines microbrewery had an excellent offer of a huge rack of ribs and a pint for $25, (the pint alone would have cost $10). Other nights had other 'specials' to enjoy without any deterioration in the quality of the food served.

As with food, Australia has made giant strides in its attitude to the consumption of alcohol in the 40+ years I've been visiting. The Barry Humphries inspired, Private Eye comic-strip image of the puking and chundering Australian beer-swiller is now almost a thing of the past. Australians drink a moderate 9.89 litres of (pure) alcohol each year putting them behind the UK, but ahead of the US. While beer is still the average Aussie's favourite tipple, per capita consumption is declining annually with the growing popularity of wine and ready-to-drink mixed spirits. What has also changed considerably is the rising popularity of micro-breweries filling the market-place with high-end beers to the disadvantage of many of the traditional suppliers. When I moved to Australia in 1972 virtually every state had its own monopoly brewery. In West Australia it was almost impossible to purchase any draught lager other than Swan, produced by the brewery of the same name.

Queensland had Castlemaine, South Australia was Coopers, Victoria was Tooheys and so on. Today many traditional suppliers have been forced by competition to invest heavily in boutique operators, especially with a number of the latter (like Manly's Four Pines) combining their brewery operations with catering ventures on the same premises. From past experience, I had no expectations of finding the perfect dark beer in the Sydney area so wasn't disappointed when I didn't. What did surprise me though, was the number of darker beers now available in what is often considered Foster's Lager Land. It isn't, Foster's is not a particularly popular drink in its own country. Most of these darker ales are produced by some of the aforementioned microbreweries: like the Four Pines 'Dark Bitter,' 'Endeavour' brewed in Sydney by Endeavour Vintage Co. and 'White Rabbit' from a Victorian micro-brewery. Even the big breweries are getting in on the act and recognizing that not everyone enjoys weak, pale lager. Tooheys, for example brews a 'Tooheys Old' while Carlton has chipped in with a 'Carlton Dark.' All of these are between 4.5% and 5.5% so aren't strong enough to meet the Manford criteria for the perfect dark beer but are nonetheless worthwhile purchases. I certainly miss my daily 'Endeavour' in the perfect setting of Manly's Wharf Bar watching the ferries come and go as the sun set in Manly Cove. All that remains, as I mentioned earlier, is to return as soon as possible to complete the Australian Sweep.

Waiting at Luna Park before the Start of the Sydney Marathon

Time to relax by Sydney Harbour after the race with Mo and Ross

REPUBLIC OF IRELAND

DUBLIN MARATHON

I've had a soft spot for Dublin ever since being captivated by J P Donleavy's novel 'The Ginger Man' while at university in the late 1960s. Once considered so raunchy it was banned in both Ireland and the USA, it follows the hedonistic, hard-drinking life of an American student living in Dublin, providing a spirited and incisive account of the city at that time. It's the one book I can read over and over again without losing interest. I am reminded by the antics of Donleavy's anti-hero, the libidinous Dangerfield, doing his drunken 'goat dance' through the streets of Dublin every time I visit. I was surprised at a friend's reaction to my decision to include this chapter in a book about foreign marathons - arguing that I couldn't include Dublin, 'Because Ireland wasn't a foreign country.' Try telling that to an Irishman and observe his reaction. The bullet holes put there during the Easter Rebellion against British rule in 1916, still visible in the Post Office building on O'Connell Street, are a constant reminder of the country's struggle for independence. Following the Irish War of Independence and subsequent Anglo-Irish Treaty, Ireland gained effective independence from the UK in 1922. Initially a dominion within the British Commonwealth, the Free State received full legislative independence in 1931. A new constitution was adopted in 1937, by which the formal name of the previous dominion became Ireland. Finally in 1948 under the Republic of Ireland Act, the country was formally declared a republic. These days the title Republic of Ireland is often used to distinguish the southern half of the island from its northern counterpart which has remained under British rule. So, 'Yes' Ireland is definitely a separate country.

At the time of writing, despite recent economic setbacks, Ireland still rates among the wealthiest countries in the world in terms of per capita GDP. In 2011 and 2013 it was ranked seventh most-developed country by the UN's Human Development Index. The country achieved considerable prosperity during the 1990's and early into the 21st century, during which time it became known as the 'Celtic Tiger.' This prosperity was halted by the 2008 financial crisis within the country. Signs of this down-turn were very much evident during this present visit with Dublin city centre in particular looking much more down-at-heel than it appeared during my previous trip there for the 2007 marathon.

Dublin is, of course, the largest city as well as the capital of the country. The Greater Dublin Area's population is expanding rapidly and is expected to reach 2 million by 2020. It has experienced a significant level of net immigration in recent years with the greatest numbers coming from the UK, Poland and Lithuania. I was surprised by the large increase in numbers of Polish shops in the centre since last visiting. Situated at the mouth of the River Liffey, Dublin is bordered to the south by a low mountain range and surrounded by flat farmland to the north and west. The river effectively divides the city into two areas unimaginatively described as the Northside and the Southside. The former is generally seen as working class while the Southside is regarded as home to the middle to upper-middle classes. Certainly, the region to the south of the Liffey appears much more affluent and genteel to that in the north. Seemingly the area around Dublin Bay has been inhabited by humans since pre-historic times and occupied in turn by both the Vikings and the Normans before the British. I'm told the name Dublin comes from 'Duibhlinn,' meaning 'black pool' – though where the black pool is I never did find out.

The Dublin region is very much the economic centre of Ireland and was at the forefront of economic expansion during the Celtic Tiger period. So much so that in 2009 it was ranked as the fourth richest city in the world by purchasing power and tenth richest by personal income. These figures surprise me; that is not the impression gained in 2014. Apart from Guinness, the brewing giants, many of the city's traditional industries have declined to be replaced by IT and global pharmaceutical companies. The likes of Google, Microsoft, Amazon, Pay Pal, Yahoo, Facebook and Twitter now have European headquarters or operational bases in the city.

I'd hardly got off the plane from the long flight back from the Melbourne Marathon in Australia in October 2014 before I was back on another one, fighting jet-lag, from Newcastle to Dublin. Fortunately this flight was to last less than an hour. On arrival it was a simple matter to connect with the Airlink Express route 747 bus to the centre. It takes 30 minutes for the 6 mile journey at a cost of 6 euros for a single ticket – the 10 euros return is better value. Buses leave at 15 minute intervals both there and back. There's also an Aircoach service for the same price. This was to be my 5th Dublin Marathon since the early 1990s and I'd particularly chosen to do this one as my friend Dave Goodwin had been selected to act as pace-maker for one of the official pace-making groups. The irony was that Dave is a 2:55 marathon runner these days and the group he'd been selected to pace was the 4:20 one. Dave was going to have to rein himself in a bit to achieve this target. I reckoned on accompanying him at my usual 10 minute per mile pace to help slow him down. The role of pace-maker in a big city marathon is not a bad job if you can get it. As well as receiving free food and hotel accommodation, Dave was given a full race kit of vest and shorts as well as a tidy cash sum for his efforts. Mind you, the job comes with responsibilities, with the organizers insisting that each mile is run at even pace throughout and that the pace-maker must finish within 30 seconds of the advertised time. No pressure there then.

This was to be the 35th, and probably final, edition of the Bank Holiday Monday event. I'd heard that the organisers were planning to move it to a Sunday slot next time (they did!). As usual, there was a group of 23 runners who'd done each one among the record-breaking field of 15,000. Having had all these years in which to practice, the organisation of virtually every aspect of the event was faultless: from the Expo, to the arrangements at the Start, the on-course marshalling of over 1,000 volunteers and the efficient handling of the congested Finish area. As usual the race Expo took place in the Royal Dublin Showground building in Ballsbridge some three miles out of town. This was no mere marketing trap; instead it contained a number of interesting exhibits like the Dublin Marathon Museum. There were talks from past winners, nutrition experts as well as hot food on offer. We were given our number/chip, towel and official Marathon bag containing assorted goodies, (like energy bars, drinks and spaghetti).

Race morning saw us separated into three different time zones according to the colour of our bibs. Each zone started 10 minutes apart with the Orange for the sub 3:50 leaving at 9 am. Then followed Green for 3:50 to 4:15 and finally Blue for 4:15 plus. Dave and I were in the latter as we were shepherded to the start line in Fitzwilliam Square. The route has changed a few times since I first did this event 20 years ago but has recently settled on the familiar course that I last ran in 2007. The only change this year, forced on the organisers due to road works in O'Connell Street, the city's main thoroughfare, meant following the south bank of the River Liffey towards the entrance to the giant Phoenix Park. Lying west of the city centre, its 11 km perimeter wall enclosing an area of over 700 hectares makes the park one of the largest walled city parks in Europe. It houses Dublin Zoo and its 700 animals as well as the historic Magazine Fort and several famous monuments, including the Papal Cross, the Wellington Monument and the Phoenix Monument. The park hosts the Irish Grand Prix, the popular Great Ireland 10K Run as well as artists such as Coldplay, Snow Patrol, the Stone Roses, Robbie Williams and the Red Hot Chili Peppers among others. Arriving in the park after 3 miles we took a slightly uphill gradient through the centre before emerging at 6 miles and losing the height we'd gained down College and Tower Roads. 8 miles brought us back into the park for a short loop to the 10 mile mark and back across the Liffey to start climbing again.

This pattern of gaining and losing height continued throughout the race. Though none of the gradients were particularly steep it did affect the ability to maintain an even pace. Dublin is certainly not a PB course because of the ups and downs and things were not helped on the day by strong swirling winds and unseasonably muggy conditions. At 13 miles we crossed the Grand Canal just before the half-way mark. Reaching this in exactly 2:10 meant that Dave had got his pacing spot-on. I'd had enough though. I don't enjoy running in a group and by this stage, though the mind was willing, the legs appeared to have been left behind on an aeroplane somewhere east of Dublin and west of Australia. Somewhat reluctantly I opted to plough a lone furrow back to the finish and struggled on through increasingly uninspiring and un-scenic urban stretches, punctuated only by a pleasant section in Bushy Park at 17 miles and a skirt around the grounds of University College at 22 to 23 miles. The final 2 miles along the dead-straight Merrion and Shelbourne Roads got me going again and it was a relief to turn into Mount Street to see the finish gantry 800 metres away in the distance. A good proportion of this was run over a blue carpet alongside thousands of cheering spectators. In fact, spectator support was one of the highlights of the event. There were numerous places on the course where large crowds had gathered to offer very vocal encouragement; in many ways reminiscent of the early days of the Great North Run.

I finished in a disappointing 4 hours 41 while Dave did what it said on the tin and got his followers home in 4:19:48. This was despite his pace-making partner throwing in the towel, unable to go any further after 20 miles. Our reward was a really nice medal and, in the tradition of the Dublin Marathon, a long-sleeved T-shirt – a much more sensible and useful gift than yet another of the ubiquitous short-sleeved ones. It was a generous goody bag too, containing chocolate, drinks and crisps among other treats.

I thought this was a brilliant event. Promoted as 'The Friendly Marathon' it certainly lives up to its name. It's one of the few big city marathons I've done recently that is just that: a marathon with no Half, 10k, 5k or fun run getting in the way. Dublin too is an exciting city to visit. There's virtually not one, but two, pubs on every corner and in every one of them you bet there's someone playing live music. That night the city was awash in a sea of lime green Dublin Marathon long-sleeved T-shirts as runners celebrated a great day out.

As I've mentioned, this was my 5th attempt at running the Dublin Marathon, (slowest too). Over the years I've gradually worked my way through the full tourist itinerary so feel at least partly qualified to make recommendations to fellow runners. Depending on your viewpoint, Dublin has the enviable/unenviable reputation as a city that likes its alcohol. Stag parties visit in their thousands drawn by the twin attractions of Temple Bar and the Guinness brewery. I find them both somewhat over-rated.

Temple Bar consists of a warren of streets just south of the Liffey. It is promoted as the cultural centre of the city and, indeed, does include many Irish cultural institutions such the Irish Film Institute, the Project Arts Centre and the Irish Photography Centre. It also includes a large number of Dublin's rowdiest pubs that, after dark, become a major centre for nightlife. It's to this area that the stag groups make a bee-line on arrival. Attracted by the live music, most of the pubs are full to the rafters with noisy revellers. At times it's difficult to be heard or to get to the bar to buy a drink. It's definitely the place for the younger crowd though, saying that, Dave, Martin Bush and I (all no spring-chickens) had a great time celebrating in Fitzsimons on finishing the marathon. For those who prefer a quieter time I'd recommend Fitzgeralds, facing the Liffey just around the corner or the authentic Oval Bar, housed in a beautiful Victorian building on Abbey Street.

The number one tourist destination in Dublin continues to be a visit to the famous Guinness Storehouse. This provides an interesting journey into the heart of the Guinness brand and company. This historical building is considered part of Ireland's heritage and, over the years, has been continually updated to create a blend of historical tradition with contemporary design. Entry on the door costs 18 euros though an Early Bird price of 14.40 euros can be booked online in advance. For the money you get to visit the Atrium and stand at the bottom of the world's largest pint glass that rises up through the centre. There's also a talk by the Master Brewer, guiding you step-by-step through the brewing process after which you are invited to sample your first drink of the visit. On the fourth floor there are lessons in how to pour the perfect pint. (I'm not sure the bartender in Fitzsimons has been to this one). You're handed a certificate to prove you can do this before being treated to one in the Perfect Pint Bar. After a visit to the Gravity Bar on the seventh floor most visitors head for the ground floor Store to spend yet more money on Guinness memorabilia, including your own personalised bottle of Foreign Extra Stout.

While still on the alcohol theme, some of the literary-minded among you might be interested in the Dublin Literary Pub Crawl. Costing 12 euros and leaving at 7.30 each night from The Duke Pub, just off Grafton Street. This takes groups of those who enjoy combining their pint with a cultural twist, on a crawl from pub to pub with professional actors performing the works of Dublin's most famous writers: Joyce, Beckett, Oscar Wilde and Brendan Behan among them. Unfortunately, you still have to pay for your own pint.

This is by no means the only walking tour available to those who prefer others to lay on their entertainment for them. For anyone interested in the history of Ireland's struggle for independence there's a '1916 Rebellion Walking Tour.' Here, the authors of 'The Easter Rising' will take you to visit relevant sites of the rebellion and provide an understanding of this historic occasion that precipitated the formation of the Irish Republic. Virtually every interest is catered for by these walking tours and they are a good way to satisfy those with specialist interests. There's an Architectural Tour, an Arts Tour, a Waterways Walking Tour and Guided Photography Tours: all for a similar price.

If it's free entertainment you're looking for, much of what's available is very much based on a cultural theme. The Visit Dublin website, for example, provides a list of the Top 10 Free Attractions in the city. These include: The National Gallery, where you can examine an original Caravaggio, The National Museum displaying an exhibition of ice-age bodies and the Science Gallery, where you can get involved in a hands-on experiment. There's also, among others, the Botanic Gardens, the National Library and the city centre

Chester Beatty Library containing artistic treasures of the great cultures and religions of the world. After visiting that little lot you'll be looking forward to the evening's Pub Crawl.

Dublin is unmistakably Ireland's cultural capital as evidenced by the numbers of books and films that have been located there. Even just walking around the place you can almost feel its cultural heritage seeping up through its streets. Apart from 'The Ginger Man,' Joyce's masterpiece 'Ulysses' is set in Dublin, as is Roddy Doyle's 'Paddy Clarke Ha-Ha-Ha,' Flann O'Brien's 'At Swim-Two-Birds' and Sheridan Le Fanu's 'The Cock and Anchor.' A number of well-known films have also been located in the city including 'Educating Rita' – set in Liverpool but filmed in Trinity and University Colleges. Roddy Doyle's Trilogy 'The Commitments,' 'The Snapper' and 'The Van' were all based in 1980's Dublin, as too was 'Once' one of the most widely loved romantic films and 'My Left Foot' the true story of Christy Brown, an artist born with cerebral palsy played by Daniel Day-Lewis.

In short, Dublin has something for everyone. It's a great city for the marathon tourist and I've hardly scratched the surface here in describing things to see and do. Grafton Street, with its famous statue of Molly Malone, (there's another of Thin Lizzy's Phil Lynott nearby), is a good place for shopping. Dublin Castle is one of its oldest landmarks while, at the centre of O'Connell Street, the giant Spire of Dublin is one of its newest. Officially titled 'The Monument of Light' this 398ft, needle-shaped, stainless steel tower is intended to mark Dublin's place in the 21st century. At night the base of the monument is lit and the top is illuminated to provide a beacon across the city. Finally, some mention must be made of Trinity College just south of the Liffey. It's worth a visit if only to see the Book of Kells; an illustrated manuscript created by Irish monks circa 800 AD.

I won't go on about food and drink in Dublin. Drink, as you can imagine, became the mandatory Guinness – certainly a dark beer, if not a perfect one. Though people wax lyrical about how they can only get the perfect pint of Guinness in Dublin, I'm not convinced. The Guinness I drink in Guardamar, (where I have my apartment in

Spain), for 3 euros a pint is just as tasty as Dublin's version that costs two euros more. Who says Guinness doesn't travel?

As for food, I could be wrong here but I doubt if Dublin has what can be called a specialized cuisine. On each of my five visits I've tended to simply stick with the simple carbohydrate diet of the marathon runner: fish and chips in a café on O'Connell Street for 8.95 euros the night before the race and Pizza, chips and salad in the restaurant virtually next door post-race for 9.95 euros. As the saying goes, 'it ain't fancy but it's cheap.'

With 100 Club legend Danny Kay before the start in Dublin

Celebrating in Temple Bar with Dave and Martin Bush

TURKEY

ISTANBUL MARATHON

The Istanbul Marathon, often referred to as the Eurasia Marathon, provides a unique opportunity to run on two Continents within the same race and within a fascinating city steeped in history and tradition. For centuries Turkey in general, and Istanbul in particular, have been said to form the dividing line between Europe and Asia. I'd never visited either previously and was anxious to find out for myself whether the time-worn cliché comparing both to 'a bridge between East and West' was, in fact, correct. Russia apart, Turkey is the only nation incorporating both Asian and European territory, though given its turbulent history of settlement from every direction many would argue that the term 'battlefield' rather than a 'bridge' is a more appropriate description.

Turkey's location at the crossroads of the two Continents, controlling the entrance to the Black Sea, makes it a country of significant geographical importance. It has been continuously inhabited and fought over for over 10,000 years, first by various ancient Anatolian civilizations, then by in succession: the Greeks, the Romans, the Byzantine Empire , the Mongols and finally by the Ottoman Empire. From the late 13th century the Ottomans united what is now known as Anatolia and created an empire incorporating much of Southeastern Europe, Western Asia and North Africa. The Empire subsequently fell into a long period of decline, resulting in 1919 Turkish War of Independence led by Mustapha Kemal Ataturk (commonly known as 'The father of modern Turkey) and the establishment of the modern Republic of Turkey with Ataturk as its first president.

The English name Turkey first appeared in the late 14th century and is believed to be derived from medieval Latin. Today's modern Turkey, post Ataturk, is a secular, constitutional republic with a diverse cultural heritage – currently undergoing a process of Westernisation of its Ottoman origins. Its official language is Turkish and is spoken by approximately 85% of the population of which about 75% are ethnic Turks. The remainder consists of various minorities, mainly Armenians, Greeks, Jews, Kurds, Albanians and Georgians. The vast majority of the population belongs to the Muslim faith. Asian Turkey, which includes 97% of the country is separated from its European counterpart by the Bosphorus, the Sea of Marmara and the Dardanelles mountain range. The Asian section has a much more mountainous landscape than the West and is the source of major rivers such as the Euphrates and the Tigris and contains the Bible's Mount Ararat, Turkey's highest point at over 5,000 metres.

Turkey is best known economically for its large automotive industry which produced over a million vehicles in 2012. Turkish shipbuilding is also highly regarded for their production of oil and chemical tankers, while brands like Beko and Vestel are among the largest producers of electronic and home appliances in Europe. Tourism too, has experienced rapid growth in recent years and is now an important part of the Turkish economy, ranking it as the 6th most popular tourism destination in the world in 2013. Turkey's growing economy and diplomatic initiatives have led to its recognition as a regional power and, having joined the European Customs Union in 1995 it has now started negotiations to become a full member of the European Economic Community. Presumably this is why the euro is quoted alongside the official currency of the Turkish Lira for some transactions in Istanbul. At the time of my visit in November 2014 the exchange rate was £1 = 3.25TL. For ease of calculation I worked on the premise that 10 lira was the equivalent of £3.

Having done my homework on the country all that now remained was to travel to its most famous city, Istanbul, for some hands-on research. My friend Dave Goodwin had recently been to

Istanbul and had returned with glowing reports of both the city and its marathon. He was also good enough to provide Mo and I with written recommendations about both. His advice to base ourselves at the Hotel Basileus in the Sultanahmet district was most useful. Not only was this an excellent hotel in a brilliant location for both sightseeing and the marathon, but the staff was amongst the friendliest and most helpful I've encountered on my travels. Nothing was too much for them and they were happy to go out of their way to ensure our stay was as comfortable as possible. Initially we were suspicious of the motives behind their seeming over-friendliness but we needed have worried; there was no hidden agenda, they weren't trying to sell tours on commission, advice was given impartially and with our best interests in mind. I'd recommend the hotel to anyone visiting Istanbul. Booking direct on the hotel's own website also includes a free airport pick-up arranged by the hotel: a saving of in the region of 25 euros on the quoted price.

We travelled to Istanbul direct from Edinburgh with Turkish Airlines on the Thursday before the race. This doesn't seem to be a popular route judging by the number of empty seats on the planes both there and back. It did allow us to travel in some comfort though with the 4 hour 15 minute flight allowing sufficient time to watch two full-length feature films and a decent meal, (and drink), in both directions. Without a pre-arranged pick-up it's possible to reach the city centre by a tiring journey by both tram and metro involving the purchase of jetons (plastic tokens) for access to the platforms. Tokens can be bought from a cashier or from an automatic dispenser on the platform that accepts lira bank notes. You'll need to purchase a 4 lira token for the 3 stops to Zeytinburnu on the red metro line in the Aksary direction, and then a further 4 lira token at the nearby tram station for the approximately 15 short stops to Sultanahmet Square. The Hotel Basileus is a short walk downhill past the Blue Mosque from there. Be warned though, both trams and metro can be ridiculously overcrowded at most times of the day with commuters squashed into carriages like sardines in a tin. Be careful too, on arrival at the airport that you don't make our mistake of reaching the passport booths without first having forked out £20 each at a nearby kiosk for an entry visa. We knew nothing about this. Perhaps this was what one of the stewardesses on the plane was mumbling about in one of her unintelligible in-flight announcements. Either way, it left a nasty first impression of the country. The only currencies acceptable at the visa booths were £GB or $US – fortunately we carried some of the former. I've since learnt that it's possible to buy visas online much more cheaply prior to departure at evisa.gov.tr/en/

If you're intending to stay in Istanbul for any length of time, a better option than continually feeding coins into machines for plastic tokens, would be to purchase an Istanbulkart. Two of the lads I met up with had done just that and found it easy to use. It's a plastic card that looks like a credit card and can be used as a ticket on trams, metro, buses, suburban trains and even the cross-Bosphorus ferries. You simply touch the card to a reader when entering the platform and top it up as and when required at designated booths around the city.

On arrival, the twin personas of Istanbul are immediately apparent. In the streets around the main shopping areas it looks very much like a European city but, away from these you enter another age and another culture. Istanbul is the only city in the world to have been capital to consecutive Christian and Islamic empires, both of which have made their own impact and left their own legacies. The difference between Sultanahmet's historical and cultural centre and the majority of the city has to be seen to be believed. Though Ankara has replaced Istanbul as Turkey's capital, the old imperial capital maintains a cultural and economic dominance and the traditional sights and ancient buildings stand in stark contrast to ever-encroaching Western influences. As a visitor from Western Europe, used to the way the McDonalds, Starbucks and KFCs have taken over our cities, I much preferred the Istanbul of the Blue Mosque, Aya Sofya and the Grand Bazaar. But, then again, I don't have to live there.

Actually, being surrounded on three sides by water makes Istanbul not such a bad city in which to live – provided, of course, you've got easy access to a shoreline. The city is divided in two by the Bosphorus, over which we were soon to run. This 30km narrow strait is one of the world's most strategic waterways, linking the Black Sea to the north with the Sea of Marmara in the south, separating Europe from Asia in the process. Flowing into the southern end of the strait from the European side is the famous Golden Horn, an inlet of water starting as two small streams about 7km from the Bosphorus itself. The city's affluent residential areas are situated along the shores of the Sea of Marmara and fronting the Bosphorus' hilly banks while light industry dominates along the Horn. This latter body effectively separates the European side of the city into two distinct city centres: the Sultanahmet district on one side and the business cum shopping centre of Taksim on the other. The iconic Galata Bridge is the joining link.

Dave Goodwin had advised us to build enough time into our itinerary to be able to take in all that Istanbul had to offer. Unfortunately, constrained by flight schedules, this just wasn't possible. After our four nights there we realized that we'd hardly scratched the city's surface and, like Dave, we'll go back to take in what we have missed. Istanbul is a truly fascinating city, perhaps the most interesting and impressive I've ever visited. There's so much to see and do at every turn, I'm not sure how long I'd need to stay to do it justice. I think that the best I can do for anyone reading this who's considering going to Istanbul is to set out what, in my opinion, are the must-see sights of the city. Bear in mind though, that in order to get maximum enjoyment from your visit you need to develop a pretty thick skin towards the hordes of persistently irritating touts that pester your every movement, either wanting to be your guide, your new best friend or offering to sell you everything at a discount from carpets to cruises and insisting that theirs is the perfect restaurant in which you should eat. Most of these can be got rid of with a firm but polite, 'no thank you.' It's the ones that don't go away that you have to worry about!

Most short stay visitors spend the majority of their time in the Sultanahmet district, home to Istanbul's major sightseeing attractions. No visit would be complete without spending some time at the following: the Topkapi Palace, heart of the former Ottaman Empire, the Sultanahmet Camii (better known as the Blue Mosque); and the Aya Sofya, the former Byzantine church converted into a mosque. These three attractions are within a stone's throw of one another on an elevated site overlooking the junction of the three major waterways mentioned earlier. A short walk away are the equally worth visiting ancient Hippodrome, the underground Basilica Cistern and the Kapah Carsi (Grand Bazaar) the largest covered bazaar in the world. With apologies to the numerous landmarks I've omitted, I'd also suggest spending time on the interesting Galata Bridge and, above all, making sure that you take one of the many boat cruises along the Bosphorus.

Of all the attractions on offer the latter interested me most. I was really keen to see more of this famous waterway than a mere run across the Bosphorus Bridge during the course of the marathon would have allowed. I wasn't interested in some of the shorter, more expensive cruises on boats of dubious sea-worthiness touted by the scam artists lining the quays. I wanted to sail all the way up to the entrance to the Black Sea and only Sehir Hatari, Istanbul's official ferry company provided this option. And good value it was too for an 8 hour trip leaving at 10.35am daily from close to the Galata Bridge - all for a mere 25 lira. Sailing to Rumeli Kavagi and Anadolu Kavagi, the two most distant villages on the European and Asian sides respectively, each way takes about 90 minutes with the ferry making about 5 short stops to let people on and off. We passed under both the Bosphorus bridges en route and it was a sobering thought, looking up, to remind myself that I'd be running over the first of these the next morning. It was interesting to observe that on either side of the strait on virtually every inch of shoreline not designated as a nature reserve, affluent Turks had managed to build their dream homes. Meanwhile giant oil tankers lumbered past us on their way to cities on the Black Sea The big disappointment of the voyage was the almost 3 hour 'lunchbreak' wasted in the truly awful Anadolu Kavagi where, on disembarking, we were immediately accosted by gangs of restaurant owners who, dependent on the boat trade for a living, simply refused to take no for an answer. In desperation, Mo and I attempted to walk out of the village to a ruined castle on a nearby hill. Rather scarily, we were followed menacingly by a large pack of feral dogs before our way was finally blocked by military installations guarded by men with very large guns. We couldn't get back on the boat quick enough. It almost ruined the day.

Arriving back in the city at 4.30pm we next explored the numerous restaurants built under the arches on both sides of the Galata Bridge. Most of these specialized in fish dishes at a reasonable price. Perhaps it was no coincidence that the parapets above were lined toe-to-toe with anglers casting into the water below. A Balik Ekmek Salata (smoked fish in a roll with salad) made a tasty afternoon snack for a mere 6 lira in the Cansun Café below the Eminonu side of the bridge.

Next it was uphill to the Grand Bazaar. I was dreading the crowds but Mo was intent on using her haggling skills to purchase accessories for her belly dancing classes that were unavailable in the UK. With sixty six streets and alleys, over four thousand shops, numerous storehouses, banks, moneylenders, a post office, a mosque, police station and health centre, the Bazaar is said to be the largest of its type in the world. You're almost certain to get lost at some stage in the labyrinth of alleyways leading off in all directions. Most of these are poorly marked and their signs are often obscured by goods hung up for sale. If you can stand the mayhem and the hurly-burly, the noise, chaos and confusion it's an incredibly atmospheric place to spend some time. Virtually everything is for sale: from rugs and carpets, to gold and jewellery to bags, materials, leather items and shoes galore. I had to laugh at a trader's sign boldly advertising 'genuine fake watches.' Mo got the things she needed at considerably less than the initial asking price. It's all a big game where, seemingly, everyone's a winner. There's another famous bazaar hidden behind the 'New' Mosque on the waterfront, known as the Spice Bazaar (for obvious reasons), that's also worth a visit. Though not as large or as atmospheric as the Grand Bazaar, you can't help to be attracted by the spicy aromas wafting out from the entrance as you approach. Spices are not the only commodity sold there. You can haggle over many of the items that are also found inside its more famous counterpart.

Most of the other attractions I've listed are all virtually within metres of Sultanahmet Square. Previously known as The Hippodrome of Constantinople, (Istanbul's former name), this large rectangular area was the sporting and social centre of Constantinople during its time as capital of the Byzantine Empire. Chariot races were held here on a regular basis with huge amounts bet on the outcome. The remains of the race track can still be seen. The Hippodrome was also the scene of the lavish circumcision ceremonies of the Sultan's many sons! Worth inspecting are the various monuments brought to the city to improve its image by the Emperor Constantine. Among these are the Serpent Column, cast to celebrate the victory of the Greeks over the Persians and the Egyptian Obelisk, brought from the Temple of Luxor.

Cross the Square to the fountain and you are confronted on either side by breathtaking vistas of what have to be two of the most beautiful architectural buildings in the world: The Blue Mosque and the Aya Sophia. At times, I found it difficult to know which way to look or even to turn away; both buildings are so inspiring. I'd been to Pisa last year for the marathon there and visited the World Heritage 'Field of Dreams,' a landscaped, walled square containing the Leaning Tower, Duomo (Cathedral), Bell Tower and Baptistry. At the time I thought it was the finest example of medieval architecture I was likely to see. I was wrong. The combination of architectural gems in Sultanahmet Square is far superior. The buildings are even more breathtaking when illuminated at night, especially when viewed through the multi-coloured water emanating from the fountain in between. I could fill pages writing about all the things they contain and still not do them justice. In truth, these mosques really do fit into the have to be seen to be believed category.

The Blue Mosque, the most visually stunning and photogenic has to be my favourite. Briefly, it was the grand project of Sultan Ahmet who died aged only 27 the year after its construction and whose tomb is located inside the building. Rather gruesomely, his wife and three sons were strangled and buried with him. Thousands of blue tiles adorn the walls and give the mosque its unofficial name. The curvaceous exterior seems to defy gravity, featuring a veritable cascade of domes, a huge courtyard and six tall minarets, (more than any other Ottoman mosque). If visiting, remember that only worshippers are admitted through the main eastern door and that females should bring a shawl to cover their heads.

Standing opposite to the Blue Mosque, the Aya Sofya, consecrated as a church and later converted to a mosque, is also considered to be one of the world's greatest buildings. It was made into a museum by Ataturk in 1934, but such were the queues whenever I visited that I never did manage to see inside. Next time perhaps?

Directly behind the Aya Sofya and situated within acres of leafy parks and gardens is the Topkapi Palace; considered famous or infamous depending on your point of view. As home to a number of rulers of the Ottoman Empire, some who were considered good, some bad and some just plain mad, the palace has been the subject of many colourful stories over the years. Most of these revolve around the various excesses of the Sultans and feature scheming courtiers, treacherous eunuchs and beautiful concubines. For those interested in the latter, it's possible to visit the original harem for an additional supplement to the entry fee.

Finally, a short walk over the tram tracks will bring you to the never-ending queues for entrance to the Basilica Cistern. This subterranean 6th century structure is the largest of several hundred ancient cisterns lying beneath the city and was built to store water for use in the nearby Topkapi Palace. Its cathedral-like underground chamber contains a forest of 336 marble columns, each 9 metres in height supporting its decorated ceiling. The uniqueness of its design has made it the location of a number of films over the years; most famously 'From Russia with Love.'

With the sightseeing over and done with it was time to turn thoughts to the business end of the trip: running the Istanbul Marathon. Costing a mere 60 Turkish Lira, (£17), to enter this has to be one of the best value-for-money big city marathons left on the running calendar. Registration takes place on the three days prior to the event in a difficult to find, large out-of-town Sports Stadium three metro stops from Ataturk Airport. This is provided of course your flight coincides with opening times. Otherwise, it's a long way back out to register via a combination of congested tram and metro.

It's well worth the effort to attend though as, like Dublin two weeks previously, this one is no mere marketing exercise. Apart from numerous diverse exhibitors, both runners and spectators alike were supplied with as much freshly cooked pasta, fruit and drink as we cared to consume. When I somewhat jokingly said that I preferred the officials' event T-shirt to the official one, they obligingly gave me one of each to add to the domestic T-shirt mountain. The £17 entry fee also included a 20 minute bus ride across the Bosphorus Bridge to the Asian side of the city on race morning. The buses left in a continuous procession from 7am onwards amid scenes of real pandemonium from outside the magnificent Blue Mosque. The buses were signalled to arrive individually at regular intervals, each arrival being greeted by a mixture of rugby scrum and riotous free-for-all. It was a miracle no one was crushed under the wheels. We were to finish in almost the identical spot later that day. I made the mistake of catching one of the earlier buses and was subsequently left standing exposed to the cold wind on the Bridge for one and a half hours before the start of the race. With nothing better to do, it was interesting to observe the numerous street vendors pushing their barrows among the throng of assembled runners, attempting to hawk all manner of stuff to their captive audience. They never miss a trick these guys; though why anyone about to run a marathon would be interested in buying a carpet at this stage is beyond me.

This was the 36th edition of the marathon that was first run in 1978 at the request of a group of 34 German marathoners. According to the organisers, this year there were over 25,000 runners representing 118 countries entered into the 3 main events: marathon, 15km and 10km plus an untimed Fun Walk. Approximately 3,200 of us completed the marathon. The marathon and 15km started simultaneously at 9am, with a great deal of pushing and shoving, following a lusty rendition of the Turkish National Anthem. The 10km set off ten minutes later over an already overcrowded Bosphorus Bridge, cluttered with what seemed like thousands of spectators anxious to take advantage of the one day in the year that the bridge is closed.

The bridge is one of two suspension bridges currently spanning the Bosphorus. The other is the Fetih Sultan Mehmet Bridge and a third one is planned. The Bosphorus Bridge was the first built in 1973 and was opened one day after the 50th anniversary of the founding of the Turkish Republic. At the time of construction it was the fourth longest suspension bridge in the world. The bridge has six lanes which are altered to suit the flow of traffic. On weekday mornings four of these run westbound into the city while, in the evening, the situation is reversed. The marathon is not the only sporting activity to have been held on the bridge, (though it is the only genuine one; the others falling into the category of mere gimmicks) For example, in 2005 Venus Williams played a show game of tennis on the bridge with a Turkish opponent, the first tennis match to be played on two Continents. In the same year, Formula One driver David Coulthard drove his Red Bull racing car back and forth across the bridge. Ironically, he was fined 20 euro for passing the toll booths without payment. His team paid the fine! Finally in 2013, as a promotion for the Turkish Open, famous golfer Tiger Woods was brought to the bridge by helicopter to hit a series of golf balls from the Asian side to the European side.

Knowing that the route had been designed to show us the best that Istanbul could offer: over famous bridges, past iconic mosques and palaces, under historic aquaducts, through beautiful parks and along scenic coastlines, I'd decided to take the camera and run this one in the guise of a marathon tourist as opposed to that of a marathon runner. I wasn't disappointed. Some of the views and architecture we saw en route were simply spell-binding and unlikely to be repeated. Anyway, it's not a course where you can aim for a fast time, Istanbul is built on 7 hills and too many of them were in the way.

The first of these confronted us as soon as we'd crossed over the bridge, putting the brakes on some of the more enthusiastic starters. The uphill didn't last long, however, and we were soon charging down the opposite slope towards Besiktas Pier and the start of the flat-as-a-pancake coast road towards the Galata Bridge. This stretch afforded views of the magnificent Dolmabahce Palace, the administrative centre of the late Ottoman Empire. Next to it is the equally impressive Dolmaahce Mosque, one of the most famous examples of 19th century mosque architecture. Just before the 10km mark we crossed the Galata Bridge across the Golden Horn. The current bridge is the fifth such bridge built on the same spot and is one of the few moveable bridges in the world that also carries electrified rail tracks. Over the centuries it has become a symbolic link between the traditional city of Istanbul proper, site of the imperial palaces, and the working districts on the other bank where a large proportion of the residents are non- Muslim.

From 10km to 17 km we ran an out-and-back section along the shore of the Golden Horn, losing the hordes of 15km runners in the process. For the Ottoman Empire, the Horn was a vital harbour supplying the trading colonies on the northern shore. The origin of its name is uncertain though rumour has it that it originated during the 15th century siege of the city, when all the gold and precious objects of the Byzantine citizens were thrown into its waters to keep them from the advancing Ottoman forces. On two separate occasions, capture of the Horn proved to be the turning point of successful military campaigns: first by the Crusaders and later by Mehmet the Conqueror who, on finding his ships blocked by a chain across the Horn simply carried them over it in the dead of night.

From 17km we climbed again, away from the Horn, and under an ancient aquaduct before descending to the coast at the Sea of Marmara. Then came the hard bit; trying to keep our concentration, as we ran through the increasing rain and mist for the next 20km on either side of the undistinguished coastal dual carriageway. All the way we had tantalizing glimpses of this inland sea that connects the Black Sea with the Aegean Sea, but never enough to get any real sense of its proximity. The final 2km were virtually all uphill, through the grounds of the Topkapi Palace, before emerging for the final sprint along the Hippodrome to the finish outside the Blue Mosque. We were handed a superb medal and yet another T-shirt (the third!) for our efforts.

It was now time to find something to eat and drink and, as usual when we visit a new country, we were anxious to try some of its specialized cuisine. Despite the encroachment of the ubiquitous fast food outlets, Turkish people still rely primarily on the rich and extensive dishes of Ottoman origin. Placing ourselves at the mercy of one of the less-pushy restaurant owners on the street leading to the central station, we explained that we wanted to eat something typically Turkish. After a great deal of discussion we both settled on Mercimek as starters; a tasty dish of lentil soup - thick enough to stand a spoon in. This was followed by a traditional Karniyarik; a Turkish and Iranian dish consisting of eggplant stuffed with a mix of chopped onion, garlic, black pepper, tomatoes and minced meat. Dessert was the fairly well-known Turkish Baklava, made with pistachio. The whole lot, washed down with a liquid yogurt (Turkish spelling) drink, came to less than 30 lira.

Being in a Muslim country, finding suitable alcohol outlets proved a little more difficult. Those who prefer British-style pubs will find two of these within the vicinity of Sultanahmet Square: the Cozy Pub next to the tram stop and the Port Shield leading down towards the quayside. We spent some time in the latter as their meals were also reasonably priced, but weren't greatly impressed by the local EFES lager at 16 lira a pint. Much better value was the same brewery's 7.5% Special Beer or 5% Malt Beer, available in cans from most corner mini-markets at considerably less cost. We did try a bottle of Turkish red wine for 20 lira, the least said about which, the better.

I have to admit that this is one of the most memorable marathons I've ever completed - in one of the world's most inspiring cities. As an event in which to combine a love of travel with a love of running, the Istanbul Marathon is second to none. My only regret is that I wasn't booked for a longer stay but, having had a taste of what the city has to offer, I'd certainly like to return for more as soon as this pandemic is over.

The Blue Mosque. Waiting for the bus to the Start.

By the iconic Galata Bridge with its famous fish sandwiches

MALTA

MALTA MARATHON

Mo and I first landed in Malta while returning by ship from Australia in 1974, returning for a holiday with our two young sons some twenty years ago. My impressions on both occasions were that the island seemed, like many of the British seaside resorts of the Victorian era, to be stuck in some sort of time-warp from which it needed to be dragged kicking and screaming into the current century. I also considered it a rather ugly island, scarred by unattractive, piecemeal development in its resorts and almost totally devoid of rivers, lakes and other forms of natural beauty. What it has got going for it, apart from almost 3,000 hours of annual sunshine, is that it's one of the few places in Europe with a February marathon. I'd been back twice since my earlier visits, for the island's marathons in 2010 and 2011. On both occasions nothing much seemed to have changed. That said, some people actually enjoy the quirky, slightly antiquated atmosphere and won't have a bad word said about the place. 2015 was to be my third attempt at the Malta Marathon – I was interested to see if there'd been any significant changes over the past few years.

On the past two visits for the marathon I'd flown with easyJet from Newcastle, flying out Saturday and returning Tuesday. These are the only two days on which flights operate on this route and, unfortunately, on both occasions the Saturday outward flight arrived too late for the registration deadline. This meant having to ask someone else to collect my number for me – something I wasn't too keen to do this time. Almost as an afterthought Mo and I took a look at the easyJet Holidays website and found a last minute deal for 7 nights' half board at Sliema's 4-star Hotel Windsor costing not much more than the price of the flights themselves. It seemed too good to miss. We went for it but it's not recommended. As usual, there was a good reason why it was cheap. The hotel was outdated and uncomfortable with a dining room that was nothing short of depressing. There are better hotels to be had in the resort of Sliema, the obvious choice for anyone entering the marathon. Buses leave from there to take runners to the start at Mdina at 6am on race morning, the race finishes on Sliema's waterfront and, until this year, pre-race Registration was always held in the resort.

We noticed the first significant change since our 2011 visit immediately on arrival at Malta International Airport, (known as Luqa after the former RAF base it now occupies). We were no longer greeted by the fleet of garishly coloured and antiquated public service buses for which Malta has long been associated. This set of 1950s exports from Britain, lit up like Christmas trees and adorned with the owner's favourite religious icons, had provided character to Malta's public transport system for decades. I had to do a double-take to confirm that I'd actually left Newcastle on seeing the customary colours of Arriva, our own local bus company, waiting for us to embark. It seems that the ancient, multi-coloured fleet of owner-operated buses were finally scrapped in July 2011 and replaced by 264 new vehicles in Arriva's livery. The irony is that Arriva ceased operations less than three years later having got themselves into financial difficulty. Their buses remain as their legacy having been nationalised as Malta Public Transport by the Maltese government before their management was handed over to a Spanish company. You couldn't make it up!

So it was onto the X2 for the 1.30 euro hour-long ride to Sliema. Don't be fooled into thinking that the X in the title stands for Express. It was one of the slowest bus rides imaginable with enough twists and turns to make anyone dizzy. The fares, though, are a real bargain – particularly the 7-day tickets at 6.50 euros, allowing you to jump on any bus to anywhere on the island, any time you wanted. Mo and I bought one of these the next day and just about wore it out. On previous visits these tickets had been 13 euros to foreigners and only half that price to locals. The EU soon put a stop to this discrimination and insisted on parity. To be fair to the government they at least reduced the overseas visitor rate to that of the locals instead of bringing the latter up to match.

Despite its faults, Malta is a fascinating country with a rich and varied history. The origin of its name is unclear with the most common explanation being that it derives from the Greek word 'meli' – meaning honey. The Ancient Greeks called the island Melite, meaning honey-sweet. This is said to be due to Malta's unique production of honey produced by a local species of bee on the island, giving it the popular name of the 'land of honey' (most tourists end up taking home a jar of the stuff – it tastes pretty nice.) The Romans went on to name it Melita, a common name found on the island today. Another theory as to the origin of its name argues that it comes from the Phoenician word 'Maleth' meaning a haven. This is thought to be in reference to the island's many bays and coves offering shelter to seafarers.

Geographically, Malta is the most southerly country in Europe, located roughly halfway between the eastern and western ends of the Mediterranean and virtually equidistant from Sicily to the north and North Africa to the south. Though only small in size at a mere 122 square miles, its strategic geographical location has been an attraction to a whole series of dominant maritime nations throughout history. Over the centuries, Malta and its two neighbouring inhabited islands of Gozo and Comino have been occupied by the Phoenicians, the Ancient Greeks, Romans and Arabs. The latter stayed for over 250 years between the 9th and 12th centuries, leaving an indelible impression of their language and culture. In 1127 Christianity returned when King Roger the Norman reconquered the islands for the Kingdom of Sicily. Malta then became an important location during the Crusades. At a time when the Ottoman Empire was the dominant power in the Mediterranean, Malta was given to the Order of St John, a military order of Knights who had attempted unsuccessfully to defend Jerusalem against the Turks. Suleiman the Magnificent mounted an unsuccessful siege against Malta in 1565 with 180 ships and 30,000

Turkish soldiers. The siege lasted several months concluding with the Knights, in charge of only 8,000 defenders, succeeding in driving the Turks away. After the siege the Order founded the city of Valletta on a peninsula fortified with the massive stone walls we see today. At this period in its history Malta had the reputation of being the world's most fortified place. The impressive walls of Valletta were even able to withstand heavy enemy bombing during the Second World War. Malta is extremely proud of the fact that it was awarded the George Cross for its heroic resistance during that war. The country's flag displaying the Cross is to be seen all over the island and on many of its souvenirs.

After the Turks it was Napoleon's turn to invade. In 1798 the French took the island without resistance when the Knights surrendered on deciding that they were unable to defend their position. French rule only lasted two years before they too surrendered – this time to Nelson's British Navy. The British then ruled the island – with some limited self-determination for its inhabitants – until Malta gained its independence in 1964. The islands were declared a republic in 1974 and became part of the European Union in 2004. Finally, in 2008, Malta abandoned its own version of the pound and converted to the euro.

With a current population of around 416,000, Malta is one of the world's smallest and most densely populated countries. Valletta, its capital, is also the smallest national capital in the European Union. It has two official languages: Maltese and English. The former, Malta's national tongue is a fairly incomprehensible ancient language related to Arabic and written in the Roman script. Fortunately for us tourists 88% of the population also speak English, 66% speak Italian and 17% speak French. This widespread knowledge of a second language makes Malta one of the most multilingual countries in the EU. It has helped the fast growing tourist industry. Although tradition still plays an important part in daily life, Malta has experienced a great deal of change since independence. Tourism in particular has become the major focus of wealth creation. Almost 1.2 million tourists visit each year – three times more than there are residents. In recent years Malta has also advertised itself as a medical tourist destination – hoping to further boost its economy by jumping on the medical tourism bandwagon. Currently, its major resource is limestone. It produces only 20% of its food requirements, has limited freshwater supplies and no domestic energy sources. This increases the economy's dependence on tourism and foreign trade where it acts as a freight trans-shipment hub).

I've been four times now and have just about seen everything the island's got to offer. On this visit Mo and I were hoping to spend a fair portion of our time just strolling in the sunshine along the miles of promenade between our base in Sliema and the nearby resort of St Julian's. With a bit of imagination this stretch can be considered Malta's equivalent to Nice's Promenade des Anglais. Unfortunately, the weather ruined our plans. Malta in February is very hit-and-miss. When I was there for the marathon in 2010 we had wall-to-wall sunshine. The following year it rained so much that us runners had to climb up and then run along a wall to avoid having to wade through one of the deeper puddles on the course. Friends tell me that last year the weather was perfect. This year it was back to being wet and windy. Over the seven days we were there it seemed to rain every time we stuck our heads out of the door. Worse still, staying in a hotel means that there's nowhere for wet clothes to dry. It meant jumping on and off buses just to stay dry – but at least we made full use of our 7-day bus pass.

Apart from the Sliema/St Julian's axis there were really only four places I was interested in re-visiting. In alphabetical order these were: Gozo, Marsaxlokk, M'dina and Valletta. The ugly, ribbon coastal development of Qawra/Bugibba/St Paul's that catered mainly to British tourists didn't interest me one bit. I'd stayed in the latter for a week way back in 1996 and found it tacky and dull despite the fact that it's the site of one of Malta's most historical events. In AD60 St Paul and St Luke were shipwrecked off an island there while travelling to Rome to appeal for the Emperor's clemency. Paul allegedly spent the winter months living in a cave at Rabat where his preaching of Christianity began the conversion of the islanders. Paul's statue dominates the barren rock, visible from the number 222 bus that makes the journey from Sliema to the Gozo ferry terminal at Cirkewwa. From here regular ferries make the thirty minute voyage across to the island of Gozo at a cost of 4.65 euros return. The ship passes the tiny island of Comino with its single hotel and a mere handful of houses. On arrival you'll find the 303 public bus waiting to take you to Gozo's ancient capital of Victoria. (Malta's bus passes are not valid on Gozo but the fare is only 1.50 return)

Gozo, Malta's smaller neighbour, has about one-fifth of Malta's population on an island less than a quarter of its size. While both islands share the same history, they are entirely different in character. Without its own airport, Gozo gets much fewer tourists, is much quieter with a much slower pace of life. With less tourism development and only ten hotels, a greater proportion of the land is used for farming. It is much hillier than Malta and much greener. The island's authorities have also had the good sense to avoid some of the worst excesses of modern development by insisting that all buildings are constructed of local sandstone, in keeping with the island's character. Victoria, the island's capital, is well worth a visit. Known for centuries as Rabat, and still called that by the locals, the name was changed in 1887 for the Queen's jubilee. There are many places of historical and cultural interest in Victoria and a visit to the fortified citadel is considered a must. The fortifications are similar, but on a smaller scale, to those at Mdina and afford superb views over the whole island. Also within the Citadel is the Gozo Cathedral, Law Courts, old prison and various museums. When you get tired of looking at ancient history and architecture the city's main square with its street cafes and open-air market is a great place to watch the world go by.

Marsaxlokk, the next place I'd recommend for a spot of marathon tourism, is on the opposite side of Malta. We used our passes to take one of the numerous buses into Valletta and then changed to the number 85 to the south east coast. Marsaxlook is a charming fishing village famous for its big Sunday fish market, brightly decorated fishing boats and numerous quayside fish restaurants. Apparently the name is derived from 'marsa' meaning port and 'xlokk' meaning south. The first Phoenicians landed here in the 9th century and set up their trade. It was here too that the Turkish fleet of 181 ships disembarked their 30,000 troops during the Great Seige of 1585. It was weird sitting there eating our octopus in garlic in one of the seafront restaurants, imagining what it must have been like watching the fleet arrive! Fortunately, the village has remained virtually unchanged, having escaped the mass tourist development of the north coast – there's not a single high-rise in sight. It's one of the few places in Malta that I'd consider staying for any length of time.

Mdina is where the marathon starts on Sunday morning. Runners are transported there by 6am bus from Sliema for a 7.30am start, leaving little time to look around. Besides, there's nothing open at such an early hour – the fascinating, ancient city merits its own sightseeing trip. Later in the week Mo and I took the 30 minute bus ride on the number 51 bus from the Valletta terminus. Stepping through the main gate into the warren of narrow streets and alleyways is like stepping back in time. In the 8th century the Arabs transformed Mdina into a fortified citadel, akin to the one mentioned earlier in Victoria (but on a much grander scale) by constructing impregnable walls to protect it from enemy attacks. Mdina, meaning literally 'the walled city' became the capital of the island until the Knights arrived and made their headquarters at Grand Harbour, (modern-day Valletta) Under the Knights, and even more so under the British, the importance of Mdina as the seat of power faded steadily and what was once known as the 'Noble City' became virtually a ghost town. Today it is referred to as 'the silent city' When the tourists go home less than 400 inhabitants remain. Still, the place itself is a pleasure to stroll around, with many of the silent alleyways giving the sense that nothing has changed for more than a millennium since the Arabs were here. The main attractions worth visiting are the cathedral named after St Paul, its museum and the enormous ramparts. There is an interesting story about the two different faces of the Cathedral clock. Apparently the reasoning was to have one clock which showed the correct time and one set up to confuse the devil.

My favourite pastime is to admire the views from the city walls stretching right down to Valletta and the distant course. It is one of the most inspiring places imaginable in which to start a marathon.

No visit to Malta would be possible without spending time in the capital, Valletta. The most enjoyable way to reach it is by taking the regular 10 minute ferry across Marsamxett Harbour from Sliema (1.50 euros each way). The journey provides excellent views of the imposing city walls and the towering St John's Co-Cathedra that dominates the skyline from miles around. Valletta, with its rich 16th century architectural heritage, was one of the earliest sites inscribed by UNESCO on the World Heritage list. As the peninsula on which it's built is only a couple of kilometres in length, the ideal way is to do everything on foot. I particularly enjoy the spectacular walk around the city walls from the ferry terminal to the Grand Harbour. Others may choose to negotiate the steep stairs through atmospheric streets to the centre of town. Most visitors are taken by the quaint, enclosed wooden balconies fronting most of the old apartment buildings. The main street is Republic Street, a busy pedestrian zone leading from the main outer gate of the city walls down to the iconic Republic Square. Most of the city's attractions, including the Cathedral, the Palace of the Grand Masters (now home to the Maltese Parliament), National Museum and National Library are located nearby. For those interested in history and culture who wish to be fed a potted audio-visual version of the island's history, I'd recommend a visit to The Malta Experience in Mediterranean Street.

2015 was to be the 30th anniversary of the Malta Marathon. The principle aim when the race started in 1986 was to increase interest in athletics on the island, particularly in road running. That year a mere 60 Maltese athletes completed the first event. In 2015 the 4,000 mark was reached for the first time. That, of course was over all three events on offer: the marathon, a half marathon and a half marathon Walkathon. Whereas in previous years participation by both local and foreign participation had grown simultaneously, this year it was the number of foreign runners that had shown a significant increase. Last year's 1,600 foreign participants had grown to 1,900 while local participation remained at 2,100. That is a staggering almost 50% of the field from overseas, something unheard of on the international marathon circuit. The UK was the country best represented with just over 600 runners, the Italians followed with 300 and then the Germans with 226. Other nationalities out in force were Poland with 89, France with 83, USA with 71, Sweden with 69 and Japan with 59.

Due to the large number of international participants the organisers altered the registration procedure for the 2015 event. Instead of everyone having to squeeze into an overcrowded shopping centre in Sliema, registration was split into two separate venues – one catering for locals, the other for foreigners. Those of us from overseas were asked to register from Thursday onwards at the 5-star Le Meridien Hotel in St Julians. Very few of us were impressed by the new arrangements. Apart from moving away from the traditional base at Sliema where most of us had booked our accommodation, registration itself was confined to a cramped, bedroom size space in the hotel and not, as envisaged, in one of the public areas. I arrived shortly after registration opened on the Thursday evening to find queues already stretching along the hotel corridor. After being admitted a few at a time we were directed from table to table to be handed a number with combined chip, goody-bag, T-shirt and pre-paid bus ticket to the start. There was nothing else in the room: no Expo and nothing to purchase like gels or drinks. The T-shirt was yet another cotton affair, just like I'd been given on my two previous visits. Very few major marathons hand out cotton T-shirts these days. On taking it home the red dye came out on the first wash and the garment shrunk to be almost unwearable. It's now in use as a duster.

Sunday morning saw us all gathered by the ferry landing at Sliema waterfront, huddled together against a vicious wind in the pre-dawn gloom. At least it had stopped raining. Buses started leaving for the start at Mdina at 6am sharp. I knew from previous occasions that it wasn't wise to take one of the earlier buses. As it's only a 20 minute journey, these left you at the start with well over an hour to spare before the off. The exposed, hillside location of

Mdina, totally devoid of shelter of any kind, is no place to have to stand shivering in the cold. Even the last bus to leave Sliema had me there with 50 minutes to hang around. Fortunately there were 12 of us there from the 100 Marathon Club with a lot of catching up to do. Among these were two American members: Rich Holmes and Robert Bishton, who'd come to Malta to add it to their growing list of countries in which they'd completed a marathon. I'd previously encountered Robert (in his alter-ego of 'Cowboy Jeff' –he always runs in a cowboy hat) at Gdansk. Both have been instrumental in the foundation of the Marathon Globetrotters, a new, largely American based, club for those, like me, who enjoy combining a love of marathon running with a love of travel. Anyone who has completed a marathon in 10 or more countries is eligible for full membership. As the philosophy of the club is very similar to my own concept of marathon tourism I decided I'd like to join. Not sure though that many of us born in the UK would agree with the inclusion of the likes of Jersey, Guernsey and the Isle of Man as official countries. However, following much discussion and debate the Globetrotters have agreed to use a list of 254 countries based on ISO-3166 (The International Standard for country codes). Those of us who are members of the club are committed to abide by these rules. Still, using that criteria, I can now add another three countries to my list!

With the countdown drowned by the sounds from an enthusiastic brass band playing on the start line we eventually set off from outside Mdina's main gate at 7.30am. The half marathon and Walkathon were to leave together at 9.15am. After a short circuit through the streets of nearby Rabat, the course wended its way steadily downhill towards Malta's international football stadium. With a strong following wind on the mainly downhill stretch, the early kilometres seemed to fly past quickly. As the course levelled out we began the first of two spirals that had us running back on ourselves with views of Mdina's fortifications and Cathedral ever-present in the distance.

Passing the Ta' Qali National Stadium for the first time I was surprised that such a small island could have such an impressive football stadium. Built in 1981 with a capacity of 18,000 people, it is not only home to the national football team but also stages most Maltese Premier League and cup matches. The construction of the stadium meant that for the first time ever, important football matches were able to be played on natural turf. The route continues through some fairly unattractive terrain until the next place of note. At 15k we reach the outskirts of the village of Mosta, a town whose major asset dominates the approaching skyline. The Rotunda of the church of Santa Maria Assunta is said to be the fourth largest dome in Europe. It's considered a masterpiece of design and construction skills, with the 51 metre high dome with walls 6 metres thick, having been completed without the aid of interior scaffolding. The church is famous for the fact that during the Second World War, a German bomb pierced the dome and fell into the church below while a service was in progress. The fact that it did not explode is considered to be in the order of a miracle. A replica of the bomb is on display in the sacristy.

After Mosta comes perhaps the hardest part of the course, a three kilometre uphill climb on a footpath next to a busy road before the national stadium is passed for a second time. At 26k we emerged once again onto the main Mdina to Valletta road just as those in the half marathon run/walk arrive directly from the start at their 5k point. It's rather demoralising to realise that you've run for so long and are still only a short distance from where the race began. Even more annoying is the fact that many of the walkers spread themselves out in groups across the road, making it difficult to pass. It's also difficult at this stage to work out who's in what event – everyone just seems to merge in to one indistinguishable mass.

Apart from a couple of dog-legs before and after Birkirkara at approximately 28k and 32k, the route largely heads east to Valletta from now on. From here-on in the strong wind that had been a significant presence from the start seemed to be permanently in our faces as we made our way towards Sliema. The second of these dog-legs through an industrial area between major highways was a truly awful part of the course. Just like four years ago, the roads were marked by potholes full of water with the strong winds whipping up spray from these into our faces. I was glad when at 37k we finally reached the outskirts of Valletta to begin the sharp descent down towards Marsamxett Harbour. This to me is the most beautiful part of the course. I always enjoy running beside water and the combination of expensive yachts, blue water and not having far to go certainly lifted spirits. The groups of walkers had long been left behind and it was only us runners sprinting along the final straight kilometre to the finish by the ferry landing, where we'd queued for buses what seemed like hours ago. (It was hours ago!) I was pleased to finish just outside my 4hour 15 minute target time and receive the rather garish, gold, specially commissioned 30th anniversary medal.

That evening I went back along to the Le Meridien hotel with colleagues Danny Kay and Gina Little for the Presentation of Awards ceremony. This was a bit of a disappointment. Amid growing murmurs of discontent, this got underway long after the officially advertised start time. There was nowhere to sit and many of the announcements for the marathon were inaudible above the background chat of those waiting for their own event to be called. For some reason finishing times were not read out. At least Gina won her Female 65 age category while Danny came second in his, (Male 70). I'm not sure that many of the winners were too impressed with what looked like a mosaic marble ashtray.

Anyone in search of traditional Maltese food during their visit will discover that it's hard to find. Maltese dishes traditionally take time to prepare and therefore don't translate well to a restaurant menu. (The island's lack of wood for stoves and fires meant that a high heat in cooking was a false economy). Limited rainfall has also meant that chefs have always had to work with what the seasons made available. Rabbits have traditionally provided the main source of protein with Fenek (rabbit stew) considered the national dish. The fact that our accommodation was on a half board basis limited our opportunities for eating out – though we couldn't resist trying the Rabbit with chips, salad and a bottle of white wine at 15.99 euros in the nearby Surfside Restaurant overlooking the

Mediterranean. We also sampled the traditional 'Bragjoli' or beef olives, courtesy of Malta Night in the hotel. This is tasty, thin beef fillets stuffed with mincemeat and onions smothered in tomato sauce. We were too early in the season for the autumnal delicacy of snails cooked in olive oil and garlic - maybe next time.

Don't expect to find any form of perfect dark beer in Malta. You're most likely to be offered a pint of the local, watery Cisk lager. Don't even expect to find any decent pubs. The best I can recommend is the Plough and Anchor on the landward side of the prom mid-way between Sliema and St Julians. This hole-in-the-wall pub, though short on space is big on atmosphere with its quirky memorabilia and beams decorated with Toby jugs. It also serves a decent pint of Farson's Blue Label. The Café Jubilee, not far from the finish line on Sliema's waterfront also provides a bit of character with your drink. Finally, there's Time Square on the prom just up from Sliema for those who want to watch wall-to-wall sport with their beer. With its huge servings of carbohydrate loaded stodge, this pub has been a long-time favourite haunt of UK runners over the years.

Next to the Finish gantry in Sliema

With Danny Kay and Gina Little at the Finish

RUSSIA

WHITE NIGHTS MARATHON, ST PETERSBURG

I'd always wanted to run a marathon in Russia and had, in fact, already booked flights to September 2015's Moscow Marathon before two friends, Roger Barrett and Sam Kimmins, wrote to say that they were going to this one in June that year. Rather than travel to Moscow on my own I decided to switch events and join them. With Lithuania to go, this would at least help me to complete the set of Baltic marathon events: Helsinki, Stockholm, Tallinn, Riga, Gdansk plus the Nordic ones of Oslo and Odense (Denmark). In case you're wondering the 'White Nights' in the title derives from the long hours of daylight stretching well into the night that this part of north western Russia experiences during the summer months.

Unfortunately, Russian bureaucracy doesn't make travel to their country easy. The whole system seems designed to make you spend time and money to get around the obstacles it creates. They've made the Visa process so difficult, so expensive and so time-consuming as to actively discourage all but those fully determined to go there. You'd be forgiven for thinking that the country had reverted to the old Communist attitude of not welcoming foreign visitors. What has always been a complicated and difficult process has been made even more so by the introduction in 2014 of new rules governing biometric fingerprinting of all applicants. Where previously an applicant could pay a visa-expediting agency to cut through the red tape, the new rules make it mandatory to attend a Russian Embassy in person to have your fingerprints taken. This is justified on the grounds of, 'improving the security of the visas issued in the context of preventing illegal migration, terrorism and other illegal activities.'

There are a number of hoops to be jumped through before you can even get to this stage. Firstly, you've got to decide on the type of visa required. This is normally the cheapest option of a Tourist visa for a single visit of up to 30 days. Simple, you'd think. But not so! You now require some sort of supporting document from within Russia 'inviting' you to visit. Generically known as Visa Support, this is best obtained by pre-booking a hotel that offers this as part of its service. This doesn't come free – we each paid 800 rubles to our hotel; M-Hotel in Sadavaya Street, to purchase our Visa Support document covering our four night stay (at the time £1 bought 80 Russian rubles). Armed with this document, and provided your passport is valid for a minimum of six months, you're now ready to go online and start all the form filling. This process has now been outsourced to a firm called VFS.GLOBAL, whose website is fairly easy to follow. There's even a Helpline number for assistance in English. It still took me hours to complete the online application form that seemed to want to know everything I'd ever done in my life up to that point. The hardest part for me was completing the section requiring details of every country visited in the last ten years, including dates of entering and leaving. That really involved some research. They also required an up-to-date passport size photograph to precise specifications. Yet more expense.

The completed document, photo and passport must then be taken in person to a Visa Application centre attached to a Russian Embassy. There are only two of these in the UK: in London and in Edinburgh. You can't make an appointment, you just have to turn up and join the queue. I took mine up to Edinburgh to be confronted by two stony-faced, monosyllabic and totally disinterested Russian dolly-birds. Having been fingerprinted like a common criminal, I was then charged £88.40 for the privilege (£50 for a 5-working day fee plus £38.40 service charge). I could also have paid an extra £9.80 to have the passport returned by secure postal delivery but opted to return one week later to collect it in person from the same lovely ladies. After a cursory glance through the files, one of these informed me that my visa wasn't among them and that I should return another day. That's when I lost my composure. I wasn't making a third trip to Edinburgh. I'd been told that the visa would be available on that day and wasn't leaving without it. I got it in the end. This was just as well – Sam's went missing in the post. I also had more luck with my Embassy visits than my two friends. They went all the way down to London only to find that the Russian Embassy was closed that day - for International Women's Day! With rail fares, passport photo fees and visa costs this was already turning out to be an expensive marathon before all the usual expenses of flights and accommodation had to be paid. Marathon entry at only 20 euros was peanuts by comparison. I later discovered after talking to the English-speaking Russian receptionists in the hotel, that that they had been forced to go through a similar process by the British authorities when visiting our country. It's a shame that these tit-for-tat formalities exist. The complexities of the visa application process give the distinctly false impression that the whole trip will somehow be riddled with bureaucracy and red tape. It's not.

So, clutching the precious visa, I boarded the KLM 6am red-eye from Newcastle to Amsterdam with a connection later that day to St Petersburg. Roger and Sam arrived on a different route from Manchester via Munich shortly afterwards. We had the choice of two ways of getting to the city centre – public transport or taxi. The first of these involved taking the number 39 bus leaving every 20 minutes from outside the terminal to connect with the nearest metro station at Moskovskaya. The bus costs 28 rubles for the 25 minute journey (pay the conductor on board). The blue line number 2 metro leaves every few minutes for a speedy seven-station ride to the city centre station of Nevsky Prospect. A single journey ticket throughout the whole metro network costs only 31 rubles and tokens can be bought at the station's ticket booth. Signs on the metro are in both Russian and English. We came back to the airport via this method without the slightest problem. Incidentally, the St Petersburg metro is the deepest in the world due to the city having been built on what was originally swampy marshland. There are four colour-coded lines and stations are marked with an M and have separate doors for incoming and outgoing passengers. Because of the horrific traffic congestion the metro is preferable to the city's buses and trams as a means of traversing the city. On arrival we decided to take a taxi direct to our hotel, figuring that this would be the quickest way to travel. We'd neglected to factor in the horrendous rush-hour traffic in St Petersburg. The 13 mile journey was one of the scariest bumper-to-bumper rides I've ever been on, with vehicles continuously changing lanes at high speed without indication. It brought to mind Bob Dylan's lines, 'Though the rules of the road have been lodged, it's only people's games you've got to dodge.' It ended up taking over one and a half hours to reach the hotel. It's important to ignore the illegal taxi touts who hang around Arrivals, pestering the life out of those who've just stepped off a plane. An outfit called Taxi Pulkova is the officially endorsed airport taxi firm. These have a booth outside the terminal with prices displayed to all areas. They'll accept both cash and credit card and, most importantly, will provide a receipt to give to the driver so there's no haggling at the end of the journey. We paid 900 rubles between the three of us – more expensive than public transport, but still cheap by British standards.

I would imagine that most people will know that St Petersburg, with over 5 million inhabitants, is Russia's second largest city after Moscow It is situated on the Neva River at the head of the Gulf of Finland on the Baltic Sea and is the most northernmost city in the world with a population in excess of one million. Founded by the visionary Tsar Peter the Great in 1703 it was the imperial capital of Russia for most of the two centuries between 1713 and 1918 before the central government was moved to Moscow. Peter the Great's original intention in choosing the city's location was to provide a seaport available to trade on a year-round basis with other maritime nations. At the time Arkhangelsk (Archangel) the nation's major seaport on the White Sea, to the north was closed to shipping during the winter months.

For such a young city St Petersburg has packed a lot into its just over 300 years of history. It has gone through several name changes over the years. In 1914, after the outbreak of World War 1, the government renounced its Germanic-sounding name and renamed the city Petrograd, meaning 'Peter's City'. Under this name the city was the cradle of the revolutions that overthrew the Tsars and brought the Bolsheviks, led by Vladimir Lenin, to power. Shortly after Lenin's death in 1924, the city was renamed Leningrad in his honour. During World War 2, the infamous Siege of Leningrad by German forces was one of the longest and most destructive sieges of a major city in modern history. During the 872 days the city was under siege the city was isolated from essential supplies resulting in the deaths from starvation of over one million of its citizens. Thousands more were either evacuated or escaped, so the city became largely depopulated. It remained as Leningrad until 1991, the year that the USSR collapsed when, by popular approval, it finally reverted back to its original name. The changes in name are celebrated in a ditty along the following lines: 'Born in St Petersburg, Went to school in Petrograd, Worked in Leningrad, Now living in St Petersburg.'

Today, St Petersburg is a major trade gateway, financial and industrial centre in Russia specialising in oil, gas, shipbuilding and aerospace industries as well as a whole host of other businesses. Most importantly for those of us in search of the perfect dark beer, it has a significant brewing and distillery industry and is known as the beer capital of Russia due to the supply and quality of its local water. 'Piter' as it's commonly called by the locals, is now often described as the most Westernised city in Russia as well as its cultural capital. Much of this is down to Peter the Great's embrace of European culture and his rejection of what he considered to be the Old Russia, centred on the former capital of 'Asiatic' Moscow. Petersburgers tend to look down on their less cultured Muscovite neighbours. The Muscovites regard them in turn as somewhat snobbish. Certainly, the city is associated with some of the most significant figures of Russian culture and history: composers such as Stravinsky, Tchaikovsky and Shostakovich, writers like Pushkin and Golgol, scientists such as Pavlov plus political heavyweights like Lenin, Trotsky and Rasputin. Even the current Russian President,

Vladimir Putin, was born in the city. Contrary to his image in the West, you get the impression that Petersburgers are quite proud of his local connections. T-shirts featuring him shooting, wrestling and riding bears are available for purchase on stalls throughout the city.

The heart of the city and the (only) bit visited by most tourists is the fan-shaped oval of land contained by the seven-kilometre long River Fontanka and the wider River Neva. This area, known as the Fontanka, is defined by a series of avenues radiating from the Admiralty, containing a number of canals crossed by imposing bridges. This watery setting has earned the city its nickname as 'The Venice of the North.' Rivers and canals make up one tenth of the city's area, with most parts being only three metres above sea level. Within the Fontanka are most of the city's greatest monuments, among them: the Winter Palace/Hermitage, the Admiralty, St Isaac's Cathedral, The Church of the Saviour on the Blood plus other world famous cathedrals, theatres and bazaars – more than enough to keep even the most discerning Marathon Tourist busy for days. The majority of these also figured prominently on the marathon route and, as there's so much to see in St Petersburg it's hard to know where to start, I'll confine my descriptions to the more iconic places we visited on our way around the city.

Roger had found us a hotel just off the main street, Nevsky Prospect, so we were well placed to visit most of these places on foot without recourse to public transport. I'd unhesitatingly recommend the M-Hotel to anyone contemplating visiting the city. Tucked away in a quiet courtyard just behind the main thoroughfare, it's an ideal base from which to explore. I paid 22,000 rubles for a single room for 4 nights. The room was clean and modern, the staff friendly and helpful and the large buffet breakfast provided a good start to the day. Additionally, Race registration took place less than ten minutes away while the event's Start/Finish was only a twenty minute walk down the main street. We were to find Nevsky Prospect a fascinating thoroughfare for all manner of reasons. We stood gaping in disbelief on one occasion as two pretty girls on horseback rode their mounts down the street at one o'clock in the morning. No one else batted an eyelid. Over 4 kilometres long and 60 metres wide, the street was constructed under Peter the Great using Swedish prisoners of war as St Petersburg's rival to the Champs Elysees and, like its French equivalent, attracts a seething mass of humanity at all hours of the day and night. Stories about the street are legion. I particularly liked the one about how, during the 19th century, its pavements were kept clean by forcing all prostitutes arrested during the night to sweep the streets at 4am. The only drawback today is the noise from the Formula 1 grid-like start every time the traffic lights changed to green. The motorbikes were the worst offenders – some of them must have been touching 100mph in the space of a few hundred metres between the lights! It seems driving rules and regulations are ignored with impunity, even if there are traffic cops around. These seemed more interested in booking motorists for being in the wrong lane at intersections than on preventing lethal speedsters. The street is littered with a host of impressive buildings, far too numerous to mention. Two in particular stand out as must see venues. These are the incredible Church of the Saviour on Spilled Blood and the Kazan Cathedral.

The church with the strange name is one of the most ornate buildings as well as one of the main attractions in St Petersburg. Built in the neo-Russian style to resemble St Basil's in Moscow, it draws crowds in their thousands to its ornately decorated onion domes and the stunning mosaics on both its exterior and interior. Alexander 3rd commissioned the construction of the church in 1883 as a tribute to his father who was murdered on the site by revolutionaries. The name reflects the murder and much of the art inside has a martyrdom theme. The tabernacle is actually over the spot where Alexander's blood stained the cobblestones. Unbelievably, for such a beautiful building, it was closed by the Communists in the 1930s and used as a storeroom. In 1970 it became a museum of mosaics before being closed again for over twenty years. Though no longer an active church it can be visited for 300 rubles from Thursday to Tuesday.

On the other side of the Nevsky Prospect sits the Russian Orthodox Kazan Cathedral, also known as the Cathedral of Our Lady of Kazan. Though not as stunning as the church with the strange name, it has an interesting history. Despite protests from the Russian Orthodox hierarchy, it was modelled on the Catholic St Peter's Basilica in Rome. Anyone who has visited the Vatican will immediately notice the similarity. After Napoleon invaded Russia shortly after its completion, the cathedral was perceived primarily as a memorial to the Russian victory. In 1837 the first political demonstration against the Tsars took place on the cathedral's steps. After the 1917 Revolution it was closed for a number of years before being reopened as a pro-Marxist 'Museum of the History of Religion and Atheism.' It has now returned to the Orthodox Church as the mother cathedral of the city.

We spent an interesting but footsore day sightseeing within the Fontanka before deciding to save our legs for Sunday's race by making use of the many water-based tours available. These go to a variety of destinations and can be booked from most of the city's bridges or from the River Neva, close to the Admiralty. Touts will pester you to take their boat and, if you stand your ground or haggle, they'll happily come down in price. We negotiated a 400 ruble price for a 600 ruble one and a quarter hour voyage on the river and through the canals, passing most of the sights I'll be describing shortly. The next day we went even further out into the Gulf of Finland to see the spectacular development at Peterhof. The forty minute hydrofoil out there cost a non-negotiable 1,200 return. I'd like to say that it was well worth the money, but I can't.

Often referred to as 'The Russian Versailles' Peterhof is another of St Petersburg's popular tourist attractions. It represents the perfect example of the self-excesses of Tsarist rule with its Great Palace, lakes, fountains, gardens, pavilions, golden statues and staircases. Not personally impressed by ostentatious displays of wealth I found it both offensive and distasteful. No wonder the peasants revolted in the end. I was also less than pleased to find, on arrival, that we had to pay a further 500 rubles just to get off the jetty and into the grounds. There were further charges to actually get inside the Palace and various ancillary buildings. It was bombed to smithereens by the Nazis in World War 2 – they had the pictures of the ruins on display. I'm only surprised that the communists went to the trouble of completely re-building such a prominent reminder of their Imperial oppressors.

Registering for the marathon was a more rewarding experience, once we'd located the hard-to-find side door of the Zimniy Stadion in which it was held. A few visible signs pointing us in the right direction would have helped. It might also have helped if the organisers had kept their promise to send a reminder before the day of the race. None of us knew our bib numbers and finding them amongst the Cyrillic script on the Start List was well-nigh impossible. We managed with a little help from the friendly Russian staff. The stadium contained an indoor running track and a few stalls promoting other Russian marathons. There was also a smattering of the usual merchandise outlets, but no bargains to be had. We also decided against the pasta on offer. This wasn't free and cost 200 rubles for a small cardboard container of unknown quality. We'd already spotted a nearby Mama Roma's Italian restaurant where a huge plate of spaghetti bolognaise was to be had in much greater comfort for only 50 rubles more.

Soon it was time for the big event. This was to be the 26th edition of the marathon, held annually in conjunction with a 10k event. From what I could gather from a not very informative and somewhat confusing website, about 4,150 had entered the marathon and 4,450 the 10k. I have to say that there seemed to be considerably less than 8,000 plus on the start line. Apparently runners from over 30 nations were represented in the two events, though British accents were few and far between. Sam was down for the 10k with Roger and I in the longer event.

We all gathered in the ceremonial Palace Square in front of the imposing Winter Palace (now the Hermitage Museum) on a beautiful warm and sunny morning. Humidity levels were high well before the 9am start so we expected a torrid time during the run. Palace Square, with the colossal Alexander Column as its centrepiece and flanked by the beautiful General Staff Building, is by far the largest and boldest of the city's public open spaces. The latter building incorporates a monumental central arch through which in the Imperial era great armies would parade into the square itself. The square has a prominent place in the history of St Petersburg. Standing in line waiting for the marathon to start this sense of history is palpable. It was here that Tsarist troops fired on unarmed strikers to spark the Bloody Sunday revolution of 1905. It also played an important part in the Bolshevik revolution of 1917, when a group of militants stormed the Winter Palace following a shot fired from the cruiser Aurora. Today, the enormous square is used for more peaceful purposes. Locals often gather here and tourists gawp at its architectural delights or stand queuing to get into the Hermitage Museum. Political rallies and official ceremonies still take place here along with concerts and festivals. The day before the race we'd watched a passing-out ceremony for army cadets in the morning while, later that day, the square had been the venue for the Piter Street Games – a series of sporting events for young people. The star attraction in the square is undoubtedly the Alexander Column, a monument to Russia's victory over Napoleonic France. The 156 ft high column topped with a statue of a smiling angel is considered a great feat of engineering, having been erected without the aid of any mechanical devices.

On the northern side of the square is the grand Baroque-style Winter Palace, the main residence of the Russian Tsars. Built around a giant quadrangle, the palace sits on the banks of the Neva River and, these days, serves as the main building for the world famous Hermitage Museum. Stories about the excesses that took place in the Winter Palace during the reins of successive Tsars are apocryphal. Check out the one about Catherine the Great and the horse! The Hermitage Museum grew out of the private art collections of Peter the Great and Catherine housed within the Winter Palace. After the October Revolution the collections became part of a state museum. With the possible exception of the Louvre, there is no museum in the world that rivals it in size and quality. It is reckoned that a visit to all 350 exhibition rooms containing over three million items would entail walking something like 10 kilometres. There's virtually a continuous queue of people willing to pay the 600 rubles it costs to enter.

On leaving the square we headed off past the magnificent St Isaac's Cathedral and the famous Statue of the Bronze Horseman to reach the embankment along the Neva River. The cathedral is named after a former Byzantine monk whose feast day just happened to fall on the birthday of Peter the Great. Its immense dome dominates the St Petersburg skyline from every angle, particularly from the water. The dome is the third highest cathedral dome in Europe and is so prominent that during World War 2 it was shown on the Luftwaffe's bombing maps as 'reference point number 1'. During our visit we climbed up the 262 steps to take in the glorious all-round views over the city from its perimeter. The dome is covered by almost 100kg of gold leaf, resulting in the deaths of 60 serfs from mercury poisoning during the gilding process. During the communist era the building was used for yet another Museum of Atheism. It has since been re-consecrated as a place of worship but is still classified as a museum. Such is the demand for entrance that the ticket office remains open until 4.30am! The park in front of the cathedral features the famous equestrian statue of Peter the Great as 'The Bronze Horseman.' The horse is meant to represent Russia rearing above the snake of treason. The statue was immortalised in Pushkin's epic poem of the same name.

Just before 2km we ran across the first of the many bridges we were to encounter en route. Apart from a few kilometres through parks and the occasional boulevard, the course was to follow canals and rivers for much of its 42k. Arriving on the opposite bank of the Neva we were to run past the Academy of Arts, Menshikov Palace, the Academy of Sciences and the city's Zoological Gardens before arriving at 4km at the Rostral Columns and Naval Museum. The 100 ft high twin columns are important landmarks in the city. Designed as navigational beacons, they are decorated with the prows of victorious Russian naval vessels.

At 5km we crossed yet another bridge to reach Petrovsky Island on what is still known as the Petrograd side of the city. On our left was Petrovsky Stadium, the home of Zenit St Petersburg – a famous name in European football. At this point we reached the first water station which turned out to be something of a disaster. It didn't seem to be ready for us, leading to unsightly scenes of runners squabbling over water bottles and even picking discarded ones up off the floor. Fortunately, the 10k runners turned off shortly after this and things settled down for the rest of the race. I'd been a bit apprehensive about my recurring knee problems coming into the race and had actually pulled out of starting three marathons I'd entered (Windermere, Newry and Edinburgh) since my last marathon in May. I'd decided on maintaining a sedate 10 minute per mile pace to reduce the impact on the knee and so far everything was holding up fine.

At 7km we passed the historic waterfront Peter and Paul Fortress containing the cathedral of the same name. Situated directly across the river from the Winter Palace this was Peter's first ever building in his new city. Built initially to secure Russia's hold on the Neva delta, the fortress has a grim history. Forced labourers perished in their thousands during its construction and later, while used as a prison, thousands were tortured within its interior, earning it the nickname of the 'Russian Bastille.' Ironically, the island containing the fortress is now used for swimming and sunbathing during the summer months. After mostly following the perimeter of Petrovsky Island for a further 15km, we finally re-crossed Dortovsky Bridge at the 22km point, close to where we started the race. This time we ran back along the embankment via the Admiralty to where the giant cruise liners are berthed. The gleaming spire of the Admiralty building is yet another of St Petersburg's prominent landmarks and the focal point of the city's three main thoroughfares. The Admiralty was one of the first structures to be built in the new city. Peter, who had a genuine, lifelong interest in shipbuilding, had it designed to be a fortified naval dockyard in the newly acquired territory around the Neva delta. It remained as Russia's naval headquarters until 1917 and is currently in use as a naval college.

The second half of the course is not as full of historic sites as the first half. That's not to say that it was boring. Far from it – we continued to run along the side of various canals containing all sorts of architectural gems – I just didn't know what they were called. I kept up my 10 minute/mile pace until the 30km drinks station. By this time the heat was stifling and I was looking for something other than water to keep me going. I only found one of the two isotonic drink stations advertised. After 30km we crossed the Fontanka River and headed off along Nevsky Prospect to its eastern end. This was about the only time that we encountered crowds along the course. I'd guess that most of these were not spectators, merely people out doing their Sunday shopping. I don't think Petersburgers have yet embraced the marathon on their doorstep despite this being the 26th year of the race. Crowd support was minimal throughout. At 33km we again reached the banks of the Neva for a final slog into a very strong headwind to the finish in Palace Square. I would imagine that the lethal combination of heat, humidity and headwind added a few minutes to everyone's times. This was confirmed by the winner's unusually slow time of over 2 hours 20 minutes. I was twice as slow (as usual) but finished feeling strong in 4.41 so have no complaints either about my performance or the course. I'll treasure the medal given at the end. And yes, there were isotonic drinks at the finish.

Speaking of drinks, we didn't have to look far to find the perfect dark beer - it found us. On our first night there we wandered into the first pub we saw (strangely called Pub Oldham) to find a drink list containing the heavenly Belgian beer, Leffe Brune at 300 rubles per pint. This is well over what most Russian draught beers cost at 100 to 150 rubles per pint but it's a beer I can't resist so who cares. Weirdly, among the other draught beers on offer in the pub was my local brew of Newcastle Brown Ale, also at 300 rubles per pint. I can't even buy this in draught form in Newcastle despite it being brewed just down the road. What a strange world! However, I hadn't come to Russia to drink Belgian beer, at least not all the time. We found the local favourite Baltica in the bar of our hotel for only 100 rubles a pint. It's a bit too light for me. I much preferred the darker Zatecky Gus for the same price. I'd tell you too about some of the strong (8%) Russian beers we bought for only 50 rubles in our local supermarket, except I don't have the letters on my keyboard to write their Cyrillic scripted names.

Finally we had, of course, to try the Russian cuisine. After a couple of nights of carbo-loading on pasta in Mama Roma's we searched long and hard for a suitable Russian restaurant. Surprisingly, there weren't too many of them about. In the end we settled on the traditional dish of Borsch with sour cream – a Ukranian soup with beef and beetroot. Roger and I followed this with Stroganoff with buckwheat – sauteed pieces of beef and mushrooms served in yet more sour cream. As a guideline, the Borsch cost 250 rubles and the Stroganoff 390 rubles. Poor Sam was short-changed by choosing the Russian dumplings which arrived looking more like large pieces of pasta. The dishes were tasty but not sufficiently man-sized enough to satisfy hungry marathon runners.

Those of you planning to visit St Petersburg should abandon any preconceptions you may have about grim Communist buildings and unfriendly Russian people. If, like me, you grew up during the Cold War era where Russia was portrayed as a no-go area of squalid apartment blocks and communists depicted as evil creatures with horns, you'll soon have these illusions shattered. Without exception, I found everyone we spoke to be both friendly and welcoming. Many were keen to know what we thought about their city and expressed concerns about the negative image they felt that Westerners had of their country. They couldn't understand why British tourists didn't seem to wish to go there. How do you explain factors like jingoism, propaganda, the Daily Mail and the UK right-wing press to someone who is struggling to converse with you in even the most basic English. I have to say that I enjoyed every minute of my four days in St Petersburg and haven't a bad word to say about the place. Contrary to expectations, I found it to be a delightful city; modern, vibrant and sophisticated with a relaxed, cosmopolitan atmosphere. I was taken by the grand boulevards and even grander architecture – all in a huge variety of pastel colours. The delightful waterway network of rivers and canals certainly made it worthy of the accolade of the 'Venice of the North.' There was also an almost total absence of the things that blight most big English cities like litter, graffiti, dog waste, beggars, drunks, tattooed louts and chavs. The citizens were in the main well-dressed and courteous, with a respect not only for their city but for themselves too. Some of the females we saw could have graced any Parisian cat-walk. St. Petersburg certainly compared with, if not surpassed, many European capitals I've visited during my time as a marathon globetrotter. I'm thinking here about cities like Paris, Prague, Stockholm, Budapest and Oslo among others. I'd much prefer to return to St Petersburg than to any of these. Where else can you come out of a pub at 1.30 in the morning to find hundreds of people queuing patiently in the daylight to take a boat ride around the city's canals. There was no obvious police presence and not a hint of trouble. Our only brush with authority came when Sam was reprimanded by a security guard for standing on the grass at Peterhof. I couldn't help comparing the scene in St Petersburg to what was probably happening in the Bigg Market, Newcastle at the same hour of the night. It's a shame in many ways that there's always new marathons to run and new cities to see – otherwise I'd be back in St Pete's next year.

Don't know what it says but it looks impressive

Palace Square and Alexander Column St. Petersburg

CROATIA

ZAGREB MARATHON

This wasn't the weekend I'd originally had planned in October 2015. My initial intention had been to run the Gothenburg Marathon in Sweden and to that end I'd booked cheap and convenient flights from Edinburgh with Ryanair. Within weeks Mr O'Leary's mob were up to their old tricks. I first heard from them to say that the advertised airport in Gothenburg was no longer available and asking if I'd accept their alternative. As both airports were virtually equidistant from Gothenburg city centre, I accepted without complaint. As race day approached a second notification of changes to the booking arrived. This time they'd altered the times of the outbound flight from a very accessible 12.35pm to a nigh on impossible to get to 6.05am. This would have required staying in a hotel in Edinburgh the night before, as well as getting up at some God-forsaken hour to get to the airport. I wasn't prepared to do that. By cancelling I got my fare back – but that's not the point. At that stage in the proceedings it's virtually impossible to book an alternative flight at anywhere near a similar cost. Ryanair know this of course but I have the feeling they couldn't care less. After all, they were now left with a spare seat that they could re-sell for even more money. It's by no means the first time Ryanair have done this to me. I'm determined it will be the last. There really ought to be some form of legal redress when this happens. Like compelling airlines to reimburse ancillary costs occurred owing to changes to flight bookings in the same way as they are now required to compensate passengers over undue delays to flight schedules. I won't hold my breath over this ever happening.

Having lost out on Gothenburg, I started to consider Zagreb as an alternative. Croatia was a country I'd never visited and Zagreb a capital I'd never run in. My friend Sam Kimmins of the oddly-named Wingerworth Wobblers Running Club (Wingerworth is actually Sam's home village) also decided that he'd like to go to Zagreb. Sam set off from Manchester with Lufthansa via Frankfurt. I left Newcastle with KLM via Amsterdam and then Croatia Airlines to Zagreb. Neither of our fares was cheap! With perfect timing we both landed at Zagreb airport within minutes of each other on the Saturday afternoon before the race. A Croatian Airlines bus waits directly outside the gate of the Arrivals Hall, leaving on the hour and half-hour for the city centre. The thirty minute journey costs 30 kuna (£3 at the rate of £1=10kn). We'd booked a twin room at the 4-star Hotel Astoria, a Best Western Premier Hotel, less than a ten minute walk from the Start/Finish area. The hotel did us proud by upgrading our accommodation at no extra cost to two single rooms without us having to ask. The comprehensive buffet breakfast alone was well worth the £30 a night it cost. I'd recommend the place to anyone considering running the city's marathon.

I'm not so sure though, that I'd recommend the marathon itself. Things went wrong from the beginning, particularly with the method of payment. The race's website was short on details and gave scant information on what most runners, particularly those travelling from abroad, need to consider before entering. For example, there was no mention initially about the dates and times of registration. This is essential information around which flights need to be booked – there's no use in getting a flight that arrives after registration has closed. (I know several runners who've found this out to their cost). Unusually too, for a big city marathon Zagreb has no online payment facilities. Though the entry fee is a mere 25 euros payment can only be made by bank transfer. Runners were allowed to enter first and then transfer the money later. I knew from experience that my bank, Barclays, charged a minimum fee of £25 regardless of the amount involved to transfer money abroad. Sam had the same problem with Santander. With this in mind I emailed the organisers requesting registration times and asking if it would be possible to pay the entry fee in cash when registering. I got no reply so headed off to Barclays to make the transfer as the website insisted that all payments must be completed by October 7th (four days before the race). It turned out that this couldn't be done. Apparently, the bank code given on the website wasn't fit for purpose. Barclays required further details, like the full names and addresses of both the recipient and the bank to which the sum was being transferred. Again, Sam had the same problem. I wrote once more to the organisers, this time in stronger terms, pointing out the deficiencies of their website and the fact that their payment system discriminated against overseas entrants whose bank costs meant that they ended up paying more than double the entry fee. Yet again they failed to reply. As with Ryanair I got the impression that they couldn't care less. It took some digging around on my part to find the information my bank needed. To add insult to injury I not only forked out the £25 transfer fee but I was charged an additional £9 fee by the receiving bank. It had cost me an extra £34 on top of the 25 euros (£19) entry fee. To say that I was angry at seeing some overseas runners paying their entry fees in cash at registration doesn't do justice to how I annoyed I felt. I couldn't blame the young ladies on the desk – they were only doing their job – but requested to see the organiser. It turned out that he was 'unavailable'. Speaking later to other overseas entrants a similar story emerged. Virtually all had experienced difficulty in making payment and in communications with the race organisation. Things had got off to a bad start and they didn't get much better. It had started raining the moment we arrived and continued unabated, getting heavier by the minute, for most of our stay – reaching almost Biblical proportions during the next day's race. More later.

I didn't know much about Croatia before entering the event having never gone down the usual tourist road of holidaying in any of the supposedly beautiful Adriatic resorts such as Split, Dubrovnik and Istria. I tried to think of the names of famous Croatians but could only come up with sportsmen like Goran Ivanisevic (tennis) and Niko Kranjcar (soccer). I did recall that Croatia had recently become a member of the European Union but like Denmark and the UK had decided to retain its own currency. For most of my lifetime Croatia had existed as part of the Republic of Yugoslavia (later to be the Socialist Federal Republic of Yugoslavia). This had its antecedents after World War 1 when the Kingdom of Serbs, Croats and Slovenes was formed. This first version of Yugoslavia, which lasted until 1941, was ruled by the Serbian Royal Family. Their natural bias towards the Serbs caused simmering resentment in Croatia. The area was invaded by Nazi Germany in 1941, giving Croatia independence under the fascist dictator Ante Pavelic. This regime was infamous for its atrocities and harsh rule – leading over 200,000 Croats to join the resistance movement under Marshall Tito which liberated the country in 1945. In November of that year, Yugoslavia was created with Tito as its leader and incorporating Croatia, Slovenia, Serbia, Bosnia & Hercegovina and Macedonia (all now newly independent countries) plus the autonomous provinces of Vojvodina and Kosovo. Breaking ties with Stalin and the USSR in 1948 Yugoslavia, unlike much of Eastern Europe, maintained ties with the West under which trade and tourism were allowed to flourish. During his lifetime Tito worked hard to quash any disagreements between the various republics as well as keeping in check any nationalistic feelings each may have had. After his death in 1981, things slowly began to change. Croatia was the first to break ranks, declaring independence in 1991 and prompting a Serbian invasion. Most of us will remember the bloody conflict that ensued in the Balkans during the early 1990s. After four years of fighting Croatia was fully liberated and enjoyed celebrating 25 years of independence in 2016.

Zagreb, with a population of nearly one million, contains almost a quarter of the entire population of Croatia. It is also the country's capital as well as its cultural, political, economic and administrative hub being home to the Croatian Parliament, Government and President. It is situated in the northwest of the country, along the Sava River at the southern slopes of the Medvednica Mountain. There are various explanations as to how the city got its name. Some sources suggest that the name derives from 'za breg' meaning 'beyond the hill'.' The hill in question may well have been the river bank of the Sava River which is believed to have previously flowed closer to the city centre. Others argue that a possible origin is the term 'za grabom' meaning 'beyond the moat' as the city was heavily fortified since its origin. I prefer the local folk legend that describes how an old Croatian warrior was returning from battle tired and thirsty and asked a young girl called Manda to scoop up some spring water for him. Apparently, the Croatian word for to scoop up water is 'zagrabiti.' There's an ornamental fountain in the middle of the main square named Mandusevac Fountain in honour of the girl. It's built above a natural spring that provided the city with drinking water right up to the 19th century. Court records mention the spring as the meeting point for Zagreb's witches during the Middle Ages.

The Zagreb of today also dates back to the Middle Ages and the settlements on two hills: secular Gradec, known as the Upper Town and ecclesiastical Kaptol, site of the city's magnificent cathedral. The two hill settlements, adversaries for centuries, were separated by the Medvescak creek that sat along the present day street of Tkalciceva, and which still runs underneath on its way to the river Sava. In the mid-13th century the Tartars ravaged nearby Hungary and their king fled to Zagreb where its citizens provided him with a refuge. In gratitude, the king gave Gradec a charter proclaiming it a royal free city. His generosity is symbolically re-enacted everyday by the firing of a cannon at noon from the Lotrscak Tower overlooking the city. For centuries the town remained under threat of attack and bells were sounded to warn citizens to return to sanctuary as the gates to the city were about to be closed and locked. In time the threats of attack subsided and the city started to spread out around the valley. A trading centre below the two settlements evolved into what is now the main square of Ban Josip Jelacic. Relationships between the two settlements gradually improved and the two finally merged in 1850 to form the unified city of Zagreb. The new city's position enabled unhindered growth and Zagreb soon spread around the valley of the Sava River. The development of industry, commerce, transport and banking during the second half of the 19th century encouraged the city's expansion. The coming of the railway in 1862 was instrumental in connecting Zagreb to other European capitals. This is when the city started to develop along gridlines, with the town planning scheme strictly outlining that all streets must be straight and of the same width, and all buildings of the same type and height. Apart from the occasional skyscraper this uniformity is apparent when walking around the city today. Further expansion after the Second World War lead to the city finally spreading over the south bank of the Sava and to the construction of some fairly ugly residential blocks. For centuries, the Sava had been flooding the valley while protecting citizens from invasion and serving as a link to distant lands. From the mid-20th century it became the border between the Old Town and Novi (New) Zagreb. Today there are twelve bridges connecting the old with the new. Unfortunately, the Sava is too far out from the city to visit on foot. One of the most noticeable aspects of my visit was the fact that, unlike most other major European capitals, Zagreb did not have a river running right through its centre.

Zagreb is now a major international trade and business centre as well as an essential transport hub at the crossroads of Central Europe, the Mediterranean and the Balkans. Almost all of the largest Croatian as well as Central European companies have their headquarters in the city. The most important industrial activities there involve the production of electrical machinery, chemical, pharmaceutical, textile and food and drink processing. Zagreb has also become an important tourist centre attracting close to one million visitors annually. It does, however, have unfulfilled potential in that many tourists visiting Croatia skip Zagreb in order to visit the beach resorts on the coast. During our visit the city seemed to be swarming with groups of umbrella-toting Asian tourists photographing anything that moved.

Zagreb is a compact city, disarmingly easy to get around on foot, with virtually everything of importance revolving around the city's central square Ban Josip Jelacic. This is where Registration for the marathon was held, where we started and finished the next day and where, due to the nature of the course, we were to pass through a further three times during the race. We weren't able to see it at its best until all the paraphernalia associated with the race, like tents and gantries, had been dismantled. Registration was held in one of the tents. Here we were given our numbers plus a string shoulder bag containing two T-shirts, a can of Red Bull, a muesli bar and an invitation to food and drink after the race. The food stopped at 3pm and as the race started at 10am with a 5 hour time limit, it didn't give runners much time to get back for it. One of the T-shirts was navy and of technical material and worth keeping. The other was white cotton, worth wearing to keep warm before the race and then discarding. Disappointingly, there was no written information about the event – nothing that runners needed to know about such things as baggage facilities or even a map of the course. I quickly surmised that if you wanted to know anything you needed to ask. That became apparent the next morning during the chaos at the start. Without having been informed otherwise, Sam and I along with friends Dave and Linda Major from the 100 Club, had positioned ourselves as usual towards the rear of the field. Virtually everyone was wearing ponchos, bin bags or other outer clothing over their numbers in the teeming rain so it was impossible to see which event the person standing next to you was in. There were three events on the day: full marathon, half marathon and 5k, all with a simultaneous start: (457 in the marathon, 1,157 in the half and 1,181 in the 5k.) The PA announcements in Croatian were inaudible as well as indecipherable. None of us were aware that the three events were meant to be segregated with the marathon getting a head start. When we finally managed to push our way towards the front I was prevented from setting off by an over-officious marshal demanding to see my number. By the time I finally got going the marathon runners were well down the road. Within seconds I was swamped by scores of fleet-footed shorter distance runners. What with this, the puddles, the tram lines, dangerously slippery leaves and the incessant rain, I had a feeling that this wasn't to be my day.

I was wrong. Once I worked out that the best place to run and avoid both the puddles and the leaves, was on the non-slip surface between the tram lines I had a thoroughly enjoyable run. The rain didn't matter. Once you're wet, you're wet – you can't get any wetter. I did feel sorry though for the poor marshals standing out in the downpour for hours and hours. The course itself was perhaps the most uninspiring I've come across on a big city marathon. It consisted of two out-and-backs from the main square. The first of these took us approximately 8.5 kilometres along a dead straight and featureless major road to the east of the city. We then turned and ran back exactly from whence we'd come. The route was devoid of atmosphere and without spectators. The only building of interest along the route was the home stadium of Dinamo Zagreb FC, Croatia's premier football team.

Arriving back at the square just before 17km, we then ran a second out-and-back loop in the opposite direction through the city's shopping district. Here, at least, there were crowds to spur us on. The half marathoners finished here. Those of us in the marathon had to do it all again. Despite the course I was able to maintain an even pace throughout and finished seconds over 4hours 15 minutes to achieve second place in the Vet70 age category. I'm convinced that the chaos at the start was responsible for not finishing sub-4:15. I had to laugh when informed that my prize of either books or T-shirt would be forwarded to the UK. Why bother? I can't read Croatian and need another T-shirt like I need a hole in the head. The medal we were handed at the finish was one of the worst I've received in a major marathon. It felt like tin and resembled a milk bottle top. All I wanted on finishing was a hot bath so, ignoring the food on offer, I picked up a pint of beer in a plastic glass and hot-footed it back to the hotel. By the time I arrived ten minutes later the alcohol content of the beer had been diluted to virtually zero by the rain filling the glass. It didn't matter though, I'd already stashed away in the hotel fridge two large bottles of Karlovacko 6% dark beer I'd found in the supermarket opposite. Sam and I spent the afternoon enjoying our beers and discussing the race. The beers had cost a mere 75p per half litre bottle.

Normally, after the race we'd have been out around the town doing a spot of marathon tourism. The rain put paid to that. Fortunately, on waking up the next morning the rain had stopped. My flight back left on the Monday evening giving a four hour window after breakfast in which to look around. I pared down my original itinerary to prioritise the sights I really wanted to see. This meant starting again at the Ban Jelacic Square. Evidence of the marathon had all disappeared by the Monday morning and I was able to see the square in all its glory. It has served as the city's commercial heart since 1641, when it was designated as a place where fairs could be held. Most of the buildings around the square date from the 19th century, and display a variety of architectural styles. The square was Zagreb's main marketplace and carried the name Harmica (Hungarian for one thirteenth) after the tax levied on goods sold there. In 1848 the square was officially renamed in honour of Ban (Governor) Josip Jelacic. Today, it stands at the centre of Zagreb's social life and the most popular meeting points are 'under the clock' or 'under the horse's tail'. The latter is a reference to the equestrian statue of Ban Jelacic that dominates the square. This statue was placed in the square in 1866 only to be removed by the communist authorities in 1947. A public petition secured the return of the statue in 1990.

Just around the corner from the square and characterized by its soaring twin towers dominating the Zagreb skyline, is the historic Cathedral of the Assumption of the Blessed Virgin Mary. It's certainly the city's most eye-catching and most visited monument. Its foundation stone was laid in 1093 but its current appearance is relatively new. After an earthquake destroyed the building in 1880, a new façade, including the 105 metres tall bell tower was constructed. The stunning exterior is as breathtaking as the interior, with no expense having been spared in its reconstruction. The cathedral, which seats 5,000, features neo-Gothic marble altars, stained glass and a beautiful pulpit. It's quite a humbling experience standing inside while mass is being celebrated.

The cathedral's defensive walls with round towers were built when the threat from the Ottoman Turks was at its height. They remain among the best-preserved Renaissance defences in Europe. After the cathedral had been reconstructed, a fountain was built in front of it. Facing it are the gold-plated statues of the Virgin Mary and four angels, the latter symbolising the Christian values of Faith, Hope, Innocence and Humility. Also close to the cathedral is the famous open-air Dolac food market. This market, known as 'the belly of Zagreb' for the range of foodstuffs on offer, was in full swing on the Monday morning. Watch your pockets as you walk around. Around the corner, next to the public library, is an alley known as the Bloody Bridge. The bridge itself disappeared in 1899 but was originally across the now submerged creek where battles took place between the inhabitants of Gradec and Kaptol.

If, like me, you enjoy learning about the history of the city you're visiting you will enjoy walking around the Upper Town north of the cathedral. Everywhere there are traces of the city's turbulent past. Entry is through the only remaining medieval gate next to a small square where residents pray and light candles. In the heart of the area is the 13th century St Mark's Church, known for its brightly coloured tiled roof. There are two museums nearby that are definitely worth a visit if time allows. The Croatian Museum of Naive Art houses a collection of 1,500 works by artists who have completely abandoned all painting conventions, creating bizarre scenes in bright colours. Less than a two minute walk away is the Museum of Broken Relationships containing dozens of ordinary artefacts, each with a story about a broken relationship. The collection is meant to underline the fact that 'love leaves us not only with beautiful, but also with, heart- breaking memories.' Nearby is the Zagreb Funicular is a 120-year-old cobalt-blue cog railway that connects Zagreb's upper town with the lower town. A ride on this fun city train takes only 64 seconds to climb 66 metres; it is used by thousands of passengers each year to travel up and down the hillside. Still in its original condition, the funicular is Zagreb's oldest means of transportation and a protected cultural monument. For the best views of Zagreb's lower city, climb the Kula Lotrscak (Burglars' Tower). The tower stands at the top of the funicular stop and was part of the old town's former fortifications.

The Lower Town doesn't have the same charisma or atmosphere as its upper counterpart. I confined myself to walking around the so-called Green Horseshoe. This line of eight green squares connects Ban Josip Jelacic in the north with the railway station to the south. One of the most popular of these, Zrinjevac, is known for its row of plane trees brought in from Italy more than a century ago. There is also a meteorological display which citizens of Zagreb use to check the time, temperature and humidity. Particularly impressive is the view faced by those arriving by train. These are greeted by lovely views of King Tomislav square, named after the first Croatian king. The views take in an equestrian statue of the king, a beautiful fountain and the Art Pavilion, a venue for special cultural events. This impressive building was originally the Croatian Pavilion at the Millenium Exhibition in Budapest in 1890. Its innovative iron construction made it possible to transport it to and reconstruct it on its present site. Continuing the green theme, the city's Botanical Gardens are located nearby. Sadly, time constraints meant that this was the limit of my sightseeing on this trip.

I can't quite put my finger on it but something about Zagreb just didn't quite gel. Maybe it was the awful weather, though I've tried to take this into consideration. Perhaps it was the lack of a river running through its centre. Who knows? It seemed to lack the elegance and style of many of the other European capitals I've visited while marathon globetrotting. There were some beautiful medieval parts of the city but too much of it appeared fairly ordinary, down at heel and in need of a good lick of paint or some plastering over the cracks. One of the positives I did take away with me was the quality and value of its food and drink. We did look for restaurants advertising traditional Croatian cuisine offering national dishes like Strukli (cottage cheese with sour cream and eggs), Brudet (a fish stew) and Turkey with Mlinci (flat, sour dumplings). We didn't find any. What we did find was an excellent Pasta and Pizza restaurant named Capuciner directly opposite the cathedral. On the night before the race we carbo-loaded with huge plates of pasta for 36kn (£3.60). The next night was even better. We had been recommended to visit the Pivnica Mali Medo (The Little Bear) on Tkalciceva. This is the street with the creek running underneath that originally separated the warring factions of Gradec and Kaptol. Today it's lined with pubs and restaurants and is very much the centre of the city's nightlife. The Little Bear not only provided giant Picante pizzas full of bacon, ham and cheese for a mere 42kn, the pub also had its own micro-brewery with a range of excellent beers. I settled on the 7% ABV Gricka Vjestica – almost the perfect extra strong dark beer at 16kn (£1.60) per half litre. Result!

Posing at Registration in Zagreb

Ban Josip Jelacic Square where the marathon starts

SWITZERLAND

LAUSANNE MARATHON

I love running by water, there's always something to see and it has such a soothing influence. So, when I heard that the Lausanne Marathon ran for 21 kilometres along the shores of Lake Geneva before turning around and running all the way back again, I knew I had to go. I'd previously completed the Geneva and Zurich Marathons, both of which had promised lots of lakeshore running, but had come away slightly disappointed on both occasions. Neither of them had actually hugged the side of the lakes I'd expected to see. As easyJet had cheap Friday to Monday weekend flights to Geneva available from Newcastle and trains ran directly from Geneva airport to Lausanne, Mo and I were on our way. Our first stroke of luck occurred when a last minute check of our hotel's website to see if the room had a kettle, found that the hotel had reduced their rates by £80 to new bookings over the length of our stay. Naturally we cancelled the original booking free-of-charge and immediately re-booked at the new rate. The £80 saved was the exact cost of two return train fares between Geneva airport and Lausanne. Even better, we found on arrival at the lakeside Hotel Aulac that our revised booking had not only saved us money, but had resulted in a room with magnificent views of Lake Geneva and the surrounding mountains instead of the inland views we'd anticipated. To cap it off, everything we needed was on hand less than 50 metres away around the corner including a Co-op supermarket, the White Horse pub and a reasonably priced (in Swiss terms) Thai restaurant. The weekend had got off to a good start.

That was how it was to continue. We couldn't have had a better time. Gorgeous autumn sunshine prevailed throughout, more than compensating for the drenching I'd had in Zagreb two weeks earlier. Lausanne's location is extremely picturesque with the city being built on three hills, surrounded by vineyard-covered slopes, with Lake Geneva sitting at its feet. Early morning mist on the lake rolled away each day revealing a riot of autumnal colours among the leaves of the lakeshore gardens, while, in the distance, the magnificent snow-capped mountains of the Savoy Alps dominated the opposing French shoreline.

Lausanne is the capital of the canton of Vaud in the French-speaking part of Switzerland. Its population of approximately 140,000 makes it the fourth largest city in the country. In the 15th century the Romans built a military camp on the site above the lake which they called 'Lousonna.' Following the fall of the Roman Empire the original lakefront site was moved to a better-defended location above the lake, which is now the site of the Old Town. During the Napoleonic Wars the city joined the Swiss Federation as capital of the newly formed canton of Vaud. When in 1915 the International Olympic Committee chose Lausanne as its headquarters it attracted with it a whole array of world governing bodies in a variety of sports (55 at the last count). Since 1994 the city has incorporated the term 'Olympic Capital' in its promotional literature. Evidence of the city's claim to this status can be seen all over Lausanne. Directly facing the hotel was a stone sculpture displaying a digital countdown in days, hours and seconds to the start of the 2016 Olympics in Rio. (285 days away on the day of the Olympic marathon). To the west of the hotel in a street featuring permanent placards of Olympic scenes sat the IOC Headquarters with its swish Olympic Museum. To the east lay a large Olympic-themed, lakeside, park with running trails and facilities for every sport imaginable.

Lausanne is regarded as one of the most beautiful of Swiss city's and has been dubbed by some as 'Switzerland's San Francisco.' I didn't see too many comparisons other than the obvious – that of topography. Like San Francisco, Lausanne sits on a series of steep hills, tiered above the lake. Anyone visiting must be prepared for a fair amount of uphill walking. There are three main levels. The first tier is at lakeshore level in the suburb of Ouchy. Once a separate fishing village, Ouchy was incorporated into the city in the mid-19th century to serve as a port on Lake Geneva. Links between the port and the centre were improved by the opening of Switzerland's first funicular railway in 1877. The line was converted to a rack railway in 1954 and then finally upgraded to be the terminus of the city's Metro line 2 in 2006. Today, Ouchy's cafes and bars have made it a popular lakeside resort. It is also the point of departure for the passenger boats that run to various locations around the lake. Ouchy is definitely the place to stay for anyone running the marathon. Registration for the event, the free Pasta Party and the race's Finish all occur at this level. The Start is only a little way uphill in the nearby Place de Milan. At the middle level are the train station and the city's main commercial districts. I found this area to be distinctly unimpressive compared to what lies above and below. The main focus of the city centre level is Place St-Francois which serves as the hub of the bus routes and the heart of the shopping district. The quarter in which St Francois stands spreads over a narrow ridge between two gorges. As the city expanded in the early 19th century, most of the slums in this area were demolished and the River Flon, running through the gorges was filled in to form the current Rue Centrale.

The fashionable shopping street of the Rue de Bourg links the centre with the Old Town in the city's highest level at the top of the hill. Dominating the city from its perch on the summit of the hill is Notre Dame Cathedral. Seen as one of the most beautiful Gothic art monuments in Europe, it attracts more than 400,000 visitors a year. The Cathedral is the biggest in Switzerland and contains some notable features: a painted portal, a rose window comprising 105 panels recounting the history of the medieval world and a modern organ boasting 7,000 pipes. The Cathedral has its own Watchman who continues the medieval tradition of crying out hourly, 'All's well' between 10pm and 2am each night. I came away underwhelmed at what I'd seen, both internally and externally. The hype surrounding the cathedral had me expecting more. Of much more interest were the squares of Place de la Palud and Place de la Riponne and the atmospheric, cobbled streets that connect them below the Cathedral.

Located in the tranquil centre of the Old Town, the Place de la Palud is the perfect spot to sit and watch the world go by in one of its many pavement cafes. This is where the city's 17th century Town Hall is situated, with its Vaudois roof, arcades and Renaissance façade decorated with two copper gargoyles in the form of dragons. In the centre of the square is the town's oldest fountain, adorned with a statue representing justice. Nearby, a clock presents the history of the region in animated scenes on the hour from 9am to 7pm. From the Place de la Pilud, the Rue de Magdeleine runs up to the much larger square of the Place de la Riponne. Lausanne is an important university city with a large student population that can make the city a lively place in the evening. The square seems to a popular meeting-place for many of these, especially on the steps of the Palais de Rumine. This huge Florentine-style building was donated to the city by the Rumine family, descended from Russian aristocracy, as a thank-you for its hospitality.

With all its ups and downs, sightseeing in Lausanne can be quite tiring. Fortunately, like in most Swiss cities any hotel guest who pays the city's overnight tax is entitled to a voucher allowing free travel on the city's bus, train and metro network. Mo and I found it easier to hop on and off the metro running from Ouchy than to keep on walking up the hills. With the opening of the second line to Ouchy, Lausanne became the smallest city in the world to have a full metro system. We wanted to get full-value out of our free travel voucher, so rode the city's two metro lines to their termini just to see what we could discover. Our journey on Line 2 to the terminus at Croisettes was a big disappointment. Croisettes, to the north of the city, turned out to be an uninteresting suburb of pharmaceutical companies whose main focus appeared to be that of a transport interchange for more distant parts. Renens at the terminus of Line 1, had even less to offer. Unfortunately, unlike in Geneva, the transport pass did not allow free rides on the boats on the lake. It did get us a big discount off the return trip across Lake Geneva to Evian-les Bains on the French shore. As a result the 35 minute each way trip cost us only CHF28 each instead of CHF46 (£1 = CHF1.40 at time). It's a good idea to take some euros across with you as Swiss Francs are not valid in France. I'd recommend the boat trip as a good way to keep the weight off your feet on the day before a marathon. Evian, off course, is where the expensive bottled water of the same name originates. Having visited the place I can now see why the water is so dear. It's very much an up-market holiday resort and spa town catering to the well-heeled, having had royalty like Kings Edward V11 and George V of the UK and King Farouk of Egypt, as well as a host of celebrities among its regular visitors. Still, it made an interesting diversion before the marathon.

I was also keen to visit the much-trumpeted Olympic Museum set in the palatial grounds of the IOC Headquarters overlooking the lake. The modern museum is an opulent affair, with bronze statues standing in landscaped gardens tumbling down to the lake. You couldn't help wondering how much of our money intended to go into sporting activities goes to its administrative costs and upkeep. For an entry fee of CHF18, state-of-the-art audiovisual, IT and robotics technology allows the visitor an interactive experience of the best moments from various Olympics and an insight into the emotions of the competitors. Along the way we are shown how sporting competitions have evolved and how technological innovations have changed certain Olympic disciplines. (It doesn't say anything about doping scandals though!). We are taken into the heart of the Olympic Village and shown how athletes prepare themselves for their event. There's even an opportunity to have an interactive dialogue with former champions. The bit I enjoyed most took place in a mock-up of a typical mid 60's living room where, on an old black and white TV, you could watch Cliff Michelmore introducing highlights from the 1964 Tokyo Olympics. How time flies. It really brought back memories of what only seemed like yesterday.

Registration for the event took place in a giant marquee directly outside our hotel in the Place de la Navigation on Ouchy's waterfront. The marathon had a 10.10am start on the Sunday and it was possible to register up to an hour beforehand. I decided to get mine over and done with early on Saturday before heading off on the boat. Initially, I was pleased with the wine coloured long-sleeve top handed out bearing the simple logo 'Lausanne Marathon' until realizing that everyone else, regardless of event entered, was getting exactly the same. Given that there were five separate events: Marathon, Half Marathon, 10k, 10K Walk and 10k Nordic Walk plus a host of children's events involving about 14,000 in total, that must have been some T-shirt order. I didn't see this as I was too busy running but Mo is convinced that everyone also received exactly the same medal at the finish of their event. If this is true, I find it disappointing. It somehow devalues all that extra effort that marathon runners put in – not to mention the fact that the cost of entry for the marathon at CHF80 was significantly higher than for all other races (10k walkers, for example, paid only CHF34). Of excellent value, though, were the free Pasta Party tickets handed out to competitors. Non runners were meant to pay CHF10 for their meal but Mo was simply given a ticket for free. The venue turned out to be superb, with the event being held on the steamer 'Lausanne' moored by the side of the lake. The views over the lake at sunset while we were enjoying our food were quite breathtaking.

The start next morning took place on the street in front of the Parc de Milan, a large public park mid-way between the station and the lake. The two 10k walking events had set off earlier at 8.45 and 8.50am respectively. The marathon was to leave in two separate waves three minutes apart from 10.10am, with the 10k race leaving at 10.45. Half Marathon runners had to wait until 13.45 for their start some twenty plus kilometers away along the lake at La Tour-de-Peilz, the turning point for the marathon. In the three main events 1274 completed the marathon, 4525 finished the half marathon and there were 5598 finishers in the 10k.

Conditions were excellent at the start with clear skies, cool temperatures and virtually no wind though it did get unseasonably hot as the day progressed. As all runners will know, there's no such thing as a flat course along the side of a lake. Lausanne was no different and there were numerous inclines and declines on the way around. The return section from Tour-de-Peilz, when temperatures were hottest and legs at their weariest seemed to go steadily uphill. The views of mountains, vineyards and lake were exceptional throughout and more than made up for any pain experienced. I'd always thought it would be difficult to find a more scenic marathon course than the UK's Great Langdale Marathon on a sunny autumn day – I found it here.

The first couple of kilometres were an easy downhill to the lakeside at Port de Pully. This was to be the first of a succession of interesting lakeside villages we were to pass through during the race. The heart of the old market town of Pully is a network of delightful little cobbled streets. These were lined by cheering spectators and a traditional Swiss band blaring out Oompah music. Despite it being a tiny town in the eastern suburbs of Lausanne, Pully has two train stations. Here the line out of the city splits with one line heading northwards toward Bern and the other heading east to the Simplon Tunnel through the Alps. Pully marks the beginnings of the vineyards of Lavaux that were to dominate the landscape along the road to Vevey and the turn before Montreux. Designated a UNESCO World Heritage Site in 2007, the vineyards of Lavaux can be traced back to the 11th century when Benedictine and Cistercian monasteries controlled the area. Down the centuries the site has preserved a unity in terms of its architecture, walls, textures and colours – giving an almost Mediterranean character to the region and earning it the accolade of the 'Swiss Riviera.' The mild climate and south facing slopes have combined to produce mainly white wines from the Chasselas grape as well as a variety of other specialities. The vineyards were to be a constant companion for the remainder of the race.

Next up was Lutry, a small medieval town of historical importance. The well-preserved heart of the town, with its narrow alleyways and merchants' and noblemen's houses dating from the 15th to 18th centuries, is under a preservation order. In 1984, during the construction of a car park an arraignment of 24 standing stones were discovered. After Lutry came Villette, another small village involved in the wine industry and then on to Cully with its historic centre of narrow streets and pretty houses dating from the 16th century. Every April the town is home to the Cully Jazz Festival offering 9 days of live music with 30 paying and 70 free concerts to 45,000 visitors. It's considered to be one of the most intimate and friendly of Switzerland's major jazz festivals with great music and fine wine from the neighbouring vineyards. The next village of St-Saphorin revealed more narrow alleyways and an unusual church tower that can be traced back to Roman times. Inside the church, a milestone dating from the year 53 bears witness to that era.

We then passed through Corseaux, a much bigger village where the actor James Mason lived until the end of his life and where Graham Greene is buried in the local cemetery. We were now close to the 19km mark and beginning to anticipate the turn-around as we approached Vevey. This is by far the largest town we encounter on the lake and is home to the world headquarters of the food giant Nestle, founded here in 1867. Milk chocolate was invented in the town by Daniel Peter in 1875. Vevey is also noted as being the final home of comedy legend Charlie Chaplin from 1952 to 1977. Other notable residents past and present include writers Fyodor Dostoevsky and Victor Hugo, philosopher Jean-Jacques Rousseau and musicians David Bowie and Shania Twain. We pass Chaplin's statue en route and the table on which Rousseau used to eat is still to be seen in the Le Clef restaurant there. The town is also the setting for Anita Brookner's Booker Prize-winning novel 'Hotel du Lac.' If, like me, you were a fan of the 70's progressive-rock band Yes, you'd be interested to know that keyboard player Rick Wakeman recorded the final organ portion of the song 'Awaken' and the organ part of 'Parallels' on the pipe organ in St Martin's Cathedral in Vevey. I thought it was a beautiful place and would have loved to have returned for a longer visit if time had allowed. With its flower-bedded lakeside promenade lined with classy hotels, paddlewheel steamers plying the lake and breathtaking views of the Alpine panorama, Vevey has been described as the Pearl of the Swiss Riviera.' I can see why. Fortunately, by turning just after the point where half marathon runners were waiting to start, we got to see it twice.

We left the outskirts of Vevey at the 25km mark to run back from whence we'd come. The route seemed a lot harder the second time round. We were also running away from the Alps so the views weren't quite as impressive. The only deviation came at the end of the race where, instead of continuing inland to the Parc de Milan, we hit the lakeshore promenade to finish immediately in front of the Olympic Museum. I'd run conservatively intent on enjoying the views rather than going for a good time. 4 hours 31 minutes did me fine. All that remained was to see if we had enough money left to sample the draught Belgian Beer in the White Horse (unfortunately it was Leffe Blonde and not Leffe Brune, but never mind). Switzerland is, of course, a very expensive country in which to eat and drink. I calculated that the plate of pasta we bought two weeks earlier in Zagreb for £3.60 would have cost on average at least £15 in Lausanne. I won't do the comparisons with the beer – it would put you off going and that would be a shame. It's certainly one of the nicest marathons that I've ever run.

Mo by the 'Lausanne.' A great venue for a Pasta Party

By the Lake at the finish of the Lausanne Marathon

FRANCE

FRENCH RIVIERA MARATHON

2015 saw the 8th edition of the popular French Riviera Marathon that takes runners on a peach of a course between Nice and Cannes on the second Sunday of November each year. I have friends who wouldn't miss it and who make booking their next year's entry the first priority when planning their annual running itinerary. Having finally got round to doing it, I couldn't agree with them more. Mo and I left the impenetrable fog and mist of the UK behind to find the clearest blue skies imaginable during our four days in Nice. It brought to mind the words of the famous artist and long-time Nice resident Henri Matisse who once remarked, 'When I realized I would see that light every morning, I could not believe my happiness ... I decided never to leave and remained here for almost my entire existence.' Who could blame him.

Nice, the capital of the Cote d'Azur (The Blue Coast) is a truly cosmopolitan tourist destination and a great place for sun lovers during its mild winter months. It first became fashionable as a winter resort in the 18th century, as aristocratic visitors from Britain and Russia in particular, made the long journey south in search of the sun. This seasonal exodus reached its zenith in the 'belle epoch' era of the late 19th century that left the legacy of the grandiose and opulent architecture visible today along the famous Promenade des Anglais (Walkway of the English). Up until the beginning of World War 1 the city was synonymous with aristocracy and wealth. Those with money to burn built huge villas here or stayed for the season in their plush hotels. After the War things changed and many of the aristocrats never returned and in their place came artists and intellectuals. Social changes after World War 2 meant that the area no longer remained an exclusive playground for wealthy foreigners. Today, the city still shows evidence of its faded glories and though, by no means a package resort, the eclectic mix of the crowds on the promenade are testament to its changing status as a popular tourist destination.

With a population of around 350,000, Nice is the capital of the Alpes Maritimes province and the fifth largest city in France after Paris, Marseille, Lyon and Toulouse. It is located on the south east coast of France on the Mediterranean Sea a few miles from the principality of Monaco. Nice has the second largest hotel capacity in the country and has become a mecca for tourists with over 4 million visitors each year. It also has the third busiest airport in France after the two main Parisian ones with an average of 39 flights arriving each day. It doesn't take long to get acquainted with the layout of the city. Overlooked by mountains that curve down to the sea east of its port, Nice divides neatly into the old and the new. Vieux (Old) Nice huddles underneath the hilltop park of Le Chateau. This is the most interesting and atmospheric part of the city with narrow alleyways, ancient buildings and a myriad of bars and restaurants. On the eastern side of Le Chateau is the city's port. This quarter is hemmed in to the west by the tram lines along the Boulevard Jean-Jaures, built over the course of the River Pallion flowing beneath. The central square Place Messina covers the former river-bed, sitting at the end of the modern city's main street, the Avenue Jean-Medecin. The city's main train station is at the other end of this street. Along the wide 5 kilometre stretch of seafront from the Old Town to the airport runs the iconic Promenade des Anglais. It's very easy to find your way around provided you remember the Chateau is to the east, the airport to the west with the Mediterranean in between.

With no direct flights available from Newcastle in the winter months, Mo and I travelled all the way down to Gatwick for an easyJet flight to Nice. The airport in Nice is built on reclaimed land jutting into the sea on the western end of the bay and landing there provides spectacular views of the coastline and hills. The airport has two terminals connected by a shuttle bus, with most international flights arriving at Terminal 2. Theoretically, it is possible to simply walk the 4 kilometres, most of it along the Promenade des Anglais, into the city centre. I guess it depends on how much luggage you're carrying. Otherwise, buses 98 and 99 run regularly from both terminals to Place Messina and Nice Train Station respectively. Both cost an over-priced 6 euros for a 30 minute single journey. I'm told that a cheaper option is to simply take a local bus costing 1.50 euro from outside the airport's gates. This option is not publicized for obvious reasons. Even when we inquired at the Tourist Information office they were not keen to give us any details. Apparently, the city's current single line tram system is shortly to be extended to the airport. We also found it difficult to find a convenient hotel in Nice that offered the extras we look for when booking: breakfast facilities, a kettle in the room and a hair-dryer (for drying wet trainers, of course). With days to go before leaving, Booking.com finally came up with a hotel that satisfied our requirements so, for the second trip in a row, we cancelled our original booking arrangements to change to a better hotel at a better price. Sometimes it pays to wait until the last minute when hotels become desperate to fill rooms. We ended up at the Hotel de Flore, a short stroll to the promenade and just around the corner from Registration and the start of the race.

After completing registration formalities on the Thursday evening we were left with two full days to look around before race day. We decided to spend one of these exploring the city and the other travelling the short distance to Monaco to see how the other half lives. Culture abounds in Nice and the city is home to a number of good museums and popular art galleries, among them: the Museum of Palaeontology, the Archaeological Museum, Museum of Fine Arts and the Museum of Modern and Contemporary Art. It also has its fair share of historic buildings, monuments and churches such as: the magnificent Lascaris Palace, the Russian Orthodox Cathedral of St. Nicolas, Notre Dame Basilica and the Cathedral of St. Reparte. With the glorious weather, however, this wasn't going to be an indoor trip. The cultural side of things will have to wait for another visit – we were much more anxious to get out and enjoy the sunshine.

Our first move was to take the almost obligatory stroll along the length of the Promenade des Anglais. The point where the now underground River Pallion flows into the sea marks the start of this famous walkway. (Incidentally, this is almost exactly where the marathon starts). The Promenade began as a coastal trail along which wealthy English residents would take their afternoon stroll. It was along here where the dancer Isadora Duncan was famously strangled by her own scarf being caught in the wheels of the car in which she was travelling. Walking along the Promenade gives you the chance to admire some of the most beautiful architecture on the Riviera coast. The Art Deco façade of the Palais de la Mediterranee and the grandiose Hotel Negresco in particular stand out. I'm told that a glass of wine in the latter costs a mere £25. At the western end of the Promenade, almost directly opposite the airport, is the Phoenix Parc Floral de Nice, the city's much visited botanical gardens and zoo. As we walked along we were surprised at the large numbers of people swimming in the sea or simply sunbathing on the pebbly beach. It's not something you still expect to see well into November.

Returning back along the Promenade we headed for the Port of Nice at the eastern edge of the city. Also known as Lympia Port after a nearby spring, this is the principal harbour on this stretch of the Mediterranean and, being the point on the French mainland nearest to Corsica, has regular ferry connections to the island. Filled with expensive yachts and pretty fishing boats and surrounded by beautiful red-ochre buildings, the port is a picturesque setting in which to sit and enjoy a meal or a drink. On the way back towards the city centre we took the time to climb the steps up to the Chateau and enjoy the extensive ocean and city views from its heights. This is where Nice began as the ancient Greek city of Nikea. The fortress that once dominated the summit was destroyed by French troops when Nice belonged to Savoy. I hadn't realized until visiting the Chateau that Nice only united with France as recently as 1860.

Our next stop was to explore the rabbit-warren of streets that make up the Old Town. Most of these are too narrow for vehicles so the whole area is virtually traffic-free, though you do have to watch out for the idiots on scooters who insist on driving around at full throttle. The Old Town's centre-piece is the atmospheric Cours Saleya where the dark streets open up into a large sunlit square that houses the city's main market. Each night during our stay a group of twelve of us from the 100 Marathon Club would meet here at Ma Nolan's Irish Bar, next to the Opera House, for a couple of pre-dinner drinks before heading off to eat in one of the street's many outdoor restaurants. Most of these offer three-course set menus in the region of 15 euro. It can become expensive when you start to order your drinks. We solved this problem by taking advantage of the 6pm to 8pm Happy Hour when most bars offered drinks at half-price. Ma Nolan's, for example, sold their beautiful Leffe Blond for a 'mere' 4.90 euros per half litre during that time – a considerable saving on restaurant prices for an inferior beer.

The following day Mo and I took the number 100 early morning public service bus from its terminus at the port to Monaco. At only 1.50 euro this has got to be one of Nice's bargains. The 45 minute journey hugs the precipitous coastal road presenting beautiful views over the rooftops of picturesque villages and ports along the route. At times the bus would disappear into tunnels hewn through the rock to emerge at yet another breathtaking vista of the Cote d'Azur. With a population of only 3,600 Monaco is the second smallest country and, some say, the most glamorous place on Earth. It's basically famous for three things: tax evasion, its Formula One race and its resident celebrities. There's a big connection between the latter two, (probably all three if truth be known) In recent years it seems to have been infiltrated by a whole host of racing drivers: Lewis Hamilton, Jenson Button, David Coulthard, Nico Rosberg and Giancarlo Fisichella to name but five. Tennis players such as Novak Djokovic and Caroline Wozniacki also have homes there and are said to be regular practice partners. Other famous residents include Shirley Bassey, Roger Moore, Ringo Star, Bono from U2, Mohamed Al Fayed and Stellios Haji-Ioannou the founder of easyJet - (now we know where our fares go). We never spotted a single one of them and I doubt very much that they were looking for us. We found Monaco a strange place. Though it was instantly recognizable through decades of constant exposure on TV and cinema screens, in truth, there didn't seem to be much to see on arrival. We eye-balled the Monte Carlo Casino and took the mandatory walk around the harbour but then came away, glad to get back to Nice. After a while you stopped being impressed. There was no one big yacht that stood out, no one super-car to admire – they were all big yachts and every car was either: a Ferrari, Rolls Royce or Maserati. Ostentatious shows of wealth were the norm rather than the exception. I don't think I would have liked to have lived there. I need space – there simply wasn't any. The whole place was over-built, with tower blocks appearing to be sitting on top of other tower blocks and buildings clinging to tiny pieces of earth while, above, the mountains seemed to fold in around the whole place. It all made me feel claustrophobic and glad to get out. I came away wondering where they could have possibly have found 26.2 miles of space on which to run the now defunct Monaco Marathon of the early 2000s.

Registration for the French Riviera Marathon took place in a specially erected tented village on the Quai des Etats -Unis at the eastern end of the Promenade on the Thursday evening and all day Friday and Saturday. It's important to note that registration was dependent on having supplied a valid medical certificate to the organizers beforehand. For my 60 euros entry fee I received an excellent rucksack and a heavy box full of fairly useless free gifts. These included a jar of curry paste and a carton of soup, both in excess of the 100ml airport –allowance. We had to leave these back in the hotel. Given that 28% of the 14,000 plus runners came from 63 separate countries, I would imagine that quite a lot of curry paste and soup never made it out of the country. The entry fee also included a 7 euros charge for the shuttle bus to transport us back from Cannes after the race. There was also a free-to-enter breakfast run at 10am on the Saturday for anyone who fancied it. I didn't. Medals and T-shirts were to be distributed on crossing the finish line. Part of the Expo within the tent contained information stalls for other international marathons. Here I was pleased to catch up with the organizers of the Lausanne Marathon I'd completed two weeks previously.

Sunday morning race day started, as usual, sunny and bright as we all lined up for the 8am start. The event also included a Marathon Relay made up mainly of corporate teams and a Pairs Marathon where each of the runners completed 21.1km of the course. Given that only 6,603 runners finished the marathon that leaves another 7,717 in the various relays. Some of the relay runners were required to run a mere 3km. I always take it with a pinch of salt when marathon organizers boast of the numbers in their event. As far as I could ascertain there was no segregation between the events and as the race progressed you had to look carefully at the bib to see which category the person running with you was competing in. I really didn't fancy the congestion in the 4 hour 15 section in which I'd been placed so made my way to the back of the field. I'd watched the video of the course before leaving the UK and had already decided that it was one to be appreciated and enjoyed as opposed to one to go flat out on.

I was too far back to hear the announcements or whatever it was that started the race, but suddenly we were off en-masse on our way to Cannes. My fears about congestion in the opening kilometres were unfounded. Runners not only followed the traffic-free road but spread out right across the wide pedestrianised section of the Promenade des Anglais itself. In that way the first 4 kilometres taking us past the airport went quite comfortably. Then we were back onto the road and into new territory. I was looking forward to seeing what lay ahead. The excellent map and video produced by the race organizers showed us as having to pass through towns with exotic names that rolled off the tongue, like Antibes and Juan-les-Pins, before arriving at the even more exotic destination of Cannes itself. With the sun on our backs, a light following breeze, a clear blue sky and the Mediterranean sparkling away to our left, it all seemed too good to be true.

After about 7k we crossed the River Var and arrived at the beautiful port of Saint-Laurent-du-Var, one of the largest ports of the Cote d'Azur. Shortly after 10k a classy-looking racecourse appeared on the right-hand side of the road. I later found out that this was the Hippodrome de la Cote d'Azur – home to the Grand Criterium, one of the great classics of the European trotting season. After this the course left the coast briefly for a short out-and-back inland section – the only real digression from the magnificent coastal scenery for the whole of the race.

At 15k the course went back on itself again to take us down to the new marina development at Baie des Anges. For the first time we could see where we were in relation to others on the course. Spotting the 4:30 pacemaker not too far ahead provided an incentive to see if I could catch up. The beautiful marina is an award winning development on a former camp site that took 25 years to complete. Fronting the marina are four giant pyramid-shaped apartment blocks, designed to resemble huge white waves. They dominate the skyline along this stretch of the coast. Several of the clientele in the up-market restaurants seemed somewhat surprised at having their peace and quiet shattered by a host of sweaty runners. After emerging from the marina we enjoyed a long straight section following the beach until just after the half-way point.

Next up was Fort Carre, a 16th century star-shaped fort of four arrow-head shaped bastions that stands on the outskirts of Antibes. During the French Revolution Napoleon was briefly imprisoned here. In 1860 the fort played an important role in France's annexation of Nice from Savoy. James Bond fans will recall it as Blofeld's fortress in 'Never Say Never Again' – Sean Connery's final appearance as Bond. Here the course narrowed considerably as we ran around the ancient walls leading towards Antibes. Antibes was a Greek fortified town named Antipolis and later a Roman town and active trading port on the Mediterranean. Today it's an attractive town and popular destination for tourists. Its port, Port Vauban, is the largest yachting harbour in Europe with room for more than 2,000 moorings. It has a long and colourful history which includes not only the Greeks but Romans and Crusaders who stopped here on their way to the Holy Land. With its busy port, 16th century ramparts and narrow cobblestone streets, it is everyone's idea of the quintessential Mediterranean town. Artists like Picasso, Max Ernst and Nicolas de Stael all stayed in Antibes, as did British author Graham Greene.

We left Antibes via Plage de la Garoupe, and shortly after this at 28k I was reduced to walking for the first time when faced with a steep hill taking us over the narrow part of the peninsular of Cap d'Antibes. The Cape separates the Bay of Nice from the Bay of Cannes and as soon as we crossed over it we were now running along the latter towards our final destination. 30k saw us at the famous resort town of Juan-les-Pins, a major holiday destination popular with the international jet-set for its casino, nightclubs and beaches. Those of a certain age may recall Peter Starstedt's 1969 number one hit song 'Where do you go to (My Lovely)' about a girl who becomes a member of the European jet-set. The song mentions that the girl spends her summer vacations in Juan-les-Pins. The resort also figures prominently in many literary works including Sartre's 'La Reprieve,' the second volume of his 'Roads to Freedom' trilogy and Charles Jackson's novel 'The Lost Weekend.' The town is also famous for its annual jazz festival 'Jazz a Juan.' The fact that Juan-les-Pins is twinned with New Orleans helps to attract a large number of internationally known American artists to the festival. A set of ceramic tiles laid into the pavement display the handprints of some of these including: Dave Brubeck, B. B. King, Ray Charles, Little Richard and Stevie Wonder. Some line-up! After the pebbled beaches of Nice the fine grained sands we ran past were most appealing.

At 35k we reached yet another marina at Golfe-Juan. This is the nearest port and seaside resort to the east of Cannes and is much quieter and far less expensive than its larger neighbour. Its main claim to fame is the fact that Napoleon landed here in 1815 with 600 men after escaping exile from the Isle of Elba 150 miles away. After being supplied with provisions by the local populace, he and his supporters marched north over the mountains – now known as Route Napoleon – to reach Grenoble in six days. From there he continued on a victorious entry into Paris. One hundred days after landing at Golfe-Juan he met his Waterloo – literally. The event is celebrated every two years in March with a colourful re-enactment on the beach. Uk Forces Sweetheart Dame Vera Lynn was one of the town's most famous residents.

Exiting Golfe-Juan we were confronted with the second significant uphill of the race. For the second time I slowed to a walk. This time I was in good company, chatting to a French couple dressed in Superman costumes. I figured that if it was too hilly for Mr. and Mrs. Superman then there was no shame in me walking alongside them. This section took us alongside a busy road with queues of cars full of angry drivers frustrated in their attempts to reach Cannes. We left the busy road at the 40k mark, turning left to take us down to the long run-in along the seafront approach to Cannes known as The Promenade de la Croisette. This long promenade lined with palm trees and pines is the natural link between the beach and the city itself. The former coastal path has become one of the best known boulevards in the world and is synonymous with the identity of Cannes. Nowadays, palaces and sumptuous residences have replaced the simple huts originally occupying this spot. Its most famous building is the Palais des Festivals et des Congress, an unimposing modern building where the annual Cannes Film Festival is held. Like most of the other towns we'd passed en route, Cannes is known for its association with the rich and famous and for the host of celebrities that turn up for the film festival held there since 1946. The final 2k along the Croisette were lined with crowds of spectators who'd made the journey to Cannes to see their favourites finish. The last few hundred metres were particularly congested - somewhat like those sections you see in the Tour de France where over-zealous spectators almost succeed in knocking competitors off their bikes.

Despite finishing with the 4:30 pacemaker my time was recorded at 4hour 33 minutes. That didn't bother me too much as I'd thoroughly enjoyed the run. The course was beautiful and the organizers had done everything expected of them. On a hot day they'd ensured that we got plenty to drink – and not just water –

there was electrolyte drinks at intervals and coca cola too. Food tables were stacked with all sorts; from fruits to chocolates to sugar lumps so no problems there. The finisher's medal and T-shirt were also of a high quality and we were handed water, ham rolls, croissants and confectionary to keep us happy on the bus back to Nice.

My plan on finishing had been to simply don the T-shirt and take a look around Cannes. Neither happened – being just after midday it was still too hot for extra clothing and the crowds put paid to any ideas I had of extra sightseeing. It's difficult to form opinions of a place when it's full to bursting with tired, sweaty runners and their families blocking the views. First impressions, though, were that it lacked the character, opulence and stately architecture of Nice, its main rival on the Cote d'Azur. I found my friend Paul Richards waiting for me on the mile long walk to where the buses were parked so simply strolled around the harbour before heading off. On the bus back I reflected on what had been the wonderful experience of running along a world famous coastline. This had been the second marathon in succession where I had been lucky enough to run in glorious scenery and I couldn't help but compare the two. While Lausanne had provided mountains, lakes and vineyards, this one had served up sea, beaches and exotic resort towns. I couldn't decide which one I'd liked best. They were both excellent marathons for different reasons. It's what makes Marathon Tourism such an enjoyable pastime.

The famous Promenade des Anglais in Nice

Before the Start of the French Riviera Marathon

ITALY

FLORENCE MARATHON

Florence is one of four marathons I've completed in Italy: Milan, Pisa, Florence and Venice in that order. They were all interesting events in historic locations but, of the four, Florence is the one that had the biggest impact. I'd last visited Florence long ago in 1974 before returning for the city's marathon in November 2015. I found it hard to believe that much has changed there in the intervening 41 years. Florence is still the quintessential medieval city of ancient buildings, beautiful squares and narrow streets crawling with tourists at all times of the day (and night). It has been ranked by Forbes as one of the most beautiful cities in the world. It is often referred to as 'the cradle of the Renaissance' and is often described at times as 'the Athens of the Middle Ages.' The Historic Centre of Florence attracts millions of tourists each year anxious to experience its culture, and its Renaissance art, architecture and monuments. One noticeable consequence of all these visitors is that just about every third building in the city seems to be a hotel. The city is also virtually an open air museum enclosed by ancient walls that safeguard world-famous masterpieces. Today's crowded streets are the same ones through which Leonardo da Vinci, Michelangelo, Dante, Galileo and many other of the most illustrious minds of all time once wended their way. Unsurprisingly, the city was declared a World Heritage Site by UNESCO in1982.

Just to give you a few brief facts: Florence, with a population of around 340,000 inhabitants, is the capital of the region of Tuscany. It sits on either side of the River Arno, between the Adriatic and the Tyrrhenian seas, almost in the middle of the Italian peninsula.

Founded by the Romans in the first century B.C. it began its rebirth after the decadence of the barbaric ages, reaching its highest pinnacles of civilization between the 11th and 15th centuries. In the latter century it came under the rule of the Medici family, who later became the Grand Dukes of Tuscany. This was the period that has left the greatest legacy on today's city. During this time Florence was at the height of its glory in art and culture, in politics and in economic power. In the 18th century the Medici dynasty was succeeded by the House of Lorraine before the city became part of the Kingdom of Italy of which it was the capital from 1865 to 1871.

As a result of the Medici legacy Florence's museums, palaces and churches house some of the greatest artistic treasures in the world. Its most famous sites are internationally renowned and their names virtually roll off the tongue. These include the magnificent cathedral the Duomo, the churches of Santa Croce and Santa Maria Novella, the Uffizi, Bargello and Accademia museums, the library of San Lorenzo and the iconic Ponte Vecchio Bridge. Using the theme 'Run in Art,' the marathon organizers had promised runners a course that took in all these sites and more. The marathon tourist in me simply had to go.

But first I had to get there. Florence's Peretola airport is a single runway affair that doesn't attract too many international flights. I believe that the only ones from the UK are from London City with either BA City Flyer or City Jet. Many UK visitors fly into the larger Pisa Airport and from there take the 70 minute train ride inland to Florence. My itinerary meant getting up at 3.00am for a 5.55am flight from Newcastle to Schiphol and then on to Florence. As things turned out the flight Gods had unwittingly sat me next to a young marathon runner from Amsterdam, Alma Vietor on the second leg of the journey. We were probably the only two of our kind on that flight. Alma, who was planning on running only her fifth marathon in Florence made great company, both on the flight and on our shared journey out to the distant Registration and Expo. From the airport we took the shuttle bus (the Volainbus) that leaves every half hour for the 20 minute trip into the city's central station of Santa Maria Novella. It's 6 euros for a single journey, payable to the driver. If you want to take advantage of the 10 euros return fare, tickets must be purchased in advance inside the terminal. On arrival at the station we jumped straight into a taxi for a shared 15 euros drive to Registration about 4 kilometres away at the giant Luigi Ridolfi Athletic Stadium in the Campo di Marte sports complex.

Being Saturday afternoon, Registration was a busy and crowded affair. Here we were handed our number/chip, programme and goody bag. The latter contained largely adverts for various running related products, a copy of Distance Running magazine, clothes bag for the next day, some powdered sports drinks and a muesli bar. It would have contained a Pasta Party ticket if I'd paid for one but, seeing the huge queues of those waiting to eat, I was glad I hadn't. The organizers had then cleverly arranged things so that we had to pass all the usual stalls of merchandise, both there and back, before we could collect our long-sleeved event T-shirt and, like Elvis, finally leave the building. Having collected a map of the city at the Expo, I was more confident of navigating my way back to the centre on foot. It also gave me the opportunity of doing some preliminary sightseeing before booking into my hotel.

Florence is a compact city easily traversed by walking and orientation is straight-forward. Using the giant, terracotta dome of the cathedral as a point of reference, it's only ten minutes from the bus and train stations to the Piazza del Duomo from where most of the major sites are within a short walking distance. Before travelling I'd identified the Duomo, the Palazza Vecchio, the Santa Croce basilica, the Ponte Vecchio Bridge and the Santa Maria Novella church as my five must-see buildings. Within two hours of leaving Registration I'd managed a cursory look at them all - in that order. The constant stream of pedestrians and those stopping dead in front of you to take photographs make walking uncomfortable at times. Even worse are those on bikes, still attempting to cycle at speed despite the crowds. Heaven knows what it must be like on these streets in summer. Even after visiting all of these magnificent sights I was fully aware that I'd only just scratched the surface of what there was to see. Most of Florence's real treasures are kept indoors, away from eyes that haven't forked out good money for the privilege of seeing them. And, judging by the size of the crowds queuing up outside each of the places mentioned, I wasn't sure that I'd have the time to join them.

The ornate beauty of each of the buildings I visited was quite breathtaking. So much so that at times I found it difficult to tear myself away. I know I felt compelled to take far more photos than I normally would have done. Over the centuries some have described physical symptoms that they attributed to the effects of the sheer beauty of what they were seeing. This has been officially recognized as a form of 'Stendhal's Syndrome' – something that occurs when an individual is exposed to overwhelming beauty, usually in the form of works of art. Affected individuals might experience symptoms such as physical or emotional anxiety, rapid or irregular heartbeat, dizziness, fainting, nausea and even hallucinations. I kid you not! The affliction is named after French author Henri-Marie Beyle, better known by his pen-name Stendhal. When Stendhal visited the Santa Croce and saw Gotti's famous frescoes for the first time in 1817 he found himself overcome with emotion. It wasn't until 1979, after local chief psychiatrist Dr G Magheri recorded the regularity with which tourists came to her hospital suffering from dizzy spells and disorientation after admiring Michelangelo's David that the syndrome was officially recognized. In her book on the subject Dr Magheri documented 106 similar cases admitted to her hospital between 1977 and 1986.

For this visit I'd changed my usual practice of locating myself close to the Start/Finish area and selected the Dedo Boutique Hotel five minutes walk from the station and one street back from the river. This meant that all I had to do was follow the river for thirty minutes, along past the Ponte Vecchio and on to the start on race morning. This was to be close to the Basilica de Santa Croce. I'm normally suspicious of anything that advertises itself using words like boutique, executive, exclusive, luxury and similar. As well as sounding pretentious such adjectives are often used to deceive purchasers and pump-up prices. The same applies to descriptions of organically grown food, gastro pubs, locally-sourced produce and writing the menu in French. Who do they think they're fooling? The hotel cost me £100 for the two nights which was quite reasonable by Florence's standards. I'm not sure what was 'boutique' about it but I've no complaints other than the fact that the key they gave me for the outer door wouldn't turn in the lock. Not good after a late night out.

Sunday morning started bright and dry, if a little on the cold side and without a breath of wind. With the temperature expected to peak at 13 degrees, it was ideal conditions for marathon running. One of the more interesting observations to be made at the start was in comparing the two large groups of African males on either side of the fenced-off area. Inside the fence were the elite African runners, there chasing the big bucks. On the outside was an entirely different, yet well organized group of Africans carrying bin-bags and standing at regular intervals apart. They were there for the more mundane task of collecting discarded clothing as their reward. Judging by the number of bags they filled they seemed to be doing pretty well.

This was to be the 32nd edition of the race that over the years has grown in popularity to be the second largest marathon in Italy after Rome. In 2015 there were 10,099 recorded entrants of whom 8,183 completed the course. I can't help thinking from my experiences at the start that the race has long passed the optimum number of participants for the nature of the course. Florence is a historic, medieval city of narrow often cobble-stoned streets not in the least bit suited to mass participation sporting events. The course, though scenic for the most part, was as convoluted as the French Riviera's had been straightforward a couple of weeks ago. I guess the frequent retracing of steps was to be expected given the difficulties in fitting 42km into a city of Florence's size and surrounded by hills on all sides.

The start is best described as organized chaos and the first few kilometres were far from comfortable as runners jostled one another for space to place their feet. I felt we were kept waiting in our pre-ordained pens based on predicted finishing times for far too long. The barriers between pens were then opened too soon, resulting in those who'd predicted a slower finish suddenly deciding they wanted to get to the head of the queue. I can't understand that mentality. At this stage runner's etiquette went out the door – I don't think I've been in a race where so many of those who passed me immediately cut diagonally across my path forcing me to stop. I can only describe it as like being corralled by sheepdogs. The only consolation was that this was a true marathon race featuring only marathon runners. There was no Half Marathon or 10k athletes to get in the way. It was a good 5 kilometres until I felt I was breathing my own air.

Once we'd found our feet and our rhythm the race turned out to be a marathon tourist's dream. The organizers definitely kept to their promise of showing us the best that Florence had to offer. First up, at about 4k was the giant, pentagonal fort of the Fortezza da Basso. This masterpiece of military Renaissance architecture was commissioned by the Medicis in the 16th century as a show of strength to deter possible insurgents. These days the hundreds of thousands of square metres of space within its impenetrably thick walls are used for more peaceful purposes as an exhibition and congress centre.

Shortly after passing the fortress we arrived for a long out-and-back section within the Parco delle Cascine, a beautiful and historic long and narrow park bordering the River Arno. The park was originally built as an agricultural and hunting estate of the Medici family. At last, the wide avenues within the park provided space in which to run as well as shade from the overhanging trees. It had turned into a sunny autumnal day and the 10 kilometres we ran within the park offered the most peaceful part of the race. Before leaving the park at 15k we passed not one but two racecourses. The first of these, La Muline, was a trotting course closed in 2012 to give back more of the park to the city of Florence. The other, the Ippodromo del Visarno, also stages pop concerts in its 15,000 capacity stadium when races are not being held. Pink Floyd's David Gilmour featured there recently.

On leaving the park we crossed the river on the first of four occasions to run along its southern bank before turning inland to the ancient gateway of Porto Romano. The 14th century gate belongs to the original city walls of Florence and is the largest and best preserved of the remaining city gates. The entrance still has the original iron doors and a marble slab with the Medici coat of arms. Turning at the gate we headed back down to and across the river to the half way mark on its northern bank. Then came the two least scenic parts of the route: a 2km stretch either side of the railway line between 25k and 27k then a 3km zig-zag around the Campo di Marte sports complex where Registration had been held. The area incorporates a large variety of sporting venues with facilities for soccer, swimming, athletics, tennis and basketball – we must have run around the lot of them. I was particularly interested in taking a look at the Stadio Artemio Franchi, the home of Fiorentina soccer club as well as to some pretty famous footballers in their time: Roberto Baggio, Gabriel Batistuta and Brian Laudrup to name but three. The 47,000 capacity stadium built in 1931 was completely renovated before the 1990 World Cup held in Italy. It hosted three group matches and the quarter final between Argentina and Yugoslavia during the tournament. The whole place was deathly quiet – not a fan in sight.

The last 8 kilometres finally brought us back into the historic centre of the city and from there on in the sights came thick and fast. Arriving along the long and narrow Via della Colonna, we first passed the National Archeological Museum and the St. Annunciata, an art-filled church renowned for its frescoes, before turning right in front of the Accademia. This is the gallery that is famous for its sculptures by Michelangelo, particularly his statue of David which was transferred here in 1873. The 5.17 metre marble statue of a standing male nude representing the Biblical hero David is considered a masterpiece of Renaissance sculpture. Because of the nature of the hero it represented, the statue soon came to symbolize the defence of civil liberties embodied in the Republic of Florence, an independent city-state threatened on all sides by more powerful enemies. In its original position outside the Pallazo Vecchio the eyes of David, displaying a warning stare, were directed to the enemy of Rome. Entrance is 12.50 euros if you don't mind the long queues.

Next up at 35k was Florence's Duomo, the city's most iconic landmark. Capped by Brunellschi's amazing red-tiled cupola, the cathedral dominates the skyline, with its eight white ribs set against a background of terracotta tiles. The building took 150 years to complete. Close up it is so huge as to be quite overwhelming. Even while running past you couldn't help admiring the breathtaking pink, white and green marble façade. Beside it stands the similarly ornate Campanile (bell tower) designed by Gotti and the Baptistery building. These three buildings are the centre-piece of the UNESCO World Heritage Site. Entry to the cathedral is free though you do have to pay if you want to ascend to the cupola. Until the development of new structural materials and new construction methods in modern times, the dome was the largest in the world. It is still the largest brick dome ever constructed. Standing inside the cathedral and looking up the cupola is an awe-inspiring sight, decorated with its elaborate series of religious paintings. Other than these, the vast interior of the cathedral appears stark and empty in comparison to its decorative exterior. Many of its treasures have been lost over time or transferred to the Museum Opera del Duomo.

We left the cheering crowds of the cathedral square behind to do a mini-tour of the city streets, heading west to a turn in front of the Stazione Leopalda at 37k. Then it was back along the riverbank to cross the river for the third time at the Ponte Santa Trinita before immediately re-crossing over the iconic Ponte Vecchio at 39k. To me, this was the highlight of the race and something that I'd been looking forward to immensely. No visit to Florence is complete without at least spending some time dawdling on the bridge. Usually the bridge is crawling with tourists making sightseeing uncomfortable. On marathon day we had it all to ourselves. The bridge spans the narrowest part of the River Arno, and doesn't really look like a bridge at all due to the overhanging shops and houses. Its uniqueness lies in the fact that it is not only a functional structure for crossing the river, but is also a combination of road, market place and shopping area that has developed in a chaotic fashion over the centuries. By remaining intact the bridge has not only succeeded in defying a river prone to serious flooding but has also defied the laws of physics. It's no coincidence that it was the only bridge that was spared by the retreating German troops in 1944. Instead of destroying it they simply isolated it by blowing up the bridge's access points. The laws at the time of construction in the mid-14th century did not allow owners to build on the pavement, so the buildings were extended over the river and held up by slender wooden stakes, making them appear to be suspended in mid-air. But the most ingenious development on the bridge is the famous Vasari Corridor, another wonder of the Renaissance period. This is a covered passageway running above the shops commissioned by Cosimo 1 de Medici as a novel way of connecting the government offices of the Uffizi with his Pitti Palace across the river. As you walk across the bridge the parade of shops is suddenly interrupted by two wide terraces opening out to magnificent views of the river. One of these includes a fountain with statue of the sculptor Benvenuto Cellini. To the annoyance of the authorities, who now impose heavy fines on anyone caught in the act, couples declare their love by attaching a lock to the statue and throwing the key into the river. The bridge is even more captivating when lit-up at night.

The final 3 kilometres threw up a host of treasures. We next ran past the Piazza della Signoria containing the magnificent Palazzo Vecchio and the Uffizi Museum. The Piazza is famous mainly for its vast array of statues. These include, among others, the equestrian statue of Cosimo 1, Ammannati's Neptune Fountain and copies of Donatello's heraldic lion and Michelangelo's David (for those who can't be bothered to queue to see the real thing). Florence's fortress-like palace, the Pallazo Vecchio with its crenellations and 94 metre-high tower dominates the square. Completed in the 14th century for the city government it remains the seat of the city's power and is home to the mayor's office and the municipal council. A visit to the top of the tower is said to give the best views over the city. In the southern corner of the square is the Uffizi, the city's former government offices now converted into one of the world's top art museums. It houses some of the most important works of the Renaissance, including works by Leonardo da Vinci, Caravaggio, Rembrandt, Botticelli and, of course, Michelangelo. The entrance fee is 12.50 euros but such is its popularity waiting times have been known to be as long as five hours during high season.

The route continued through the narrow and very crowded streets taking us back to the Piazza del Duomo. This time we emerged on the opposite, eastern side of the cathedral before continuing along the final couple of kilometres to the finish in the Piazza Santa Croce. The devastating flood of 1996 is said to have permanently changed the area around the square. Prior to then it had been one of the more densely populated parts of the city but, flood damage resulted in many of the residents moving away from the river. The square in which we finished has traditionally been one of the city's main areas for festivities. The Medici used it for pageants while during the years when Savonarola was preaching his own particular brand of religion, it was the principal site for the ceremonial execution of heretics. Dominating the square is the Franciscan Basilica de Santa Croce, another beautifully ornate neo-Gothic building decorated by varying shades of coloured marble. The church takes its name from a splinter of the Holy Cross donated to it by King Louis of France in 1258. Most visitors come to see the tombs of Michelangelo, Galileo and Ghilberti inside the church and to admire Gotti's frescoes decorating the chapels next to the altar - the ones that Stendhal swooned over!

On finishing, the organizers led us away from the square past tables full of food and drink and down to the baggage storage next to the river. High fences similar to those at the start ensured that the runners were kept separate from the surging crowds of spectators. Apart from the congestion mentioned earlier it had been an enjoyable day on an interesting course around a wonderful city. I'd been impressed by what was on offer on our way around: a choice of water, isotonic drinks and hot tea with fruit and confectionary throughout, sponges at intermediate drinks stations and even gels at the 30k mark. I was happy too with my medal and my time of 4 hours 22. My priority now was to sample some of the local food and drink before heading off home.

When eating in Florence remember the golden rule is that the closer you are to the historic old town, the higher the price. Many of the best restaurants in the city can be found in the Santa Croce district. If you're looking for something cheaper there are numerous fast food outlets near the station. Incidentally, the central station of Santa Maria Novela is the one obvious blot on the city's architectural heritage. It was built in the 1930s after a design competition to replace Brunel's original station. It resembles an ugly oblong box, variously described as 'a packing case' and 'a prison refrigerator.' I'd eaten there the previous night when all I wanted was something/anything with chips before the marathon. After the race I was looking for authentic Tuscan cuisine and had been recommended to try the 11 Latini restaurant in Via dei Palchetti, close to the Ponte Vecchio Bridge. Booking is advisable so I'd made one beforehand – just as well as the place was packed. I better not say how much the meal cost in case Mo is reading this. Believe me, it was a lot more than I would normally pay when eating on my own. My recommendation is to not to eat too much of the bread basket before the real food arrives. First up were plates of meats, melons and caprese salad. Next followed three different pastas: including a meat sauce fusili, gnocchi with rabbit and a cheese-stuffed ravioli. Then came the house speciality of Bistecca Florientina, a two-inch giant lump of steak served with potatoes and spinach. After this three desserts were offered: a raspberry tart, Tiramisu and finally a plate of biscotti. It all came with a carafe of the local house wine that could be topped up on request. It was an expensive but wonderful meal.

Finding somewhere to get a decent drink was not as easy. As I'd previously found after the Milan Marathon most alcohol in Italy is served in café-bars. You know the type of place I mean – pretty little spots full of biscuits and cakes where the beer is brought to your table by a guy in a white shirt and tie who hovers around expecting a tip. These places have no atmosphere and simply don't appeal. I took a long time searching the side streets until I eventually discovered The Joshua Tree, something resembling a British pub, close to the central station. There are also two Irish bars in the city centre, both in prestige locations. One, which I think is simply called The Irish Pub is opposite the Baptistery in the Piazza del Duomo. The other, The Michael Collins, that I visited for a Guinness is in the centre of the Piazza della Signoria. Most of its beers seemed to cost 6 euros per pint.

While it didn't have the same affect on me as it did on our friend Stendhal, I still came away from Florence enthralled by what I'd seen. A weekend's visit simply doesn't do the place justice. I'm aware that I only scratched the surface of what there is to see and do in this fascinating city. I won't leave it another 41 years before returning.

Florence's magnificent Duomo. Part of the Marathon course

Dismantling the Finish gantry outside the Basilica de Santa Croce

EGYPT

EGYPTIAN MARATHON

On reaching my 230th marathon early in 2015 I started to begin thinking of somewhere 'different' where Mo and I could go to celebrate the landmark 250th. I figured that by running my usual twenty or so marathons each year I could choose between Dubai, Egypt, Tel Aviv or possibly Boston in early 2016. We decided on Egypt. Neither of us had been before and the chance to visit what remained of the splendours of the Ancient Egyptian civilisation appealed the most. Rather than make it a rushed trip we chose to indulge ourselves by combining the marathon with a two-week, all-inclusive holiday in a 5-star hotel on the banks of the Nile in Luxor. We'd no sooner paid our holiday in full when the unthinkable happened and ISIS succeeded in blowing a Russian passenger jet out of the sky at nearby Sharm-el-Sheik. This resulted in UK airlines refusing to fly to that part of the world and to all sorts of confusion as to whether our holiday was likely to be cancelled or, indeed, whether or not it was still safe to travel. Though Luxor is on the opposite side of the Red Sea to where the plane was downed it also has an unenviable reputation for a major terrorist atrocity. As recently as 1997, 64 people, including 59 visiting tourists, were massacred at Luxor's Temple of Hatshesput in what was at the time the worst terrorist attack in Egypt. (Ironically, this same Temple was to be the Start and Finish point of the marathon I'd just agreed to enter). Thompson Holidays, with whom we were due to travel, assured us that the booking would be honoured. Unfortunately, other passengers who'd booked on our flight from Manchester had been having second thoughts about the wisdom of continuing with their holiday plans so Thompson pulled the plug on the flight, citing insufficient demand. In the end they amalgamated the Manchester departure with a same-day flight from Gatwick so we were on our way – albeit with the added inconvenience of overnight stays out-and-back in London we could well have done without. A 30 day visa is required for all tourist visitors to Egypt. This can be purchased at the airport on arrival for £20 or $25 – just make sure that in all the chaos you end up in the right queue.

The fact that I'd had so much hassle entering the marathon in the first place strengthened my determination to go regardless of any safety concerns. I wouldn't say that it's an easy event to get in to. Early versions of the event website gave little in the way of useful information and the link to the entry process didn't appear to work. My entry was made by email correspondence with Event Sports, the Cairo based race organisers. The whole process appeared to revolve around taking their marathon package that involved staying for a minimum of two nights (before and after the race) at their event hotel, the 5-star Maritim Jolie Ville, located on an island in the Nile south of Luxor. It was put to me that it was easier to do this and be taken by the organiser's transport to the early morning start (and return) on the opposite bank of the Nile than to attempt to make my own arrangements. The package also included an early morning wake-up call and breakfast plus a post-race special presentation dinner for the athletes after the race. Having thought about it, I'm sure I could have made alternative and possibly cheaper independent arrangements but I rather fancied the idea of being part of a group and having everything sorted out beforehand. It was, after all, meant to be a celebration of a landmark marathon. In the end I paid out 315 euros for the full package for Mo and myself, with Mo being an invited guest to the post-race meal. Of this amount 95 euros constituted the race entry fee.

Egypt has been a country I've always dreamed of visiting. Its history can be traced back to prehistoric times when the Sahara Desert was formed in around 8,000 BC. This prompted early civilisations to move closer towards the fertile banks of the Nile to catch fish and grow crops. However, it's the Pharaoh's Egypt that began some 5,000 years ago that really captures everyone's imagination. The Pharaonic period, also known as the Dynastic era because Egypt was ruled by a series of 30 different dynasties, has left a truly remarkable impact on civilised history. The Pharaohs oversaw more than 3,000 years of progress and achievement. They created strong government, military and religious structures, held court and ruled the land with unquestioned authority. They were worshipped as Gods by their people and lavished their phenomenal wealth on building temples and monuments in their honour – the same structures that visitors from all over the world now come to gaze at in awe and incomprehension. Their lives, cultures and phenomenal knowledge of mummification, mathematics and astronomy have created iconic images of an ancient Egypt that continue to fascinate overseas visitors.

Geographically, Egypt enjoys a strategic location in North Africa close to the Middle East. Known officially as the Arab Republic of Egypt, it borders Libya to the west, Sudan to the south and Israel and the Gaza Strip to the east via the Sinai Peninsula. The country has long played an important role in connecting Africa with Asia and the Mediterranean with the Indian Ocean. It is a vast country, four times the size of the UK and twice the size of France yet its major cities of Cairo, Aswan and Luxor all hug the shores of the River Nile, while Alexandria, the second largest city after Cairo sits on the Nile Delta at its Mediterranean outlet. The importance of the Nile on Egyptian civilisation simply cannot be over-estimated. It has been said that without the Nile there would be no Egypt. The very name Egypt meaning 'Black Land' derives from the colour of the silt deposited following the flooding of the Nile.

Luxor, the host city to the Egyptian Marathon, straddles the Nile more than half way between Cairo and Aswan. Visiting the city today it is hard to believe that Luxor was for several centuries one of the most important cities in the world as well as the centre of political, economic, religious and military life in Ancient Egypt. Luxor derives from the Arabic al-uqsur meaning 'the palaces' and refers to the appearance of the town until the 19th century when it lay largely within the remains of the palace-like Temple of Luxor that still dominates the surrounding area. Though the ancient Egyptians named their city Waset ('The City' – greatest of all capitals) it is best known as Thebes, the name given to it by Greek historians. Thanks to the imperial conquests of Egypt's warrior kings the wealth and talent of the world poured into Thebes. Ships from Phoenicia and Nubia tied up at its quays to unload cargoes from the Mediterranean and Africa or to deliver tributes to the Pharaoh of gold, ebony, ivory, slaves and grain. At its height Luxor's population reached over one million and the wealth, knowledge and technical abilities of its inhabitants made it a centre of the ancient world for more than half a millennium.

By contrast, the Luxor of today is in a sorry state. Its population has dwindled to less than 400,000 and due to the political instability since the Egyptian Revolution of 2011 visitors no longer arrive in their thousands to boost its flagging economy. Some hotels were closed and abandoned and one at least remained open with only a single guest. Our own hotel was operating at less than 20% capacity. We found the city centre consisting of, at most, three main shopping streets to be squalid, dirty and unattractive. After a couple of early forays in search of food and drink we soon abandoned the idea of going out in the evening and confined ourselves to our hotel's buffet meals – after all, we'd already paid for these as part of the all-inclusive package. Fortunately for us we really liked the Iberotel in which we were staying. In the absence of other guests and without us requesting it, the management had upgraded us to a top floor room with views to die for overlooking the Nile. The large balcony afforded magnificent vistas of sunrise and sunset over the river and across to the Theban hills. The hotel's landscaped gardens were terraced right down to the river banks and the swimming pool sat in a floating pontoon over the river itself – no wonder some of our fellow guests never left the sanctuary of the hotel for the duration of their stay. That's not the way Mo and I operate, however, and we spent much of the time we had when not visiting the sights, strolling along the three kilometre Corniche

(Promenade) that follows the Nile from Luxor to Karnak. I also enjoyed several early morning training runs along the Corniche just as the sun was rising and before the crowds woke up – the atmosphere was magical with reminders everywhere of how you were virtually running through history.

Any tourist not up and out before 8am is in big trouble. Once breakfast-time is over it's virtually impossible to escape the confines of your hotel without suffering serious harassment from swarms of locals wanting to sell you something/anything as soon as your feet touch the pavement. These touts, for want of a better word, surround and molest all westerners like flies around a honey-pot. Deprived of their income from the tourist dollar for the past four years, they are desperate in demanding their share of your holiday spending money. The harassment borders at times on the obnoxious and many will simply not take no for an answer. Much of their patter is quite ingenious and the scams they attempt have to be seen to be believed. Their persistence can be so wearing that some of our fellow guests refused to leave their hotel bubble. They simply couldn't deal with the constant harassment. The irony of this whole scenario is that these touts refuse to recognise that they're their own worst enemy. They excuse their molestation by explaining that business is bad because tourists are no longer coming, without realising that their own offensive behaviour is what is turning tourists away. It's certainly the one thing about Luxor that would make us have second thoughts about returning. Touts aside, we found the vast majority of Egyptians with nothing to sell and with no particular axe to grind among the friendliest and most genuinely welcoming people we've ever met. At no stage during our visit did we feel threatened or unsafe – and that included a three and a half hour ride each way on a local train between Luxor and Aswan where, on both legs, we were the only westerners on the train. Even the touts were never aggressive. After a week of hearing a polite but firm 'No Thank You' from us they eventually learned to leave us alone.

Just to amuse ourselves, Mo and I drew up an imaginary League Table of the worst offenders by occupations. Well on top of the league were the caleche (horse carriage) drivers who consistently followed us along the streets insisting that we take a ride with them for 'the good of the horse!' Even crossing the road to avoid them brought little respite – they merely did a full U-turn and followed in the opposite direction. A close second were the felucca (sailing boat) boatmen forever pestering you to go on 'my lovely boat' usually to Banana Island (wherever that might be). Next up were the horn-tooting taxi drivers who refused to believe that some of us just like to walk. Then it's the unofficial, self-appointed tour guides who latch on to you both inside and outside temples, tombs and museums expecting to be paid for pointing out the bleeding obvious. One of the highlights of our whole trip was watching a fist fight develop between one of these 'guides' and a Japanese tourist who'd refused to pay his rip-off demands, deep in the bowels of Ramesses 11's tomb. Finally, making up the league table are the hotel staff, each with his own gimmick to extract extra cash (it has to be a 'he' – there were no females employed in our hotel). Their behaviour becomes more and more ingratiating the closer it gets to check-out (tipping) time. In a (junior) league of their own were the scores of insistent children who, lacking the sophistication of their adult counterparts, simply thrust outstretched hands in our faces demanding 'back-sheesh' (money).

Despite the touts and its tawdry appearance, Luxor nevertheless justifies its description as the 'world's greatest open-air museum and archaeological site.' It offers visitors the chance of seeing almost a third of the ancient antiquities known to man in just a few kilometres. It would take more than a mere fortnight's holiday to take-in all the temples and structures that have stood for thousands of years and have been beautifully preserved in the dry desert air, but we gave it our best shot. Luxor's sights are set on both the east and west banks of the Nile on which it sits. The urbanised East Bank is home to most of Luxor's tourist infrastructure and the world-famous temples of Karnak and Luxor as well as the recently built Luxor Museum and a separate Mummification Museum. I'd recommend a visit to each of these during your stay but don't be fooled by signing-up for any of the ridiculously over-priced guided tours on offer. Each of these four sites are located on the Corniche within walking distance from our hotel so Mo and I simply made our own way to each, paid the entrance fee and had a good look around while consulting our guide book bought as a present before leaving the UK. We literally saved hundreds of Egyptian Pounds (exchange rate was £1 = E£11 at the time). For those unfamiliar with Ancient Egyptian history, Karnak is perhaps the largest religious complex ever constructed. Centred on the Temple of Amun, over the course of two millennia, it was enlarged by consecutive Pharaohs to serve not only as a spiritual centre but also as an economic hub containing administrative offices, treasuries, palaces, bakeries, breweries, granaries and schools. Much of it is still intact and to visit is truly awe inspiring. In ancient times an avenue of sphinxes connected it to Luxor Temple some three kilometres away. Luxor Temple itself is a strikingly beautiful monument right in the heart of the modern town. The temple is dedicated to the Theban triad of Gods: Amun, Mut and Khonsui and is best visited when lit up at night to create an eerie atmosphere long remembered. Nearby, the purpose-built Luxor Museum is another must-see experience and the perfect place to view artefacts that once belonged to the great kings and queens of ancient Thebes, including several exquisite objects from Tutankhamun's tomb. Finally, the Mummification Museum sited on the Corniche has a graphic display of how the ancient Egyptians would mummify not only humans, but also crocodiles, household pets and even fish.

The tombs and memorials on the West Bank are a different proposition. This area is also referred to as the Theban Necropolis. It's basically a giant burial ground for the ancient rulers of Luxor and includes such iconic sites as the Valley of the Kings, the Valley of the Queens, the Tombs of the Nobles and much, much more. Moving around the West Bank requires much more planning – not least because you've first got to get across the river. That can be done via the government passenger ferry for the small sum of E£1each way. You're then faced with the problem that the sites you might want to see are so spread out that it would require a succession of taxis to reach them. Also, the tickets for each have first to be purchased from a central ticket office. We thought that on this occasion it was best to go on one of the organised tours and paid E£325 each for the privilege. We didn't regret it. It saved us a lot of hassle and not only was our guide interesting and knowledgeable, he also took the time to drive us around the marathon course so I could see what lay in store later in the week. As things turned out the course actually ran past many of the places we'd wanted to visit so I'll leave my descriptions of these until I get to the marathon itself.

Like a lot of things in Egypt, the marathon wasn't exactly what we had been led to believe. Despite this being the 23rd edition of an officially recognised AIMS' event featured regularly in the Distance Running magazine the race's profile within Luxor was so low-key as to be virtually anonymous. No one we spoke to knew of its existence and that included the officials in both of the city's central Tourist Offices. One of these did give me a brochure in which it was featured (and I quote) as 'attracting some 2,000 participants each year.' Even the event's own website boasted, 'Number of participants in Marathon is 1,874 runners.' Did they mean the aggregate number of runners in the previous 22 editions of the race? Who knows? I was aware in advance that actual numbers were to be very different courtesy of a friend Rob Harris, who had run it the previous year together with a mere 22 other finishers. Some difference! I wasn't in the least bit surprised, therefore, on turning up at Registration to find the official entry lists pinned on a notice board showing the Marathon as having 18 entrants, the 22km Luxor Run with 40 entrants and a 12km Ramsis Run with 13 competitors. I was the only one from the UK registered for the marathon that also included in the 13 finishers a German, an Austrian, two Americans, a Japanese runner, an Italian, a Spaniard, two Frenchman, a Canadian and a couple of Egyptians. There were also a number of ex-pat, largely American, runners from a Cairo based running club, most of who seemed to be taking part in the 22km event. The lack of entrants didn't particularly bother me. I knew what I was coming to and, as I said earlier, I was looking for somewhere 'different' on this occasion. This certainly fitted the bill.

The small field and the fact that most of us had taken the option of staying at least two nights in the race hotel meant a friendly, social atmosphere prevailed. I particularly enjoyed the company of the Cairo based German runner Gerhart Lichtenthaler and his American wife Debra who became close companions during our stay. I also have to compliment the race organisers for the way they reacted on finding out that I'd chosen their event for my 250th marathon. They not only went out of their way to ensure that I enjoyed the event but also presented me with a special memento, a commemorative silver plaque, at the post race Awards Dinner.

The race headquarters at the 5-star Maritim Jolie Ville hotel provided a touch of opulence to the proceedings. Set in a bungalow complex on its own private island in the Nile some 4 kilometres south of the city, the place was as different from Luxor as Mars is from Pluto. With two infinity pools, tennis courts, a gym, zoo, bars, restaurants, prayer areas and extensive gardens in which it grew its own vegetables, the hotel was the ultimate in conspicuous luxury. It even had a measured jogging track around its perimeter for those who wanted to stretch their limbs pre-race. It brought to mind an upmarket Butlin's holiday camp reserved for royalty. Access and egress was by a single bridge where armed guards stopped and searched everything that moved, placing bomb-detectors under all vehicles seeking entry. While it was nice for a couple of days I wouldn't have liked to have stayed there any longer. I found it just too perfect, confined and claustrophobic and was happy to return to the mayhem of Luxor after the event.

Race day started with a 4.30 am wake-up call and a 5 am breakfast. A bus was meant to leave for the start at 5.30 am but those of us who'd bothered to be punctual were forced to sit and wait in the dark for over 20 minutes while the more thoughtless enjoyed an extended breakfast. Not a good start to the day. We then travelled for 40 minutes across the recently built Luxor Bridge to the 7 am start outside Queen Hatshepsut's Temple on the West Bank of the Nile. This funerary temple of a well-loved Queen sits in a commanding position at the base of the rugged limestone cliffs rising nearly 300 metres above the desert plain. Almost entirely reconstructed in recent times it's unlike any other temple in appearance with a long, ceremonial approach that is reputed to have extended all the way across the Nile to connect with the temples at Karnak. While waiting for the race to start it was difficult not to reflect on what happened on this spot in November 1997. In a mid-morning attack, six gunmen disguised as members of the security forces massacred 59 foreign nationals and several Egyptians. Having first killed the two armed guards patrolling the entrance to the temple they then commenced systematically killing the tourists trapped inside. The assault lasted 45 minutes during which time many bodies, especially of women, were mutilated with machetes, with a note praising Islam being placed inside one of the disembowelled bodies. After hijacking a bus most of the attackers evaded a shoot-out with police and armed forces and made their escape to the hills where their bodies were subsequently found in a cave. A sobering thought on which to start a marathon race.

Immediately behind the Temple of Hatshepsut, in the folds of the Theban Hills, lies the iconic Valley of the Kings. In 1979 this was made a World Heritage Site and remains one of the most important and famous archaeological sites in the world. It is believed to have been used as a royal burial site for over 500 years and contains the tombs, some yet undiscovered, of kings and nobles from the 18th to the 21st dynasties. The Pharaohs who chose the site as their graveyard had astonishing tombs built deep into the hillside in the hope that the artefacts they'd selected to accompany them to the afterlife would remain undisturbed. Over 60 tombs have been discovered, including the most famous of them all, that of Tutankhamun. Sadly most of the tombs have been robbed over time and the treasures removed. Don't let that put you off visiting – simply entering one of the tombs is an unforgettable experience. To go to the marathon without seeing the Valley of the Kings would be like going to Paris and not seeing the Eiffel Tower. The marathon route comes close in taking runners up to a dog-leg turn on the approach road to the Valley on each of the 4 laps.

The race begins with a once-only one kilometre downhill from Hatshepsut's Temple before turning onto the first of the four 10 kilometre rectangular laps around the West Bank. At 2km we passed under what remains of the village of Gurna – a collection of brightly coloured mud houses belonging to workers now resettled elsewhere since the discovery of further tombs on the site. These are the Tombs of the Nobles – mainly priests and high officials who served their Pharaoh. Nearby too, is Deir El-Medina, the workers' village where there are tombs of artisans and workmen who laboured in the Valley of the Kings. On the opposite side of the road at this stage is the Ramesseum, the funerary temple of Ramesses 11. Though largely ruinous it is famous for its fallen colossal statue of the King. At 3.5km we followed the road in the direction of the Valley of the Queens before turning sharply to descend towards the central ticket office and along a long, straight stretch towards the Nile. This brought us at 5.5km to the famous Colossi of Memnon with its tourist buses on our left. These two giant statues are all that remain of the funerary temple of Pharaoh Amenophis 111. The statues, which once guarded the outer gates of the temple, represent the enthroned and divinised Amenophis himself. Over time all memory of Amenophis was forgotten and the Greeks decided the statues were of Memnon, son of Tuthonus a legendary Egyptian king, and of Eos the Dawn. Both Greek and Roman tourists were especially attracted to the Colossus on the right hand side which, after being shattered by earthquakes and lightning, would sometimes emit a musical note as the sun rose over Thebes. Readable Greek and Roman graffiti still adorn the base of the statue.

After the Colossi we were to get a break from Egyptology overload for most of the rest of each lap. At 7km we reached the village of New Gurna where most of the displaced workers have been resettled. We turned there to run another arrow-straight 2 kilometre stretch alongside a canal with fields of sugar cane on our left hand side. This brought us at 9.5 km to yet another, busier village whose name I was never able to find out. After that it was slightly uphill, past Howard Carter's house and on to the first of the four turning points. Carter was the discoverer of Tutankhamun's tomb in 1922 – an event that triggered the subsequent mania for Egyptology that continues today.

The first two laps through the villages were no problem. Most of the inhabitants had yet to wake up and the early morning temperatures of about 13 degrees were perfectly manageable. Things changed by the start of the third lap. Mainly the villagers just stared, bemused by these strange, profusely sweating westerners running past (though one man did step out and try and sell me a map of the Nile!) Gangs of children, however, insisted on running alongside repeatedly wanting to know our names. Then the traffic arrived – men on motor bikes, push bikes, donkeys, trucks and cars kept on getting in the way despite the heavy police presence. Normal road rules appeared non-existent. At first it was tolerable but as tiredness set in and temperatures rose into the mid-twenties it ceased to be amusing. I was grateful to reach the end of the fourth lap with only the one kilometre uphill back to the finish to have to negotiate. I was pleased with my 4 hours 28 minute finishing time for 1st (and only) Vet 65/70 and, in particular, with the warm applause I received on crossing the line from those who'd already finished. It had been a great day, one I will long remember and the perfect way to celebrate a special, landmark marathon.

While happy with the event it would be remiss of me to ignore some of the things I feel the organisers should address to improve their current arrangements. Some of these revolve around the transport facilities. Basically, there was far too much hanging around – either waiting for latecomers before the event or with what happened afterwards. On finishing, most of us had to sit around for ages in the sun waiting for the back-markers to complete their race before the bus could return to base. I waited for over an hour for the four runners still on the course to come in. When they finally arrived not a single one of them was taking the transport provided. The wait had been for nothing and some of the earlier finishers, including the winner, had sat for up to two hours in the hot sun before the bus departed. A simple clerical procedure involving ticking off the names of those who were, or were not, taking the bus could have avoided all the hanging around.

Incidentally, the final finisher was the only and thereby the first lady in the race. Her time of 5 hours 35 minutes earned her the female winner's trophy. The men's race had been won in 3 hours 30 minutes. Both times are indicative of the quality of the field. I also find it difficult to believe that the organisers couldn't have provided a tent or similar in which we could wait out of the sun at the finish. The same tent could also have given us somewhere to leave our bags and get changed. As it was, bags were simply dumped in an unsecure area behind the timekeeper and there was nowhere with a modicum of privacy for us runners to change out of our sweaty clothes.

The accuracy of the course was another subject of much discussion after the race. I can't comment too much on this because I don't run with a Garmin. Everyone who did complained that the course was short – up to one kilometre in some cases. If this is true it shouldn't happen on what is advertised as an 'AIMS measured course.' Certainly something needs to be done about the course marking. Simply placing signs reading 5, 15, 25 and 35km and 10, 20, 30 and 40km in the same spots cannot possibly be an accurate reflection of the distance covered. It totally ignores the one kilometre stretch from and to Hatshepsut's Temple at the start and finish of the race. It would have been nice, too, to have been given something other than the lukewarm water to drink on the way around. Questions also have to be asked as to why so few Egyptians take part in their country's one and only marathon. The answer, of course, has everything to do with money. I was told that while many locals would like to enter the race they are effectively prevented from doing so by the high cost of the full race package the organisers try to get everyone to take. It's hard to argue against this point of view. I don't want to be too critical as nothing I've mentioned here detracts from my overall enjoyment of the event. Though improbable, I'd definitely return if circumstances permit.

That evening came the piece de resistance – something you're unlikely to encounter in any other marathon event. This was the Gala Dinner for runners and invited guests where medals and certificates were distributed and awards handed out. Cynics might say that this was an unnecessary ploy to extract more money out of us by forcing us to attend. They're probably right but, again, I've no complaints. No one twisted my arm behind my back and I enjoyed socialising with my fellow competitors. They were a nice bunch of people who I probably would never have met otherwise. The dinner took the form of an Egyptian folkloric evening in a huge indoor/outdoor setting in what was possibly a Bedouin tent (I could be wrong on this). There were belly dancers, whirling dervishes, stick men, musicians, folk dancers and even a magician to keep us entertained. The latter managed to shove a dagger through Mo's wrist without her having a clue as to how he did it. The food too was excellent with barbecued beef, chicken and kofti sausages as well as a whole array of Egyptian specialities. Our favourite was Koshari, a national dish made from macaroni, rice, lentils and chickpeas served with a thick garlic and tomato sauce topped with fried onions and herbs. We also enjoyed the Foul Medames, a dish of beans served with boiled eggs plus the ever-popular falafel, a dish of spicy beans mashed together and fried with herbs. Most of the desserts were delicious, drenched with honey and very fattening. It all made a welcome change from the westernised dishes we'd been served at our hotel. The only extra to be paid for was the alcohol. We'd already had a week of free Egyptian wine and brandy in the hotel so confined ourselves to a couple of the local Stella beers at E£25 per bottle (twice the price that it is elsewhere). Still, it was a great night and an excellent ending to an enjoyable couple of days. I'd promised myself somewhere exotic for my 250th marathon and have no regrets in choosing this event.

Finished! The Egyptian Marathon is hot and thirsty work.

The centre of Luxor (Nobody knew about the Marathon)

ISRAEL

TEL AVIV MARATHON

I'd always promised myself a trip to the Holy Land to visit the sites that were drummed into us daily during school Religious Education lessons. Jerusalem, Bethlehem and the Sea of Galilee in particular, with their obvious Biblical connections, were high on my list of must-see places to go. Initially I planned to combine the visit with running the annual Jerusalem Marathon held in mid-March each year. However, running friend Kate Taylor, who has connections in Tel Aviv spoke highly of that city's marathon at the end of February as an alternative event well worth considering. It seemed the perfect follow-up to the Egyptian Marathon I'd run the previous month as well as a chance to compare and contrast the two locations. Fortunately, easyJet had just started a new route from Luton to Tel Aviv with fares considerably less than on offer elsewhere. We were on our way – hopefully to a week in the sun.

Lining up at the boarding gate at Luton airport for our Sunday morning flight it was immediately apparent that Mo and I were among the few northern Europeans on the plane. Almost 75% of those boarding were dressed in the traditional outfits of the Hasidic Jews – the men in their black jackets and trousers, white shirts and black 'stovepipe' hats, with long beards and curly ringlets and the women with their wigs. A few hours into the flight we witnessed something I've never seen on a plane before. An announcement was made that prayers would be held at the back of the aircraft, limited to groups of ten at a time. At intervals, groups of men started putting on their black jackets and hats and made their way to the rear of the plane where chanting commenced. While it didn't particularly bother us we couldn't help wondering whether the airline affords this privilege to other religious groups (or any other groups at all for that matter) that might be travelling with them. After our experience on the flight out we fully expected to see large numbers of similarly dressed individuals on the streets of Tel Aviv. In fact, we hardly saw any – they were conspicuous by their absence. We travelled back on a Saturday, the Jewish Sabbath, and, for obvious reasons, there wasn't a single Hasidic Jew on the flight.

Anyone flying to Tel Aviv's Ben-Gurion Airport should prepare themselves for the slow process of passport control, both when arriving and leaving. The State of Israel Border Control authorities issue a 3-month Stay Permit that includes your passport photo on entering and a similar Exit Permit on leaving. These can take some time to produce. The blue Stay Permit is very important and should be retained at all times not least because, by proving that you're a foreign citizen, it exempts you from having to pay hotel taxes required from the locals. There is easy access to the city from the airport via a connecting train service one level below the Arrivals Hall. Trains run in the direction of Nahariya at 05 and 35 minutes past the hour with a single journey costing 13.50 ILS (Israeli Shekel). At the time of our visit £1 was worth 5.42ILS. Trains stop at all four Tel Aviv stations with the exception of late night trains that stop only at Tel Aviv Merkaz/Savidor station – the city's central rail station. The stations in order from the airport are: HaHagana (8 minutes travel), HaShalom (13 minutes), Merkaz/Savidor (18 minutes) and University (25 minutes). Unfortunately there is no service from Friday afternoon until Saturday evening because of the Jewish Sabbath. Our return taxi on the Saturday cost a whopping 140 ILS.

As I'm sure you're well aware, Israel is the only state in the world with a majority Jewish population. This came about by intent rather than by accident. Following the suffering under the Holocaust, the division of the former British Mandate of Palestine and the creation of the State of Israel after the War was the culmination of the aim of the Zionist movement. This entailed a homeland for Jews hitherto scattered all over the world. The State of Israel is seated on a portion of land in the Middle East, known from 1920 to 1948 as Palestine. The area is considered a 'Holy Land' for a number of religions including Judaism, Christianity, Islam, Druze and Baha'I Faith. Modern Israel is bordered by the Mediterranean Sea to the west and the northern shore of the Gulf of Aqaba in the Red Sea. It shares land borders with Lebanon to the north, Syria, in the northeast, Jordan to the east, Egypt to the southwest and the Palestinian Territories of the West Bank and the Gaza Strip. Enmity from its neighbours has affected Israel from the time of its independence in 1948 since when it has been locked in conflict with the Palestinians and its Arab neighbours over ownership of land considered holy by each of them. Currently, Israeli jurisdiction over the holy city of Jerusalem is the focus of international dispute and conflict over its occupation of Palestinian territories has shaped the country's internal political and social structure as well as its international relations. These have been dominated by the conflict with its Arab neighbours, including full-scale regional wars in 1948, 1967 and 1973. Despite the tensions we found Tel Aviv a relaxed, safe place to visit with no extra visible security presence than would be found in any European city of comparative size. Things were slightly different when visiting Jerusalem and Bethlehem with armed soldiers patrolling the streets and security searches before entering holy places. While we were there an Israeli serviceman was shot by his fellow soldiers while attempting to protect him from a knife attack.

Aware of Tel Aviv's reputation as one of the best beach-cities in the world we had chosen our accommodation carefully before setting out. High-rise hotels and apartment blocks line the busy beachside promenade that runs for around 8 kilometres from the city's Port in the north to the ancient settlement of Jaffa in the south. We wanted to be near the northern end to keep us close (or so we thought) to Registration for the marathon and the Start and Finish of the race. Most of the hotels located on the beachfront like the Hilton, Sheraton and Renaissance were beyond our pocket. Just opposite the Marina and across the road from the beach we found the small Olympia Hotel at value-for-money rates of around £60 per room per night. The room came with a delightful all-you-can-eat buffet breakfast and free-to-use, 24 hour coffee and fruit juice machines. We loved the fresh tuna, raw fish, omelettes and pancakes served each day with side dishes of hummus, cottage cheese plus a variety of salads, yoghurts and dips. No one seemed to mind you putting up a few sandwiches or rolls for lunchtime so effectively we only had our evening meals to worry about during our stay. Here an American guest pointed us in the right direction by recommending the low-cost Falafel restaurant, a short walk away on Bugrashov Street. We ended up there most evenings consuming one of the thick bean or red lentil soups before moving on to the falafel pitta, hummus and salad. The cost was negligible by Tel Aviv standards: soup and falafel cost 45 ILS while the help-yourself salad came free. To give you a comparison of the cost, even the most basic of pizzas would set you back around 65ILS while an average 3-course meal with drinks would leave you with no change from 100 ILS.

Tel Aviv (meaning 'Hill of Spring') was founded just over a century ago by a group of Jewish residents of the ancient port city of Jaffa. Naming it after the Utopian town envisioned by Zionist author Theodore Herzi in his novel 'Altneuland' (The Old New Land) they had plans to establish a European-style garden suburb with wide streets and boulevards in contrast to the cramped conditions within Jaffa's walls. Moving out of the Arab dominated town represented their belief in the Jewish National Movement of Zionism. Subsequent Arab attacks on Jewish properties in Jaffa in 1921 encouraged thousands of fellow Jews to leave Jaffa for the newly established suburb. Within a decade Tel Aviv had become a city and the centre of culture, commerce and industry for the entire Jewish population. 1938 saw the opening of Tel Aviv's own port – an important step signalling the end of its dependency on Jaffa. By this time, Tel Aviv was the biggest city in the country with over 130,000 inhabitants. After Israel's declaration of independence in 1948, Jaffa became a district of Tel Aviv and the city's name was changed to Tel Aviv-Yafo.

Today the city is the thriving heart of a modern, prosperous nation. Over 3 million people live in the 25 kilometre sprawl along the Mediterranean coast with around 400,000 in Tel Aviv itself making it Israel's second city after Jerusalem (over 760,000 inhabitants) While the latter is Israel's capital city where most government departments are situated, Tel Aviv is the nation's economic and cultural centre. It has a deserved reputation as Israel's party town and has been dubbed 'the city that never stops.' It was not uncommon while we were there to see revellers making their way home while I was heading for an early morning jog along the beach. Tel Aviv also has a reputation as the most liberal city in Israel with its easy-going lifestyle and tolerance of minority issues and activist movements. With its liberalism comes a sense of detachment and sophistication some find upsetting. It is often described as 'The Bubble' or 'Medinat Tel Aviv' (the State of Tel Aviv) by ultra-Orthodox Israelis who consider the city a modern day Sodom and Gomorrah due to its hedonistic lifestyle. I have to say that after the restrictive atmosphere and constant harassment at my previous marathon in Luxor I found the sense of freedom in Tel Aviv quite exhilarating.

The city attracts over a million international visitors annually with its beaches and promenade playing a major role in its attraction. It was ranked by Lonely Planet as the third hottest city in the world (after New York and Tangier) in 2011 and the world's ninth-best beach city by National Geographic. It's a very easy city to get around on foot with most places of interest to tourists confined in a rectangle between the Yarkon River to the north, the beaches to the west, Jaffa to the south and the railway line to the east. We tended to spend our time, when not on the beach, walking along Dizengoff and Ben Yahuda streets where most of the shops and restaurants can be found. In 2003 Tel Aviv was declared a UNESCO World Heritage site due to the numerous Bauhaus style buildings constructed between 1930 and 1950. This style emphasises simplicity and the colour white, hence Tel Aviv's nickname of the 'White City.'

In his welcome address in the race programme the city's Mayor asserts that the Marathon is Israel's largest sporting event with over 40,000 participants. He's talking here about all events on the day: the marathon, half marathon, 10k, 5k, a hand cycle race (wheelchair, I think) and probably the series of Kids Mini Marathon held two days before the main events. He promises that 'the marathon route will take you through a tour of Tel Aviv-Yafo and let you experience the energy of our city.' Firstly you've got to register. Number, chip and T-shirt distribution takes place in a huge tented area in the centre of Rabin Square right in the heart of the city. Registration is open from midday on the Sunday and between 10am and 9pm each day until Wednesday evening. Initially we were required to have a stamped and signed medical certificate from our doctor. The Israeli Court ruled this unnecessary on December 15th, shortly after I'd succeeded in finally getting a medical appointment after a 3-week's wait! As Expos go this was one of the better ones with other things to do instead of just look at merchandise. You could race a virtual runner along a measured course, enjoy a beer at the bar or eat your way through a variety of free yoghurts. There was also a Pasta Party on the (Thursday) evening before race day for anyone wanting to pay the extra.

I only wish Rabin Square had been where the race started and finished. I think they got this all wrong. Getting to the 7am start on Friday morning turned out to be a major problem. In previous years the race had started in a large park on the seafront but has since been moved to an almost inaccessible spot close to the University Campus and the Israeli Fair and Convention Centre. This was in the northeast of the city - way outside the city limits, across the river and on the 'wrong' side of the rail and motorway section. To be fair to the organisers I think they realised the difficulties runners faced in reaching the new start area and made several suggestions in the race programme and website as how to get there. These included ideas like hiring a bike or taking one of the early morning trains to University station. Neither of these was feasible, especially the train option - all roads were closed from 4am so it was just as impossible to get a bus or taxi to the station as it was to the actual start. None of the taxi firms would take our booking because they were unable to reach any of the beach hotels. We were advised to set off early and attempt to flag down any passing taxi we saw. We left the hotel at 5.15am in the pitch darkness but neither of the two taxis we encountered would take our fare. The first pretended he didn't know the location of the start. The second was more honest and said he couldn't get near the place. Through the darkness we kept observing groups of other unsuners runners getting into and then out of the same taxi. In the end we just put our heads down and walked the 6 or 7 kilometres to the start line. One and a half hours later we arrived just before the off! Even then there was confusion in trying to find the entrance to the starting lane and the lead runners were already down the road before, without any pre-race preparation whatsoever, I was able to give chase. The ordeal of getting to the start soured my experience of the whole event leaving me both angry and frustrated and definitely in no condition, either physically or mentally, to run a good time. I'd seriously suggest that if the organisers intend to continue with their current starting venue they should give careful consideration to laying on a pre-booked shuttle bus service from either the coastal hotels or Rabin Square (preferably both). Incidentally, of the other events starting from the same spot, the hand cycle race commenced at 06.50, the 10k left in three stages between 07.20 and 07.50, the half marathon departed in two groups at 08.10 and 08.25 while the 5k runners enjoyed a nice lie-in until 11.00. Event closing time was 1pm giving the marathoners 6 hours to get round the course. Just over 1,600 finished the marathon so the other races must have been pretty full.

    Initially we followed Rokach Boulevard westwards for 3 kilometres heading towards the coast and the highly visible chimney of the Reading Power Station. Turning north onto Eshkol Street took us past the smart apartment blocks of the northern suburbs to a 2km out-and-back section on the landward side of the city's second airport Sde Dov. The airport, which sits directly on the seafront on prime beachfront land, mainly handles domestic flights to Eliat and Ovda. It is expected to be closed permanently in 2018 with the land being re-zoned for expensive residential apartments. Just before the 10km mark we reached the wide coastal cycle path on the seaward side of the airport fence. From here things took a turn for the better as we continued all the way down the coast to the 20km turn just after Jaffa. First we crossed the Yarkon River over a wooden pedestrian bridge to reach the Port of Tel Aviv. The river is the largest coastal river in Israel at 27.5 km in length. It became increasingly polluted during the 1950s with many blaming this on the sewage outlet from the nearby power station. Eventually the Yarkon River Authority was established to revitalize the river and make it suitable for swimming and other recreational purposes. It took an unexpected tragedy, however, to speed up the process. The world in general first heard of it in 1997 when a temporary pedestrian bridge over the river collapsed under the Australian delegation to the Maccabiah Games. More than 60 athletes were injured and four died as a result of fungal infection caused by aspiration of the heavily polluted water. This tragedy led to the Australian branch of the Jewish National Fund to donate 15 million ILS to accelerate the clean-up operations. Today, from its outlet at the coast, both banks of the river are covered in beautiful parkland with cycling and jogging paths stretching far into the interior. The park has hosted concerts by some internationally famous artists in recent years including: the Rolling Stones, Paul McCartney, Elton John, Guns N' Roses, David Bowie and many others of that stature. Mo spent the hours while I was otherwise engaged walking and sunbathing in the park. The port area we ran through has also been subjected to a recent facelift. The Port has played a very important part in the establishment of the State of Israel and the subsequent mass migrations from around the world. As containerized shipping became the standard way of transporting goods, bigger ports were built elsewhere and Tel Aviv became derelict. The original developers have now restored the Port and recreated it as an area of leisure facilities with the old warehouses being converted into trendy restaurants, shops and nightclubs. It's now one of the most popular places to go and be seen by the more affluent residents of Tel Aviv. A huge wooden deck shaped like waves in the sea covers 14,000 square metres of the dockside and acts a unique promenade running along the seafront.

Shortly after leaving the Port at 13km we were joined briefly by the pacesetters in the half marathon race before they turned off into the city at our 15km mark. We had the road to ourselves again for the next ten kilometres as we ran between the blocks of high-rise hotels on the beachfront before emerging into the relative sanity of the magnificent old port of Jaffa. Spending time in Jaffa was one of the highlights of our time in Israel. Mo and I had taken a leisurely stroll there earlier in the week and been impressed by its history and its beauty. The Old Jaffa Port is reputed to be one of the oldest ports in the world and, allegedly, the port from which Jonah set off in the famous Biblical story involving the whale. For over 7,000 years it has been actively used, predating Muslims, the Crusaders, Jews and even the Egyptians. It has a long and fascinating history as a strategic port in the Eastern Mediterranean before new ports were built at Ashod, Tel Aviv and Haifa to cater for modern shipping methods. Today it still functions as a small fishing port but is largely a recreational zone with restaurants and cafes. Nearby attractions well worth visiting include an interestingly huge Flea Market, the restored original railway station that once connected it to Jerusalem and St Peter's Church. (The Bible records several of the deeds of the Apostle Peter in Jaffa such as his stay at the house of Simon and his journey up the coast to Caesaria). The park in its centre provides wonderful views up the coast to Tel Aviv and eastwards to the hills of Jerusalem.

After leaving Jaffa at 23km the remainder of the route proved much less inspiring. At 25km we turned inland through hot and dusty streets lined with crowds going about their everyday business. By now the temperature was climbing steadily to the forecast 26 degrees and there were no longer the coastal breezes to cool us down. Fortunately, water was provided in small bottles every three kilometres – most of which went into the hat and onto the head. There was isotonic drink and gels on offer but only on a couple of occasions. An 8 kilometre loop around the city brought us back out on to the coast again at 33km. This time we ran northwards back to Tel Aviv Port before turning on the busy Dizengoff Street down towards Rabin Square. This is the city's biggest public square with an ecological pond filled with lotus flowers and koi, a fountain that's floodlit at night and some trendy cafes around its perimeter. Its northern side is dominated by the 1960s communist-style tower block of City Hall The square used to be called Malchei Israel (Kings of Israel) Square but was renamed after the assassination of Prime Minister Yitzhak Rabin in 1995. There's a small memorial on Ibn Gabirol Street, next to City Hall marking the spot where he was shot. We arrived at Rabin Square shortly after the 37km mark. All that was left was to negotiate the long, straight, two kilometre stretch north on Ibn Gabirol, cross the bridge over the Yarkon River and make our way through the park to the finish, medal and goody bag. Considering the heat and the energy expended in getting to the start I was reasonably satisfied with a 4 hour 42 minute finish that placed me 6th out of 15 in my Vet 70 age-group. I was disappointed though to see that the free bar had run out of beer. That aside, I'd had an enjoyable day out on a course through a lovely city and would certainly come and do it all again (maybe next time bringing my own tent and sleeping in the park next to the start).

As I said earlier, my motivation in coming to the marathon was to fulfil a life-long ambition of visiting the Holy Land and seeing all those places we read about in the Bible. Rather than go into the unknown on our own Mo and I decided that, this time, we'd go on one of the organised tours with a reliable, well-informed guide. There's any number of these tours on offer and every hotel stocks their advertising material. They're all much of a much-ness with very little difference in prices or itineraries. We actually booked a Jerusalem and Bethlehem tour via a link on the marathon website to Israeli Experts. We've got no complaints – both our guides were interesting, experienced and professional (you have to be handed over to a Palestinian guide for the Bethlehem visit). I'd have no hesitation in recommending them to fellow runners. Other tours on offer consisted mainly of visits to: Massada and the Dead Sea, Highlights of Galilee (Nazareth, Sea of Galilee, Capernaum and

Jordan River) and Western Galilee (Caesaria, Haifa, Acre and Rosh Hanrika). If time had allowed we would have gone on every one of them. The sense of history in the place is overwhelming and simply makes you want to see more. We did manage to squeeze in a quick visit to the Sea of Galilee. I believe there's a marathon there in Tiberius each January. One for the future!

Tel Aviv Marathon. I missed the Start – not so great!

Tel Aviv's beautiful seafront (Part of the marathon course)

UNITED STATES OF AMERICA

BOSTON MARATHON

I'd lived and worked in Boston for a few months on a student visa as long ago as 1969 but had never been back since (not even to the USA for that matter). My main memory of the place is of toiling for long hours of back-breaking work on double shifts in the factory of the city's premier ice-cream manufacturer. Being summer, demand for the product was high and the work was hot and sweaty. I stuck at it for the length of my contract, lost a lot of weight and made a lot of money. My only other significant memory was of hearing the opening chords of 'Honky Tonk Woman' for the first time in the entrance to Macey's department store in downtown Boston. I didn't enjoy my stay. It was the time of the Vietnam War, student unrest and inner-city race riots. Boston in the late '60s was not a great place to be. I was mugged at knifepoint one day in broad daylight on Boston Common. The guy only wanted my watch – he didn't get it but it shook me up. I've had no real desire to return and certainly never envisaged standing on the start line of a marathon there some 47 years later. However, the pull of the Boston Marathon eventually proved irresistible. It's the oldest and most prestigious marathon in the world and for some time now has been up there with Athens as a must-do on my marathon bucket list.

The Boston Marathon is considered by many runners to be the crown jewel in the world's marathon calendar. There are bigger, faster and certainly more scenic races out there but none with the charisma that Boston possesses. It's one of the six World Marathon Majors and is one of only four important events in the US to have been held continuously throughout both World Wars (The Kentucky

Derby, Rose Parade and Westminster Kennel Club Dog Show are the others, in case you're wondering). Starting with only 18 participants when first run in 1897 and held every year since, the event now attracts an average of about 30,000 competitors each year. The Centennial Boston Marathon in 1996 established a record as the world's largest marathon with 38,708 entrants. In 2014, the year after the infamous bombings near the finish line, there was a post-centennial, one-off expansion of the field to 36,000 runners. Inspiration for the event came from The Boston Athletic Association, the race organiser from the outset. They had been encouraged to put on a marathon race in the city after the distance's debut in the 1896 Olympic Games. Initially they chose a 24.5 mile route from Ashland, Massachusetts to the centre of Boston. Then, in 1924, when the marathon distance was standardized at 26 miles 385 yards, they moved the start line farther west to the village of Hopkinton, where it remains today. From 1897 until 1968, the marathon was held on Patriot's Day, April 19th, a holiday commemorating the start of the Revolutionary War against the British and recognised only in the states of Massachusetts and Maine. In 1969, the holiday was officially moved to the third Monday in April and since then the race has always been held on that day.

The Boston Marathon was originally a local event, but its fame and status now attracts runners from all over the globe. For most of its history, the marathon was a free event with the only prize for winning being a wreath woven from olive branches. The first corporate-sponsored cash prize for winning the marathon was awarded in 1986 when organisers realised that professional athletes were beginning to boycott the event in the absence of financial incentives. Women weren't officially allowed to enter the race until 1972, although Roberta 'Bobbi' Gibb did manage to become the first female unofficial finisher in the three years from 1966 to 1968 after famously joining the race after hiding in the bushes near the start line. Another unforgettable incident occurred in 1967 when Katherine Switzer, who did not clearly identify herself as a female on the entry form, was given an official race number.

Most of us will have seen the memorable photo of race official Jock Semple attempting unsuccessfully to rip off her race number and eject her from the event. How times have changed – in 1996 the B.A.A. retroactively recognised as champions the unofficial women's leaders of 1966 through to 1971 and these days about 46% of the field is female. I met Katherine Switzer signing copies of her book at this year's (2016) race and Bobbi Gibb was also present in an official capacity - 50 years on from the bushes incident.

The Boston Marathon is unlike most other marathons in that you can't just sign up and enter. Since 1970, the main way for runners to secure a place in the event is by achieving the Boston A.A. prescribed qualifying time for your age group. That qualifying time has to have been run within a set date range on a certain type of course. In the US, marathons must be run on a course certified by US Track & Field while overseas marathons must be certified by that country's athletic federation. The qualifying standards have changed over the years but have always been seen as a challenge for everyday runners (a bit like the 'good-for-age' requirements in London). For many, getting a Boston qualifier (BQ) is considered a lifetime running achievement. Registration for the following April's marathon usually opens in mid-September and the qualifying time has to have been achieved at a recognised event within the previous 12 months. For example, I achieved the qualifying time of sub 4 hours 25 minutes for my Vet 70 age category in Melbourne in October 2014 and used this when applying in September 2015 to get into the April 2016 event. I improved on my Melbourne time of 4 hours 18 at a few other events and could have, if I'd been bothered, submitted the faster time to improve my seeding in the race. For the past few Boston Marathons there have been more qualifiers seeking a bib number than places available. For the 2016 event, 28,594 time qualifiers submitted an entry of which 4,562 were not accepted. On this occasion runners needed to better their age and gender qualifying mark by 2 minutes 28 seconds or more, proving that achieving a BQ time doesn't necessarily guarantee entry. Of the race's 30,000 entrants, roughly 80% are time qualifiers and 20% are charity runners. Once your qualifying time has been vetted and approved, registration takes place on a rolling basis – with the fastest qualifiers being allowed to register first. Bib numbers are assigned and posted to the entry list page in early March. In early April, the coveted Boston Marathon Runner Passport containing comprehensive race instructions is posted to all participants.

Having completed all the above formalities and with official passport, Runner Passport and ESTA (visa) documents in hand, Mo and I set out with Aer Lingus via Dublin for a six day break in Boston. We hadn't realised that Dublin airport has a compulsory Pre-Clearance entry facility for travellers to the USA and almost missed our connection while standing in the endless queue to be fingerprinted and photographed. In the end, this proved a blessing in disguise. We simply walked off the flight without further formality on arrival in Boston and, within minutes, were on the free Silver Line Shuttle bus stopping directly outside our hotel. The shuttle is part of the MBTA's '(Massachusetts Bay Transport Authority) extensive network. The shuttle connects to South Street Station from where you can pick up any of the city's four colour-coded metro lines to reach just about any destination in the urban area. Single-journey tickets cost $2.65 and can be purchased from machines inside the stations using coins, cards or notes. Unfortunately, only the inbound journey from the airport is free – you'll have to buy a ticket when leaving for your return flight. Boston is an easily walk-able city and apart from a trip out to my old haunts in Cambridge and a couple of harbour cruises on MBTA ferries we hardly used public transport during our stay.

On the recommendation of friends Paul Richards and Dave Goodwin who'd stayed there the previous year, we'd booked ourselves into the Seaport Hotel in the new Seaport District of the city. When I was last in Boston the area was all derelict wharves and swampy marshland. Now it's a spanking new harbour-side residential and hotel district of high-rise chrome and glass. Like most of the hotels in the city the Seaport goes out of its way to attract runners on marathon weekend. For example, they provided an all-you-can-eat pasta buffet on the evening before the race, a special early-morning runner's breakfast on race day, free bottles of water, energy gels, bananas and sunscreen plus, best of all, a free shuttle service to the race buses leaving from Boston Common. The shuttle turned out to be a chauffeur-driven, gleaming black, blacked-out window, luxury Mercedes Benz more suited to a Presidential cavalcade than to a bunch of under-dressed runners. There were even free massages waiting for us on our return. An additional bonus was the view from our top floor room looking directly over the harbour. I haven't got a bad word to say about the place.

Our plane landed at 1pm on the Friday and two hours later we walked into the John Hynes Convention Centre on downtown Boylston Street for Registration. The organisers had sensibly kept number pick-up separate from the huge Expo on the floor below, so there were no queues. That doesn't mean that collecting my race number was easy – far from it. You'd think that a UK passport would be sufficient proof of identity, wouldn't you? Not to the lady behind the counter who, unfortunately, turned out to be a real jobsworth. She insisted on seeing my driving licence or something 'official showing my address' before she'd hand over anything. I don't carry the former and wasn't prepared to return to the hotel for the latter, pointing out that the race information regarding number collection simply asked for 'a photo ID.' She didn't seem to think that a mere passport fulfilled that requirement. After a long stand-off the number was finally and reluctantly handed over. Not a good start! I was beginning to think I'd made a mistake returning to Boston.

My mood didn't improve on visiting the adjacent Expo. This appeared little more than a glorified merchandising outlet cum spend-fest with runners queuing to hand over $110 at a time for one of this year's event jackets as if they were going out of fashion. In a sense they were, due to the B.A.A.'s clever marketing ploy of producing a different colour of jacket for each year's event, with the year featured prominently on the back. I was happy to collect my event long-sleeved T-shirt, bits & bobs and runners-only tickets to the pre-race dinner and post-race party. Non runners were expected to pay $25 admission to each of these. I attended the pre-race dinner in the City Hall Plaza on the Sunday afternoon but gave the after-race party in the legendary Fenway Park baseball stadium a miss. The dinner was excellent with a plentiful supply of all the necessary carbohydrates. We even got a pint of the local Samuel Adam's Brewery's (one of one of the race sponsors) Boston Marathon 26.2 Ale, specially brewed for the event. Mo ate elsewhere, which was just as well as - good as it was, I'm not sure she would have found value-for-money for her $25.

With formalities over I was anxious to take a good look around Boston and see if I could rediscover old haunts. Founded by Puritan settlers from England in 1630, Boston is the capital and largest city in the State of Massachusetts. It's known to most people as the home of the Kennedy dynasty and the scene of several key events of the American Revolution. I won't go into detail as I'm sure everyone will be familiar with the significance of the Boston Tea Party, the Boston Massacre, the Battle of Bunker Hill and the Siege of Boston during America's struggle for independence. The city's leading role in American Independence from Great Britain gives it a rich sense of history not found in many American cities. Following independence Boston continued to be an important port and manufacturing hub, as well as a centre for education and culture (think Harvard University and the Massachusetts Institute of Technology). Because of the city's prominent role in the American Revolution, several historic sites relating to that period are preserved as part of the Boston National Historical Park. Most are found along the Freedom Trail - a tour of these sites made by following a red line of bricks embedded in the ground. The Trail attracts millions of visitors to the city each year and I'd recommend anyone with limited time in Boston to make walking the Trail your number one sightseeing priority. The 2.5 mile Trail runs from Boston Common across the Charles River to the Bunker Hill Monument and can take from one to three hours depending on your interest. The part I enjoyed most was the stretch through the old North End of town, home to the city's large Italian community and some excellent pubs and pasta restaurants. The area was also the home of the famous American patriot and folk hero Paul Revere, an ardent colonialist who took part in the Boston Tea Party and devised a system of lanterns shone from the local church to warn of the British invasion. His famous night time ride to Lexington in 1775 to warn Samuel Adams and John Hancock of the approaching British (commemorated later in Longfellow's famous poem) earned him a special place in American history. The Trail visits his house, the church from which he sent signals and the iconic statue of Revere on his horse. Also worth visiting on the Trail is the historic Faneuil Hall, a market place and meeting hall since 1743. It was the site of several speeches by patriots Samuel Adams, James Otis and others encouraging independence from Great Britain. The hall is often referred to as 'The Cradle of Liberty' and was rated number 4 in America's Most Visited Tourist Sites by Forbes Traveller in 2008. While you're there you must visit the food stalls in next door Quincy Market for an excellent but inexpensive selection of meals.

There was plenty else to do and see in Boston to keep us occupied for the next few days but, first, the no-small matter of the city's marathon had to be considered. The Boston Marathon is respected (and feared) as much for its course as its history. The course has a well-earned reputation as one of the more difficult marathon courses because of its rolling nature and the series of hills near Newton, one of the eight towns passed on the quirky point-to-point route. Infamous among these is the aptly named Heartbreak Hill, the last of the Newton Hills near Boston College. The series of four hills between the 16 and 21 mile marks is considered among the most challenging in any popular marathon. Though Heartbreak Hill itself is only 0.4 miles long and rises only 88 feet (27 metres), it comes at a point on the course between the 20 and 21 mile mark where glycogen stores are most likely to be depleted. The hill is named after an incident that occurred during the 1936 event. It was on this hill that defending champion John Kelley overtook rival Ellison Brown, giving him a consolatory pat on the shoulder as he passed. This gesture invigorated (or should that be infuriated) Brown who rallied, overtook Kelley and went on to win the race – something that is said, to have broken Kelley's heart.

Everything about the Boston Marathon is conducted with the efficiency of a well-drilled military operation – after all they've had 120 years in which to get it right. It starts with the ordered timetabling of the entry procedure, continues with the bombardment of emails detailing race information, can be seen in the marshalling of the queues at the pre-race dinner and, best of all, in the smooth scheduling of the transport to the start in Hopkinton on race morning. As runners wait on Boston Common early on Sunday morning, whole fleets of local school buses swarm down Tremont Street like a plague of yellow locusts. We left at 8.35am – precisely on schedule. After an hour's drive the buses reached Hopkinton where we were off-loaded at the newly constructed, tented Athlete's Village on its perimeter. It was such a beautiful, hot morning that the tents were unnecessary on this occasion. Stalls within the village dispensed water, Gatorade, energy bars, gels and all manner of goodies while runners waited the call to leave for the start according to the colour of their race number. The start was arranged in four waves with the fastest qualifiers starting first at 10am. I was placed in the Yellow (4th) wave to start at 11.15am. Even within that wave there were 8 separate corrals. I left with the second of these precisely as planned at 10.30am to walk the long mile to the start line in the centre of town. On our way we walked through streets that were deathly quiet and seemingly devoid of people. That's because the whole town was waiting for us at the start with flags, banners, music and placards – I doubt if I've ever seen such an enthusiastic bunch of spectators. It was satisfying too, to observe those who'd attempted to sneak into the wrong corrals being denied access by race officials and re-directed to where they were meant to start – that's proper marshalling.

Hopkinton is 26 miles and a whole world away from big city Boston. I was impressed by its colonial architecture, neat white, weatherboard houses and historic centre. The first couple of miles of the course following Route 135 are largely downhill. From an initial elevation of 472 feet the route drops into the village of Ashland, site of the original starting line from 1897 to 1923. Crowd support here is as enthusiastic as it was in Hopkinton and you soon realise that this is going to be a prominent feature in the race. The course continues to lose altitude until around the 5 mile mark before traversing the first of seven sets of railway tracks approaching the 10km timing mat at Framingham. Apparently it was here in 1907 that several members of the lead pack got separated from the eventual winner by a slow-moving freight train. The course undulates as it skirts Lake Cochituate and proceeds into the centre of Natick. At 8.5 mile at the intersection of Mill Street and Route 135 in Natick, we pass the workshop of Henry Wilson, a local cobbler who went on to be Ulysses S Grant's vice president. Most of us are too pre-occupied with the heat to notice. Next up is Wellesley College at 12.5 miles. You know you're approaching it well before you get there by the sounds of shrieking coming from the college's 3,600 students. Considering that we're the fourth wave of runners to reach them it's amazing how they'd kept this up for so long.

At this stage we felt the first stirrings of a breeze coming from the coast. This soon turned into a pretty stiff headwind, giving us something else to think about as the Newton Hills approached. On its way into Newton Lower Falls, Route 135 drops 150 feet in half a mile, the steepest drop since leaving Hopkinton. What makes it worse is the punishing climb up over the bridge over Route 128. The strengthening wind really hit hard here. At 17.5 miles the course takes a sharp turn, bearing right towards the first of the infamous hills. The first of these is pretty long but has the gentlest gradient. The second hill rears up just past the statue of John Kelley opposite Newton City Hall. And then it's on to the big one; Heartbreak Hill itself. Crowd support here is the most welcome on the route with spectators reaching out to touch you as if to help lift you up the hill. I particularly enjoyed reading some of the innovative placards being waived at us. One reading 'Pain is only the French word for bread' made me laugh but I wasn't sure what to make of another held up by an attractive young female carrying the message, 'Finish the race and you can sit on my face.'

At mile 23 the course plummets downhill towards Boston College and yet more frantic shrieking from hordes of the College's students. After that, trolley tracks paralleling Commonwealth Avenue on the left keep supporters at arm's length for a while through the suburb of Brookline. Kenmore Square MBTA stop near mile 25 is where infamous race-cheat Rosie Ruiz is said to have walked out of the station and entered the field for her ill-gained 'first place' finish in 1980. A long straight stretch down Commonwealth Avenue takes you to a right onto Hereford Street and a final short incline before turning sharp left into Boylston Street and a sprint to the line in front of Boston Public Library. Like most finishers I spoke to afterwards my time was around 20 minutes slower than the qualifying time I'd submitted for entry. We all conveniently put this down to the heat, the hills and the unfavourable headwind - as opposed to saying we didn't try hard enough!

Having collected your medal and the various refreshments on offer don't even think of trying to exit the finish area by any other than the designated route – it really is that efficiently organised. Rightly so, spectators were packed tighter than sardines, while no less than two separate film crews were in the vicinity shooting crowd scenes for their forthcoming films about the Boston Bombings. I'm not sure of their titles but watch out for one starring Mark Wahlberg and the other featuring Jake Gyllenhaal – they'll be coming soon to a cinema near you (as they say). Having had enough of crowds for the day and not being a fan of baseball, I'd no intention of going to the post-race party in Fenway Park. I'd already decided on my own refuelling strategy for the evening, one that I'd recommend to all future Boston Marathon runners. This consisted of consuming a giant bowl of the city's speciality dish, the delicious Clam Chowder, served inside a huge hollowed-out bread roll and washed down with a pint of Samuel Adam's tasty Red Brick Ale. The Chowder can be bought almost anywhere in Boston for around $7.25, though I preferred the dishes served in the Quincy Markets.

The Red Brick Ale is also easy to find for around $7 a pint – Boston is a city of thirsty Irishmen and we were fortunate in that two good Irish bars; O'Connor's and The Whiskey Priest were both located a short walk from our hotel.

I loved Boston – both the city and the marathon. Though the former has changed beyond recognition since I was last there, most of the changes have been for the good. I've never been to a marathon that takes over a whole city in the way that the Boston Marathon does. It has become an institution of which everyone is proud and in which everyone gets involved – even more so since the 2013 bombings. There's a defiance and determination evident in the T-shirts and placards bearing the message, 'This is our f*****g city and we'll run where and when we like.' Discussions about the marathon dominate every conversation, every news bulletin and every TV weather forecast. For days before and after the event the city is swamped with runners sporting their various multi-coloured Boston Marathon jackets while the crowd support is simply inspirational. This is an event that should be on the wish list of everyone who calls himself a marathon runner.

The Boston Marathon Finish line on Boylston Street

Boston city skyline

NORTH MACEDONIA

SKOPJE MARATHON

This country was simply called Macedonia when I went there in May 2016. It was a country I'd never previously run in, never visited and one about which I knew very little. The only living Macedonian whose name came to mind was Darko Pancev (a former European Golden Boot winning soccer player). I wasn't even certain how to get there. The Hungarian airline Wizz Air is the major sponsor of the Skopje Marathon and has direct flights to the country's capital solely from Luton in the UK. As none of their flight times were suitable I initially gave up on the idea of going and booked instead to spend the month of May at our flat in Spain. Niggling away at the back of my mind, however, was the thought that I'd rather be in Skopje running their marathon. Almost by chance, while in Spain I found a connection from Alicante via Milan Bergamo for such a ridiculously low fare that, in the end, I couldn't resist interrupting the holiday to spend a few days in Macedonia's capital. It cost me the princely sums of £24.99 to fly from Alicante to Milan with Ryanair from where I picked up a £8.41 Wizz Air flight to Skopje, returning with Wizz Air to Barcelona for £16 and then taking a £14 train ride back down the coast to Alicante to resume the holiday. At those prices, how could I resist? Because Wizz Air is the marathon's main sponsor, the more expensive of their flights was reduced by 20 euros using a voucher given as part of the 16 euros marathon entry fee. You don't have to be a mathematical genius to work out that the fee was more than covered by savings on the air fares. The only problem was that my plane from Milan didn't arrive in Skopje until 6pm on the Saturday evening and Registration at the inner-city

Congress Hall closed at 7pm. Concerned that any flight delay might mean missing Registration I wrote to the organisers asking if an emergency number pick-up arrangement was available. Without hesitation they told me not to worry as they'd simply deliver the race package to my hotel. Even when I offered to take a taxi to any address they might provide they were insistent on delivering the number personally. How often do you get this kind of service from race organisers? I was already beginning to like the place before setting off.

In deciding to go to the 2016 event I was hoping for a little more luck than my friends Jack Brooks and Roger Biggs had experienced the previous year when, for safety reasons, the race was cancelled at the very last minute with runners already assembled on the start line. The official organiser of the marathon, The Sport Union of Skopje, subsequently released a statement stating, 'As a result of the new situation in the country and for safety reasons, regretfully for the many sports lovers who eagerly awaited this event, this year's traditional Wizz Air Skopje Marathon was cancelled at the request of the competent institutions.' I've never really got to discover the precise explanation behind what occurred, what exactly were the safety reasons, or even who were the competent institutions. The statement did continue, giving a hint of what might have happened by adding, 'We express our deep regret at the current situation and we sympathize with the families of the deceased soldiers.' A decision was taken to compensate those affected by the cancellation by scheduling a free-to-enter 5km race in the city in the following September. All disappointed marathoners and half marathoners were additionally offered free entry to any of the three subsequent marathon/half marathons of their choosing – all very generous gestures by the organisers. Of some concern to me during April 2016 as I prepared for the race, was TV newsreel footage of crowds of refugees attempting to access the Balkans via Macedonia and battling with police on the country's borders. I was keeping my fingers crossed that bad luck couldn't happen twice in succession and that the deteriorating refugee situation would have no effect on this year's race.

North Macedonia is a small nation with a complex and fascinating history. It has been described as part Balkan, part Mediterranean and rich in Greek, Roman and Ottoman history. It is also said to offer 'impressive ancient sites side by side with buzzing modernity' as well as 'managing to pack in much more activity and natural beauty than would seem possible for a country its size'. It all sounded a bit too good to be true. The country is one of the successor states of the former Yugoslavia, from which it declared independence in 1991. It became a member of the United Nations in 1993, but, as a result of an ongoing dispute with Greece over the use of the name Macedonia (the reason for the subsequent addition of 'North' to its name) it was admitted under the provisional description of the Former Yugoslav Republic of Macedonia (abbreviated to FYROM), a term that was also used by international organizations such as the European Union, the Council of Europe and NATO. North Macedonia is a landlocked country, bordered by Kosovo to the northwest, Serbia to the north, Bulgaria to the east, Greece to the south and Albania to the west. It shares the historical region of Macedonia with Bulgaria, Albania and, more significantly, Greece. To the latter, Macedonia is an ancient region within Greece and for the new republic to have called itself as such is considered by many Greeks as claiming a stake on their territory. The two countries also appear to be at odds over the claiming of Alexander the Great as their national hero. It was put to me while in Skopje that, as Alexander's father was Macedonian and his mother Greek, he must be considered as more Macedonian than Greek. However there's no disputing the birthplace of Skopje's other famous former inhabitant, Mother Teresa, as evidenced by the brass plaques containing one or more of her famous sayings decorating every public building in the city.

When Yugoslavia fell apart, the former republic of Macedonia retained the currency, the dinar - which, to distinguish it from the Serbian version, is spelt 'denar'. One of the main problems I had in making arrangements to travel was in obtaining currency for the trip. None of the travel outlets I normally use (Thomas Cook, Thomson, Post Office) dealt in Macedonian denars while the cashier on the foreign exchange counter at Newcastle Airport looked at me as if I was crazy. However, the currency that counts is the euro. The best plan is to take plenty of them as cash, in low denominations (nothing bigger than 20 euros) and change them locally as and when you need to. You should get around 55 denars per euro which in the cheaper bars will be enough to buy a beer. Little and often is the rule for currency transactions, because you don't want to be left with denars when you leave the country. The US dollar is also welcome – as I had a few left over from the previous month's visit to Boston, I took them along too.

Skopje has an international airport, Skopje Alexander the Great Airport. It is located in Petrovec, some 20 km east of the city. Vardar Ekspres operates buses between the airport and the city centre. The journey takes approximately 30 minutes and costs MKD 175. Tickets can be purchased from the booth in the airport and must be paid for in local currency, which can be obtained from exchange offices or ATMs in the airport. The bus stops at the International Bus Station and the Holiday Inn hotel. Buses leave the airport every day at 01:00; 02:50; 04:30; 09:00; 10:30; 13:30; 15:50; 18:30; and 20:30. Alternatively, the Airport Taxi firm is the only outfit authorised to take passengers from the airport. Their price lists are displayed at the exit to the airport and within the vehicle. It currently costs 1220 denar or 20 euros into the city centre. Make sure you get into a white vehicle numbered from 1 to 65.

With approximately 700,000 inhabitants, Skopje is the country's capital and largest city as well as its political, cultural and economic centre. The fact that it has been occupied by many different civilisations since its foundation is evidenced by the presence of a number of Byzantine churches and monasteries as well as several historic Roman sites. It was the Ottomans, however, who left the greatest mark on the city. They ruled North Macedonia for hundreds of years, building a large number of mosques and bazaars still in use today. The city is located in the Skopje Valley along the Vardar River and is surrounded by beautiful mountain ranges to the north and south. While there, I found that you could escape the restricted feeling of being in a city simply by looking upwards at the mountain slopes.

The city experienced rapid development after the Second World War during which Skopje had been occupied by Bulgarian forces fighting for the German cause. This development was altered by the disastrous earthquake of 1963 which caused enormous damage to the city. The disaster killed over 1,000 citizens, injuring 3,300 others. Over 16,000 people were buried alive in the ruins and 70% of the population lost their homes. Prior to the earthquake the prosperous city had boasted many neoclassical buildings laid out in a harmonious Central European style and an international competition was held to redesign the city and restore it to its former splendour. This was won by a Japanese architect whose designs produced an imaginative, futuristic style. Some of his creations, such as the National Theatre with its sloping roof, have reshaped Skopje's modern skyline. Though, to this day, the clock on the remaining wall of the old railway station stays stuck at 5:17 – the moment that the earthquake struck. Partial reconstruction was completed by 1980 with many elements never built as funds became exhausted. When the economic situation improved in the new millennium, many landmarks were restored under the Skopje 2014 project. The project, launched in 2010 ostensibly to improve the appearance of the city centre by that date, has not received universal approval. Many critics see it as merely an expensive and frivolous display of nationalism designed to annoy Greece and North Macedonia's population of ethnic Albanians.

Having had my race package delivered to my hotel as promised I had no need to attend the race Expo in the Alksander Makedonski Congress Hall. This was just as well, considering the heavy thunderstorm that greeted my arrival. My hotel, the Hotel City Central, proved an excellent choice for 44 euros per night with breakfast. My room overlooked the start line and the Macedonian Gate leading to the famous Square of the same name. All I had to do was tumble out of bed in the morning, descend a few steps and I was ready to run. According to the Mayor's address in the race programme this was to be the 12th edition of the race (the same programme, however, only displayed results from 2008). As well as the Marathon, events included a Marathon Relay, Half Marathon and a 5K race. Though we were meant to line up in that order with marathon runners setting-off first, there appeared to be little official control of who went where and I found myself starting with runners from all four events. Altogether, there were something like 6,500 runners entered on the day: 234 in the Marathon, 63 teams of 4 in the Marathon Relay, 1,309 in the Half Marathon and 4,771 in the 5K. The marathon was to be two laps of the half marathon course with a 5 hours and 15 minutes time limit.

We left at 8.45am to turn into Macedonian Square, running under the colossal statue that dominates the centre of the Square and has come to be recognised as the new symbol of the city. Though not officially named after him, the statue is taken to depict Alexander the Great, the country's most famous son. The monument was built in Florence and officially completed in September 2011 to commemorate 20 years of the Republic's independence. The bronze sculpture is huge: 14.5 metres tall, sitting on a cylindrical column which itself is 10 metres in height. This column stands in a fountain and at its base are 8 bronze soldiers each 3 metres tall. There are also 8 bronze lions around the fountain's edges, four of which act as part of the fountain, releasing water from their mouths. The fountain is also said to play music from time to time. Sadly, like a number of other monuments in the city, the column is currently daubed with paint from those protesting against the country's current regime.

Almost immediately we then crossed the River Vardar via the ancient Stone Bridge, whose narrowness resulted into something of an initial bottleneck. The Bridge, constructed in the 6th century by the Byzantine emperor Justinian, is the second instantly recognisable symbol of Skopje. Virtually every ruler of the city has tried to leave his mark on the 13-arched bridge at some stage or other with the biggest reconstruction being made by the Ottomans during the 15th century. The stone fence and guard tower were added then. The guard tower fell down during its most recent restoration and is waiting to be reconstructed. Despite several new bridges being built across the Vardar in recent years, the old Stone Bridge is still the main connection between Macedonia Square to the south and the Old Bazaar area to the north of the city.

Turning left over the bridge we ran between the National Theatre and the Holocaust Museum. The latter is an ultra-modern, futuristic building designed in remembrance of the 4,000 Jewish citizens who were transported to Treblinka by the Nazis during the Second World War. Virtually every single one of them died in the death-camp. Immediately to our right was Kale Fortress atop the highest hill in the valley and offering great views of the city. The oldest section of the fortress is within the present-day fortifications and this too was built by Justinian. Most of the current fortifications were built during the 10th century and reinforced by the construction of over 70 towers during the Ottoman occupation of the city. The fortress was the last important landmark we passed before heading out to the western suburbs on a long, wide open road. There was no further congestion from thereon in but neither was there anything of particular interest to be see – just suburbia and then….more suburbia. In many ways the course reminded me of the one I'd run on some six months earlier in Zagreb: an out-and-back loop to one side of the city then an out-and-back to the other side of the city – both repeated twice. Not exactly thrilling.

Crowd support was minimal on most of the course until the city centre was approached again at 12km, 21km, 33km and the finish. As soon as we'd turned away from the half marathons to skirt the Square for the start of our second lap the race turned into a lonely slog for the remaining 21 kilometres. The main difference from Zagreb was the contrast in the weather. Instead of the torrential rain of Zagreb we had heat and humidity. I can't recall running anywhere quite as humid. The previous evening's thunderstorms had resulted in a heaviness and high level of humidity that became apparent early in the race. Fortunately the organisation of the drink stations was spot-on, with lots of water, oranges, bananas and, especially welcome, the isotonic drinks on the second lap of the course.

I've never been a hot weather runner so abandoned all hope of a fast time and concentrated solely on survival. I'm not complaining, I'm quite content at plodding along on my own and don't really need to be surrounded by other runners or cheering crowds to enjoy an event. There's a real satisfaction to be had in running somewhere foreign, somewhere different, somewhere you never dreamt you'd get to and just observing what's there in front of you. It's not the organisers' fault that the course lacked the iconic landmarks of other big city marathons. Given the topography of the place I'm sure they chose the only route that was fit for purpose. After all, who would want the alternative of running round and round Macedonia Square or over and over the bridges until you got dizzy. I was happy enough with running through Macedonia Gate (Skopje's own Arc de Triumph) and up to the finish in the shadow of Alexander's horse. I enjoyed the event and was pleasantly surprised to find that my slow 4 hours 39 minutes was good enough to make me 1st Vet 70, as well as being faster than anyone in the Vet 65 age group too. I'll value the medal and its saucy Wizz Air pink ribbon, if not the far-too-small similarly coloured T-shirt (a perfect fit for Mo). I enjoyed, too, sitting in the hot sun next to the paint-spattered lions by Alexander's fountain and watching other runners finish. There was no shortage of people to provide a really good atmosphere at the end.

After the race I went looking as usual for the best places to eat and drink. For the former, I'd recommend visiting the Old Bazaar area to the north of the river. Though some parts of the bazaar have been destroyed to make streets and parking areas, it's still the largest bazaar in the Balkans and well worth a visit. It's a labyrinth of streets lined with small shops intended as a contact zone for both the Christian and Muslim populations living in their separate areas of the town. The whole area is surrounded by markets, split for hygiene reasons according to produce on offer. If the food smells emanating from some of the many outdoor restaurants aren't enough to pull you in then the prices certainly will. I'd heard that local prices were cheap but hadn't reckoned on them being quite so cheap and still of such good quality. A huge pre-race dish of

Spaghetti Bolognaise cost only 170 denars (about 3 euro) while the next night's massive pizza was even less at 150 denars. The cost of a pint of lager ranged between 70 to 110 denar depending on how close to the city centre or how classy the establishment considered itself to be. I was happy to pay the more expensive price at Paddy's Irish bar on the south bank just so I could have an informed conversation with the local manager who held some very interesting views about the current political situation in his country.

I found Skopje one of the most unusual cities I've ever visited. I think part of that is down to the fact that the place seems uncertain of its own identity. I get the impression that it's trying too hard to turn itself into something that it's not. At the moment it appears neither fish nor fowl. If I lived there I'd be concerned that those in control of the purse strings are in danger of turning the city into a Las Vegas-style parody of what they consider to be a modern city. Skopje appears unfinished and in a constant state of redevelopment and reconstruction. Even its centrepiece, the iconic Macedonia Square, had no less than four separate buildings around its perimeter covered in scaffolding. All along the nearby river banks there were works in progress. Some of these simply didn't fit the environment in which they stood. For example, of what relevance are the two reconstructed Spanish galleons (with another under construction) to a landlocked Balkan capital city? On the opposite, north bank the parade of opulent, extravagant government buildings and museums just seemed over-the-top and out of context. They looked too large, too new and somehow not quite right for their location. Perhaps they'll weather and bed-in as time goes on but at the moment they stick out like sore thumbs. And why does the city need to be continually building new bridges to cross a half-kilometre stretch of riverbank? You could virtually throw a blanket over the five that are already there and there's another on the way. Again, it just seems over-the-top construction for construction's sake. I'm sure concerned citizens must be asking as to where all the money is coming from for all the public building infrastructure in the nation's capital. Nothing is more self-indulgent, however, than the forest of statues that has sprung-up in recent years. I can't imagine anywhere with as many statues – not even Louis XIV's Versailles or Peter the Great's spread at St. Petersburg. The place is like 'The Land of a Thousand Statutes.' The things are everywhere with one bridge, the Bridge of Art, hosting no fewer than 35 of them. With time on my hands after the race I set out to count them all but gave up when I got to sixty. North Macedonians I spoke to jokingly claim that there's a statue for every person in the country. Others reckon that the only reason that bridges keep getting built is to provide somewhere to erect more statues. It really is that ridiculous – they've just taken what started as good ideas far too far. There are too many statues, too many bridges, too many Spanish galleons and far too many plaques of Mother Teresa's quotes.

Despite what I've said, I found Skopje's quirkiness attractive and would definitely like to return. There was a pleasant, relaxed and, surprising, air of affluence about the city centre. My initial reservations were groundless as I saw no evidence of the refugee situation on its borders having any impact on the day-to-day life of the city. I'm not sure though that the events that resulted in the cancellation of last year's marathon have entirely gone away. There was a sizeable, peaceful protest march in the centre on the day I arrived and I get the impression that a large number of citizens are very unhappy with those in office. However, Skopje does need to improve its tourist infrastructure if it wants to succeed in its intention of attracting more overseas visitors. Things you take for granted in other foreign capitals appeared lacking in the city. A few things stood out. For example, I found no Tourist Information Offices on my visit, my hotel wasn't even able to provide the usual city map and there were no information brochures or pamphlets on display. Likewise, the location and times of airport buses aren't sign-posted or easy to find. Little things, I know – but essential to every visitor.

Start/Finish area at Skopje

Alexander the Great's statue looks down on the Start

LUXEMBOURG

ING NIGHT MARATHON

.

This was another new country to the list. I'd never previously run in Luxembourg and, having never before visited the country, had been looking forward to going to a place whose name brought back happy memories of teenage evenings spent glued to the radio station of the same name. Radio Luxembourg broadcasting at 208 on the dials of our old battery operated radios was the station in the late 50s and early 60s on which those of my generation cut our musical teeth. At the time, the BBC with its broadcasting monopoly on British territory devoted itself to mediocre, middle-of-the-road musical schmaltz. This was the era before pirate and commercial radio was ever invented and only Radio Luxembourg could be relied upon to deliver the very latest of the new rock n' roll sounds coming out of the United States. It alone provided us with music from the likes of Chuck Berry, Buddy Holly, the Everly Brothers, Jerry Lee Lewis and Little Richard among others – music that means as much to me now as it did then. I'll be forever grateful to those who worked so hard on Radio Luxembourg back then for the part they played in bringing us what, at the time, was considered revolutionary music. Though the 208 wavelength was finally closed down in December 1992 the musical memories linger long. I wondered whether I'd be as impressed by the country as I had been by its radio station.

As race day drew nearer, I approached this event with a great deal of apprehension. Despite the desire to add Luxembourg to the growing list of countries in which I'd run a marathon I began to have nagging doubts as to whether I was wise to go ahead with the trip. Firstly and most importantly, I had concerns about my health. How many times do we, as runners, tell ourselves that we should listen to our bodies only to simply ignore what they're telling us when the message becomes inconvenient. I'd been well and truly laid low with some sort of debilitating stomach bug in the week leading up to the race and scarcely had the energy to get out of bed on the day I was due to fly to Luxembourg. I'd been in a similar situation two years previously when setting off for the Stockholm Marathon and was mindful of the wasted journey I'd made when the illness forced me to pull out on the start line on that occasion. Though I didn't want a repeat of that experience, we runners are an optimistic bunch, so two weeks after Skopje, I headed off to Amsterdam for a connecting flight hoping for, but not expecting, some sort of 24-hour miracle recovery.

The second doubt was very much connected to the first. I wasn't aware, for example, of how popular this event had become and how quickly it sells out – the marathon entry limited was reached as early as February in 2016. The organisers had been very helpful in assisting me to find a place in their already sold-our event. I didn't want not to turn up and leave them thinking I was unappreciative of their assistance. I was hoping that I liked what I saw when I got there. I didn't want to appear ungracious or over-critical in writing this account of the race but, at the same time, was determined to remain both objective and impartial in my comments.

Another doubt concerned the timing of the event. This is a night marathon and I've never really enjoyed other night marathons that I've run. I've nothing against night marathons per se – there's absolutely no reason why marathon races shouldn't be held late in the day and I'm sure that many other marathon runners thoroughly enjoy the experience. Unfortunately, as I've documented elsewhere (see the chapter on the Bilbao Night Marathon in 'Marathon Tourism in Spain') I've never performed well in an evening race. My body clock is very much set on morning time and has never been suited to running late in the day. I've always been an early morning runner who prefers to get the running over and done with as early in the day as possible. I don't like the long wait until an evening run. My body prefers to be relaxing - or in the pub.

I tried to put those doubts behind me when setting off for Luxembourg. I hoped that: my illness would allow me to start, I hoped I'd enjoy the event, I hoped that I'd conquer my aversion to an evening start and I hoped to see as much of the city as I could in the time available. But first, I needed to brush up on my knowledge of where I was going. Research revealed that Luxembourg was founded in 963, when Count Siegfried bought the fortress of Luxembourg from the Holy Roman Empire. It has a complicated history. For some three centuries different European countries including Spain, France and Austria held it at various times. In 1815, after Napoleon's defeat Luxembourg's future was uncertain. The Congress of Vienna declared it a Grand Duchy, and handed it to the Netherlands. There were more squabbling and land grabs, but in 1867, what was left of Luxembourg gained full independence. Despite declaring its neutrality, Luxembourg was occupied by Germany during both World Wars. After renewed occupation in the Second World War, Luxembourg abandoned its neutrality and became an enthusiast for international co-operation.

Today, it's the only Grand Duchy left in the world and operates as a hereditary constitutional monarchy, headed by Grand Duke Henri Albert Gabriel Félix Marie Guillaume. While small in terms of land area, Luxembourg could be considered 'The Heart of Europe' Its strategic position, a healthy mix of cultures, and a powerful economy give it more influence than you might expect from such a tiny country. Along with economic and cultural strength, the Grand Duchy served as a founder of the EU, leading the way in the recent creation of an overall politically stronger Europe. Luxembourgers are a very independent lot. Despite, or perhaps because of the heavy influence of major European powers on all sides (Luxemburg is a land-locked country bordered by neighbours France, Germany and Belgium) its national motto is 'Mir wëlle bleiwe, war mir sin' which means 'We want to remain what we are.' Luxembourgers enjoy one of the highest per capita GDPs in the world, ranking second (after Qatar) in 2014. The steel industry made the country rich in the 19th century, but when that collapsed in the late 1970's, Luxembourg evolved into a major financial centre. Today, there are about 150 banks in a country that's smaller than some English counties. Its reputation as a tax haven made it attractive to all kinds of foreign investment. For example, Amazon and Skype have headquarters there. In their 2015 World Happiness Report, the United Nations ranked Luxembourg number 17 out of 158, not bad for a country with a population of about half a million. The report cites the high GDP, which translates into purchasing power, as the biggest factor. It also did well in social support - the country is very generous with its citizens, spending about 1/3 of its revenue on social services and universal, free health care.

The city of Luxembourg in which the marathon takes place is the capital of the Grand Duchy and the country's most populous commune. As of January 2016, the commune had a population of over 115,00, which was more than three times the population of the country's second most populous commune. Standing at the confluence of both the Alzette and Pétrusse rivers in southern Luxembourg, the city lies at the centre of Western Europe, situated 213 km by road from Brussels, 372 km from Paris, and 209 km from Cologne. Due to its location and natural geography, Luxembourg has through history been a place of strategic military significance. The first fortifications were built as early as the 10th century and the city contains Luxembourg Castle, established by the Franks in the Early Middle Ages, around which a settlement developed.

The city centre occupies a picturesque site perched high on precipitous cliffs that drop into the narrow valleys of the two rivers. The Unesco-listed Old Town is considered one of Europe's most scenic capitals, thanks largely to its unusual setting. The 70 metre deep gorges cut by the rivers are spanned by many bridges and viaducts, including the Adolphe Bridge, the Grand Duchess Charlotte Bridge, and the Passerelle. Although Luxembourg City is not particularly large, its layout is complex, as the city is set on several levels, straddling hills and dropping into the two gorges (something that we'd have to face while running the marathon course). The capital is said to have a fairy-tale quality to its Unesco-listed historic core, memorably perched along a dramatic cliff top. The Chemin de Corniche the pedestrian promenade at the top of the cliff has been hailed as 'Europe's most beautiful balcony.' It winds along the route of the 17th-century city ramparts with views across the river canyon towards the hefty fortifications of the Wenceslas Wall. The rampart-top walk continues along Blvd Victor Thorn

Luxembourg is officially divided into 24 districts, but the visitor really needs to know only four: Ville Haute ('High City'), the medieval town core, Ville Basse ('Low City'), situated in the gorge that cuts itself across the city and the most picturesque area, Gare ('Station'), the location of the train station and the Hotel Empire I'd booked directly opposite, a 15 min walk south of Ville Haute and home to many restaurants and cafés and finally Kirchberg, the modern city full of banks and European Union buildings. This is where the marathon starts and finishes. It's a soulless, character-less sort of place with nothing symbolising this glassed-in corporate quarter more than the 'Giant Banker' statue on Avenue JFK. It is a seat of several institutions of the European Union, including the European Court of Justice, the European Court of Auditors, and the European Investment Bank.

The easiest way to reach Luxembourg City from the airport is by bus. The bus station is right outside the terminal, and lines 16 and 29 both reach the centre within 20–25 minutes. Single journey tickets cost 2 euros from machines at the bus stop. Buses run every 10 minutes on Monday to Friday, every 20 minutes on Saturdays, and every 30 minutes on Sundays. Alternatively, taxis charge around 25 euros for the 10 to 15 minute drive to the city. If you arrive on a flight during registration opening hours it's possible to get off bus 16 directly next to the Luxexpo venue after only two stops. Public transportation is one of the few things that are actually cheap in Luxembourg is. A day-ticket valid for all buses/trains in the entire country costs just 4 euros. Luxembourg City's bus system is also very efficient, with 31 lines operating each day. A 2-hour ticket costs 2 euros, while a 10-ticket card costs 16 euros – both sold at ticket machines at bus stops. There is no charge whatsoever for buses within the city centre on a Saturday – something worth bearing in mind when making plans to travel to Registration. However, due to the city's small size and beautiful scenery, the best way to appreciate it is on foot. In a few hours (or dividing your trip in two days like I did) you can get to know the whole city by walking around. The city also operates a self-service bike scheme and the stations can be found in various locations around the city centre. Useful guidelines on how to make best use of the city's bicycles is given in the event's Runner's Handbook.

A lot of thought has obviously been put into the compilation of this Handbook, downloadable from the event website and available in booklet form at Registration. It provides detailed information on all aspects of the event, not just for runners but for spectators too. 2016 was the 11th edition of this annual night marathon in Luxembourg that was held for the first time in 2006 as the Europe Marathon. Race headquarters including Start and Finish are located on the premises of Luxexpo, a huge, modern conference and exhibition centre designed to host events and seasonal fairs, situated in the Kerchberg district approximately 7 kilometres to the north east of the central station. This is a somewhat inconvenient distance for those staying in the city centre. As far as I could see, there are no hotels within what I'd consider the immediate vicinity of the Expo (ie. walking distance) so my initial concern centred round how I was going to get back to a bed on finishing in the early hours of the morning. The organisers have solved this problem by providing an efficient fleet of shuttle buses running to and from all areas of the city throughout the Saturday (race day), both before and after the race. Entry fees for the marathon are fixed on an upwardly sliding scale from 51 euros before the end of November to 56 euros to the end of January and 63 euros until April 24th. There's an extra charge of 13 euros, 5 euros of which is refunded, for those who don't have their own chip. As I said earlier, however, this event sells out fast so don't do what I did and think you can still enter nearer the time. For the cost of entry you will receive: start number and safety pins, a ticket for the pre-race Pasta Party and kit bag for clothing check-in containing a gel and other assorted goodies. On finishing runners receive a souvenir medal, certificate and results, a massage service and entry to the finish area buffet. There's no T-shirt included in the package, these have to be purchased separately. I'll leave you to decide whether what you get is value for what you pay. Personally, I couldn't care less about a T-shirt, I've got enough to last me a lifetime – I'd prefer the entry fee went on the not inconsiderable cost of the shuttles provided as well as on the quantity and quality of what you're given at the drink stations en route.

Unfortunately, arriving in Luxembourg late Friday evening didn't allow enough time to take a public bus back out to the Expo to register before closing. This not only meant missing the Pasta Party but also gave me several hours of simply sitting around the next day. I didn't want to have to make two journeys out-and-back to Luxexpo by registering early in the day. As Registration closed at 4pm on the Saturday, I figured that I needed to take the number 18 bus from the station to be at the Expo with time to spare and avoid the last minute crowds. It was such a beautiful day when I arrived shortly after 3pm that sitting out in the sun for four hours before race started didn't appear to be too much of a chore. Registration was un-crowded and the whole process took only a matter of minutes. It didn't take much longer to walk around the stalls to see what was on offer – largely running merchandise and promotions from other, mainly French, marathons. Unfortunately, the heavens opened shortly afterwards bringing a fierce thunderstorm and sending everyone scurrying indoors. Soon the place was filled to capacity with runners sprawled on the floor in their thousands as the rain beat on the tin roof. Conditions soon became uncomfortable and what should have been a pleasant wait turned into a nightmare, reinforcing all those feelings I have about sitting around waiting for an evening start. Our clothing bags had to be handed in by 6pm just as the rain was beginning to relent and we were finally able to step tentatively outside. I felt really sorry for all those outside stall-holders selling kebabs, chips and the likes. Their profits must have taken a nose dive.

The ING Night Marathon, to give it its official title, includes a number of other events aside from the marathon itself: there's a Half Marathon, a Marathon Team Relay, a 5K Run for Success and a children's Mini Marathon. The first three of these start at the same time at 7pm in front of the Luxexpo building with the other two starting at 8pm and 7.40pm respectively. Unusually for once, the marathon is not simply two laps of the half marathon distance, and the races are separated at two points at about 15 km and again at approximately 36 km on the marathon route. Marathon runners are allowed 6 hours in which to complete the course. Runners in the three main events are given colour-coded bibs dependent on expected finishing times. Though I'd predicted a 4 hour 30 finish when entering that was when I was fit and keen to run. Given how I felt on the day I knew I could never get anywhere near that time. My stomach felt worse, not better, and the big decision I had to make was whether I was going to start at all. I don't want to make too much of the illness thing. There's nothing worse than runners who bang-on about illness and injury. It happens to all of us at some time or other. I prefer the 'No excuses' philosophy of 'Just get on with it.' I mention it only because it affects what follows. I'd read in the Handbook that pacemakers had been provided up to 5:29 but wondered if I was even capable of that pace. While I stood at the very back of the field pondering all this, a lady wandered past me carrying a balloon displaying 6:00. I asked if she was an official pacemaker and in her broken English she assured me that she was and that she'd even been interviewed to do the job. On explaining my situation, this lovely lady called Anja promised that if I stuck with her she'd ensure that I completed the course. This gave me the confidence to start – I knew that there was a preliminary loop of 5k bringing us almost back to where we'd started from. I'd see how I went on that and if I had to drop out then so be it.

It took us 12 minutes to cross the starting line to an unrelenting and deafening background of noise from those who'd come to see us off. The crowd support over the first five kilometres was brilliant with many of the spectators wearing the bright orange cowboy hats and waving the similarly coloured huge, orange hands distributed by the sponsors. Their exuberance certainly encouraged me to continue and I'd soon left Anja behind and caught up with and settled in behind the 5:29 pacemakers. There then followed a quieter downhill section through the roads of the business district before reaching the outskirts of the city after 8km. Here the crowds reappeared in number and remained pretty constant through the twists and turns to the north of the city. We reached the first dividing point at approximately 15km while passing through the noisy and busy Place Guillame. Those of us near the back of the field were not to see the half marathon runners again – most of these had already finished by the time the two courses rejoined at 36km.

Without the company of the thousands of half marathoners the remainder of the race took on a different complexion. At this stage the marathon route headed out westwards as runners ploughed a lonely furrow through a complicated and convoluted section of the course for the next 13 or so kilometres. We ran back and forth through what was largely a residential area with only the odd smattering of curious residents watching our progress. The near-empty streets took on an eerie quality as dusk descended. I was grateful for the presence of those in the Team Relay who swelled the numbers on the course and even more grateful for the street-corner bands whose persistent drumming could be heard from miles away and at least helped to create some sort of atmosphere on this section.

We returned towards the city at 28km before reaching what to me was the most memorable part of the course. After crossing the Avenue de la Liberte we commenced a long, descent under the walls of the old fortress into the Petrusse gorge. The sky was dark by now but the course was lit by paper lanterns with what looked like powerful candles adding to the glow. Even more beautiful (and definitely atmospheric) was the haunting blue light that seemed to emanate from the water itself. The words fairy-tale, mystical and magical come to mind. I don't think I've ever seen anything quite like it on a marathon course. The only problem is that, looking up, you can see the outline of a bridge over which people are running and you realise that you too have got to get up there somehow. Fortunately, the ascent is nowhere near as steep as the descent, involving merely a long, steady incline away from the river.

This brought us eventually back into the heart of the old city for the second time. This time the crowds have had a couple of more hours in which to enjoy their Saturday evening drinks and the support becomes even more boisterous with slaps on the back and alcohol being offered in passing. It was the night of the Champions League Final between Athletico and Real Madrid which was being shown in all the bars en route. Knowing that a fast time was out of the question, I'd already stopped at a couple of these to find out the score. However, the match had lasted almost as long as the marathon, going to extra time and penalties. I arrived into the fourth bar I visited just in time to see Ronaldo scoring the winning penalty.

Leaving the city for the final time we re-crossed the river at the 37km mark for the last 5k uphill slog to the finish through the deathly silent business district. There were no crowds, no atmosphere and very little light. It didn't matter, the fact that we were so close to the finish made it all bearable. I'd long since abandoned following any pacemakers and had simply been running according to how I felt – and I felt strong (the marathon cure for ill health!) passing a number of those who I thought were away and out of sight. The finish itself was something entirely different and altogether very enjoyable. After circling the Expo building in near darkness we were suddenly plunged into an indoor arena that appeared like something between a fairground and a disco with music blaring, lights flashing, gyrating dancers and cheering crowds. Many runners who'd finished earlier stayed on until late in the night to enjoy the food and drink at the After Race Party. I wished I'd had the stomach to join them but could manage only one celebratory beer. The shuttle bus to the station pulled up right on cue – there was no waiting around even at 2 o'clock in the morning.

Anyone thinking of going to this event shouldn't be put off by the course profile that oscillates up and down like an out of control electro-cardiograph. Though varied and challenging in parts it's not really that hilly. To me, there appeared more down than up on the way around. It must have been difficult for the organisers to find 42.2 kilometres of fairly flat road in such a small city with such an uneven topography – hence all the turning back and forth on the marathon course. I have to say that I didn't enjoy some of these sections but I guess an alternative, more scenic route, would have been too hilly. The city's size appears more suited to a half marathon as opposed to the full distance and I'm surprised that the organisers haven't found a course where marathoners simply repeat the half marathon route as happens in so many other big city events. I'm sure they've considered this so there must be good logistical reasons for the current arrangement. Certainly, the half marathon is by far the more popular of the two events with over 6,400 finishers as opposed to only 1,172 in the marathon. Apparently over 14,000 runners registered for all the races on offer – a record for the event. The overall organisation was faultless, as befits eleven years of practice. The organisers had thought of everything and had somehow managed to successfully combine a competitive marathon race for those at the front with an exuberant party-like experience for those of us who took it less seriously. This year the course record was broken by the Kenyan winner whose 2:12:57 showed just what it was possible to achieve on this course. Those with less ambitious goals had the opportunity of registering a friend or family member to run with them over the last 2.5 kilometres. Called 'Go-Go Boys' (or Girls) these individuals were equipped with special T-shirts to make them visible to those they planned to support. It's that type of event! Aid stations were plentiful and evenly spaced with virtually every one of them providing isotonic drinks and usually a choice of bananas and oranges. The route was very well-marshalled (it needed to be as the night progressed and the drinks took hold of some of the spectators) with hundreds of volunteers and police on the course until well after midnight. I did feel a bit sorry for those on the quieter parts of the course between 15 and 28km and again during the last 5km as they stood stoically at their posts as the back-markers trickled by. Would I do it again? I'm not sure - perhaps if it was a day-time event. I haven't lost this long-standing aversion to running late in the day. My 5:19 finishing time was well over an hour slower than my fastest time this year so I'd certainly like to see what I can do on the course when fully fit.

Despite not getting to bed until almost 3am I was determined to do the full marathon tourist thing and see as much as possible of Luxembourg before I left later that day. I'd already toured the Old City taking in a number of the historic sites. These included the Grand Ducal Palace, the official residence of the Grand Duke of Luxembourg where he performs most of his duties as head of state of the Grand Duchy. It also houses the country's Parliament and Chamber of Deputies. A short walk away is the Cathedral de Notre Dame built by the Jesuits in the early 17th century and considered a noteworthy example of gothic architecture. Nearby is the Gelle Fra (literally 'Golden Lady') – a golden figure of a woman holding a wreath as symbol of victory. It was removed by the Nazis during occupation but has been reinstated as a memorial to those who gave their lives during the Second World War. Also within strolling distance is the historic Place de Guillaume. This is one of the busiest little squares in the city, hosting colourful open-air markets each Wednesday and Saturday morning. It's well worth a visit, whether for shopping or simply walking around and meeting people. The market at Place Guillaume is a mass of vibrant, interesting stalls selling fresh vegetables, fruit, fish, cheese and flowers, with many of the produce being organically grown. The centre of Place Guillaume is dominated by a bronze statue of King and Duke William XI of Nassau-Orange, seated on a horse. William XI ruled the Duchy from 1840 to 1849. Also worth a look is the Town Hall, located at one side of Place Guillaume, notable for its bronze lion statues. The Town Hall dates back to 1830, having been built using stone from the Franciscan monastery that stood on the site previously.

On the Sunday I was determined to revisit those parts of the course that had caught my interest when running through in the dark. In particular, I wanted to see the Petrusse Valley in daylight and then walk along the Passerelle viaduct linking the train station with the Old City. The Petrusse Park is a beautiful place to relax after a race. The paths winds through the old town, overlooking the city's cliffs, bridges and the river carving its way through the valley. Top of the agenda, however, was a visit to the famed Casemates du Bock, the 17km of underground tunnels beneath the city's old castle. For over four centuries, the best military engineers from Burgundy, Spain, France, Austria and Germany ended up turning the Bock promontory into one of the most fortified places on earth – the so-called 'Gibraltar of the North' with around 40,000 square metres of bomb shelters lodged in the city's rock. These were able to shelter not only thousands of defenders, including their horses and equipment, but also artillery, workshops, kitchens, bakeries, abattoirs and so forth. The Casemates are open from 10am until 5.30. The 4 euros entry fee is great value for money in providing a lasting final memory of an interesting weekend in Luxembourg.

Preparing for the Start in Luxembourg

The indoor Finish of the Luxembourg Night Marathon

SWEDEN

STOCKHOLM MARATHON

I had two goes at this event before succeeding in completing it. Such is the popularity of the Stokholm Marathon that on both occasions I entered it the day entries were opened. Both times almost a year before the race. True to form interest in the event on both occasions was greater than ever; the race filling up quickly each time with almost 22,000 runners from 93 countries taking part. These were the highest figure in the race's long history. I'd last visited western Sweden over forty plus years ago with stays in both Gothenburg and Malmo. Lots of things have changed since then. Not only have Abba come and gone while the Volvo keeps on going; but the country is now connected to Denmark by a bridge-tunnel across the Oresund that I'd seen whilst in Copenhagen en route to the Hans Christian Anderson marathon. I'd yet to make it as far as Stockholm on the east coast and had certainly never before run a marathon in Sweden; I was therefore looking forward to the trip immensely.

Briefly, a bit of background: Sweden is the largest of the Scandinavian countries and the third largest in Western Europe behind France and Spain. It's also twice the size of Britain but with a population of only 9.6 million giving it an extremely low population density of 54 per square mile; space to breathe for everyone - provided that is, you don't live in one of the urban areas where 85% of the inhabitants are concentrated, (especially on marathon day!). The remainder of the country is principally a land of lakes and forests and lots of elk.

For centuries Sweden was inhabited by various Germanic tribes who eventually emerged as the Vikings. It unified as a country during the Middle Ages and expanded its territories during the 17th century to form the Swedish Empire, one of the great powers of Europe. The Empire declined rapidly during the following two centuries with territories like Finland being lost to Russia. Since its last battle with neighbour Norway in 1814, Sweden has led a peaceful existence as a neutral state. Today, it's a parliamentary democracy and constitutional monarchy with the world's eighth highest per capita income. It also continuously ranks highly in numerous surveys comparing a country's performance in areas such as quality of life, prosperity and economic competitiveness. A member of the European Union since 1995, it voted against joining the Eurozone in 2003 and still retains the Swedish kroner as its currency. Currently (2021) £1 equates to 12.01SEK.

Stockholm, the nation's capital, boasts an idyllic location, sitting on fourteen different islands connected by fifty seven bridges where the freshwater of Lake Malaren meets the Baltic Sea. Its location is an almost perfect combination of water, green open spaces and fresh clean air, leading it to be often described as one of the world's most beautiful cities. It is also the most populous city in Sweden with almost 900,000 people in the metropolitan area most of whom work in the service industry where it's a major IT and financial centre. Its lack of heavy industry combined with the fact that, thanks to Sweden's neutrality, it escaped damage during World War 2, has resulted in it being an attractive city in which to live. In recent years, tourism has played an important part in the city's economy, ranking it tenth largest visitor destination in Europe.

With it being a Saturday lunchtime marathon, on our initial visit in 2014, Mo and I decided to travel from Thursday to Sunday, flying with Norwegian Airlines from Edinburgh airport and intending to meet up with friends Dave Goodwin and Paul Richards on arrival. The main airport is at Arlanda 23 miles north of the city and while it's possible to take the cheaper and more time-consuming Flygbussama coach into the city centre, we decided instead on catching the Arlanda Express high-speed train service that makes the journey in a mere 20 minutes at speeds of over 200 km per hour. We had an early return flight on the Sunday morning and the Express return fare was the best way of making this. Pre-purchase of tickets on the internet is the most convenient and cheapest way of booking what is by any standards a costly journey – an expensive introduction to a very expensive city. If two people are travelling together between Thursdays and Sundays return tickets cost only 2 x 280 SEK, as opposed to 2 x 490 SEK if purchased separately – a saving of well over £30! Once you've used your credit card to make the booking, all you have to do on boarding the train is to show the same card to the ticket inspector.

Not for the first time, I had to reflect on the advantages of modern technology. Not only could we buy our train tickets online, we were also able to select and pay for the specific boat we wanted to use for a cruise around Stockholm's waterways. As usual, before going to a new city, we also used Google's Street View to walk their little man along the very streets we were to take from the Central Station to our hotel and, later, from the hotel to the Olympic Stadium. Doing this virtual walk allowed us to identify supermarkets, bars/restaurants and points of interest en route. Although such facilities make travel these days so much easier, some would point out that it takes away some of the excitement of seeing everything with 'fresh eyes' on arrival. Personally, given that a lot of the pleasure of travel these days has been taken away by the cattle-class nature of the low-cost airlines plus the incessant queues and security measures at airports; I'm all for anything that makes the whole experience a little more pleasurable.

As things transpired, the central location of our hotel meant that we could easily walk anywhere we needed to go and had no need to make use of the extensive public transport system within the city. For those a little less centrally located the quickest and most useful form of transport is the Tunnelbana - abbreviated to T-bana and symbolized with a blue T on a white round sign. This is Stockholm's equivalent of the Tube with exactly 100 stations on 3 main lines, (red, green and blue). It's certainly not cheap in comparison with other European cities but will get you virtually anywhere you need to go within the metropolitan area much quicker than the local buses that are often much less direct due to the city's layout.

I'd mentioned in my earlier chapter on the Hans C. Andersen Marathon about staying in the Cabinn chain of hotels based on the concept of the cabin accommodation on a boat. It seems that this is something of a growing trend, or should it be 'fad,' in Scandinavia as we were to find out in Stockholm. Virtually all hotels in the city had been pre-booked for the marathon weekend and on being offered a cabin room (without window) and shared bathroom for 895 kroner per night for 3 nights, we initially baulked at the idea. Unfortunately, beggars can't be choosers and the inability to find anything else suitable meant we were forced to accept. This was a bad mistake and one I won't repeat. Unlike the ones in Denmark that have windows, furniture and, most of all, space; this had none of these. It was more of a cupboard than a cabin: both cramped and claustrophobic with a lot less room than you'd find in your average prison cell. (And most prison cells have windows). How on earth do they get away with it? £45 each per night for a bunk bed within a tomb, however well you gloss it up, is pure daylight robbery. Even an upgrade to a cupboard with en-suite facilities was little better. The fact that we were both suffering badly from flu; coughing and spluttering all night without access to fresh air, only made everything worse leading to the inevitable consequence I'll be coming to shortly. Paul and Dave, who weren't arriving until the next day, had at least a room with a window to look forward to for an extra 20 kroner or so each.

We arrived early on the Thursday afternoon to brilliant sunshine not realizing that it wasn't going to last for much longer. The plan was to register early and then walk around most of the first loop of the course that co-incidentally included most of the sights we would have aimed for anyway. Registration was held in a specially erected tented village behind the Olympic Stadium on an area that I guess would have incorporated the warm-up track for the 1912 Games. Is it just me or are these Expos becoming less and less fun to visit and more and more like cynical marketing opportunities designed to maximize sales of technicolour merchandise to a captive audience of runners? This one was nothing more than a glorified shop where we were forced to go to pick our numbers up. There were no tempting free samples of food or drink, no bargain items of clothing, nothing in the way of entertainment; just a succession of stalls selling expensive running gear. We were given number and chip only – no T-shirt until after the race. The Pasta Party ticket wasn't valid until the next day and given the rain and how I felt at the time, the thought of standing in long queues for lukewarm pasta just didn't appeal. The only other item of interest was the fact that our race number allowed us free transport in the metro area on race day – no big deal if you were within walking distance of the Stadium.

The Stadium itself is a classic sports arena. Built for the 1912 Stockholm Olympics, it looks similar today to what it looked over 100 years ago. Over the years a number of major sporting events have also been held there including ice hockey world championships, national football matches and, oddly enough, the 1956 Olympic Equestrian events despite the Olympics that year being in Melbourne! Apparently, quarantine regulations at the time made it impossible to take horses to Australia. Over the years, no fewer than 83 world records in athletics have been broken on the track – a world record of world records no less. After a quick tour of the Stadium, I left Registration weighing up the pros and cons between what we were given and what we forked out - from memory, something like 112 euros. You can guess my conclusion.

We've moved a long way away from the original concept of the marathon where the focus was on the let-the-best-man-win contest between runners prepared to test themselves over an irritatingly difficult distance. Nowadays your average big city marathon as Van Morrison would say, 'Is all show biz!' Contrast the build-up to this year's event with Stockholm's first marathon in 1979. The story behind this is often quoted to prove the point that, with enough determination, almost anyone can set up a marathon. (I know - I have). Despite lots of entrenched opposition, Anders Olsson a former sports journalist inspired by an article about the New York Marathon, decided that Stockholm needed its own event to boost the profile of distance running in Sweden. Just over 2,000 runners entered the first event with the field more than doubling in 1980. Among the finishers that year was Bjorn Ulvers of Abba fame, (the one married at the time to the gorgeous blond Agnetha). Bjorn finished in the highly respectable time of 3 hours 23 minutes, proving that some people not only have all the luck, they're also blessed with considerable talent. The following year numbers almost doubled again with Sweden's former world heavyweight boxing champion, Ingemar Johansson being among the finishers in 4 hour 40. Surprisingly, the men's course record of 2 hour 11:37 set by Britain's Hugh Jones in 1983 hasn't been broken since. 2014's Kenyan winner, Benjamin Bitok recorded 2 hour 13:21. The female record was also set in the 1980s by the legendary Grete Waitz and stands at 2 hour 28:29 – a full 4 minutes faster than the 2014 Swedish winner. There can't be too many big city marathons these days whose course records have stood for so long.

Our plan to walk around the first loop of the course after registering, took a lot longer than intended. The loop encompasses most of the iconic sights of the city making it very much a stop/start affair. If I was asked for a must-see itinerary suitable for a weekend visit to Stockholm, I'd suggest spending some time in each of the following four areas: Norrmalm, Gamla Stan, Sodermalm and Djurgarden. Norrmalm is what I think of as the mainland site of the city (the other three are on nearby islands) and is considered to be its commercial hub and major shopping area, bustling with crowds at all times of the day. It had little to distinguish it from the usual city centre and, having had its heart ripped out by the proponents of the concrete and glass, 1960's architectural philosophy, reminded me very much of similar developments in a number of UK cities. The centre piece appeared to take the form of a huge, circular hole in the ground resembling an up-market bomb crater into which many of the shops seemed to have fallen as casualties.

Gamla Stan (The Old Town) was an altogether different proposition. This small island, a short walk across a bridge from downtown modernity is where Stockholm was founded in 1252 and remains one of the largest and best preserved medieval city centres in Europe. All of Gamla Stan and the adjacent island of Riddarholm are like a living, pedestrian-friendly museum of attractions with their restaurants, cafes, bars and souvenir shops. The narrow, winding cobblestone streets, with their buildings in many different shades of gold, give the Old Town its unique character. There are several beautiful churches and museums, including Sweden's national cathedral and the Nobel Museum. Dominating the island is the Royal Palace, one of the largest in the world with over 600 rooms. Equally impressive is the Swedish Parliament building in front of the Palace. This is where Sweden's much-envied welfare state was shaped and formed during the post-war years.

Behind the Old Town, over yet another bridge, is the much larger island of Sodermalm. This is worth a visit if only to take in the district known as So-Fo, the handful of streets lined with cafes and restaurants that has become the new 'in place' to be seen. Benny the other male in the ABBA quartet, instead of running marathons like his mate Bjorn, has opened his own hotel, 'Rival' in the area. (I wonder if there's anything to be read into the choice of name).

Finally, Djurgarden a 3km long finger-shaped forested island to the east of the city is an excellent place to escape the congestion of downtown. This former royal hunting ground, probably Stockholm's most enjoyable city park, can be reached by a steady hike around the inner harbour. Most tourists come to the island to visit Skansen, a vast authentic open-air museum with 150 reconstructed buildings from a whole town square to farms, manor homes and windmills, all laid out on a region-by-region basis. There's also a zoo containing Nordic animals like elk, reindeer and brown bears. All the above places I've mentioned are best approached by water and there's a variety of boat options available for this. As well as the local ferry service, Stockholm Sightseeing offers several different guided tours. There's a Royal Canal Tour that takes you around the eastern parts of the city and through the Djurgarden canal for 150SEK for the 50 minute trip. For those with more time on their hands, there's also a 3 hour boat ride out into the islands of the

Stockholm Archipelago for 250SEK. Mo and I chose the 225SEK, 1hour 50 minute 'Under the Bridges Trip' on the Friday morning. The boat travels under fifteen bridges and passes through two locks connecting the Baltic Sea with Lake Malaren while sailing past a number of islands and iconic buildings. The on-board commentary in English, both interesting and informative, was well worth the expense.

As luck would have it, it poured throughout the rest of Friday and we both ended up in precisely the situation we didn't want: being soaked to the skin with no facilities in the broom cupboard room to dry our wet clothes. Sleeping that night in an uncomfortable damp atmosphere did nothing for our collective colds. As soon as I awoke the next morning, fighting for breath and barking like a seal, I knew I wasn't in any fit state to run 26.2 miles. It's not like me to pull-out if there's a chance of completing the course – I certainly hadn't done so in 220 marathons to that point. Sometimes though you just have to let discretion overcome valour and admit defeat. I talked it over with Mo, Dave and Paul and all three thought that, in the condition I was in, I'd be silly to run. Showing a measure of commonsense with which I'm not normally associated, I agreed. I preferred a DNS rather than a DNF against my name and wasn't prepared to struggle around trying to get within the 6 hour time limit to possibly end up with a 6 hour finish on my marathon CV. Reluctantly, I gave my chip to Paul to hand in and set out to walk ahead of the runners to see as much of the course as I could manage.

It was scant consolation that I was by no means the only one to drop out: of the 21,500 entrants only 16,075 completed the race. These left in two starting pens from outside the Olympic Stadium at 12:00 and 12:10 respectively. Oddly enough given that the starts were seeded according to time, pacemakers aiming for the same finishing times started from both groups. The heavens opened again to thoroughly soak everyone on the very congested start line but fortunately that was the last major shower of the day and conditions improved as the race progressed. The marathon route consisted of two separate, unequal laps. The first 16+ km involved a circular tour around the city's perimeter including the islands of Gamla Stan and Soderman mentioned earlier. After 18km the course spent the next 10 km or so meandering around the parklands of Ladugardsgardet and Djurgarden before reconnecting with the original lap again at 28km and repeating the remainder of this to culminate in a Stadium finish. Spectator support on the two city laps was plentiful with Saturday shopping crowds helping to swell the ranks of bystanders. Support on the middle section, however, was thin on the ground and very reminiscent of the riverside stretch on the Amsterdam Marathon.

For those who'd bothered to read the organiser's comments about the course there were some interesting aspects other than the obvious to look out for en route. Shortly after hitting the waterfront at 3km the course continues past Normalmstorg, the square where a famous bank robbery in 1973 gave name to the psychological state known as Stockholm Syndrome, based on the behaviour of the victims who continued to defend their captors even after their six days as hostages were over. Just after 5km, after running around the east side of Gamla Stan, the course passes through Slussen, (the Lock), where boats are raised and lowered between Lake Malaren and the Baltic Sea. It was here that the lead group of seven East Africans came steaming past; seemingly in a race of their own and already over two minutes ahead of the rest of the field. At 8km the toughest ascent of the race takes you over Vasterbron, Sweden's largest arched road bridge. The crossing of this reaches the main city beaches on Kungsholmen (King's Island) usually crowded in the summer months, but not as I stood and watched. At 12km the route approaches City Hall, a romantic masterpiece with three gold crowns, the ancient symbol of Sweden at the top. The prestigious Nobel Prize ceremony is held there each year.

The course now continues back into the city, past the Central Station and away from the waterfront, descending at 14 to 15km past the Public Library and back towards the Stadium via Sturegatan; the little park used as the site for common graves for victims of the plague. Turning away from the Stadium without entering, at just over 18km the parkland loop begins by entering the diplomatic district, past the West German embassy occupied by a terrorist group in 1975. Two of the hostages were killed as their demands were refused by the German government and more people died when the explosives installed by the terrorists exploded. The next landmark, standing in splendid isolation among all the greenery, is the 500-feet high Kaknas Tower with its radio antenna, one of the tallest buildings in Northern Europe. The 24km mark brings runners over the canal, scene of the 1912 Olympic rowing, and on to Djurgarden, (meaning the Animal Garden). As well as entertaining the deer hunting royals, lions and bears were used here in animal fights in the 17th century. Just before rejoining the inner city loop for the second time at 28km the route passes the famous Vasa Museum dedicated to the warship of the same name. When the Vasa set sail in 1628 she was reputed to be the world's most powerful warship with 64 cannons and 300 men. Sadly, she sank on her maiden voyage but was raised with great difficulty in 1961 and restored as a fully rigged ship.

This time round the race goes into the Olympic Stadium instead of skirting away from it, finishing directly on the home strait in front of a fairly packed grandstand. Finishers are then led out of the stadium to receive medals, T-shirts and goody bags. The medal in 2014 was a substantial affair depicting the entrance to Skansen, the open-air museum mentioned earlier, while the shirt was a mid-blue with a green motif of a runner crossing the finish line. The goody bag contained drinks, (pepsi and an isotonic), cashew nuts, raisins, banana, chocolate bar and a plastic Stockholm Marathon water bottle. Dave had finished in 3 hour 16 and Paul in 4 hour 1 minute and I was anxious to seek their opinions from a runner's perspective. Both were reasonably happy with the organisation of the event. Aid stations were plentiful and evenly spaced with adequate water and energy drinks throughout – though both were given in cups. The stations were also equipped with bananas, glucose tablets, coffee, cake, flap jacks and, for some reason, gherkins! Both also enjoyed the atmosphere created by various bands, DJs and dancers around the course. Their misgivings centered around the level of congestion on the course and the lack of running etiquette shown by many of their fellow competitors. It seems pushing and shoving and a general disregard for fellow runners was endemic at times. Naturally, these are things you don't see when you're simply strolling around the course. Both Paul and Dave felt that the race has reached its optimum capacity and that entries should either be reduced or, on no account exceed the current level. They also felt that the entry to the starting pens was poorly controlled, allowing runners to simply walk into pens to which they hadn't been assigned. This, of course, usually works to the disadvantage of the faster runners and shouldn't be allowed to happen. Their final reservation, not a major one, concerned the long walk after finishing within the stadium to the point in the registration area where medals etc were given out.

Nothing my friends said would have put me off entering the event in future years. I'd some unfinished business with Stockholm. Due to illness, I'd missed out on adding Sweden to the list of countries in which I've run. Having just walked around the course there's no way I could count the 2014 race as a completed marathon. It's very disappointing, especially as I'd been entered for the race for almost a year. I accept that you can't do much about ill health. It creeps up on the best of us and I've been fortunate to have avoided it for most of my running career. As marathon runners we chose our races well in advance, pay our entry fees, book flights and accommodation at considerable expense and then keep our fingers crossed that we're fit and well enough to take part on the day. Usually it works – occasionally it doesn't. There's always the next one to look forward to.

I returned to Stockholm in 2016 to complete the marathon – this time fully fit and housed in a decent hotel with windows. I also came away from it in full agreement with the comments my friends had made two year's earlier. The marathon simply has too many participants for it to be a comfortable running experience. I won't be back.

Before leaving for Stockholm for our initial visit Mo and I fully expected restaurant menus to be dominated by offers of smorgasbord-type meals. Smorgasbord is, rightly or wrongly, universally considered to be the Swedish national dish. Literally translated it means 'bread and butter table' and consists of a number of hot and cold dishes served buffet style. The term has become world famous for a collection of various foods served all at once and traditionally includes, among other things: herring, smoked eel, roast beef, boiled potatoes and layered potato dishes of onions and cream topped with anchovies and Swedish meatballs. Surprisingly, these types of restaurants are thin on the ground and it wasn't until our second evening that we came across a smorgasbord restaurant in Gamla Stan. Like everything in Stockholm it wasn't cheap and severely depleted our weekend spending budget. We should have followed the advice given in the guide books to try, if possible, to eat your main meal of the day at lunchtime when restaurant prices are considerably cheaper. For example, the next day's buffet meal in a Thai restaurant cost 95SEK at lunchtime as opposed to 150SEK for the same meal in the evening. For anyone happy to settle for the ubiquitous fast-food option of burgers, pizzas and kebabs, as a rough guide, most of these came in at just under £10.

Drinking is also expensive in Sweden, especially in bars and restaurants. It's much cheaper to buy your alcohol in one of the state run liquor shops, the Systembolaget. Supermarkets do sell alcohol but are limited by law to an alcohol content of 3.5%. Because of our respective colds and flu, neither of us was particularly interested in drinking on our first visit trip so the quest for the perfect dark beer had to be put on hold that time. (Two years later I was in and out of the city in a day so had no time to look). I guess we saved ourselves a fortune. The only occasion that we spent any time in a pub was with Paul and Dave after the marathon. I was less than impressed by the bog-standard Swedish lager served flat for 55SEK per pint. It was so bad I can't remember its name. Ironically, in the same pub and for the same price I was able to buy a decent pint of draught Newcastle Brown Ale. This is something I can't even do at home even though it's brewed less than thirty miles away from where I live.

Checking out the Stockholm course

Stockholm's Olympic Stadium

LITHUANIA

KAUNAS MARATHON

I'd wanted to run in Lithuania for some time in order to add to my collection of running in each of the Baltic marathons along with Tallinn (Estonia), Riga (Latvia). Stockholm, Helsinki and Gdansk (Poland). Mo and I had been booked to go to Vilnius the capital of Lithuania the previous September but the date had clashed with the only available date for the Christening of our first Grandson. We couldn't not go to that so missed out on the Vilnius marathon instead. In the process we ended up forfeiting our non-refundable flight costs and entry fee for the race. As soon as I found out that there was a marathon in Kaunas, Lithuania's second city, in June of the following year (2016) the decision to go was inevitable. At that stage what I knew about Lithuania could have been written on the back of a postage stamp. I needed to do some research on the place.

Lithuania is the southernmost of the three Baltic States and the largest and most populous, with an estimated population of 2.9 million people as of 2015. Its capital and largest city is Vilnius, whose marathon I'd initially intended to run. The country is situated along the south-eastern shore of the Baltic Sea, to the east of Sweden and Denmark and is bordered by Latvia to the north, Belarus to the east and south, Poland to the south, and Kaliningrad Oblast (a Russian exclave) to the southwest. The country is predominantly flat (as we were to find out on a bus journey we took between Kaunas and Vilnius) with a few low hills in the western uplands and eastern highlands with forests covering just over 30% of the country. Lithuanians are a Baltic people and the official language, Lithuanian, along with Latvian, are the only two living languages in the Baltic branch of the Indo-European language family. Apparently, the first unified Lithuanian state, the Kingdom of Lithuania, was created as far back as 1253. During the 14th century, the Grand Duchy of Lithuania was the largest country in Europe with present-day Lithuania, Belarus, Ukraine, and parts of Poland and Russia all part of its territory at that time. With the Lublin Union of 1569, Lithuania and Poland formed a voluntary two-state union, the Polish–Lithuanian Commonwealth. The Commonwealth lasted more than two centuries, until neighbouring countries systematically dismantled it - with the Russian Empire annexing most of Lithuania's territory.

As World War I neared its end, Lithuania's Act of Independence was signed declaring the establishment of a sovereign State of Lithuania. During the Second World War, Lithuania was occupied first by the Soviet Union and then by Nazi Germany. Towards the end of the Second World War the Soviet Union reoccupied Lithuania. The Soviets then engaged in massive deportations of many of its citizens to Siberia with complete nationalization and collectivization together with general Sovietisation of everyday life. After the war approximately 100,000 Lithuanian partisans fought a guerrilla war against the Soviet system. An estimated 30,000 partisans and their supporters were killed, and many more were arrested and deported to Siberian gulags. It is estimated that, during World War II, Lithuania lost 780,000 people.

The advent of perestroika and glasnost in the late 1980s allowed the establishment of Sąjudis, an anti-Communist independence movement. The Sąjudis proclaimed Lithuania's independence in March 1990, becoming the first Soviet republic to do so. The Soviet Union attempted unsuccessfully to suppress the secession by imposing an economic blockade. After a transition from a planned economy to a free market one, Lithuania became a full member of NATO and the European Union in the spring of 2004. Since then Lithuania has been among the fastest growing economies in the

European Union. On 1 January 2015, it adopted the euro as the official currency and became the 19th member of the Eurozone.

Armed with all this newly-acquired information we made our way from Edinburgh to Kaunas with one of those awful early morning Ryanair flights that require you staying awake for most of the night in case you miss your alarm. Our troubles began the second we stepped off the plane. It was pouring down on arrival – really pouring down – the type of rain that soaks you to the skin before you can finish the short walk to the arrivals hall where we stood in line for what seemed like hours waiting for our passports to be inspected. On exiting the terminal the number 29 City Bus (a misnomer if ever there was one) was just disappearing into the distance. The driver on the next bus didn't speak a word of English and hadn't a clue where we wanted to be dropped off. Words like Old Town, Town Hall, Market Square and City Centre simply didn't register with him, nor did it do us any good trying to show him on a map. He simply took our 80 cents fare and pointed us to an empty seat. It was at this stage that we met the first of several 'helpful' individuals whose attempts at practising their English on us left us worse off than before we started. These were mainly young, pleasant, student types full of good intentions (no one over thirty seemed to speak anything but Lithuanian). Avoid them like the Plague, they invariably provide misinformation – it's better to try to work things out for yourself. Following a lengthy conversation with the driver, one of our new found friends on the bus assured us that he'd sorted out where we needed to be dropped off. By now the bus windows were so steamed up no one had a clue where they were. Eventually the driver called out that it was our stop. It wasn't. Our new friend had mistaken our request for 'Centre' with the 'Centre Hotel.' This was yet another misnomer as it was anything but central. We ended up in the middle of nowhere in teeming rain that made short shrift of our only map. An hour later we finally arrived bedraggled at our hotel looking as if we'd reached it by swimming down the river. And, I'd still got to go back out in the deluge to walk the 2.5 kilometres to Registration.

The hotel, the 4-star, Amberton Cozy just behind the Town Square, turned out to be the second disappointment and the third misnomer of the day. Cosy it was not – unless you happened to be less than about 3-feet tall. The room we were given was in the attic, up four flights of a dark and dingy, death-trap of a staircase and required bending over double to get from one side of it to the other. Mo still laughs about me having to back-away from the sink every time I cleaned my teeth or washed my hands to avoid bumping my head on the eaves at either side. It wasn't funny at the time though. Who on earth hands out these 4-star ratings? The hotel's only asset was its proximity to the start and finish of the race. Even then there's a story involved. That evening while settling down to our pasta dinner at a restaurant around the corner in the Town Square, our friendly, 'helpful' English-speaking waiter blithely told me that I'd got it all wrong in thinking that the marathon started and finished in the Square outside. According to our second best new friend of the day, the race only finished there but started in another Square that I'd never even heard of some 20 minutes away. He even wrote down the name of the Square for us. We couldn't find it on our newly acquired hotel map. By this time it was only a few hours before the early morning start next day and the waiter's insistence and apparent sincerity had me wondering whether I'd misinterpreted the event's website instructions (there'd been no written instructions handed out at registration). The uncertainty ensured that I couldn't enjoy the meal before sorting out the confusion over the start. In the end I was right and the waiter was wrong. The race did start in the Square metres away from the waiter's workplace. I made a point of returning the following evening to point this out to him without making the mistake of eating there again. To add insult to injury, the same helpful waiter had also managed to serve us the wrong pasta dishes (seafood instead of bolognaise) and had then succeeded in totalling the bill incorrectly (in the restaurant's favour). Incidentally, in case I forget, don't bother making the long walk to Registration at the out-of-town Zalgiris Sports Arena particularly if it's pouring down, there's nothing there worth seeing. What the organisers had neglected to mention in their regular email up-dates was that race numbers and T-shirts could be picked up at the start line prior to the 8.00am start on race day. They'd also neglected to mention that they hadn't ordered sufficient size large T-shirts. I wasn't happy at being fobbed off with a smaller size.

Reading this you're probably thinking that we didn't enjoy our time in Kaunas. You'd be wrong. We awoke next morning to beautiful sunshine that remained with us for the rest of our stay. With the sun beaming down on it the city turned out to be a pleasant, inoffensive sort of place with a laid-back, low-key, small-town atmosphere. Kaunas is located 100 kilometres from the capital Vilnius and 212 kilometres from the country's major seaport Klaipeda. It is the second-largest city in Lithuania with around 310,000 inhabitants and has historically been a leading centre of Lithuanian economic, academic, and cultural life. It has a reputation as a city of young people with over 35,000 students (the largest number in Lithuania) studying at one of its seven universities. In the Russian Empire it was the capital of the Kaunas Governorate from 1843 to 1915. It has the distinction of being the only temporary capital city in Europe during the inter-war years when Polish forces occupied Vilnius.

An old legend claims that Kaunas was established by the Romans in ancient times. These Romans were supposedly led by a patrician named Palemon, who had three sons: Barcus, Kunas and Sperus. Palemon fled from Rome because he feared the mad Emperor Nero. Palemon, his sons and other relatives travelled all the way to Lithuania. After Palemon's death, his sons divided his land. Kunas got the land where Kaunas now stands. He built a fortress near the confluence of the Nemunas and Neris rivers, and the city that grew up there was named after him. There is also a suburban region in the vicinity named Palemonas.

The Old Town area around which the day's events were centred sits in a V-shaped jumble of cobbled and pedestrianised streets formed by the confluence of the Nemunas and Neris rivers, the two largest in Lithuania. The centre follows the same blueprint that I'd seen when running in cities such as Tallinn, Riga, Krakow, Poznan and the like with a large, picture-postcard, medieval market square dominated by the city's historic Town Hall and Cathedral. The only difference being, nice though it is, Kaunas's Square is smaller and less-impressive than any of the aforementioned. The streets leading to/from the Square are lined with some beautiful pastel coloured, chocolate-box buildings many of which double up as outdoor restaurants and pavement cafes. Unfortunately, too many of these close to the Square are in desperate need of repair or in the very least a major paint-job. Too many are derelict with peeling plaster, broken or boarded windows and detract badly from the overall aesthetic feel of the place. The further you go from the city centre the worse it gets with the grey, concrete block legacy of the Soviet era architecture becoming much more prominent. Both of the city's major transport hubs are too far out for ease of use. For example, the new bus station is tucked away behind the Akropolis shopping centre some 2.5 kilometres out of town while the main train station is even further away at 4 kilometres along the same road. We took the bus to Vilnius from the former, returning by train to the latter and faced a long walk on both occasions. We also had to return to the bus station the next day to catch the airport bus – it probably stops somewhere closer to the Old Town but we couldn't find out where and nobody could tell us. To tell you the truth we didn't dare ask.

Whatever you do don't travel to Kaunas thinking that you're visiting an exciting tourist destination and don't let the nice people in the city's only Tourist Information Office try to convince you otherwise. There's really nothing of any great significance to see. The city centre is defined by two pedestrian streets: the 2-km-long Laisvės alėja (Liberty Avenue), a central street of the city, lined by linden trees, and its continuation, Vilnius Street, leading to the oldest part, the Old Town of Kaunas. Some of the most prominent features in Kaunas include: Kaunas Castle which was built in the middle of the 14th century and is the oldest building in Kaunas. Today the round tower houses an art gallery. The castle is open to tourism, and hosts occasional festivals. The castle sits on a small mound in the pleasant Santakos Park, behind the City Hall at the confluence of the two rivers. Kaunas City Hall was built in the mid-16th century, at the time when Kaunas was flourishing city of merchants and is a good example of renaissance architecture. Locals unofficially call it The White Swan. In 1836 it was reconstructed and the residence for Russian czars was made there. The Wedding Hall (marriage registration office) was opened on the ground and first floors in 1973. The cellars are used by a Kaunas Ceramics museum. The museum collection consists of archaeological findings from the Old Town and surroundings of Kaunas. The collection contains craftsmen-made crockery, tile stove ornaments, and roof tiles of impressive size. The exposition also reflects the lifestyle of the townsmen of the time. Adjacent to the City Hall is the Kaunas Cathedral Basilica mentioned in written sources as early as 1413. This was shrouded in scaffolding during our visit. Also worth seeing are the two still functioning funiculars in Kaunas. The Zaliakalnis Funicular on Putvinskio Street is an electrically operated funicular railway, the oldest funicular in Lithuania and one of the oldest in Europe. It was constructed by AEG and began operating on 5 August 1931. The funicular has wood panelled coachwork and is serviced by an English speaking operator in uniform. It climbs the 75 m up from behind the Vytautas the Great War Museum to the Church of the Resurrection for some of the best views in Kaunas. Another funicular, the Aleksotas Funicular, built in 1935, near Aleksotas (or Vytautas) bridge, that connects the Old Town with Aleksotas district, takes people up to Aleksotas hill. From here is probably the best view of Kaunas downtown. There are other things to see, of course, and other places to go but most of these involve visits to either museums or churches. Call me a Philistine if you like but I much prefer seeing real live places and events to exhibits and artefacts so gave them all a miss on this occasion. The highlight of the trip was undoubtedly the day we spent sightseeing in Vilnius – a much larger, more up-market and more interesting city than Kaunas - as befits the capital of the country.

The Kaunas Marathon turned out to be one of the cheapest I've ever entered thanks to a generous 40% discount on entries for anyone over 65. I've a receipt showing that I paid a mere 11.40 euros to enter – though entries jumped from 19 to 50 euros from July to race day for younger runners. This was to be the fourth edition of the event that first started in 2013 and the marathon formed only part of a day-long festival of running that also included a Half Marathon, 10K, 5K and 1.5K races. The full and half marathons started simultaneously at 8am with the other races at staggered intervals to ensure that the Town Square continued to buzz throughout the day. The Kaunas Marathon is described as being not just about running, it's intended as a festival for the whole city with food stalls, live music, dancers and even BMX riders entertaining the crowds in the Square. 242 runners completed the full distance, 792 ran the half marathon with 695 in the 10K at 3pm, 1158 competitors in the 2pm 5K and 418 finishers in the 1.5K that started at 1.00pm - grand total of 3,306 over all five events.

Those of us in the marathon were given five and a half hours in which to complete the race. As soon as I saw the course I knew I was going to enjoy the day. This consisted of 2 laps of the Half Marathon course which in itself involved 2 out-and-back loops from the city centre. Both loops followed closed roads and cycle paths along the city's two rivers. It was the perfect sunny day to be running alongside sparkling fresh water. Once the half marathoners had disappeared on our return to the Square, those of us still running had the second half and the scenery all to ourselves. Basically, the route followed the road eastwards along the Nemunas River through the grounds of the Zalgiris Arena for 7 kilometres before dropping down to the riverside cycle path and returning to the city at the 14k mark. We then began the second loop along the path next to the River Neris to a second turn at 18k and then back down the adjacent road into the Square. Running over the mat at the Half Marathon finish gantry gave us our only timed split in the race – there were no timing mats at 5 kilometre intervals like you see in other big city marathons. It seems that some runners were aware of that and, sadly, were prepared to take advantage of the fact on the second lap. With big gaps appearing between runners and no on-course supervision on this lap, it was an easy matter to simply cross unseen down the embankment from the road on to the cycle path thus taking out 7 kilometres of the course. I can recall at least two runners who were quite clearly behind me at the 18k turning point who mysteriously appeared in front of me on the cycle path. I'm aware of the old adage about 'only cheating themselves' but seeing the practice in operation still leaves a nasty taste. Of course, the whole thing could have been avoided with a couple of strategically placed timing mats at the turns. With those in situe it would have been impossible to take short cuts.

I wasn't going to let a couple of suspicious incidents ruin what had been an enjoyable run on a very good course. I find it so much more pleasurable running in low-key events with a small field than say the 20,000 plus I'd gone round Stockholm with on the previous weekend. Also, after the debacle at Luxembourg two weeks earlier where I'd struggled with illness it was reassuring to know that, at my age, I could still post what is considered to be a reasonable time. On this occasion I managed to run the full distance, stopping only to unpeel the bananas offered at drink stations and wash them down with an isotonic drink. Though well-off the pace of the two guys in front of me in my age category I was still pleased with my 4:26 finish. Incidentally, the Kenyan winner's finishing time of 2:26:29, though slow by comparison with that of most major marathons was still a record for the course and earned him a 600 euros bonus.

There was a quality medal waiting at the finish with a well-stocked goody bag plus a couple of cans of alcohol-free beer, excellent value for money for the small entry fee. Actually, we found everything in Lithuania very good value for money particularly transport costs and food and drink. For example, fares for the 100+ kilometre journey to Vilnius cost a mere 6 euros whether by bus or train, while a decent main course in a quality restaurant could be bought for no more than 5 euros. That's what we paid for our spaghetti bolognaise in our friendly (but ill-informed) waiter's restaurant fronting the Main Square. Even cheaper was the full-size pizza plus beer at 3 euros we enjoyed in one of the local pizza outlets. We didn't want to leave, however, without trying the Lithuanian cuisine so on our final night splashed out on a dish of Juka (blood soup) – not what you're thinking but a cabbage soup flavoured with carrots, ham and onions in which we dipped Rugine duona, a tasty, dark rye bread. This was followed by a main course of Saltnosiuka – the omnipresent dumplings and potatoes in what appeared to be a sour cream sauce. For dessert we had Spurgos – Lithuanian doughnuts filled with jam all washed down with a glass of 5% Lithuanian liquor, a thick syrupy drink made from fermented bread and raisons. The whole package cost less than 10 euros each. I never did find the perfect dark beer in Kaunas though I looked damned hard. There were a couple of English/Irish style bars in Vilnius Street just off the Main Square whose names I can't recall (I think one was typically called The Shamrock). The best these came up with was Grimbergen Dubbel (Double) a dark, malty Belgian Abbey beer at 6.5% for 2.99 euros per half litre. Average prices per pint were much cheaper than that of course. My particular favourite tipple was the local Lithuanian brew of Tauras Tradicininus at 6.4% at a mere 74 cents a pint if purchased in a can from the local mini-market.

I'm pleased I went to Kaunas. It compensates for having missed out on the Vilnius Marathon the previous year. By all accounts this is a much bigger and much more competitive event. Never mind, I can now happily add Lithuania to the growing list of countries in which I've run a marathon.

Marathon route by the river. (Photo by Misael Silvera on Unsplash)

Kaunas Marathon Finish in the Town Square

SOUTH AFRICA

CAPE TOWN MARATHON

Cape Town has a justifiable reputation of being one of the most beautiful cities in the world. It is a top global travel destination, known universally for the quality of its tourism infrastructure, outstanding attractions and an abundance of natural beauty. It was named the best place in the world to visit by the New York Times in 2014, appointed World Design Capital in the same year, featured second in Travel and Leisure's list of top holiday destinations and also won the Telegraph reader's survey award as the best to visit for three years in a row. Writing in a Telegraph article about the award, travel journalist Pippa de Bruyn reckons that, 'You really can't overstate the case for visiting Cape Town,' and goes on to extol the, 'in-your-face beauty of the backdrop of Table Mountain and the city's pristine white beaches.' It is certainly a place I've always fancied seeing since I was a kid, inspired by stories of sailing ships rounding the Cape of Good Hope on their voyages to Australia and the East. The Cape Town Marathon which is staged each year on the Sunday nearest to the 24th September, South Africa's Heritage Day, provides an excellent opportunity to see what the city has to offer.

Mo and I travelled there in September 2016, flying KLM from Newcastle to Amsterdam before changing planes to fly directly to Cape Town. Eleven hours after leaving Amsterdam we landed at Cape Town International Airport, the second-busiest airport in the country and the main international gateway to the Cape Town metropolitan area. The airport is approximately 20 kilometres from the city centre, accessible from the N2 freeway. Transport to and from the airport is also provided by metered taxis and various private shuttle companies. Touch Down Taxis is the officially authorized taxi company at the airport, charging between R260 to R310 for the journey to central Cape Town destinations. (£1 is approximately 20 South African Rand). For those preferring local transport options the MyCiTi bus rapid transit system provides a shuttle service connecting the airport with the Civic Centre bus station in the city centre. Buses depart every 20 minutes from 04:20 to 22:00. Wanting to reach our hotel as quickly as possible on our late evening arrival we took a taxi from the airport but used the much cheaper and very reliable bus when returning for our departure flight. We'd done our homework on where best to stay for our week-long visit. We wanted somewhere on the coast, south east of the city centre and, preferably within walking distance of the marathon's early morning start. The Peninsula All Suite Hotel on Beach Road in the seaside suburb of Sea Point proved ideal at £571 for an 8-night, bed and breakfast stay. After a hard-day's sightseeing it was great to be able to return to our balcony and enjoy the Atlantic Ocean sunsets while sharing a bottle of wine. The rear of the hotel had magnificent views over the aptly-named Lion's Head and up towards Table Mountain. Even better, was the fact that it was connected by a pleasant stroll along the ocean promenade that connected the hotel to the marathon start and iconic Victoria and Albert Waterfront complex. The hotel also offered a regular, free shuttle bus service to most of the important points of interest within the Cape Town area including: Table Mountain, the city centre, the Waterfront complex and the beautiful Camps Bay beach. We made maximum use of this service during our stay.

For those who've never been: Cape Town is the southernmost city on the African continent. Located on the shore of Table Bay, it was first developed by the Dutch East India Company as a supply station for Dutch Ships sailing to East Africa, India and the Far East. Jan van Riebeek's arrival in 1652 established the first European settlement in South Africa. Cape Town quickly outgrew its original purpose as the first European outpost in the area, becoming the economic and cultural centre of the newly established Cape Colony. The Witwatersrand Gold Rush in 1886 led to it being replaced by Johannesburg as the largest city in South Africa. Today, it ranks third among the most populous areas in the country after Johannesburg and Durban. It is also the tenth most populous city in Africa and home to approximately 64% of the Western Cape's population. It is regarded as one of the world's most multicultural cities, reflecting its role as a major destination for immigrants and expatriates. It has always been the most cosmopolitan of South Africa's cities. The Dutch who planted the first gardens were followed by the French who imported their wine-making skills. Malay slaves brought spices and mosques, the English left Georgian mansions and Victorian terraces, while immigrants from all over Africa have introduced their own particular lifestyles on the city. As the seat of the National Parliament Cape Town is also the legislative capital of the country as well as the economic hub of Western Cape Province. It serves as a major regional manufacturing centre with fishing, clothing and textiles, wood products, electronics, tourism, finance and business services among its major industries. The city has recently enjoyed a booming real estate and construction market following the 2010 World Cup with many people relocating there or purchasing summer homes. Cape Town is also not only the most popular international tourist destination in South Africa, but in Africa as a whole. This is due to its excellent climate, natural setting and well-developed infrastructure. The city has several world famous natural features especially the iconic Table Mountain that continue to attract tourists. Fortunately, most of these can be seen during the course of the marathon there.

Prior to existing in its current format, the Cape Town Marathon was organised by Celtic Harriers running club. It started and finished in Pinelands, and was introduced in 1994. In 1996, the Cape Town Marathon was won by Josia Thugwane, who went on to win the men's Olympic Marathon at the 1996 Summer Olympics in Atlanta, Georgia. This was then followed by a separately organised marathon, which was also held in Cape Town in 2005 and 2006. The first Cape Town Marathon (in its current format) was run in

September 2007. From 2007 to 2009 the race was organized by Western Province Athletics, under a corporate sponsorship agreement with the national federation, Athletics South Africa. From 2014 its name changed to the Sanlam Cape Town Marathon and, following a new partnership with the City of Cape Town plus the endorsement of South African sporting legends Elana Meyer and Francois Pienaar, the event began to attract a larger and larger field of runners allowing it to develop into an international event showcasing the city as a world class destination for major sporting events. In 2014 and 2015 it was accredited with IAAF Silver Label status and in 2017 it was the first African Marathon to achieve IAAF Gold Label Status. The Men's course record was set in the year I ran it, 2016 (but not by me!) at 2:08:41 by Asefa Negewo (Ethiopia) and the Women's by Isabella Ochinchi (Kenya) in 2015 with a time of 2:30:20. Today's Cape Town Marathon is intended to provide first-time runners with a race devoid of steep hills and unnecessary turns and to aid more experienced runners in achieving fast times to enable qualification for South Africa's two most prestigious events: the Comrades and Old Mutual Two Oceans Marathons. The organisers' intentions have been unambiguous since re-branding, to present a route 'to take in the famous natural beauty of Cape Town's mountains and sea, as well as many of the city's great attractions in a running celebration of South Africa's oldest Mother city.'

The event consists of five separate distances: the marathon, a 22km race, 12km race, a 10km event and a 4.2km fun run. The maximum number of runners accepted across all distances is 7,000. Only the 10km and the marathon are held on the Sunday with the 10km leaving at 6.50am and the marathon at 7.00am. The remaining races take place on the Saturday morning. Registration and Expo takes place at The Lookout situated on the Cape Town Waterfront. This glass-sided venue affords magnificent views of iconic landmarks like Cape Town Stadium, Table Bay, Lion's Head, Robben Island as well as the breathtaking Table Mountain. Registration is open all day on the Friday and Saturday before the race. We went on the Friday morning. There were no queues.

Neither were there any views – it didn't stop raining that morning – the only rain during the week of our stay. Entry fees are considerably higher for overseas athletes at R1,000 for race entry, timing chip, Asics T-shirt and temporary South African athlete registration. South African registered local entrants pay a mere R200. Entries close two weeks before race day with no late entries being accepted. 4,300 runners had completed the marathon distance the previous year (2015) with times ranging from 2 hours 11:41 for the Kenyan winner to 6 hours 58:45 for the final runner. Marathon runners are given a generous 7-hour time limit to take in all the sights on the course during the race.

The marathon starts on the corner of Beach Road and Grainger Road, close to the V & A Waterfront. In the end I decided to avoid tiring myself out by walking the 45 minutes to the start in pitch darkness and took a taxi instead. For runners who prefer to stay in the centre of town there's a free MyCiTi shuttle service that runs every 20 minutes between the Civic Centre and the Start from 5am to 6.15am. The return journey is only made until 2pm – leaving late finishers in a bit of a rush to get back. From memory, the 2016 course had been changed from the previous year. To provide an overview: this year we began with a short loop around the Green Point headland before running past Cape Town Harbour, then back into the city before heading out into the leafy southern suburbs. Running in the shadow of Devil's Peak we then headed past landmarks like the Liesbeek River, Rondebosch Common, Newlands Cricket Ground, Groote Schuur and the University of Cape Town. From there it was back into the city in the shade cast by Table Mountain with views of Table Bay and Robben Island before passing the Castle of Good Hope, the City Hall, the Houses of Parliament, St George's Cathedral, Green Market Square and the Mandela Rhodes Building among other attractions. In the final stretch the route turned in the direction of the V & A Waterfront before making its way back towards Cape Town Stadium to the finish at the Green Point Athletics Track. In short, the course is a Marathon Tourist's dream, incorporating virtually everything any visitor to Cape Town would want to see.

To give a more detailed description of the course: shortly after the start we passed the magnificent new Cape Town Stadium – familiar, I'm sure, with football fans who enjoyed watching the 2010 World Cup. This replaced the Green Point Stadium, which was the name of the previous stadium on the site. Confusingly, this name was also used frequently during World Cup media coverage. Despite hosting concerts by internationally famous artists like Ed Sheeran, Kings of Leon, Coldplay and Lady Gaga it would seem that this 55,000-seater showpiece stadium is in danger of turning into a white elephant. Effective utilization and use of the stadium is something of a political issue in South Africa with several individuals and groups having called for the stadium to be demolished due to its under-utilization after the World Cup. At 1km we came to the Green Point Lighthouse, the square, candy red and white striped beacon standing on the edge of Mouille Point. It is said to be the very first 'solid' lighthouse on the South African coast having been first lit in 1824. Turning north after 2km onto Helen Suzman Boulevard we then headed towards the Port of Cape Town. It's reported that the Port competes with Alexandria for recognition as the most famous port in Africa. It's certainly got to be one of the most scenic harbours in the world with its backdrop of Table Mountain and its mountainous Peninsular. The Port is situated on one of the world's busiest trade routes giving it a lasting strategic and economic importance. Today it's the country's second busiest container port after Durban. As we left the Port and made our way to the turn back towards the city at 10km it was impossible not to notice the scores of make-shift dwellings lining the road's perimeter.

At 14km the course turned again to take us along Newmarket Street and into the Southern Suburbs beneath Devil's Peak. The Peak is the spire that forms part of the mountainous natural amphitheatre around Cape Town. I found an interesting story about the Peak in Cape Town Magazine. Legend has it that around 1700 a Dutchman named Jan van Hunks who lived at the foot of the mountain had a smoking contest with a mysterious stranger. Jan was so busy bragging about how much he could smoke he failed to notice that his opponent had two horns and a forked tail. Before he knew it he'd struck a deal with the devil and a ferocious smoking contest ensued that Jan won but which resulted in the mountain being covered in a Table Cloth cloud of smoke. From that day Charles Mountain became known as Devil's Peak (and Jan's wife moved to Australia in protest!)

Next up was the Liesbeek River, the first river that van Riebeeck named after settlement. The first free burghers of the Dutch East India Company were granted land to farm along the river. Shortly after the half-way mark we completed a loop around Rondebosch Common, a valuable 40 hectare block of public open space surrounded by established homes, schools and hospitals. These days it's popular with joggers and dog-walkers but in the past was used as a military camp. In 1805 the local Dutch farmers rallied here before the decisive Battle of Blaauwberg. The land was proclaimed a National Monument in 1961. At 27km the route then passes Newlands Cricket Ground reputedly one of the world's most picturesque cricket venues with its panoramic views of Table Mountain and Devil's Peak The ground hosted its first Test Match in 1889 when England defeated South Africa by an innings and 202 runs. Since then, over 50 official Tests have been played at the ground. For lovers of Rugby, nearby is the equally well-known Newlands Rugby Stadium. The course then reached Groote Schuur Hospital at around 30km. This is the house that formerly belonged to Cecil Rhodes and which he bequeathed to the nation along with vast tracts of nearby mountainside. Groote Schuur (Dutch for 'Big Barn') was built around 1657 by the Dutch East India Company as part of the company's granary. After being restored by Rhodes it was used for a long period from 1911 to 1994 as the official Cape residence of eleven South African Prime Ministers.

We then turned back under Table Mountain towards the city centre. I'm not sure what Cape Town would be without this iconic landmark that dominates the city from every angle. As you run around Cape Town it seems to remain visible no matter where you are. It's reportedly one of the oldest mountains in the world and, at

1,084 metres, is said to be still growing. The cableway to the summit (a must for every visitor) was opened in 1929. At least one couple each week get married on the mountain which has been nominated as one of the new Natural Seven Wonders of the World. The course at this point also gives magnificent views of Table Bay and Robben Island. The latter needs no introduction regarding its significance in the history of South Africa. The late Nelson Mandela spent 18 of the 27 years of his incarceration imprisoned on the island, turning it into possibly the most well-known island prison on the planet. The island, a World Heritage Site some 9km offshore, was dubbed 'Robben' (the Dutch word for seal) island by the early settlers. Over the centuries it has housed a prison, a hospital, a leper colony, a mental institution and acted as a military base.

Arriving back in the city centre, we ran past a number of famous landmarks. First of these was The Castle of Good Hope, the oldest building in South Africa. Built by van Riebeeck and the Dutch East India Company, the building is an example of a 'star fort.' Its 18th century décor has been restored and today it functions as a popular museum showcasing the Cape's early history. Next up was Cape Town's City Hall built in Italian Renaissance style and one of the last Victorian-style sandstone structures in the city. It was from the City Hall balcony that Nelson Mandela first addressed the world after his release from prison. On that day in 1990, 250,000 people came to the Grand Parade to celebrate the release of the country's future President. The same Grand Parade in front of the City Hall was the setting for the FIFA Fan Fest during the 2010 World Cup. More than 25,000 fans were comfortably able to watch live matches there on a giant screen during the duration of the tournament. Nearby are the South African Houses of Parliament, scene of some pretty dramatic debates over the years. Some of the most stirring of these occurred during the apartheid era when opposition party members stood up to hold the Nationalist government to account for the disastrous effects of that policy. In 1994 the building witnessed a major landmark in South African history when Mandela was introduced as President after the country's first democratic elections.

After passing City Gardens and St George's Cathedral we made our way via Three Anchor Bay to the finish at the A track in the recently redeveloped Green Point Park – one of the most significant legacies of the 2010 World Cup. At the finish there is stadium seating for spectators, club gazebos, big screen TV with live streams from the race, vending stalls, a beer garden and live entertainment. It's a great place to finish the race, especially as the famous V & A Waterfront is only a short stroll away. While many runners headed there afterwards I was content to merely to meet up with Mo and make a slow walk back to the hotel in the sunshine along the lovely Beach Road promenade. I felt I'd had a good run and felt strong throughout. Despite the ever-increasing heat I'd managed to run without stopping in well under my expected finishing time of four and a half hours. Time to put my feet up on the balcony with that bottle of good South African wine!

Though the most important, the marathon was only one aspect of our trip. We were there for 8 days and wanted to experience everything that Cape Town had to offer. The city's two most obvious attractions: a cable car ride up Table Mountain and a visit to Robben Island were the most prominent on our list. Unfortunately, the first of these was something of an anti-climax. Figuring to avoid the long queues for the cable car up to the top of Table Mountain we'd already purchased our tickets online before taking the hotel shuttle bus to the cable car station early on a sunny morning. Morning tickets, valid from 9am until 1pm cost R380 online. Afternoon tickets (1pm until closing) are cheaper at R300. (The Cableway can also be reached by public transport. The MyCiTi bus route that runs from Camps Bay stops close by on route number 106 and 107 from the Civic Centre to Camps Bay). Our plan was to spend the rest of the morning hiking around the summit trails, taking-in the magnificent views.

The journey from the base of the Cableway to the summit of Table Mountain only takes roughly 4 to 5 minutes. Initially the views back to the coast were excellent but on arrival at the summit a thick mist suddenly decided to descend as we joined the queue for the first of the 30-minute hiking tours that take place on the hour from 09:00 to 15:00 daily. Departing from the Twelve Apostles Terrace (below the Café), these are free, guided walks conducted by staff, who share the story of Table Mountain and the Cableway. Within minutes the cloying, wet mist obscured everything but the hand in front of your face. It simply wasn't worth staying on the summit and so, with great reluctance, we were soon back in the cable car to continue our walk at a lower level – in full sunshine, of course!

We had better luck with our trip to Robben Island. The Island, a desolate outcrop five miles offshore and home to the notorious prison that held Nelson Mandela is considered a testament to courage and fortitude in the face of brutality and a must-see for any visitor to South Africa. The national and UNESCO World Heritage site is one of South Africa's most visited attractions. Tours leave Cape Town four times a day at 9am, 11am, 1pm and 3pm, and the trip, which costs R600, includes a bus tour of the island and a visit to the prison. The ferries depart from the Nelson Mandela Gateway at the V & A Waterfront and the whole tour takes 3.5 hours including the ferry trip to and from the Island. The journey across Table Bay takes approximately 40 minutes and offers outstanding views of Table Mountain in both directions.

The island was first used as a political prison in the mid-1600s; Dutch settlers sent slaves, convicts and indigenous Khoikhoi people who refused to bend to colonial rule. In 1846 the island was turned into a leper colony. From 1961 to 1991, a maximum-security prison here held enemies of apartheid. In 1997, three years after apartheid fell, the prison was turned into the Robben Island Museum. The most powerful part of the tour is a visit to Mandela's cell, a 7-by-9-foot room where a bulb burned day and night over his head for the 18 years he was jailed here, beginning in 1964. Many of the guides are themselves former prisoners, including the one who conducted our tour who spoke openly about the brutality of his life inside the gaol. It's probably one of the most inspirational and best-value tours I've taken on any of my overseas trips.

We also made use of our free hotel shuttle to visit a couple of Cape Town's popular beach resorts. Camps Bay, just over the headland from where we were staying is one of the more accessible beaches close to the city and a hotspot for both surfers and celebrities. It boasts a beautiful, long stretch of white sand bordered by a promenade full of upmarket restaurants, clubs, and hotels. The setting is absolutely gorgeous, with the towering Twelve Apostles mountain range making for a craggy backdrop. From Camps Beach we jumped on the coastal service bus to the seaside suburb of Hout Bay 20 kilometres south of the city. The sheltered bay of Hout Bay has a beautiful white sand beach as well as one of the busiest fishing harbours in the Western Cape with a well-established tuna, snoek and crayfish industry. It's a great place for those who enjoy their seafood – the fish and chips were delicious.

When not travelling around we spent most of our time eating and drinking at The V&A Waterfront. This modern tourist development attracts roughly 24 million visitors each year, making it South Africa's most-visited destination. It's almost as synonymous with Cape Town as the iconic mountain whose feet at which it sits. While the Waterfront has become a busy shopping, dining and entertainment area, it's also still a working harbour and visitors can sit watching fishing boats bringing in their catch as large container vessels dock nearby. There is also a little something for the history buffs. The waterfront is named after Prince Alfred, who began construction on the harbour in 1860, and his mother Queen Victoria. The V&A Waterfront encompasses 22 landmarks, including the Chavonnes Battery Museum, which dates back to 1725 and is the harbour's oldest heritage site. You can opt to do a self-guided walking historical tour, which starts at the Information Centre, or you can take the 90-minute guided tour that departs daily from the Chavonnes Battery Museum at 11am and 2pm. Check out the infamous Breakwater Prison (dating back to 1860), the Robinson Dry Dock (one of the oldest operating dry docks in the world) or you can brush up on your marine history at the Iziko Maritime Centre. For something a little more recent, visit Nobel Square, which boasts bronze sculptures of South Africa's Nobel Peace Prize winners, or the Springbok Experience Rugby Museum, which immerses you in the history of the nation's rugby team. There's food stalls, food markets and restaurants of every variety. There's also some pretty decent bars in which to just sit in the sun and watch the world go by while gazing up to wonderful views of Table Mountain. Mitchell's Brewery was our particular favourite.

With so many beautiful coastal venues to visit we didn't spend much time in the actual city centre. In the same way that out-of-town shopping malls have affected traditional city outlets, most of Cape Town's thunder appears to have been stolen by the emergence of the V & A complex. We spent an afternoon visiting (in a more leisurely fashion) most of the attractions seen during the last two kilometres of the marathon. The whole place seemed a little tired and jaded. It made us pleased that we'd chosen to stay in a hotel on the coast.

Photo at Registration against Table Mountain backdrop

The V & A Waterfront. Cape Town

ROMANIA

BUCHAREST MARATHON

Romania is situated in the north of the Balkan Peninsula on the western shores of the Black Sea and is the largest country in South Eastern Europe and the twelfth-largest in Europe. According to The Blue Guide 'it is one of the most beautiful countries of Southeast Europe,' with both diversity and a rich cultural heritage. The beautiful Carpathian Mountains dominate the centre of Romania, with 14 mountain ranges reaching above 6,600 ft. while the Danube River forms a large part of the border with Serbia and Bulgaria, and flows into the Black Sea, forming the Danube Delta, the best-preserved delta in Europe. The country's name which derives from the Latin 'romanus' meaning 'citizen of Rome' has been officially in use for around 150 years. When the principalities of Wallachia and Moldavia - for centuries under the suzerainty of the Turkish Ottoman Empire - secured their autonomy in 1856; they were formally united in 1862 under the new name of Romania. The country gained recognition of its independence in 1878. It joined the Allied Powers in World War I and acquired new territories - most notably Transylvania - following the conflict. In 1940, Romania allied with the Axis powers and participated in the 1941 German invasion of the USSR. Three years later, overrun by the Soviets, Romania signed an armistice.

The post-war Soviet occupation led to the formation of a communist People's Republic in 1947 and the abdication of the king. The decades-long rule of dictator Nicolae Ceausescu, who took power in 1965, and his Securitate police state became increasingly oppressive and draconian through the 1980s. Running a neo-

Stalinist police state from 1967–1989, Ceausescu wrapped the iron curtain tightly around Romania, turning a moderately prosperous country into one on the brink of starvation. To repay his $10 billion foreign debt in 1982, he ransacked the Romanian economy of everything that could be exported, leaving the country with desperate shortages of food, fuel, and other essentials. An army-assisted rebellion in Dec. 1989 led to Ceausescu's overthrow, trial, and execution. Prominent among the charges for which he was executed was 'genocide by starvation!'

Former communists then dominated the government until 1996 when they were swept from power. Romania, a slower developer than other former communist countries of Eastern Europe, next took a major step away from its past when it was one of seven countries to join NATO in late March 2004. Its strategic location and Black Sea air and naval bases make it attractive to the alliance. Failure to push ahead sufficiently with reforms meant that the country was slow in being accepted among the list of new EU members, eventually joining the union in January 2007. The Romanian economy suffered badly in the global financial crisis of 2008, prompting the government to launch a draconian austerity programme in 2010. This led to major street rallies and clashes with police in January 2012, which brought down the government of Prime Minister Emil Boc and ushered in a period of political instability. Since then, the country has seen a slow but steady economic recovery. Things for which Romania is said to be famous include: the Carpathian Mountains, medieval fortresses, painted monasteries, Dacia cars, Dracula, stuffed cabbage leaves, the Black Sea coast, gymnast Nadia Comaneci, footballer Gheorghe Hagi and the Danube Delta.

Bucharest is the capital and largest city of Romania, as well as its cultural, industrial, and financial centre. It is located in the southeast of the country on the banks of the Dambovița River, less than 60 km north of the Danube River and the Bulgarian border. It became the capital of Romania in 1862 and is the centre of Romanian media, culture, and art. In the period between the two World Wars, the city's elegant architecture and the sophistication of its elite earned Bucharest the nickname of 'Little Paris.' Its architecture is a mix of neo-classical, Bauhaus and art deco, communist-era and modern. Although buildings and districts in the historic city centre were heavily damaged or destroyed by war, earthquakes, and above all Nicolae Ceaușescu's program of systematisation, many survived. Finding a 300 year old church, a steel-and-glass office building and Communist-era apartment blocks next to one another is a common sight. According to the 2011 census almost 2 million inhabitants live within the city limits making Bucharest the sixth-largest city in the European Union by population within city limits, after London, Berlin, Madrid, Rome, and Paris.

In recent years, the city has been experiencing an economic and cultural boom with many large infrastructure projects changing the old face of the city. It has benefited from an economic boom along with the EU grants that have helped rebuild neglected parts of the city, such as the historic Lipscani area. Today Bucharest has become a very interesting mix of old and new and offers some excellent attractions that make it well worth visiting. It has gradually cultivated a sophisticated, trendy, and modern image that is to be expected from a European capital. Given the generally bad press it receives in the UK, I'm sure many first time visitors will, like me, be surprised by the city's vibe and energy.

Romania's capital has an undeservedly poor reputation. Prior to visiting I came across various horror stories of what might lie in store. Most of these revolved around psychopathic taxi drivers, aggressive beggars, ubiquitous pickpockets and the very real possibility of attack by feral dogs! Knowing that my flight wasn't due to arrive until the early hours of the morning I was concerned to read about the apparently regular taxi scams perpetrated upon unsuspecting tourists. I read of new arrivals being driven to a remote forsaken place and being forced to pay up if they want to be taken to their destination. There were stories of how seconds before setting off, another man jumps in the car, and together with the driver, threatens tourists out of their money. I read somewhere that a Japanese tourist was fatally injured during one of these scams. I saw warnings about the numbers of pickpockets on public transport and the dangers of being accosted by beggars who refuse to take no for an answer. It all sounded rather scary. Just to top things off, it was also reported that Bucharest has perhaps the largest population of stray dogs for any city in eastern Europe. These are said to remain a threat to safety especially at night when they tend to form packs thus greatly increasing their danger. As someone who's been threatened by a pack of feral dogs in Asia this was particularly unsettling. In the end I needn't have worried. The stories were purely scaremongering. I pre-booked a hotel shuttle for arrival thus by-passing any potential taxi scam. On returning to the airport the English-speaking driver provided pleasant conversation and charged only the metred fare. Pickpockets and beggars were conspicuous by their absence (according to the Daily Mail they're all now in the UK!) and I doubt if I even saw a dog during my stay.

After a long train journey down to Luton, I arrived in Bucharest on a Romanian airline called Blue Air – a new one to me – but a useful to know budget airline that charged a mere £16.99 for the flight out. The return flight was also ridiculously cheap but other commitments meant returning with Ryanair via Stansted for £8 extra. That, of course, involved yet another tiring train journey back to my home in North Northumberland – the sacrifices we have to make to satisfy our ambitions as marathon globetrotters! I'd booked for 3 nights into the 4-star Hotel Parliament for £131 on the basis that it was walking distance to the Start/Finish area. While it was a decent enough hotel I wouldn't recommend it to others travelling to the marathon. It was in an isolated location with no amenities nearby – no shops, no restaurants, no pubs. To make the most of your stay in Bucharest you need to be close to the Lipscani district (named after the long street that bisects it.) This is where everything happens in the city – it's home to all the best places to eat and drink as well as all the stag-night orientated strip clubs and bars. Friends Dave and Linda Major had sensibly booked into the Europa Royale Hotel there along with fellow 100 Club members Roger Biggs and Rich Holmes. All the amenities were on their doorstep. I had a 30 minute walk through dark and deserted streets to get there with the possibility of being pursued en-route by packs of feral canines.

On arrival in Bucharest all scheduled flights including those operated by low cost airlines, land at Henri Coanda International Airport located in Otopeni, 18 km north of downtown. Confusingly the airport is often referred to only as Otopeni on airline bookings, because of its location. There are several options to get from the airport to Bucharest. Using public transport, Express bus 783 goes from the airport to downtown Bucharest. It runs approximately every 20 minutes, daily, including weekends and holidays (every 40 minutes during the night). Expect the trip with bus 783 to be about 40 minutes long (from Piata Unirii to the airport) or even longer during rush hour traffic. A second Express bus 780 links the airport with the main train station, Bucuresti Nord (Gara de Nord). It runs approximately every 40 minutes, daily (including weekends and holidays) from 5.30am to 11pm. When taking the 780 bus from Gara de Nord train station to Otopeni airport, note carefully that Gara de Nord is not the end of the bus route, hence, the 780 buses that pass Gara de Nord actually run in two directions. Therefore, to catch the 780 that takes you to the airport, you need to catch it from the 780 bus-stop that requires crossing a road, i.e. not the 780 bus stop that is directly outside the Nord station. Confusing or what! Best to ask locals where the correct bus stop is. Lowest price option for any of these express buses is 7 lei - two rides uploaded on an Activ card. (£1 gets you approximately 5.2 lei at the time of writing). Cards can only be purchased from the booth in front of either the Arrivals or Departures terminals (respectively on the return trip from ticket booths in stations along their route). They can't be bought from the driver. A 'to and fro' ticket (without Activ card) from the Airport to city centre and back costs 8.6 Lei, which is also cheap. (Normal transport passes do not work on these Express buses). There is a ticket machine in front of the Arrivals terminal in service 24 hours a day. Remember to always validate your ticket on boarding the bus as these two bus lines are a prime target for ticket inspectors.

In the past taking a taxi from Bucharest Henri Coanda airport was a hazardous experience as described earlier. I understand that the long running scam with tourists has now been resolved through the introduction of the ticketing system where taxi customers should get a ticket from the booths when coming out of the arrivals hall. Once you have a ticket wait for the taxi with your number on the side to arrive outside and after that the fare should be as per the meter (usually 1.39 lei per kilometre or around 30 lei to the centre of Bucharest). The safest way to get a low cost taxi is to order one using the electronic touch-screen kiosks on the Arrivals level. This will provide you with a printed ticket (which you should be sure to keep) for a specific taxi which will arrive within minutes. You're meant to show the ticket and keep the ticket for complaining if you have 'surprises.' You're advised to never give the ticket to the driver and to check the rate before getting in (it should be written on the taxi's doors) and also check that the meter is turned on. To avoid last minute stress, you can pre-book online between 30 days and 1 hour in advance.

The Bucharest Marathon, organised by the Bucharest Running Club, in cooperation with the Romanian Athletic Federation has been held every October since 2008. The event consists of competitive races (Team Relay, Half Marathon and Marathon plus Wheelchair races) and non-competitive races (Children Run and Fun Run). The course is certified by AIMS and IAAF with the time limit for the Half Marathon being 3 hours and 6 hours for the Marathon. The event, which celebrated its 10th edition in 2017, attracts over 15 000 participants from over 50 countries. When I ran the event in 2016 there were 927 finishers in the Marathon, 2781 in the Half, 14 Wheelchair contestants over both events and a whopping 774 Relay Teams, each with four runners, also in the Marathon event. Start and finish line are in the same place, in front of the Parliament Palace (former Ceausescu Palace) - the biggest building in Europe and the second biggest in the world. All runners receive adidas running T-shirts as well as a quality medallion. Early-bird entry fee for the marathon was 38 euros rising to 56 euros closer to race day. Registration takes place on the Friday and Saturday before the

Sunday's race in a specially erected tented-village in Constitution Square immediately opposite the Parliament Palace. The Registration area was a busy affair with all sorts of amenities on offer including stalls for food and drink as well as entertainments for the children. I arrived early on the Saturday morning to find huge numbers already in attendance watching the children's races that were already in full-swing. It would have been nice to stay and watch and soak in the atmosphere but I was already thoroughly soaked to the skin by the heavy persistent rain that continued relentlessly throughout the day. This made the sightseeing I'd planned difficult and, on occasions, impossible.

No trip to Bucharest would be complete without a visit to the Palace of Parliament, the craziest and crassest tribute to dictatorial megalomania you'll probably ever see. This unmistakable building, due to its immense physical, psychic and historic stature, is perhaps the most controversial building in Romania. Meant to be the crowning achievement of Centrul Civic (Civic Centre) - Communist leader Nicolae Ceausescu's ambitious urban development plan - the Palace of Parliament represents one of the most extravagant and expensive building projects of the last century. Claimed to be the world's second-largest building by surface area (after the US Pentagon), the Palace of Parliament is one of Romania's biggest tourist attractions, despite popular disdain. Ceausescu achieved the idea for 'The People's House' after a visit to North Korea's Kim Il-sung in 1972. The 'People's House' would be the largest, most lavish palace in the world and would hold all the functions of his socialist state, as well as serve as a handsome residence for he and his wife Elena. Leading to the Palace would be Boulevard 'Victory of Socialism' (now called Boulevard Unirii), the Champs Elysees of Bucharest, deliberately designed to be 1 metre wider on each side and 6 metres longer than Paris' thoroughfare, stretching from Piata Alba Iulia to the Palace premises. This Boulevard features prominently on the marathon route. To build the Palace and Centrul Civic, Ceausescu set about demolishing most of Bucharest's historic districts apart from Lipscani, including 19 Orthodox Christian churches, 6 synagogues and Jewish temples, 3 Protestant churches (plus eight relocated churches), and 30,000 homes in two neighbourhoods alone. In total, one-fifth of central Bucharest was razed for the project. As a result, a popular joke of the time was that the 'Victory of Socialism' Ceausescu had engendered was over the city itself.

It's said that some 20,000 workers toiled in 24-hour shifts, seven days a week, to build the 12 stories tall, 1,100 room Palace that also includes an undisclosed number of underground levels (at least 8)meant to double-up as nuclear bunkers to house thousands of people. To finance the project, Ceausescu had to take on enormous foreign debts. It's reported that in order to repay these debts he systematically starved the Romanian people, exporting all of the country's agricultural and industrial production as the standard of living in Romania sank to an all-time low. Food-rationing, gas electric and heating blackouts became everyday norms; people lived in squalor and poverty as the Ceausescu's themselves exhibited outrageous extravagance. The Romanian Revolution of 1989 broke out just as the People's Palace was nearing completion. Following Ceausescu's arrest and execution with his wife, (apparently there was no shortage of volunteers for the firing squad) the new government moved its functions into his maniacal mansion and it was renamed the Palace of Parliament. Today it also houses the National Museum of Contemporary Art (MNAC), however most of the premises remain unoccupied.

The Palace of the Parliament is opened for the public between 10 am and 4 pm daily. Buying tickets is said to be difficult (thought there didn't appear to many visitors while I was there) and it's recommended that you book these by phoning ahead in advance as parliamentary business means the official opening hours are subject to change. You will also need to bring your passport, driving license or other form of internationally-accepted ID. And request that you want an English-speaking guide. You can buy different tickets that allow you to visit a certain number of chambers, the basement and the main balcony with prices ranging between 25-45 lei, depending on the ticket. In order to take pictures inside the building you have to pay 30 lei. This all seemed rather complicated to me so I booked my ticket before travelling to Bucharest via the getyourguide.co.uk website. This provided a Guided tour with hotel pick-up for about £20 and included the main rooms, hallways and balcony from which Ceausescu had optimistically intended to address the crowds. This was somewhere I particularly wanted to see having read that none other than the late Michael Jackson had stood there in 1992 while performing in the city. The story goes that on hearing that Jackson was inside the building people had gathered in large numbers hoping to see him on his way out. Seeing the crowds from inside, Jackson decided to do an unplanned appearance on the balcony and thus became the first person to pronounce a speech from there. Apparently 'Hello Budapest' was all he managed to get out! The Bucharest crowd was not very impressed.

Another interesting fact I learned during the visit was that the Ceausescus were the last people to be executed in Romania before the abolition of capital punishment in January 1990. Despite the execution being filmed and the images of the dead Ceaușescus being videotaped and shown on Romanian television, that wasn't the end of the affair. In July 2010, forensic scientists exhumed the bodies to perform DNA tests to prove conclusively that they were indeed the remains of the Ceausescus. The body believed to be Elena's had decayed too much to allow for a positive identification, but Nicolae was easily identifiable, wearing the bullet-riddled black winter coat he had been wearing when he was killed. DNA was able to conclusively prove his identity. His family organized a funeral service for the couple and they were reburied together at Ghencea, under a modest tombstone.

By this stage I'd become totally fascinated by what I'd been hearing about the eccentric dictator. When it was explained that his former residence was open to the public that afternoon I abandoned pre-arranged plans (which largely involved walking around in the rain) in favour of taking a taxi to have a look at the property. On the way we stopped at another of the iconic symbols of Bucharest – the city's version of the famous Arc de Triomphe. Though smaller than the original it's still an impressive structure. The initial, wooden, triumphal arch was hurriedly built on the site, after Romania gained its independence in 1878, so that the victorious troops could march under it. Another temporary arch was built on the same site, in 1922, after World War I. This was demolished in 1935 to make way for the current arch under which military parades take place on every 1st December – Romania's national holiday.

Set in 3.5 acres of grounds in Bucharest's desirable Primaverii (Spring) neighbourhood, the luxurious 80-room residence of the former dictator was designed in the mid-1960s to the exact specifications of Ceausescu and his wife, who reportedly personally picked the chandeliers and mosaics. The Ceausescus lived here for around two decades up until their end in 1989. After the Romanian revolution the building, known as Palatul Primaverii (Spring Palace) was taken over by the state and only rarely used to host official delegations. It was put up for sale in 2014 but attracted no buyer. Now everything has been returned to its former state, including the couple's bedroom and the private apartments of the three Ceausescu children. Highlights include a cinema in the basement, Elena's opulent private chamber and the back garden and swimming pool. The building is open from Wednesdays to Sundays with an entry fee of 45 lei for an English-speaking guide. Those who want to splash out 200 lei by pre-booking a 2 hour private tour will also get to see Ceausescu's private room, his bunker and trophy room, as well as visit to the Underground Tunnel and the portrait gallery.

The rest of the day was spent wandering around the city in the rain. I headed first for the old part of town centred on the Liscanti district. Although much of the area remains agreeably tatty, a massive regeneration project has transformed many of its previously run-down streets and buildings. The area, stretching between the Dambovita river to the south, Calea Victoriei to the west, Calea Moşilor to the east and Regina Elisabeta boulevard to the north, contains an assortment of middle 19th century buildings, ruins of the Wallachian princes' medieval court, churches, bank headquarters, a few hotels, clubs, restaurants and shops. Narrow cobblestoned streets retain the names of the ancient guilds that resided on them. What struck me most as I made my way north to the enormous University Square were the number of British/Irish themed pubs in the area: The Explorers, The Vintage, Trinity College Pub, Jack's Pub. There was even a nightclub curiously named 'Bastards.' Opposite the Old Town on the edge of Unirii Square sat McDonalds and a KFC. It was difficult to believe that you'd left the UK. Just to confirm that I had (and to get out of the rain) I went into the nearby Romanian National History Museum and spent an hour or so in this huge building containing Romanian historical artefacts from prehistoric times up to modern times. The permanent displays include a plaster cast of the entirety of Trajan's Column and the Romanian Crown Jewels. After that it was time to eat. I decided on a Jazz-themed restaurant, the 55Jazz Music Bar, I'd spotted in Strada Franceza (the street with the big Kebab shop on the corner). Though Jazz is not the music of my taste the place had atmosphere and the pasta dishes were excellent value for less than a fiver.

Sunday morning started surprisingly warm and sunny after yesterday's downpours as we all lined up in Constitution Square for the 9.30am start under the looming shadow of the gigantic Parliament building. All three of the main events started simultaneously with the Wheelchair racers having left ten minutes earlier. The event gives runners the chance to discover Bucharest while running, as the route includes some of the largest boulevards in the Romanian capital as well as some of its most well-known squares. The first 3 kilometres took us in a clockwise loop around the Parliament and its grounds. That should give you some idea of how big the place is. Kilometres 4 and 5 had us circling Unirii Square, one of the largest squares in central Bucharest. Located right in the centre of the city, it is bisected by Unirii Boulevard, originally built during the Communist era as the Boulevard of the Victory of Socialism, and renamed after the Romanian Revolution of 1989. The square is a significant transport hub, containing the Piața Unirii metro station and a major interchange for local buses; there is also a tram terminal near the southwest corner. Bucharest's largest shopping centre with the Cocor department store and a large taxi rank are located on the east side of this square. The centre of the square boasts a small park and fountains which are particularly popular with commuters and passers-by in the hot summer months. There were plans to build the Romanian National Salvation Cathedral in the park, but the idea proved technically impossible due to the busy underground network and lack of popularity among local citizens and therefore the location was changed.

The route then heads north through the busiest part of the city – though, fortunately on traffic-free streets. Between 6 and 7 kilometres the course bisects the Romanian National Museum of Art and the Roman Athenaeum. The latter is an important building to Romanians and is considered as symbolic of the national culture. It was built with money collected publicly, following a national lottery (500.000 tickets were issued, costing one lei each). Since completion in the heart of Bucharest 120 years ago as a building dedicated to art and science the Athenaeum has become the architectural and spiritual landmark of the nation. Runners can't fail to notice that the facade is inspired by the architecture of ancient Greek temples and consists of a row of columns which support a triangular pediment. The interior is arranged after the model of an ancient Greek-Roman amphitheatres. Today, the ornate, domed, circular building is the city's main concert hall and home of the George Enescu Philharmonic and of the George Enescu annual international music festival. The building was placed on the list of the Label of European Heritage sites in 2007.

The course turns back on itself at 8km and progresses slightly downhill past the George Enescu Museum, the Romanian Academy and the Museum of Art Collections. As you'll have gathered the name Enescu features prominently in Bucharest. Enescu was one of the most prodigiously gifted musicians of the 20th century: he not only distinguished himself as a violinist, conductor and composer, but was also an accomplished pianist, able cellist and a famous violin teacher. His reputation places him as one of the most remarkable men of culture of the 20th century. He played a prominent part as a music ambassador both in his country and worldwide. He also involved himself actively in promoting

Romanian music, composers, conductors and performers internationally and is regarded as one of the greatest composers of the 20th century and Romania's most important musician. The Romanian Academy has an interesting remit. According to its bylaws, its main goals are the cultivation of Romanian language and Romanian literature, the study of the national history of Romania and research into major scientific domains. Some of the academy's fundamental projects are the Romanian language dictionary, the dictionary of Romanian literature, and the treatise on the history of the Romanian people. The Academy also operates its own publishing house. The Art Collections Museum, meanwhile, works as a branch of the National Museum of Art and is housed in the Romanit Palace. Its collections showcase international artists like Gustave Courbet, van Gogh and Pissarro but with special emphasis placed on the works created by Romanian artists. You're probably also thinking by now that the marathon course is becoming something of a cultural procession. You're right! Next up, set back from the road close to the 10km mark is the Sala Palatului - a conference centre and concert hall immediately behind the National Museum of Art of Romania, the former royal palace in the heart of the city. It was built during the communist era and in recent years has featured performers such as Demis Roussos, Nana Mouskouri, Engelbert Humperdinck, Tom Jones, Elvis Costello, Bryan Ferry, John Mayall, Status Quo and Mark Knopfler. Quite an eclectic mixture.

By 11km, just when we're thinking we've left all the culture behind to follow the banks of the Dambovița River for a kilometre or so, the course makes a 3 kilometre dog-leg up to the Palace of the National Military Circle (or the 'Central House of the Army' as it was known during the communist period). Today, the beautiful building fronted by an ornate fountain, is considered a historic and architectural monument. It represents the central cultural institution of the Romanian army and it is also used for various cultural events and for representation and protocol purposes. The restaurant and the terrace are open to the public. The river is crossed for the first time just after 15km when we ran along its opposite bank until the 17km mark. Shortly after this a right turn took us back past the start and out on to an undistinguished 8 kilometre loop around the south western suburbs. There's very little to see on this section and very few spectators other than when approaching the relay change-over.

Returning again to Constitution Square at 25km, runners begin a long, straight stretch heading east along Unirii Boulevard – Ceausescu's would-be rival to the Champs Elysees. The water features along the boulevard at least offer some respite in the heat. The monotony is broken at 28km when running around the gigantic Alba Iulia Square traffic circle and into Decebal Boulevard towards the turn shortly after 31km. Just when you're settling in for a straight run back to the finish, the course makes an unexpected diversion to complete a 1 kilometre loop around the National Stadium at 32km. The gleaming new stadium opened in 2011, replaced the former National Stadium on the same spot. It was built for the Romania national football team, hosting its games as well as the Romanian Cup Final and the Romanian Supercup. The 2012 UEFA Europa League Final was held at the new stadium - the first final of a major European football club competition hosted by Romania. It has also been chosen as one of the venues for group-stage matches at the UEFA Euro 2020 Finals. The highest audience for a football game was achieved at the 2014 FIFA World Cup qualification match between Romania and Netherlands in 2012, when 53,329 people attended. There must have been something taking place inside as we ran around it judging by the large crowds milling about. I'd been running fairly comfortably up until this stage and was well under a sub-4:30 finish. However, as is usual with me, when the temperature rises the pace begins to fall and the last 10 kilometres became something of a struggle. This time it was all I could do to restrain myself from jumping into one of the fountains as we ran back along the Unirii Boulevard.

The final sting in the tail as we arrived at Unirii Square with the finish in sight close to the 38km mark, was to be re-directed northwards for a last 4km loop along the river and over the same bridge we'd crossed hours earlier. Mentally, that was hard! I finished just outside the 4:30 I'd been hoping for. An interesting side-line to this is the fact that initially I was awarded 1st Vet Over-70 position — I've even got a certificate and print-out showing no fewer than eleven recorded split times proving this. As there was no prize money or trophies involved I thought nothing of it at the time. It was only some months later while reviewing the results for this chapter that I found that I'd been downgraded to 2nd place. Curiously, the new winner of the age- category had no recorded split times and there was no differential between his official (gun) time and real (crossing the line) time. More in hope than expectation, I contacted the organisers for an explanation. They replied that the winner's chip had malfunctioned and that they'd viewed photos from around the course to verify their decision. I fully accepted their explanation and can only admire the guy who ran 3:55 in that heat — it's an excellent time for someone over 70 years of age.

While in Bucharest I was determined to try some Romanian cuisine. The problem was we rarely hear about it in the UK where Romanian restaurants are few and far between so I asked the friendly receptionists in the hotel what to look for. Not only did they tell me what to order (though I didn't much like the sound of the tripe soup) they also both recommended going to La Mama, part of a modern restaurant chain specialising in Romanian cuisine, located near the Romanian Athenaeum. I headed there as soon as I'd showered and changed after the race. Apparently, Romanian meals traditionally begin with a soup, often a 'sour' one called ciorba. The sourness derives from vinegar or lemon added during preparation. I tried their Ciorba de Perisoare a meatball soup with minced meat, celery, parsley and parsnip, carrot, onion, bell pepper and green beans costing 14 lei. For a main course I was advised to order the traditional favourite 'Sarmale' - a dish made of rolled minced meat (pork usually) mixed with rice and herbs and covered in cabbage leaves. For 24 lei I had the Sarmalute Cu Mamaliguta, the house speciality with ground beef and pork, smoked bacon, onion, sauerkraut, rice, tomato paste and pepper. Very nice it was too. I'd like to have finished with some of the local brew but surprisingly for a restaurant specialising in national dishes, all they had on the menu were the usual Carlsberg, Tuborg and Holsten, The Cuba Libre went down well enough for 14 lei.

I was still anxious to taste some of the local brew before leaving Bucharest. Before travelling I'd read that some of the most popular Romanian beers are: Ursus, Timisoreana (named after the city of the same name), Stejar, Bergenbier, Ciuc and Silva. Silva and Ursus are also said to brew a dark lager variety. That's what I went looking for having been advised to visit one of the two 'Beer O'Clock' pubs in Bucharest. The one on Gabroveni Street, in the heart of the Old Town, being the main venue has probably the biggest selection of bottled beers, ales and ciders in the city with brews from all over the world. It's worth visiting this place to try the local brewed beers from the Ground Zero factory. Also they have a huge selection of Belgian beers and the staff will help you pick a beer suited for your taste. Obviously, I put in a request for the perfect dark beer and ended up trying an Ursus Black at 6% ABV and a much tastier Hop Hooligan Dumpster Bear at 7%. Neither of them were perfect but were at least a better than what was on offer at La Mama. To round off a great weekend, later that evening I went to the Explorer Pub to meet up with 100 Club colleagues Dave and Linda and, briefly, Roger and Rich, for – you guessed it – more of the same!

The Marathon HQ opposite the huge Parliament building

21 hours before the start. My, didn't it rain!

SLOVENIA

LJUBLJANA MARATHON

Though I love the peace, tranquillity and beautiful coastal scenery of my home in Northumberland (and wouldn't want to live anywhere else in the UK) I'm sometimes envious of those of my fellow runners who find themselves living close to one of the country's major airports. It opens up endless opportunities for visiting more and more countries for a spot of marathon globetrotting. Ljubljana, for example, proved one of the more difficult places to get to from the North East of England in 2016. EasyJet is the only one of the low-cost airlines that fly there on a regular basis from the UK and that, for me, meant getting up before the crack of dawn for a 6 am train to Stansted via Kings Cross for the 1 pm flight. I met up at the airport with 100 Club colleague Roger Biggs who'd had a much easier time getting there – simply driving the short distance from his home in well under an hour. Coming back I had the choice of returning the same way or taking a Wizz Air flight from Ljubljana to Brussels and then on to Edinburgh for a much shorter train ride down the coast to home. I chose the latter – just for a change. I was getting bored with travelling back and forth to London for connections to events. It's easy to be put-off travelling when faced with the difficulties involved but, in the end, I'm always pleased to have made the effort. The memories you bring back of the places you've visited last far longer than the temporary discomforts you face on the journey (like the six-hour wait in Brussels on this one). Anyway, I'd been enthusiastically looking forward to visiting Ljubljana for some time. Everyone I'd met who'd been there had returned with glowing accounts of a unique, picture-postcard size capital city surrounded by mountains and in a glorious riverside setting. They weren't wrong.

With a population of around 300,000, Ljubljana is the capital of Slovenia and one of the smallest capital cities in Europe. Slovenia itself only has around 2 million inhabitants – not much more than some of the UK's larger cities. Known as 'Slovenes' these are a South Slavic people with a unique language (though virtually everyone under 30 prides themselves on speaking English). Situated in southern Central Europe, Slovenia borders Italy to the west, Austria to the north, Croatia to the south and southeast, and Hungary to the northeast. The north of this small country is dominated by the Alps, while in the southwest, the Karst Plateau is a region filled with limestone caves and gorges. Slovenia also has a coastline of 46.6 km by the Adriatic Sea between Italy and Croatia. Because of its size and the variety of its landscapes one of the proud boasts of the Slovenian tourist industry is that it's a country where it's possible to ski in the morning and swim in the afternoon.

For most of its history, Slovenia was largely controlled by the Habsburgs of Austria, who ruled the Holy Roman Empire and its successor states, the Austrian Empire and Austria-Hungary. In addition, coastal portions were held for a time by Venice. In October 1918, the Slovenes exercised self-determination for the first time by co-founding the State of Slovenes, Croats and Serbs. In December 1918, they merged with the Kingdom of Serbia into the Kingdom of Serbs, Croats and Slovenes (renamed Kingdom of Yugoslavia in 1929). During World War II, Slovenia was occupied and annexed by Germany, Italy, and Hungary, with a tiny area transferred to the Independent State of Croatia, at that time a Nazi puppet state. Afterward, it was a founding member of the Federal People's Republic of Yugoslavia, later renamed the Socialist Federal Republic of Yugoslavia, a communist state which was the only country in the Eastern Bloc never a part of the Warsaw Pact. In June 1991, after the introduction of multi-party representative democracy, Slovenia split from Yugoslavia and became an independent country. Unlike Croatia or Bosnia-Herzegovina, Slovenia's independence from Yugoslavia was almost bloodless. In 2004, it entered NATO and the European Union; in 2007 became the first formerly communist country to join the Eurozone. The country also found the transition from a state economy to the free market easier than most. It had a reputation as one of the best-performing new EU members before being dragged into a deep recession by the European financial crisis in 2012. Slovenia is becoming an increasingly popular tourist destination, especially for adventurous travellers who love the outdoors. The country offers plenty of opportunities for hiking, kayaking, rafting, cycling, skiing and climbing, making activity holidays really popular.

We arrived in Slovenia at Ljubljana's Joze Pucnik Airport (commonly referred to as Brnik Airport) located 27 km north of the city centre. The country's other main airport is at Maribor, Slovenia's second city. From the airport the cheapest ways to the city are by regular public buses costing around 4 euros for the 50 minute journey to the main Ljubljana bus and train stations. These are located next to each other in the city centre a short distance from the Marathon Expo making it perfectly possible to register before making your way to your hotel. Bus tickets can be bought from the driver and detailed timetables are available on the airport website. Alternatively, a metered taxi from the airport to the centre will cost in the region of 30 euros. Roger had already pre-booked our ride into town for this amount. I'd booked bed and breakfast for 3 nights at the city-centre Hotel Emonec for 192 euros. With a sense of pride, our driver explained the origins of the hotel's name. It seems the Roman city of Emona, a major military base, was established on Ljubljana's present location as a gateway from the Roman Empire to the Balkans and to Eastern Europe. Though burned down by Huns in 452 AD, you can still see Roman walls, town gates and cemeteries some of the remains of which are incorporated into city architecture. He also explained that with the hotel being in a pedestrianised street he was unable to take us directly to the door, but hadn't factored in that surrounding streets were also closed due to children's races being held nearby as part of the marathon weekend. After several false starts and lots of stopping and asking directions we eventually found the hotel tucked into an alleyway very close to both the main square and the race's start and finish. The hotel's location was about its only asset. It was tired, dated, noisy and not particularly comfortable – but it served its purpose in providing somewhere to sleep for a few hours each night. The rest of the time was spent finding out what Ljubljana had to offer the marathon tourist. And that was quite a lot. The term 'hidden gem' is often used when talking about Ljubljana - Lonely Planet, for example, named it the second best place in Europe to visit in 2014 and the city was nominated as the European 'Green Capital' for 2016.

As Slovenia's capital and largest city it has been the cultural, educational, economic, political, and administrative centre of independent Slovenia since 1991. Its central geographic location within Slovenia, its transport connections, concentration of industry, scientific and research institutions, and cultural tradition are contributing factors to its leading position. It's known for its university population and green spaces, including the expansive Tivoli Park. It is a charming city full of artists, museums, and galleries. Car traffic is restricted in the centre, leaving the leafy banks of the emerald-green Ljubljanica River, which flows through the city's heart, free for pedestrians and cyclists. In summer, cafes set up terrace seating along the river which flows through the centre of town, past Baroque buildings and under the ramparts of the ancient castle on the hill. It has managed to retain traces from all periods of its rich history; from the legacy of Roman Emona; through to the Renaissance, Baroque and Art Nouveau periods characterised in the house fronts and ornate doorways of the city centre, the romantic bridges adorning the river, the lopsided rooftops and a park reaching deep into the city centre. The new city and modern-day commercial core lies to the west of the river, while the old city and the castle are located on the east side of the river. Ljubljana is very much a people-friendly city. Categorised as a medium-sized European city, it offers everything a metropolis does yet manages to preserve its small-town friendliness. I took an instant liking to the place and couldn't wait to explore. Our first priority, however, was to register for the forthcoming marathon.

This involved an easy 30 minute walk on the Friday evening following the city's main thoroughfare north to what appeared to be a modern conference centre (or similar) type building close to the bus and train stations. The venue was both spacious and well set-out with all sorts of stalls of interest to most marathon runners. It wasn't simply a cynical merchandising sales pitch – there was lots to see and do including quite a few freebies and even an exotically dressed samba dancer who looked like she could have been representing the Rio Carnival. I still haven't worked out why she was there! The whole thing was excellent value for the 35 euros entry fee. Except it wasn't just 35 euros – I forgot to factor in the extra £20 it cost to enter by bank transfer. Why on earth events that like to consider themselves as 'international' marathons can't just simply set-up a secure online method of entry payment continues to baffle me. While wanting to attract overseas entrants they do nothing to make things easier for us to get into their event. For our pains we were given a quality long-sleeved T-shirt and the most useful rucksack I've had from any event. With a larger capacity than most it easily fits an extra pair of trainers and everything needed on an overseas trip. It's become indispensable and now accompanies me everywhere I go.

Further value-for-money was there in the Pasta Party held in the same venue that Roger and I returned to the following night. I like it when you are allowed to have as many refills of spaghetti bolognaise as you're able to manage. The Expo is open for registration from 9 am to 7 pm for three days before the race starting on Thursday and even opens early on Sunday morning for those arriving late into town. For 2017 entry fees remained at 35 euros until mid-August, rising to 40 euros before the race. The prices includes single use chip. If a participant has his own Champion Chip, then he doesn't need to pay 3 euros for the chip. Anyone leaving things until the last minute will only get a number and chip – no T-shirt, no rucksack. 2016's event was to be the 21st edition of the race that was first held in 1996 with a mere 153 participants in the marathon, 327 in the half marathon and a further 193 in a recreational event. This year (2016) almost 2,000 entered the full distance and close to 7,500 runners took part in the half marathon. In total more than 22,000 entered all events on the race programme. These included a well-attended 10K recreational run and wheelchair races early on the Sunday morning as well as a wide variety of children's races held throughout the day on Saturday. So, basically something for everyone to get involved in.

On returning from the Expo we stumbled across Halliday's, a British style pub on the same street that provided our introduction to Slovenian beer. Unfortunately, beer in Slovenia is dominated by the pale lager market with the most commonly known brands of Slovenian beer, Lasko and Union now united under the same parent company, though smaller breweries do exist. The beers are very similar with Lasko being slightly more bitter. I'm told that Union is the main beer of the capital city, Ljubljana while Lasko is mostly drunk elsewhere. I remembered that if you want a dark beer it's necessary to ask for 'pivo' otherwise you'll invariably be sold one of the paler brews. Trying both varieties from each of the main breweries left me no nearer to ending my search for the perfect dark beer. The best I found was Crni Baron 6% (Black Baron) a rich caramel drink that can only be purchased in 33cl bottles. Fortified by a couple of these I opted against returning to the hotel with Roger in favour of a late night stroll along the riverbanks attempting to find a restaurant specialising in Slovenian food for when we were joined by Paul Richards and Dave Goodwin on the following night. Despite the late October chill most of the restaurants appeared to be doing good business with many of the clientele eating under heaters or else swaddled in blankets. There was a cheerful, friendly ambience about the place that I hadn't found in too many European capitals.

Saturday was devoted to sightseeing – an easy task with most of the city's attractions located a stone's throw from one another. The place to start is in the lovely Preseren Square, Formally a meeting place for several roads in front of one of the old entrance gates to the city, and a public square since Ljubljana's original defensive walls were torn down in the middle of the 19th century, this is one of the city's most important landmarks. Named after Slovenia's national poet France Preseren, it's both a popular meeting place under the large statue of the man after whom the square is named and a site for concerts and events during the summer. The poet's statue is symbolically faced by the statue of Julija Primic, his great love, mounted on the facade of a building located across the square. The charming little public space is ringed by a number of interesting sights including the magnificent Art Nouveau façade of the Urbanc House. The imposing pink-coloured Franciscan church of the Annunciation was built within the square during the 17th century. The church, built by the Augustinians, is today one of the main symbols of the city due to its location in the centre of the square and its striking colour. Its triple staircase which faces the square is a popular spot for street artists, locals and visitors, having as it does a great view of the Triple Bridge, the square and those strolling by. When the architect Joze Plecnik's Triple Bridge was built, the square extended to the other side of the Ljubljanica River and assumed its present appearance. All manner of things took place in the square during our stay, not least the marathon making its way back to the finish just after the 40 kilometre mark.

Connecting Preseren Square and the newer areas of the city with the Old Town and the Market is the famous Triple Bridge, one of the most unusual and the most frequently crossed bridges in Ljubljana. Starting out as a wooden structure that served as an entrance to the fortified medieval town of Ljubljana it was replaced by a stone structure in 1842 that today forms the present central bridge of the three. The final adjustment was completed in 1931 when architect Joze Plecnik added the side pedestrian bridges to the existing main one to keep pedestrians separate from increased traffic and a busy tram line. Instead of building a new bridge Plecnik decided to keep the central bridge and to add pedestrian bridges on either side. Two staircases leading down to the embankment of the river were added to each of the pedestrian bridges, which gives an impression of portals and a Mediterranean touch that Plecnik wanted to give Ljubljana. With the two pedestrian bridges and the balustrades, the bridge got the name Triple Bridge. The Bridge is a perfect place to stop, feel the pulse of the city and watch the world go by.

We visited the city's main Tourist Office located directly across the bridge to see what else was on offer. The most appealing of the suggestions made was the one involving an afternoon's boat trip along the Ljubljanica River. Before that though we wanted to visit the city's ancient castle that dominates the city skyline. There are many pathways leading up the hill to the castle, all involving around 10 minutes of hard walking. The most popular are the ones leading from the old town square or the one from the Central market. The nearby funicular railway appeared a more attractive option though both of us hesitated initially at having to fork out the 10 euros return fare until it was pointed out discreetly that, as obvious old-age pensioners, we were entitled to a 25% discount. The castle of Ljubljana is just one of the castles in the city but certainly the biggest one and also the most visited. Built in the middle of the 15th century, today it is a popular tourist destination for locals and foreigners also. Small wonder. It offers an outstanding view over the city, a romantic atmosphere and is a place of numerous cultural events. We first climbed to the top of the tower to take in the outstanding views and could actually watch the runners in the children's events taking place below. We also took advantage of the free 'Virtual Castle,' a documentary about the history of the castle in a variety of languages, discovering that it was built by the Hapsburgs to defend against Turkish invasions and peasant rebellions. In the 17th and 18th century the castle had the function of a military hospital and an arsenal. Napoleon's occupation in 1809 brought a brief period of freedom and cultural and national enlightenment to the citizens of Ljubljana. After the French left, the Habsburgs used the castle for jails. The jail period lasted until the end of the Second World War, when first Italians and after their capitulation Germans took over the management of the castle. Until 1963 ostracised citizens of Ljubljana lived on the castle in terrible conditions before renovations commenced in the 1970s.You don`t have to pay anything to enter the castle courtyard, where you can relax with a cup of coffee, glass of wine or a piece of cake or you can visit numerous art exhibitions which take place in different parts of the castle and are usually also free. I particularly enjoyed a visit to the cells and seeing the horrific conditions in which prisoners were kept. We could easily have stayed longer but there was more to see before the boat trip.

Next up we wanted to visit the city's Central Market. Being Saturday the place was buzzing with people squashed into the narrow alleyways between the stalls selling everything from cheeses, fresh fruit and vegetables to take-away hot food. The Central Market is more than just a place to shop. Traditionally, it has also been a place for the locals to meet and enjoy themselves. It consists of an open-air market, located in the Vodnik and Pogacarnev squares, plus a covered market situated in between the two squares, and a series of small food shops along the river Ljubljanica, known as 'Plecnik's Covered Market.' This is a two-storey range of market halls within a colonnade designed by Ljubljana's famous architect Joze Plecnik. The market building stretches between the Triple Bridge and the Dragon Bridge, following the curve of the Ljubljanica River. At the covered market, you can get dry-cured meat products, fresh meat, homemade bread baked in the wood-fired oven, homemade biscuits and other sweet baked goods. The homemade bread was both delicious and inexpensive. Both the market and Vodnik Square are listed as cultural monuments of national significance and are well worth visiting even if you don't wish to purchase anything.

Situated next to the market is the Cathedral of St. Nicholas, the main church of Ljubljana and by far the biggest. More than 300 years old it replaced a much earlier church on the same spot he first church in this same spot built by Ljubljana boatmen and fishermen in honour of their patron St. Nicholas, the patron Saint of fishermen. Its green dome and twin towers make it highly visible from all over the city. Though not particularly impressive from the outside, particularly on market day when the crowds and stalls spill all over onto its steps, the pink-marbled interior is something special. After a quick look inside we fought our way through the throng to see two of Ljubljana's other main attractions, first the Dragon Bridge and then the Butcher's Bridge – both mere metres away.

The symbol of the city is the Ljubljana Dragon. It is depicted on the top of the tower of Ljubljana Castle in the Ljubljana coat of arms and on one of the important river-crossings; the Dragon Bridge. It's said to symbolise power, courage, and greatness. As usual, there are several explanations as to the origin of the Ljubljana Dragon. The one I'd like to believe (but don't) involves the Greek legend of Jason and the Argonauts. This says that on their return home after having taken the Golden Fleece they found a large lake surrounded by a marsh between the present-day towns of Vrhnika and Ljubljana. It was there that Jason struck down a monster, believed to be a dragon. As a Ljubljana trade-mark, the Dragon Bridge is one of the most well-known sights of the city. The chief attraction of the bridge are four sheet-copper dragon statues, which stand on pedestals at its four corners. The dragons are said to wave their tails when the bridge is crossed by a virgin. There was no tail-wagging while we were there.

The nearby Butchers' Bridge is a recently constructed footbridge crossing the river connecting the Ljubljana Central Market with the opposite embankment. The construction of a bridge with the same name, Butchers' Bridge, was planned as early as the late 1930s by the architect Joze Plecnik. According to his plans, the bridge was to be covered, and was to be a part of the Market. However, due to the outbreak of World War II, the bridge was never built. For more than fifty years, an empty spot in the middle of the Central Market marked the place where the bridge was meant to be built. The modern bridge, features a staircase at its left entry, glass walking belts at the sides and two fences with steel wires and wide top shelves. Shortly after the opening of the bridge hundreds of padlocks of couples in love started appearing on the steel wires. The largest sculptures on the bridge represent figures from Ancient Greek and Christian/Jewish mythology including a grotesque statue of Prometheus, running and disembowelled, in punishment for having given knowledge (of fire) to mankind.

That afternoon we caught up with 100 Club friends Gina Little and partner Ray watching the children's races in Congress Square, the headquarters for all the weekend's events. The square is one of the most important centres of the city. It was built in 1821 for ceremonial purposes such as the Congress of Ljubljana after which it was named. Since then it became an important venue for political ceremonies, demonstrations and protests, such as the ceremony at creation of the Kingdom of Yugoslavia, the ceremony of the liberation of Belgrade and protests against Yugoslav authority in 1988. The square also houses several important buildings, such as the University of Ljubljana, the Philharmonic Hall and the Ursuline Church of the Holy Trinity. Star Park, in the middle of the square, was packed to capacity with families enjoying watching the free entertainment. We left them to head off with Gina and Ray for one of the highlights of the weekend; the boat trip along the river. At 8 euros per head this was excellent value for the hour-long journey in the beautiful autumnal sunshine. Being off-season, we virtually had the boat to ourselves. As we sailed away from the centre the surroundings were even more impressive with grandiose building and tree-line boulevards on both sides – all on a human scale. It's easy to see why Ljubljana has developed a reputation as a 'people-friendly' city. I'd been told to look out for wild otters swimming in the river but didn't spot any. That evening Paul and Dave's arrival meant more catching-up with good friends; this time in the Cutty Sark pub over a few more pints of Union Pivo. With a marathon to run the next day we were fortunate (or not) that as the evening progressed the volume of the music increased, drowning out conversation and giving us the perfect excuse to make an early exit.

Marathon day started freezing cold with an eerie mist hanging over the river and blanketing the sun. For some reason the main events didn't start until 10.30 am leaving us with too much time on our hands to wait around. Being the last weekend in October the clocks had been put-back an hour which somehow made the wait seem even longer. I attempted to kill time by walking around the corner to Congress Square to watch the 8.30 am start of the 10K Recreation Run with close to 6,000 runners taking part. The cold had me soon scurrying back to the warmth of the hotel. Fortunately, the sun had burnt off the mist before it was time for us to run. We lined up wherever we fancied with the half marathoners on the edge of the Square. It was one large free-for-all. Though there were signs indicating zones based on predicted times, no one checked your entry and runners just stood wherever they wanted to. With around 9,500 starters over both events it meant that those at the back of the field, crossing the start line after 10 minutes or so, would have to pace themselves carefully to finish under the 5-hour limit.

I'd love to give a full course description – unfortunately I can't. The route was largely non-descript, anonymous and without outstanding features and I've little recollection of where it took us. The marathon course was one large, anti-clockwise circuit around the city's perimeter with the half marathon returning to the centre at its southern edge. They were lucky; the first section of the two was the most interesting. Leaving the Square we ran arrow-straight for over 4 kilometres along the main entrance to the city heading north. We then returned south, following the railway line to the 8km mark before heading north-west along a different railway line to 11km. From 14km to 17km we ran the only bit of the course I really enjoyed - in rural surroundings through the western end of the giant Tivoli Park. Apparently, in previous years the marathon had been two laps of the half marathon course. They should have left it at that. That way we would have at least run twice through the park.

The second half was (to me) a tough, winding slog through unattractive suburban streets. By this time we were well into the afternoon, the sun was at its hottest and I was beginning to struggle. It was only when we approached the city again after the 40 km mark that the surroundings became of interest. My abiding memory is of passing the cathedral before crossing the Triple Bridge for a final short loop through city streets and back to the finish gantry in a crowded Congress Square. As well as a top quality medal we were handed an excellent running vest instead of the usual T-shirt. (Don't forget, we'd already received a long-sleeved running top at Registration). I hung around waiting for Roger to finish, disappointed with my time of an inglorious 4:44:34. At least it was well inside the enforced 5 hour limit. Roger was not so lucky; problems with a long-term Achilles injury meant that he'd had to step off the course. It's a long way to go for a DNF but at least he'd had the consolation of seeing a beautiful city – with the bonus of a trip to scenic Lake Bled to look forward to the next day - while I returned home.

That evening the six of us visited a Serbian/Slovenian restaurant just around the corner from Congress Square to try the local cuisine. It would seem that Slovenian dishes have been heavily influenced by those from surrounding countries such as Italy, Austria and Hungary. The latter cuisine has gifted the local one with goulash while sausage (Carniolan sausage is the best known Slovenian speciality) and Wiener Schnitzel come from Austria with the usual pasta and pizza dishes from Italy. It's no exaggeration to say that, between us, we probably tasted the lot of them. All main courses cost between 8 to 10 euros. To be honest I was expecting something a bit more exotic. I tried the goulash but came away disappointed feeling that in no sense had I eaten anything uniquely Slovenian. Perhaps we chose the wrong restaurant. We made no mistake with our choice of where to drink; returning to Halliday's for some serious sampling of the local dark beer.

Ljubljana Castle in background

Marathon Start

CUBA

HAVANA MARATHON

This is one marathon that had been on my bucket list for a long, long time. As a 14 year-old in 1959, I can clearly remember when the news came through that Fidel Castro and his revolutionary forces had succeeded in banishing the corrupt American-backed Batista regime from Cuba and establishing the first Communist outpost close to American soil. I followed developments on the island with interest including the subsequent unsuccessful Bay of Pigs Invasion, allegedly conducted by the CIA, followed by the nuclear stand-off that scared the world to death during the Cuban Missile Crisis. Later, while at University I'd elected to study Cuba's particular brand of communism as a component of my Political Science degree. Like most students at the time my room was decorated with posters of Castro and especially, his side-kick Che Guevara. I even wore one of those trendy Che Guevara T-shirts much favoured by middle class would-be revolutionaries most of whom end up as affluent bankers, accountants and estate agents in later life. In short, the place meant something to me. It was always a country that I wanted to visit. Unfortunately, in those days Cuba was a no-go area for us decadent capitalists in the West. In fact, up until 1997, it was actually illegal for locals to mingle with international tourists. Of late, relationships between Uncle Sam and the Cuban government have much improved and Cuba, in desperate need of the tourist dollar, now welcomes us to its shores.

Cuba is the largest and with over 11 million inhabitants, the most populous of the Caribbean islands – roughly the size of England. It is the most westerly of what is known as the Greater

Antilles group, lying a mere 90 miles, though a world away, from the south of Florida. When Columbus reached there in 1492 declaring it, 'The most beautiful land human eyes have ever seen,' he encountered three indigenous groups – all three of which were wiped out by disease within the next 50 years. In addition to disease subsequent Spanish and French settlers introduced sugarcane and later slaves. Both sugar and Cubans of African descent continue to help define the character of the island with the racial make-up of the country being a mosaic of these three separate waves of inhabitation.

Two wars of independence marked 19th century Cuba. The first, between 1868 and 1878 ended in stalemate. The second ended when the USA was drawn into the conflict in 1898 when Cuba was initially occupied for two years by US forces. After their withdrawal in 1901, the USA maintained effective political control, allowing Cuba to be governed by a series of corrupt dictators culminating in the infamous Fulgencio Batista. The excesses of the Batista regime led to its eventual overthrow in 1959 by Fidel Castro and his revolutionary army and to the establishment of the socialist state that has defined Cuba's position in World politics ever since. Castro expropriated all US businesses resulting in the US severing all diplomatic links between the two countries. Thereafter, Cuba accelerated relations with the Soviet Union and the USA instituted a full economic and financial blockade on the island. These events have effectively frozen the island in time. Vintage American cars seemingly repaired to oblivion, still roll through the deteriorating streets of Havana where beautifully restored colonial buildings sit side-by-side with the rundown tenements of its citizens. Contrary to the general consensus of opinion in the West, not everything about Castro's reign is considered negative. For example, Cuba has the highest literacy rate in the Americas – something like 99.98% as opposed to the 40% prior to the revolution. In addition, Cuba has the highest doctor-to-patient ratio in the world. Since the Revolution the Cuban government has made healthcare a priority and twelve schools produce thousands of doctors each year. This has raised the number of doctors from 0.92 per thousand people in

1958 to 6.72 per thousand today – more than any other country in the world. Also, all medical transactions are free to Cuban citizens, from doctors' visits to medicines and every kind of surgery – even penis enlargement and sex reassignment surgery are free!

In the years since Castro came to power and established a socialist state the relationship between Cuba and the Western World has been plagued by distrust and antagonism. During the half century that followed, successive U.S. administrations pursued policies intended to isolate the island country economically and diplomatically. One of the consequences of US policy was to turn Cuba into an isolated, economic backwater whose citizens existed in near-Third World poverty in what had become a 50s 'time warp.' Though the United States has imposed sanctions against Cuba longer than any other country, things started to change during the Obama administration when Presidents Barack Obama and Raul Castro, who replaced his brother as Cuban leader in 2008, took some extraordinary steps to normalize bilateral relations, meeting with each other, restoring full diplomatic ties, and easing travel restrictions. The thaw in relations continued in the months that followed. The Obama administration eased travel and trade restrictions on Cuba, and removed it from an official list of terrorism sponsors. The two governments also reopened their embassies. In early 2016, President Obama took another significant step down the normalization path, visiting Havana in what was the first trip to Cuba by a sitting U.S. president since 1928. That same week the Rolling Stones made history by becoming the first major international rock band to play in Cuba when more than 100,000 people attended their free concert at a run-down sports complex on the road to the airport. There's an interesting story of how for years, following the revolution, rock music was banned on Cuban state TV and radio. Cubans who wore long hair and beards faced harassment from officials, including Fidel Castro who told them to dress like men. Music by the Beatles was initially banned as being too decadent for socialist tastes. In 2000 Castro changed his mind, declaring John Lennon a working class revolutionary and attended the unveiling of a statue to Lennon in the newly created John

Lennon Park. We watched tourists queue up to have their photos taken next to the statue that is usually missing his iconic spectacles, stolen by souvenir hunters. The park guards keep spare pairs on hand to give everyone the perfect picture.

The visits of Obama and The Stones were taken as signs that Cuba was about to step out of its self-imposed exile and join in with the 'normal' world. Now that the five-decade embargo with the United States is starting to thaw, Americans are beginning to put Cuba on their travel radar again. Initially, they were restricted to family visits and packaged cultural tours but, despite ex-President Trump's best efforts to turn back the clock, it seems only a matter of time before common sense prevails, relations normalise and a wave of curiosity tourism flocks to this unique island. Though it will likely take decades for the inevitable impact of mass tourism to destroy Havana's unique character and charm, this time-warp nation is already showing signs of change. I thought it best to get there before mass tourism of the US-variety changed the place beyond all recognition. How ironic, that after all those years, the great man himself Fidel Castro should choose to die during our stay!

Mo and I flew to Havana with British Airways for a 2-week visit in November 2016. We'd arranged to stay for 7-nights at the centrally-situated Hotel Telegrafo, a short walk from Havana's Capitol building and the start and finish of the marathon. The second week was to be spent at the all-inclusive Breezes Resort located in Varadero, the start of 20-km long sand-spit jutting out into the Atlantic in the north of the island. I figured that if Mo was prepared to accompany me all the way to Cuba for a marathon she at least deserved a bit of luxury during her stay. The whole fortnight cost us around £1,500 each. The second week in Varadero was a big mistake. Despite being forewarned about the decrepit architecture, the 1950s automobiles and the food shortages we'd enjoyed our week in Havana so much that we didn't want to leave. We'd grown accustomed to the decadence and had accepted the fact that there was virtually nothing in any of the shops worth buying, that supermarkets sold little but biscuits and that when ordering staple commodities like chicken or even bread from restaurant menus we'd usually be told that these weren't available. The city had much more interesting compensations. Our hotel was excellent and only a short stroll from Havana's famous Malecon sea promenade and its harbour where we sat and watched the cruise ships arrive as well as to the restaurant area around the two main streets of O'Reilly and Obispo. Varadero, by contrast, was so untypically Cuban that it could have been any other luxury resort on the planet. It was basically a giant Butlin's holiday camp in the sun full of loud-mouthed, obese, largely North American tourists there to take maximum advantage of the all-you-can-eat and, especially, all-you-can-drink facilities. Their concessions to dress rules in the restaurants was to turn up either dripping wet from the swimming pool or to sit with baseball caps turned back-to-front, dirty, crumpled sleeveless vests, shorts and flip flops. Their table manners were atrocious. I'm no snob or stickler for etiquette but their behaviour had us both anxious to leave. Mid-way through our stay Castro's death was announced and the whole country went into nine days of mourning. In most of the country this meant that restaurants, bars were closed and all forms of entertainment were cancelled. It also meant that concerts by Cuban dancers and singers that had been the only highlight of our stay in Varadero no longer took place. Perversely, with Breezes being an international resort catering solely to overseas visitors the drinking was allowed to continue unabated.

Known as the Marabana, Havana's marathon has been held on the third Sunday in November since 1987. The entire weekend is meant as a celebration of sports and coincides with The National Day of Physical Culture and Sports in Cuba. These days it's possible to enter in advance via the race's official website with entry fees of 50 euros until the end of July, 60 euros until the end of October and 75 euros from then until 5 days before the race. Curiously, the same fee is charged for all three races: Marathon, Half Marathon and 10k. In 2015 only 380 out of 3,365 finishers from 64 countries took part in the marathon. There is an overall limit of 5,000 participants for all three events. For many years all entrants were required to collect their numbers in person from inside the Kid Chocolate building in front of the city's Capitol – the huge white building on the main Paseo de Prado. Anyone who has visited Washington D.C. will do a double take when they first see the beautiful El Capitolio (the Capital) due to its likeness to the American building of the same name. It was the seat of government in Cuba until after the 1959 Revolution and is now home to the Cuban Academy of Sciences. The Paseo del Prado on which it sits is considered by many to be the most beautiful street in Havana. The terrace with its marble benches, bronze lions and iron lampposts impart the feel of a grand boulevard from a bygone era and was once the home to some of Havana's wealthiest families. Elegant old cinemas, mansions and hotels from the 19th and 20th centuries line the street – many of which have been fully restored.

In 2016 for some reason, registration close to the Capitol was only available to local entrants, foreign entrants were compelled to make the 7 kilometre trip to the out-of-town Melia Hotel. Rather than take a taxi, on the Friday before the race Mo and I enjoyed a pleasant stroll along the Malecon to the sea-front hotel unaware of the nightmare we had to face. Registration was being held in one of the smallest rooms the organisers could have chosen and the place was already full to overflowing with entrants for all three events. There were no orderly queues and no signage to indicate where the numbers for the different races were being issued. Consequently, some runners had queued for ages at one side of the single desk only to be told that registration for their particular race was at the other end of the room. There was pushing, shoving, shouting, fighting and tears on a scale I've never encountered at any previous marathon. At one stage I almost packed the whole thing in (and probably would have too, if it hadn't been for the fact that I'd have to repeat the process the following day). After an hour and a half I finally got to the front of the desk only to find that the guy next to me was there to collect a whole list of race numbers for those in some tour group. As only a single overworked individual issued the marathon numbers it took me another half an hour before finally being served. Mo, meanwhile, thinking that she'd missed me leaving due to the crowds, was outside searching along the Malecon for me. The whole thing, as well as being a total disgrace, was also deeply insulting to all the overseas athletes who'd paid so much and travelled so far for the event. The simple fact is – it all could have been avoided with a modicum of planning and forethought. Hours later I'd calmed down sufficiently to laugh at section 19 of the official regulations reading, 'All the runners are required to wear appropriate clothing to run, without phrases of profanity, offensiveness or inappropriateness for a sporting event.' So leave that mankini at home for this one!

All three races start simultaneously at 7am in front of the same Capitol building with a 5-hour time limit imposed on marathon runners. The event has a warm, friendly pre-race vibe with a colourful opening ceremony, a choir, an Afro-Cuban tribal dance, plus lots of music and dancing in the warm-up activities. Despite the early morning start, the temperature was already close to 20 degrees and humidity levels were high. It was going to be a difficult run in these conditions. The half marathon-distance course is a huge, anti-clockwise loop around the city. Marathon runners have to do this twice. The route heads down towards the Malecon seafront boulevard initially reaching the port after about one mile. It follows the Malecon along the waterfront for a further three miles with runners often getting drenched with spray from the breaking waves. This was my favourite part of the course. The first few miles along the coast is flat, after that you turn inland on more undulating terrain. The route then goes through a number of the city's neighbourhoods and past historical sites such as the National Sports Stadium and Revolution Square before returning to the Old Town via the Malecon and the finish of the half marathon outside the Capitol.

Towards the latter part of the first lap I felt a sudden pain in the groin area that forced me to stop. Every time I attempted to re-start running the pain got worse. Examination of the area showed a large protruding lump. I'd developed a hernia! The question now was whether to continue or to pull-out of the race. On reaching the half-way point Mo was waiting with a worried look on her face. I'd taken over 15 minutes longer than my usual half marathon time so she knew that something must be wrong. I hadn't the heart to tell her, knowing that not only would she be upset, she'd also quite sensibly force me to pull out. That was out of the question. I hadn't travelled all this way for nothing and who knew if I'd ever get the chance to return. The second lap was a slow painful affair during which I limped my way around in almost three hours. My finishing time of 5:23 was well outside the 5-hour deadline but I was still nowhere near the last to finish. I can only think that the organisers took pity on those of us who struggled in the high humidity and temperatures that had reached 30 degrees by midday. Almost everyone I've spoken to who has run the Marabana has spoken in warm terms of their experience. Most accept its faults as something to be expected in a country that has been isolated from mainstream tourism for decades and are happy to file these in the 'different and quirky' category. My abiding memory on finishing (pain aside) was of the scores of young and not-so-young Cubans queuing up to ask us for our trainers. Actually, this happened on a number of occasions throughout our stay. All manner of individuals would approach, strike up what initially appeared to be nothing more than a friendly conversation and then, before departing, would ask if it was possible to have the trainers I had on my feet. Quite how they expected me to return to the hotel shoe-less didn't seem to come into the equation.

    The character and atmosphere in Havana make it a tourist attraction without parallel. Despite being a victim of the economic meltdown that followed the Revolution, the city retains an energy and vitality hard to find in its more prosperous counterparts. 'Anything is possible in Havana,' wrote Graham Green and today, the fascinating sights in Cuba's capital captivate travellers at every turn. It's a city made for strolling around, taking in the salsa sounds and rumba beats while visiting the restaurants in which Hemmingway once dined or inhaling the salty air of the famous Malecon. Old Havana is a UNESCO world heritage site, oozing the charm of days gone by. Highlights worth visiting among its cobbled streets and squares include: the Catedral de San Cristoba a celebration of the Cuban Baroque style; the ancient Castillo de la Real Fuerza - an impressive military fortress and the squares of Plaza Vieja and Plaza de Armas. Strolling along Havana's famous sea front boulevard the Malecon with the locals at sunset is definitely one of the best ways to soak up the city's atmosphere. The boulevard is overlooked by a colourful collection of well-preserved 20th century buildings in a mix of architectural styles. Among them the historic Hotel Nacional de Cuba, a World Heritage Site and National Monument with a long history of glamorous former guests, including Frank Sinatra, Marlene Dietrich and Marlon Brando.

The day following the marathon had been set aside for sightseeing. By this stage the hernia was giving so much pain that it was difficult to walk. The solution was to take the Havana Hop-on, Hop-off Bus Tour, one of the best ways of getting to see all the sights in relative comfort. At only 10 CUC it's excellent value for money. A word here about the Cuban currency. Cuba's dual-currency system seems to cause a great deal of confusion with some travellers. The official currency that locals use is the Cuban Peso (CUP), however Cuban Convertible Peso (CUC) is the new 'tourist' currency that most foreign visitors use. (£1 currently buys 33 CUC). Money should only be changed at a bank or official Cadeca Casa de Cambio (exchange bureau), but there are plenty of people offering to exchange with you on the streets. Be careful, as some try to rip you off. Even shop keepers are notorious for short-changing transactions, taking advantage of tourist confusion and switching CUP for CUC. We joined the bus directly opposite our hotel and rode on the sunny top deck all the way to the coast at Playas Del Este Beach. Without disembarking, it's almost a 2-hour trip. Our route covered a fair proportion of the marathon course by taking us all the way along the Malecon, through the Plaza de la Revolution, the impressive Colon Cemetery, Parque Almendares, Miramar Trade Centre, the Capitol and Grand Theatre as well as to the beach. Though there was a guide on board giving information in English the noise from the traffic often droned out what was being said. Another point worth noting is that the bus cannot enter the

'Old Havana' part of town due to traffic restrictions but this area can easily be visited on foot. I'd highly recommend it as a cheap and affordable alternative to private taxis with a day-long ticket costing the same as a single fare allowing you to spend as much or as little time exploring on foot as you're comfortable with. We rode the bus for several hours, getting to take in all the major attractions.

While in Havana it's worth becoming acquainted with Cuba's recent troubled history by visiting both the Museum of the Revolution and the Jose Marti Memorial in Revolution Square. Housed in a former presidential palace, the Museum contains a multitude of displays on Cuba's struggle for independence. These include life-size wax figures of Che Guevara and Camilio Cienfuengos as well as the yacht 'Granma' that brought Castro and his group to Cuba from Mexico. Also on display is a plane shot down during the unsuccessful Bay of Pigs invasion. The Plaza de la Revolucion, formerly the Plaza Civica, deserves a brief stop due to its historical significance. More than a million people have gathered here for Castro's speeches while in 1998, during a visit to Cuba, Pope John Paul 11 celebrated mass in the square.

Also worth visiting are the sources behind the twin icons of the Cuban economy: cigars and rum. The cigar is one of Cuba's most enduring images and even a non-smoker like myself was interested in seeing how the product is made. (It's a little known fact that hours before the USA's trading ban went into effect President Kennedy bought 1,200 Cuban cigars). Tours can be easily booked to visit a local cigar factory to watch workers rolling tobacco by hand. This tour can be arranged with a continuation to a nearby rum factory to observe how Cuba's other staple product is produced. One of my favourite tipples, Bacardi Rum was founded in Cuba in 1862, but the family-run company ended up getting exiled after the Revolution. Luckily they had already built plants in Mexico and Puerto Rica. Though you won't find any Bacardi in Cuba these days, all your rum needs are catered for by the Havana Club brand. This tour was more to my taste – particularly the sampling of the different brands that comes at the end of the visit.

We thoroughly enjoyed out time in Havana (if not in Varadero) and would return to the city at the drop of a hat. It will be interesting to see how relationships with the US develop now that Trump has gone. Hopefully, Cuba will get that influx of American tourists after all. And, who knows, the marathon organisers might even work out a system of issuing race numbers that doesn't involve wholesale chaos and fisticuffs. I won't be holding my breath!

One Hour before the start of the Havana Marathon

Havana's seafront: the famous Malecon

UNITED ARAB EMIRATES

DUBAI MARATHON

I visited Dubai in the summer of 2014, stopping over for two nights on the way to Australia. At the time I described it as soulless, characterless and artificial. I remember writing in my book 'Marathon Tourism' that, 'The whole place seemed like a nightmare vision of a futuristic hell on earth: of cities judged on how tall they can build their skyscrapers and how fast, straight and congested they can get their motorways.' The fact that we were there in August with temperatures of 42 degrees didn't help. Dubai was like a ghost town with barely a soul on the streets. Who can blame them in that sort of heat! Everyone appeared to be living an air-conditioned existence – scurrying from air-conditioned homes to air-conditioned cars before driving to air-conditioned offices and air-conditioned shopping malls. So what's changed? Why would I want to go back? The answer is simple – it has a marathon. Not only that. It's the only marathon that I can easily get to in a part of the world in which I'd yet to run via direct flights from Newcastle. Even better, it's where the sun still shines in January - but with an intensity that not only makes life pleasant but does away with the reliance on air-conditioning.

Dubai, the most populous city of the United Arab Emirates is considered by many as a brash, modern city known for its luxury shopping, ultramodern architecture and lively nightlife. It is located in the Persian Gulf and is one of seven Emirates that make up the UAE. There are a number of theories about the origin of its name. I prefer the one that links it to a word meaning 'money.' It somehow seems appropriate. People from Dubai were said to be rich due to its position as a thriving trade centre. An Arabic proverb reads, 'Dada Dubai' meaning 'They came with a lot of money.' The impact of the discovery of oil in 1966 accelerated the city's phenomenal growth though, contrary to popular opinion, its supplies are low and oil revenue today is less than 5% of GDP. Today its main revenues come from tourism, aviation, real estate and financial services. In recent times it has become synonymous with its many large-scale construction projects as well as its sporting events. It has also attracted negative attention recently for human rights violations concerning the living conditions of the city's largely South Asian workforce. This problem emphasises the contrast between the super-rich and the super-poor in Dubai. The local born Emiratis who make up about 12% of the population are among the former while a huge working class population predominantly from the Indian sub-continent make up the latter. Sitting somewhere in between the two groups is a growing band of expats, mostly from the West, who continue to profit from the city's equivalent of the Gold Rush.

The Dubai Marathon has been held in January each year since 2000. In 2007 it was declared as the world's richest long distance running event, with one million US dollars on offer for a world record and $250,000 for first place for both men and women. Unsurprisingly, such generous prize-money has attracted some of the world's greatest marathon runners. Haile Gebrselassie and Kenenisa Bekele are among those who've tried and failed to set a world record on the course. Of the two, Gebrselassie came the closest with a time of 2:04:53 in 2008, the second fastest in the world at the time. Bekele had an injury and struggled to finish. Four years later in 2012 a record of four athletes ran under two hours and five minutes in the men's race. On that same occasion the top three female runners came in under two hours twenty minutes for the first time in history. Though prize-money for the top ten athletes now ranges from a 'mere' $200,000 to $8,000 and the world record incentive has dropped to only $100,000 there are many who believe that the event is still too much of an elitist race with the needs of average runners being neglected by the organisers.

I went back to Dubai in January 2017 with running friend Ivan Field. Unfortunately, I was suffering from the hernia mentioned in the previous chapter at the time and waiting, very impatiently, for corrective surgery. As flights, accommodation and entry fees had already been paid well in advance, I travelled largely to keep Ivan company – never thinking that I'd a snowball's chance in Hell of taking part in the race. We flew from Newcastle with Emirates for a 3-night stay at the Holiday Inn Express in Dubai's Internet City area, directly opposite the internationally famous Palm Jumeirah resort. Travelbag's flights and accommodation package with bed and breakfast cost a very reasonable £442 each. We'd deliberately chosen the Holiday Inn due to its relative proximity to the event's starting area. Unfortunately, long queues at passport control on arrival in Dubai meant that our taxi didn't reach our hotel until well into the middle of the first night. Not a good start.

It was up bright and early the next morning for yet another taxi to Registration in the Turf Suite at the city's Meydan racecourse. Home to the Dubai World Cup Carnival, Meydan is an extremely futuristic-looking racecourse that has even been used as a Star Trek filming location. It has the distinction of having the longest grandstand in the world, and can accommodate 60,000 spectators. The whole stadium simply radiated opulence and luxury. It's certainly the most impressive location I've visited to collect a race number.

With our numbers in our bags along with the event T-shirt, Ivan and I now had the afternoon free for a spot of sightseeing. Dubai is famous for its skyscrapers and I guess while you're in Dubai for the marathon you might as well go and visit the most famous one of all. Travelling by the Dubai Metro, we took the Red Line to Burj Khalifa Station. From there you can take the F13 bus and get off at the next stop, which is the Dubai Mall Bus Stop. (There are two lines that run through the metro in Dubai: the Red Line and the Green Line. The Red Line runs from Al Rashidiya metro station to UAE Exchange metro station and vice-versa, whilst the Green

Line runs from Etisalat to Creek and vice-versa). Soaring above the city like a giant needle-shaped spacecraft is the 830 metre high Burj Khalifa, the tallest building, on the planet. This 167-storey skyscraper is one of the wonders of modern technology. The opportunity to view the city from the observation deck on the 134th floor is an opportunity not to be missed, particularly at night with buildings lit up beneath you. The entry fee for visits to the higher floors of the Burj Khalifa is around AED533 per person. (£1 = 5.20 UAE Dirham). Tickets bought online in advance offer a considerable savings over the instant access tickets on the door.

I'm not normally a big fan of indoor (or outdoor) shopping malls but the Dubai Mall is also something else. The shopping and eating aspects are virtually a side attraction. The mall is simply huge and features a 22-screen cinema, an outdoor theme park, a world for children called Kidzania, a giant Aquarium with an underwater zoo and a full-sized ice rink. The mall even offers an opportunity to ski in the desert, boasting a ski run of 1,300 feet. You can rent all the ski gear you need but it is expensive. Outside the mall is the famous Dubai Fountain, built to rival that at the Bellagio in Las Vegas. Shows on site start at 6pm each evening.

Nearby and not to be missed is the sail-shaped Burj Al Arab hotel located on the coast close to the start and finish of the race. Often described as 'the world's only 7-star hotel' (not true, that's the certified seven-star Town House Galleria in Milan) it stands on an artificial island offshore from Jumeirah beach. The shape of the structure is meant to mimic the sail of a ship. While it is reputed to be the third tallest hotel in the world, almost 40% of it is non-occupiable space. Since its construction several well-publicised events have taken place on its rooftop helipad, all designed to attract media attention - Andre Agassi and Roger Federer playing tennis, Tiger Woods teeing off and David Coulthard driving in circles in a Formula 1 race car. Whatever next!

It was up early again the next morning (Friday) for our pre-booked taxi to the 6.30am start of the marathon on Umm Suqem Road opposite the Madinat Jumeirah opposite the Burj Al Arab. Taxi is about the only way to arrive at the start unless you're prepared to walk (and that I wouldn't recommend – those streets aren't made for walking!) The early morning ride in the dark turned out quite surreal. In an obvious attempt to scam us for more money, our driver headed-off in the opposite direction to where we needed to go. Fortunately, we knew the route and politely but firmly pointed out that we weren't there for the fleecing. Eventually he 'found' the correct drop-off point on the Al Wasi Road from where it was only a short walk to the starting pens. While waiting to go into the pens it was possible to watch the elite athletes going through their warm-up routines on the other side of the barriers. Prominent among these was multiple global champion and world record holder Kenenisa Bekele, rumoured to be making another attempt on the marathon world record during the race. At this stage I still had no intention of attempting to run the marathon distance. However, since arrival in Dubai I'd seen that the first 5 kilometres of the race passed immediately in front of our hotel before turning and heading-off in the opposite direction. Having travelled so far, the least I could do was to see if I could manage this section of the course. I could always just stop at the hotel if the hernia became painful. If not, I had 7 hours in which to limp around the course.

With that in mind I joined the other 24,000 runners on the start line for the 6.30am start. The event also included a 10k race with 14,500 runners starting at 9am and a 4k Fun Run containing 7,300 participants that started at 11am. Altogether, 149 nationalities were said to have contested the three events. The marathon itself is classed as an IAAF Gold Label event – the only one of its kind in the Middle East. Online entry only was advertised initially for all three events, though I understand that entries were still being taken at Registration. Marathon entry cost USD$120.

Both the marathon and 10k began in the shadow of the iconic Burj Al Arab building close to the ocean. It's hard to imagine a flatter or straighter marathon course exists. The whole course is designed solely to produce fast times, especially for the elite runners. With temperatures between 10 to 15 degrees at the start, water stations are placed every 2.5 kilometres with sponge stations in between and isotonic drinks at 5 kilometre intervals after the first 10km. Basically the route follows the Al Sufouh Road along to the turn at Palm Island at 5km before heading back on the same road to the famous Jumeirah Beach Road, running past the Burj Al Arab at 12km. It then continues arrow-straight along this road to another turn at 26km before running back past the Grand Mosque to the Burj Al Arab again at 41k. A left turn here leads towards the finish just before the Dubai Police Academy. Simple and uncomplicated but it still attracts criticism. Many runners find the course monotonous and boring, bemoaning the lack of spectator support and the absence of landmarks other than the aforementioned Burj Al Arab. Though I'm inclined to agree with this point of view, I'm still glad that I took part. I'm even more delighted that I finished. There's something to be said about having no expectations and no real pressure to finish in a 'respectable' time. There was something surreal about plodding along the deserted streets of Dubai as dawn was breaking between the skyscrapers. The first 5 kilometres went well – albeit at a jog/walk pace – with no temptation to step off the course when passing our hotel. To my surprise (and relief) I managed to keep this going the whole distance, while elite athletes hurtled past going in the opposite direction along the seemingly endless out-and-back stretch on Jumeirah Beach Road. Ivan had also passed in the opposite direction, shouting encouragement and promising to be waiting at the finish.

I got back in 05:12:21 – dreadful under normal conditions but perhaps the most satisfying time I've recorded given the circumstances. At least, unlike Kenenisa Bekele, I managed to finish. His much heralded world record attempt suffered an early blow after he fell at the start. After being held up in the pack while the leaders accelerated away at world record pace, Bekele never got back on terms and the injuries sustained in the fall caused him to drop out just after halfway. It's the second time that Bekele has dropped out of the Dubai Marathon, having suffered a hamstring injury two years previously. 'I was at least in the same shape as in Berlin and ready for something special today, said Bekele, 'but after a hard fall just after the start, my body was out of balance and I got cramps in my left calf trying to run at world record pace. I like to prepare for many scenarios, but this was definitely not one of them!' Tamirat Tola of Ethiopia broke the course record, clocking 2:04:11, while compatriot Worknesh Degefa made it a sixth consecutive Ethiopian double by winning the women's race in 2:22:36.

Having heard all sorts of stories in the media about the difficulties in both getting to and getting away from this event, Ivan and I were safely in a taxi and heading back to the hotel within minutes of me finishing. After a quick shower and a refuelling visit to the nearby London Fish and Chip shop, it was time for a final sightseeing session. Internet City is one of the many stops of the Dubai Tram, a 14.6km-long route that runs in a loop that mainly follows the Al Sufouh Road, linking Madinat Jumeirah and the Mall of the Emirates with Dubai Marina and the Jumeirah Beach Residence. We took this to visit the two artificial islands of Palm Jumeirah and Palm Jebel Ali. Both take the forms of a palm tree and contain a large number of residential properties aimed at the very rich and famous (David Beckham and Michael Owen have bought here) plus leisure and entertainment centres. Together they add a total of 520 kilometres of non-public beaches to the city of Dubai. Their residential addresses are considered a status symbol in this wealth-obsessed city. We wanted to visit Atlantis, a famous luxury hotel resort located at the apex of the Palm Jumeirah. This hotel's pink, palatial structure towers over its neighbours, with soaring turrets and a distinctive Arabian archway. It's the epitome of Dubai: big, brassy and bold with over 1,500 rooms and suites. To get there it's necessary to take the Gateway Monorail situated a 5 minute walk from the Palm Jumeirah Tram stop. It's quite a spectacular ride passing over the palm-shaped islands as they spread out on either side of the monorail. The nicest part of Atlantis is the sea views from the promenade facing away from the place!

From there we took the tram further up the coast to Dubai Marina, yet another of the entirely man-made developments designed to attract the big spenders to the area. The Marina is a skyscraper-packed artificial canal city carved along the Gulf shoreline south of The Palm Island. At its heart is a 3-kilometre waterway framed by residential blocks, hotels, shops, restaurants, and entertainment venues. When fully complete the complex will accommodate more than 120,000 people in residential towers and villas. Anyone who's ever been to Vancouver will recognise the similarities with the Concord Pacific Place development there. (It's where you go to pick your numbers up for the Vancouver Marathon). Ivan and I enjoyed a leisurely stroll around its perimeter before settling down to two of the biggest and cheapest pizzas on offer in one of the plush waterside bars.

If like me you quickly tire of all these artificial, moneyed creations and want to see at least one thing natural during your visit to Dubai I suggest you spend some time at Dubai Creek. The creek is the original, bustling heart of the city and the site of the oldest settlement in the city. Here you can see Dubai as it once was. During our stay in 2014, Mo and I spent virtually a whole day criss-crossing the creek on the abras (water taxis) watching dhows being loaded and made ready to sail, visiting mosques and souks as well as simply strolling along the waterfront admiring the coffeehouses, handicraft shops and barasti (palm-frond) huts. It was the most enjoyable experience of the whole trip.

As you've probably guessed I consider some of the 'attractions' to be found in Dubai bordering on the bizarre. One of the good things about being a discerning marathon globetrotter is that you can look beyond the obvious - the things that people want you to see - and look for some of the less publicised but more interesting aspects about where you're visiting. For example, one of the things the guide books don't tell you about the Burj Khalifa is that the height of the half-mile tower means that Muslims who live in the upper floors have to wait longer to break their fasting during Ramadan because they can see the sun for longer than those on the ground. Muslim clerics advise residents above the 80th floor to wait an extra two minutes and those above the 150th floor to wait for three minutes before breaking their fast during the holy month.

Other interesting stories concern the plans afoot to construct the world's first multi-room underwater hotel, the Hydropolis. The lower levels of the huge jellyfish-shaped hotel will contain suites situated 20 metres under the Persian Gulf. Many luxury amenities such as a grand ballroom, cinema, bars and beauty spas are also planned for the development. Also in the pipeline are plans to outdo Disney with the city's own Dubailand, expected to open in 2020 the year Dubai hosts the World Expo. (Originally scheduled from October 2020 to April 2021 but postponed due to the COVID-19 pandemic. The new dates are October 2021 to March 2022. Despite being postponed, organizers intend to keep the name Expo 2020 for marketing and branding purposes. It is the first time that a World Exposition has been postponed to a later date rather than cancelled). Dubailand is intended to be twice the size of Walt Disney World Resort, housing multiple theme parks, retail and entertainment outlets, hotels and sporting attractions. You've got to admit, the place does think big. Unsurprisingly, during the pre-2008 property boom Dubai was dubbed the crane capital of the world. The skyline was littered with towering cranes as construction projects progressed throughout the city. At one stage over 30,000 of the world's 125,000 cranes were at work in Dubai.

While finishing on the subject of biggest is best, I'm told that the city's police force employ a fleet of top of the range vehicles in pursuit of speeding lawbreakers. McLarens, Lamborghinis, Aston Martins, Bentleys and Ferraris painted in the city's white and green patrol some of Dubai's highways. And, it's just so typical of the place that there are actually gold dispensing machines operable in Dubai. These 'Gold to Go' machines dispense gold items such as bars, jewellery and customised coins in exchange for market value prices. The machines have an internet connection and their prices are updated every ten minutes. Some of the items are dispensed in gift boxes with a certificate and an anti-counterfeit hologram label. You couldn't make it up!

Registration at the Meydan Racecourse

The Burj Al Arab (close to the Start line)

FAROE ISLANDS

TORSHAVN MARATHON

The Torshavn Marathon takes place annually in June in the beautiful and stunning scenery surrounding Torshavn, one of the smallest capitals in the world. I'm not entirely sure when the event was first held as the event website only shows results from the past three years (2016, 2017 and 2018) but also features photos from 2015. A true story: on telling a fellow runner that I was travelling to the Faroes to run this race in 2017 his immediate reply was, 'You wouldn't catch me going there, there's too many terrorists in Egypt these days.' I kid you not, I just hope he doesn't get to read this book! The Faroe Islands, in fact, are much closer to the UK than my geographically-challenged friend suspects. This self-governing archipelago, part of the Kingdom of Denmark, comprises 18 rocky, volcanic islands in the middle of the North Atlantic Ocean, northwest of Scotland and halfway between Iceland and Norway. These days, most of the islands are connected by road tunnels, ferries, causeways and bridges.

I first heard of this event from fellow guests in our hotel while in Reykjavik for the marathon there in 2015. These were a couple of Faroese nationals who'd recently run a half marathon over part of the course taken by the full distance race. Both were good ambassadors for their country, proud of the fact that it now had its own marathon and anxious to welcome overseas visitors.

At that time the Faroes could only be reached from the UK via indirect flights via Denmark or Iceland making travel difficult, though not impossible. Shortly afterwards Atlantic Airways began flying directly to the Faroes from Edinburgh. I was determined to go

– even more so when friends Sam Kimmins and Roger Barrett encouraged me to accompany them in 2017. First, though, I had to recover from my long-awaited hernia operation that had kept me from any worthwhile exercise for the past six months. Despite the gap of less than the required month's convalescence between surgery and marathon day I decided to chance it. We flew from Edinburgh on the Thursday returning on Sunday for a 3-night stay in Torshavn. Return tickets cost me 1952 Danish Krone (£231 at the rate £1 = DKK 8.44). Sam and Roger, who'd booked their flights much earlier than me, paid considerably less. We weren't the only runners on the flight. I was pleased to see friends Dave and Linda Major among the passengers as well as a smattering of other marathoners from various parts of the UK. The 1 hour 25 minutes flight was all going smoothly until our approach to Vagoy Island on which the Faroes' airport is situated. Dense fog down to ground level meant that we were unable to land. We circled round and round in a total black-out, burning fuel and praying that the fog would lift. Bets were soon being taken on whether we'd be diverted to Iceland or back to Scotland when, finally, the pilot announced that he'd got one last chance of getting through the fog. He did, but I couldn't help thinking that if these were the conditions in early June, how on earth did any planes manage to fly there in the winter months.

    Local bus service 300 connecting the towns of Torshavn and Sorvagur stops at the airport around seven times each day. Anyone unlucky enough to have a long wait for the bus will need to find a taxi. Vagoy Island connects to the main island of Streymoy in which Torshavn is situated via a recently constructed lengthy, undersea tunnel. (Though with the fog persisting, the whole journey was like being in a tunnel). The bus takes about one hour. Though my friends had booked budget out-of-town accommodation I preferred being close to the city centre and stayed for three nights at the Hotel Torshavn next to the harbour and, more importantly, very close to the start and finish of the race. The room cost DKK 899 (£106) per night with a good breakfast. Pricey, I know, but that's the going rate in these places. I had no complaints. Lots of other runners were also booked here, including Dave and Linda, so there was always someone around to chat to.

The Faroe Islands is a fascinating country. The Islands were first colonized by Norwegians Vikings in the 9th century. The Viking settlers established their own parliament with local courts in different areas of the islands and the main court on Tinganes in Torshavn. Around the year 1000, Christianity came to the Islands and shortly after this they came under the control of the Norwegian kings. Much later the Norwegian crown came under the Danish monarchy, and with the Reformation, the Danish king took control of the islands by establishing the Royal Trade Monopoly. The islands were then governed directly from Copenhagen. The Faroese population has largely descended from these settlers with recent DNA analyses revealing that Y chromosomes, tracing male descent, are 87% Scandinavian. By contrast, the DNA studies tracing female descent show that this is 84% Scottish. Make of that what you will!

Although the Islands are a self-governing island territory of Denmark, they politically aim for higher independence. Faroese, the national language, is rooted in Old Norse and the Faroese government prints its own currency, the krona - although Danish coins are used. The exchange value is equivalent to the Danish krone, and Danish notes are equally acceptable as the Faroese krona throughout the country. The Faroes have a population of nearly 50,000, and a language and culture of their own. For generations the locals lived off the land and the animals that are on the islands as not much grows in the severe climate. Today the islands have one of the smallest independent economic entities in the world. The fishing industry accounts for over 80% of the total export value of goods, which are mainly processed fish products and fish farming. Tourism is the second largest industry, followed by woollen and other manufactured products.

When visiting the Islands you are never more than 3 miles away from the ocean. The countryside is dominated by steep mountains and there are about 70,000 sheep and some 2 million pairs of seabirds, including the largest colony of storm petrels in the world. The Islands are undeniably beautiful: green, rugged and wind-swept. First impressions are very similar to what you experience by visiting the remoter sections of the West Coast of Scotland and its Outer Isles. The Faroese tourist season is very short. It begins in May and ends by September when the Islands are at their best. Hikers and bird-watchers in particular are attracted to the island's mountains, valleys and grassy heathland, and steep coastal cliffs that are home to thousands of seabirds. It's worth pointing out that, in a recent survey of 111 island communities throughout the world conducted by National Geographic magazine, the Faroe Islands came out on top as the most appealing destination in the world. The Faroes received top marks for its preservation of nature, historic architecture and national pride from a panel of 522 experts in sustainable tourism, rating ahead of such exotic islands such as Bermuda and Hawaii in the process.

Torshavn, the largest town on the Faroes with a population of only 20,000, is one of the world's smallest capitals. Named after the Nordic god Thor, it's known for its old town, Tinganes, crammed with wooden turf-roofed houses on a small peninsula. Nearby is Torshavn Cathedral, rebuilt in the 19th century. I was pleasantly surprised by the place and found it a quiet, peaceful town, certainly not lacking in the usual amenities along the main shopping strip of Niels Finsens gota. The harbour area was a particularly relaxing place for a stroll or to sit in one of the pavement cafes and admire the yachts and small boats bobbing on the Atlantic swell. Nearby, you can also observe the loading-and-unloading of the giant containerships which supply the Faroes or watch the ferries come and go to the other islands in the group.

Entry levels for the Torshavn Marathon have remained fairly constant for the three years for which results have been published. It's a small, low-key event with 131 finishers in 2016, 134 in 2017 in 146 in 2018. It's held simultaneously with a half marathon run and a half marathon walk for which separate results are given. This can be a bit confusing as some of the walkers end up finishing much faster than the slower runners. It seems 358 finished both half marathons in 2016, 304 in 2017 and 349 in 2018. I notice that for the 2019 edition, two shorter distance races have been added to the programme. Online entry for the 2017 edition of the marathon cost me DKK 550 (about £65). Numbers were collected at the Faroes' largest shopping complex, the SMS Shopping Centre, Torshavn between 10am and 6pm on the Friday before the Saturday's race. The shopping centre is not difficult to find (nothing's difficult to find in Torshavn) just head north away from the harbour and you're there. Disappointingly, there was no event T-shirt, just a number and separate chip. Remember to hand this in when you finish!

Both the full and half marathons start in the centre of Torshavn at 1pm on the first Saturday in June each year. There's an excellent video of the marathon course on the event website – so you know exactly what you're in for. It looks tough, and it is. But, it's also beautiful and filled with dramatic scenery. Just the sort of course I like. After the rain and fog of the previous two days we started in crisp sun of around 10 degrees which felt colder due to a strong wind blowing from the sea. Basically, the course can be summed up as a city loop of around 8 kilometres followed by an out-and-back section of 34km that hugged the shoreline on either side of the beautiful Kaldbak fjord via 'settlements' (settlements! – there was hardly anyone there) at Hoyvik, Hvitanos and Sund. This is the hilliest and literally most breathtaking part of the route. On reaching the village of Kalbak on the opposite shore the route returned directly to the city centre finish.

The race has a particularly welcoming feel to it in the first few kilometres as runners pass through Torshavn to the cheers of support from locals. This all stops once the town loop is completed. From thereon-in totally disinterested sheep are the only living creatures other than fellow runners. This was definitely the best part of the race. The roads were closed to traffic making it feel so quiet and relaxing. After passing Hoyvik, it was nothing but mountains and rushing waterfalls to the left and ocean to the right. This section took us running down some pretty steep hills for many kilometres. We understood, of course, that this meant running up those same hills on the way back. Something I wasn't looking forward to given that the wind that was now on our backs would be in our faces on the return. At 18km we came to the head of the fjord and turned right off the main road for a short 5.5k out and back to the village of Kaldbak. At the bottom of the fjord, the mountain Sornfelli rises into the sky like a giant shield. Kaldbak itself is a small, isolated village of around 230 inhabitants. Though it was a nice, sunny day with views to die for over the offshore island of Nolsoy, I couldn't help wondering how it must be living there once the winter set in. We turned at around the 23km mark (an honour system turnaround with no timing mat) to be greeted by an aid station loaded with a plentiful supply of very filling cakes and pastries – just what was needed for the mostly uphill journey back. Despite a recent background of very little training, I was still running well at this stage but knew I'd struggle to maintain the same pace – the return leg was as tough as the outward leg had been relatively 'easy.' It wasn't until reaching the outskirts of Torshavn that we could finally relax on the final downhill section to the finish.

I finished in 4:53; nothing to write home about I know but on a hilly course and after over six months of virtually no running, I had to be pleased. There was no Vet 70 category, not even a Vet 60 – the Vets' categories stopped at 50+. Just to put my time into perspective I checked the results for the following year when a Vet 60 category was introduced. There were 9 finishers in this age group that year with the winner's time being 5:15. One of the more memorable features of the event was the post-race refreshment area to which we all adjourned. The hospitality here was as good as I've encountered anywhere else in the world. The friendly locals dished up as much as you could eat and drink in the way of sandwiches, cake soup and beer. The hot, thick and extremely nourishing fish soup has become a tradition of the event. The guy who made it seemed impressed by the fact that someone in his 70s (his own age) could complete such a marathon and insisted on continually topping up my empty soup bowl. I enjoyed listening to his account of how it was made and he even offered to take me out on his boat with him the next day to see where he caught the fish. I would have gone, too, if flight times had allowed.

As I said earlier, most visitors come to the Faroes to hike or to bird-watch. The latter doesn't appeal and, while I enjoy hiking, it's not the perfect activity immediately prior to any marathon. Sam, Roger and I decided instead on seeing more of the islands. The best way to do this is my local bus. There's connections to most of the islands from Torshavn and fares are relatively cheap. We spent the one free day of our stay on the 400 bus to Klaksvik, the second city in the Faroes, about a one and a half hour's drive from the capital. The town is located on Borooy, which is one of the northernmost islands in the chain. The opening of the Leirvík sub-sea tunnel in 2006 provided Klaksvík with a physical link with the mainland of the Faroe Islands, leading to its development as one of its key ports. It now boasts an important harbour with fishing industry and a modern fishing fleet and I'm told, occasionally plays host to passing cruise ships. The Foroya Bjor brewery in Klaksvík is a Faroese family brewery, founded in 1888 and is now the only surviving producer of beer and soft drinks in the Faroe Islands. Of course, we had to try a pint or two. While Klaksvik is an interesting place to visit, the undoubted highlight of the trip was the journey there and back. The mixture of spectacular, untamed scenery and wild seascapes was simply incredible.

Our evenings were divided between the Cafe Natur with its Faroese beers and an Irish-themed pub, simply called The Irish Pub. Of the two this was our preferred destination, mainly due to the size and quality of its evening meals – real marathon runner's grub! On the Saturday night after the race the pub was full to bursting, not only with thirsty marathon runners, but with some well-oiled locals enjoying the Real Madrid v Juventus Champions League Final. It almost looked as if things were going to turn nasty as the night went on and some got the worse for wear but, in the end, the troublemakers were evicted leaving Dave, Linda and I celebrating until close to dawn. (Remember, there's no night in June in these latitudes). An early morning walk around the old town admiring the colourful turf-roofed houses in incessant drizzle soon cured our hangovers. It had been an excellent weekend at a welcoming, well-organised event. If you can, make sure you put this one on your bucket list.

With Sam and Roger at the start of the Torshavn Marathon

The scenery was nothing short of spectacular all the way around

BELARUS

INTERNATIONAL FRIENDSHIP MARATHON

This is a unique and interesting cross-border marathon that has taken place annually for the past six years between the cities of Grodno in Belarus and Druskininkai in Lithuania. The start and almost 80% of the route is within Belarus with the finish and final 20% in Lithuania. There are several marathons around the world that offer such a unique experience, but almost all of them are between countries that have border regulations that allow people to cross from one country to another without too much hassle (The Niagara Falls Marathon, for example). This event crosses one of the strictest borders in Europe and the logistics require a lot more organisation than the usual marathon. A number of different organisations have worked together to make it possible. The event has developed thanks to long-lasting co-operation between the Athletics Federations of both countries which inspired them to search for common opportunities to implement joint projects. After jointly organising smaller projects, the federations decided to convert the co-operation into the first 'Marathon of Friendship, Grodno-Druskininkai' in 2011. The Organizing Committee consists of a wide spectrum of organisations from both countries, each with their own responsibilities to ensure the successful execution of the marathon. Included among these are no fewer than 15 ministries, departments, national agencies, state authorities, non-governmental and sports organizations such as: the Belarusian Ministry of Sport and Tourism; the Lithuanian Academy of Physical

Culture and Sports Department; the Belarus and the Lithuanian National Olympic Committees of the republics; the Belarusian and Lithuanian Athletics Federation; the Grodno Region Executive Committee of Physical Culture, Sport and Tourism Division; the Grodno City Executive Committee; the Druskininkai municipality; both the Grodno and Lithuanian border groups and both the Grodno and Lithuanian customs services. If you're thinking that's an awful lot of bureaucracy, you're spot on – as we were soon to find out!

The day-to-day running of the event appears to fall on the public institution named 'Sportbalt' whose email address is given as the first point of contact. (I assume the title translates as 'Baltic Sports' or similar). The event website sets out the main objectives of the marathon as primarily: to strengthen friendly relations between people of the Republic of Belarus and the Republic of Lithuania; to strengthen relations between establishments and administrations of Belarus and Lithuania, the development of trans-regional relations and integration; to improve the image of Belarus and Lithuania Republics and to present Grodno and Druskininkai as the places suitable for the important European sport events. Also listed are a number of purely running-related objectives such as: to develop physical activities including running race; to strengthen friendly relations between youth, runners, and veterans of physical culture of both states: to promote running, physical activities and sports as educational measures for physical, spiritual and moral education; to promote the social values and healthy lifestyle and to improve the skills of Belarus and Lithuanian athletes. All very impressive and worthwhile objectives.

Though I'd known about the event's existence for a number of years there were too many factors related to entering that I'd found off-putting. Foremost among these were the visa requirements for travelling to Belarus. I'd had a bad experience in getting a visa for the St Petersburg Marathon in Russia and wasn't prepared to put myself through that again. Nor was I happy at having to present a Health Certificate at Registration, (have you tried booking a doctor's appointment these days?) Another thing that irritated was the fact that the organisers expected foreign runners to pay the 25 euros entry fee via bank transfer. This, I'm afraid, is one of my pet hates. As I've described elsewhere, it effectively penalises overseas athletes in forcing us to, at times, pay almost double the cost of entry in international bank transfer fees. I feel strongly that any event that advertises itself as 'international' or that seeks to attract runners from abroad should at least have an online entry system in place. It's so easy to set up. Finally, the sheer logistics of getting to the start line in an isolated part of southern Lithuania/western Belarus did nothing to inspire. It was going to be a difficult journey whichever way I went. With these considerations in mind I 'forgot' about the event until circumstances forced me to search around for the 50th country in which to run a marathon. I'd meant to achieve this in Belgrade in April but hadn't been able to do so following a hernia operation. Trawling the internet for somewhere to run I rediscovered this event and was surprised to read that Belarus had recently revised its strict visa requirements. Under the new rules all British passport holders (except those entering on a diplomatic or official passport) could now enter Belarus for a maximum of 5 days without a visa (the day you arrive counts as day one, regardless of arrival time). Unfortunately, entry and exit is only be allowed by flying both into and out of Minsk International Airport, somewhere virtually impossible from where I live. These new regulations mean that you can`t cross the Belarus Republic border in any other place. In other words, participating in the marathon would be an infringement of the Belarus Border Guard Service Act! Further reading of the event's website showed that the organisers had made special arrangements to resolve the visa problem on the spot in Druskininkai for marathon entrants. It seemed that now all you had to do was to send a photocopy of the photo page of your passport to Sportbalt for a visa to be arranged. Even better, Organisers would meet runners in Druskininkai and then bus the Friendship Marathon participants across the border to Grodno on the day before the race for registration there. A hotel in Grodno had also been reserved for competitors at about 20 USD per person.

Encouraged that one of the major obstacles to participating had all but disappeared I e-mailed Sportbalt for up-to-date information; mentioning in passing my disappointment at the bank transfer system of payment. Almost by return I received a very helpful reply from Vytautas Lucinskas explaining that I could pay the entry fee on arrival and that a self-certification health form was now all that was required. Three down, only one obstacle to overcome – the journey. I have to admit that at times I was on the verge of giving up on this – nothing seemed to fall in place easily. Either the right flight times were on the wrong day or connecting buses or trains simply didn't connect. The organisers had suggested flying into either Vilnius or Kaunas in Lithuania, both 128 miles from Druskininkai in opposite directions. I was unable to find a suitable flight to either from any nearby airport. In the end I had to settle for one of Ryanair's new routes from Glasgow to Palanga on the Lithuanian Baltic coast, close to the Latvian border and more than 350km from where I needed to be. To be honest I was so determined to get my 50th marathon country over and done with I'd have gone via the North Pole if necessary. I went on my own. On this occasion Mo declined to accompany me on this odyssey – and who can blame her. My itinerary panned out as follows: Thursday July 6th – 3 hour journey to Glasgow Airport by train and bus, overnight in Hotel Muza, Palanga. Friday July 7th – five and a half hours by bus across Lithuania to Druskininkai, overnight in the Hotel Europa Royale. Saturday July 8th – two and a half hours border crossing on organiser's bus to Belarus, overnight in the Hotel Belarus, Grodno. Sunday July 9th – run a marathon back across the border to Lithuania, overnight in Hotel Europa, Druskininkai. Monday July 10th – two and a half hours by bus from Druskininkai to Kaunas, overnight at Hotel Magnus. Tuesday July 11th – 30 minute bus journey to Kaunas Airport, flight to Edinburgh, one and a half hours to home by bus and train. Who said marathon globetrotting was meant to be easy!

On the plus side, one of the unexpected bonuses of being a marathon tourist is that you occasionally come across somewhere that exceeds all expectations. Palanga was such a place. Though it is the busiest summer resort in Lithuania it's still a beautiful, relaxed, upmarket seaside town. Tourists from all over Lithuania and abroad come for its idyllic 10km sandy beach backed by sand dunes and scented pines. Despite the crowds and encroaching neon, Palanga oozes charm, with wooden houses and the ting-a-ling of bicycle bells and pedal-powered taxis in the air. For the past few years Palanga's International Airport, the third largest in Lithuania, has offered connecting flights to Scandinavia, Germany, United Kingdom, Poland and to Riga, Latvia. Fortunately, the place hasn't yet attracted the tattooed hordes or the swarms of stag night drunks. I arrived just in time to join in the annual carnival centred on Jonas Basanavicius Street, which is a pedestrian only thoroughfare during the high season. There are dozens of restaurants, bars, rides, and other forms of entertainment to be enjoyed. I had an evening and almost the whole of the next day there before leaving on the five and a half hour bus ride to Druskininkai. Fortunately, despite Mo's protestations that it was a 'woman's book' I'd picked up Rosanna Ley's 'Last Dance in Havana' (a legacy of our trip to the Havana Marathon) to keep my mind occupied during the journey. With close to 500 pages it retained my interest for the full ride. A long, solitary journey is so much easier with something to occupy the mind.

It didn't take me long to warm to the beautiful resort of Druskininkai - a spa town on the Nemunas River in southern Lithuania, close to the borders of Belarus and Poland. The city, with a population of around 23,000, is situated in a picturesque landscape with rivers, lakes, hills and forests. Formerly a popular Soviet Union all-year-round health resort it suffered economic difficulties following the dissolution of the Soviet Union due to the lack of many of its former tourists. Druskininkai has begun a revival since 2001 when unemployment reached record levels. Sanatoriums, spas and the city's infrastructure have been renovated by both the local government and privately owned businesses. The first water park in Lithuania was opened in Druskininkai in 2006 while the new Snow Arena is one of the biggest indoor skiing slopes in Europe. Tourists can visit it by cable car, enjoying panoramic views of Druskininkai en route. I was delighted to bump into 100 Club friend Jack Brooks at breakfast on arrival and thoroughly enjoyed the two days I spent there before and after the marathon. Jack had suffered an even more difficult journey to get there than I had. He'd initially booked to fly into Minsk and out from Vilnius. The new visa regulations had made that impossible so not only did Jack lose the money he'd spent on his inward flight, he'd also been compelled to sit around in Vilnius airport for six and a half hours awaiting the delayed arrival of Rich Holmes, his American travelling companion. In the end the organisers had to arrange for them to be picked up in Vilnius and brought to Druskininkai for the visa formalities.

Having run the Kaunas Marathon twelve months previously I was quite familiar with Lithuania but knew very little about Belarus (who does?) before entering the event. The Republic of Belarus, formerly known by its Russian name Byelorussia or Belorussia, is a landlocked country in Eastern Europe bordered by Russia to the northeast, Ukraine to the south, Poland to the west, and Lithuania and Latvia to the northwest. Its capital and most populous city is Minsk. Over 40% of the country is forested. Its strongest economic sectors are service industries and manufacturing. Belarus's two official languages are Russian and Belarusian; Russian is the main language, used by 72% of the population, while Belarusian, the official first language, is spoken by around 12%. Minorities also speak Polish, Ukrainian and Eastern Yiddish. In the aftermath of the 1917 Russian Revolution, Belarus declared independence as the Belarusian People's Republic, which was then conquered by Soviet Russia. The Socialist Soviet Republic of Byelorussia became a founding constituent republic of the Soviet Union in 1922 and was renamed as the Byelorussian Soviet Socialist Republic (Byelorussian SSR). Much of the borders of Belarus took their modern shape in 1939, when some lands of the Second Polish Republic were reintegrated into it after the Soviet invasion of Poland, and were finalised after World War II. During that war, military operations devastated Belarus, which lost about a third of its population and more than half of its economic resources.

The country became independent in 1991, following the collapse of the Soviet Union. In the Soviet post-war years, Belarus had become one of the most prosperous parts of the USSR, but with independence came economic decline. Long-serving President Lukashenko has steadfastly opposed the privatisation of state enterprises. Private business is virtually non-existent and foreign investors stay away. The Lonely Planet guidebook believes that, 'While the rest of Eastern Europe has charged headlong into capitalism' Belarus has remained 'Eastern Europe's outcast …. Taking its lead from the Soviet Union rather than the European Union … determined to avoid integration with the rest of the continent at all costs.' Belarus' Soviet-style economy is subsidised by cheap Russian gas and a key oil and gas pipeline from Russia to Europe runs through the country which remains heavily dependent on Russia to meet its own energy needs. More than two decades after independence the sense of national identity is weak, international isolation continues and the nature of political links with Russia remains a key issue. According to the BBC's country profile, 'The country has been ruled with an increasingly iron fist since 1994 by President Alexander Lukashenko who has often been dubbed as 'Europe's last dictator'. Opposition figures are said to be subjected to harsh penalties for organising protests. (As recently as May 2021 the Belarusian authorities has been accused of 'hijacking' a civilian airliner by forcing a Ryanair passenger flight to land in the country using a fake bomb threat so that a prominent critic of its authoritarian leader Alexander Lukashenko could be arrested). No surprise then that, as early as 2005, Belarus was listed by the US as Europe's only remaining 'outpost of tyranny'.

The hijacking incident aside, there has recently been small signs of change following increasing public protest against the Lukashenko regime. Since 2014, following years of embrace of Russian influence in the country, Lukashenko has pressed a revival of Belarusian identity, following the Russian annexation of Crimea and military intervention in Eastern Ukraine. For the first time, he delivered a speech in Belarusian (rather than Russian, which most people use), in which he said, 'We are not Russian — we are

Belarusians,' and later encouraged the use of the Belarusian language. The recent relaxation of visa requirements appears to be a further indication of this change.

Before leaving home I'd tried to find out as much as I could about the marathon. The fact that the event website hadn't been updated didn't help. It seems that this was to be the 7th edition of the race which changes the direction in which it is run each year – Grodno to Druskininkai one year, the opposite direction the next. The first event was held in 2011 with only 42 participants. In 2013 86 runners finished out of 102 at the start. 2014 saw 123 athletes from 12 countries take part. As news of the event spread, in 2016.the organisers received 15 applications on the first registration day. Among the applicants were citizens of the UK, the USA, Czech Republic and Germany. This year (2017) close to 190 competitors entered the event. Most of these were from either Lithuania, Belarus or Russia apart from a handful of us from 'overseas'. These included 2 from the UK (Jack and myself), 2 from the USA, 3 Finns, 1 Dane and 1 German. We made our way in a group clutching our passports to the Druskininkai Cultural Centre at 1pm on the Saturday afternoon to hopefully collect our visas for Belarus. Following a spot of form-filling these were available as promised: one for entry to Belarus, one for exit and a rather large, certificate-like page in who-knows-what language for who-knows-what purpose. (I can't recall anyone asking to see it but I could be wrong. It's still in my possession). Then it was on to the bus and we were on our way to the border. Firstly, we had to negotiate an exit from Lithuania. That didn't take too long – the border authorities were mainly interested in the non-EU members of our party – the two Americans. Getting through to Belarus was a much more prolonged and unpleasant experience. At border control our bus was boarded by a dour, unsmiling female official who disappeared with our passports and entry visa. After what seemed like hours she eventually returned and handed back the passports, duly stamped, and minus one of our entry forms. We proceeded into Belarus past a long queue of stationary heavy goods vehicles stretching at least a kilometre into the distance. A further 40 minutes or so of driving along the road on which we were to run the next day brought us to the Olympic Reserve Hockey Centre in Grodno for Registration.

Registration started off with yet more form filling – as far as I could see it was a duplication of the details we'd already given when entering online. I was asked for my medical certificate, something that I didn't possess, having already been informed by Sportbalt that only self-certification was necessary. This resulted in me being pointed towards a long queue where other runners were lining up to have their blood pressure recorded. Anyone who failed the test was then being led away for further medical examination. By this stage my blood pressure was already beginning to rise - in annoyance. I wasn't having any of this medical examination lark so dug out my medical insurance forms and pointed out the bit where it said that I was covered for marathon running. This seemed to satisfy them enough that I was allowed to proceed without further formality. I collected my event T-shirt but there was no chip as advertised – everything was done by hand-timing, I presume as a cost-cutting measure. The lack of a chip was one of only two promises that the organisers failed to fulfil. The other was that they failed to send us the promised pre-race email with details of our start number. Other requirements for registration listed on the website were largely ignored. These included: the need to show documentary evidence of medical insurance to the value of 10,000 euros and funds equivalent to 25 euros per day plus a printed document that participants were supposed to receive after payment of the entry fee.

Despite the complicated logistics of getting us to this stage of the proceedings everything had run fairly smoothly to date – other than the periods of interminable hanging-around, designed to test the patience of the proverbial Saint. Much of the credit for the success of the event is due to the two young English-speaking members from the Grodno Department of Tourism who went out of their way to look after the interests of overseas runners. Unfortunately, being part of a group meant that we had to wait around at registration until the last member was ready to leave. By then we'd been on the go for over four hours without food or drink since breakfast and most of us were desperate to eat. Eventually, after 5pm the handful of overseas entrants were taken as a group the short distance to our hotel. One of the problems with being locked into a group situation is that you can't choose your own company. It makes it hard to escape anyone you'd prefer to avoid!

The Hotel Belarus in Grodno deserves a chapter all on its own. I've stayed in some soul-less and character-less places throughout the world but never anywhere as drab and depressing as this hotel. It was a relic of the worst type of Soviet-era architecture with an antiquated reception system, antiquated decor, antiquated rooms, antiquated service and an antiquated lift. It served neither food nor drink, had no entertainment and, apart from our small group, appeared to be totally empty. The organisers had advertised that the room cost was approximately $20 so many in the group had brought US dollars with them with which to pay. Problem was – they would only accept Belarusian rubles or credit card payment. None of us had rubles and the receptionist wasn't able to accept card payment until our passports had been 'processed.' To get the key to our room we had then to go through a second-stage of registration involving someone in an office on the 3rd floor in charge of handing-out keys. This process had to be reversed on leaving. I've never been so happy to stay only one night at any hotel.

As soon as all formalities had been completed Jack, Rich and myself walked the kilometre or so into Grodno in search of sustenance. What should have been a simple, pleasant transaction turned into something resembling a Brian Rix farce. As Jack is a vegetarian and Rich and I will eat anything that's dead we allowed Jack the choice of restaurant. He chose a pizza outlet after first confirming with the waiter that they would be prepared to serve him a ham and sausage pizza topped with mushrooms and cheese without the first two ingredients. Their first attempt produced the ham and sausage without the mushrooms and cheese. This was returned. Next up came a sausage-only creation. This too was returned with demonstrations of what was required. By now Rich and I had finished our pizzas and Jack must have been starving. They almost got it right at the third attempt except that the only topping was cheese – no mushrooms. Back went Jack before finally throwing in the towel when informed that mushrooms weren't available. By this stage I was on to my second meal of spicy sausage and chips (I was that hungry) and quietly enjoying a pint of tasty Belarusian dark beer. The menu was written in Cyrillic script so I may have the translation incorrect but I believe it was called Ledckoe. Whatever it was it came close to the criteria of the perfect dark beer I'm always looking for and at the equivalent of only 1.50 euros per pint. In fact, my two meals plus the beer came to only 18 rubles – about 9 euros. Good value. But we didn't leave a tip!

We tried to see something of Grodno before returning to the hotel but the rain that had been threatening during the day's humidity finally came down in buckets. According to the tourist brochure, Grodno is a regional centre in the country located on the banks of the Neman River and an important tourist attraction in Belarus. It has something of a reputation as an open-air museum city, having the largest number of historical and cultural monuments in the country apart from the capital, Minsk. One of its main attractions is said to be the Old Castle with its series of fortified walls and towers. We confined ourselves to a stroll along Soviet Street, Grodno's version of the ever-popular pedestrian street that almost all former Soviet cities have. The stroll seemed like a walk along a timeline as you go from the Polish-Lithuanian era of the 15th century New Castle to the more recent Russian and Soviet era. Soviet Street eventually leads to Lenin Square, where the monument to Vladimir Lenin still dominates today. (Most of the great man's statues have long since disappeared from the streets of the neighbouring Baltic States). I'm afraid that, due to the rain, our sightseeing didn't do the place justice. Maybe next time or, more like it, maybe not!

We were up and out of Grodno's version of the Outlook Hotel early next morning for the final series of the visa processing by border control officials. These lay in wait for us at the entrance to the Olympic Stadium. This time there appeared to be something amiss with my passport. I stood for ages while a young female officer sporting a snazzy peaked cap scrutinised its every page before handing the document to a senior officer (with an even larger peaked cap). I watched while he made a phone call to who-knows-where, looking and pointing in my direction as he spoke. Finally and without explanation, I was allowed through. At this stage all of our passports were retained by border control for reclaiming at the end of the race. A sticker displaying our bib number had been affixed to the back of the document. This number was our identification while passing through the barriers at the border during the race. All we had to do now was place our personal belongings into a numbered bin-bag and these were taken by bus to await us at the finish.

At 7.50am all runners gathered at the start line for a series of indecipherable speeches by unknown dignitaries and at 8am we were off and running. We had 6 hours in which to get to the finish in Druskininkai. By now the early morning rain had stopped and it was turning into a beautiful hot but humid day. After leaving the western suburbs of Grodno at about 5km, the marathon route took us into miles and miles of forests on long, straight roads where every mile seemed to be the same as the one before. Every kilometre was marked and at numerous intervals officials were sighted noting our race number as we passed. Drink stations were frequent and well-stocked with water, isotonic drink and bananas. The road was partially closed to traffic throughout with police leading vehicles in single-file convoys in one direction at a time. Although the scenery was incredibly monotonous, it felt good to know I'd soon be completing my gaol of running a marathon in 50 different countries. I ran for a couple of kilometres with two Minsk-based Belarusian athletes. They were both businessmen who worked for foreign companies that required them to have a fluency in English. I learned quite a bit from them about conditions in their country. They told of a long-standing Belarusian joke about the difficulties at their border crossings. Basically it goes, 'Why did the Germans take so long to invade Belarus? Answer: Because they couldn't get through the border controls!'

Most of the race passed without incident though there were a couple of things that I found amusing. The first of these concerned the ambulance that had driven along doggedly beside me for about the first ten kilometres. In the beginning I paid it no heed until its continual presence began to annoy. Then it dawned on me that perhaps it was deliberate and that it was under instructions to follow me as I was by far the oldest runner in the event. I hadn't asked for it and certainly didn't welcome its presence. In the end I stepped out in front of the vehicle forcing it to stop and explained to the driver firmly but politely that I was unlikely to require his assistance and that perhaps it was time that he followed someone else. He did. I came across him later at the border checkpoint with his ambulance pointing back in the direction of Grodno. He didn't acknowledge me and I didn't acknowledge him. Also at the border checkpoint, 31 kilometres into the race, there seemed to be the same long queue of HGVs that we'd passed the day before, with what looked like the same set of drivers standing disconsolately by the side of the road. Again there was no acknowledgement as we passed. Perhaps they blamed us runners for their delay. In what seems to be a prominent theme in this event, the legions of suited and booted border guards milling around the border control area showed a similar poker-faced disinterest in the runners as we came through. By this stage humidity levels had risen considerably to the extent that it felt like running through treacle. Worse still were the hundreds of flies that poured out of the forests attracted by our sweat. I've never seen so many on a race – not even while running through outback Australia. For long periods of the race most of my energy seemed to be directed towards making windmill gestures with my hands to keep the little blighters out of eyes, ears, nose and mouth.

Once on the other side of the border, the monotonous forests and countryside continued until we got to the turn-off taking us into the suburbs of Druskininkai. After passing through its outskirts, we finally arrived at the café-filled streets of the city centre and into the finish in a park where many of the pedestrians seemed oblivious to the marathon despite the finish line, an award stage and runners with race numbers all over the place. There were 141 finishers plus a number of DNFs out of the 190 or so who had entered the race. To me that seemed a poor return for all the effort that the organisers had put into their event, particularly when you think of all the border personnel, admin staff, medical staff, soldiers, police, volunteers as well as all the unknown others who had given up their time to ensure that the marathon could take place. It was certainly excellent value at 25 euros per head (15 euros if you entered early). The post-race meal was almost worth that, not to mention the cost of buses, medal, T-shirt and all the other expenses involved. I'd come in 127th in a very slow time of 5:08:02. This didn't bother me one bit – I always struggle in hot and humid conditions. More importantly, I'd got the 50-country monkey off my back at last. I'll go faster in the next one.

We finished the day, joined by my two Belarussian friends, sitting in the sun at the outside tables of the excellent Kolonada Restaurant in the park – all free and courtesy of the event organisers. And this was no pasta-in-a-box affair. The restaurant did us proud with a generous serving of traditional Lithuanian food: cabbage soup with sour cream for starters followed by stuffed dumplings, more sour cream, traditional salad and lots of tasty black bread. After that we needed a drink and what better than the Volfas Engelman dark lager from its Kaunas brewery -only 4.2% but a lovely malty taste. Later that evening I came across the same brewery's Horn Disel – not dark but almost perfect. It provided an excellent ending to what had been a memorable few days.

The Start in Grodno

One of the best post-race meals (with Jack, Rich and two runners from Belarus)

UKRAINE

KIEV MARATHON

Prior to entering this event my knowledge of both the country and the city in which it is held bordered on negligible. If you'd asked me what I knew about Ukraine I'd probably have blurted out something along the lines of the old schoolboy-geography mantra about it having been 'the bread-basket of the former Soviet Union' plus some highly uninformed comments about recent protest demonstrations in Kiev and the Russian incursion into Crimea. The more I delved into the history and politics of this enormous country the more I learned and the more fascinated I became.

Ukraine is actually Europe's second largest country, bordering the Black Sea, between Poland, Romania, and Moldova in the west and Russia in the east. According to the BBC Country Profile, the Ukrainian Republic was, after Russia, the most important economic component of the former Soviet Union, producing about four times the output of the next-ranking republic. Its fertile black soil generated more than one-fourth of Soviet agricultural output, and its farms provided substantial quantities of meat, milk, grain, and vegetables to other republics. Likewise, its diversified heavy industry supplied unique equipment, such as, large diameter pipes and vertical drilling apparatus, and raw materials to industrial and mining sites in other regions of the former USSR. Ukraine gained independence after the collapse of the Soviet Union in 1991 and has since veered between seeking closer integration with Western Europe and being drawn into the orbit of Russia which, it's said, sees its interests as threatened by a Western-leaning Ukraine.

Ukraine has a long history of being subjugated by foreign powers. This is even reflected in its name, which many scholars believe means 'borderland' and is part of why it used to be called 'the Ukraine' as opposed to simply Ukraine. (Other interpretations of the name give it as meaning 'homeland.') The country is also said to be deeply divided by language, by history and by politics. A significant minority of the population uses Russian as its first language, particularly in the industrialised east. In Crimea, an autonomous republic on the Black Sea that was part of Russia until 1954, ethnic Russians make up about 60% of the population. One-third of the country speaks Russian as its native language, and in practice even more use it day-to-day. The Russian-speakers mostly live in one half of the country; the Ukrainian-speakers live in another. I've read that it's not just that Ukraine has two halves that predominantly speak different languages. They are said to have different politics – and different visions for their country. While Ukraine and Russia share common historical origins, the west of the country has closer ties with its European neighbours, the eastern side with its Russian neighbours. My understanding of the current situation is that these divisions came to the fore in 2013 when moves to reach an association agreement with the EU, seen as a key step towards eventual EU membership, threatened to damage Ukraine's traditional economic ties with Russia. Russia is its largest individual trading partner and Ukraine depends on Russia for its gas supplies and forms an important part of the pipeline transit route for Russian gas exports to Europe. A prolonged crisis in Ukraine began in November 2013, when then-president Viktor Yanukovych suspended preparations for the implementation of the association agreement with the European Union. It's been reported that he'd been offered 'sweeteners' by Russia to backtrack on the EU agreement. (Corruption is reported to be endemic in Ukraine).This decision resulted in mass demonstrations by its proponents with tens of thousands of protesters eventually forcing the collapse and flight of the Yanukovych government in violent chaos four months later. Russia reacted to Ukraine's domestic turmoil by sending troops to annex the former Russian territory of Crimea while stoking separatist sentiment in eastern Ukraine and plunging European into its worst diplomatic crisis since the Cold War.

Though tensions have quietened down of late this background of potential civil unrest ensured that Paul Richards, Dave Goodwin and I wanting to run the marathon in Kiev made a beeline to the UK Government's Advice for Travellers website before sending in our entry fees for the 2017 event. It read, 'The situation in Kyiv and other areas outside Donetsk and Luhansk is generally calm. Public demonstrations regularly take place at Maydan Nezalezhnosti (Independence Square), in and around government buildings such as the Verkhovna Rada (parliament building) and the National Bank of Ukraine as well as elsewhere in Kiev. Although most are peaceful, public demonstrations can flare up and turn violent with little warning. Policing of these demonstrations may include road closures. Avoid all demonstrations and take extra care in public gatherings. You should remain vigilant throughout Ukraine.' With that in mind, there seemed no reason not to go especially as EU citizens no longer require a visa for stays of up to 90 days.

When Mo decided she'd like to see Kiev too the decision travel was easy. Unfortunately, as with most journeys these days things don't always go as smoothly as planned. The start and end of the journey were both unpleasant but, fortunately, the middle and most important bit made it all worthwhile. We'd booked to go with KLM from Newcastle with a very short turn-around in Amsterdam before changing to a Ukrainian Airlines flight to Kiev. Conditions in Amsterdam meant that our first plane was delayed by over an hour and wasn't due to arrive in time in time for the connecting flight. Deeply disappointed, we'd already made plans to simply return to Newcastle rather than hope for space on the next day's flight to Kiev. On arriving at the Customer Services desk at Schiphol we heard news that the Ukranian Airlines flight had also been delayed and that there was still a possibility of boarding if we could manage the equivalent of a four-minute mile dash through the transit terminal. We made it with seconds to spare! Coming back, our problems were of our own making. You'd think four seasoned travellers would be too street-wise to fall for any form of taxi scam.

Wrong! None of us saw what was coming as the 'taxi' driver sitting outside the entrance to our hotel systematically and, to be fair, somewhat ingeniously took us to the cleaners. I won't go into too much detail: it involved a dismountable taxi sign on the roof of the vehicle, a fake portable 'meter' that fell off the dashboard en route and appeared to be connected to some sort of mobile phone app, and a baseball cap that was suddenly pulled over the driver's eyes as he approached the terminal. I can laugh about it now but the upshot was that it cost us twice as much to return to the airport in Kiev than it had on our arrival there three days earlier when we'd sensibly taken the fixed-price fare of 428 UAH offered by the airport's authorised taxi concession. Forewarned is forearmed: so be careful – these taxi scammer guys are experts. Incidentally £1 gets you about 30 UAH (hryvnia) – a closed currency that you can purchase at the airport on arrival. I worked on the basis that 100 hryvnia was about £3 when calculating expenses in Kiev.

Of course, we could have avoided taxi drivers altogether using public transport. Though there's no rail link or metro station at the airport there is a Sky Bus service. It costs 80 UAH for the 19 mile journey into Kiev Train Station, stopping en route at Kharkivska Metro Station (Green line). The complete journey takes just under an hour and buses operate around the clock with departures every 15 minutes or so during day and 30 minute intervals during night. The bus leaves from just outside Arrivals in Terminal D. Tickets from driver or from ticket office in Arrivals hall. It's not recommended for first time arrivals to Kiev as Kiev train station isn't near any of the major hotels so likely you'll have to take the adjacent Vokzalna Metro Station (Red line) or catch a taxi. Taxi drivers at the station tend to charge more. All bus, trolleybus and tram tickets normally need to be validated by being 'punched' when boarding and on the spot fines are served on anyone travelling with a ticket that has not been validated. We figured that the extra hassle just wasn't worth the money saved particularly as our hotel was a fair distance from the Sky Bus terminus. We stayed at the magnificent, Soviet-era Hotel Ukraine overlooking the start and finish of the marathon in Independence Square. What a bargain-for-the-money this placed turned out to be. This palatial, centrally situated hotel with gorgeous views plus all services included cost Mo and I less than £25 per person per night with a good hot and cold buffet breakfast. We couldn't help comparing its value with the underground bunker of a room with shared bathroom we'd stayed in while attending the Warsaw Marathon two weeks earlier.

This year (2017) was to be the 8th edition of the Kiev Marathon that first started in 2010. On that occasion 546 runners took part with only 144 of these running the marathon distance. The race has grown steadily rather than spectacularly over the years, with overseas participation growing year on year. The second edition in 2011 was attended by more than 1,000 runners. 1,693 participants registered in 2013, and in the spring of 2014 nearly three and a half thousand athletes from 32 countries started the officially titled 'Wizz Air Kyiv City Marathon.' It became an autumn event in 2015 with 3,800 participants from 38 countries. The marathon route became the special feature of this race since for the first time it was mapped as one lap through the city. More than 6600 athletes from 50 countries participated in the various events in 2016. This year events and their entry limits included: Marathon (1,000 limit) Half marathon (2,000) Marathon Relay (500) 10K (1,200) 5 km (1,200) Children's 1000 metre race (350) Children's 500 metre race (300) Children's 100 metre race (350). The fact that there were so many races with runners arriving at the finish throughout the day made it interesting for spectators like Mo and others who had come simply to watch. Entry fees for the marathon ranged from 500 UAH to 770 UAH depending on when you entered. For this we were given a medal and a 20 euro voucher for a Wizz Air flight valid for one year. There was no 'free' T-shirt while tickets for the Pasta Party cost 55 UAH, payable at Registration. The Expo is open on the Friday and Saturday before the race from 12:00 pm to 8:00pm Friday and 10:00am to 8:00pm Saturday. Citizens of foreign countries participating in the marathon or half marathon are required to provide health insurance that covers participation in sports activities or accident insurance. A Certificate of Health is only necessary for local residents. The fact that all our running bibs had been overprinted with the German as opposed to the British flag provided some amusement (or should it be bemusement) for our small group of UK runners.

One of the few disappointments about the event was that runners were required to collect their starter's packages at an out-of-town venue almost 6 kilometres away from the city centre start and finish. There's obviously a good explanation for this (I suspect that, as usual, it has a lot to do with maximising marketing opportunities) but none of us enjoy being forced into the outer suburbs for registration when there appears to be much more convenient sites nearby. Independence Square, for example, is a huge public space where organisers had already erected numerous tents for other purposes. Never mind, while some of our friends took taxis out to Registration at SportExpoUA 2017 at 40 Peremogy Avenue, Pushkin Park, Mo and I were determined to master the complexities of the Kiev metro system. In fact, the system is not the least bit complex. The Metro is one of the pleasures of Kiev. It is a clean, fast subway system, and it is easy to navigate once you realize that all three metro lines (red, blue and green) go through the city centre. In total there are 52 stations, with ambitious plans for extension. All station signs and metro maps are in Cyrillic and English. When you enter the Metro, you must purchase an entrance token from the cash desk (Kasa) or from a special ticket machine. One token is valid for one trip, no matter how far you go. A token is UAH5 and one needs to be inserted into the turnstile to enter. This gets you one journey, including interchanges. Additionally, every station has got its unique three-digit number, with the first digit showing the number of line (M1 for red, M2 for blue, and M3 for green). Once on board, every station is announced by loud speakers and TV screens. It was an 11 minute, 5 stop journey from our nearest station Khreshchatyk to the Shuliavska station, a 10 minute walk from Pushkin Park.

While at the Expo I took the opportunity of catching up with Ilona Sekevich, a lovely lady I'd met manning the Run Ukraine stall at the Warsaw Marathon two weeks previously. Ilona is 'Manager of Communications with International Participants' for Run Ukraine and had showed genuine interest and pleasure when I informed her in Warsaw that a group of us were travelling to her event. She took my email address and forwarded lots of information and video links about a range of Run Ukraine events. She was waiting in the pouring rain to greet me at the finish line at the end of the marathon and ensured that I received all available goodies and space blanket. She even joined me while walking the stiffness out of my legs; all the time showing real concern as to my opinions on the race. Better still, she went out of her way to ensure that I received the magnificent trophy I'd won as First Vet 70. (I hadn't attended the Awards Ceremony thinking that my very slow time of 4:52 couldn't have possibly merited an age-group place). Besides, I'd been running in freezing rain for the past two hours and desperately needed a hot shower. No sooner had I got out of the shower than hotel reception rang our room to say that there was someone in the lobby with a trophy for me. It was a very drenched Ilona. Without her kindness I'd have returned to the UK minus a tangible memento of an excellent event. It didn't end there – on returning home there was a Ukranian language email (marked as spam) stating that I was entitled to a monetary award of about £40 and requesting details of my credit card for payment. Ilona was able to verify its authenticity and ensured that I received the money. She's definitely the go-to person for anyone from the UK wanting to travel to this event. I really can't thank her enough for her kindness and for helping to make it such a memorable weekend.

With the Expo out of the way it was down to some serious sightseeing. We were anxious to experience what Kiev had to offer. Ukrainians are very proud of their capital's role in establishing European civilisation in Eastern Europe. Kiev is one of the oldest cities in Eastern Europe, dating back to the 5th century, although settlements at this location existed much earlier. The city was founded on the banks of Dnipro (aka Dnieper) River. The translation of the city's name from Ukrainian is 'Kyiv', and this variation is used in official English language materials in Ukraine, major English-speaking countries and international organizations. The city's name spelling is said to be a sensitive political topic for many Ukrainians, since the outdated 'Kiev' spelling is based on the Russian translation that was prevalent during the Soviet occupation and therefore reminds of Russian influence over Ukraine. It's recommended to use Kyiv when in Ukraine not to hurt anybody's feelings. The marathon, for example, uses the spelling Kyiv in its title.

Kiev/Kyiv is the capital and largest city of Ukraine, located in the north central part of the country and situated on the Dnieper River. With a population of around 3 million it ranks as the 7th most populous city in Europe. According to my old friend Wikipedia, 'Kiev is an important industrial, scientific, educational, and cultural centre in Eastern Europe …. and is home to many high-tech industries, higher education institutions and world-famous historical landmarks.' The city's name is said to derive from the name of Kyi, one of its four legendary founders. During its history, Kiev, passed through several stages of great prominence and relative obscurity. Following the collapse of the Soviet Union and Ukrainian independence in 1991, Kiev remained the capital of Ukraine and experienced a steady migration influx of ethnic Ukrainians from other regions of the country. During the country's transformation to a market economy and electoral democracy, Kiev has continued to be Ukraine's largest and richest city. Its armament-dependent industrial output fell after the Soviet collapse, adversely affecting science and technology. But, new sectors of the economy such as services and finance have facilitated Kiev's growth as well as providing continuous funding for the development of housing and urban infrastructure. Since independence Kiev has emerged as the most pro-Western region of Ukraine and parties advocating tighter integration with the European Union dominate during election.

During our visit it certainly impressed as an affluent, westernised and cosmopolitan city with plenty to offer the tourist - from its historical heritage to inspiring architecture and modern commerce centres. The city features many places of worship with golden-domed monasteries, orthodox churches and cathedrals. The most famous ones include the Kiev Pechersk Lavra, one of Ukraine's most important monasteries and founded in 1077 by St Antoniy.

The other is St Sophia's Cathedral housing the world's largest collection of frescoes and mosaics from the 11th century onwards. It is also very rich in the people's history. Over 40 different museums are visited by millions of guests every year. Foremost among these is the Museum of the Great Patriotic War with a stunning, more than 100 metres high monument of 'Mother Motherland' that I was looking forward to running beneath during the course of the marathon.

Saturday was a beautiful, sunny autumnal day; ideal for seeing the city in its best light. We started off by walking the length of the conker strewn Khreshchatyk Street, the city's main thoroughfare. With its designer-label stores we could have been in any of the major cities in Western Europe. Much more interesting than the above-ground shops were the scores of smaller outlets located underground in the numerous pedestrian subways that provided the only safe passage across this busy street. At the street's intersection with Tarasa Shevchenko Boulevard we encountered the huge indoor Bessarabsky Market – something of an anomaly among its up-market neighbours. At one end of the market is an array of popular food stalls. Spotting a well-dressed crowd queuing at one of the noodle outlets we decided to investigate, ending up with the tastiest meal of the whole weekend. We thought the 60 UAH for a large bowl of spicy chicken and noodles, less than half of the cost in the nearby Noodle Doodle chain of restaurants, was an incredible bargain. After eating our fill we returned in the opposite direction and into the Cross Park at the eastern end of Khreschatyk Street. We wanted to see the famous Rainbow Arch, whose image is incorporated into the marathon's logo, as well as take in the views of the nearby Dnieper River. Officially titled the 'Friendship of Nations Arch.' Dedicated to the unification of Russia and Ukraine, the arch was built in 1982 during the Soviet era to celebrate this unification and to commemorate the 60th anniversary of the USSR and the celebration of the 1,500th Anniversary of Kiev. In May 2016 the Ukrainian government announced plans to dismantle the arch as part of its de-communisation policy. In its place is planned a memorial dedicated to veterans of the War in Donbass. Normally a dull titanium structure the arch was revitalised in honour of 2017's Eurovision theme: Celebrate Diversity. For that year's Eurovision Song Contest held in Kiev, the arch was temporarily painted into a rainbow and renamed the Arch of Diversity. At night, the arch illuminates as a rainbow as well. Passing under the giant arch brings you to a well-placed Observation Deck affording great views over the river and down to Park Bridge, a pedestrian bridge that connects the city with Trukhaniv Island.

Leaving the park we walked down the historic St Andrew's Descent to the lower commercial district of Podil in order to take the funicular back up to St Michael's Golden Dome Monastery and the Upper Town. The Kiev funicular is one of only two funicular railways in Ukraine (the other is in Odessa). The ride is short but interesting, only costs 3 UAH and gives great views back across the river. The sky-blue St. Michael's Cathedral, with its fabulously shining domes, is one of the most beautiful and important Orthodox temples in Ukraine. The current building is a remake of the destroyed St. Michael's Cathedral, which stood on the territory of the oldest monastery of Kievan Rus (a loose federation of East Slavic tribes in Europe from the late 9th to the mid-13th century) for over eight centuries. The Cathedral is famous for its unique mosaics and frescos, which are rightfully considered to be the greatest creations of the Old Russian monumental painting. Its mosaics are nicknamed 'glimmering,' because of their exquisiteness and shine. When the temple was completely demolished by the Soviets in 1937, the valuable mosaics were rescued. Some of them were kept in nearby St. Sophia Cathedral, others were taken to the Hermitage Museum in St. Petersburg and the Tretyakov Gallery in Moscow. After the buildings reconstruction, all of them were returned. You can visit the museum there for only 9 UAH.

A short walk to the west brought us to Saint Sophia Cathedral, an outstanding architectural monument that is one of the city's best known landmarks and the first heritage site in Ukraine to be inscribed on the World Heritage List along with the Kiev Cave Monastery complex. The Cathedral has world biggest ensemble of frescoes and mosaics dating from 11th century, Its 13 golden domes provide a stunning, almost breath-taking, sight. The site stopped being an active church in 1934, and has since been operated as government owned museum. Green-robed ladies maintain order and prevent visitors from planning to take a photo. The gatehouse and other restorations were completed in the 17th century. Outside the gates, in the square where the city's Christmas Markets are held, there is a statue commemorating Bohdan Khmelnytskyi, who liberated Kyiv in the 17th century... then gave the city to the Russian Empire. It costs 60 UAH for admission to the complex and church. Additional charges to climb the bell tower, visit the museum and have a guided tour. It's well worth the cost. Our final stop in this heritage quarter of the city was at the Golden Gate of Lyov on the corner of Volodymyr Street and Yaroslaviv Val Street. This was the main gate in the 11th century fortifications of Kiev and was named in imitation of the Golden Gate of Constantinople and described by Mussorgski in 'Pictures of an Exhibition'. The structure was dismantled in the Middle Ages, leaving few vestiges of its existence but, amid much controversy, was completely rebuilt by the Soviet authorities in 1982. It is quite a nice spot to visit and learn about the town walls.

With sightseeing over for the day it was time to prepare for the next morning's marathon. Though heavy rain had been forecast, the day started sunny but cold as we waited on the start line next to Independence Square. As early risers we had plenty of time to take in the majesty of our surroundings where a whole tented village had been erected for marathon purposes. The Square, (Maidan Nezalezhnosti in Ukrainian) is the central square in Kiev as well as the most beautiful one. Parades, concerts, demonstrations, festivals and other city arrangements and holidays take place on this square. It contains six fountains, Independence Column and artificial waterfall. The left side of the square is covered with granite and splendid panoramic view of Old Kiev opens from the upper floors of the square's buildings, including from our hotel. Visible are the domes of Sofia Cathedral, Andreevskaya Church, City Parliament, the Central Mall, and various administrative buildings. A large number of shops, hotels and cafes are situated in the Globus complex beneath the square. Two metro stations, Kreschatik and Maidan Nezalezhnosti, are also situated nearby. One of the fountains of the square is decorated with statues of legendary brothers Kie, Schek, Horiv and their sister Libed. According to Nikon's Russian Primary Chronicle they chose the place for the city foundation and decided to name it in honour of the elder brother Kie. One of the best notable decorations of the central square is the Independency Column topped with a statue of the Archangel Mikhail, who is considered to be the saint patron of Kiev. In front of the column, at the end of the square there is an arch decorated with the statue of Archangel with sword and shield. Placed all around the square are picture shrines to those who lost their lives during the political demonstrations of only three years earlier. It was a hard fact to take in while waiting for a marathon!

Of the four main events, the marathon and half marathon and marathon relay set off simultaneously at 9 am with the 10K starting ten minutes later. All four followed the same course with the 10K turning at the 5K mark and the full and half marathons completing the same 21.1km lap to the south of the city before returning to Independence Square. Those of us running the full distance were then required to complete a second lap – this time around the northern suburbs of Kiev. We had 6 hours in which to complete the race. I was a little apprehensive about the joint start but needn't have worried. It was well organised with checks to ensure that runners entered their correct starting gate. The course itself had its good bits and its bad bits (I suppose like any other big city marathon). At times we found ourselves running by World Heritage sites, past picture-postcard, colourful onion domed Cathedrals and iconic monuments. At other times, particularly on the second lap of the race, us marathon runners found ourselves ploughing a lonely furrow through some highly unimpressive, graffiti littered suburbs. On balance I enjoyed it. The good out-weighed the bad – though most of us were not impressed by the long stretches of cobbles we encountered en route (at least four of them during the marathon). When the rain came down heavily after midday these stretches were no fun. It certainly wasn't an easy course or a place to run a PB – there were far too many hilly sections for that.

Highlights of the course included passing the Dynamo Stadium complex within the first couple of kilometres. The stadium holds 16,873 spectators, and has been home to Dynamo Kiev, Ukraine's most successful soccer club and a familiar name to those of us interested in European football, since 1934. These days, due to a high demand for tickets at European fixtures Dynamo play a majority of their home fixtures at Kiev's and Ukraine's largest stadium, the 84,000 capacity Olimpiyskiy National Sports Complex. At 5 kilometres the course took us around the gigantic Motherland Monument close to the banks of the Dnieper. This was something we'd glimpsed in awe on our taxi ride in from the airport and something I definitely wanted to revisit. Known locally as 'Brezhnev's Daughter' the monument is a giant titanium statue visible from all parts of the city that celebrates the Soviet Union's victory over Nazi Germany. At 62 metres high it's most certainly the city's most distinctive feature. The sword in the statue's right hand is 16 metres long weighing 9 tons, with the left hand holding up a 13 by 8 metre shield with the State Emblem of the Soviet Union. The sculpture is a part of the Museum of The History of Ukraine in World War II, Kiev. The Memorial hall of the Museum displays marble plaques with carved names of more than 11,600 soldiers and over 200 workers of the home-front honoured during the war with the title of the Hero of the Soviet Union and the Hero of Socialist Labour. There is also a large open air partly free exhibition of tanks and other military equipment (tanks, planes, rocket launchers etc.) on the way to the museum. In modern-day Kiev, the statue remains controversial, with some claiming it should be pulled down and its metal used for more functional purposes. Financial shortages mean that the flame, which uses up to 400 cubic metres of gas per hour, can only burn on the biggest national holidays, and rumours persist that the statue is built on unstable foundations, something strongly denied by the Kiev local government. In April 2015, the parliament of Ukraine outlawed Soviet and Communist symbols, street names and monuments, in an attempt at de-communisation. But World War II monuments are excluded from these laws and the monument looks as if it's there to stay. Another highlight was when we crossed and then re-crossed a bridge over the River Dnieper between 6 and 13 kilometres. This got us out of the concrete and provided a close look of the river landscape. After that it was mainly gradually uphill back towards Independence Square and the end of the first lap. Highlights of the second lap largely came in the section through the heritage quarter. These have been described earlier but it was still nice to revisit the area around the main Cathedrals.

We set out for Kiev with our usual plans of trying the local cuisine. This proved more difficult than it sounds. Restaurants advertising authentic Ukrainian dishes were thin on the ground and the language didn't help. Virtually all the menus were in Cyrillic script with few concessions to English visitors. Fair enough, I doubt if you'd find too many menus in the UK printed in Ukranian. We'd been told to look out for dishes like: Potato Varenyky (Potato Dumplings), Holubtsi (Stuffed Cabbage Rolls), Kartoplia Solimkoi (Deep-Fried Straw Potatoes), Cabbage Borshch and Nachynka (Cornbread Stuffing). Mo would have been very happy with some Kotlety Po-Kyivskomy - authentic Chicken Kiev in the city its named after. Eventually we gave up looking and settled instead for the old fall-back option of pizza and pasta in a restaurant very close to our hotel. SoloPizza in Khreshchatyk Street, next door to the hotel of the same name, served marathon-runner size dishes at very affordable prices from an extensive menu. Don't be deceived by the exterior, the inside was warm and cosy and, above all, the pleasant waitress spoke excellent English. At around 100 UAH per main course and good local beer at 39 UAH a pint, Dave, Paul, Mo and I were happy to eat there on consecutive nights. We had much better luck in our continual search for the perfect dark beer by stumbling across The Cooper Bar, located downstairs in the right hand corner of Independence Square (facing away from the Ukraine Hotel). We were joined in here by friends Dave and Linda Major and spent a couple of pleasant evenings drinking their lovely, malt-flavoured Dunkel beer of unknown origins. To be truthful, the volume of the music played in the bar was too high to have a conversation about the beer's origins. Though dunkel is the German word meaning dark, when ordering at a bar 'dunkel' is likely to mean whatever dark beer the bar has on tap, or sells most of. Who cares! At 44 UAH a pint I wasn't going to quibble about where it came from. All things considered it had been a brilliant weekend. Kiev is a city I'd be happy to revisit and would certainly recommend to all fellow Marathon Tourists.

View from our hotel of Independence Sq. and the Marathon Finish

With Ilona Sekevich at Registration

BULGARIA

SOFIA MARATHON

This was to be the second of four marathons I'd got planned to run on successive weekends during October 2017. Kiev had been the first and there were Novi Sad, Serbia and Podgorica, Montenegro to complete the set. Things didn't go well from the start in Sofia. With my Wizz Air flight from Doncaster not due to arrive until 1.30 in the morning, I'd followed the airport website's advice and pre-booked one of the official OK Taxis to meet me on arrival. Or at least I thought I had. Shortly before setting-off I realised I'd received no official confirmation of the booking. Subsequent emails to OK Taxis all went unanswered and I arrived in Sofia at an ungodly hour to find no taxi waiting for me. Fortunately, the taxi firm's airport office was still open with a real, live human being behind the counter to help me get to my city centre Best Western Art Plaza Hotel.

Despite it being well after 2.00am on arrival at the hotel, for some reason the receptionist demanded that I pay the bill upfront. Only problem was that his card machine wouldn't accept my one and only debit card. The receptionist insisted on keeping on inserting the card into the card-reader when it was quite clear (to me) that the machine didn't work. Eventually he suggested that I go and get the money from an outside ATM. Searching for an ATM in a strange city in the middle of the night was something I just didn't fancy doing. And, besides, if my card didn't work in the hotel it was unlikely to work anywhere else. I awoke later that morning to find a message from Mo to say that Barclays' Fraud Squad had already contacted home to report 'unusual activity' on my card. Effectively I was stranded in Sofia without recourse to funds. The joys of being a

Marathon Globetrotter! The next day's new receptionist admitted that the hotel had been having problems with its card-reader terminals during the night and the transaction eventually went through without any further problems. I still had to deal with the Fraud Squad on returning home. Despite the issues with the card I'd certainly recommend the Art Plaza as a convenient place to stay for the marathon. Its location was excellent just around the corner from Vitosha Boulevard, the city's main thoroughfare and within easy walking distance to Registration and the event's start and finish. The breakfasts were huge.

Bulgaria was one of those countries where I didn't really know what to expect when visiting. I hadn't really developed any preconceived ideas about the country and because of all the other marathons I'd got planned around that time my research on this one had been very limited. I would have liked to have run in Sofia the previous year when my friend Gary O'Brien had completed his 100th marathon but had already booked flights and hotel for the Bucharest Marathon that particular weekend. Gary is one of the increasing number of foreigners with property in Bulgaria and regularly runs this event. Though I knew little about Bulgaria, Gary's enthusiasm for both the country and its capital city had encouraged me to come and see the place for myself.

Bulgaria is situated in the Balkans on the western side of the Black Sea surrounded by Romania to the north, Serbia to the northwest, the Republic of Macedonia to the southwest, Greece to the south, and Turkey to the southeast. Being located close to the Turkish Straits means the key land routes from Europe to Middle East and Asia pass through Bulgaria. Over the years the country has become a cultural melting pot with Greek, Slavic, Ottoman, and Persian influences. The Bulgars, a Central Asian Turkic tribe, merged with the local Slavic inhabitants in the late 7th century to form the first Bulgarian state. In succeeding centuries, Bulgaria struggled with the Byzantine Empire to assert its place in the Balkans, but by the end of the 14th century the country was overrun by the Ottoman Turks. Northern Bulgaria attained autonomy in 1878 and all of Bulgaria became independent from the Ottoman Empire in

1908. Having fought on the losing side in both World Wars, Bulgaria fell within the Soviet sphere of influence and became a People's Republic in 1946. Communist domination ended in 1990, when Bulgaria held its first multiparty election since World War II. During Communist times, the Bulgarian Black Sea Coast was a favourite destination for travellers behind the Iron Curtain, hence the name 'Red Riviera.' Now, increasing numbers of western Europeans travel throughout the country, and many have bought vacation houses near the Black Sea or in picturesque villages. During the 2008 global financial crisis, Bulgaria marked a decline in its economy of 5.5% but quickly restored positive growth levels, in contrast to other Balkan countries. That said, the Bulgarians have the distinction of boasting the strongest and most stable currency in Eastern Europe. The country joined NATO in 2004 and became a full member of the European Union in 2007. Despite significant economic advances, the country is the poorest member of the European Union. It is reported that corruption combined with a weak judicial system and the presence of organised crime remain significant long-term challenges for the country's development and economic prospects. The currency in Bulgaria is the Lev (plural Leva). You will also see the abbreviation lv. or the ISO code - BGN. The currency exchange rate is fixed at 1 EUR = 1.95583 BGN. The exchange rate to any other currency except for the euro is not fixed directly. During my visit £1 bought 2.1BGN.

Sofia is the capital and biggest city in Bulgaria with about 1.7 million citizens. It didn't become a capital until 1879, a year after the Russians liberated the country from 500 years of Ottoman rule. The oldest buildings, a mix of stately Viennese, neo-Renaissance and other grand styles, date to the late 1800s. Unattractive prefabricated apartment blocks from the post-World War II Soviet era rise from many of the city's suburbs. The city is located at the foot of Vitosha Mountain in the western part of the country. Being in the centre of the Balkan peninsula, it is midway between the Black Sea and the Adriatic Sea, and closest to the Aegean Sea. Being Bulgaria's premier city, it is home to many of the major local universities, cultural institutions and commercial companies. I've seen it described as a 'dynamic Eastern European capital, distinguished by its unique combination of European and Communist-style architecture as well as many beautiful orthodox churches.' Though Sofia is often overlooked by visitors heading straight to the coast or the ski resorts, it is one of the few European capitals with beautiful scenery and a developed ski-resort so close to it. The Vitosha Mountain is a magnificent landmark rising just south of the capital easily accessible by public transport for day trips on sunny days or for skiing in the winter. The city was voted by Trip Advisor as Europe's most affordable capital to visit in 2013.

For those arriving by air in Sofia, the best way to travel between the airport and the city centre is to take Sofia Metro Line 1 (Red) which operates service from the airport between 5:30am and midnight. The stop is located in the eastern part of Terminal 2. The journey to Serdika station in the city centre takes 20-30 minutes. Those wishing to travel to the central bus station will need to transfer to the Blue Line Metro Line 2 at Serdika. A single ticket costs 1.60 lev but you don't need a new ticket when making the transfer from one metro line to another. Ticket machines for metro tickets are located at Sofia Airport Metro Station. These accept Bulgarian banknotes and coins, and one of them accepts credit cards as well. I'm told that any piece of baggage exceeding 60x40x40 cm requires a separate ticket. There are Public Bus services (84 and 184) operating between both terminals and the city centre but the Metro is the most convenient and exactly the same price as the bus. If you have to take a taxi you're recommended to book at OK Supertrans office within the airport terminal to avoid being pestered by touts. (Just don't try booking it online before travelling!) My fare to the city cost 15 lev as opposed to the 12lev I paid on the return journey when booking through the hotel.

This was to be the 34th edition of the Sofia Marathon: a fact that surprised me somewhat given that I'd heard very little about the event before entering. The event attracts little publicity and appears to have been under the radar for much of that time. Even a thoroughly extensive search of the internet failed to find any information about the race's history. This low-key nature of the marathon was reflected in the Registration process held in a newly erected tent in a parking lot opposite the city's Vasil Levski Stadium to the south of the city centre. The whole thing was a virtual non-event and I was in and out inside 5 minutes on the Saturday before the race. The fact that I was able to provide proof of insurance specific to marathon running spared me the compulsory pre-competition medical exam. Apart from our race number with attached chip we were given a choice of T-shirt in 3 colours (lime green, bright orange and grey – I chose the latter – it was too short), a red poncho and a 20 euro Wizz Air flight voucher. Given that it had only cost the same amount to enter I think that I came out ahead.

This year there were 2,648 entrants spread over the four events on offer: a 3K Fun Run starting at 9.40am, the marathon at 10.00am, a half marathon at 10.00am and a 10.55K race at 10.20am. The latter 3 events all followed the same lap course with the 10K running a single lap, the half marathon completing 2 of these laps and the full marathon going round the same laps four times. Marathon runners were given 5 hours and 30 minutes to complete the course: 400 of us finished of which 313 were males and 77 females. This was definitely not a course for the Marathon Tourist – the route went nowhere near the centre of the city or past any of its famous landmarks. Instead, we plodded our mind-numbing way four times around the perimeters of two gigantic parks seeing virtually nothing of interest en route (unless you count glimpses of the exterior of the Vasil Levski Stadium and the city's Palace of Culture). Named after Bulgarian national hero and revolutionary Vasil Levski, the former is the country's second largest stadium. The Bulgaria national football team's home matches and the Bulgarian Cup finals are held at the venue, as well as athletics competitions. It was used as the home venue for Levski Sofia's Champions League games, and is often used for important derbies between the big clubs from Sofia, instead of their own home stadiums. The stadium was the proposed venue for the Opening and Closing Ceremonies in Sofia's bid for the 2014 Winter Olympics and has hosted concerts music shows by some world-famous stars such as Metallica, Madonna, Bon Jovi, Guns N' Roses and AC/DC. The National Palace of Culture meanwhile, abbreviated in Bulgarian as NDK, was built in 1981 to mark the country's 13th centennial and is the largest multifunctional congress, conference, convention and exhibition centre in Southeastern Europe as well as Sofia's most prominent modern landmark. It houses concert halls, exhibition space, offices, shops and restaurants and hosts a variety of cultural events from classical to avant garde; concerts, film festivals, art exhibits, fashion shows and trade fairs as well as major conferences.

Race day started unseasonably hot for mid-October and got hotter as the day progressed. I don't run well in heat and the repetitive nature of the course did nothing to inspire. Things weren't helped by the fact that we were only given water en route – isotonic was promised but where did that go? By the beginning of the fourth lap I'd lost the desire to continue and the final 10.5 kilometres were pure drudgery enlivened by the occasional chat with others in the same predicament. With no Vet 70 category (not even a Vet 65) to aim for I abandoned all ambitions of a respectable finishing time and ended up walking while simultaneously chucking water over my head for most of the last lap. My only concerns were to finish within the event's time limit. I did this with half an hour to spare - desperate to taste something that wasn't water. Water was all they had on offer. I won't be returning to this one.

I have similar feelings towards Sofia as a city. I can't put my finger on exactly why but I came away totally underwhelmed by the place. Perhaps it was the lack of a decent size river running through the centre – I'd got used to seeing the Danube, the Vistula, the Dnieper or similar while running in Eastern Europe. Sofia had nothing similar. Neither did it have the atmosphere or buzz of a big city capital or the range of iconic buildings, statues, monuments and landmarks that I'd found elsewhere. It felt more like a provincial city than a major European capital. Don't get me wrong here, there was nothing really to dislike about the place – it was a pleasant enough, compact, inoffensive city with lots of green spaces

– it just seemed to be lacking that certain something that makes a city memorable.

I tried not to be too judgemental in my sight-seeing trips on Saturday and Monday. Trouble was, most of the Tourist Office's recommendations involved visits to churches, museums, galleries and government buildings – none of which particularly interested me. Most of these appeared to be squeezed into a narrow corridor heading east from Serdaka metro station towards the historic Alexander Nevski Cathedral. This is truly the one awe-inspiring building in the city. Named after St. Alexander Nevski, a Russian Tsar who saved Russia from invading Swedish troops in 1240 and the patron saint of Tsar Alexander II, who was also referred to as Bulgaria's Tsar Osvoboditel (Liberator), since it was his troops that finally brought about Bulgaria's liberation from Ottoman rule. Built in the early 20th century in memory of the 200,000 Russian, Ukrainian, Belorussian and Bulgarian soldiers, who died in the Russo-Turkish War of 1877–1878 it has Neo Byzantine style typical of Russian churches. The huge cathedral is said to hold up to 7000 people while the belfry alone is 52 metres high and houses 12 bells. Some of Russia and Bulgaria's best artists of the time worked on the interior with its five aisles and three altars. The spectacular external golden domes were covered in gold leaf, donated by Russia in 1960 and have recently been re-gilded. It is reputedly one of the largest Eastern Orthodox cathedrals in the world. While walking down 'Tsar Osvoboditel' street towards the cathedral you will also see the beautiful gold domes of the so-called 'prettiest church in Sofia.' This is the Russian Church of St. Nicholas the Miracle-Maker with its high dome, surrounded by four smaller domes, all made of gold to harmonize perfectly with the roof of the church which is covered with green majolica tiles.

Other points of interest include the restored Ancient Roman complex of Serdica, located between the Council of the Ministers and the Presidency close to Serdica metro. Among the most important attractions of ancient Serdica, which now forms the largest open-air museum in Bulgaria, is the Decumanus Maximus, the main road of the Roman city, which prospered between the

First and Sixth centuries AD. Visitors can walk around preserved foundations of antique buildings, roads and a Christian basilica. The 2000-year-old pavement of the road has been preserved almost entirely. Under a glass dome on the same site sits the remains of an ancient Roman amphitheatre which was among the biggest in the eastern part of the Roman Empire and the largest in what is today Bulgaria. It lay outside the city walls of Serdica and hosted fights between gladiators and wild beasts, which were advertised at the entrance of the city. Overlooking the remains, standing in the same spot that for many years had featured a statue of Lenin, is the St Sofia Monument a striking 24 metre-high bronze statue of the city's patron saint. Soon after the fall of Communism, a famous local artist was commissioned to create a new statue that would fill the iconic spot and serve as a symbol of the city. The monument was unveiled in 2001 to mixed reception. Many felt that the statue strayed away from Orthodox Christian symbolism, and showed, what some considered, disturbing pagan influences. Apparently, Sofia means 'wisdom' in Greek – that's why she's holding an owl (a symbol of wisdom) in her left hand. In her right hand she holds a laurel wreath – a powerful symbol for Greeks and Romans meaning peace and success.

I guess what I enjoyed most in Sofia was simply sitting in the sunshine outside one of the numerous cafes on the pedestrianised Vitosha Boulevard taking in the distant view of the mountains while engaging in a favourite hobby of people watching. All forms of humanity are represented in the street from Bulgaria's rich and famous, to stag groups dressed as kangaroos and to the occasional aggressive beggar who refuses to leave you in peace. It's a great place to eat – you're virtually spoiled for choice. Apart from the ubiquitous McDonald's and KFC there's an abundance of pizza and pasta at the Spaghetti Company restaurant in the Serdica Centre and some pretty decent noodle dishes at the nearby, strangely-titled Wok to Walk. I tried them both and particularly enjoyed the latter and their 5.95 lev meals (about £3). The best value pizza could be had at the Garden House restaurant opposite the NDK Metro station. Here, the enterprising owner has found a way to make a fortune without even attracting anyone inside his premises by setting up a stall outside selling giant pizza slices for only 2.50 lev. Each slice is so filling it's almost a meal in itself. Of course, I had to have at least one attempt at the local cuisine while in Bulgaria so on my last night I ate in the Shtasliveca (I think it means 'Lucky Man') restaurant on Vitosha. Don't ask me to spell the Bulgarian names of what I had but I started with a Thick Yoghurt and Chopped Cucumber Soup called Tarator which I'm told came with two types of cow milk, radish, garlic, spring onions, roasted hazelnuts and walnuts. This was followed by an unpronounceable traditional Bulgarian dish consisting of meatballs made from smoked pork served with fries, roasted sweet red peppers and olive oil with herbs. The soup cost 6.80 lev and the meatballs 9.90 lev. These were washed down with a couple of draught Shumensko beers at 3.50 lev a pint and a glass of Rakia at 2.80 lev. I had to try this as Rakia, at an average 40% ABV and produced by distillation of fermented fruit, is widely considered to be the country's national drink. It wasn't bad.

Later that evening I visited the Fox and Hounds, a cosy British-style pub in the street next to my hotel. It's a good place to go if you want to hear English spoken or to watch Premier League football. I got there just in time to see Newcastle earn a creditable draw at Southampton. I won't be back for the beer though – their local brew was no nicer than that I'd had in the restaurant at exactly the same price. There were no dark beers on offer. Fortunately I'd had the foresight to buy a couple of much cheaper but more rewarding Solichno Bocks from the local supermarket – lovely 6.5% almost perfect dark beers that were sitting waiting for me in the hotel fridge.

Sofia Course Map – Round and Round the Parks!

Vitosha Boulevard and the distant mountains

SERBIA

NOVI SAD MARATHON

I'd been looking forward for some time to participating in the 30th edition of the Belgrade Marathon in April 2017. This was intended to be a special, landmark event for me. As I'd never previously visited Serbia it would have been the 50th different country in which I'd run a marathon. Prior to that though I had to finish a race in country number 49 at the Seychelles Marathon in February of that year. Unfortunately, the hernia I'd suffered during the Havana Marathon in November 2016 resulted in me having to travel to pre-booked holidays at the Lanzarote, Funchal and Seychelles events between December and February without being able to run. I did manage to somehow manage to hobble around the Dubai course in January 2017 but that only exacerbated the hernia to the point where surgery was inevitable. The operation took place the week before the Belgrade Marathon so running was totally off the agenda. That still left me with the problem of not having run a marathon in Serbia. To correct that Mo and I travelled to the country in October that same year for the less well-known Novi Sad Marathon held in the country's second largest city about an hour away from Belgrade.

For the October trip we flew KLM from Newcastle via Amsterdam to Belgrade and return. This cost us a lot more than the easyjet flights we'd booked in April but it was by far the easiest way to arrive at Belgrade's Nikola Tesla airport without having to make an overnight stop en route. Renamed in 2006 in honour of scientist and inventor Nikola Tesla, Belgrade's airport is the largest and busiest in Serbia, situated 18 km west of the centre near the suburb of Surcin. For those wanting to base themselves in Belgrade during their trip, Public Bus Line 72 leaves from the airport every 24 minutes to Belgrade central station. Ticket price is RSD 89 (Serbian dinars) if bought in the airport kiosk or RSD 150 if bought on the bus. (£1 = RSD 140 approx.) Travel time is about 30 to 40 minutes. Taxicab prices are divided into 6 different zones priced by kilometres travelled, with a fixed amount of about RSD 700 added to travel the 20 minutes from the airport to the city centre. From central Belgrade there are regular bus services to take you to Novi Sad. These cost as little as 3 euros and depart every two hours each day. The journey takes approximately 1h 40m. Rather than make the journey in and out of Belgrade, we decided to pre-book an online taxi shuttle direct from the airport to our hotel in Novi Sad that cost us 30 euros for the 37 mile journey. The Hotel Putnik, where we'd booked a 3-night stay, was conveniently placed just around the corner from the city's main square where the marathon both started and finished.

I have to admit knowing very little about Novi Sad before travelling there. It was just a city in Serbia that hosted a marathon. And I desperately wanted to run a marathon in that country. Lying on the banks of the River Danube, upriver from Belgrade and downriver from Budapest, Novi Sad (meaning 'new plantation' in Serbian) was founded in 1694 when Serb merchants formed a colony across the Danube from the giant Petrovaradin Fortress, a strategic Habsburg military post that towers over the city. Sitting on the right bank of the Danube, Petrovaradin is considered one of Europe's best-preserved fortresses. Its history as a military stronghold, complete with dungeons, treasure troves and 16km of (still tour-able) underground tunnels, has given way to its modern-day use as the home to Serbia's famous annual music festival 'EXIT'. In subsequent centuries, Novi Sad became an important trading, manufacturing and cultural centre. In the 19th and early 20th century it was the capital of Serbian culture, earning it the nickname 'the Serbian Athens'. During that time, almost every

Serbian novelist, poet, jurist, and publisher had lived or worked in Novi Sad at some point in their career. In the first half of the 19th century Novi Sad has grown into a city which many described as the most beautiful town on the lower Danube. The city's progress was interrupted when it was heavily devastated in the 1848 Revolution. The people of Novi Sad refused to accept Hungarian authority and opened cannon fire on the Petrovaradin Fortress, where the Hungarian army was stationed. From the fortress the Hungarians bombarded Novi Sad, which was then almost completely destroyed. From about 2800 houses only 800 remained, and most residents were killed or fled. It took 20 years to return Novi Sad city to the state before the bombing. Consequently, most of the buildings, monuments, cultural and other buildings are no more than 150 years old. Novi Sad also suffered badly during the Balkan's Conflict when in 1999 NATO bombing destroyed all three bridges across the Danube together with oil refineries, electric power facilities and many other buildings in the city and its surroundings. Our taxi driver, who was living in the city at the time of the NATO bombings, had a lot to say on this – none of it complimentary towards NATO, who he considered to be 'worse than war criminals.' Today, along with the Serbian capital city of Belgrade, Novi Sad has recovered to be an industrial and financial centre important to the Serbian economy.

Since 2000, the number of tourists visiting Novi Sad each year has steadily risen. During the annual EXIT music festival in July, the city is full of young people from all over Europe. In 2017, over 200,000 visitors from 60 countries came to the festival, attending about 35 concerts. The tourist port, near Varadin Bridge in the city centre, welcomes cruise boats from across Europe that travel the Danube River. A visit to the city's historic centre is a must. Many of its magnificent buildings date from the end of the XIX century when Novi Sad was the leader of cultural progress in the region. In the Old Town's Liberty Square allows visitors to admire the architecture of the City Hall and the Name of Mary Catholic Church, plus a host of other heritage buildings. The city has been named as a European

Capital of Culture 2022 (it was postponed for a year due to the coronavirus pandemic).

The Novi Sad Marathon has been on the calendar since 1993 and, pandemic permitting, will be celebrating its 29th edition on October 10, 2021. Surprisingly, it's not the only marathon held in the city. The Novi Sad Night Marathon (with different race organisers) traditionally takes place on the last weekend in June and is currently on to its 12th edition. Try as I might, I found it difficult to glean much information about either event from their respective Serbian language-only websites. All I knew was that there would be 5 distance options for the October event: Marathon, 33km, 25km, 10.5km and 5km. I paid 25 euros for my marathon entry for which I received the usual T-shirt and medal. It also got both Mo and I into a pretty decent eve of race Pasta Party following Registration in the once sumptuous but now decidedly fading Hotel Vojvodina, the city's oldest hotel fronting the main square. Included with the race-pack was one of the most confusing Course Maps that I've seen for any of the marathons I'd run to date. This was also in Serbian but included English sub-titles that just didn't make sense. What already seemed to be a complicated route was made even more difficult by errors lost in translation. The inclusion of symbols for a 10-stage Marathon Relay to the map just added further to the complication. The course had no fewer than 8 turns to make up 42 kilometres over its total length of 13.5 kilometres through the city and its suburbs. Most of these loops occurred within the first 6 kilometres of the race as we ran past the newly constructed bridges along the banks of the Danube. I knew it was going to require concentration and, as events unfolded, I was proved to be right.

143 of us in the marathon set off from in front of the Cathedral across from the Hotel Vojvodina at 10am on a warm Sunday morning. The first kilometre took us through the city and out on to the wide boulevard that skirted the river. The first turn was meant to be at 1.6km and that's where it all started to go wrong. Many of the front runners simply ploughed straight ahead instead of turning. I could be wrong but I didn't see any marshals in place to

prevent this happening. Only a few locals, presumably knowing the course from previous years actually turned and headed back correctly from where we'd come. It was all very strange watching runners going in different directions. I just kept on going with the pack, knowing deep down that I'd need to make up the distance nearer the end of the race. Fortunately, the other turning points were much more obvious and much better manned by the time we got to them. Nevertheless, it was dispiriting to realise that instead of turning for the finish in Liberty Square on returning from the suburbs I faced either running the missing or loop or automatic disqualification. I ran the missing loop! Others didn't and were subsequently disqualified. At 3pm on the dot, 5 hours after the start, the course was closed and workers began dismantling the finish gantry.

After the race we had time for a good look around to see what the city had to offer. There wasn't that much to see – apart from the Square and Dunavska (Danube) Street, an east to west partly pedestianised avenue that linked Liberty Square to the Bishop's Palace. It's said that Novi Sad's residents have been coming to this classy thoroughfare to amble and meet friends for as long as the city has stood. Many of the old buildings on Dunavska are protected cultural monuments from the middle of the 19th century, built after Novi Sad was damaged in the 1848 Revolution against the Austrian Empire. These are painted in pastel shades and host upmarket restaurants, ancient inns, bookshops, boutiques and outdoor cafes to while away the hours in the sunshine. Mo and I enjoyed exploring the cobbled laneways running off the street, containing quirky pubs serving excellent local beers. It was here for the first time that I came across what has turned out to be my favourite dark beer – the oddly-named 'Niksicko,' brewed in nearby Montenegro, where fortunately we were heading to later that week. We also took the opportunity to sample the local cuisine in one of the 'kafanas' (traditional Serbian taverns) behind the main street. Among the various Serbian dishes we tried were: Sarma - pickled cabbage, minced meat and rice, Cevapi - grilled finger-shaped mincemeat served with chopped onions and Prebranac - a simple dish made from beans with bacon or grilled sausages. Of the three the latter was by far the most filling. All were ridiculously inexpensive.

We couldn't leave Novi Sad without visiting its most famous building, the Petrovaradin Fortress. Towering over the river on the opposite bank to the city on a 40m-high volcanic slab the mighty fortress, considered Europe's best-preserved citadel is aptly nicknamed the 'Gibraltar on the Danube'. Constructed using slave labour between 1692 and 1780, its dungeons have held notable prisoners including Karađorđe (leader of the first Serbian uprising against the Turks and founder of a royal dynasty) and Yugoslav president Tito. The fortress is open daily and is free to visit with plenty to see in addition to the building itself; there's the onsite City Museum of Novi Sad, the Fight of Deer sculpture, the quirky 'drunken clock' with its back-to-front hands and the underground tunnel tour. The mysterious 16km of subterranean tunnels that goes four floors below the ground was built in the late 18th century makes the fortress even more interesting. It was intended for the lodging of soldiers and keeping of weapons. Stories about the treasure of the Habsburg family, about a monster from Petrovaradin fortress, the enigma of a Maltese cross on a wall of a dead-end corridor and the guessing about a tunnel under the Danube are constant topics of numerous explorations and writings. The crew of the show 'Ghost Hunters International' from the American channel SF filmed a documentary about the underground's mythology. The most stunning part of the fortress, however, is the Clock Tower at the Ludwig bastion. The clock is peculiar for its clock-hands: a little hand indicates minutes, while the big hand represents hours. This unusual clock was constructed in this way so that people, and especially the boatmen on the Danube, could read the time from far away. Even without these attractions, the views of the Danube and across to the city are quite spectacular and well-worth the uphill walk to get there.

Next morning we were up bright and early for our shuttle back to Belgrade Airport and onward flight to the Adriatic resort of Tivat on the Montenegro Riviera for a 5-night holiday prior to the following weekend's Podgorica Marathon. As I've said elsewhere, 'It's a hard life being a Marathon Tourist!'

Dunavska (Danube) St. Novi Sad's main thoroughfare

Waiting for the Start in Novi Sad

MONTENEGRO

PODGORICA MARATHON

The marathon in Novi Sad, Serbia's second city, the weekend before this one in Podgorica provided the perfect excuse to stay in the area between the two events and sample the delights of the Montenegrin coastline that we'd heard so much about. The day after running in Novi Sad we took a Montenegro Airlines flight from Belgrade to the town of Tivat on the Montenegro Riviera for a four nights' stay. And what a beautiful place Tivat turned out to be! Located in the middle of a huge fjord-style inlet and surrounded by high mountains it was the perfect place to recover before making our way inland to the Podgorica Marathon on the following weekend. Be warned though, Tivat is being repackaged as an upmarket tourist resort designed to attract those with deep pockets (which, unfortunately, we haven't got). Still, it was nice to stroll around in the sun (with hands in pockets) and admire the numerous Russian-oligarch style enormous yachts moored like floating apartment blocks in the prestigious, newly developed Porto Montenegro. Even nicer were the cheap local bus rides around the spectacular fjord to such places as the indescribably beautiful ancient Venetian walled city and fortress town of Kotor, a World Heritage Site sitting at the fjord's head. Marathon Tourism at its very best.

The 9 euros bus journey from Tivat to Podgorica at the end of our stay was an adventure in itself as the bus climbed the steep hairpin bends above the cloud line and away from the coast before dropping onto the plain on which Podgorica is located. I would imagine that the two other marathon entrants from the UK would have used the more conventional option of flying there from Stansted with Ryanair (or perhaps not given the airline's recent problems). If considering this be aware that there aren't many transportation options to get from the airport into the city. We were advised to avoid the airport taxis at all costs as they are totally overpriced and to book a taxi through your hotel or hostel beforehand at a fraction of the price and have the driver meet you at the airport. We did this for our return flight home for a reasonable 10 euros. We'd also booked ourselves into the City Hotel, Podgorica – a 4-star hotel that acted as the marathon's Race Headquarters for the weekend and offered reduced prices to those taking part.

As is usually the case with these newly-created countries, I knew very little about Montenegro before deciding to run in its capital Podgorica. Montenegro is a Balkan country on the Adriatic Sea bordering Croatia and Bosnia and Herzegovina to the north, Serbia to the northeast, Kosovo to the east, and Albania to the south. To the west is the Adriatic Sea. For a long while considered an unsafe no-go area, the country is now being deservedly promoted as the new dream holiday destination. Its charm lies in its picturesque medieval towns and villages, its timeless river valleys, beautiful beaches, glassy lakes and towering mountains. The high mountains in the north of Montenegro include some of the most rugged terrain in Europe averaging more than 7,000 feet in elevation. Formerly a part of Yugoslavia, Montenegro was embroiled in the ethnic and civil unrest that plagued the region in the 1990s. After peace was brokered Montenegro was joined to Serbia as a combined state before emerging as a sovereign state in 2006 after a referendum in which just over 55% of the population opted for independence. Apparently the breakup happened peacefully. I've read one description comparing it to a marriage that just wasn't working in that there was some anger but no big fight. Though Montenegro's tourism suffered greatly from Yugoslavia's tragic civil war, the stabilized situation in the region has seen tourism beginning to recover and Montenegro being re-discovered by tourists from around the globe.

In contrast to most of Montenegro, Podgorica lies in a mainly flat area at the northern end of the Zeta plain. Though small in size compared to other European capitals its population of around 200,000 inhabitants constitutes almost one-third of the national population. The name Podgorica translates from Serbian as 'under the Gorica' where Gorica means 'little hill' (referring to the cypress-covered hill that overlooks the city centre). The city is located in central Montenegro approximately 15 kilometres north of Lake Skadar. The Moraca and Ribnica rivers flow through the city, while the Zeta, Cijevna, Sitnica and Mareza flow nearby. Podgorica suffered heavily during World War II; being bombed over 70 times, razing it to the ground and causing the deaths of over 4,100 people. Two years after liberation in 1944 it became the capital of the Socialist Republic of Montenegro (one of the republics of the Socialist Federal Republic of Yugoslavia) under the name Titograd. A period of unprecedented expansion followed; as in the rest of Yugoslavia, the population increased dramatically, the city was heavily industrialised, infrastructure was improved, and health, educational, and cultural institutions were founded. To accommodate the growing population, several residential and business blocs were erected in the style typical of the Eastern Bloc countries at the time. While these 'Tito styled' structures provided needed housing, they were criticized for their bleak and depressing appearance. The progress halted again in the 1990s with the breakup of Yugoslavia when the entire country was greatly affected by severe economic stagnation due to international sanctions. The name of Podgorica was reinstated in 1992, when Serbia and Montenegro became a joint federal state. Today Podgorica is the seat of Montenegro's Parliament and government, but not of the country's President, who resides in the former royal capital Cetinje. In recent years Podgorica's cityscape has seen a lot of urban development, including the introduction of more modern buildings and landmarks creating an interesting mixture of old and new.

The Podgorica Marathon was first held on 8 October 1994 and though it has been held annually on the last Sunday in October since then I'd met very few runners who'd actually taken part in the event. When I first discussed coming here with fellow members of the 100 Marathon Club of similar age most were put-off by the event's 4 hour 30 minute time limit. A group of Finnish runners I'd met at the Belarus Marathon in July had warned me how they'd been quizzed on arrival at the half-way point in 2 hours 15 as to whether they'd be able to finish within the limit (they did). I'd yet to break 4:30 in the short time since the hernia operation but decided that I'd enter and take my chances on a DNF on the day. As it happened I needn't have worried – on arrival in Podgorica I found that they'd unexpectedly extended the limit to a more reasonable 5 hours 30 minutes - though they did have a pull-out point for anyone who hadn't reached the 36 kilometre mark by a specified time. For some unfathomable reason this was 4 hours 30 for male runners and 5 hours for females. Can you understand the maths behind this? No, neither can I.

For 20 years the Podgorica Marathon has incorporated the national championship in both Marathon and half marathon for men and women and has twice hosted the Balkan Marathon Championships. Technical organisation is done by the Podgorica Marathon Running Club, while the City of Podgorica is the de facto sponsor through the full support it gives to the race. Similarly, the Danilovgrad Municipality which hosts the start of the half marathon has traditionally extended full support to that event. Since 1996 the marathon has been included in the calendar of the European Athletics Association, and in 2010 it became a full member of AIMS with international certification of the course.

According to the event's literature, the Podgorica Marathon has become a trade mark of the city, and of Montenegro itself. It is a sporting, cultural and touristic event which attracts more and more participants and supporters from throughout Montenegro, neighbouring countries and overseas. Over 541 runners from 35 countries had taken part in the previous edition of the event which offers a choice of the marathon, a half marathon, 5K and 10K Fun Runs and a 1K Eco run for the youngest runners. Course records stand to Petko Stefanov of Bulgaria, who recorded 2:11:41 and to Serbia's Olivera Jevtic, who ran 2:31:18. To date, two male Serbian runners, have run every edition of the Podgorica Marathon which awards winners in each five-year age category upwards from age 35 to 65+. The first three male and female finishers in the Marathon win cash prizes, trophies, medals and certificates. Awards extend to 10th place in the men's race and eighth place in the women's. The race has an unusual entry system in that no payment is required after completion of the online entry form. You simply hand over the ridiculously cheap 10 euros entry fee when collecting your race number. Incidentally, the euro is the official currency in Montenegro – which certainly made things easier than it had been the week before in Novi Sad.

I found the registration process something of a disappointment. Basically they needed a bigger venue. Registration took place from 10am to 9pm on Saturday in a tiny room in the bowels of the City Hotel where we were staying. On arriving just before the 10am opening I found no orderly queue but a scrum of people pushing and jostling one another in a stairwell littered with luggage. For some reason the needs of a coach-load of athletes from a particular Serbian athletics club had been given priority and the rest of us were expected to simply stand around in silence. The whole atmosphere was so claustrophobic I almost turned around and left but, that would have been counter-productive and besides there was no space in which to turn. The race pack consisted of a bib, safety pins, a fill-it-in-yourself certificate and a white cotton T-shirt. I'm not complaining, remember entry was only 10 euros. I had to ask for the food vouchers for the post-race lunch and then had to return later in the day on discovering the existence of a race programme full of essential information that hadn't been given to me. By then the crowds had cleared and I was able to finally see that my year of birth was incorrectly recorded by four years on the start list. This would have made a real difference to the results if there'd been a Vet 70 category (as there should have been) in this event.

The marathon started at 9am on a sunny Sunday morning in Republic Square in conjunction with both the 5K and 10K events. There were 205 entrants on the marathon start list but only 133 finishers in the published results where 72 runners were listed as DNF. That's over 35% of the field – an almost unprecedented percentage of non-finishers. I'd prefer to think that most of these were no-shows who having not been required to pay in advance simply didn't bother to turn up, than accept the thought that many of these were pulled out at the 36 kilometre mark. 87 runners completed the 5K race, 68 finished the 10K and a further 207 runners completed the half marathon event that was run on a separate course. I have to say that, be-decked in flags for the marathon, Republic Square looked a lot more colourful than it normally does. I was surprised to learn that the square, formerly known as Ivan Milutinovic Square after a famous Montenegrin communist politician, military general and national hero, had undergone a massive reconstruction in 2006, the year of Montenegrin Independence. It was widened, paved, a big central fountain was constructed and the area was turned into a car-free zone. The square was also decorated with colonnades, palm trees and water channels in a project costing around 2.5 million euros. So why does it appear so outdated?

This is not a course for the Marathon Tourist. On leaving the square there's little to see of any significance on the single, anti-clockwise lap around the Zeta Plain. Within the first couple of kilometres we ran across the new Millennium Bridge, visible on most tourist literature as the new symbol of Podgorica. A more recent addition to the cityscape, this stark white piece of modern architecture stands as one of Podgorica's most notable landmarks. The elaborate and innovative cable bridge spanning the Moraca River, has one main 57 metre high pylon, with 12 cables on one side supporting the roadway deck and 24 cables on the other side acting as counter balances. The official opening of the bridge on July 13, 2005, Montenegro's National Day, coincided with the anniversary of the Uprising in Montenegro, when the local communist party staged a revolt against occupying Italian troops. The bridge is seen at its best when taking a stroll across the nearby pedestrian Moscow Bridge capturing views of the river below and the snow-capped mountains off into the distance. Next up we ran past the imposing Cathedral of the Resurrection of Christ, a Serbian Orthodox Church in the 'New Town' area on the western bank of the river before reaching the giant statue of St. Peter close to the University centre. After that runners in the 5 and 10K races gradually disappeared from the course as they made their respective turns for home leaving those of us left in the marathon to plough our own lonely furrows around the remaining 37 kilometres or so of the course.

From 5km to 16 km we ran virtually arrow-straight along a flat, wide and empty dual carriageway, passing the airport as we made our way south. On arriving at the village of Golubovci the route turned eastwards past the half-way mark to bring us to the smaller village of Mataguzi. From here the course headed north again back in the direction of the city. This second half of the course was much more rural than the first and on much narrower roads running through agricultural settlements with their fresh farm smells. I loved every minute of it. We were in turns chased and encouraged by local children, many of them enjoying the freedom of playing on their bikes on the traffic-free roads. At this stage you couldn't help staring in awe at the beautiful mountain scenery dominating the horizon every time you looked up from the road. I ran conservatively just taking in the atmosphere on a lovely warm autumnal day but still managed to reach the 36km pull-out point with over half an hour to spare. Reaching the outskirts of Podgorica I felt strong enough to increase the pace and ended up passing other runners for the first time in the race to finish in my targeted time of 4:45. This got me 2nd Vet 65 position that came with a gold medal award and a 30 euros cash prize. Not bad for an event that only cost 10 euros to enter. The post-race pasta meal back at the hotel was in itself worth more than that. It had been a thoroughly enjoyable day out in a lovely part of the world. Despite a few hiccups at Registration I'd recommend this event to anyone wanting to run somewhere 'different' for a change.

Podgorica certainly fits into the 'different' category. Though Montenegro's tiny capital is slowly changing for the better, it isn't one of Europe's most visited capital cities. It can be difficult to pin a label on the city; its streets are a strange mixture of Ottoman remnants, depressing communist-bloc apartments and shiny new shopping malls with none of the big-city atmosphere or urgency of many other European capitals. It appears to be a city searching for its own identity. This is unsurprising given that it's undergone five name changes, passed through the hands of everyone from the Romans to the Turks to the Austro-Hungarians, and twice been wiped off the map entirely. Some regard it as unattractive and drab, and on first sight it's rather easy to jump to that conclusion. Unfortunately, Podgorica's city centre does nothing to dispel that impression. The area around the show-piece Republic Square resembles one of those awful 1960's 'new-town' developments now falling to bits throughout the UK. It looks tired and badly in need of a major face-lift. The whole square requires updating to bring it into line with some of the iconic city-centre showpieces found in most European capitals. It's far more pleasant to focus on the wonderful vistas of the surrounding mountains than to look at what is immediately in front of you. When you compare it to the beauty of some of the towns that line the Adriatic coast, like Tivat, Budva and Kotor, it's understandable why many don't spend much time in the capital. To be fair, there are a number of rather pleasant tree-lined streets immediately to the west of the square between it and the river. This is where most of the outdoor cafes and restaurants are situated and where we spent most of our evenings. The city's parks and areas along the riverbanks are also peaceful places to visit. The longer I was there the more I came to appreciate it for what it is: a quiet, low-key city in a beautiful location that allows you to go skiing in the mountains in the morning and sunbathing on the beach in the afternoon. There aren't too many capital cities that offer that. I'd like to return someday to see how it develops.

One of our first tasks on arriving in Podgorica was to visit the local tourist office for advice on where to find the best Montenegrin cuisine. We were directed to what the assistant called 'The National Restaurant' close to the city's historic Clock Tower, one of the few remaining Turkish landmarks in Podgorica that wasn't destroyed during WWII. This impressive 16 metre-high tower in the centre of Becir Beg Osmanagic Square, was constructed in 1667. The clock, said to have been imported from Italy, was the only public clock in the city and signalled times for the Muslim call to prayer. We nearly gave up looking for the 'National Restaurant' until someone explained that it was officially called Pod Volat. Open daily from 7 a.m. to midnight this is the place to eat in Podgorica. Pod Volat serves up traditional Balkan fare and is filled with a good mixture of locals and tourists. Their large menu offers up plenty of options and the portions are huge. On our first visit I tried the Njeguski Steak, a pork steak stuffed with Montenegrin cream cheese (kajmak) and prosciutto, rolled up and typically served with fries and vegetables. Mo had the Karadjordjeva Schnitzel: basically the same dish but this time served crumbed and fried. This dish is also known as 'djevojacki san' or 'maiden's dream' – allegedly because of its phallic shape! The next night we shared dishes of Cevapi and Pljeskavica, minced meat dishes which are found throughout the Balkans. Cevapi are little sausages and pljeskavica are burger patties. Both come with french fries and salad at a very affordable price.

Finally, for those of you aware of my search for the perfect strong, dark beer. I think I've found it in Montenegro in the shape of Niksicko Tamno Pivo (Dark Beer). We first came across it in a pub in Novi Sad sold on draught at not much more than £1 a pint. It's a beautiful tasty 6.2% ABV malty drink brewed by the Trebjesa Brewery, the only brewery in Montenegro. The brewery is based in the town of Niksic (hence the unfortunate name) to the north west of Podgorica and is owned by Molson Coors. Beer from Trebjesa brewery is by far most popular and most consumed beer in Montenegro as well as enjoying significant popularity in Croatia, Slovenia, Albania and Bosnia and Herzegovina. Look out for it on your travels!

Podgorica's River and Mountains

Podgorica Marathon Start

MOLDOVA

CHISINAU MARATHON

The Chisinau Marathon was held for the first time in 2015. In that year the non-governmental organization 'Sporter' took the initiative in undertaking the organisation of an annual international marathon race in Chisinau. The idea was supported by important sports organizations, including the Ministry of Youth and Sports, the National Olympic and Sports Committee of Moldova and the Athletics Federation of Moldova. The marathon was initially held in April but now takes place in late September or early October. According to the event website in 2015 there were 1000 finishers in one of the three races on offer over distances of 10K, 21.1K and 42.2K. Of these there were 106 marathon finishers, less than half of the 257 runners who completed the marathon distance in 2019, the last time it was held prior to the Covid pandemic. In the second Chisinau marathon in April 2016, it is claimed that 15,000 people took part. (This seems a totally exaggerated figure. I would imagine most of these were spectators!) On this occasion a 5K race and a 1.5K Fun Run were added to the existing programme. There were 239 entrants in the marathon, 651 in the half marathon and 1322 in 10.5k event. I needed to run this one to complete the full set of advertised road marathons in every country in Eastern Europe (see my book 'Marathon Tourism in Eastern Europe' for full details). The opportunity finally arrived to go to Moldova in September 2019 when I travelled there with 100 Club colleague and friend Paul Richards.

Chisinau is not a particularly easy place to get to from the UK. Taking into consideration Paul's work commitments we basically had only two options: fly overnight with Wizz Air from Luton arriving Chisinau at 5.20am on the Saturday morning or, have a good night's sleep at a cheap Birmingham Airport hotel before catching a 6.10am Lufthansa flight via Frankfurt to arrive in Chisinau at 1.45 pm on the Saturday afternoon. Both options cost in the region of £200 with return flights. As we'd arrive refreshed and with plenty of time for Registration, we chose the latter. A twin room with breakfast for two nights at the Hotel Astoria, less than half a mile from the start, added another £40 each to the bill. On arrival you can travel the 13 kilometres into the city from Chisinau International Airport by taking the No. 30 Express Bus Service to its terminus at Dimitrie Cantemir Square. Buses run regularly between 6.00am and midnight with the fare costing 2MDL. (The Moldovan Leu is the currency of Moldova. At the time of writing £1 = 25 leu). Another, similarly-priced, option is to use the 15-seater Minibus Taxi No 165 from outside the arrivals hall. The drawback with this is that you have to wait for the minibus to be full. A third option is to order a regular taxi directly from the airport's taxi agency desk for approximately 100 leu. Despite our experience with taxi scammers in Kiev, we decided to ignore all three options while Paul practised his bargaining skills with the unlicensed drivers hunting customers outside the terminal. (When will we ever learn?) Within minutes we were ensconced in a dodgy looking red van and, we hoped, on our way to Registration.

When planning our itinerary Paul and I both agreed on one thing: we both knew very little about the country or its capital. A little bit of research found some surprising facts about the country. For example, Moldova has the dubious distinction of being the poorest country in Europe with a per capita GDP of just $5,327, according to the IMF. The second lowest is Ukraine's, at $8,305 (Moldova's neighbour Romania's is $20,326, while the UK's is $42,480). It's also the least visited country in Europe. Only 121,000 foreigners are reported to have entered the country in 2016 (according to the UN World Tourism Organisation). By far the vast majority of these were from Romania, Ukraine, and Russia. This means that the number of visitors coming from countries other than its neighbours is very, very small. On a global scale only Bangladesh and Guinea are less touristy destinations (taking into account number of visitors per resident), according to Priceonomics. Moldova is technically a landlocked country. Though, in a bid to gain access to the Black Sea, Moldova negotiated a territorial exchange with Ukraine in 2005, giving the country access to a 600m stretch of the River Danube, which flows into the Black Sea. It also has its own breakaway territory. The region known as Transnistria declared independence from Moldova in 1990, precipitating the War of Transnistria which secured a de facto independence for the territory. Finally, its capital city Chisinau was almost totally destroyed in 1940. Having been invaded by the Red Army in June that year, Chisinau then suffered a deadly earthquake measuring 7.3 on the Richter scale in October which destroyed much of the city. As if that wasn't enough, the following year the Luftwaffe arrived and blew what was left of the city to smithereens.

Sandwiched between Romania and Ukraine, Moldova emerged as an independent republic following the collapse of the Soviet Union in 1991. According to the BBC Country Profile it is regarded as one of the poorest countries in Europe, with its economy relying heavily on agriculture. Two-thirds of Moldovans are said to be of Romanian descent. The languages are virtually identical and the two countries share a common cultural heritage. Present Moldova used to be part of a region named Bessarabia, which belonged to Romania but got annexed to the Soviet Union in 1940. After the Soviet Union dissolved in 1991, Moldova attempted to join Romania but, for several reasons, mainly because of the pro-Russian people from Transnistria and Gagauzia, it didn't happen and Moldova became an independent country. The industrialised territory to the east of the Dniester, generally known as Trans-Dniester, was formally an autonomous area within Ukraine before 1940, when the Soviet Union combined it with Bessarabia to form the Moldavian Soviet Socialist Republic. This area is mainly inhabited by Russian and Ukrainian speakers. As people there became increasingly alarmed at the prospect of closer ties with Romania during the twilight years of the Soviet Union, Trans-Dniester unilaterally declared independence from Moldova in 1990. Fierce fighting followed. To all outward appearances, Transnistria is a sovereign state, albeit one that leans heavily towards Russia. Its flag includes the hammer and sickle and often flies alongside Russian flags. The Transnistrian ruble bears the images of Russian figures like General Alexander Suvorov and Catherine the Great. An enormous statue of Lenin guards the entrance to the Supreme Soviet, its parliament building. Pictures of Stalin and Putin are almost as ubiquitous as those of Transnistrian president Yevgeny Shevchuk. In return, Russia provides free gas and supplements residents' pensions. It also provides more than 1,000 troops - to the consternation of those in Ukraine. Still, Russia has not formally recognized the breakaway state, and does not appear inclined to. Nor does Moldova. In fact, despite having its own currency and border controls, Transnistria is not officially recognised by a single member of the United Nations. The region has existed in a state of limbo ever since. Currently, The Republic of Moldova actively pursues EU membership but the level of poverty in the country is proving a stumbling block to accession while the fact that the Trans-Dniestrian dispute has yet to be resolved is also a major obstacle.

Chisinau, also known by the Russian name Kishinev, is the capital and largest city of the Republic of Moldova with a population of around 600,000 inhabitants. The origin of the city's name is unclear, but in one version the name comes from the archaic Romanian word chisla (meaning 'spring' or 'source of water') and nou ('new') because it was built around a small spring, at the corner of Puskin and Albisoara streets The city is Moldova's main industrial and commercial centre, and is located in the middle of the country, on the river Bic. Chisinau is regarded as by far Moldova's largest and liveliest city and its main transport hub. While the city's origins date back six centuries to 1420, much of Chisinau was levelled during WWII and in the tragic earthquake that struck in 1940. The city was rebuilt in Soviet style from the 1950s onwards, and both the centre and outskirts are dominated by utilitarian and unattractive buildings. According to the Lonely Planet guide, 'the centre does have a few architectural gems remaining, and is surprisingly green and peaceful.' While Chisinau does not have a reputation as a tourist destination for overseas visitors there are a number of visitor attractions that are reportedly worth seeing. Like Paul and I, most visitors confine their stay to the centre, defined by two large, diagonally opposed parks: Cathedral Park, and Stefan cel Mare Park. The best museums, hotels, restaurants and cafes are a short walk away. The impressive main artery, Stefan cel Mare Boulevard, cuts right through the axis of the two parks. Cathedral Park - better known as Central Park, is in the very centre of the city. The centre is adorned with the Nativity Cathedral, the main church for the city. To the Southwest is the Triumphal Arch constructed in 1841 which is the centre piece of The Great National Assembly Square where the marathon starts and finishes. Across Stefan cel Mare Boulevard is the Government House. The city's biggest flower market is on the north side of the park along Banulescu Bodoni Street. At the intersection of Stefan cel Mare and Banulescu Bodoni is a statue of Stefan cel Mare (Stephen III of Moldovia) who in the 15th century achieved European fame by resisting the Turkish advances. The monument is the gateway to the beautiful park of the same name. We were to see lots of these two parks as we passed them out-and-back on our loops around the city.

We arrived for registration in the flag-bedecked General Assembly Square at around 3pm on a sweltering hot Saturday afternoon. There were posters, bunting and decorations everywhere but very few people. Within seconds we'd picked up our a starter pack, which included bib number, a disposable timing chip, a commemorative T-shirt, branded backpack and route maps together with a detailed schedule of the event. At the finish line all participants receive commemorative medals. All very good value for the 25 euros entry fee. Returning to the square at 5pm for the Pasta Party you could hardly move for the queues of hungry runners who suddenly appeared as if from nowhere. Once they'd had their food, they just as quickly disappeared. The absence of people seemed to be a recurring theme of the weekend as, once the marathon had finished, Chisinau took on the appearance of a ghost town.

There were plenty of people around on Sunday morning though as we lined up next to the Triumphal Arch for the 9am start of all five events on the programme. The time limit is 6 hours. The route is set around the central streets of Chisinau with the start and finish line located next to the Triumph Arch in Great National Assembly Square. The Marathon covers 4 out-and-back laps of 10+ kilometres around the city centre on an undulating course with elevations between 70m and 110m. Most of the elevation occurs on a 2 km a steadily uphill stretch between the 2km and 4km sections of each lap. The upshot of this, of course, was that we ran the same stretch downhill once we'd turned to run back into the city. The course was quite busy for the first two laps as we ran accompanied by those in the shorter distance races. After that huge gaps appeared in the field and we had the city to ourselves. As the heat built up during the day the hill got longer and harder. I knew I wasn't in condition to do a respectable time so simply ambled around chatting to the 5-hour pacemakers – both of whom spoke perfect English (as well as Russian and Romanian) and expressed surprise that anyone would want to travel all the way from the UK to their event. I'd no idea on finishing that such a slow time had got me first position in the Vet 70 age category so missed out on collecting the award at the end. I was too busy elsewhere, enjoying the post-race hospitality. The outdoor area where the Pasta Party had been the night before had been turned into a bar for which we'd been given a token for our first pint. As no one asked for the token and no one seemed to mind how many pints we had, four pints later I was sitting blissfully drinking in the sun as the Award Ceremony took place. On leaving the bar, I gave my unused token to a beggar who looked in need of a drink!

I probably wouldn't have enjoyed Chisinau if the weather hadn't been so nice while we were there. All it seemed to consist of was one main street and the area around the two parks mentioned previously. Away from this there was little else of interest. Whoever it was that described Moldova as 'the most boring country in Europe' knew what they were talking about. Saturday night in Chisinau was as dull as ditchwater. Paul and I trawled the city searching for somewhere lively to have a drink – even walking deep into the back streets to visit a bar that Paul had seen recommended on some social media site. We needn't have bothered, the result was still the same. We found ourselves to be the only customers in each of the places we visited. And, this was Saturday night in a European capital city. Sunday night was little better. You'd have thought the bars would have been packed with thirsty marathon runners after the race. They weren't. In fact, the only signs of life came from a group of middle-aged, non-running English guys whose sole purpose for being in Chisinau was to visit Transnistria and have their passports stamped. Their recommendation was that we should go to the nearby Robin Pub for a lively atmosphere and a decent pint. We did. Guess what? We were the only ones there. Giving up on the idea of a celebratory drink among fellow runners, we headed instead to Andy's Pizza restaurant we'd spotted earlier next to Cathedral Park. At least the place was busy, the pizzas were good and the bottles of Moldovan wine even better. We could have done with them again the following day when we missed our flight back to Birmingham due to a bomb scare at Frankfurt Airport. The add-on effect of this entailed the extra costs of having to book a last-minute overnight stay in Birmingham as well as an early morning train home the following day. It was a disappointing end to an even more disappointing trip. Sometimes this Marathon Tourism just doesn't work out right!

Paul Richards at the Chisinau Marathon Start line

Chisinau's Nativity Cathedral and Triumphal Arch

CHINA

SHANGHAI INTERNATIONAL MARATHON

Running the Shanghai Marathon was an afterthought to a trip Mo and I had planned in November 2019 to spend Christmas with our son Ross and his wife in Australia. Having already booked a 15-day cruise from Singapore to Sydney on November the 25th, I couldn't resist the opportunity of finding somewhere new to run en-route. Both the Shanghai and Penang Bridge Marathons on consecutive weekends (November 17 and November 24th) fitted perfectly into our plans. We wanted to break our journey with a week or so stopover in Asia, preferably somewhere we'd never previously visited and that could allow us to include a marathon (or two) into the itinerary.

One of the good things about a quick, in-and-out visit to Shanghai was that, under current visa rules, it was no longer necessary to go to the expense and inconvenience of having to arrange a full Chinese visa for our stay. Under the current 144-hour Visa-free Transit Policy visitors do not have to have a Chinese visa to run the Shanghai Marathon. You can stay in Shanghai for up to 6 days if you meet certain conditions. These are: you are passport holder of one of the eligible 51 countries of which the UK is included, you have valid air tickets with a confirmed seat in the next 144 hours to the a country or region. (The 144-hour period starts to count at 00:00 the next day upon your arrival in China. Technically this makes your actual stay longer than 144 hours) and you must fly out of China to a third country or region, not where you come from.

I figured that by staying in Shanghai for less than 6 days and then moving on to Penang in Malaysia for the marathon there on the following weekend, I could add two new countries to my list of countries in which I'd completed marathons.

Launched as recently as 1996, the Shanghai International Marathon has established itself as the marquee running event on China's Marathon calendar. Every November the marathon takes tens of thousands of runners through many of the city's iconic landmarks, such as the Bund, Customs House, Shanghai Museum, Shanghai Grand Theatre, Shanghai Exhibition centre, Jing'an Temple, Nan Pu Bridge, Lu Pu Bridge, Long Hua Temple, and Shanghai Stadium. The course records were both set in 2012 as Kenya's Sylvester Kimeli Teimet set the men's standard of 2:09:01 hours and Ethiopian Feyse Tadese broke the women's record with 2:24:08 hours. Participation also reached a new high that year, as over 30,000 runners competed in the marathon. At the 2018 event, 720 runners finished the full marathon within three hours, which was a record among all marathon events around the country, according to Zhou Jin, general manager of organizer, Shanghai Donghao Lansheng Event Management Company.

In 2019, online registration opened for general runners from August 1st to 12th. Slots were distributed through a lucky draw and the results announced on August 23. The registration fee for the full marathon was 100 yuan (US$ 14.50) for Chinese and 300 yuan for foreigners. Registration for the 10-kilometre and 5.5-kilometre events was 60 yuan for Chinese and 200 yuan for foreigners. The event, which took place on Nov 17 that year, featured three races – a full marathon, a 10-kilometre run and a 5.5-km run. The full marathon was restricted to 25,000 runners, while the 10-km and 5.5-km runs were capped at 6,000 and 7,000 participants respectively. For elite runners, there is a green channel to assure them entry. Elite runners include the top 200 finishers of the 2019 Shanghai International Women's Half Marathon, the top 600 male and 300 female finishers of the 2019 Shanghai International Half Marathon, as well as top finishers of last year's Shanghai International Marathon.

The Shanghai International Marathon has been rated as a golden-label road race by the IAAF (International Association of Athletics Federations). The organiser's next goal is to build the annual event into a platinum-label race, a higher road race category IAAF introduced in 2019. All the funds raised are donated to Shangma Charity Fund established by the Shanghai Sports Development Foundation. The donated funds are used to help the vulnerable groups to stay healthy and promote the development of mass-participation sports.

For something that describes itself as an 'international' event, I found the English version of the website sadly lacking in the most basic information. There were a number of things that bothered me from what I could gather from the website. For a start, there was no guarantee that I'd be successful in the ballot-style entry system. Even if I was, I wouldn't know this until late August and as Shanghai was only one component of a much longer, much more complicated itinerary, I needed everything firmed up long before then. There was also the language problem to consider. I didn't speak a word of Mandarin and, if the website was anything to go by, there was very little concession made for this up to and during the event. Also all the essential elements of the event appeared to be located in different parts of a very crowded and complicated foreign city. Registration was in one area, the start in another area and the finish in yet another part of the city – like the three points of a triangle. Getting from one to another of these appeared to be a nightmare. I understand that plans are afoot to update the information on the Shanghai Marathon website but, at the time, the paucity of detail meant that I didn't feel confident in booking without experienced help. This was one of the very few times in my marathon career that I've used the services of a sport's travel specialist. In this case, the highly-recommended Manchester based Sports Tours International Ltd (STI). These seemed to be offering what I was looking for: guaranteed race entry, the company of other English-speaking runners, transfers to and from the airport, the opportunity of having my race packet delivered to my hotel and the chance to be met on the finish line and delivered back across town to my hotel.

With these things in mind, Mo and I committed ourselves to a 4 night/5 day itinerary with STI at the 4-star Greenland Jiulong Hotel in Shanghai about one mile walk away from the marathon start on the city's iconic Bund area. The alternative accommodation on offer, the 5-star Huating Hotel, was located close to the finish in Shanghai Stadium. As Shanghai is such a large and complex city we also took up the group guided tour option allowing us the services of a tour guide and driver to show our group the sights of Shanghai and, hopefully, make the visit less stressful and more rewarding. The whole package, including airport transfers, guided tours and hotel B & B accommodation cost £569 each, (not including flights). Marathon entry was an extra £40.

Mo & I flew with Emirates from Newcastle to Dubai and then on to Pudong International Airport Shanghai, arriving late afternoon on the Thursday before the race. We were surprised how easily the visa-free 6-day entry rule allowed us to circumvent the lengthy queues faced by those who had visas to present. Our driver was there as arranged and we were soon on our way to our hotel, weaving through wall-to-wall traffic on wide motorways flanked by high-rise apartment blocks as far as the eye could see in every direction. The one hour drive to the hotel was to be our introduction to what became a common theme of our stay: traffic congestion and the difficulties encountered in making any sort of above-ground journey within the city area. I guess that's not surprising considering that Shanghai has a total population of over 24 million of which almost 90% live in the urban areas. I read that there are something like 40,000 taxis and 3.40 million private cars in the city. Unfortunately, most of these appeared to be on the road at the same time! The driver told us that new vehicle regulations were introduced in June 2016 to limit the growth of automobile traffic and alleviate congestion. Under these, new private cars cannot be driven without a licence plate which are sold in monthly licence plate auctions for around 90,000 Chinese Yuan. That's about £10,000 to fork out in addition to the price of the car! (£1 = CNY9).

Only locally registered residents and those who have paid social insurance or individual income taxes for over three years are eligible to be in the auction.

Fortunately, there are useful alternatives to using Shanghai's highly congested road network. The city boasts the first and the fastest commercial high-speed Maglev train in the world. With a maximum operation speed of 267 mph, the train can complete the 19 mile journey between Longyang Road Station and Pudong International Airport in 7 minutes 20 seconds. This compares well to the 32 minutes by Metro Line 2 and up to an hour by car. A one-way ticket costs CNY50, (or CNY40 for those with airline tickets or public transportation cards). For journeys within the city, the fast-growing Shanghai Metro network has 14 lines (with others under construction), with nearly all lines operating underground. Line 1, the first and busiest metro line in Shanghai is the city's main tourist line, connecting Shanghai Railway Station, People's Square, South Huangpi Road and popular shopping areas like South Shanxi Road, and Xujiahui as well as South Railway Station. Being on a guided tour with transport provided meant that we only had to use the Metro once during our stay. It appeared fast, cheap, air conditioned and fairly user-friendly with most signs and station arrival announcements bilingual in Mandarin and English, but the trains can get packed during rush hour. Fares range from CNY3 to CNY9 depending on distance.

Traffic problems aside, we found Shanghai to be a fascinating city with an equally fascinating history. Shanghai, which literally means the 'City on the Sea,' lies on the southern estuary of the Yangtze River, (with the Huangpu River flowing through it), at the point where China's main waterway completes its long journey to the Pacific. Situated on China's central coast, it's the country's biggest city and the third most populous city in the world. It's also a global centre for things like finance, research, technology, manufacturing, and transportation. The Port of Shanghai is the world's busiest container port. At the heart of the city is the Bund, a famed waterfront promenade lined with colonial-era buildings. Across the Huangpu River rises the Pudong district's futuristic skyline, including 632m Shanghai Tower and the Oriental Pearl TV Tower, with distinctive pink spheres. Until 1842 Shanghai's location made it merely a small fishing village. After the first Opium War, however, the British named Shanghai a treaty port, opening the city to foreign involvement. The village was soon turned into a city carved up into autonomous concessions administered concurrently by the British, French, and Americans, all independent of Chinese law. Each colonial presence brought with it its particular culture, architecture, and society. This history has shaped Shanghai's cityscape significantly. British-style buildings can still be seen on The Bund, while French-style buildings are still to be found in the former French Concession. The old racetrack in the British area has given way to what is now People's Park, with a major metro interchange underneath. Other metro stops include the railway station at the edge of what was once the American area, and Lao Xi Men and Xiao Nan Men, (Old West Gate and Small South Gate respectively), named for two of the gates of the old Chinese walled city.

This mixing of cultures shaped Shanghai's openness to Western influence. Shanghai became an important industrial centre and trading port that attracted not only foreign businesses but also Chinese migrants from other parts of the country. In its heyday, Shanghai was the place to be. Christened 'The Paris of the East' it had the best art, the greatest architecture, and the strongest business in Asia together with dance halls, brothels, glitzy restaurants and international clubs. Shanghai was occupied by the Japanese in 1937 after a bitter battle lasting several months. After the war, the autonomous concessions were not re-imposed and though trade did resume, it was never at pre-war levels. After the Communist victory in the civil war in 1949, many of the people involved in the entertainment industry and many business people fled to Hong Kong and Taiwan. Shanghai's days of glory were over. Closed off from the outside world with which it had become so comfortable, Shanghai fell into a period of hibernation. Fashion, music, and romance gave way to uniformity and the stark reality of Communism. In the beginning of the 1990s, the Shanghai government launched a series of successful strategies to attract foreign investment. The biggest move was to open up Pudong, once a rural area of Shanghai but now a major destination for corporate headquarters housed in numerous skyscrapers, including the World Financial Centre – the 3rd tallest in the world. According to Kristin Baird Rattini's 'A Short History of Shanghai' in the New York Times Travel Guide, 'Today Shanghai has once again become one of China's most open cities ideologically, socially, culturally, and economically, striving to return to the internationalism that defined it before the Revolution.'

These comments are very much in-line with our own conclusions. Shanghai is a super modern, cosmopolitan city full of foreign tourists, with an air of prosperity and an openness about it that we hadn't expected to find prior to arrival. English education in Shanghai is reputed to be amongst the most advanced in China, meaning that most of the citizens, especially the younger ones can speak good English. Also, with a lot of foreign residences in Shanghai, most of the street signs and transportation signage are written in English. We knew before leaving that we were the only ones from the UK to book the Shanghai trip with Sports Tours International that year (it had already been removed from the STI website before our departure), so weren't expecting to find other English speaking runners at our hotel. We didn't – but there was one Italian runner. Together we were added to a much larger group of Danish and German runners with different tour companies who'd chosen to stay at the Huating Hotel mentioned earlier. Unfortunately, pick-up and drop-off arrangements between the two hotels involved a continual back-and-forth coach ride across the city every time the amalgamated group went anywhere together. We were disappointed on our arrival to find that the final itinerary we'd received had been changed without us having being notified. There was no 'pick up (of) your race packets from the hotel reception when you check in' and the Saturday's itinerary did not include a visit to, 'Shanghai Stadium: the marathon finish area,' as promised. We were being taken to the Expo to collect our own race packets instead – something that I'd been hoping to avoid by booking this whole trip in the first place. Post-race arrangements had also changed without us having been informed. We were no longer being met at the finish line area as advertised but, instead, had to make our own way to the lobby of the nearby Huating Hotel. I can only think that these unexpected changes had been made to fit in with the interests of the German/Danish group. They weren't major inconveniences but it wasn't what we'd been led to expect when we booked initially. The response from Sports Tours International when I pointed this out to them was very gracious. I don't blame them in any way for the mix up. It just got the whole visit off on the wrong foot. I'd certainly think twice about booking trips to future overseas events without a rock-solid guarantee that the itinerary was the one I'd paid for. As things turned out our fellow marathon runners from Denmark and Germany all spoke very good English in our company and just accepted us as part of their group.

I've no complaints about our two tour guides Cherry and Andrew. Both were knowledgeable, informative spoke perfect English and did their utmost to ensure that we enjoyed what their city had to offer. I do think, though, that their employers need to vary their tours to cater for the specific needs of their clientele. Most marathon runners need some time to put their feet up and rest before a race. Plus, some time to get their breath back and recover afterwards. This didn't appear to be a consideration in the itinerary. For example, after travelling for around 24 hours to get there, the last thing that Mo and I wanted early next morning was to have to get on a tour bus and drive through congested traffic for over an hour to visit an even more congested tourist attraction - before having to turn around and drive all the way back again. The excursion took us to Zhujiajiao, said to be the best-preserved ancient water town among the four ancient towns in Shanghai. Zhujiajiao, also called 'The Venice of Shanghai', features lovely waterways, curved rock bridges, old streets cemented with stone, and over 10,000 buildings dating back to the Ming and Qing dynasties. It was an interesting enough place to visit, if only to see the busy markets and Buddhist temples. It is also very much a tourist trap and not somewhere I'd have gone to that day. The highlight of the day came after a gondola trip on a canal was the communal meal overlooking one of the canals. This was to be the first of several meals where the whole group sat around a large circular table with Chinese dishes heaped on a revolving circular tray. With a group full of hungry marathon runners you had to be quick before all the popular meat specialities disappeared on to someone else's plate.

After this, the original itinerary had us returning to our hotel for an afternoon's free time. This was something Mo and I had been looking forward to and had made our own plans for. Instead, we had to go with the others to join the lengthy queues at the Shanghai New International Exhibition Centre to collect our race packets in person. The fact that this is a totally different building to the original Shanghai Exhibition Centre located on the opposite bank of the river makes it all very confusing. I wonder how many of the foreign marathon runners unfamiliar with the city ended up at the wrong venue! Free at last from the day's travel, we spent our evening doing what we'd wanted to do during the day and walked from the hotel to see the famous Bund.

For centuries now the Bund has been the most famous tourist destination in Shanghai, making it a must-visit place and the pride of Shanghai. The Bund (meaning 'embankment) is a legendary, kilometre-long waterfront located on the western bank of the Huangpu River famous for its grand, Western-style buildings that were built in the late 19th and early 20th Centuries. The buildings feature architectural styles from Neoclassical to Beaux-Arts to Gothic to Baroque. The Bund is noted for its controversial history of Western colonialism. Briefly, after the Chinese lost the first Opium War in 1842, the Western powers demanded trading rights in China, and they were granted settlements or concessions. Soon wharves and trading houses were set up on the Bund along the Huangpu River by the Americans and, mainly, the British. The first decades of the Bund saw modest offices built. Then in the late 19th century, larger neo-classical and British colonial style buildings were erected. At first trading companies dominated the Bund, but soon they gave way to financial institutions as trade in Shanghai increased. By the early 20th century, financial institutions were the biggest industry in the Bund. Banks like the Hong Kong Shanghai Banking Corporation (HSBC) established themselves on the Bund. From 1920-1937, the architectural style was grander and gaudier, and the Bund reached its peak. Alongside the banks, social clubs like the highly exclusive Shanghai Club and glamorous hotels were built to accommodate wealthy tourists. The Bund became synonymous with alcohol, jazz, celebrity, and capitalism. After the war, the new Communist government cleared out the area. Considering it a symbol of Western colonialism, greed, and capitalism, the government kicked out many of the banks and put government ministries into these buildings instead.

The Bund, with its rich history, culture, and tradition, has a lot of things to offer visitors. We enjoyed a leisurely stroll along its length, observing the buildings and the crowds while gazing across the Huangpu River to the massive and gleaming financial towers in Pudong – recognised universally as a symbol of Shanghai's modernity. The Bund Sight Seeing Tunnel is a subterranean passageway connecting The Bund to the Pudong District. It is a great way to get to the other side of the river and is a popular tourist attraction. On the Bund's northernmost tip overlooking the river-bend is Shanghai's oldest park. It is a triangle of green in the urban jungle. There is the Shanghai People's Heroes Monument built, a grandiose edifice which is dedicated to its local revolutionary heroes. Beneath the monument, there is the Bund Historical Museum, where you can journey to the Bund's past through photographs and artefacts. We found the best time to visit is after sunset when the towers of the Pudong skyline are lit up in a dazzling display of flashing scenes and colours. Although the day view of the Bund is phenomenal, the night view is simply breathtaking. It's probably, the most spectacular night-time scenery of any major city on the globe.

We were back on the tour bus battling the traffic early again on the Saturday morning. Our reward this time was to stand in the long queues for entry into the famous Shanghai Museum. Situated on the People's Square in the Huangpu District of Shanghai, the museum is considered one of China's first world-class modern museums. Designed to resemble the shape of an ancient Chinese ding (a three-legged cooking vessel), the museum is home to one of the most impressive collections in the land. Famous for its large collection of rare cultural pieces, it houses over 120,000 precious historical relics in twelve categories, including Chinese bronze, ceramics, paintings, furniture, calligraphy, seals, jades, ancient coins, and sculptures. All well and good if you're into these sorts of things. Call me a Philistine if you like but I've always preferred living, moving objects to those from the past. The gardens were nice though! After that it was the bus versus traffic combination once again for an hour of sightseeing on the Bund – something that we'd already done the night before.

Following another round table group lunch the tour took us to the iconic Yu Garden and the Old Town Bazaar. Yu Garden is a classical garden dating back to the Ming Dynasty (1368-1644). Yu in Chinese means pleasing and satisfying, and this garden was specially built for his parents by a government officer named Pan Yunduan as a place for them to enjoy a tranquil and happy time in their old age. It was anything but tranquil while we were there. Once again, I got the impression of being in a gigantic tourist trap, surrounded cheek-to-jowl by jostling crowds. It was probably the last place that my body wanted to be on the afternoon before a major marathon. No, I'll take that back. What came next was probably even more tiring – being expected to wander around the nearby Bazaar - an overcrowded shopping centre on a busy Saturday afternoon. By this stage I'd given up and simply sat in the sun next to an artificial water feature. Saturday evening was programmed for a pre-race briefing by the tour guides at yet another round table meal. I guess none of us could complain about not being well fed, though I have to say that the quality of these meals was no better than the cuisine provided at the Chinese restaurant close to my holiday home in Spain.

It was quite a relief on Sunday morning to be able to simply stroll to the marathon start and then just run for a few hours on a course mercifully free of traffic of any kind. It was a beautiful warm morning as we waited on the Bund watching the crimson sun rise slowly between the towers on the opposite bank. As usual with Shanghai the start area was wall-to-wall crowded long before the 7 am start of both the full marathon and 10km events (I never did find out where the 5.5km Fun Run started). The 10km runners were meant to start at the back of the field behind the various time zones for the marathoners. I'm not sure how many of them did – there was a great deal of changing of positions before the start. I never think it's a good idea to start potentially faster, short distance athletes behind slower, longer distance runners in any race. It's simply asking for trouble. After the gun went it took quite a while for those of us slower runners to reach the start line. This was followed by this stop-start effect for a kilometre or so with everyone striving for space to put their feet. Eventually, things sorted themselves out as the roads widened and there was room to run. The slow start didn't bother me too much given the marathon cut-off time of 6:15:00 (with roads opening on a rolling basis). I just settled down and determined to take in as much as possible of this weird and wonderful city.

The Marathon is a flat point-to-point course starting at the Bund and finishing inside the Shanghai Stadium, or more commonly known by the locals as '80,000 audience stadium.' On leaving the Bund, the course then goes to Nanjing Road, the busiest pedestrian-only shopping street. It passes the Shanghai Museum between 3km and 4km before reaching the original Shanghai Exhibition Centre at around 6km. Between these two buildings we passed the 40-metre tall Shanghai Grand Theatre in the city's political and cultural centre. As a symbolic landmark for the city, the Grand Theatre has staged over 6,000 operas, musicals, ballets, symphonies, chamber music concerts, spoken dramas and various Chinese operas since the its opening in 1998. Next up is Jing'an Temple, a thousand-year-old Buddhist temple located in West Nanjing Rd, the flourishing downtown area of Shanghai. After the 10km runners finish the course then heads to the river, reaching the Nan Pu Bridge just after 15km. The impressive construction was the first bridge over the Huangpu River in central Shanghai, and the fourth biggest cable-stayed bridge in the world. Turning back on itself, the course passes the Lu Pu Bridge at 23km and follows the newly constructed city running trails for several kilometres. The final major landmark, the Long Hua Temple is met at both the start and finish of a long out-and-back section from 26km to 39km. The Temple together with the adjacent Longhua Pagoda one of the best preserved temples in Shanghai and the oldest, largest and most majestic Buddhist building in the lower reaches of the Yangtze River Delta. This religious attraction is famous for its old temple, old tower, temple fair and evening chimes, with collections of various sutras, golden seal, and figures of Buddha from Tang, Ming and Qing dynasties.

By this stage the humidity levels had risen considerably, with a number of runners requiring medical attention. The final few kilometres end in a large loop approaching the finish in the new, saddle-shaped roof Shanghai Stadium, built in 1997 to serve as the flagship venue for the 1997 National Games of the People's Republic of China. The purpose-built stadium also hosted several games during the 2008 Olympic football tournament. On finishing, runners are then led directly out of the stadium to collect their finisher's goodies: a beautiful boxed medal, slippers and a special marathon towel. This seemed such a waste of a stadium finish. The huge stadium was completely empty except for runners and totally without atmosphere. As one competitor commented on the website marathonguide.com, 'Why not issue some family passes and pack out the stadium for a rousing finish? That would be truly memorable and worth returning for.'

At the finish I met up with Franco, the Italian runner from our hotel, so that we could make our way together to the Huating Hotel where our lift to the Jiulong was waiting. We'd hardly had time to shower and rest at the hotel before it was back on the coach again for the post-race gala dinner at yet another circular table establishment. This was followed by what was meant to be the highlight of the tour: an evening river cruise on the Haungpu River. What seemed at the time like a perfectly good idea was ruined by the length of time spent queuing to get on the boat. Once on board we found that there was no place to sit. Standing for an hour or more whilst being pushed and jostled by fellow passengers was definitely not what I wanted after a hard marathon. Even worse was being in a closely confined space and being subjected to the truly disgusting Chinese habit of spitting in public. I lost count of the number of times many of our fellow passengers simply spat on the floor in front of us and walked away. I was informed by our guide that this was considered an accepted part of their lifestyle. It seems that, in China, many people view spitting as a cleansing action for the body. Apparently, many Asian cultures see the Western act of blowing or sneezing in public into a handkerchief and then putting that into a pocket as equally disgusting if not much worse than spitting. Cultural attitudes towards spitting in public aside, I would have preferred to have not been on that boat. My ideal ending to a busy day would have involved enjoying exactly the same views of the spectacular Shanghai evening skyline while relaxing with a beer or two on one of the outdoor venues on the Bund.

We got out of Shanghai just in time. Not long after our visit news started to quietly filter through about a new, deadly coronavirus strain emanating from nearby Wuhan City in Hubei Province. We all know what happened after that.

Registration at the International Exhibition Centre Shanghai

Shanghai's world-famous skyline

MALAYSIA

PENANG BRIDGE INTERNATIONAL MARATHON

This marathon offered something I'd never done before: a run in the dead of night over a major suspension bridge across the Penang Strait linking the island of Penang to the mainland of Malaysia. It also provided the opportunity of adding another country to the list of those in which I'd run a marathon. Penang is home to the popular Penang Bridge International Marathon, an annual event held at the iconic bridge that connects Penang Island to the Penang Mainland.

Penang Bridge may not be an official sightseeing spot in Penang but it is the sight that greets most visitors to the island. It is considered a major Penang landmark, with locals often curiously comparing it to London Bridge. (I can't see why. They're totally different in all ways imaginable).The 8.4 mile-long suspension bridge connects Perai on the mainland side of the state with Gelugor on Penang Island, crossing the Penang Strait. The bridge was the first and, until 2014, the only road connection between the peninsula and the island. It's the second-longest bridge in Malaysia and the fifth-longest in Southeast Asia, with a length over water of 5.2 miles. Before the bridge was opened the only way to get to the mainland was via the state-owned Penang Ferry Service that runs between Butterworth and George Town. Today the toll bridge, with fees paid only when heading to the island is one of the busiest freeways in the country. The only time it closes is for the annual Penang Bridge International Marathon.

The Penang Bridge International Marathon (PBIM for short), the largest mass-participation sporting event in Penang that brings tens of thousands of runners out onto the streets each year, is organised by Penang State Tourism Development office (PETACH) and fully supported by the Penang State Government. The race is known as the biggest event in the country. During the competition, participants run over the bridge and along a scenic coastal highway. The event started in 1984 as a Road Race from Esplanade to Gurney Drive on the island of Penang. The completion of the original Penang Bridge in 1985, has seen it held there annually in late November since 1986. In 2006, after a break for a number of years, the Penang Bridge International Marathon was revived as a combination of the Penang International Marathon, which was last held in 1999, and the Penang Bridge Run, which had been held from 1992 to 2003. The only year since then when it hasn't been run over the Penang Bridge was in 2014. In that year the race attracted 60,000 runners. This unprecedented entry arose because it was held for the first and only time on the newly-opened 'Second Penang Bridge' — the 24km-long Sultan Abdul Halim Muad'zam Shah Bridge – the longest in South-East Asia.

The event also incorporates a half-marathon race and a 10K run. The competition also had an 8K fun run event, but it was removed in 2018 as part of rebranding exercise. In that same year, the 10K race with over 11,000 participants was cancelled for the first time due to heavy rain and lightning making conditions dangerous on the bridge (though both the marathon and half marathon were allowed to finish). All registered runners were given finisher medals as a consolation. The organiser originally planned to also remove the 10K run competition as well by 2020, but chose to continue due to popular demand. The event was rebranded again in 2020 with the introduction of the new logo as well as the tagline 'The Asian Challenge,' reflecting the vision of making it into an internationally acknowledged marathon event. (Unfortunately, the 2020 in-person edition of the race was cancelled due to the coronavirus pandemic, with all entries automatically transferred to 2021).

Penang, the second smallest Malaysian state by land mass is located on the northwest coast of Peninsular Malaysia, by the Malacca Strait. It has two parts: Penang Island, where the capital city George Town is located, and Seberang Perai on the Malay Peninsula. They are connected by Malaysia's aforementioned two longest road bridges, the Penang Bridge and the Sultan Abdul Halim Muadzam Shah Bridge. The history of modern Penang was shaped by British colonialism, beginning with the acquisition of Penang Island from the Sultanate of Kedah by the British East India Company in 1786. Developed into a free port, the city state was subsequently governed as part of the Straits Settlements, together with Singapore and Malacca. The state capital, George Town, briefly became the capital of this political entity between 1826 and 1832. By the end of the 19th century, George Town prospered and became one of the major ports in Southeast Asia. During World War II, Penang was conquered and occupied by the Japanese Empire from 1941 to 1945. At the end of the war, Penang was also the first state in the Malay Peninsula to be liberated by the British, under Operation Jurist. The Straits Settlements was dissolved in the following year and Penang was merged into the Federation of Malaya. In spite of a secessionist movement within Penang, the merger with Malaya went ahead and the federation attained independence from the British Empire in 1957. Malaya later evolved into the present-day Malaysia in 1963. Noteworthy as the only state in Malaysia to have a Chinese majority population, Penang's sub-culture is a mixture of Asia itself. Rather than feeling mono-ethnic, it exemplifies the country's colonial past and mixed-heritage future. It isn't Malaysia's most beautiful state yet it does possess a certain charm. The oldest of the British Straits settlements, this state is said to be one of its most tolerant and cosmopolitan. Today, Penang is Malaysia's most tourist-visited destination. The island manages to embrace modernity while retaining its colonial traditions; due to its well-preserved heritage buildings. Penang's capital, Georgetown, has been accorded a listing as a UNESCO World Cultural Heritage Site.

Mo and I flew to Penang via Kuala Lumpur the day after I completed the Shanghai International Marathon in China. One of the conditions of our 6-day visa-free entry into Shanghai was that it was necessary to fly to 'a third country' (not the city of origin) after our visit. Because of its proximity to Singapore, Malaysia suited us fine. Although we'd previously spent time in the country many years ago most of that had been in the Kuala Lumpur area. Penang Island, with its beautiful beaches and stunning scenery, seemed an ideal place to pass the six days that remained before embarking on our ship from Singapore to Sydney. We arrived at Penang International Airport late on the Monday evening with a 5-night stay booked at the beachfront Royal Copthorne Hotel, west of Georgetown. Located in Bayan Lepas about 20 minutes away (10 miles) from Georgetown, the Penang International Airport (previously known as the Bayan Lepas International Airport) is the island's only terminal for flights in and out of Penang. Taxis at the airport operate on a coupon system, making it necessary to buy a coupon beforehand from inside the terminal. A trip to Georgetown costs between RM40 - RM 60, depending on the taxi size. (£1 sterling = 5.69 Malaysian Ringgits). Most overseas visitors tend to be heading to the beach resorts on the north of the island close to the main resort of Batu Ferringhi. This is about 20 miles away - a 55-minute taxi journey from the airport. For those in no hurry, Penang has a fairly comprehensive public transportation system and there are a number of bus lines available from the airport. There's even a Rapid Penang bus that goes into the city. This runs every 30 minutes, between 06:35 and 23:00 but due to its many stops, it takes quite a while to make its way into Georgetown. If you are in a hurry, or if like us you arrive too late for the last bus, it's easy enough to grab a cab.

Though we were mainly in Penang to enjoy a relaxing beach holiday prior to the marathon, there are a few interesting sights worth seeing on any visit to the island. Georgetown, Penang's capital city has a multitude of attractions to appease the curious visitor. Located on the north-eastern corner of the island, Georgetown is dotted with idiosyncratic Chinese shops, narrow roads, old-fashioned colonial-era mansions, clan houses, numerous schools, ornate temples and Little India districts. The city is a mainstay on the Malaysian tourist scene yet it is also a popular expat enclave; besides that, the food here– a hotchpotch of Indian curry and Chinese noodles – is for many the best in Malaysia. Bordering the conurbation is a landscape of beaches, forests and lakes. We passed some of Penang's finest beaches on the local coastal bus that took us into town. The main bus station connects directly with the city's ferry terminal. Ferries run between Georgetown and Butterworth on the mainland every 20 minutes from 06:00 to 00:30 – the fare is RM1.20 per adult. We were keen to make the trip across the Penang Strait, if only to get our first views of the impressive Penang Bridge that dominated the southern skyline. First thoughts were that it was an awfully long bridge to have to run across in the dark (or in the daylight, come to that).

On returning to Georgetown we jumped on the free hop-on-hop-off tourist bus that provides the easiest way to see all the sights in one go. Central Area Transit (or CAT, for short) is a free shuttle service that operates every 15 to 20 minutes from 6.00am to 11.40pm. Starting at the Weld Quay Bus Terminal, it travels along the major streets in George Town and drops passengers off at 19 designated bus stops (stations) that are mere walking distance to major attractions. Stations 3, 5, 8 and 18 are among the most visited. Station 3 is Little India, a small Indian enclave in the city and one of the favourite places for lovers of Indian food. You can eat in small stalls along the streets, buy snacks from street vendors or sit down in one of the many restaurants. As soon as you walk into the area, you are hit by the aromatic smell of spices and the sounds of the latest Bollywood hits blaring out on loud speakers from all the colourful shops of the area. The main tourist sight is the Sri Mariamman Hindu Temple along Queen Street (the oldest Hindu Temple in Penang). Station 5: Bank Negara, allows passengers to visit the City Hall, Town Hall and the War Memorial. If your main incentive in Penang is to cover the religious and shopping aspects of the town, Station 8 is within walking distance from Benggali Mosque and Chowrasta Market. Finally Station 18: Kota Cornwallis, allows visits to the city's historical fort, Fort Cornwallis and the nearby Queen Victoria's Memorial Clock Tower.

Fort Cornwallis, the largest standing fort in Malaysia, stands on the site where Captain Francis Light first set foot in 1786 on the then virtually-uninhabited Penang and took possession of the island from the Sultan of Kedah. He then established a free port to lure trade from Britain's Dutch rivals. Set close to the Esplanade and Jubilee Clocktower, the star-shaped fort is one of the oldest structures in Penang. Named after Marquis Charles Cornwallis, only a set of ten-foot high outer walls remain, with an enclosed park within. It is a surreal experience to hear the 1812 Overture playing over the speaker system while a Malaysian man dressed in full British regalia stands at the gate. Located south of Fort Cornwallis, the Moorish-style Queen Victoria Memorial Clock Tower is a testament to Penang's royal connections. Commissioned in 1897 by a local millionaire, Cheah Chen Eok, to commemorate Queen Victoria's Diamond Jubilee, it stands 60ft-high, with each foot representing a year of the Queen's 60-year reign. The Tower's main claim to fame is that, due to wartime bombing, it's meant to lean like the Leaning Tower of Pisa. I couldn't see it myself and am not sure it's worth a visit in its own right - but you might as well take a look while you're at the Fort.

We made two other trips of note during our short stay. The first was to Penang Hill, one of Penang's most popular attractions rising 821 metres above sea level. The best way to reach the summit is to ride on the funicular train that travels all the way up in half an hour, presenting visitors with breathtaking views of the whole island all the way to the top. Apart from providing a welcome break from the near-constant humidity, highlights at the peak include a pretty Hindu temple, church, mosque and even a snake show where you can take photos with a tame python for a fee. The other outing was to the beach resort of Batu Ferringhi, Penang's second most popular destination after Georgetown. The resort consists of a long stretch of soft, white sandy beach along a winding road filled with a host of accommodation and dining options. Though Batu Ferringhi has a beautiful seashore coupled with beach activities for tourists in the morning, it's the evening activities centred around its night market that have become a legendary tourist attraction. An area stretching 1km from the McDonald's restaurant comes alive every night as vendors set up stalls along it after dusk, offering everything from fake designer bags to dirt-cheap pirated DVDs and home deco items to souvenirs. Many tourists visit just to stroll through the stalls enjoying the atmosphere of this gigantic outdoor flea market. Unfortunately, we timed our visit to coincide with one of that week's heaviest tropical downpours. There was no atmosphere. Just lots of puddles.

At the end of the week we changed our hotel to the more upmarket Eastin Hotel in Bayan Lepas on the eastern side of the island, only a short walk from the marathon start line. Race entry fee cost RM 90. Registration was held from 9am to 8pm on the Saturday in the large outdoor car park of the nearby Queensbay Shopping Mall - the largest shopping centre in Penang. Minutes away from the Penang Bridge, the waterfront complex is home to mid-level restaurants, branded clothing stores, electronics shops and a large Golden Screen Cinemas complex. There's plenty of fast-food outlets like McDonald's, KFC and Burger King for fuelling stops. The big problem was filling in the rest of the day before having to return to the car park after midnight for the 1.30am start. Wandering around wasting energy in the heat and humidity was out of the question. While the Mall's air-conditioning provided some form of refuge, the venue soon became packed with runners seeking respite from the temperature outside. Attempts to sleep for a few hours in the sanctuary of the hotel room proved equally futile. It was going to be a very long night!

It was a strange experience waiting near the start line watching thousands of runners warming-up in the dark. Many had taken advantage of specially arranged bus shuttle services linking with revised ferry times from the mainland to get them to the venue. I was already sweating profusely from the short walk from the hotel and felt no need to follow their example. The Full Marathon was flagged-off by Chief Minister Chow Kon Yeow at 1.30am followed by the Half Marathon at 3am and the 10K Run later in the morning at

6.30am. Marathon runners were given a much-needed 7 hours in which to complete the race.

On leaving Queen's Bay Mall, the course first turned onto the Tun Dr Lim Chong Eu Expressway, which runs along the eastern coast of Penang Island. We ran about 5 kilometres south before turning north and retracing our steps, passing the entrance to the bridge en route. A further turn back to the south finally brought us to what we'd all been waiting for - the on-ramps to the iconic bridge. It was an even stranger experience running across the Penang Strait in total darkness. There was little sense of running over water and virtually no evidence of the eagerly anticipated breeze to counteract the humidity. By this stage I was totally lathered in sweat — almost as if I'd been immersed in water for hours. Fortunately, the drink stations throughout the course were both regular and well-stocked. We'd only run a short distance on the bridge before arriving at the point where the half marathon and 10K competitors would have to turn later that night. (Neither of them get to spend much time on the bridge). It was only after cresting the bridge's 'hump' at the halfway point that lights on the distant shore became visible. It was a case of heads-down and make for there. Shortly after crossing the 8.4 mile bridge, a large roundabout turned the runners around and sent us back over the bridge in the opposite direction. By this point dawn became a faint light in the sky, making it possible to recognise ships navigating the Strait. We finally reached the off-ramp on the island side from where it was only a couple of kilometres back to the finish at the Mall. We approached among a sea of 10K runners, half-way through their race. It had been a tough night — possibly one of the toughest I've had due to the unrelenting humidity. I never dreamt that conditions could have been so de-energising. I now know why we'd been given 7 hours in which to finish the marathon!

Over 25,000-strong participants from 65 countries had taken part in the three events, with Kenyans emerging as winners in most of the categories. Kenyans Moses Kiptoo Kurgat and Peninah Kigen were the champions in the Men's and Women's Open categories. However, a local married couple stole the headlines by separately winning the full marathon's 'Malaysian category'. Husband Nik Fakaruddin Ismail finished the men's marathon in first place with 2 hours, 40 minutes and 53 seconds; while his wife Nur Amelia Musa finished the women's in 3 hours, 18 minutes and 51 seconds to clinch the top spot. I would have liked to have stayed around for the Presentation ceremonies and some after-race socialising. Unfortunately, there was barely time for a quick wash before it was off to the airport for our early morning flight on to Singapore (and, hopefully, another marathon in New Zealand in two weeks' time).

At Registration for the Marathon

Penang. The old and the new side-by-side

EPILOGUE

My last overseas marathon was in Malaysia in late 2019 just before the Covid pandemic wreaked havoc on everyone's lives and overseas travel became nigh-on impossible. I've subsequently missed out on planned marathons in new countries like Oman, Kuwait, Jordan, Kenya and New Zealand (among others), as well as having had to suffer cancellations of pre-booked island-based marathons in Ibiza, Cyprus and Rhodes. I'm sure that there are many of you reading this with similar tales to tell. Who knows if we'll ever get the chance to go to any of these events. Though the future looks bleak I can't wait to get back on the road.